The World Treasury of
Modern Religious Thought

The World Treasury of Modern Religious Thought

EDITED BY
JAROSLAV PELIKAN

With a Foreword by
Clifton Fadiman, General Editor

LITTLE, BROWN AND COMPANY

BOSTON   TORONTO   LONDON

FIRST EDITION

Acknowledgments of permission to reprint
previously copyrighted material appear on pages 631–635

Library of Congress Cataloging-in-Publication Data

The World treasury of modern religious thought / edited by Jaroslav
Pelikan: with a foreword by Clifton Fadiman, general editor. — 1st
ed.
         p.   cm.
     ISBN 0-316-69770-2
     1. Religion. I. Pelikan, Jaroslav Jan, 1923–   II. Fadiman,
Clifton, 1904–
     BL25.W69   1990
     200'.9'034 — dc20   89-37290
                                                                      CIP

MV PA

Designed by Robert G. Lowe

Published simultaneously in Canada
by Little, Brown & Company (Canada) Limited
PRINTED IN THE UNITED STATES OF AMERICA

To my son Martin,
who has helped me to discover a universal vision

Contents

II. THE WILL TO BELIEVE

III. THE GRANDEUR OF GOD

IV. REVERENCE FOR LIFE

V. THE RECONSTRUCTION OF TRADITION

VI. LOVE ABIDES

VII. VISIONS OF THE OTHER WORLD

VIII. FAITH AND FREEDOM

Foreword

THIS VOLUME forms one of a continuing series of World Treasuries published in cooperation with the Book-of-the-Month Club. Each of these Treasuries gathers, from as many literatures as possible, previously published, high-order writing of our time, fiction or nonfiction. Each covers a specific field or genre of general interest to the intelligent reader. Each has been constructed and edited by a recognized authority in the field.

The underlying purpose of the series is to meet the expectations of the thoughtful modern reader, one conscious of the striking change that has taken place in our view of the world. That change has run counter to parochialism. It recognizes the contribution made by thinkers and prose artists of the Orient as well as the Occident, of those who use languages other than English. Hence *World* Treasuries.

The series is planned to cover a great variety of fields, from the life sciences to religious thought, from science fiction to love stories to mystery and detection, and will be issued over the next several years.

Clifton Fadiman
General Editor

Preface

As a scholar who has devoted most of his research and writing for more than forty years to the history of religious thought in far earlier centuries, I have, I must confess, found it a bit daunting to put together a volume with such a presumptuous-sounding title as *The World Treasury of Modern Religious Thought*. Not only are the criteria of selection for the modern period considerably more elusive than they are for ancient Christianity or the Middle Ages or the Reformation, but the need to bring the time limits of the material down to the present day necessarily meant that some of my own teachers, friends, and colleagues would suddenly become part of a book for which I was responsible. The exponential increase in the sheer amount of such material during the nineteenth and twentieth centuries complicates the problem still further: it is probably accurate to estimate that in any given decade of these two centuries more was written about religion in German scholarship alone than had been produced in an entire century of the early church. No one can claim to have read even all the monuments of modern religious thought, not to mention the literally thousands of less celebrated works, in which there may well be lurking some gems for such a "treasury" as this.

Inevitably, everyone will have certain favorite authors, and certain favorite articles or chapters by those authors, whose absence from these pages will be surprising, if not indeed shocking. I know that this is true of me. There are at least a dozen pieces of modern religious thought — several of them, as I have suggested, by my own teachers, friends, and colleagues, together with other classics by other thinkers — that I deeply cherish and that, if someone else had been editing the book, I would have expected to find in it; and I probably would have complained if I could not find them here. Yet I have not been able to include them, because of the constrictions of space or the restrictions of copyright or both. Even in those that are included, moreover, I have sometimes felt obliged to select certain passages on the basis of their appropriateness to this book. On the other hand, as I have been telling myself, the sheer plethora of material has helped to assure the happy result that while not every treasure could get in, every essay that did get in is, in some sense, a genuine treasure.

The obligation to make this treasury a world treasury, as its title promises, has further complicated my task as its editor. For although I have, I suppose, ranged more widely in my own studies than some of my colleagues have, it is on the history of Christian doctrine through the centuries that I have concentrated, as is evident in my recently completed five-volume lifework, *The Christian Tradition: A History of the Development of Doctrine.* This concentration has, of course, required me to come to terms historically with the relations between Christian doctrine and other traditions, particularly the Jewish and the Greco-Roman (and, in some periods, the Muslim), all of which have decisively affected the development of Christian doctrine, and in a positive as well as in a negative way. Nevertheless, there is no gainsaying that I do know the history of other faiths chiefly through the work of other scholars and not firsthand. Fortunately, I have had the opportunity to draw on the work of such scholars, not merely for these texts themselves but for the identification of the texts in the first place. Among the many scholars who have generously shared with me their expertise in modern religious thought, I must mention at least (in alphabetical order): Charles J. Adams, Julia Ching, Joseph Mitsuo Kitagawa, and Hajime Nakamura. I have considered all of their nominations seriously, even though, for the reasons already stated, I have finally been obliged to leave out some of their (and my) favorites.

The experience of crossing these ancient and formidable boundaries, even with the kind of diplomatic passport that scholarship provides, has impressed me yet again with the urgency for our own time of relating the particularity of each of the several traditions to the universality of the one true God. It has also made me recognize that, within the Christian tradition that I study, I myself have always been drawn most to those thinkers whose faith in the universality of the one true God has compelled them, in one way or another, to say Both/And rather than Either/Or in speaking about other traditions. And at a time when extremists on both sides seem to be insisting to us that our choice today lies between a religious conviction that leads to persecution and a religious toleration that is based on skepticism, I find myself looking instead for a definition of toleration that is based on religious conviction rather than on theological (or antitheological) indifference; and I find that in each of the major traditions there are positive resources for just such a definition. It is my hope and earnest prayer that *The World Treasury of Modern Religious Thought* may make its own modest contribution to that urgent need.

It remains only to thank my colleagues in the publishing world for their encouragement and support: the original publishers of the selections, from all parts of the world, as listed in the acknowledgments at the end of the book; Clifton Fadiman (whose translation of Nietzsche I read as a student); and the editors at Little, Brown and Book-of-the-Month Club, Ellen Denison and Maron L. Waxman.

The World Treasury of
Modern Religious Thought

Introduction

Eᴀᴄʜ of the five key terms in the title of this *World Treasury of Modern Religious Thought* has decisively shaped the book, and taken together they perform the function of defining its content and purpose.

To begin with the most equivocal of them, the term *religious* as used here refers to what has been defined as "the experience of the Holy" or as "ultimate concern." Regrettably, but also unavoidably, we often tend to interpret so basic a phenomenon of human life as religion on the basis of our own traditions and of our personal relation to them. To someone who stands in the tradition of Judeo-Christian monotheism, for example, it may seem obvious that religion presupposes a revelation from the one true and transcendent god (or God), as that revelation has been enshrined in a holy book (or Bible) and maintained by a sacred community (or Church). But in fact most religions in human history have worshiped more than one god and have not ascribed that sort of metaphysical transcendence to any of these gods, while some have worshiped no god at all. Many of them, moreover, do not have either a holy book or a sacred community or a historical revelation, at least not in the sense in which Western religious thought has conventionally understood these concepts. Yet almost everyone would agree that it would be cultural snobbery of the most egregious sort to conclude from the absence of one or more of these elements that these movements and traditions are not entitled to be called religious.

At the same time, the term *religion* as it is being used here is exclusive as well as inclusive. Not everything that religious people say or do is automatically to be labeled religious. Especially misleading is the widespread tendency to suppose, simply because of the centrality of concepts like "law" and "love" in many religions, that the essential content of any religion is its code of conduct, and thus to use religion and morality interchangeably: to "get religion" during the revivals on the American frontier often meant little else than to take the pledge of total abstinence from alcohol. While it is true that an external religious observance that has no effect on moral behavior and on society has evoked the denunciation of the religious prophets of many traditions, including Martin Luther King's unforgettable "Letter from Birmingham City Jail," it is quite possible for someone to be morally upright without any specifically religious faith or devotion, as, to name only one modern example from among many, both the life and the thought of Sigmund Freud showed. The converse of the confusion between religion and morality is the habit of calling any vague sentiment "religious," just as long as the feeling is intensely subjective and somehow satisfying. At least as it is being used here, religion does involve a reverence for someone or something as holy or sacred. Sacred things, sacred places, sacred times, sacred persons, sacred actions, sacred meals — the variety of these and other objects of reverence seems to be almost infinite in the history of religions. But what they all have in common is the identification of something or someone as hallowed or set apart from the ordinary and common-place. As applied to the decision about what to include in this book, then, this definition implies that one component of any selection must be that it refer, implicitly or explicitly, to the sacred dimension of life and reality.

It must also belong to the genre of religious *thought*. It is probably undeniable that nothing is more authentically and universally religious, as we are using the term here, than the language of prayer (despite the great variety of the ways in which people pray). For the purposes of this book, however, what qualifies for inclusion is not a particular prayer, for example the Vedic hymns of Hinduism or the Lord's Prayer in Christianity, but reflective thought about prayer, like the essay of Friedrich Heiler printed here. Reflective thought, in turn, should help to illumine the particular prayers by relating them to the individual and corporate experience of the Holy and by placing them into the context of prayer across the whole spectrum of the religions, from the prayer wheel of the Eastern religions to the "Jesus prayer" of the Greek Orthodox monks on Mount Athos to the silent prayer and "inner light" of the Quakers. There is a kind of dialectic between religious worship and religious thought, by which each influences the other and acts as a check upon its excesses. Critical thought can be a means of rescuing worship from superstition and formalism, while participation in concrete acts of devotion and liturgical worship can help to prevent the reflections of the intellectual or the speculations of the scholar from being "sicklied o'er with the pale cast of thought."

The most formal and technical kind of religious thought is that which we associate with theology. Although it has sometimes been asserted categorically that only Christianity has produced a technical theology, this assertion is refuted by the mass of literature, coming out of the several religious traditions, for which "theology" is the only appropriate term. Sarvepalli Radhakrishnan's "Mysticism and Ethics in Hindu Thought," taken from his book *Eastern Religions and Western Thought,* would certainly seem to qualify as theology by any reasonable definition. For religious thought to be theological in the sense implied here, there must ordinarily exist a structured religious community with an identifiable tradition of witness, worship, and reflection. Theology serves that community not only when it provides the curriculum for the training of its future professional leaders, but even more when it critically examines the apparent contradictions within the tradition and proposes a resolution of them. Because the theological deposit left by earlier generations is sometimes our only means of access to their faith and life as a whole, the data it provides can be indispensable to an understanding of how the faith and life have developed also among ordinary believers. Even where that is not the case, moreover, the theologian's strenuous insistence upon clarity can make a work of systematic theology a key to the deeper meaning beyond the conventional interpretations that have been based upon the institutions and structures, the postures and gestures, and the words and actions of almost any religious tradition.

Even where it enjoys privileged status, however, theology does not hold a monopoly on religious thought. Somewhere behind almost every theological issue looms a philosophical question, and the two are often so closely intertwined that the facile distinction between theology and philosophy seems to break down. Are Confucius and Plato among ancient thinkers, or Maimonides and Thomas Aquinas among medieval thinkers, or Alfred North Whitehead and Martin Buber among modern thinkers, to be classified as theologians or as philosophers? The right answer would seem to be "Yes," for each of them was both. An anthology laying claim to the title of religious thought must therefore cast its net much more widely than the circle of the professional theologians, so that a seminal article like "The Will to Believe" by William James can stand right alongside essays by orthodox theologians who would not have had anything to do with William James could they have helped it. The other major source of religious thought, beyond both theology and the philosophy of religion, is comparative religion (now usually called the history of religions), which is in its present form a creation of the nineteenth and twentieth centuries. For if religion is to be defined as we are defining it, religious thought must include not only the thought, whether philosophical or theological, about a particular religious tradition by those who stand within it, but also the thought of scholars, historians, and anthropologists about those religious traditions that have not produced systematic reflections on their own. These include not only the earlier stages of some religions in which theology eventually did arise, but especially those earlier developments to which, not without a touch of condescension, we ordinarily apply such terms as "primitive religion" and "magic." An especially provocative example of scholarly thought about primitive religious phenomena is the chapter excerpted here from Jane Ellen Harrison's *Prolegomena to the Study of Greek Religion,* in which a brilliant modern scholar combined technical philology with a sensitivity to ritual in an examination of the latent religious presuppositions of the familiar and, as read by many previous critics, supposedly not very religious monuments of ancient Greek philosophy and drama.

A further stipulation provided by the title is that the religious thought be *modern.* It is by no means as obvious as many of our contemporaries seem to suppose that what is modern is necessarily superior to what is ancient. That supposition is probably true in the case of medical care or the means of transportation and communication, but as various of these essays suggest, the argument in favor of "newer is better" is much more difficult to make when one compares, say, the genius of Saint Augustine, who died in 430 C.E., with the system of any other Western religious thinker, regardless of denomination or theological position, during the fifteen centuries since Augustine. The grounds for concentrating on modern religious thought here, consequently, do not lie in a simplistic theory of inevitable progress. On the contrary, they are to be sought precisely in the recognition that there has not been unilinear progress and that in our religious thought we moderns in both the East and the West are in many ways living off our inheritance without adding as much to the principal as we are taking down from it. Yet for that very reason, those who have shared our existential situation and who have sought to come to terms with it in a sensitive and informed way may have something special to say to us about the problems of religious thought in the context of modern culture.

The chronological boundaries of modernity are notoriously difficult to fix, and the task has not been made any easier now that many observers have begun to speak about the present as a "postmodern era." In computer science, this week's latest memory chip seems to make all previous hardware and software obsolete and therefore "premodern," while in certain academic circles the time limits go back considerably further: the late M. David Knowles was Regius Professor of *Modern* History at Cambridge University, although his field of scholarly concentration was the history of monasticism during the Middle Ages, because in the rather quaint nomenclature of Cambridge whatever history was not "ancient" had to be "modern." For the purpose of understanding religious thought, it would appear to be a defensible procedure to define modernity as the period since the Enlightenment of the seventeenth and eighteenth centuries and hence to make the modern era roughly equivalent to the nineteenth and twentieth centuries.

For if the Enlightenment was, in the celebrated definition of Immanuel Kant, "the exodus of humanity from its self-imposed tutelage," nowhere was the tutelage more comprehensive or the exodus more traumatic than in the area of religious thought. Daring to think for oneself about the issues of ultimate concern — about God, free will, and immortality, to use Kant's own triad — set the thinkers of the Enlightenment and their disciples apart from their predecessors as perhaps no other feature of modern thought has done. Their break with the religious past had as one of its standard corollaries the search for a "natural theology," the assigned theme of the celebrated Gifford Lectures in Scotland (which several of our authors have delivered): an interpretation of the nature and destiny of the world that did not depend on the particular beliefs of any one historic religious system but could be abstracted from one or more of them as common to them all. The missionary enterprise was to yield to mutual understanding and toleration, competition was to be replaced by cooperation and sharing. This has increasingly been the setting within which all the religions of the world have had to function in the modern age, whatever their own positions might be. And when they have not faced anticlericalism and downright persecution, they have confronted the even more deadly peril of indifference and deliberate ignorance. Not only their answers but their questions have been deemed irrelevant, and they have had to redefine themselves in fundamental ways. "Is Religion Possible?" is the original title of the essay by the distinguished Muslim philosopher Muhammad Iqbal presented here, and *The Reconstruction of Religious Thought* is the original title of the book from which it is taken. He was speaking for believers from every tradition of religious thought in asking that question and in looking to tradition — and at the same time beyond tradition — for the possibilities of reconstruction.

Increasingly, believers of every tradition have found themselves sharing the predicament of fellow believers who stand in other traditions, which is why the term *world* is indispensable not only to the title of this collection but to its contents. Religious belief is notorious for encouraging a sense of "us" against "them" and for producing a narrowness of perspective, as the etymology of our English word "parochialism" (from the Greek and then the Latin original of the word "parish") suggests. The convictions that religion fosters and the sense of a particular community that it inculcates can quickly become a wall of separation. Therefore the words of the hypocrite in the New Testament, "God, I thank thee that I am not as other men are," are, unfortunately, a prayer that has been uttered, or at any rate felt, everywhere. Yet the very recognition of how universal this kind of parochialism is can itself become the beginning of wisdom — but only if it leads to a serious attempt at understanding and respecting the religious faith of others. More than any other period in world history, the modern era has been the time when this attempt at understanding and respect has claimed the attention of thoughtful people everywhere, even as the modern era, including its most recent decades, has been a time when the failure to understand and to respect the religious faith of others has continued to be a major cause of hatred and bloodshed.

One of the most important by-products of the modern quest for religious understanding has been the work of scholars dedicated to making the major religious traditions of the world accessible to those who could not read the ancient languages in which those traditions are enshrined. The fifty-one volumes of *The Sacred Books of the East,* published in England by Friedrich Max Müller of Oxford between 1879 and 1910, were the most massive example of this labor of editing and translating, but they were part of a general movement that has found acceptance everywhere during the nineteenth and twentieth centuries. Anyone who has ever undertaken the translation of a sacred text can testify, in Max Müller's words, "how almost impossible it is to find in English a sufficient number of nouns and adjectives to render the superabundant diction" of another religious language (in this case, Sanskrit). It is a formidable assignment to select equivalents in one language, shaped by one religious tradition, for the central terms of another language and another religious tradition; philology and philosophy but also dogmatism and prejudice will play a part in that process of selection. For reasons that lie deep in the cultural, political, and commercial history of the colonialist and Christian West, the great bulk of such translating and interpreting of the world religions has been done in Western countries and into Western languages. Except for missionary literature by Westerners using native vernaculars, the volume of Asian or African publication on Western religious traditions has been comparatively small, at least until the past two or three generations. The lopsided balance of trade suggested by that situation has inevitably made itself evident in the table of contents of this volume as well, where perforce works by Western thinkers (even about Eastern topics) tend to predominate — although the ratio of Western to non-Western writers, and for that matter of male to female writers, is probably significantly lower here than it would be in most library card catalogs. One ironic result of this trend in the history of scholarship has been that students who themselves stood in the tradition of a non-Western religion have frequently been obliged to learn French or German or English if they wanted to understand even their own sacred scriptures in a historical and critical way.

Another result, however, is that there exists in these Western languages, including English, a very substantial body of scholarly literature on which Western students of the world religions — and Western readers of this volume — are able to draw. Those religions that have no canon of sacred scripture, perhaps not even a written language at all, form a special case. Knowledge of them has been derived from the early accounts of Western explorers, who were succeeded by Western missionaries, who have been succeeded in turn by Western anthropologists. Each set of foreign observers has superimposed upon those "primitive" cultures a different set of presuppositions and has, not surprisingly, found the presuppositions confirmed in those cultures. As recent debates among anthropologists indicate, this has been no less true of social scientists than it was of evangelists, and modern readers have properly learned to be wary. Yet several selections in this volume show how unwarranted it would be to conclude from this that the efforts of Western thinkers and scholars to understand non-Western and non-literary religions are nothing more than "Eurocentric" theological narcissism. Interpreters of these religions from within have frequently testified, for example, how helpful the analyses of Mircea Eliade have been in their own quest for self-understanding. As his researches also suggest, it is necessary, even and especially in a modern age that regards itself as secular, to try to understand, as though from the inside, the systems of belief and practice cherished by our fellow inhabitants of the globe.

To that end, this volume has been designed to be a *treasury*. From the vast body of existing literature on religious thought produced in the modern world, we have intended to select several dozen passages that can, for one reason or another, be called classic statements. The opening passage, "The Grand Inquisitor," from Dostoyevsky's *Brothers Karamazov,* is a classic in several senses of that overworked label. As it happens, it also formulates dramatically most of the major issues involved in any consideration of religious thought in the nineteenth and twentieth centuries, documenting both the language of the believer and the questions of the skeptic with force and authenticity. Therefore it introduces the various themes of the volume as perhaps no other text could have done. Partly because it contains echoes of Dostoyevsky but chiefly because it summarizes many of these same themes in a powerful and innovative voice of its own, the closing selection, Aleksandr Solzhenitsyn's Nobel Lecture on Literature, "Beauty Will Save the World," seems appropriate as the other "bookend." But the criteria involved in determining what should appear in this *World Treasury of Modern Religious Thought* are complex.

Some of the passages are included because they are representative of the religious thought of an author whose distinction in an important dimension of modernity makes such a statement of ultimate concern particularly striking. What Albert Einstein thought about God, religion, and the universe stands out from similar statements by others, simply because of Einstein's towering position as a scientist in the history of the modern effort to understand the central forces in the universe. Seyyed Hossein Nasr's discussion of the Prophet and prophetic religion, which is devoted to *the* Prophet as confessed and honored in Islam, illustrates a second criterion, more operative in selecting some passages than others: the representative character of the statement as a guide to the religious tradition in which the author stood or about which the author wrote. This does not imply some kind of "Noah's ark" principle of picking two from each species, but it does imply that to be a world treasury, such a collection as this, edited and published in the West though it certainly is, must make a point of doing justice to traditions that are non-Western. Conversely, also those passages chosen principally for their representative confessional character must manage at the same time to speak in an accent to which those outside that tradition can somehow resonate. Abraham Heschel's "The Spirit of Judaism" is unmistakably a Jewish essay, and yet those who adhere to another faith or to no faith at all can read it with sympathy or even with empathy; and the "visions of the other world" described in *Black Elk Speaks* became the best possible source for the title of our entire section on mysticism and the vision of God.

In the case of other passages, it has been their eloquence and beauty as literary statements of religious faith and thought that has determined their inclusion; thus both at the beginning and at the end of the book, and within each of the eight sections of the book as well, the poets and the men and women of letters have been encouraged to have their say. That criterion applies not only to the haunting lines of "God's Grandeur" by the Jesuit poet Gerard Manley Hopkins, but to such pieces as Rabindranath Tagore's "The Four Stages of Life" and "The Unbeliever" by Albert Camus. There are also some selections that have been included because the scholarship of their author makes them deserving of consideration even by someone who does not share their outlook. The stature of Adolf von Harnack as probably the most influential historian of Christianity in the modern era gives his proposals about what constitutes "the essence of Christianity" additional force. Sometimes it has been the ethical authority, not the scholarly credentials, of the author, that argued for a particular passage; so it was, for example, with the paragraphs culled from Mahatma Gandhi's autobiography, which carry the weight of his remarkable moral force and of his dynamic personality. Gandhi's standing as a public figure certainly adds interest to his reflections on the relation between the several religions of India. Something similar is true of the piece by Dietrich Bonhoeffer, who was martyred for his part in a plot to assassinate Adolf Hitler.

Thus the paths by which these authors have come to this anthology are almost (but not quite) as diverse as the paths by which the several religious faiths of humanity have traveled in their quest for God. For readers who themselves are still engaged in that existential quest, as most of us are, these testimonies may serve as a source of instruction and encouragement from fellow pilgrims who are likewise still on the way. Conversely, for readers to whom the very idea of that quest is no more than an "illusion" or at best the confession of a "failure of nerve," this anthology may provide data about the puzzling question of why such antiquated modes of thought should continue to retain such a hold on so many of our contemporaries. And those readers, if any, who cannot understand why there should have to be any quest at all for the answers about which they themselves and their own tradition are so invincibly certain will surely find many of these selections initially disturbing. But even they should be enlightened and edified by the sheer variety and depth of this search for "the unknown god"; and perhaps eventually they, too, will come to acknowledge the fellowship, across historic lines of separation, of a communion of saints transcending theological divisions in the mystery of the One and the All.

F. M. DOSTOYEVSKY

The Grand Inquisitor

Fyodor Mikhaylovich Dostoyevsky (1821–1881) devoted his entire life as a writer to probing the depths of human misery and grandeur. His last great novel, *The Brothers Karamazov,* sounds the themes of faith and doubt, of decadence and nobility, in counterpoint, and nowhere more provocatively than in Ivan Karamazov's parable, "The Grand Inquisitor."

"AND BEHOLD, He deigned to appear for a moment to the people, to the tortured, suffering people, sunk in iniquity, but loving Him like children. My story is laid in Spain, in Seville, in the most terrible time of the Inquisition, when fires were lighted every day to the glory of God, and 'in the splendid *auto da fé* the wicked heretics were burnt.' Oh, of course, this was not the coming in which He will appear according to His promise at the end of time in all His heavenly glory, and which will be sudden 'as lightning flashing from east to west.' No, He visited His children only for a moment, and there where the flames were crackling round the heretics. In His infinite mercy He came once more among men in that human shape in which He walked among men for three years fifteen centuries ago. He came down to the 'hot pavement' of the southern town in which on the day before almost a hundred heretics had, *ad majorem gloriam Dei,* been burnt by the cardinal, the Grand Inquisitor, in a magnificent *auto da fé,* in the presence of the king, the court, the knights, the cardinals, the most charming ladies of the court, and the whole population of Seville.

"He came softly, unobserved, and yet, strange to say, every one recognised Him. That might be one of the best passages in the poem. I mean, why they recognised Him. The people are irresistibly drawn to Him, they surround Him, they flock about Him, follow Him. He moves silently in their midst with a gentle smile of infinite compassion. The sun of love burns in His heart, light and power shine from His eyes, and their radiance, shed on the people, stirs their hearts with responsive love. He holds out His hands to them, blesses them, and a healing virtue comes from contact with Him, even with His garments. An old man in the crowd, blind from childhood, cries out, 'O Lord, heal me and I shall see Thee!' and, as it were, scales fall from his eyes and the blind man sees Him. The crowd weeps and kisses the earth under His feet. Children throw flowers before Him, sing, and cry hosannah. 'It is He — it is He!' all repeat. 'It must be He, it can be no one but Him!' He stops at the steps of the Seville cathedral at the moment when the weeping mourners are bringing in a little open white coffin. In it lies a child of seven, the only daughter of a prominent citizen. The dead child lies hidden in flowers. 'He will raise your child,' the crowd shouts to the weeping mother. The priest, coming to meet the coffin, looks perplexed, and frowns, but the mother of the dead child throws herself at His feet with a wail. 'If it is Thou, raise my child!' she cries, holding out her hands to Him. The procession halts, the coffin is laid on the steps at His feet. He looks with compassion, and His lips once more softly pronounce, 'Maiden, arise!' and the maiden arises. The little girl sits up in the coffin and looks round, smiling with wide-open wondering eyes, holding a bunch of white roses they had put in her hand.

"There are cries, sobs, confusion among the people, and at that moment the cardinal himself, the Grand Inquisitor, passes by the cathedral. He is an old man, almost ninety, tall and erect, with a withered face and sunken eyes, in which there is still a gleam of light. He is not dressed in his gorgeous cardinal's robes, as he was the day before, when he was burning the enemies of the Roman Church — at that moment he was wearing his coarse, old, monk's cassock. At a distance behind him come his gloomy assistants and slaves and the 'holy guard.' He stops at the sight of the crowd and watches it from a distance. He sees everything; he sees them set the coffin down at His feet, sees the child rise up, and his face darkens. He knits his thick grey brows and his eyes gleam with a sinister fire. He holds out his finger and bids the guards take Him. And such is his power, so completely are the people cowed into submission and trembling obedience to him, that the crowd immediately make way for the guards, and in the midst of deathlike silence they lay hands on Him and lead Him away. The crowd instantly bows down to the

earth, like one man, before the old inquisitor. He blesses the people
in silence and passes on. The guards lead their prisoner to the close,
gloomy vaulted prison in the ancient palace of the Holy Inquisition
and shut Him in it. The day passes and is followed by the dark,
burning 'breathless' night of Seville. The air is 'fragrant with laurel
and lemon.' In the pitch darkness the iron door of the prison is
suddenly opened and the Grand Inquisitor himself comes in with a
light in his hand. He is alone; the door is closed at once behind
him. He stands in the doorway and for a minute or two gazes into
His face. At last he goes up slowly, sets the light on the table and
speaks.

" 'Is it Thou? Thou?' but receiving no answer, he adds at once, 'Don't
answer, be silent. What canst Thou say, indeed? I know too well
what Thou wouldst say. And Thou hast no right to add anything
to what Thou hadst said of old. Why, then, art Thou come to hinder
us? For Thou hast come to hinder us, and Thou knowest that. But dost
Thou know what will be to-morrow? I know not who Thou art and
care not to know whether it is Thou or only a semblance of Him, but
to-morrow I shall condemn Thee and burn Thee at the stake as the
worst of heretics. And the very people who have to-day kissed Thy feet,
to-morrow at the faintest sign from me will rush to heap up the embers
of Thy fire. Knowest Thou that? Yes, maybe Thou knowest it,' he
added with thoughtful penetration, never for a moment taking his eyes
off the Prisoner. . . .

" 'Hast Thou the right to reveal to us one of the mysteries of that
world from which Thou hast come?' my old man asks Him, and
answers the question for Him. 'No, Thou hast not; that Thou mayest
not add to what has been said of old, and mayest not take from men
the freedom which Thou didst exalt when Thou wast on earth.
Whatsoever Thou revealest anew will encroach on men's freedom of
faith; for it will be manifest as a miracle, and the freedom of their faith
was dearer to Thee than anything in those days fifteen hundred years
ago. Didst Thou not often say then, "I will make you free?" But now
Thou hast seen these "free" men,' the old man adds suddenly, with a
pensive smile. 'Yes, we've paid dearly for it,' he goes on, looking sternly
at Him, 'but at last we have completed that work in Thy name. For
fifteen centuries we have been wrestling with Thy freedom, but now
it is ended and over for good. Dost Thou not believe that it's over for
good? Thou lookest meekly at me and deignest not even to be wroth
with me. But let me tell Thee that now, to-day, people are more
persuaded than ever that they have perfect freedom, yet they have

brought their freedom to us and laid it humbly at our feet. But that has been our doing. Was this what Thou didst? Was this Thy freedom? . . .

" 'The wise and dread spirit, the spirit of self-destruction and non-existence,' the old man goes on, 'the great spirit talked with Thee in the wilderness, and we are told in the books that he "tempted" Thee. Is that so? And could anything truer be said than what he revealed to Thee in three questions and what Thou didst reject, and what in the books is called "the temptation"? And yet if there has ever been on earth a real stupendous miracle, it took place on that day, on the day of the three temptations. The statement of those three questions was itself the miracle. If it were possible to imagine simply for the sake of argument that those three questions of the dread spirit had perished utterly from the books, and that we had to restore them and to invent them anew, and to do so had gathered together all the wise men of the earth — rulers, chief priests, learned men, philosophers, poets — and had set them the task to invent three questions, such as would not only fit the occasion, but express in three words, three human phrases, the whole future history of the world and of humanity — dost Thou believe that all the wisdom of the earth united could have invented anything in depth and force equal to the three questions which were actually put to Thee then by the wise and mighty spirit in the wilderness? From those questions alone, from the miracle of their statement, we can see that we have here to do not with the fleeting human intelligence, but with the absolute and eternal. For in those three questions the whole subsequent history of mankind is, as it were, brought together into one whole, and foretold, and in them are united all the unsolved historical contradictions of human nature. At the time it could not be so clear, since the future was unknown; but now that fifteen hundred years have passed, we see that everything in those three questions was so justly divined and foretold, and has been so truly fulfilled, that nothing can be added to them or taken from them.

" 'Judge Thyself who was right — Thou or he who questioned Thee then? Remember the first question; its meaning, in other words, was this:"Thou wouldst go into the world, and art going with empty hands, with some promise of freedom which men in their simplicity and their natural unruliness cannot even understand, which they fear and dread — for nothing has ever been more insupportable for a man and a human society than freedom. But seest Thou these stones in this parched and barren wilderness? Turn them into bread, and mankind will run after Thee like a flock of sheep, grateful and obedient, though for ever trembling, lest Thou withdraw Thy hand and deny them Thy bread." But Thou wouldst not deprive man of freedom and didst reject the offer, thinking, what is that freedom worth, if obedience is bought with bread? Thou didst reply that man lives not by bread alone. But dost Thou know that for the sake of that earthly bread the spirit of the earth will rise up against Thee and will strive with Thee and overcome Thee, and all will follow him, crying, "Who can compare with this beast? He has given us fire from heaven!" Dost Thou know that the ages will pass, and humanity will proclaim by the lips of their sages that there is no crime, and therefore no sin; there is only hunger? "Feed men, and then ask of them virtue!" that's what they'll write on the banner, which they will raise against Thee, and with which they will destroy Thy temple. Where Thy temple stood will rise a new building; the terrible tower of Babel will be built again, and though, like the one of old, it will not be finished, yet Thou mightest have prevented that new tower and have cut short the sufferings of men for a thousand years; for they will come back to us after a thousand years of agony with their tower. They will seek us again, hidden underground in the catacombs, for we shall be again persecuted and tortured. They will find us and cry to us, "Feed us, for those who have promised us fire from heaven haven't given it!" And then we shall finish building their tower, for he finishes the building who feeds them. And we alone shall feed them in Thy name, declaring falsely that it is in Thy name. Oh, never, never can they feed themselves without us! No science will give them bread so long as they remain free. In the end they will lay their freedom at our feet, and say to us, "Make us your slaves, but feed us." They will understand themselves, at last, that freedom and bread enough for all are inconceivable together, for never, never will they be able to share between them! They will be convinced, too, that they can never be free, for they are weak, vicious, worthless and rebellious. Thou didst promise them the bread of Heaven, but, I repeat again, can it compare with earthly bread in the eyes of the weak, ever sinful and ignoble race of man? And if for the sake of the bread of Heaven thousands and tens of thousands shall follow Thee, what is to become of the millions and tens of thousands of millions of creatures who will not have the strength to forego the earthly bread for the sake of the heavenly? Or dost Thou care only for the tens of thousands of the great and strong, while the millions, numerous as the sands of the sea, who are weak but love Thee, must exist only for the sake of the great and strong? No, we care for the weak too. They are sinful and rebellious, but in the end they too will become obedient. They will marvel at us and look on us as gods, because we are ready to endure the freedom

which they have found so dreadful and to rule over them — so awful
it will seem to them to be free. But we shall tell them that we are Thy
servants and rule them in Thy name. We shall deceive them again, for
we will not let Thee come to us again. That deception will be our
suffering, for we shall be forced to lie.

" 'This is the significance of the first question in the wilderness, and
this is what Thou hast rejected for the sake of that freedom which
Thou hast exalted above everything. Yet in this question lies hid the
great secret of this world. Choosing "bread," Thou wouldst have
satisfied the universal and everlasting craving of humanity — to find
some one to worship. So long as man remains free he strives for
nothing so incessantly and so painfully as to find some one to worship.
But man seeks to worship what is established beyond dispute, so that
all men would agree at once to worship it. For these pitiful creatures
are concerned not only to find what one or the other can worship, but
to find something that all would believe in and worship; what is
essential is that all may be *together* in it. This craving for *community*
of worship is the chief misery of every man individually and of all
humanity from the beginning of time. For the sake of common
worship they've slain each other with the sword. They have set up gods
and challenged one another, "Put away your gods and come and
worship ours, or we will kill you and your gods!" And so it will be to
the end of the world, even when gods disappear from the earth; they
will fall down before idols just the same. Thou didst know, Thou
couldst not but have known, this fundamental secret of human nature,
but Thou didst reject the one infallible banner which was offered Thee
to make all men bow down to Thee alone — the banner of earthly
bread; and Thou hast rejected it for the sake of freedom and the bread
of Heaven. Behold what Thou didst further. And all again in the name
of freedom! I tell Thee that man is tormented by no greater anxiety
than to find some one quickly to whom he can hand over that gift of
freedom with which the ill-fated creature is born. But only one who
can appease their conscience can take over their freedom. In bread
there was offered Thee an invincible banner; give bread, and man will
worship Thee, for nothing is more certain than bread. But if some one
else gains possession of his conscience — oh! then he will cast away
Thy bread and follow after him who has ensnared his conscience. In
that Thou wast right. For the secret of man's being is not only to live
but to have something to live for. Without a stable conception of the
object of life, man would not consent to go on living, and would rather
destroy himself than remain on earth, though he had bread in abun-

dance. That is true. But what happened? Instead of taking men's freedom from them, Thou didst make it greater than ever! Didst Thou forget that man prefers peace, and even death, to freedom of choice in the knowledge of good and evil? Nothing is more seductive for man than his freedom of conscience, but nothing is a greater cause of suffering. And behold, instead of giving a firm foundation for setting the conscience of man at rest for ever, Thou didst choose all that is exceptional, vague and enigmatic; Thou didst choose what was utterly beyond the strength of men, acting as though Thou didst not love them at all — Thou who didst come to give Thy life for them! Instead of taking possession of men's freedom, Thou didst increase it, and burdened the spiritual kingdom of mankind with its sufferings for ever. Thou didst desire man's free love, that he should follow Thee freely, enticed and taken captive by Thee. In place of the rigid ancient law, man must hereafter with free heart decide for himself what is good and what is evil, having only Thy image before him as his guide. But didst Thou not know he would at last reject even Thy image and Thy truth, if he is weighed down with the fearful burden of free choice? They will cry aloud at last that the truth is not in Thee, for they could not have been left in greater confusion and suffering than Thou hast caused, laying upon them so many cares and unanswerable problems.

" 'So that, in truth, Thou didst Thyself lay the foundation for the destruction of Thy kingdom, and no one is more to blame for it. Yet what was offered Thee? There are three powers, three powers alone, able to conquer and to hold captive for ever the conscience of these impotent rebels for their happiness — those forces are miracle, mystery and authority. Thou hast rejected all three and hast set the example for doing so. When the wise and dread spirit set Thee on the pinnacle of the temple and said to Thee, "If Thou wouldst know whether Thou art the Son of God then cast Thyself down, for it is written: the angels shall hold him up lest he fall and bruise himself, and Thou shalt know then whether Thou art the Son of God and shalt prove then how great is Thy faith in Thy Father." But Thou didst refuse and wouldst not cast Thyself down. Oh! of course, Thou didst proudly and well, like God; but the weak, unruly race of men, are they gods? Oh, Thou didst know then that in taking one step, in making one movement to cast Thyself down, Thou wouldst be tempting God and have lost all Thy faith in Him, and wouldst have been dashed to pieces against that earth which Thou didst come to save. And the wise spirit that tempted Thee would have rejoiced. But I ask again, are there many like Thee? And couldst Thou believe for one moment that men, too, could face such a temptation? Is the nature of men such, that they can reject miracle, and at the great moments of their life, the moments of their deepest, most agonising spiritual difficulties, cling only to the free verdict of the heart? Oh, Thou didst know that Thy deed would be recorded in books, would be handed down to remote times and the utmost ends of the earth, and Thou didst hope that man, following Thee, would cling to God and not ask for a miracle. But Thou didst not know that when man rejects miracle he rejects God too; for man seeks not so much God as the miraculous. And as man cannot bear to be without the miraculous, he will create new miracles of his own for himself, and will worship deeds of sorcery and witchcraft, though he might be a hundred times over a rebel, heretic and infidel. Thou didst not come down from the Cross when they shouted to Thee, mocking and reviling Thee, "Come down from the cross and we will believe that Thou art He." Thou didst not come down, for again Thou wouldst not enslave man by a miracle, and didst crave faith given freely, not based on miracle. Thou didst crave for free love and not the base raptures of the slave before the might that has overawed him for ever. But Thou didst think too highly of men therein, for they are slaves, of course, though rebellious by nature. Look round and judge; fifteen centuries have passed, look upon them. Whom hast Thou raised up to Thyself? I swear, man is weaker and baser by nature than Thou hast believed him! Can he, can he do what Thou didst? By showing him so much respect, Thou didst, as it were, cease to feel for him, for Thou didst ask far too much from him — Thou who hast loved him more than Thyself! Respecting him less, Thou wouldst have asked less of him. That would have been more like love, for his burden would have been lighter. He is weak and vile. What though he is everywhere now rebelling against our power, and proud of his rebellion? It is the pride of a child and a schoolboy. They are little children rioting and barring out the teacher at school. But their childish delight will end; it will cost them dear. They will cast down temples and drench the earth with blood. But they will see at last, the foolish children, that, though they are rebels, they are impotent rebels, unable to keep up their own rebellion. Bathed in their foolish tears, they will recognise at last that He who created them rebels must have meant to mock at them. They will say this in despair, and their utterance will be a blasphemy which will make them more unhappy still, for man's nature cannot bear blasphemy, and in the end always avenges it on itself. And so unrest, confusion and unhappiness — that is the present lot of man after Thou didst bear so much for their

freedom! Thy great prophet tells in vision and in image, that he saw
all those who took part in the first resurrection and that there were of
each tribe twelve thousand. But if there were so many of them, they
must have been not men but gods. They had borne Thy cross, they
had endured scores of years in the barren, hungry wilderness, living
upon locusts and roots — and Thou mayest indeed point with pride
at those children of freedom, of free love, of free and splendid sacrifice
for Thy name. But remember that they were only some thousands; and
what of the rest? And how are the other weak ones to blame, because
they could not endure what the strong have endured? How is the
weak soul to blame that it is unable to receive such terrible gifts? Canst
Thou have simply come to the elect and for the elect? But if so, it
is a mystery and we cannot understand it. And if it is a mystery, we
too have a right to preach a mystery, and to teach them that it's not
the free judgment of their hearts, not love that matters, but a mystery
which they must follow blindly, even against their conscience. So we
have done. We have corrected Thy work and have founded it upon
miracle, mystery and *authority*. And men rejoiced that they were again
led like sheep, and that the terrible gift that had brought them such
suffering, was, at last, lifted from their hearts. Were we right teaching
them this? Speak! Did we not love mankind, so meekly acknowledging their feebleness, lovingly lightening their burden, and permitting
their weak nature even sin with our sanction? Why hast Thou come
now to hinder us? And why dost Thou look silently and searchingly
at me with Thy mild eyes? Be angry. I don't want Thy love, for I love
Thee not. And what use is it for me to hide anything from Thee? Don't
I know to Whom I am speaking? All that I can say is known to Thee
already. And is it for me to conceal from Thee our mystery? Perhaps
it is Thy will to hear it from my lips. Listen, then. We are not working
with Thee, but with *him* — that is our mystery. It's long — eight
centuries — since we have been on *his* side and not on Thine. Just
eight centuries ago, we took from him what Thou didst reject with
scorn, that last gift he offered Thee, showing Thee all the kingdoms
of the earth. We took from him Rome and the sword of Caesar, and
proclaimed ourselves sole rulers of the earth, though hitherto we
have not been able to complete our work. But whose fault is that?
Oh, the work is only beginning, but it has begun. It has long to
await completion and the earth has yet much to suffer, but we shall
triumph and shall be Caesars, and then we shall plan the universal
happiness of man. But Thou mightest have taken even then the sword
of Caesar. Why didst Thou reject that last gift? Hadst Thou accepted

that last counsel of the mighty spirit, Thou wouldst have accomplished all that man seeks on earth — that is, some one to worship, some one to keep his conscience, and some means of uniting all in one unanimous and harmonious ant-heap, for the craving for universal unity is the third and last anguish of men. Mankind as a whole has always striven to organise a universal state. There have been many great nations with great histories, but the more highly they were developed the more unhappy they were, for they felt more acutely than other people the craving for worldwide union. The great conquerors, Timours and Ghenghis-Khans, whirled like hurricanes over the face of the earth striving to subdue its people, and they too were but the unconscious expression of the same craving for universal unity. Hadst Thou taken the world and Caesar's purple, Thou wouldst have founded the universal state and have given universal peace. For who can rule men if not he who holds their conscience and their bread in his hands? We have taken the sword of Caesar, and in taking it, of course, have rejected Thee and followed *him*. Oh, ages are yet to come of the confusion of free thought, of their science and cannibalism. For having begun to build their tower of Babel without us, they will end, of course, with cannibalism. But then the beast will crawl to us and lick our feet and spatter them with tears of blood. And we shall sit upon the beast and raise the cup, and on it will be written, "Mystery." But then, and only then, the reign of peace and happiness will come for men. Thou art proud of Thine elect, but Thou hast only the elect, while we give rest to all. And besides, how many of those elect, those mighty ones who could become elect, have grown weary waiting for Thee, and have transferred and will transfer the powers of their spirit and the warmth of their heart to the other camp, and end by raising their *free* banner against Thee. Thou didst Thyself lift up that banner. But with us all will be happy and will no more rebel nor destroy one another as under Thy freedom. Oh, we shall persuade them that they will only become free when they renounce their freedom to us and submit to us. And shall we be right or shall we be lying? They will be convinced that we are right, for they will remember the horrors of slavery and confusion to which Thy freedom brought them. Freedom, free thought and science, will lead them into such straits and will bring them face to face with such marvels and insoluble mysteries, that some of them, the fierce and rebellious, will destroy themselves, others, rebellious but weak, will destroy one another, while the rest, weak and unhappy, will crawl fawning to our feet and whine to us: "Yes, you were right, you alone possess His mystery, and we come back to you, save us from ourselves!"

" 'Receiving bread from us, they will see clearly that we take the bread made by their hands from them, to give it to them, without any miracle. They will see that we do not change the stones to bread, but in truth they will be more thankful for taking it from our hands than for the bread itself! For they will remember only too well that in old days, without our help, even the bread they made turned to stones in their hands, while since they have come back to us, the very stones have turned to bread in their hands. Too, too well they know the value of complete submission! And until men know that, they will be unhappy. Who is most to blame for their not knowing it, speak? Who scattered the flock and sent it astray on unknown paths? But the flock will come together again and will submit once more, and then it will be once for all. Then we shall give them the quiet humble happiness of weak creatures such as they are by nature. Oh, we shall persuade them at last not to be proud, for Thou didst lift them up and thereby taught them to be proud. We shall show them that they are weak, that they are only pitiful children, but that childlike happiness is the sweetest of all. They will become timid and will look to us and huddle close to us in fear, as chicks to the hen. They will marvel at us and will be awe-stricken before us, and will be proud at our being so powerful and clever, that we have been able to subdue such a turbulent flock of thousands of millions. They will tremble impotently before our wrath, their minds will grow fearful, they will be quick to shed tears like women and children, but they will be just as ready at a sign from us to pass to laughter and rejoicing, to happy mirth and childish song. Yes, we shall set them to work, but in their leisure hours we shall make their life like a child's game, with children's songs and innocent dance. Oh, we shall allow them even sin, they are weak and helpless, and they will love us like children because we allow them to sin. We shall tell them that every sin will be expiated, if it is done with our permission, that we allow them to sin because we love them, and the punishment for these sins we take upon ourselves. And we shall take it upon ourselves, and they will adore us as their saviours who have taken on themselves their sins before God. And they will have no secrets from us. We shall allow or forbid them to live with their wives and mis- tresses, to have or not to have children — according to whether they have been obedient or disobedient — and they will submit to us gladly and cheerfully. The most painful secrets of their conscience, all, all they will bring to us, and we shall have an answer for all. And they will be glad to believe our answer, for it will save them from the great anxiety and terrible agony they endure at present in making a free decision for themselves. And all will be happy, all the millions of creatures except the hundred thousand who rule over them. For only we, we who guard the mystery, shall be unhappy. There will be thousands of millions of happy babes, and a hundred thousand sufferers who have taken upon themselves the curse of the knowledge of good and evil. Peacefully they will die, peacefully they will expire in Thy name, and beyond the grave they will find nothing but death. But we shall keep the secret, and for their happiness we shall allure them with the reward of heaven and eternity. Though if there were anything in the other world, it certainly would not be for such as they. It is prophesied that Thou wilt come again in victory, Thou wilt come with Thy chosen, the proud and strong, but we will say that they have only saved themselves, but we have saved all. We are told that the harlot who sits upon the beast, and holds in her hands the *mystery*, shall be put to shame, that the weak will rise up again, and will rend her royal purple and will strip naked her loathsome body. But then I will stand up and point out to Thee the thousand millions of happy children who have known no sin. And we who have taken their sins upon us for their happiness will stand up before Thee and say: "Judge us if Thou canst and darest." Know that I fear Thee not. Know that I too have been in the wilderness, I too have lived on roots and locusts, I too prized the freedom with which Thou hast blessed men, and I too was striving to stand among Thy elect, among the strong and powerful, thirsting "to make up the number." But I awakened and would not serve madness. I turned back and joined the ranks of those *who have corrected Thy work*. I left the proud and went back to the humble, for the happiness of the humble. What I say to Thee will come to pass, and our dominion will be built up. I repeat, to-morrow Thou shalt see that obedient flock who at a sign from me will hasten to heap up the hot cinders about the pile on which I shall burn Thee for coming to hinder us. For if any one has ever deserved our fires, it is Thou. To-morrow I shall burn Thee. Dixi.' "

*   *   *   *   *

"When the Inquisitor ceased speaking he waited some time for his Prisoner to answer him. His silence weighed down upon him. He saw that the Prisoner had listened intently all the time, looking gently in his face and evidently not wishing to reply. The old man longed for Him to say something, however bitter and terrible. But

He suddenly approached the old man in silence and softly kissed him on his bloodless aged lips. That was all his answer. The old man shuddered. His lips moved. He went to the door, opened it, and said to Him: 'Go, and come no more. . . . come not at all, never, never!' And he let Him out into the dark alleys of the town. The Prisoner went away."

1 THE UNBELIEVER

If, as Robert Burns suggested, the ability to "see ourselves as others see us" is a gift from "some Power," religious faith during the modern period has been receiving that gift in generous supply. After many centuries of underground existence in the various religious cultures of the world, unbelief has acquired intellectual stature and social respectability. Thomas Aquinas in the Paris of the thirteenth century wrote a *Summa against the Gentiles* when there were very few "Gentiles" or "pagans" to be found in Europe, but the Paris of the nineteenth and twentieth centuries has acquired a reputation (unearned in part) as the seedbed of a new paganism. And in such traditionally religious cultures as Hindu India and Muslim Turkey, public figures and intellectuals have managed, practically with impunity, to confess their inability to affirm the traditional faith.

The perspective of the "unbeliever" on the traditional forms of belief has seldom been welcomed with any enthusiasm inside the communities of faith, but in spite of that it has provided an invaluable service to them. If one were to write the history of modern reform movements within the several world religions, the critical outsider would have to be accorded a substantial position in such a history. Sometimes the outsider has been a disenchanted former believer, sometimes a member of an alien group who has found all the systems of faith unacceptable. Because of the role that tradition plays in many religions, modern critics have also given considerable attention to the romanticism with which present-day believers tend to view their heritage of faith. In the harsh light of historical reality, many of those traditions emerge as far more ambiguous than they have been portrayed — or even as pious frauds. Probably the most powerful witness rendered by these unbelievers has been their pointing to the contradictions between profession and practice among religious people. But in the modern period that criticism has gone on to question the very fundamentals both of profession and of practice, by making public the unholy alliances between religious institutions and the structures of social oppression or by laying bare the false props that religious experience often provides for the self-deception of making the worse appear the better reason.

The immediate responses of believers, whether clergy or laity, have ranged from defensive to militant. Less obvious, but in the long run more important, has been the process by which such criticism has succeeded in making its point and thus has gained acceptance even within the ranks of the devout. For as Robert Burns also observed in the same context, the gift of seeing ourselves as others see us can free us "from many a blunder," and from many a "foolish notion" as well.

ALBERT CAMUS

The Unbeliever

Albert Camus (1913–1960) was born in Algeria but lived most of his life in France. His works include *The Stranger* and *The Plague*. Camus was the spokesman for an entire generation of intellectuals, both Eastern and Western, in his recognition that the conventional modern treatment of moral issues was no longer acceptable. In 1948 he was invited by the Dominican monks of Latour-Maubourg to address them on the topic "What Unbelievers Expect from Christians"; this essay was his response to that invitation.

INASMUCH as you have been so kind as to invite a man who does not share your convictions to come and answer the very general question that you are raising in these conversations, before telling you what I think unbelievers expect of Christians, I should like first to acknowledge your intellectual generosity by stating a few principles.

First, there is a lay pharisaism in which I shall strive not to indulge. To me a lay pharisee is the person who pretends to believe that Christianity is an easy thing and asks of the Christian, on the basis of an external view of Christianity, more than he asks of himself. I believe indeed that the Christian has many obligations but that it is not up to the man who rejects them himself to recall their existence to anyone who has already accepted them. If there is anyone who can ask anything of the Christian, it is the Christian himself. The conclusion is that if I allowed myself at the end of this statement to demand of you certain duties, these could only be duties that it is essential to ask of any man today, whether he is or is not a Christian.

Secondly, I wish to declare also that, not feeling that I possess any absolute truth or any message, I shall never start from the supposition that Christian truth is illusory, but merely from the fact that I could not accept it. As an illustration of this position, I am willing to confess this: Three years ago a controversy made me argue against one among you, and not the least formidable. The fever of those years, the painful memory of two or three friends assassinated had given me the courage to do so. Yet I can assure you that, despite some excessive expressions on the part of François Mauriac, I have not ceased meditating on what he said. At the end of this reflection — and in this way I give you my opinion as to the usefulness of the dialogue between believer and unbeliever — I have come to admit to myself, and now to admit publicly here, that for the fundamentals and on the precise point of our controversy François Mauriac got the better of me.

Having said that, it will be easier for me to state my third and last principle. It is simple and obvious. I shall not try to change anything that I think or anything that you think (insofar as I can judge of it) in order to reach a reconciliation that would be agreeable to all. On the contrary, what I feel like telling you today is that the world needs real dialogue, that falsehood is just as much the opposite of dialogue as is silence, and that the only possible dialogue is the kind between people who remain what they are and speak their minds. This is tantamount to saying that the world of today needs Christians who remain Christians. The other day at the Sorbonne, speaking to a Marxist lecturer, a Catholic priest said in public that he too was anticlerical. Well, I don't like priests who are anticlerical any more than philosophies that are ashamed of themselves. Hence I shall not, as far as I am concerned, try to pass myself off as a Christian in your presence. I share with you the same revulsion from evil. But I do not share your hope, and I continue to struggle against this universe in which children suffer and die.

*   *   *   *   *

And why shouldn't I say here what I have written elsewhere? For a long time during those frightful years I waited for a great voice to speak up in Rome. I, an unbeliever? Precisely. For I knew that the spirit would be lost if it did not utter a cry of condemnation when faced with force. It seems that that voice did speak up. But I assure you that millions of men like me did not hear it and that at that time believers and unbelievers alike shared a solitude that continued to spread as the days went by and the executioners multiplied.

It has been explained to me since that the condemnation was indeed voiced. But that it was in the style of the encyclicals, which is not at all clear. The condemnation was voiced and it was not understood! Who could fail to feel where the true condemnation lies in this case and to see that this example by itself gives part of the reply, perhaps the whole reply, that you ask of me. What the world expects of Christians is that Christians should speak out, loud and clear, and that they should voice their condemnation in such a way that never a doubt, never the slightest doubt, could rise in the heart of the simplest man. That they should get away from abstraction and confront the blood-stained face history has taken on today. The grouping we need is a grouping of men resolved to speak out clearly and to pay up personally. When a Spanish bishop blesses political executions, he ceases to be a bishop or a Christian or even a man; he is a dog just like the one who, backed by an ideology, orders that execution without doing the dirty work himself. We are still waiting, and I am waiting, for a grouping of all those who refuse to be dogs and are resolved to pay the price that must be paid so that man can be something more than a dog.

*   *   *   *   *

And now, what can Christians do for us?

To begin with, give up the empty quarrels, the first of which is the quarrel about pessimism. I believe, for instance, that M. Gabriel Marcel would be well advised to leave alone certain forms of thought that fascinate him and lead him astray. M. Marcel cannot call himself a democrat and at the same time ask for a prohibition of Sartre's play. This is a position that is tiresome for everyone. What M. Marcel wants is to defend absolute values, such as modesty and man's divine truth, when the things that should be defended are the few provisional values that will allow M. Marcel to continue fighting someday, and comfortably, for those absolute values. . . .

By what right, moreover, could a Christian or a Marxist accuse me, for example, of pessimism? I was not the one to invent the misery of the human being or the terrifying formulas of divine malediction. I was not the one to shout *Nemo bonus* or the damnation of unbaptized children. I was not the one who said that man was incapable of saving himself by his own means and that in the depths of his degradation his only hope was in the grace of God. And as for the famous Marxist optimism! No one has carried distrust of man further, and ultimately the economic fatalities of this universe seem more terrible than divine whims.

Christians and Communists will tell me that their optimism is based on a longer range, that it is superior to all the rest, and that God or history, according to the individual, is the satisfying end-product of their dialectic. I can indulge in the same reasoning. If Christianity is pessimistic as to man, it is optimistic as to human destiny. Well, I can say that, pessimistic as to human destiny, I am optimistic as to man. And not in the name of a humanism that always seemed to me to fall short, but in the name of an ignorance that tries to negate nothing.

This means that the words "pessimism" and "optimism" need to be clearly defined and that, until we can do so, we must pay attention to what unites us rather than to what separates us.

*   *   *   *   *

That, I believe, is all I had to say. We are faced with evil. And, as for me, I feel rather as Augustine did before becoming a Christian when he said: "I tried to find the source of evil and I got nowhere." But it is also true that I, and a few others, know what must be done, if not to reduce evil, at least not to add to it. Perhaps we cannot prevent this world from being a world in which children are tortured. But we can reduce the number of tortured children. And if you don't help us, who else in the world can help us do this?

Between the forces of terror and the forces of dialogue, a great unequal battle has begun. I have nothing but reasonable illusions as to the outcome of that battle. But I believe it must be fought, and I know that certain men at least have resolved to do so. I merely fear that they will occasionally feel somewhat alone, that they are in fact alone, and that after an interval of two thousand years we may see the sacrifice of Socrates repeated several times. The program for the future is either a permanent dialogue or the solemn and significant putting to death of any who have experienced dialogue. After having contributed my reply, the question that I ask Christians is this: "Will Socrates still be alone and is there nothing in him and in your doctrine that urges you to join us?"

It may be, I am well aware, that Christianity will answer negatively. Oh, not by your mouths, I am convinced. But it may be, and this is even more probable, that Christianity will insist on maintaining a compromise or else on giving its condemnations the obscure form of the encyclical. Possibly it will insist on losing once and for all the virtue of revolt and indignation that belonged to it long ago. In that case Christians will live and Christianity will die. In that case the others will in fact pay for the sacrifice. In any case such a future is not within my province to decide, despite all the hope and anguish it awakens in me.

I can speak only of what I know. And what I know — which sometimes creates a deep longing in me — is that if Christians made up
their minds to it, millions of voices — millions, I say — throughout
the world would be added to the appeal of a handful of isolated
individuals who, without any sort of affiliation, today intercede almost
everywhere and ceaselessly for children and for men.

EDWARD GIBBON

The Progress
of the Christian Religion

> Edward Gibbon (1737–1794) was born and reared as a
> member of the Church of England, but as a young man he
> was for a brief time an adherent of Roman Catholicism.
> Eventually he turned away from all traditional religion; and
> in his *History of the Decline and Fall of the Roman Empire,*
> from whose controversial fifteenth and sixteenth chapters
> these excerpts are taken, he combined erudition and irony
> to explain what he called "the progress of the Christian
> religion" in purely naturalistic terms.

A CANDID but rational inquiry into the progress and establishment of
Christianity may be considered as a very essential part of the history
of the Roman empire. While that great body was invaded by open
violence, or undermined by slow decay, a pure and humble religion
gently insinuated itself into the minds of men, grew up in silence and
obscurity, derived new vigour from opposition, and finally erected the
triumphant banner of the cross on the ruins of the Capitol. Nor was
the influence of Christianity confined to the period or to the limits of
the Roman empire. After a revolution of thirteen or fourteen centuries,
that religion is still professed by the nations of Europe, the most
distinguished portion of human kind in arts and learning as well as in
arms. By the industry and zeal of the Europeans it has been widely
diffused to the most distant shores of Asia and Africa; and by the means
of their colonies has been firmly established from Canada to Chili, in
a world unknown to the ancients.

But this inquiry, however useful or entertaining, is attended with
two peculiar difficulties. The scanty and suspicious materials of ecclesiastical history seldom enable us to dispel the dark cloud that

hangs over the first age of the church. The great law of impartiality too often obliges us to reveal the imperfections of the uninspired teachers and believers of the gospel; and, to a careless observer, *their* faults may seem to cast a shade on the faith which they professed. But the scandal of the pious Christian, and the fallacious triumph of the Infidel, should cease as soon as they recollect not only *by whom,* but likewise *to whom,* the Divine Revelation was given. The theologian may indulge the pleasing task of describing Religion as she descended from Heaven, arrayed in her native purity. A more melancholy duty is imposed on the historian. He must discover the inevitable mixture of error and corruption which she contracted in a long residence upon earth, among a weak and degenerate race of beings.

Our curiosity is naturally prompted to inquire by what means the Christian faith obtained so remarkable a victory over the established religions of the earth. To this inquiry, an obvious but satisfactory answer may be returned; that it was owing to the convincing evidence of the doctrine itself, and to the ruling providence of its great Author. But, as truth and reason seldom find so favourable a reception in the world, and as the wisdom of Providence frequently condescends to use the passions of the human heart, and the general circumstances of mankind, as instruments to execute its purpose; we may still be permitted, though with becoming submission, to ask not indeed what were the first, but what were the secondary causes of the rapid growth of the Christian church. It will, perhaps, appear that it was most effectually favoured and assisted by the five following causes: I. The inflexible, and, if we may use the expression, the intolerant zeal of the Christians, derived, it is true, from the Jewish religion, but purified from the narrow and unsocial spirit which, instead of inviting, had deterred the Gentiles from embracing the law of Moses. II. The doctrine of a future life, improved by every additional circumstance which could give weight and efficacy to that important truth. III. The miraculous powers ascribed to the primitive church. IV. The pure and austere morals of the Christians. V. The union and discipline of the Christian republic, which gradually formed an independent and increasing state in the heart of the Roman empire.

*   *   *   *   *

The progress of Christianity was not confined to the Roman empire; and, according to the primitive fathers, who interpret facts by prophecy, the new religion within a century after the death of its divine author, had already visited every part of the globe. "There exists not," says Justin Martyr, "a people, whether Greek or barbarian, or any other race of men, by whatsoever appellation or manners they may be distinguished, however ignorant of arts or agriculture, whether they dwell under tents, or wander about in covered waggons, among whom prayers are not offered up in the name of a crucified Jesus to the Father and Creator of all things." But this splendid exaggeration, which even at present it would be extremely difficult to reconcile with the real state of mankind, can be considered only as the rash sally of a devout but careless writer, the measure of whose belief was regulated by that of his wishes. But neither the belief nor the wishes of the fathers can alter the truth of history. It will still remain an undoubted fact that the barbarians of Scythia and Germany who afterwards subverted the Roman monarchy were involved in the darkness of paganism; and that even the conversion of Iberia, of Armenia, or of Æthiopia, was not attempted with any degree of success till the sceptre was in the hands of an orthodox emperor. Before that time the various accidents of war and commerce might indeed diffuse an imperfect knowledge of the gospel among the tribes of Caledonia, and among the borderers of the Rhine, the Danube, and the Euphrates. Beyond the last-mentioned river, Edessa was distinguished by a firm and early adherence to the faith. From Edessa the principles of Christianity were easily introduced into the Greek and Syrian cities which obeyed the successors of Artaxerxes; but they do not appear to have made any deep impression on the minds of the Persians, whose religious system, by the labours of a well-disciplined order of priests, had been constructed with much more art and solidity than the uncertain mythology of Greece and Rome.

From this impartial, though imperfect, survey of the progress of Christianity, it may, perhaps, seem probable that the number of its proselytes has been excessively magnified by fear on the one side and by devotion on the other. According to the irreproachable testimony of Origen, the proportion of the faithful was very inconsiderable when compared with the multitude of an unbelieving world; but, as we are left without any distinct information, it is impossible to determine, and it is difficult even to conjecture, the real numbers of the primitive Christians. The most favourable calculation, however, that can be deduced from the examples of Antioch and of Rome will not permit us to imagine that more than a twentieth part of the subjects of the empire had enlisted themselves under the banner of the cross before the important conversion of Constantine. But their habits of faith, of zeal, and of union seemed to multiply their numbers; and the same causes which contributed to their future increase served to render their actual strength more apparent and more formidable.

Such is the constitution of civil society that, whilst a few persons are distinguished by riches, by honours, and by knowledge, the body of the people is condemned to obscurity, ignorance, and poverty. The Christian religion, which addressed itself to the whole human race, must consequently collect a far greater number of proselytes from the lower than from the superior ranks of life. This innocent and natural circumstance has been improved into a very odious imputation, which seems to be less strenuously denied by the apologists than it is urged by the adversaries of the faith; that the new sect of Christians was almost entirely composed of the dregs of the populace, of peasants and mechanics, of boys and women, of beggars and slaves; the last of whom might sometimes introduce the missionaries into the rich and noble families to which they belonged. These obscure teachers (such was the charge of malice and infidelity) are as mute in public as they are loquacious and dogmatical in private. Whilst they cautiously avoid the dangerous encounter of philosophers, they mingle with the rude and illiterate crowd, and insinuate themselves into those minds, whom their age, their sex, or their education has the best disposed to receive the impression of superstitious terrors.

*   *   *   *   *

If we seriously consider the purity of the Christian religion, the sanctity of its moral precepts, and the innocent as well as austere lives of the greater number of those who, during the first ages, embraced the faith of the gospel, we should naturally suppose that so benevolent a doctrine would have been received with due reverence, even by the unbelieving world; that the learned and the polite, however they might deride the miracles, would have esteemed the virtues of the new sect; and that the magistrates, instead of persecuting, would have protected an order of men who yielded the most passive obedience to the laws, though they declined the active cares of war and government. If, on the other hand, we recollect the universal toleration of Polytheism, as it was invariably maintained by the faith of the people, the incredulity of philosophers, and the policy of the Roman senate and emperors, we are at a loss to discover what new offence the Christians had committed, what new provocation could exasperate the mild indifference of antiquity, and what new motives could urge the Roman princes, who beheld, without concern, a thousand forms of religion subsisting in peace under their gentle sway, to inflict a severe punishment on any part of their subjects, who had chosen for themselves a singular, but an inoffensive, mode of faith and worship.

The religious policy of the ancient world seems to have assumed a more stern and intolerant character, to oppose the progress of Christianity. About fourscore years after the death of Christ, his innocent disciples were punished with death, by the sentence of a proconsul of the most amiable and philosophic character, and according to the laws of an emperor, distinguished by the wisdom and justice of his general administration. The apologies which were repeatedly addressed to the successors of Trajan, are filled with the most pathetic complaints, that the Christians, who obeyed the dictates, and solicited the liberty, of conscience, were alone, among all the subjects of the Roman empire, excluded from the common benefits of their auspicious government. The deaths of a few eminent martyrs have been recorded with care; and from the time that Christianity was invested with the supreme power, the governors of the church have been no less diligently employed in displaying the cruelty, than in imitating the conduct, of their Pagan adversaries. To separate (if it be possible) a few authentic, as well as interesting, facts from an undigested mass of fiction and error, and to relate, in a clear and rational manner, the causes, the extent, the duration, and the most important circumstances of the persecutions to which the first Christians were exposed, is the design of the present chapter.

The sectaries of a persecuted religion, depressed by fear, animated with resentment, and perhaps heated by enthusiasm, are seldom in a proper temper of mind calmly to investigate, or candidly to appreciate, the motives of their enemies, which often escape the impartial and discerning view even of those who are placed at a secure distance from the flames of persecution. A reason has been assigned for the conduct of the emperors towards the primitive Christians, which may appear the more specious and probable as it is drawn from the acknowledged genius of Polytheism. It has already been observed that the religious concord of the world was principally supported by the implicit assent and reverence which the nations of antiquity expressed for their respective traditions and ceremonies. It might therefore be expected that they would unite with indignation against any sect of people which should separate itself from the communion of mankind, and, claiming the exclusive possession of divine knowledge, should disdain every form of worship, except its own, as impious and idolatrous. The rights of toleration were held by mutual indulgence; they were justly forfeited by a refusal of the accustomed tribute. As the payment of this tribute was inflexibly refused by the Jews, and by them alone, the consideration of the treatment which they experienced from the Roman magistrates will serve to explain how far these speculations are justified by facts, and will lead us to discover the true causes of the persecution of Christianity.

Without repeating what has been already mentioned of the reverence of the Roman princes and governors for the temple of Jerusalem, we shall only observe that the destruction of the temple and city was accompanied and followed by every circumstance that could exasperate the minds of the conquerors, and authorize religious persecution by the most specious arguments of political justice and the public safety. From the reign of Nero to that of Antoninus Pius, the Jews discovered a fierce impatience of the dominion of Rome, which repeatedly broke out in the most furious massacres and insurrections. Humanity is shocked at the recital of the horrid cruelties which they committed in the cities of Egypt, of Cyprus, and of Cyrene, where they dwelt in treacherous friendship with the unsuspecting natives; and we are tempted to applaud the severe retaliation which was exercised by the arms of the legions against a race of fanatics, whose dire and credulous superstition seemed to render them the implacable enemies not only of the Roman government, but of human kind. The enthusiasm of the Jews was supported by the opinion that it was unlawful for them to pay taxes to an idolatrous master; and by the flattering promise which they derived from their ancient oracles, that a conquering Messiah would soon arise, destined to break their fetters and to invest the favourites of heaven with the empire of the earth. It was by announcing himself as their long-expected deliverer, and by calling on all the descendants of Abraham to assert the hope of Israel, that the famous Barchochebas collected a formidable army, with which he resisted, during two years, the power of the emperor Hadrian.

Notwithstanding these repeated provocations, the resentment of the Roman princes expired after the victory; nor were their apprehensions continued beyond the period of war and danger. By the general indulgence of polytheism, and by the mild temper of Antoninus Pius, the Jews were restored to their ancient privileges, and once more obtained the permission of circumcising their children, with the easy restraint that they should never confer on any foreign proselyte that distinguishing mark of the Hebrew race. The numerous remains of that people, though they were still excluded from the precincts of Jerusalem, were permitted to form and to maintain considerable establishments both in Italy and in the provinces, to acquire the freedom of Rome, to enjoy municipal honours, and to obtain, at the same time, an exemption from the burdensome and expensive offices of society. The moderation or the contempt of the Romans gave a legal sanction to the form of ecclesiastical police which was instituted by the vanquished sect. The patriarch, who had fixed his residence at Tiberias, was empowered to appoint his subordinate ministers and apostles, to exercise a domestic jurisdiction, and to receive from his dispersed brethren an annual contribution. New synagogues were frequently erected in the principal cities of the empire; and the sabbaths, the fasts, and the festivals, which were either commanded by the Mosaic law or enjoined by the traditions of the Rabbis, were celebrated in the most solemn and public manner. Such gentle treatment insensibly assuaged the stern temper of the Jews. Awakened from their dream of prophecy and conquest, they assumed the behaviour of peaceable and industrious subjects. Their irreconcileable hatred of mankind, instead of flaming out in acts of blood and violence, evaporated in less dangerous gratifications. They embraced every opportunity of over-reaching the idolaters in trade; and they pronounced secret and ambiguous imprecations against the haughty kingdom of Edom.

Since the Jews, who rejected with abhorrence the deities adored by their sovereign and by their fellow-subjects, enjoyed, however, the free exercise of their unsocial religion; there must have existed some other cause, which exposed the disciples of Christ to those severities from which the posterity of Abraham was exempt. The difference between them is simple and obvious; but, according to the sentiments of antiquity, it was of the highest importance. The Jews were a *nation;* the Christians were a *sect;* and, if it was natural for every community to respect the sacred institutions of their neighbours, it was incumbent on them to persevere in those of their ancestors. The voice of oracles, the precepts of philosophers, and the authority of the laws, unanimously enforced this national obligation. By their lofty claim of superior sanctity, the Jews might provoke the Polytheists to consider them as an odious and impure race. By disdaining the intercourse of other nations they might deserve their contempt. The laws of Moses might be for the most part frivolous or absurd; yet, since they had been received during many ages by a large society, his followers were justified by the example of mankind; and it was universally acknowledged that they had a right to practise what it would have been criminal in them to neglect. But this principle which protected the Jewish synagogue afforded not any favour or security to the primitive church. By embracing the faith of the Gospel, the Christians incurred the supposed guilt of an unnatural and unpardonable offence. They dissolved the sacred ties of custom and education, violated the religious institutions of their country, and presumptuously despised whatever their fathers had believed as true, or had reverenced as sacred. Nor was this apostacy (if we may use the expression) merely of a partial or local kind; since the pious deserter who withdrew himself from the temples of Egypt or Syria would equally disdain to seek an asylum in those of Athens or Carthage. Every Christian rejected with contempt the superstitions of his family, his city, and his province. The whole body of Christians unanimously refused to hold any communion with the gods of Rome, of the empire, and of mankind. It was in vain that the oppressed believer asserted the inalienable rights of conscience and private judgment. Though his situation might excite the pity, his arguments could never reach the understanding, either of the philosophic or of the believing part of the Pagan world. To their apprehensions, it was no less a matter of surprise that any individuals should entertain scruples against complying with the established mode of worship, than if they had conceived a sudden abhorrence to the manners, the dress, or the language of their native country.

The surprise of the Pagans was soon succeeded by resentment; and the most pious of men were exposed to the unjust but dangerous imputation of impiety. Malice and prejudice concurred in representing the Christians as a society of atheists, who, by the most daring attack on the religious constitution of the empire, had merited the severest animadversion of the civil magistrate. They had separated themselves (they gloried in the confession) from every mode of superstition which was received in any part of the globe by the various temper of polytheism; but it was not altogether so evident what deity or what form of worship they had substituted to the gods and temples of antiquity. The pure and sublime idea which they entertained of the Supreme Being escaped the gross conception of the Pagan multitude, who were at a loss to discover a spiritual and solitary God, that was neither represented under any corporeal figure or visible symbol, nor was adored with the accustomed pomp of libations and festivals, of altars and sacrifices. The sages of Greece and Rome, who had elevated their minds to the contemplation of the existence and attributes of the First Cause, were induced, by reason or by vanity, to reserve for themselves and their chosen disciples the privilege of this philosophical devotion. They were far from admitting the prejudices of mankind as the standard of truth; but they considered them as flowing from the original disposition of human nature; and they supposed that any popular mode of faith and worship which presumed to disclaim the assistance of the senses would, in proportion as it receded from superstition, find itself incapable of restraining the wanderings of the fancy and the visions of fanaticism. The careless glance which men of wit and learning condescended to cast on the Christian revelation served only to confirm their hasty opinion, and to persuade them that the principle, which they might have revered, of the divine unity was defaced by the wild enthusiasm, and annihilated by the airy speculations, of the new sectaries. The author of a celebrated dialogue which has been attributed to Lucian, whilst he affects to treat the mysterious subject of the Trinity in a style of ridicule and contempt, betrays his own ignorance of the weakness of human reason, and of the inscrutable nature of the divine perfections.

It might appear less surprising that the founder of Christianity should not only be revered by his disciples as a sage and a prophet, but that he should be adored as a God. The Polytheists were disposed to adopt every article of faith which seemed to offer any resemblance, however distant or imperfect, with the popular mythology; and the legends of Bacchus, or Hercules, and of Æsculapius had, in some measure, prepared their imagination for the appearance of the Son of God under a human form. But they were astonished that the Christians should abandon the temples of those ancient heroes who, in the infancy of the world, had invented arts, instituted laws, and vanquished the tyrants or monsters who infested the earth; in order to choose, for the exclusive object of their religious worship, an obscure teacher who, in a recent age, and among a barbarous people, had fallen a sacrifice either to the malice of his own countrymen or to the jealousy of the Roman government. The Pagan multitude, reserving their gratitude for temporal benefits alone, rejected the inestimable present of life and immortality which was offered to mankind by Jesus of Nazareth. His mild constancy in the midst of cruel and voluntary sufferings, his universal benevolence, and the sublime simplicity of his actions and character were insufficient, in the opinion of those carnal men, to compensate for the want of fame, of empire, and of success; and, whilst they refused to acknowledge his stupendous triumph over the powers of darkness and of the grave, they misrepresented, or they insulted, the equivocal birth, wandering life, and ignominious death of the divine Author of Christianity.

The personal guilt which every Christian had contracted, in thus preferring his private sentiment to the national religion, was aggravated, in a very high degree, by the number and union of the criminals. It is well known, and has been already observed, that Roman policy viewed with the utmost jealousy and distrust any association among its subjects; and that the privileges of private corporations, though formed for the most harmless or beneficial purposes, were bestowed with a very sparing hand. The religious assemblies of the Christians, who had separated themselves from the public worship, appeared of a much less innocent nature: they were illegal in their principle and in their consequences might become dangerous; nor were the emperors conscious that they violated the laws of justice, when, for the peace of society, they prohibited those secret and sometimes nocturnal meetings. The pious disobedience of the Christians made their conduct, or perhaps their designs, appear in a much more serious and criminal light; and the Roman princes, who might perhaps have suffered themselves to be disarmed by a ready submission, deeming their honour concerned in the execution of their commands, sometimes attempted by rigorous punishments to subdue this independent spirit, which boldly acknowledged an authority superior to that of the magistrate. The extent and duration of this spiritual conspiracy seemed to render it every day more deserving of his animadversion. We have already seen that the active and successful zeal of the Christians had insensibly diffused them through every province and almost every city of the empire. The new converts seemed to renounce their family and country, that they might connect themselves in an indissoluble band of union with a peculiar society, which everywhere assumed a different character from the rest of mankind. Their gloomy and austere aspect, their abhorrence of the common business and pleasures of life, and their frequent predictions of impending calamities, inspired the Pagans with the apprehension of some danger which would arise from the new sect, the more alarming as it was the more obscure. "Whatever," says Pliny, "may be the principle of their conduct, their inflexible obstinacy appeared deserving of punishment."

The precautions with which the disciples of Christ performed the offices of religion were at first dictated by fear and necessity; but they were continued from choice. By imitating the awful secrecy which reigned in the Eleusinian mysteries, the Christians had flattered themselves that they should render their sacred institutions more respectable in the eyes of the Pagan world. But the event, as it often happens to the operations of subtile policy, deceived their wishes and their expectations. It was concluded that they only concealed what they would have blushed to disclose. Their mistaken prudence afforded an opportunity for malice to invent, and for suspicious credulity to believe, the horrid tales which described the Christians as the most wicked of human kind, who practised in their dark recesses every abomination that a depraved fancy could suggest, and who solicited the favour of their unknown God by the sacrifice of every moral virtue. There were many who pretended to confess or to relate the ceremonies of this abhorred society. It was asserted, "that a new-born infant, entirely covered over with flour, was presented, like some mystic symbol of initiation, to the knife of the proselyte, who unknowingly inflicted many a secret and mortal wound on the innocent victim of his error; that, as soon as the cruel deed was perpetrated, the sectaries drank up the blood, greedily tore asunder the quivering members, and pledged themselves to eternal secrecy, by a mutual consciousness of guilt. It was as confidently affirmed that this inhuman sacrifice was succeeded by a suitable entertainment, in which intemperance served as a provocative to brutal lust; till, at the appointed moment, the lights were suddenly extinguished, shame was banished, nature was forgotten; and, as accident might direct, the darkness of the night was polluted by the incestuous commerce of sisters and brothers, of sons and of mothers."

But the perusal of the ancient apologies was sufficient to remove even the slightest suspicion from the mind of a candid adversary. The Christians, with the intrepid security of innocence, appeal from the voice of rumour to the equity of the magistrates. They acknowledge that, if any proof can be produced of the crimes which calumny has imputed to them, they are worthy of the most severe punishment. They provoke the punishment, and they challenge the proof. At the same time they urge, with equal truth and propriety, that the charge is not less devoid of probability than it is destitute of evidence; they ask whether any one can seriously believe that the pure and holy precepts of the Gospel, which so frequently restrain the use of the most lawful enjoyments, should inculcate the practice of the most abominable crimes; that a large society should resolve to dishonour itself in the eyes of its own members; and that a great number of persons of either sex, and every age and character, insensible to the fear of death or infamy, should consent to violate those principles which nature and education had imprinted most deeply in their minds. Nothing, it should seem, could weaken the force or destroy the effect of so unanswerable a justification, unless it were the injudicious conduct of the apologists themselves, who betrayed the common cause of religion, to gratify their devout hatred to the domestic enemies of the church. It was sometimes faintly insinuated, and sometimes boldly asserted, that the same bloody sacrifices, and the same incestuous festivals, which were so falsely ascribed to the orthodox believers, were in reality celebrated by the Marcionites, by the Carpocratians, and by several other sects of the Gnostics, who, notwithstanding they might deviate into the paths of heresy, were still actuated by the sentiments of men, and still governed by the precepts of Christianity. Accusations of a similar kind were retorted upon the church by the schismatics who had departed from its communion; and it was confessed on all sides that the most scandalous licentiousness of manners prevailed among great numbers of those who affected the name of Christians. A Pagan magistrate, who possessed neither leisure nor abilities to discern the almost imperceptible line which divides the orthodox faith from heretical pravity, might easily have imagined that their mutual animosity had extorted the discovery of their common guilt. It was fortunate for the repose, or at least for the reputation, of the first Christians, that the magistrates sometimes proceeded with more temper and moderation than is usually consistent with religious zeal, and that they reported, as the impartial result of their judicial inquiry, that the sectaries who had deserted the established worship appeared to them sincere in their professions and blameless in their manners; however they might incur, by their absurd and excessive superstition, the censure of the laws.

GILBERT MURRAY

Failure of Nerve

George Gilbert Aimé Murray (1866–1957) was a classical philologist at Glasgow and then at Oxford, known for his editions and translations of the Greek dramatists. His *Five Stages of Greek Religion,* from which this excerpt is taken, was a survey of Greek religious belief and practice from the classical period into the Hellenistic age, during which Christianity and other alien faiths challenged basic Greek assumptions.

Any one who turns from the great writers of classical Athens, say Sophocles or Aristotle, to those of the Christian era must be conscious of a great difference in tone. There is a change in the whole relation of the writer to the world about him. The new quality is not specifically Christian: it is just as marked in the Gnostics and Mithras-worshippers as in the Gospels and the Apocalypse, in Julian and Plotinus as in Gregory and Jerome. It is hard to describe. It is a rise of asceticism, of mysticism, in a sense, of pessimism; a loss of self-confidence, of hope in this life and of faith in normal human effort; a despair of patient inquiry, a cry for infallible revelation; an indifference to the welfare of the state, a conversion of the soul to God. It is an atmosphere in which the aim of the good man is not so much to live justly, to help the society to which he belongs and enjoy the esteem of his fellow creatures; but rather, by means of a burning faith, by contempt for the world and its standards, by ecstasy, suffering, and martyrdom, to be granted pardon for his unspeakable unworthiness, his immeasurable sins. There is an intensifying of certain spiritual emotions; an increase of sensitiveness, a failure of nerve.

Now this antithesis is often exaggerated by the admirers of one side or the other. A hundred people write as if Sophocles had no mysticism and practically speaking no conscience. Half a dozen retort as if St. Paul had no public spirit and no common sense. I have protested often against this exaggeration; but, stated reasonably, as a change of proportion and not a creation of new hearts, the antithesis is certainly based on fact.

My description of this complicated change is, of course, inadequate, but not, I hope, one-sided. I do not depreciate the religions that followed on this movement by describing the movement itself as a "failure of nerve." Mankind has not yet decided which of two opposite methods leads to the fuller and deeper knowledge of the world: the patient and sympathetic study of the good citizen who lives in it, or the ecstatic vision of the saint who rejects it. But probably most Christians are inclined to believe that without some failure and sense of failure, without a contrite heart and conviction of sin, man can hardly attain the religious life. I can imagine an historian of this temper believing that the period we are about to discuss was a necessary softening of human pride, a *Praeparatio Evangelica* [preparation for the gospel].

I am concerned in this paper with the lower country lying between two great ranges. The one range is Greek Philosophy, culminating in Plato, Aristotle, the Porch and the Garden; the other is Christianity, culminating in St. Paul and his successors. The one is the work of Hellas, using some few foreign elements; the second is the work of Hellenistic culture on a Hebrew stock. The books of Christianity are Greek, the philosophical background is Hellenistic, the result of the interplay, in the free atmosphere of Greek philosophy, of religious ideas derived from Egypt, Anatolia, Syria, and Babylon. The preaching is carried on in Greek among the Greek-speaking workmen of the great manufacturing and commercial cities. The first preachers are Jews: the central scene is set in Jerusalem. I wish in this essay to indicate how a period of religious history, which seems broken, is really continuous, and to trace the lie of the main valleys which lead from the one range to the other, through a large and imperfectly explored territory.

The territory in question is the so-called Hellenistic Age, the period during which the Schools of Greece were "hellenizing" the world. It is a time of great enlightenment, of vigorous propaganda, of high importance to history. It is a time full of great names: in one school of philosophy alone we have Zeno, Cleanthes, Chrysippus, Panaetius, Posidonius. Yet, curiously enough, it is represented in our tradition by something very like a mere void. There are practically no complete

books preserved, only fragments and indirect quotations. Consequently in the search for information about this age we must throw our
nets wide. Besides books and inscriptions of the Hellenistic period
proper I have drawn on Cicero, Pliny, Seneca, and the like for evidence
about their teachers and masters. I have used many Christian and
Gnostic documents and works like the Corpus of Hermetic writings
and the Mithras Liturgy. Among modern writers I must acknowledge
a special debt to the researches of Dieterich, Cumont, Bousset, Wend-
land, and Reitzenstein.

The Hellenistic Age seems at first sight to have entered on an inheritance such as our speculative Anarchists sometimes long for, a *tabula
rasa,* on which a new and highly gifted generation of thinkers might
write clean and certain the book of their discoveries about life — what
Herodotus would call their *"Historiê."* For, as we have seen in the last
essay, it is clear that by the time of Plato the traditional religion of the
Greek states was, if taken at its face value, a bankrupt concern. There
was hardly one aspect in which it could bear criticism; and in the kind
of test that chiefly matters, the satisfaction of men's ethical requirements and aspirations, it was if anything weaker than elsewhere. Now
a religious belief that is scientifically preposterous may still have a long
and comfortable life before it. Any worshipper can suspend the scientific part of his mind while worshipping. But a religious belief that
is morally contemptible is in serious danger, because when the religious emotions surge up the moral emotions are not far away. And the
clash cannot be hidden.

This collapse of the traditional religion of Greece might not have
mattered so much if the form of Greek social life had remained. If a
good Greek had his Polis, he had an adequate substitute in most
respects for any mythological gods. But the Polis too, as we have seen
in the last essay, fell with the rise of Macedon. It fell, perhaps, not from
any special spiritual fault of its own; it had few faults except its fatal
narrowness; but simply because there now existed another social
whole, which, whether higher or lower in civilization, was at any rate
utterly superior in brute force and in money. Devotion to the Polis lost
its reality when the Polis, with all that it represented of rights and laws
and ideals of Life, lay at the mercy of a military despot, who might, of
course, be a hero, but might equally well be a vulgar sot or a corrupt
adventurer.

What the succeeding ages built upon the ruins of the Polis is not our
immediate concern. In the realm of thought, on the whole, the Polis

triumphed. Aristotle based his social theory on the Polis, not the nation. Dicaearchus, Didymus, and Posidonius followed him, and we still use his language. Rome herself was a Polis, as well as an Empire. And Professor Haverfield has pointed out that a City has more chance of taking in the whole world to its freedoms and privileges than a Nation has of making men of alien birth its compatriots. A Jew of Tarsus could easily be granted the civic rights of Rome: he could never have been made an Italian or a Frenchman. The Stoic ideal of the World as "one great City of Gods and Men" has not been surpassed by any ideal based on the Nation.

What we have to consider is the general trend of religious thought from, say, the Peripatetics to the Gnostics. It is a fairly clear history. A soil once teeming with wild weeds was to all appearance swept bare and made ready for new sowing: skilled gardeners chose carefully the best of herbs and plants and tended the garden sedulously. But the bounds of the garden kept spreading all the while into strange untended ground, and even within the original walls the weeding had been hasty and incomplete. At the end of a few generations all was a wilderness of weeds again, weeds rank and luxuriant and sometimes extremely beautiful, with a half-strangled garden flower or two gleaming here and there in the tangle of them. Does that comparison seem disrespectful to religion? Is philosophy all flowers and traditional belief all weeds? Well, think what a weed is. It is only a name for all the natural wild vegetation which the earth sends up of herself, which lives and will live without the conscious labour of man. The flowers are what we keep alive with difficulty; the weeds are what conquer us.

It has been well observed by Zeller that the great weakness of all ancient thought, not excepting Socratic thought, was that instead of appealing to objective experiment it appealed to some subjective sense of fitness. There were exceptions, of course: Democritus, Eratosthenes, Hippocrates, and to a great extent Aristotle. But in general there was a strong tendency to follow Plato in supposing that people could really solve questions by an appeal to their inner consciousness. One result of this, no doubt, was a tendency to lay too much stress on mere agreement. It is obvious, when one thinks about it, that quite often a large number of people who know nothing about a subject will all agree and all be wrong. Yet we find the most radical of ancient philosophers unconsciously dominated by the argument *ex consensu gentium* [on the basis of universal agreement]. It is hard to find two more uncompromising thinkers than Zeno and Epicurus. Yet both of them, when they are almost free from the popular superstitions, when they have constructed complete systems which, if not absolutely logic-proof, are calculated at least to keep out the weather for a century or so, open curious side-doors at the last moment and let in all the gods of mythology. True, they are admitted as suspicious characters, and under promise of good behaviour. Epicurus explains that they do not and cannot do anything whatever to anybody; Zeno explains that they are not anthropomorphic, and are only symbols or emanations or subordinates of the all-ruling Unity; both parties get rid of the myths. But the two great reformers have admitted a dangerous principle. The general consensus of humanity, they say, shows that there are gods, and gods which in mind, if not also in visual appearance, resemble man. Epicurus succeeded in barring the door, and admitted nothing more. But the Stoics presently found themselves admitting or insisting that the same consensus proved the existence of daemons, of witch-craft, of divination, and when they combined with the Platonic school, of more dangerous elements still.

I take the Stoics and Epicureans as the two most radical schools. On the whole both of them fought steadily and strongly against the growth of superstition, or, if you like to put it in other language, against the dumb demands of man's infra-rational nature. The glory of the Stoics is to have built up a religion of extraordinary nobleness; the glory of the Epicureans is to have upheld an ideal of sanity and humanity stark upright amid a reeling world, and, like the old Spartans, never to have yielded one inch of ground to the common foe.

The great thing to remember is that the mind of man cannot be enlightened permanently by merely teaching him to reject some particular set of superstitions. There is an infinite supply of other superstitions always at hand; and the mind that desires such things — that is, the mind that has not trained itself to the hard discipline of reasonableness and honesty, will, as soon as its devils are cast out, proceed to fill itself with their relations.

Let us first consider the result of the mere denial of the Olympian religion. The essential postulate of that religion was that the world is governed by a number of definite personal gods, possessed of a human sense of justice and fairness and capable of being influenced by normal human motives. In general, they helped the good and punished the bad, though doubtless they tended too much to regard as good those who paid them proper attention and as bad those who did not.

Speaking broadly, what was left when this conception proved inadequate? If it was not these personal gods who made things happen, what was it? If the Tower of Siloam was not deliberately thrown down by the gods so as to kill and hurt a carefully collected number of wicked people, while letting the good escape, what was the explanation of its falling? The answer is obvious, but it can be put in two ways. You can either say: "It was just chance that the Tower fell at that particular moment when So-and-so was under it." Or you can say, with rather more reflection but not any more common sense: "It fell because of a definite chain of causes, a certain degree of progressive decay in the building, a certain definite pressure, &c. It was bound to fall."

There is no real difference in these statements, at least in the meaning of those who ordinarily utter them. Both are compatible with a reasonable and scientific view of the world. But in the Hellenistic Age, when Greek thought was spreading rapidly and superficially over vast semi-barbarous populations whose minds were not ripe for it, both views turned back instinctively into a theology as personal as that of the Olympians. It was not, of course, Zeus or Apollo who willed this; every one knew so much: it happened by Chance. That is, Chance or Fortune willed it. And Tyche became a goddess like the rest. The great catastrophes, the great transformations of the mediterranean world which marked the Hellenistic period, had a strong influence here. If Alexander and his generals had practised some severely orthodox Macedonian religion, it would have been easy to see that the Gods of Macedon were the real rulers of the world. But they most markedly did not. They accepted hospitably all the religions that crossed their path. Some power or other was disturbing the world, that was clear. It was not exactly the work of man, because sometimes the good were exalted, sometimes the bad; there was no consistent purpose in the story. It was just Fortune. Happy is the man who knows how to placate Fortune and make her smile upon him!

It is worth remembering that the best seed-ground for superstition is a society in which the fortunes of men seem to bear practically no relation to their merits and efforts. A stable and well-governed society does tend, speaking roughly, to ensure that the Virtuous and Industrious Apprentice shall succeed in life, while the Wicked and Idle Apprentice fails. And in such a society people tend to lay stress on the reasonable or visible chains of causation. But in a country suffering from earthquakes or pestilences, in a court governed by the whim of a despot, in a district which is habitually the seat of a war between alien armies, the ordinary virtues of diligence, honesty, and kindliness seem to be of little avail. The only way to escape destruction is to win the favour of the prevailing powers, take the side of the strongest invader,

flatter the despot, placate the Fate or Fortune or angry god that is
sending the earthquake or the pestilence. The Hellenistic period pretty
certainly falls in some degree under all of these categories. And one
result is the sudden and enormous spread of the worship of Fortune.
Of course, there was always a protest. . . . Most interesting of all
perhaps, there is the first oration of Plutarch on the Fortune of
Alexander. A sentence in Pliny's *Natural History,* ii. 22, seems to go
back to Hellenistic sources:

> Throughout the whole world, at every place and hour, by
> every voice Fortune alone is invoked and her name spoken:
> she is the one defendant, the one culprit, the one thought in
> men's minds, the one object of praise, the one cause. She is
> worshipped with insults, counted as fickle and often as blind,
> wandering, inconsistent, elusive, changeful, and friend of the
> unworthy. . . . We are so much at the mercy of chance that
> Chance is our god.

The word used is first *Fortuna* and then *Sors*. This shows how little
real difference there is between the two apparently contradictory
conceptions. — "Chance would have it so." "It was fated to be." The
sting of both phrases — their pleasant bitterness when played with,
their quality of poison when believed — lies in their denial of the value
of human endeavour.

Yet on the whole, as one might expect, the believers in Destiny are
a more respectable congregation than the worshippers of Chance. It
requires a certain amount of thoughtfulness to rise to the conception
that nothing really happens without a cause. It is the beginning,
perhaps, of science. Ionic philosophers of the fifth century had laid
stress on what we should call the Chain of causes in Nature. After the
rise of Stoicism Fate becomes something less physical, more related
to conscious purpose. It is not *Anankê* but *Heimarmenê*. Heimarmenê,
in the striking simile of Zeno, is like a fine thread running through the
whole of existence — the world, we must remember, was to the Stoics
a live thing — like that invisible thread of life which, in heredity,
passes on from generation to generation of living species and keeps the
type alive; it runs causing, causing for ever, both the infinitesimal and
the infinite. It is the Reason of the World or the mind of Zeus, rather
difficult to distinguish from the Pronoia or Providence which is the
work of God and indeed the very essence of God. Thus it is not really
an external and alien force. For the human soul itself is a fragment or
effluence of the divine, and this Law of God is also the law of man's

own Phusis. As long as you act in accordance with your true self you are complying with that divine Fate or Providence, whose service is perfect freedom. Only when you are false to your own nature and become a rebel against the kingdom of God which is within you, are you dragged perforce behind the chariot-wheels. The doctrine is implied in Cleanthes' celebrated Hymn to Destiny and is explained clearly by Plotinus.

That is a noble conception. But the vulgar of course can turn Kismet into a stupid idol, as easily as they can Fortune. And Epicurus may have had some excuse for exclaiming that he would sooner be a slave to the old gods of the vulgar, than to the Destiny of the philosophers.

So much for the result in superstitious minds of the denial, or rather the removal, of the Olympian Gods. It landed men in the worship of Fortune or of Fate.

LUDWIG FEUERBACH

The Essence of Religion

Ludwig Andreas Feuerbach (1804–1872) broke with the German Idealism in which he had been schooled and propounded a radical materialism that influenced, among others, Karl Marx. As part of that materialism, Feuerbach here in the twelfth lecture of *The Essence of Religion* set forth the thesis that man had created God in his own image — the precise reverse of the creation story — and that therefore religion was to be explained on the basis of psychology rather than of theology.

IN THE LAST LECTURE I elucidated by the example of man one of the first and most common proofs of the existence of God, the so-called cosmological proof, to the effect that everything in the world is finite and dependent and therefore presupposes something infinite and independent. My conclusion was that although man was originally a child, he is at the same time a father, that although he is effect he is also cause, that though dependent he is also independent. But, obvious differences aside, what is true of man is also true of other beings. For all its dependency on other beings, each being is an independent self; each being has the ground of its existence in itself — to what purpose would it otherwise exist? Every being has come into existence under conditions and through causes — regardless of their nature — which could have given rise to no other being; each being owes its existence to a set of causes which would not be operative without it. Every being is both effect and cause. Without water there would be no fish, but without fish, or some other animals capable of living in water, there would also be no water. The fish are dependent on water; they cannot exist without it; they presuppose it; but the ground of their dependence is in themselves; in their individual nature, which precisely makes water their need, their element.

Nature has no beginning and no end. Everything in it acts upon everything else, everything in it is relative, everything is at once effect and cause, acting and reacting on all sides. Nature does not culminate in a monarchic summit; it is a republic. Those who are accustomed to a monarchy cannot conceive of a human society without a prince, and likewise those who have grown up with the idea of a Father in Heaven find it hard to conceive of nature without a God. But it is just as possible to conceive of nature without a God, without an extranatural and supernatural being, as of a state or nation without a royal idol situated outside and above it. Indeed, just as the republic is the historical task, the practical goal of man, so his theoretical goal is to recognize the republican constitution of nature, not to situate the governing principle of nature outside it, but to find it grounded in nature. Nothing is more absurd than to regard nature as a single effect and to give it a *single cause* in an extra-natural being who is the effect of no other being. If I cannot refrain from spinning out fantasies, from looking further and further afield, if I am unable to stop with nature and content my intellectual need for causes with the universal action and interaction of nature, what is to prevent me from going beyond God? What is to prevent me from looking for a ground and cause of God as well? Do we not in God find the same situation as in the concatenation of natural causes and effects, the very situation that I wished to remedy by positing the existence of a God?

If I conceive of God as the cause of the world, is He not dependent on the world? Is there any cause without an effect? What is left of God if I omit or think away the world? What becomes of His power if He does nothing; of His wisdom, if there is no world for Him to govern? Where is His goodness if there is nothing for Him to be good to — where His infinity, if there is nothing finite? For He is infinite only in contrast to finiteness. Thus if I omit the world, nothing remains of God. Why then should we not confine ourselves to the world, since in any case we cannot go above or outside it, since even the idea and hypothesis of God throws us back on the world, since if we take away nature, we deprive the world of all reality and consequently negate even the reality of God insofar as He is conceived as the cause of the world?

Thus the difficulties arising from the question of the beginning of the world are only postponed or thrust aside or glossed over by the notion of a God, a being outside the world; they are *not solved*. Is it not then more reasonable to assume that the world always was and always will be, and consequently that it has the ground of its existence within itself. "We cannot dispel but neither can we endure the thought," says Kant in his *Lectures on the Philosophy of Religion,* "that a being whom we conceive of as the highest of all possible beings says to himself as it were: I am from eternity to eternity; outside of me there is nothing except for that which is something through my will; but *whence then am I?*" In other words, where does God come from? What obliges me to stop at God? Nothing; I cannot help inquiring into His origin. And that is no secret: the cause of what for the theists, theologians, and so-called speculative philosophers is the first and universal cause of all things — is the human intellect. The intellect rises from the individual and particular to the universal, from the concrete to the abstract, from the determined to the undetermined. It also rises from real, definite, particular causes, and goes on rising until it comes to the concept of *cause as such, the* cause that produces no real, definite, particular effects.

God is not, at least not directly as the theists suppose, the cause of thunder and lightning, of rain and sunshine, of fire and water, sun and moon; all these things and phenomena have only particular, special, sensuous causes; He is merely the universal first cause, the cause of causes; He is the cause that is not a definite, sensuous real cause, the cause that is abstracted from all sensuous matter, from all special determinations. In other words, He is *cause as such,* the concept of cause personified as an independent being. Just as the intellect personifies as one being the concept of being, abstracted from all the definite properties of being, so it personifies the concept of cause abstracted from all the characteristics of real, determinate causality in a First Cause. Just as man, operating on the plane of reason disengaged from the senses, subjectively and quite logically sets the species above individuals, color above colors, mankind above men, so he sets "cause" above causes. "God is the ground of the world" means: *"cause"* is the ground of causes; without "cause" there can be no causes; the *first* in logic, in the intellectual order, is "cause"; the second and subordinate term is causes or *kinds* of cause; in short, the first cause reduces itself to the concept of cause and the concept of cause is a product of the intellect, which abstracts the universal from particular real things and then, in accordance with its own nature, sets this abstracted universal over them as the First.

But for that very reason, because the First Cause is a mere intellectual concept or entity without objective existence, it also is not the cause of my life and existence. *This* cause is of no use to me; the cause of my life is the sum of *many different, definite* causes; the cause, for example, of my breathing is subjectively my lungs, objectively the air; the cause of my vision is objectively the light, subjectively my eyes. In short, the First Cause is an unprofitable abstraction. From this first cause that causes nothing I therefore turn back to the more profitable theme of nature, the sum of real causes, and try once again to prove that we must confine ourselves to nature as the ultimate ground of our existence; that all derivations from nature which transcend nature to arrive at a nonnatural being are mere fantasies and delusions. The proofs are both direct and indirect; the direct proofs are drawn from nature and relate to it directly; the indirect ones show the contradictions involved in the contrary assumption and the absurd consequences that follow from it.

Our world — not only our political and social world, but our learned, intellectual world as well — is a world upside down. The great achievement of our education, of our culture, our science, our erudition has been, above all, to stray as far as possible from nature, from the simple palpable truth. It is a universal principle of this upside-down world that God manifests Himself in nature, whereas we should say the opposite, namely, that originally at least nature manifests itself to man as a God, that nature makes on man an impression which he calls God, which he becomes conscious of and objectifies under the name of God. It is a universal doctrine in our upside-down world that nature sprang from God, whereas we should say the opposite, namely, that God was abstracted from nature and is merely a concept derived from it; for all the predicates, all the attributes or determinations, all the realities, as the philosophers say, that is, all the essences or perfections which are summed up in God, or whose totality is, or is called, God — in short all those divine predicates that are not borrowed from man, are derived from nature, so that they objectify, represent, illustrate nothing other than the essence of nature, or nature pure and simple. The difference is only that God is an abstraction, that is, a mere notion, while nature is concrete, that is, real; but the essence, the substance, the content are the same; God is nature in the abstract, that is, removed from physical perception, transformed into an object or concept of the intellect; nature itself is sensuous, real nature as directly revealed and communicated to us by the senses.

If we now consider the attributes of the Godhead, we shall find that they are all rooted in nature, that they are meaningful only if we relate them to nature. One attribute of God is power: He is a powerful being, the most powerful of beings; according to late conceptions, He is all-powerful. Power is the first predicate of the Godhead or rather, it is the first god. But what is this power? What does it express? Nothing other than the power of natural phenomena. As we have seen in the first lectures, thunder and lightning, the phenomena that make the most powerful, most terrible impression on man, are the effects of the highest, most powerful god, or they are one with him. Even in the Old Testament, thunder is the voice of God, and in many passages lightning is "the face of God." But what is a God whose voice is thunder, whose face is lightning, other than the essence of nature, or of thunder and lightning? Even Christian theists identify the power of their God, for all His spirituality, purely and simply with the sensuous power of nature. The Christian poet Triller, for example, writes in his "poetic reflections":

> Is it not so, confess,
> That your heart trembles in your breast,
> When with shattering power the thunder
> Rolls and roars and crashes?
> What can be the cause of your fear,
> What else, if not that your mind
> Tells you that with the might of His thunder
> And with the sulphurous flames of His lightning
> God might suddenly snatch you from the earth?
> Thus there can be no doubt
> *That thunder and lightning are a sign*
> *Of God's being and God's omnipotence.*

And even in Christian views that do not make the power of nature so palpably evident as the divine Triller makes the thunder and lightning, it remains the underlying factor. The Christian theists, whose guiding principle is abstraction, hence remoteness from the truth of nature, who look upon nature as dead, inert matter, regard God's power or omnipotence as the cause of motion in nature. God, they say, has conferred, implanted, impressed motion upon matter, and they marvel at God's vast power, which has enabled Him to set this enormous mass or machine in motion. But this power by which God set body or matter in motion — is it not abstracted from the force or power by which one body imparts its motion to another? The diplomatic theists deny, to be sure, that God moved matter by means of a thrust, or any immediate contact; as a spirit, they claim, He did so by His will alone. But they do not really conceive God as pure spirit — at the same time they conceive of Him as a material and sensuous, or better still, cryptomaterial and cryptosensuous being. And by that same token He did not induce motion by sheer force of will. Will is nothing without power, without a positive material capacity. The theists themselves expressly distinguish God's power from His will and reason. But what is this power distinguished from will and reason if not the power of nature?

The notion of power as a divine predicate or god springs chiefly from a comparison of the works of nature with the works of man. Man cannot produce plants and trees, he cannot make storms, thunder, and lightning. Vergil therefore calls Jupiter's thunderbolt "inimitable," and in Greek mythology Salmoneus is struck by Zeus' lightning for his presumption in trying to make thunder and lightning. Such works of nature are beyond man's strength, they are not in his power. That is why the being who produces such effects and phenomena is *superhuman* and therefore divine. But all these effects and phenomena express nothing other than the *power of nature.* Christian theists, to be sure, attribute these effects *indirectly,* or in their ultimate source, to God, to a being distinct from nature and endowed with will, reason, and consciousness; but this is only an explanation, and what concerns us here is not whether a spirit is or is not, can or cannot be, the source of these phenomena, but solely the fact that the natural phenomena, the natural forces which even a Christian, at least a rational enlightened Christian, does not look upon as immediate actions of God, but, in accordance with the real facts, as effects of nature, are the model from which man originally derived the notion and concept of a superhuman divine power.

An example: If a man is struck down by lightning, a Christian says or thinks that this has not happened by chance or simply in the course of nature; he attributes it to a divine decision; for "God's eye is on the sparrow." God wanted the man to die, and to die in just this way. His will is the cause, the last or first cause of the man's death; the immediate cause is the lightning, or as the ancients believed, the lightning is the instrument with which God Himself killed the man, or according to modern faith, the instrumental cause which by God's will, at least with His permission or consent, brought about the man's death. But this shattering, killing, searing power is the power of lightning itself, just as the power or effect of the arsenic with which I poison somebody is not an effect of my will, of my power, but the power and effect inherent in the arsenic itself. Thus from the theist or Christian standpoint we distinguish the power of *things* from the power or rather the will of God. We do not regard the effects and hence the properties — for we know the properties of things only by their effects — of electricity, of magnetism, of air, water, and fire as the properties and effects of God; we do not say: God burns and gives warmth, we do not say or think that God makes something wet; we say that water makes it wet; we do not say that God is thundering and lightning, no, we say: *it* is thundering and lightning, etc. But it is precisely from these phenomena, properties, and effects of nature, incompatible with the spiritual God conceived by Christians, that man derives his conception of divine, superhuman power, and because of which, so long as he remains faithful to his original, ingenuous view and does not split nature into God and the world, he worships nature itself as God.

Apropos of the word superhuman, I cannot refrain from a digression. One of the most frequent laments heard from the religious and learned bewailers of atheism is that it destroys or ignores an essential need of man, the need to revere something higher than himself, and therefore turns man into a presumptuous egoist. But in annulling what is Above Man theologically, atheism does not annul what is ethically and naturally Higher. The ethically Higher is the ideal that every man must pursue if he is to make anything worthwhile of himself; but this ideal is and must be a human ideal and aim. The naturally Higher is nature itself, and in particular, the celestial powers on which our existence, our earth depend; for the earth itself is only a part of the "celestial powers" and is what it is only by virtue of the position it occupies in our solar system. Even the supraterrestrial and superhuman God owes His origin only to the physical, optical being-above-us of the sky and the heavenly bodies. According to Cyril, Julian proved the divinity of the stars by pointing out that everyone raises his hands to heaven when he prays or swears or in any way invokes the name of the Godhead. Even Christians put their "spiritual, omnipresent" God in the sky; and they put Him there for the same reasons which originally caused the sky itself to be regarded as God. Aristo of Chios, a pupil of Zeno, founder of Stoicism, said expressly: "Over us is [or goes] the Physical [nature], for it is impossible to know, and brings us no benefit." But this Physical is mainly the celestial. More than anything else it was the objects of astronomy and meteorology that aroused the interest of the first scientists and natural philosophers. Socrates rejected physics as something beyond the powers of man and directed men's minds from physics to ethics; but by physics he meant chiefly astronomy and meteorology, hence the well-known saying that he brought philosophy down from heaven to earth; and this is also why he spoke of all philosophizing that exceeded the powers and vocation of man as *meteorologein* (i.e., concern with celestial, supra-terrestrial things).

But just as The Power, the superhuman, the highest or higher being above us — among the Romans the gods were called *Superi* — was originally a predicate of nature, so were eternity and infinity also predicates of nature. In Homer, for example, "infinite" is an epithet for the sea and the earth, in the philosopher Anaximenes for the air; in the Zend Avesta eternity and immortality are predicates of the sun and stars. Even Aristotle, the greatest philosopher of antiquity, imputes immutability and eternity to the heavens and the heavenly bodies in contrast to the transience and mutability of earthly things. And even a Christian infers (that is, derives) the greatness and infinity of God from the greatness and infinity of the world or nature, though he immediately proceeds (for a reason that is readily understood but need not be discussed here) to make nature disappear behind God. In agreement with innumerable other Christians, Scheuchzer, for example, writes: "Not only the unfathomable greatness of the world and of the heavenly bodies but even the tiniest grain of dust, is a sign of His infinite greatness." And elsewhere the same scholar and pious naturalist writes: "The Creator's *infinite* wisdom and power shine forth not only from the *infinite magna,* from the mass of the universe and from the great bodies that float free in the heavens . . . but also from the *infinite parva,* from the grains of dust and tiny organisms. . . . Each grain of dust contains an infinite number of infinitesimal worlds." The concept of infinity coincides with the concept of all-embracing universality.

God is no particular and hence finite being, He is not confined to this or that nation or locality, but neither is nature. Sun, moon, sky, earth, and sea, said a Greek philosopher, are common to all, and a Roman poet (Ovid) said that nature gave no one exclusive possession of sun, air, or water. God is "no respecter of persons," but neither is nature. The earth brings forth its fruits not for this or that chosen person or nation; the sun shines not only on Christian or Jew, but illumines all men without distinction. Precisely because of this infinity and universality of nature the ancient Jews, who regarded themselves as the chosen people and believed that the world had been created for their sake, could not understand why the good things of life had not been made available to them alone, but to idolaters as well. When asked why God did not destroy idolatry, Jewish scholars therefore answered that He would destroy the idolaters if they did not worship things that were necessary to the world; but that since they worshiped the sun, the moon, the stars, water, and fire, why should He destroy the world for the sake of a few fools? In other words: God must spare the causes and objects of idolatry, because without them the Jews could not endure.

Here we have an interesting illustration of certain essential features of religion. First of all, an illustration of the contradiction between theory and practice, faith and life, implicit in every religion. This natural sharing of earth, light, and water with idolaters was diametrically opposed to the theory and faith of the Jews; since they wished to have nothing in common with the heathen and their religion forbade it, they should not have shared the blessings of life with them. If they had been consistent, they should have excluded either the heathen or themselves from the enjoyment of these blessings. Secondly, we have here an illustration of the fact that nature is far more liberal than the God of the religions, that man's natural view is far more universal than his religious view which separates man from man, Christian from Jew, Jew from heathen, and that consequently the unity of the human race, the love that embraces all men, is by no means grounded on the concept of the heavenly father or, as modern philosophers say, on the concept of Spirit, but far more on nature, which originally was indeed its sole foundation. The universal love of man is by no means of Christian origin. It was already taught by the pagan philosophers; but the God of the pagan philosophers was nothing other than the world, or nature.

Christians, on the contrary, held the same belief as the Jews; they too believed and said that the world was created and preserved *for their sake alone*. They were as consistently incapable as the Jews of finding an explanation for the existence of infidels and of heathen in general. For if the world exists only for the sake of Christians, why and to what end are there other people who are not Christians and do not believe in the Christian God? The Christian God accounts for the existence only of Christians, and not of pagans and infidels. The God whose sun shines on the just and the unjust, believers and unbelievers, Christians and pagans alike is indifferent to such religious distinctions, He knows nothing of them; this God, in truth, is nothing other than nature. Thus the Biblical words that God makes His sun shine on good and evil alike, contain a vestige or evidence of a nature religion, or else the good and the evil are taken as men who may differ from one another morally but not dogmatically, for the dogmatic, Biblical God strictly distinguishes the sheep from the goats, Christians from Jews and heathen, believers from unbelievers; to the goats He promises hell, to the sheep heaven. He condemns the sheep to bliss and eternal life, and the goats to eternal misery and death. But this is precisely why the existence of such men condemned to nothingness cannot be derived from Him; there is no way of explaining the thousands and thousands of contradictions, perplexities, difficulties, and inconsistencies in which religious belief involves us, unless we acknowledge that the original God was a being abstracted from nature and accordingly replace the mystical, ambiguous name and being of God with the name and being of nature.

FRIEDRICH NIETZSCHE

Beyond Good and Evil

Friedrich Wilhelm Nietzsche (1844–1900) was born and educated in Germany but became a Swiss citizen and a professor of Greek in Basel, Switzerland; for some years he was a disciple of Richard Wagner. In a series of writings of great literary power and almost prophetic intensity, of which *Beyond Good and Evil* is one of the most important, he announced that the God of traditional European belief was dead and that the future belonged to a new ethic of superior power rather than of Christlike meekness.

THERE IS A GREAT LADDER of religious cruelty, with many rounds; but three of these are the most important. Once on a time men sacrificed human beings to their God, and perhaps just those they loved the best — to this category belong the firstling sacrifices of all primitive religions, and also the sacrifice of the Emperor Tiberius in the Mithra-Grotto on the Island of Capri, that most terrible of all Roman anachronisms. Then during the moral epoch of mankind, they sacrificed to their God the strongest instincts they possessed, their "nature"; *this* festal joy shines in the cruel glances of ascetics and "anti-natural" fanatics. Finally, what still remained to be sacrificed? Was it not necessary in the end for men to sacrifice everything comforting, holy, healing, all hope, all faith in hidden harmonies, in future blessedness and justice? Was it not necessary to sacrifice God himself, and out of cruelty to themselves to worship stone, stupidity, gravity, fate, nothingness? To sacrifice God for nothingness — this paradoxical mystery of the ultimate cruelty has been reserved for the rising generation; we all know something thereof already.

Whoever, like myself, prompted by some enigmatical desire, has long endeavoured to go to the bottom of the question of pessimism and free it from the half-Christian, half-German narrowness and stupidity in which it has finally presented itself to this century, namely, in the form of Schopenhauer's philosophy; whoever, with an Asiatic and super-Asiatic eye, has actually looked inside, and into the most world-renouncing of all possible modes of thought — beyond good and evil, and no longer like Buddha and Schopenhauer, under the dominion and delusion of morality, — whoever has done this, has perhaps just thereby, without really desiring it, opened his eyes to behold the opposite ideal: the ideal of the most world-approving, exuberant and vivacious man, who has not only learned to compromise and arrange with that which was and is, but wishes to have it again *as it was and is,* for all eternity, insatiably calling out *de capo,* not only to himself, but to the whole piece and play; and not only the play, but actually to him who requires the play — and makes it necessary; because he always requires himself anew — and makes himself necessary. — What? And this would not be — *circulus vitiosus deus* [the vicious circle as God]?

The distance, and as it were the space around man, grows with the strength of his intellectual vision and insight: his world becomes profounder; new stars, new enigmas, and notions are ever coming into view. Perhaps everything on which the intellectual eye has exercised its acuteness and profundity has just been an occasion for its exercise, something of a game, something for children and childish minds. Perhaps the most solemn conceptions that have caused the most fighting and suffering, the conceptions "God" and "sin," will one day seem to us of no more importance than a child's plaything or a child's pain seems to an old man; — and perhaps another plaything and another pain will then be necessary once more for "the old man" — always childish enough, an eternal child!

Has it been observed to what extent outward idleness, or semi-idleness, is necessary to a real religious life (alike for its favourite microscopic labour of self-examination, and for its soft placidity called "prayer," the state of perpetual readiness for the "coming of God"), I mean the idleness with a good conscience, the idleness of olden times and of blood, to which the aristocratic sentiment that work is *dishonouring* — that it vulgarises body and soul — is not quite unfamiliar? And that consequently the modern, noisy, time-engrossing, conceited, foolishly proud laboriousness educates and prepares for "unbelief" more than anything else? Amongst these, for instance, who are at present living apart from religion in Germany, I find "free-thinkers" of diversified species and origin, but above all a majority of those in whom laboriousness from generation to generation has dissolved the religious instincts; so that they no longer know what purpose religions serve, and only note their existence in the world with a kind of dull astonishment. They feel themselves already fully occupied, these good people, be it by their business or by their pleasures, not to mention the "Fatherland," and the newspapers, and their "family duties"; it seems that they have no time whatever left for religion; and above all, it is not obvious to them whether it is a question of a new business or a new pleasure — for it is impossible, they say to themselves, that people should go to church merely to spoil their tempers. They are by no means enemies of religious customs; should certain circumstances, State affairs perhaps, require their participation in such customs, they do what is required, as so many things are done — with a patient and unassuming seriousness, and without much curiosity or discomfort; — they live too much apart and outside to feel even the necessity for a *for* or *against* in such matters. Among those indifferent persons may be reckoned nowadays the majority of German Protestants of the middle classes, especially in the great laborious centres of trade and commerce; also the majority of laborious scholars, and the entire University personnel (with the exception of the theologians, whose existence and possibility there always give psychologists new and more subtle puzzles to solve). On the part of pious, or merely church-going people, there is seldom any idea of *how much* good will, one might say arbitrary will, is now necessary for a German scholar to take the problem of religion seriously; his whole profession (and as I have said, his whole workmanlike laboriousness, to which he is compelled by his modern conscience) inclines him to a lofty and almost charitable serenity as regards religion, with which is occasionally mingled a slight disdain for the "uncleanliness" of spirit which he takes for granted wherever any one still professes to belong to the Church. It is only with the help of history (*not* through his own personal experience, therefore) that the scholar succeeds in bringing himself to a respectful seriousness, and to a certain timid deference in presence of religions; but even when his sentiments have reached the stage of gratitude towards them, he has not personally advanced one step nearer to that which still maintains itself as Church or as piety; perhaps even the contrary. The practical indifference to religious matters in the midst of which he has been born and brought up, usually sublimates itself in his case into circumspection and cleanliness, which shuns contact with religious men and things; and it may be just the depth of his tolerance and humanity which prompts him to avoid the delicate trouble which tolerance itself brings with it. — Every age has its own divine type of naïveté, for the discovery of which other ages may envy it: and how much naïveté — adorable, childlike, and boundlessly foolish naïveté is involved in this belief of the scholar in his superiority, in the good conscience of his tolerance, in the unsuspecting, simple certainty with which his instinct treats the religious man as a lower and less valuable type, beyond, before, and *above* which he himself has developed — he, the little arrogant dwarf and mob-man, the sedulously alert, head-and-hand drudge of "ideas," of "modern ideas"!

Whoever has seen deeply into the world has doubtless divined what wisdom there is in the fact that men are superficial. It is their pre-servative instinct which teaches them to be flighty, lightsome, and false. Here and there one finds a passionate and exaggerated adoration of "pure forms" in philosophers as well as in artists: it is not to be doubted that whoever has *need* of the cult of the superficial to that extent, has at one time or another made an unlucky dive *beneath* it. Perhaps there is even an order of rank with respect to those burnt children, the born artists who find the enjoyment of life only in trying to *falsify* its image (as if taking wearisome revenge on it); one might guess to what degree life has disgusted them, by the extent to which they wish to see its image falsified, attenuated, ultrafied, and de-ified; — one might reckon the *homines religiosi* amongst the artists, as their *highest* rank. It is the profound, suspicious fear of an incurable pessimism which compels whole centuries to fasten their teeth into a religious interpretation of existence: the fear of the instinct which divines that truth might be attained *too soon,* before man has become strong enough, hard enough, artist enough. . . . Piety, the "Life in God," regarded in this light, would appear as the most elaborate and ultimate product of the *fear* of truth, as artist-adoration and artist-intoxication in presence of the most logical of all falsifications, as the will to the inversion of truth, to untruth at any price. Perhaps there has hitherto been no more effective means of beautifying man than piety; by means of it man can become so artful, so superficial, so iridescent, and so good, that his appearance no longer offends.

To love mankind *for God's sake* — this has so far been the noblest and remotest sentiment to which mankind has attained. That love to mankind, without any redeeming intention in the background, is only an *additional* folly and brutishness, that the inclination to this love has first to get its proportion, its delicacy, its grain of salt and sprinkling of ambergris from a higher inclination: — whoever first perceived and "experienced" this, however his tongue may have stammered as it attempted to express such a delicate matter, let him for all time be holy and respected, as the man who has so far flown highest and gone astray in the finest fashion!

The philosopher, as *we* free spirits understand him — as the man of the greatest responsibility, who has the conscience for the general development of mankind, — will use religion for his disciplining and educating work, just as he will use the contemporary political and economic conditions. The selecting and disciplining influence — destructive, as well as creative and fashioning — which can be exercised by means of religion is manifold and varied, according to the sort of people placed under its spell and protection. For those who are strong and independent, destined and trained to command, in whom the judgment and skill of a ruling race is incorporated, religion is an additional means for overcoming resistance in the exercise of authority — as a bond which binds rulers and subjects in common, betraying and surrendering to the former the conscience of the latter, their inmost heart, which would fain escape obedience. And in the case of the unique natures of noble origin, if by virtue of superior spirituality they should incline to a more retired and contemplative life, reserving to themselves only the more refined forms of government (over chosen disciples or members of an order), religion itself may be used as a means for obtaining peace from the noise and trouble of managing *grosser* affairs, and for securing immunity from the *unavoidable* filth of all political agitation. The Brahmins, for instance, understood this fact. With the help of a religious organisation, they secured to themselves the power of nominating kings for the people, while their sentiments prompted them to keep apart and outside, as men with a higher and super-regal mission. At the same time religion gives inducement and opportunity to some of the subjects to qualify themselves for future ruling and commanding: the slowly ascending ranks and classes, in which, through fortunate marriage customs, volitional power and delight in self-control are on the increase. To them religion offers sufficient incentives and temptations to aspire to higher intellectuality, and to experience the sentiments of authoritative self-control, of silence, and of solitude. Asceticism and Puritanism are almost indispensable means of educating and ennobling a race which seeks to rise above its hereditary baseness and work itself upward to future supremacy. And finally, to ordinary men, to the majority of the people, who exist for service and general utility, and are only so far entitled to exist, religion gives invaluable contentedness with their lot and condition, peace of heart, ennoblement of obedience, additional social happiness and sympathy, with something of transfiguration and embellishment, something of justification of all the commonplaceness, all the meanness, all the semi-animal poverty of their souls. Religion, together with the religious significance of life, sheds sunshine over such perpetually harassed men, and makes even their own aspect endurable to them; it operates upon them as the Epicurean philosophy usually operates upon sufferers of a higher order, in a refreshing and refining manner, almost *turning* suffering *to account,* and in the end even hallowing and vindicating it. There is perhaps nothing so admirable in Christianity and Buddhism as their art of teaching even the lowest to elevate themselves by piety to a seemingly higher order of things, and thereby to retain their satisfaction with the actual world in which they find it difficult enough to live — this very difficulty being necessary.

To be sure — to make also the bad counter-reckoning against such religions, and to bring to light their secret dangers — the cost is always excessive and terrible when religions do *not* operate as an educational and disciplinary medium in the hands of the philosopher, but rule voluntarily and *paramountly,* when they wish to be the final end, and not a means along with other means. Among men, as among all other animals, there is a surplus of defective, diseased, degenerating, infirm, and necessarily suffering individuals; the successful cases, among men also, are always the exception; and in view of the fact that man is *the animal not yet properly adapted to his environment,* the rare exception. But worse still. The higher the type a man represents, the greater is the improbability that he will *succeed;* the accidental, the law of irrationality in the general constitution of mankind, manifests itself most terribly in its destructive effect on the higher orders of men, the conditions of whose lives are delicate, diverse, and difficult to determine. What, then, is the attitude of the two greatest religions abovementioned to the *surplus* of failures in life? They endeavour to preserve and keep alive whatever can be preserved; in fact, as the religions *for sufferers,* they take the part of these upon principle; they are always in favour of those who suffer from life as from a disease, and they

would fain treat every other experience of life as false and impossible.
However highly we may esteem this indulgent and preservative care
(inasmuch as in applying to others, it has applied, and applies also to
the highest and usually the most suffering type of man), the hitherto
paramount religions — to give a general appreciation of them — are
among the principal causes which have kept the type of "man" upon
a lower level — they have preserved too much *that which should have
perished*. One has to thank them for invaluable services; and who is
sufficiently rich in gratitude not to feel poor at the contemplation of
all that the "spiritual men" of Christianity have done for Europe
hitherto! But when they had given comfort to the sufferers, courage
to the oppressed and despairing, a staff and support to the helpless,
and when they had allured from society into convents and spiritual
penitentiaries the broken-hearted and distracted: what else had they
to do in order to work systematically in that fashion, and with a good
conscience, for the preservation of all the sick and suffering, which
means, in deed and in truth, to work for *the deterioration of the
European race?* To *reverse* all estimates of value — *that* is what they
had to do! And to shatter the strong, to spoil great hopes, to cast
suspicion on the delight in beauty, to break down everything autonomous, manly, conquering, and imperious — all instincts which are
natural to the highest and most successful type of "man" — into
uncertainty, distress of conscience, and self-destruction; forsooth, to
invert all love of the earthly and of supremacy over the earth, into
hatred of the earth and earthly things — *that* is the task the Church
imposed on itself, and was obliged to impose, until, according to its
standard of value, "unworldliness," "unsensuousness," and "higher
man" fused into one sentiment. If one could observe the strangely
painful, equally coarse and refined comedy of European Christianity
with the derisive and impartial eye of an Epicurean god, I should think
one would never cease marvelling and laughing; does it not actually
seem that some single will has ruled over Europe for eighteen centuries in order to make a *sublime abortion* of man? He, however, who,
with opposite requirements (no longer Epicurean) and with some
divine hammer in his hand, could approach this almost voluntary
degeneration and stunting of mankind, as exemplified in the European Christian (Pascal, for instance), would he not have to cry aloud
with rage, pity, and horror: "Oh, you bunglers, presumptuous pitiful
bunglers, what have you done! Was that a work for your hands? How
you have hacked and botched my finest stone! What have *you* presumed to do!" — I should say that Christianity has hitherto been the

most portentous of presumptions. Men, not great enough, nor hard enough, to be entitled as artists to take part in fashioning *man;* men, not sufficiently strong and far-sighted to *allow,* with sublime self-constraint, the obvious law of the thousandfold failures and perishings to prevail; men, not sufficiently noble to see the radically different grades of rank and intervals of rank that separate man from man: — *such* men, with their "equality before God," have hitherto swayed the destiny of Europe; until at last a dwarfed, almost ludicrous species has been produced, a gregarious animal, something obliging, sickly, mediocre, the European of the present day.

SIGMUND FREUD

The Future of an Illusion

> Sigmund Freud (1856–1939), who was born in what is now
> Czechoslovakia but lived in Vienna, founded modern psy-
> choanalysis, revolutionizing forever the very definition of
> human nature. In the course of doing so, he also attacked
> the Judaism out of which he had come (*Moses and Mono-
> theism*) and religion in general (*Totem and Taboo*); and in
> *The Future of an Illusion* he delivered his most thorough-
> going critique of all religious faith as grounded in a need for
> dependency that should now be addressed by other means.

WHAT IS THE PSYCHOLOGICAL SIGNIFICANCE of religious ideas and how
can we classify them? The question is at first not at all easy to answer.
Having rejected various formulas, I shall take my stand by this one:
religion consists of certain dogmas, assertions about facts and conditions of external (or internal) reality, which tell one something that
one has not oneself discovered and which claim that one should give
them credence. As they give information about what are to us the most
interesting and important things in life, they are particularly highly
valued. He who knows nothing of them is ignorant indeed, and he who
has assimilated them may consider himself enriched.

There are of course many such dogmas about the most diverse
things of this world. Every school hour is full of them. Let us choose
geography. We hear there: Konstanz is on the Bodensee. A student
song adds: If you don't believe it go and see. I happen to have been
there, and can confirm the fact that this beautiful town lies on the
shore of a broad stretch of water, which all those dwelling around call
the Bodensee. I am now completely convinced of the accuracy of this
geographical statement. And in this connection I am reminded of
another and very remarkable experience. I was already a man of
mature years when I stood for the first time on the hill of the Athenian

Acropolis, between the temple ruins, looking out on to the blue sea. A feeling of astonishment mingled with my pleasure, which prompted me to say: then it really is true, what we used to be taught at school! How shallow and weak at that age must have been my belief in the real truth of what I heard if I can be so astonished to-day! But I will not emphasize the significance of this experience too much; yet another explanation of my astonishment is possible, which did not strike me at the time, and which is of a wholly subjective nature and connected with the peculiar character of the place.

All such dogmas as these, then, exact belief in their contents, but not without substantiating their title to this. They claim to be the condensed result of a long process of thought, which is founded on observation and also, certainly, on reasoning; they show how, if one so intends, one can go through this process oneself, instead of accepting the result of it; and the source of the knowledge imparted by the dogma is always added, where it is not, as with geographical statements, self-evident. For instance: the earth is shaped like a globe; the proofs adduced for this are Foucault's pendulum experiment, the phenomena of the horizon and the possibility of circumnavigating the earth. Since it is impracticable, as all concerned realize, to send every school child on a voyage round the world, one is content that the school teaching shall be taken on trust, but one knows that the way to personal conviction is still open.

Let us try to apply the same tests to the dogmas of religion. If we ask on what their claim to be believed is based, we receive three answers, which accord remarkably ill with one another. They deserve to be believed: firstly, because our primal ancestors already believed them; secondly, because we possess proofs, which have been handed down to us from this very period of antiquity; and thirdly, because it is forbidden to raise the question of their authenticity at all. Formerly this presumptuous act was visited with the very severest penalties, and even to-day society is unwilling to see anyone renew it.

This third point cannot but rouse our strongest suspicions. Such a prohibition can surely have only one motive: that society knows very well the uncertain basis of the claim it makes for its religious doctrines. If it were otherwise, the relevant material would certainly be placed most readily at the disposal of anyone who wished to gain conviction for himself. And so we proceed to test the other two arguments with a feeling of mistrust not easily allayed. We ought to believe because our forefathers believed. But these ancestors of ours were far more ignorant than we; they believed in things we could not possibly accept to-day; so the possibility occurs that religious doctrines may also be in this category. The proofs they have bequeathed to us are deposited in writings that themselves bear every trace of being untrustworthy. They are full of contradictions, revisions, and interpolations; where they speak of actual authentic proofs they are themselves of doubtful authenticity. It does not help much if divine revelation is asserted to be the origin of their text or only of their content.

*   *   *   *   *

One must now mention two attempts to evade the problem, which both convey the impression of frantic effort. One of them, high-handed in its nature, is old; the other is subtle and modern. The first is the *Credo quia absurdum* [I believe it because it is absurd] of the early Father. It would imply that religious doctrines are outside reason's jurisdiction; they stand above reason. Their truth must be inwardly felt: one does not need to comprehend them. But this *Credo* is only of interest as a voluntary confession; as a decree it has no binding force. Am I to be obliged to believe every absurdity? And if not, why just this one? There is no appeal beyond reason. And if the truth of religious doctrines is dependent on an inner experience which bears witness to that truth, what is one to make of the many people who do not have that rare experience? One may expect all men to use the gift of reason that they possess, but one cannot set up an obligation that shall apply to all on a basis that only exists for quite a few. Of what significance is it for other people that you have won from a state of ecstasy, which has deeply moved you, an imperturbable conviction of the real truth of the doctrines of religion?

The second attempt is that of the philosophy of "As If." It explains that in our mental activity we assume all manner of things, the groundlessness, indeed the absurdity, of which we fully realize. They are called "fictions," but from a variety of practical motives we are led to behave "as if" we believed in these fictions. This, it is argued, is the case with religious doctrines on account of their unequalled importance for the maintenance of human society. This argument is not far removed from the *Credo quia absurdum*. But I think that the claim of the philosophy of "As If" is such as only a philosopher could make. The man whose thinking is not influenced by the wiles of philosophy will never be able to accept it; with the confession of absurdity, of illogicality, there is no more to be said as far as he is concerned. He cannot be expected to forgo the guarantees he demands for all his usual activities just in the matter of his most important interests. I am

reminded of one of my children who was distinguished at an early
ageby a peculiarly marked sense of reality. When the children were
told a fairy tale, to which they listened with rapt attention, he would
come forward and ask: Is that a true story? Having been told that it was
not, he would turn away with an air of disdain. It is to be expected that
men will soon behave in like manner towards the religious fairy tales,
despite the advocacy of the philosophy of "As If."

But at present they still behave quite differently, and in past ages,
in spite of their incontrovertible lack of authenticity, religious ideas
have exercised the very strongest influence on mankind. This is a fresh
psychological problem. We must ask where the inherent strength of
these doctrines lies and to what circumstance they owe their efficacy,
independent, as it is, of the acknowledgement of the reason.

I think we have sufficiently paved the way for the answer to both these
questions. It will be found if we fix our attention on the psychical
origin of religious ideas. These, which profess to be dogmas are not
the residue of experience or the final result of reflection; they are
illusions, fulfilments of the oldest, strongest and most insistent wishes
of mankind; the secret of their strength is the strength of these wishes.
We know already that the terrifying effect of infantile helplessness
aroused the need for protection — protection through love — which
the father relieved, and that the discovery that this helplessness would
continue through the whole of life made it necessary to cling to the
existence of a father — but this time a more powerful one. Thus the
benevolent rule of divine providence allays our anxiety in face of life's
dangers, the establishment of a moral world order ensures the fulfilment of the demands of justice, which within human culture have so
often remained unfulfilled, and the prolongation of earthly existence
by a future life provides in addition the local and temporal setting for
these wish-fulfilments. Answers to the questions that tempt human
curiosity, such as the origin of the universe and the relation between
the body and the soul, are developed in accordance with the underlying assumptions of this system; it betokens a tremendous relief for
the individual psyche if it is released from the conflicts of childhood
arising out of the father complex, which are never wholly overcome,
and if these conflicts are afforded a universally accepted solution.

When I say that they are illusions, I must define the meaning of the
word. An illusion is not the same as an error, it is indeed not necessarily an error. Aristotle's belief that vermin are evolved out of dung,
to which ignorant people still cling, was an error; so was the belief of

a former generation of doctors that *tabes dorsalis* was the result of sexual excess. It would be improper to call these errors illusions. On the other hand, it was an illusion on the part of Columbus that he had discovered a new sea-route to India. The part played by his wish in this error is very clear. One may describe as an illusion the statement of certain nationalists that the Indo-Germanic race is the only one capable of culture, or the belief, which only psycho-analysis destroyed, that the child is a being without sexuality. It is characteristic of the illusion that it is derived from men's wishes; in this respect it approaches the psychiatric delusion, but it is to be distinguished from this, quite apart from the more complicated structure of the latter. In the delusion we emphasize as essential the conflict with reality; the illusion need not be necessarily false, that is to say, unrealizable or incompatible with reality. For instance, a poor girl may have an illusion that a prince will come and fetch her home. It is possible; some such cases have occurred. That the Messiah will come and found a golden age is much less probable; according to one's personal attitude one will classify this belief as an illusion or as analogous to a delusion. Examples of illusions that have come true are not easy to discover, but the illusion of the alchemists that all metals can be turned into gold may prove to be one. The desire to have lots of gold, as much gold as possible, has been considerably damped by our modern insight into the nature of wealth, yet chemistry no longer considers a transmutation of metals into gold as impossible. Thus we call a belief an illusion when wish-fulfilment is a prominent factor in its motivation, while disregarding its relations to reality, just as the illusion itself does.

If after this survey we turn again to religious doctrines, we may reiterate that they are all illusions, they do not admit of proof, and no one can be compelled to consider them as true or to believe in them. Some of them are so improbable, so very incompatible with everything we have laboriously discovered about the reality of the world, that we may compare them — taking adequately into account the psychological differences — to delusions. Of the reality value of most of them we cannot judge; just as they cannot be proved, neither can they be refuted. We still know too little to approach them critically. The riddles of the universe only reveal themselves slowly to our enquiry, to many questions science can as yet give no answer; but scientific work is our only way to the knowledge of external reality. Again, it is merely illusion to expect anything from intuition or trance; they can give us nothing but particulars, which are difficult to interpret, about our own mental life, never information about the questions that are so lightly answered by the doctrines of religion. It would be wanton to let one's own arbitrary action fill the gap, and according to one's personal estimate declare this or that part of the religious system to be more or less acceptable. These questions are too momentous for that; too sacred, one might say.

At this point it may be objected: well, then, if even the crabbed sceptics admit that the statements of religion cannot be confuted by reason, why should not I believe in them, since they have so much on their side — tradition, the concurrence of mankind, and all the consolation they yield? Yes, why not? Just as no one can be forced into belief, so no one can be forced into unbelief. But do not deceive yourself into thinking that with such arguments you are following the path of correct reasoning. If ever there was a case of facile argument, this is one. Ignorance is ignorance; no right to believe anything is derived from it. No reasonable man will behave so frivolously in other matters or rest content with such feeble grounds for his opinions or for the attitude he adopts; it is only in the highest and holiest things that he allows this. In reality these are only attempts to delude oneself or other people into the belief that one still holds fast to religion, when one has long cut oneself loose from it. Where questions of religion are concerned people are guilty of every possible kind of insincerity and intellectual misdemeanour. Philosophers stretch the meaning of words until they retain scarcely anything of their original sense; by calling "God" some vague abstraction which they have created for themselves, they pose as deists, as believers, before the world; they may even pride themselves on having attained a higher and purer idea of God, although their God is nothing but an insubstantial shadow and no longer the mighty personality of religious doctrine. Critics persist in calling "deeply religious" a person who confesses to a sense of man's insignificance and impotence in face of the universe, although it is not this feeling that constitutes the essence of religious emotion, but rather the next step, the reaction to it, which seeks a remedy against this feeling. He who goes no further, he who humbly acquiesces in the insignificant part man plays in the universe, is, on the contrary, irreligious in the truest sense of the word.

It does not lie within the scope of this enquiry to estimate the value of religious doctrines as truth. It suffices that we have recognized them, psychologically considered, as illusions. But we need not conceal the fact that this discovery strongly influences our attitude to what must appear to many the most important of questions. We know approximately at what periods and by what sort of men religious doctrines were formed. If we now learn from what motives this happened, our attitude to the problem of religion will suffer an appreciable change. We say to ourselves: it would indeed be very nice if there were a God, who was both creator of the world and a benevolent providence, if there were a moral world order and a future life, but at the same time it is very odd that this is all just as we should wish it ourselves. And it would be still odder if our poor, ignorant, enslaved ancestors had succeeded in solving all these difficult riddles of the universe.

KARL MARX

Religion, the Opium of the People

Karl Marx (1818–1883), although himself a German Jew, turned against Judaism perhaps even more than against Christianity, as his treatise *On the Jewish Question* (1844) made clear. In the same year he published this essay, *Contribution to the Critique of Hegel's "Philosophy of Right,"* which contains the famous definition of religion from which our title for the piece has been taken.

FOR GERMANY, the *criticism of religion* has been largely completed; and the criticism of religion is the premise of all criticism.

The *profane* existence of error is compromised once its *celestial oratio pro aris et focis* has been refuted. Man, who has found in the fantastic reality of heaven, where he sought a supernatural being, only his own reflection, will no longer be tempted to find only the *semblance* of himself — a non-human being — where he seeks and must seek his true reality.

The basis of irreligious criticism is this: *man makes religion;* religion does not make man. Religion is indeed man's self-consciousness and self-awareness so long as he has not found himself or has lost himself again. But *man* is not an abstract being, squatting outside the world. Man is *the human world,* the state, society. This state, this society, produce religion which is an *inverted world consciousness,* because they are an *inverted world.* Religion is the general theory of this world, its encyclopedic compendium, its logic in popular form, its spiritual *point d'honneur,* its enthusiasm, its moral sanction, its solemn complement, its general basis of consolation and justification. It is *the fantastic realization* of the human being inasmuch as the *human being* possesses no true reality. The struggle against religion is, therefore, indirectly a struggle against *that world* whose spiritual *aroma* is religion.

Religious suffering is at the same time an *expression* of real suffering and a *protest* against real suffering. Religion is the sigh of the oppressed creature, the sentiment of a heartless world, and the soul of soulless conditions. It is the *opium* of the people.

The abolition of religion as the *illusory* happiness of men, is a demand for their *real* happiness. The call to abandon their illusions about their condition is a *call to abandon a condition which requires illusions*. The criticism of religion is, therefore, *the embryonic criticism of this vale of tears* of which religion is the *halo*.

Criticism has plucked the imaginary flowers from the chain, not in order that man shall bear the chain without caprice or consolation but so that he shall cast off the chain and pluck the living flower. The criticism of religion disillusions man so that he will think, act, and fashion his reality as a man who has lost his illusions and regained his reason; so that he will revolve about himself as his own true sun. Religion is only the illusory sun about which man revolves so long as he does not revolve about himself.

It is the *task of history,* therefore, once the *other-world of truth* has vanished, to establish the *truth of this world*. The immediate *task of philosophy,* which is in the service of history, is to unmask human self-alienation in its *secular form* now that it has been unmasked in its *sacred form*. Thus the criticism of heaven is transformed into the criticism of earth, the *criticism of religion* into the *criticism of law,* and the *criticism of theology* into the *criticism of politics*.

The following exposition — which is a contribution to this undertaking — does not deal directly with the original but with a copy, the German *philosophy* of the state and of right, for the simple reason that it deals with Germany.

If one were to begin with the *status quo* itself in Germany, even in the most appropriate way, i.e. negatively, the result would still be an *anachronism*. Even the negation of our political present is already a dusty fact in the historical lumber room of modern nations. I may negate powdered wigs, but I am still left with unpowdered wigs. If I negate the German situation of 1843 I have, according to French chronology, hardly reached the year 1789, and still less the vital centre of the present day.

German history, indeed, prides itself upon a development which no other nation had previously accomplished, or will ever imitate in the historical sphere. We have shared in the restorations of modern nations without ever sharing in their revolutions. We have been restored, first because other nations have dared to make revolutions, and secondly because other nations have suffered counter-revolutions; in the first case because our masters were afraid, and in the second case because they were not afraid. Led by our shepherds, we have only once kept company with liberty and that was on the *day of its internment*.

A school of thought, which justifies the infamy of today by that of yesterday, which regards every cry from the serf under the knout as a cry of rebellion once the knout has become time-honoured, ancestral and historical, a school for which history shows only its *a posteriori* as the God of Israel did for his servant Moses — the *Historical school of law* — might be supposed to have invented German history, if it were not in fact itself an invention of German history. A Shylock, but a servile Shylock, it swears upon its bond, its historical, Christian-Germanic bond, for every pound of flesh cut from the heart of the people.

On the other hand, good-natured enthusiasts, German chauvinists by temperament and enlightened liberals by reflection, seek our history of liberty beyond our history, in the primeval Teutonic forests. But how does the history of our liberty differ from the history of the wild boar's liberty, if it is only to be found in the forests? And as the proverb has it: what is shouted into the forest, the forest echoes back. So peace upon the primeval Teutonic forests!

But *war* upon the state of affairs in Germany! By all means! This state of affairs is *beneath the level of history, beneath all criticism*; nevertheless it remains an object of criticism just as the criminal who is beneath humanity remains an object of the *executioner*. In its struggle against this state of affairs criticism is not a passion of the head, but the head of passion. It is not a lancet but a weapon. Its object is an *enemy* which it aims not to refute but to *destroy*. For the spirit of this state of affairs has already been refuted. It is not, in itself, an object worthy of our thought; it is an *existence* as contemptible as it is despised. Criticism itself has no need of any further elucidation of this object, for it has already understood it. Criticism is no longer an end in itself, but simply a means; *indignation* is its essential mode of feeling, and *denunciation* its principal task.

It is a matter of depicting the stifling pressure which the different social spheres exert upon each other, the universal but passive ill-humour, the complacent but self-deluding narrowness of spirit; all this incorporated in a system of government which lives by conserving this paltriness, and is itself *paltriness in government*.

What a spectacle! Society is infinitely divided into the most diverse races, which confront each other with their petty antipathies, bad conscience and coarse mediocrity; and which, precisely because of their ambiguous and mistrustful situation, are treated without exception, though in different ways, as merely tolerated existences by their masters. And they are forced to recognize and acknowledge this fact of being *dominated, governed* and *possessed,* as a *concession from heaven!* On the other side are the rulers themselves, whose greatness is in inverse proportion to their number.

The criticism which deals with this subject-matter is criticism in a hand-to-hand fight; and in such a fight it is of no interest to know whether the adversary is of the same rank, is noble or *interesting* — all that matters is to *strike* him. It is a question of denying the Germans an instant of illusion or resignation. The burden must be made still more irksome by awakening a consciousness of it, and shame must be made more shameful still by rendering it public. Every sphere of German society must be depicted as the *partie honteuse* of German society; and these petrified social conditions must be made to dance by singing their own melody to them. The nation must be taught to be *terrified* of itself, in order to give it *courage.* In this way an imperious need of the German nation will be satisfied, and the needs of nations are themselves the final causes of their satisfaction.

Even for the modern nations this struggle against the limited character of the German *status quo* does not lack interest; for the German *status quo* is the open *consummation of the ancien régime,* and the *ancien régime* is the *hidden defect of the modern state.* The struggle against the political present of the Germans is a struggle against the past of the modern nations, who are still continually importuned by the reminiscences of this past. It is instructive for the modern nations to see the *ancien régime,* which has played a *tragic* part in their history, play a *comic* part as a German ghost. The *ancien régime* had a *tragic* history, so long as it was the established power in the world while liberty was a personal fancy; in short, so long as it believed and had to believe in its own validity. So long as the *ancien régime,* as an existing world order, struggled against a new world which was just coming into existence, there was on its side a historical error but no personal error. Its decline was, therefore, tragic.

The present German régime, on the other hand, which is an anachronism, a flagrant contradiction of universally accepted axioms — the nullity of the *ancien régime* revealed to the whole world — only imagines that it believes in itself and asks the world to share its illusion. If it believed in its own *nature* would it attempt to hide it beneath the *semblance* of an alien nature and look for its salvation in hypocrisy and sophistry? The modern *ancien régime* is the comedian of a world order whose *real heroes* are dead. History is thorough, and it goes through many stages when it conducts an ancient formation to its grave. The last stage of a world-historical formation is comedy. The Greek gods, already once mortally wounded in Aeschylus' tragedy *Prometheus Bound,* had to endure a second death, a comic death, in Lucian's dialogues. Why should history proceed in this way? So that mankind shall separate itself *gladly* from its past. We claim this *joyful* historical destiny for the political powers of Germany.

But as soon as criticism concerns itself with modern social and political reality, and thus arrives at genuine human problems, it must either go outside the German *status quo* or approach its object indirectly. For example, the relation of industry, of the world of wealth in general, to the political world is a major problem of modern times. In what form does this problem begin to preoccupy the Germans? In the form of *protective tariffs,* the *system of prohibition,* the *national economy.* German chauvinism has passed from men to matter, so that one fine day our knights of cotton and heroes of iron found themselves metamorphosed into patriots. The sovereignty of monopoly within the country has begun to be recognized since *sovereignty vis-à-vis foreign countries* was attributed to it. In Germany, therefore, a beginning is made with what came as the conclusion in France and England. The old, rotten order against which these nations revolt in their theories, and which they bear only as chains are borne, is hailed in Germany as the dawn of a glorious future which as yet hardly dares to move from a cunning theory to a ruthless practice. While in France and England the problem is put in the form: *political economy* or the *rule of society over wealth;* in Germany it is put in the form: *national economy* or the *rule of private property over nationality.* Thus, in England and France it is a question of abolishing monopoly, which has developed to its final consequences; while in Germany it is a question of proceeding to the final consequences of monopoly. There it is a question of the solution; here, only a question of the collision. We can see very well from this example how modern problems are presented in Germany; the example shows that our history, like a raw recruit, has so far only had to do extra drill on old and hackneyed historical matters.

If the *whole* of German development were at the level of German *political* development, a German could have no greater part in contemporary problems that can a *Russian*. If the individual is not re-stricted by the limitations of his country, still less is the nation liberated by the liberation of one individual. The fact that a Scythian was one of the Greek philosophers did not enable the Scythians to advance a single step towards Greek culture.

Fortunately, we Germans are not Scythians.

Just as the nations of the ancient world lived their pre-history in the imagination, in mythology, so we Germans have lived our post-history in thought, in *philosophy*. We are the *philosophical* contemporaries of the present day without being its *historical* contemporaries. German philosophy is the *ideal prolongation* of German history. When, there-fore, we criticize, instead of the *oeuvres incomplètes* of our real history, the *oeuvres posthumes* of our ideal history — *philosophy*, our criticism stands at the centre of the problems of which the present age says: *that is the question*. That which constitutes, for the advanced nations, a *practical* break with modern political conditions, is in Germany where these conditions do not yet exist, virtually a *critical* break with their philosophical reflection.

The German *philosophy of right and of the state* is the only German history which is *al pari* with the *official* modern times. The German nation is obliged, therefore, to connect its dream history with its present conditions, and to subject to criticism not only these existing conditions but also their abstract continuation. Its future cannot be restricted either to the direct negation of its real juridical and political circumstances, or to the direct realization of its ideal juridical and political circumstances. The direct negation of its real circumstances already exists in its ideal circumstances, while it has almost outlived the realization of its ideal circumstances in the contemplation of neighbouring nations. It is with good reason, therefore, that the *practical* political party in Germany demands the *negation of philosophy*. Its error does not consist in formulating this demand, but in limiting itself to a demand which it does not, and cannot, make effective. It supposes that it can achieve this negation by turning its back on philosophy, looking elsewhere, and murmuring a few trite and ill-humoured phrases. Because of its narrow outlook it does not take account of philosophy as part of *German* reality, and even regards philosophy as beneath the level of German practical life and its theories. You demand as a point of departure real germs of life, but you forget that the real germ of life of the German nation has so far sprouted only in its *cranium*. In short, *you cannot abolish philosophy without realizing it*.

The same error was committed, but in the opposite direction, by the *theoretical* party which originated in philosophy.

In the present struggle, this party saw *only* the *critical struggle of philosophy against the German world.* It did not consider that *previous philosophy* itself belongs to this world and is its complement, even if only an ideal complement. Critical as regards its counterpart, it was not self-critical. It took as its point of departure the presuppositions of philosophy; and either accepted the conclusions which philosophy had reached or else presented as direct philosophical demands and conclusions, demands and conclusions drawn from elsewhere. But these latter — assuming their legitimacy — can only be achieved by the *negation of previous philosophy,* that is, philosophy as philosophy. We shall provide later a more comprehensive account of this party. Its principal defect may be summarized as follows: *it believed that it could realize philosophy without abolishing it.*

The criticism of the *German philosophy of right and of the state* which was given its most logical, profound and complete expression by Hegel, is at once the critical analysis of the modern state and of the reality connected with it, and the definitive negation of all the past *forms of consciousness in German jurisprudence and politics,* whose most distinguished and most general expression, raised to the level of a *science,* is precisely the *speculative philosophy of right.* If it was only Germany which could produce the speculative philosophy of right — this extravagant and abstract thought about the modern state, the reality of which remains in the beyond (even if this beyond is only across the Rhine) — the *German* representative of the modern state, on the contrary, which leaves out of account the *real man* was itself only possible because, and to the extent that, the modern state itself leaves the *real man* out of account or only satisfies the *whole* man in an illusory way. In politics, the Germans have *thought* what other nations have *done.* Germany has been their *theoretical consciousness.* The abstraction and presumption of its philosophy was in step with the partial and stunted character of their reality. If, therefore, the *status quo* of the *German political system* expresses the *consummation of the ancien régime,* the thorn in the flesh of the modern state, the *status quo* of *German political science* expresses the *imperfection of the modern state* itself, the degeneracy of its flesh.

As the determined adversary of the previous form of German political consciousness, the criticism of the speculative philosophy of right does not remain within its own sphere, but leads on to *tasks* which can only be solved by *means of practical activity.*

The question then arises: can Germany attain a practical activity *à la hauteur des principes;* that is to say, a revolution which will raise it not only to the *official level* of the modern nations, but to the *human level* which will be the immediate future of those nations.

It is clear that the arm of criticism cannot replace the criticism of arms. Material force can only be overthrown by material force; but theory itself becomes a material force when it has seized the masses. Theory is capable of seizing the masses when it demonstrates *ad hominem,* and it demonstrates *ad hominem* as soon as it becomes radical. To be radical is to grasp things by the root. But for man the root is man himself. What proves beyond doubt the radicalism of Germany theory, and thus its practical energy, is that it begins from the resolute *positive* abolition of religion. The criticism of religion ends with the doctrine that *man is the supreme being for man.* It ends, therefore, with the *categorical imperative to overthrow all those conditions* in which man is an abased, enslaved, abandoned, contemptible being — conditions which can hardly be better described than in the exclamation of a Frenchman on the occasion of a proposed tax upon dogs: "Wretched dogs! They want to treat you like men!"

Even from the historical standpoint theoretical emancipation has a specific practical importance for Germany. In fact Germany's *revolutionary* past is theoretical — it is the *Reformation.* In that period the revolution originated in the brain of a monk, today in the brain of the philosopher.

Luther, without question, overcame servitude through devotion but only by substituting servitude through *conviction.* He shattered the faith in authority by restoring the authority of faith. He transformed the priests into laymen by turning laymen into priests. He liberated man from external religiosity by making religiosity the innermost essence of man. He liberated the body from its chains because he fettered the heart with chains.

But if Protestantism was not the solution it did at least pose the problem correctly. It was no longer a question, thereafter, of the layman's struggle against the priest outside himself, but of his struggle against his *own internal priest,* against his own *priestly nature.* And if the Protestant metamorphosis of German laymen into priests emancipated the lay popes — the *princes* together with their clergy, the privileged and the philistines — the philosophical metamorphosis of the priestly Germans into men will emancipate the *people.* But just as emancipation will not be confined to princes, so the *secularization* of property will not be limited to the *confiscation of church property,* which was practised especially by hypocritical Prussia. At that time, the Peasant War, the most radical event in German history, came to grief because of theology.

Today, when theology itself has come to grief, the most unfree phenomenon in German history — our *status quo* — will be shattered by philosophy. On the eve of the Reformation official Germany was the most abject servant of Rome. On the eve of its revolution Germany is the abject servant of those who are far inferior to Rome; of Prussia and Austria, of petty squires and philistines.

But a *radical* revolution in Germany seems to encounter a major difficulty.

Revolutions need a *passive* element, a *material* basis. Theory is only realized in a people so far as it fulfils the needs of the people. Will there correspond to the monstrous discrepancy between the demands of German thought and the answers of German reality a similar discrepancy between civil society and the state, and within civil society itself? Will theoretical needs be directly practical needs? It is not enough that thought should seek to realize itself; reality must also strive towards thought.

But Germany has not passed through the intermediate stage of political emancipation at the same time as the modern nations. It has not yet attained in practice those stages which it has transcended in theory. How could Germany, in *salta mortale,* surmount not only its own barriers but also those of the modern nations, that is, those barriers which it must in reality experience and strive for as an emancipation from its own real barriers? A radical revolution can only be a revolution of radical needs, for which the conditions and breeding ground appear to be lacking.

But if Germany accompanied the development of the modern nations only through the abstract activity of thought, without taking an active part in the real struggles of this development, it has also experienced the *pains* of this development without sharing in its pleasures and partial satisfactions. The abstract activity on one side has its counterpart in the abstract suffering on the other. And one fine day Germany will find itself at the level of the European decadence, before ever having attained the level of European emancipation. It will be comparable to a fetishist who is sickening from the diseases of Christianity.

If the *German governments* are examined it will be found that the circumstances of the time, the situation of Germany, the outlook of German culture, and lastly their own fortunate instinct, all drive them to combine the *civilized deficiencies* of the *modern political world* (whose advantages we do not enjoy) with the *barbarous deficiencies* of the *ancien régime* (which we enjoy in full measure); so that Germany must participate more and more, if not in the reason at least in the unreason of those political systems which transcend its *status quo.* Is there, for example, any country in the whole world which shares with such naïveté as so-called constitutional Germany all the illusions of the constitutional régime without sharing its realities? And was it not, of necessity, a German government which had the idea of combining the torments of censorship with the torments of the French September laws which presuppose the liberty of the Press? Just as the gods of all the nations were to be found in the Roman Pantheon, so there will be found in the Holy Roman German Empire all the *sins* of all the forms of State. That this eclecticism will attain an unprecedented degree is assured in particular by the *politico-aesthetic gourmandise* of a German king who proposes to play all the roles of royalty — feudal or bureaucratic, absolute or constitutional, autocratic or democratic — if not in the person of the people at least in his *own* person, and if not for the people, at least for *himself. Germany, as the deficiency of present-day politics constituted into a system,* will not be able to demolish the specific German barriers without demolishing the general barriers of present-day politics.

It is not *radical* revolution, *universal human* emancipation, which is a Utopian dream for Germany, but rather a partial, *merely* political revolution which leaves the pillars of the building standing. What is the basis of a partial, merely political revolution? Simply this: a *section of civil society* emancipates itself and attains universal domination; a determinate class undertakes, from its *particular situation,* a general emancipation of society. This class emancipates society as a whole, but only on condition that the whole of society is in the same situation as this class; for example, that it possesses or can easily acquire money or culture.

No class in civil society can play this part unless it can arouse, in itself and in the masses, a moment of enthusiasm in which it associates and mingles with society at large, identifies itself with it, and is felt and recognized as the *general representative* of this society. Its aims and interests must genuinely be the aims and interests of society itself, of which it becomes in reality the social head and heart. It is only in the name of general interests that a particular class can claim general supremacy. In order to attain this liberating position, and the political direction of all spheres of society, revolutionary energy and consciousness of its own power do not suffice. For a *popular revolution* and the *emancipation of a particular class* of civil society to coincide, for *one* class to represent the whole of society, another class must concentrate in itself all the evils of society, a particular class must embody and represent a general obstacle and limitation. A particular social sphere must be regarded as the *notorious crime* of the whole society, so that emancipation from this sphere appears as a general emancipation. For *one* class to be the liberating class *par excellence*, it is necessary that another class should be openly the oppressing class. The negative significance of the French nobility and clergy produced the positive significance of the bourgeoisie, the class which stood next to them and opposed them.

But in Germany every class lacks the logic, insight, courage and clarity which would make it a negative representative of society. Moreover, there is also lacking in every class the generosity of spirit which identifies itself, if only for a moment, with the popular mind; that genius which pushes material force to political power, that revolutionary daring which throws at its adversary the defiant phrase: *I am nothing and I should be everything*. The essence of German morality and honour, in classes as in individuals, is a *modest egoism* which displays, and allows others to display, its own narrowness. The relation between the different spheres of German society is, therefore, not dramatic, but epic. Each of these spheres begins to be aware of itself and to establish itself beside the others, not from the moment when it is oppressed, but from the moment that circumstances, without any action of its own, have created a new sphere which it can in turn oppress. Even the *moral sentiment of the German middle class* has no other basis than the consciousness of being the representative of the narrow and limited mediocrity of all the other classes. It is not only the German kings, therefore, who ascend their thrones *mal à propos*. Each sphere of civil society suffers a defeat before gaining the victory; it erects its own barrier before having destroyed the barrier which opposes it; it displays the narrowness of its views before having displayed their generosity, and thus every opportunity of playing an important role has passed before it properly existed, and each class, at the very moment when it begins its struggle against the class above it, remains involved in a struggle against the class beneath. For this reason, the princes are in conflict with the monarch, the bureaucracy with the nobility, the bourgeoisie with all of them, while the proletariat is already beginning its struggle with the bourgeoisie. The middle class hardly dares to conceive the idea of emancipation from its own point of view before the development of social conditions, and the progress of political theory, show that this point of view is already antiquated, or at least disputable.

In France it is enough to be something in order to desire to be everything. In Germany no one has the right to be anything without first renouncing everything. In France partial emancipation is a basis for complete emancipation. In Germany complete emancipation is a *conditio sine qua non* for any partial emancipation. In France it is the reality, in Germany the impossibility, of a progressive emancipation which must give birth to complete liberty. In France every class of the population is *politically idealistic* and considers itself first of all, not as a particular class, but as the representative of the general needs of society. The role of liberator can, therefore, pass successively in a dramatic movement to different classes in the population, until it finally reaches the class which achieves social freedom; no longer assuming certain conditions external to man, which are none the less created by human society, but organizing all the conditions of human life on the basis of social freedom. In Germany, on the contrary, where practical life is as little intellectual as intellectual life is practical, no class of civil society feels the need for, or the ability to achieve, a general emancipation, until it is forced to it by its *immediate* situation, by *material* necessity and by its *fetters themselves.*

Where is there, then, a *real* possibility of emancipation in Germany?

This is our reply. A class must be formed which has *radical chains,* a class in civil society which is not a class of civil society, a class which is the dissolution of all classes, a sphere of society which has a universal character because its sufferings are universal, and which does not claim a *particular redress* because the wrong which is done to it is not a *particular wrong* but *wrong in general.* There must be formed a sphere of society which claims no *traditional* status but only a human status, a sphere which is not opposed to particular consequences but is totally opposed to the assumptions of the German political system; a sphere, finally, which cannot emancipate itself without emancipating itself from all the other spheres of society, without, therefore, emancipating all these other spheres, which is, in short, a *total loss* of humanity and which can only redeem itself by a *total redemption of humanity.* This dissolution of society, as a particular class, is the *proletariat.*

The proletariat is only beginning to form itself in Germany, as a result of the industrial movement. For what constitutes the proletariat is not *naturally existing* poverty, but poverty *artificially produced,* is not the mass of people mechanically oppressed by the weight of society, but the mass resulting from the *disintegration* of society and above all from the disintegration of the middle class. Needless to say, however, the numbers of the proletariat are also increased by the victims of natural poverty and of Christian-Germanic serfdom.

When the proletariat announces the *dissolution of the existing social order,* it only declares the *secret of its* own existence, for it *is* the *effective* dissolution of this order. When the proletariat demands the *negation of private property* it only lays down as a *principle for society* what society has already made a principle *for the proletariat,* and what the *latter* already involuntarily embodies as the negative result of society. Thus the proletarian has the same right, in relation to the new world which is coming into being, as the *German king* has in relation to the existing world when he calls his people *his* people or a horse *his* horse. In calling the people his private property the king simply declares that the owner of private property is king.

Just as philosophy finds its *material* weapons in the proletariat, so the proletariat finds its *intellectual* weapons in philosophy. And once the lightning of thought has penetrated deeply into this virgin soil of the people, the *Germans* will emancipate themselves and become *men.*

Let us sum up these results. The emancipation of Germany is only possible *in practice* if one adopts the point of view of that theory according to which man is the highest being for man. Germany will not be able to emancipate itself from the *Middle Ages* unless it emancipates itself at the same time from the *partial* victories over the Middle Ages. In Germany *no* type of enslavement can be abolished unless *all* enslavement is destroyed. Germany, which likes to get to the bottom of things, can only make a revolution which upsets *the whole order* of things. The *emancipation of Germany* will be an *emancipation of man.* *Philosophy* is the *head* of this emancipation and the *proletariat* is its *heart.* Philosophy can only be realized by the abolition of the proletariat, and the proletariat can only be abolished by the realization of philosophy.

WILLIAM ERNEST HENLEY

Invictus

William Ernest Henley (1849–1903), English poet and man of letters, was the editor of several journals, and, with Robert Louis Stevenson, the coauthor of several dramatic works; he also edited the collected works of the Scottish poet Robert Burns. But he is perhaps best known for his volumes of poetry, and among his poems the best known is almost certainly this bitter and defiant outcry, "Invictus."

OUT OF THE NIGHT that covers me,
    Black as the pit from pole to pole,
I thank whatever gods may be
    For my unconquerable soul.

In the fell clutch of circumstance
    I have not winced nor cried aloud.
Under the bludgeonings of chance
    My head is bloody, but unbow'd.

Beyond this place of wrath and tears
    Looms but the Horror of the shade,
And yet the menace of the years
    Finds and shall find me unafraid.

It matters not how strait the gate,
    How charged with punishments the scroll,
I am the master of my fate:
    I am the captain of my soul.

II THE WILL TO BELIEVE

Despite the notes of dissent and criticism heard in the preceding section of this book, the modern period has repeatedly witnessed the phenomenon of a resurgence of religious faith throughout the world. What William James called "the will to believe" has proved to be more durable — and more adaptable — than its gainsayers, or even perhaps its exponents, had imagined. Secularization has not necessarily been followed by the disappearance of faith, hope, and charity. On the contrary, in every continent the followers of the historic systems of faith have found a new voice in the nineteenth and especially in the twentieth century.

Part of the reason, it seems clear, is that Enlightenment critics East and West underestimated the depth of the religious dimension in the human spirit. Despite what they used to say, there does appear to be what Dietrich Bonhoeffer once called a "God-shaped blank in the soul." And when the gods of the historic religions have been expelled from that blank, their place is not always taken by the rationality and tolerance for which the Enlightenment had hoped, but sometimes by demonic forces from the abyss, which are able to claim an intense loyalty and devotion but do not carry the redemptive grace that has been the theme of the old-fashioned world views. Confronted by that demonic reality, many children of Enlightenment skepticism have been moved to reconsider their facile repudiation of tradition, and in Islam and Buddhism no less than in

Judaism and Christianity they have looked again to the rock from which they were hewn.

It would be a mistake, however, to overlook the positive contributions that modern thought has made to the reconstruction of the will to believe. The picture of the universe bequeathed to us by modern cosmology and astrophysics is one in which many of the traditional religious attitudes of awe have acquired a new appropriateness. In the arts and in music, the themes of the religious traditions have taken on new and more meaningful forms, often by crossing (in both directions) the conventional boundaries between Eastern and Western culture. When literature has sought to set itself free from the corrosive effects of nihilism and despair, it has echoed the very quality of affirmation in the midst of despair that the scriptures of many religions had articulated. As the biting satire of Enlightenment critics had mercilessly ridiculed the priestcraft and superstition of ancient faiths, so, in the hands of satirists like C. S. Lewis, the same weapons could be employed against those who had fashioned them. And the psychological study of human behavior has reaffirmed the soundness of some of the deepest values of compassion and forgiveness, as well as the need for peace and serenity, about which Gautama Buddha and Jesus of Nazareth had spoken to all the world.

WILLIAM JAMES

The Will to Believe

> William James (1842–1910), an American minister's son, was a professor at Harvard and one of the founders of psychology as a science; as a philosopher, he was also one of the founders of American pragmatism. But in his Gifford Lectures, *The Varieties of Religious Experience,* and in his well-known essay, "The Will to Believe," James strove to bring his science and his philosophy together in a positive assessment of religious faith.

IN THE RECENTLY PUBLISHED Life by Leslie Stephen of his brother, Fitz-James, there is an account of a school to which the latter went when he was a boy. The teacher, a certain Mr. Guest, used to converse with his pupils in this wise: "Gurney, what is the difference between justification and sanctification? — Stephen, prove the omnipotence of God!" etc. In the midst of our Harvard freethinking and indifference we are prone to imagine that here at your good old orthodox College conversation continues to be somewhat upon this order; and to show you that we at Harvard have not lost all interest in these vital subjects, I have brought with me to-night something like a sermon on justification by faith to read to you, — I mean an essay in justification *of* faith, a defence of our right to adopt a believing attitude in religious matters, in spite of the fact that our merely logical intellect may not have been coerced. "The Will to Believe," accordingly, is the title of my paper.

I have long defended to my own students the lawfulness of voluntarily adopted faith; but as soon as they have got well imbued with the logical spirit, they have as a rule refused to admit my contention to be lawful philosophically, even though in point of fact they were personally all the time chock-full of some faith or other themselves. I am all the while, however, so profoundly convinced that my own position is correct, that your invitation has seemed to me a good occasion to make my statements more clear. Perhaps your minds will be more open than those with which I have hitherto had to deal. I will be as little technical as I can, though I must begin by setting up some technical distinctions that will help us in the end.

I

Let us give the name of *hypothesis* to anything that may be proposed to our belief; and just as the electricians speak of live and dead wires, let us speak of any hypothesis as either *live* or *dead.* A live hypothesis is one which appeals as a real possibility to him to whom it is proposed. If I ask you to believe in the Mahdi, the notion makes no electric connection with your nature, — it refuses to scintillate with any credibility at all. As an hypothesis it is completely dead. To an Arab, however (even if he be not one of the Mahdi's followers), the hypothesis is among the mind's possibilities: it is alive. This shows that deadness and liveness in an hypothesis are not intrinsic properties, but relations to the individual thinker. They are measured by his willingness to act. The maximum of liveness in an hypothesis means willingness to act irrevocably. Practically, that means belief; but there is some believing tendency wherever there is willingness to act at all.

Next, let us call the decision between two hypotheses an *option.* Options may be of several kinds. They may be — 1, *living* or *dead;* 2, *forced* or *avoidable;* 3, *momentous* or *trivial;* and for our purposes we may call an option a *genuine* option when it is of the forced, living, and momentous kind.

1. A living option is one in which both hypotheses are live ones. If I say to you: "Be a theosophist or be a Mohammedan," it is probably a dead option, because for you neither hypothesis is likely to be alive. But if I say: "Be an agnostic or be a Christian," it is otherwise: trained as you are, each hypothesis makes some appeal, however small, to your belief.

2. Next, if I say to you: "Choose between going out with your umbrella or without it," I do not offer you a genuine option, for it is not forced. You can easily avoid it by not going out at all. Similarly, if I say, "Either love me or hate me," "Either call my theory true or call it false," your option is avoidable. You may remain indifferent to me, neither loving nor hating, and you may decline to offer any judgment as to my theory. But if I say, "Either accept this truth or go without it," I put on you a forced option, for there is no standing place outside

of the alternative. Every dilemma based on a complete logical dis-
junction, with no possibility of not choosing, is an option of this forced
kind.

3. Finally, if I were Dr. Nansen and proposed to you to join my
North Pole expedition, your option would be momentous; for this
would probably be your only similar opportunity, and your choice
now would either exclude you from the North Pole sort of immortality
altogether or put at least the chance of it into your hands. He who
refuses to embrace a unique opportunity loses the prize as surely as
if he tried and failed. *Per contra,* the option is trivial when the
opportunity is not unique, when the stake is insignificant, or when the
decision is reversible if it later prove unwise. Such trivial options
abound in the scientific life. A chemist finds an hypothesis live enough
to spend a year in its verification: he believes in it to that extent. But
if his experiments prove inconclusive either way, he is quit for his loss
of time, no vital harm being done.

It will facilitate our discussion if we keep all these distinctions well
in mind.

II

The next matter to consider is the actual psychology of human
opinion. When we look at certain facts, it seems as if our passional and
volitional nature lay at the root of all our convictions. When we look
at others, it seems as if they could do nothing when the intellect had
once said its say. Let us take the latter facts up first.

Does it not seem preposterous on the very face of it to talk of our
opinions being modifiable at will? Can our will either help or hinder
our intellect in its perceptions of truth? Can we, by just willing it,
believe that Abraham Lincoln's existence is a myth, and that the
portraits of him in McClure's Magazine are all of some one else? Can
we, by any effort of our will, or by any strength of wish that it were
true, believe ourselves well and about when we are roaring with
rheumatism in bed, or feel certain that the sum of the two one-dollar
bills in our pocket must be a hundred dollars? We can *say* any of these
things, but we are absolutely impotent to believe them; and of just
such things is the whole fabric of the truths that we do believe in made
up, — matters of fact, immediate or remote, as Hume said, and relations between ideas, which are either there or not there for us if we
see them so, and which if not there cannot be put there by any action
of our own.

In Pascal's Thoughts there is a celebrated passage known in liter-

ature as Pascal's wager. In it he tries to force us into Christianity by
reasoning as if our concern with truth resembled our concern with the
stakes in a game of chance. Translated freely his words are these: You
must either believe or not believe that God is — which will you do?
Your human reason cannot say. A game is going on between you and
the nature of things which at the day of judgment will bring out either
heads or tails. Weigh what your gains and your losses would be if you
should stake all you have on heads, or God's existence: if you win in
such case, you gain eternal beatitude; if you lose, you lose nothing at
all. If there were an infinity of chances, and only one for God in this
wager, still you ought to stake your all on God; for though you surely
risk a finite loss by this procedure, any finite loss is reasonable, even
a certain one is reasonable, if there is but the possibility of infinite gain.
Go, then, and take holy water, and have masses said; belief will come
and stupefy your scruples, — *Cela vous fera croire et vous abêtira.* Why
should you not? At bottom, what have you to lose?

You probably feel that when religious faith expresses itself thus, in
the language of the gaming-table, it is put to its last trumps. Surely
Pascal's own personal belief in masses and holy water had far other
springs; and this celebrated page of his is but an argument for others,
a last desperate snatch at a weapon against the hardness of the
unbelieving heart. We feel that a faith in masses and holy water
adopted wilfully after such a mechanical calculation would lack the
inner soul of faith's reality; and if we were ourselves in the place of the
Deity, we should probably take particular pleasure in cutting off
believers of this pattern from their infinite reward. It is evident that
unless there be some pre-existing tendency to believe in masses and
holy water, the option offered to the will by Pascal is not a living
option. Certainly no Turk ever took to masses and holy water on its
account; and even to us Protestants these means of salvation seem
such foregone impossibilities that Pascal's logic, invoked for them
specifically, leaves us unmoved. As well might the Mahdi write to us,
saying, "I am the Expected One whom God has created in his efful-
gence. You shall be infinitely happy if you confess me; otherwise you
shall be cut off from the light of the sun. Weigh, then, your infinite
gain if I am genuine against your finite sacrifice if I am not!" His logic
would be that of Pascal; but he would vainly use it on us, for the
hypothesis he offers us is dead. No tendency to act on it exists in us
to any degree.

The talk of believing by our volition seems, then, from one point of
view, simply silly. From another point of view it is worse than silly,

it is vile. When one turns to the magnificent edifice of the physical sciences, and sees how it was reared; what thousands of disinterested moral lives of men lie buried in its mere foundations; what patience and postponement, what choking down of preference, what submission to the icy laws of outer fact are wrought into its very stones and mortar; how absolutely impersonal it stands in its vast augustness, — then how besotted and contemptible seems every little sentimentalist who comes blowing his voluntary smoke-wreaths, and pretending to decide things from out of his private dream! Can we wonder if those bred in the rugged and manly school of science should feel like spewing such subjectivism out of their mouths? The whole system of loyalties which grow up in the schools of science go dead against its toleration; so that it is only natural that those who have caught the scientific fever should pass over to the opposite extreme, and write sometimes as if the incorruptibly truthful intellect ought positively to prefer bitterness and unacceptableness to the heart in its cup.

> It fortifies my soul to know
> That, though I perish, Truth is so —

sings Clough, while Huxley exclaims: "My only consolation lies in the reflection that, however bad our posterity may become, so far as they hold by the plain rule of not pretending to believe what they have no reason to believe, because it may be to their advantage so to pretend [the word "pretend" is surely here redundant], they will not have reached the lowest depth of immorality." And that delicious *enfant terrible* Clifford writes: "Belief is desecrated when given to unproved and unquestioned statements for the solace and private pleasure of the believer. . . . Whoso would deserve well of his fellows in this matter will guard the purity of his belief with a very fanaticism of jealous care, lest at any time it should rest on an unworthy object, and catch a stain which can never be wiped away. . . . If [a] belief has been accepted on insufficient evidence [even though the belief be true, as Clifford on the same page explains] the pleasure is a stolen one. . . . It is sinful because it is stolen in defiance of our duty to mankind. That duty is to guard ourselves from such beliefs as from a pestilence which may shortly master our own body and then spread to the rest of the town. . . . It is wrong always, everywhere, and for every one, to believe anything upon insufficient.evidence."

III

All this strikes one as healthy, even when expressed, as by Clifford, with somewhat too much of robustious pathos in the voice. Free-will and simple wishing do seem, in the matter of our credences, to be only fifth wheels to the coach. Yet if any one should thereupon assume that intellectual insight is what remains after wish and will and sentimental preference have taken wing, or that pure reason is what then settles our opinions, he would fly quite as directly in the teeth of the facts.

It is only our already dead hypotheses that our willing nature is unable to bring to life again. But what has made them dead for us is for the most part a previous action of our willing nature of an antagonistic kind. When I say "willing nature," I do not mean only such deliberate volitions as may have set up habits of belief that we cannot now escape from, — I mean all such factors of belief as fear and hope, prejudice and passion, imitation and partisanship, the circum-pressure of our caste and set. As a matter of fact we find ourselves believing, we hardly know how or why. Mr. Balfour gives the name of "authority" to all those influences, born of the intellectual climate, that make hypotheses possible or impossible for us, alive or dead. Here in this room, we all of us believe in molecules and the conservation of energy, in democracy and necessary progress, in Protestant Christi-anity and the duty of fighting for "the doctrine of the immortal Monroe," all for no reasons worthy of the name. We see into these matters with no more inner clearness, and probably with much less, than any disbeliever in them might possess. His unconventionality would probably have some grounds to show for its conclusions; but for us, not insight, but the *prestige* of the opinions, is what makes the spark shoot from them and light up our sleeping magazines of faith. Our reason is quite satisfied, in nine hundred and ninety-nine cases out of every thousand of us, if it can find a few arguments that will do to recite in case our credulity is criticised by someone else. Our faith is faith in some one else's faith, and in the greatest matters this is most the case. Our belief in truth itself, for instance, that there is a truth, and that our minds and it are made for each other, — what is it but a passionate affirmation of desire, in which our social system backs us up? We want to have a truth; we want to believe that our experiments and studies and discussions must put us in a continually better and better position towards it; and on this line we agree to fight out our thinking lives. But if a pyrrhonistic sceptic asks us *how we know* all this, can our logic find a reply? No! certainly it cannot. It is just one volition against another, — we willing to go in for life upon a trust or assumption which he, for his part, does not care to make.

As a rule we disbelieve all facts and theories for which we have no use. Clifford's cosmic emotions find no use for Christian feelings.

Huxley belabors the bishops because there is no use for sacerdotalism in his scheme of life. Newman, on the contrary, goes over to Romanism, and finds all sorts of reasons good for staying there, because a priestly system is for him an organic need and delight. Why do so few "scientists" even look at the evidence for telepathy, so called? Because they think, as a leading biologist, now dead, once said to me, that even if such a thing were true, scientists ought to band together to keep it suppressed and concealed. It would undo the uniformity of Nature and all sorts of other things without which scientists cannot carry on their pursuits. But if this very man had been shown something which as a scientist he might *do* with telepathy, he might not only have examined the evidence, but even have found it good enough. This very law which the logicians would impose upon us — if I may give the name of logicians to those who would rule out our willing nature here — is based on nothing but their own natural wish to exclude all elements for which they, in their professional quality of logicians, can find no use.

Evidently, then, our non-intellectual nature does influence our convictions. There are passional tendencies and volitions which run before and others which come after belief, and it is only the latter that are too late for the fair; and they are not too late when the previous passional work has been already in their own direction. Pascal's argument, instead of being powerless, then seems a regular clincher, and is the last stroke needed to make our faith in masses and holy water complete. The state of things is evidently far from simple; and pure insight and logic, whatever they might do ideally, are not the only things that really do produce our creeds.

IV

Our next duty, having recognized this mixed-up state of affairs, is to ask whether it be simply reprehensible and pathological, or whether, on the contrary, we must treat it as a normal element in making up our minds. The thesis I defend is, briefly stated, this: *Our passional nature not only lawfully may, but must, decide an option between propositions, whenever it is a genuine option that cannot by its nature be decided on intellectual grounds; for to say, under such circumstances, "Do not decide, but leave the question open," is itself a passional decision, — just like deciding yes or no, — and is attended with the same risk of losing the truth.* The thesis thus abstractly expressed will, I trust, soon become quite clear. But I must first indulge in a bit more of preliminary work.

V

It will be observed that for the purposes of this discussion we are on "dogmatic" ground, — ground, I mean, which leaves systematic philosophical scepticism altogether out of account. The postulate that there is truth, and that it is the destiny of our minds to attain it, we are deliberately resolving to make, though the sceptic will not make it. We part company with him, therefore, absolutely, at this point. But the faith that truth exists, and that our minds can find it, may be held in two ways. We may talk of the *empiricist* way and of the *absolutist* way of believing in truth. The absolutists in this matter say that we not only can attain to knowing truth, but we can *know when* we have attained to knowing it; while the empiricists think that although we may attain it, we cannot infallibly know when. To *know* is one thing, and to know for certain *that* we know is another. One may hold to the first being possible without the second; hence the empiricists and the absolutists, although neither of them is a sceptic in the usual philosophic sense of the term, show very different degrees of dogmatism in their lives.

If we look at the history of opinions, we see that the empiricist tendency has largely prevailed in science, while in philosophy the absolutist tendency has had everything its own way. The characteristic sort of happiness, indeed, which philosophies yield has mainly consisted in the conviction felt by each successive school or system that by it bottom-certitude had been attained. "Other philosophies are collections of opinions, mostly false; *my* philosophy gives standing-ground forever," — who does not recognize in this the key-note of every system worthy of the name? A system, to be a system at all, must come as a *closed* system, reversible in this or that detail, perchance, but in its essential features never!

Scholastic orthodoxy, to which one must always go when one wishes to find perfectly clear statement, has beautifully elaborated this absolutist conviction in a doctrine which it calls that of "objective evidence." If, for example, I am unable to doubt that I now exist before you, that two is less than three, or that if all men are mortal then I am mortal too, it is because these things illumine my intellect irresistibly. The final ground of this objective evidence possessed by certain propositions is the *adæquatio intellectûs nostri cum rê* [correspondence of our intellect with reality]. The certitude it brings involves an *aptitudinem ad extorquendum certum assensum* [capacity to elicit a sure assent] on the part of the truth envisaged, and on the side of the subject a *quietem in cognitione* [serene confidence in knowledge], when once the object is mentally received, that leaves no possibility of doubt behind; and in the whole transaction nothing operates but the *entitas ipsa* [very being itself] of the object and the *entitas ipsa* of the mind. We slouchy modern thinkers dislike to talk in Latin, — indeed, we dislike to talk in set terms at all; but at bottom our own state of mind is very much like this whenever we uncritically abandon ourselves: You believe in objective evidence, and I do. Of some things we feel that we are certain: we know, and we know that we do know. There is something that gives a click inside of us, a bell that strikes twelve, when the hands of our mental clock have swept the dial and meet over the meridian hour. The greatest empiricists among us are only empiricists on reflection: when left to their instincts, they dogmatize like infallible popes. When the Cliffords tell us how sinful it is to be Christians on such "insufficient evidence," insufficiency is really the last thing they have in mind. For them the evidence is absolutely sufficient, only it makes the other way. They believe so completely in an anti-christian order of the universe that there is no living option: Christianity is a dead hypothesis from the start.

VI

But now, since we are all such absolutists by instinct, what in our quality of students of philosophy ought we to do about the fact? Shall we espouse and indorse it? Or shall we treat it as a weakness of our nature from which we must free ourselves, if we can?

I sincerely believe that the latter course is the only one we can follow as reflective men. Objective evidence and certitude are doubtless very fine ideals to play with, but where on this moonlit and dream-visited planet are they found? I am, therefore, myself a complete empiricist so far as my theory of human knowledge goes. I live, to be sure, by the practical faith that we must go on experiencing and thinking over our experience, for only thus can our opinions grow more true; but to hold any one of them — I absolutely do not care which — as if it never could be reinterpretable or corrigible, I believe to be a tremendously mistaken attitude, and I think that the whole history of philosophy will bear me out. There is but one indefectibly certain truth, and that is the truth that pyrrhonistic scepticism itself leaves standing, — the truth that the present phenomenon of consciousness exists. That, however, is the bare starting-point of knowledge, the mere admission of a stuff to be philosophized about. The various philosophies are but so many attempts at expressing what this stuff really is. And if we repair to our libraries what disagreement do we discover! Where is a certainly true answer found? Apart from abstract propositions of comparison (such as two and two are the same as four), propositions which tell us nothing by themselves about concrete reality, we find no proposition ever regarded by any one as evidently certain that has not either been called a falsehood, or at least had its truth sincerely questioned by some one else. The transcending of the axioms of geometry, not in play but in earnest, by certain of our contemporaries (as Zöllner and Charles H. Hinton), and the rejection of the whole Aristotelian logic by the Hegelians, are striking instances in point.

No concrete test of what is really true has ever been agreed upon. Some make the criterion external to the moment of perception, putting it either in revelation, the *consensus gentium* [universal consensus of the nations], the instincts of the heart, or the systematized experience of the race. Others make the perceptive moment its own test, — Descartes, for instance, with his clear and distinct ideas guaranteed by the veracity of God; Reid with his "common-sense"; and Kant with his forms of synthetic judgment *a priori.* The inconceivability of the opposite; the capacity to be verified by sense; the possession of complete organic unity or self-relation, realized when a thing is its own other, — are standards which, in turn, have been used. The much lauded objective evidence is never triumphantly there; it is a mere aspiration or *Grenzbegriff* [concept on the boundary], marking the infinitely remote ideal of our thinking life. To claim that certain truths now possess it, is simply to say that when you think them true and they *are* true, then their evidence is objective, otherwise it is not. But practically one's conviction that the evidence one goes by is of the real objective brand, is only one more subjective opinion added to the lot. For what a contradictory array of opinions have objective evidence and absolute certitude been claimed! The world is rational through and through, — its existence is an ultimate brute fact; there is a personal God, — a personal God is inconceivable; there is an extramental physical world immediately known, — the mind can only know its own ideas; a moral imperative exists, — obligation is only the resultant of desires; a permanent spiritual principle is in every one, — there are only shifting states of mind; there is an endless chain of causes, — there is an absolute first cause; an eternal necessity, — a freedom; a purpose, — no purpose; a primal One, — a primal Many; a universal continuity, — an essential discontinuity in things; an infinity, — no infinity. There is this, — there is that; there is indeed nothing which some one has not thought absolutely true, while his neighbor deemed it absolutely false; and not an absolutist among them seems ever to have considered that the trouble may all the time be essential, and that the intellect, even with truth directly in its grasp, may have no infallible signal for knowing whether it be truth or no. When, indeed, one remembers that the most striking practical application to life of the doctrine of objective certitude has been the conscientious labors of the Holy Office of the Inquisition, one feels less tempted than ever to lend the doctrine a respectful ear.

But please observe, now, that when as empiricists we give up the doctrine of objective certitude, we do not thereby give up the quest or hope of truth itself. We still pin our faith on its existence, and still believe that we gain an ever better position towards it by systematically continuing to roll up experiences and think. Our great difference from the scholastic lies in the way we face. The strength of his system lies in the principles, the origin, the *terminus a quo* of his thought; for us the strength is in the outcome, the upshot, the *terminus ad quem*. Not where it comes from but what it leads to is to decide. It matters not to an empiricist from what quarter an hypothesis may come to him; he may have acquired it by fair means or by foul; passion may have whispered or accident suggested it; but if the total drift of thinking continues to confirm it, that is what he means by its being true.

VII

One more point, small but important, and our preliminaries are done. There are two ways of looking at our duty in the matter of opinion, — ways entirely different, and yet ways about whose difference the theory of knowledge seems hitherto to have shown very little concern. *We must know the truth;* and *we must avoid error,* — these are our first and great commandments as would-be knowers; but they are not two ways of stating an identical commandment, they are two separable laws. Although it may indeed happen that when we believe the truth A, we escape as an incidental consequence from believing the falsehood B, it hardly ever happens that by merely disbelieving B we necessarily believe A. We may in escaping B fall into believing other falsehoods, C or D, just as bad as B; or we may escape B by not believing anything at all, not even A.

Believe truth! Shun error! — these, we see, are two materially different laws; and by choosing between them we may end by coloring differently our whole intellectual life. We may regard the chase for truth as paramount, and the avoidance of error as secondary; or we may, on the other hand, treat the avoidance of error as more imperative, and let truth take its chance. Clifford, in the instructive passage which I have quoted, exhorts us to the latter course. Believe nothing, he tells us, keep your mind in suspense forever, rather than by closing it on insufficient evidence incur the awful risk of believing lies. You, on the other hand, may think that the risk of being in error is a very small matter when compared with the blessings of real knowledge, and be ready to be duped many times in your investigation rather than postpone indefinitely the chance of guessing true. I myself find it impossible to go with Clifford. We must remember that these feelings of our duty about either truth or error are in any case only expressions of our passional life. Biologically considered, our minds are as ready to grind out falsehood as veracity, and he who says, "Better go without belief forever than believe a lie!" merely shows his own preponderant private horror of becoming a dupe. He may be critical of many of his desires and fears, but this fear he slavishly obeys. He cannot imagine any one questioning its binding force. For my own part, I have also a horror of being duped; but I can believe that worse things than being duped may happen to a man in this world: so Clifford's exhortation has to my ears a thoroughly fantastic sound. It is like a general informing his soldiers that it is better to keep out of battle forever than to risk a single wound. Not so are victories either over enemies or over nature gained. Our errors are surely not such awfully solemn things. In a world where we are so certain to incur them in spite of all our caution, a certain lightness of heart seems healthier than this excessive nervousness on their behalf. At any rate, it seems the fittest thing for the empiricist philosopher.

VIII

And now, after all this introduction, let us go straight at our question. I have said, and now repeat it, that not only as a matter of fact do we find our passional nature influencing us in our opinions, but that there are some options between opinions in which this influence must be regarded both as an inevitable and as a lawful determinant of our choice.

I fear here that some of you my hearers will begin to scent danger, and lend an inhospitable ear. Two first steps of passion you have indeed had to admit as necessary, — we must think so as to avoid dupery, and we must think so as to gain truth; but the surest path to those ideal consummations, you will probably consider, is from now onwards to take no further passional step.

Well, of course, I agree as far as the facts will allow. Wherever the option between losing truth and gaining it is not momentous, we can throw the chance of *gaining truth* away, and at any rate save ourselves from any chance of *believing falsehood,* by not making up our minds at all till objective evidence has come. In scientific questions, this is almost always the case; and even in human affairs in general, the need of acting is seldom so urgent that a false belief to act on is better than no belief at all. Law courts, indeed, have to decide on the best evidence attainable for the moment, because a judge's duty is to make law as well as to ascertain it, and (as a learned judge once said to me) few cases are worth spending much time over: the great thing is to have them decided on *any* acceptable principle, and got out of the way. But in our dealings with objective nature we obviously are recorders, not makers, of the truth; and decisions for the mere sake of deciding promptly and getting on to the next business would be wholly out of place. Throughout the breadth of physical nature facts are what they are quite independently of us, and seldom is there any such hurry about them that the risks of being duped by believing a premature theory need be faced. The questions here are always trivial options, the hypotheses are hardly living (at any rate not living for us spectators), the choice between believing truth or falsehood is seldom forced. The attitude of sceptical balance is therefore the absolutely wise one if we would escape mistakes. What difference, indeed, does it make to most of us whether we have or have not a theory of the Röntgen rays, whether we believe or not in mind-stuff, or have a conviction about the causality of conscious states? It makes no difference. Such options are not forced on us. On every account it is better not to make them, but still keep weighing reasons *pro et contra* with an indifferent hand.

I speak, of course, here of the purely judging mind. For purposes of discovery such indifference is to be less highly recommended, and science would be far less advanced than she is if the passionate desires of individuals to get their own faiths confirmed had been kept out of the game. See for example the sagacity which Spencer and Weismann now display. On the other hand, if you want an absolute duffer in an investigation, you must, after all, take the man who has no interest whatever in its results: he is the warranted incapable, the positive fool. The most useful investigator, because the most sensitive observer, is always he whose eager interest in one side of the question is balanced by an equally keen nervousness lest he become deceived. Science has organized this nervousness into a regular *technique,* her so-called method of verification; and she has fallen so deeply in love with the method that one may even say she has ceased to care for truth by itself at all. It is only truth as technically verified that interests her. The truth of truths might come in merely affirmative form, and she would decline to touch it. Such truth as that, she might repeat with Clifford, would be stolen in defiance of her duty to mankind. Human passions, however, are stronger than technical rules. "La cœur a ses raisons," as Pascal says, "que la raison ne connaît pas" ["The heart has its reasons that reason knows not of"]; and however indifferent to all but the bare rules of the game the umpire, the abstract intellect, may be, the concrete players who furnish him the materials to judge of are usually, each one of them, in love with some pet "live hypothesis" of his own. Let us agree, however, that wherever there is no forced option, the dispassionately judicial intellect with no pet hypothesis, saving us, as it does, from dupery at any rate, ought to be our ideal.

The question next arises: Are there not somewhere forced options in our speculative questions, and can we (as men who may be interested at least as much in positively gaining truth as in merely escaping dupery) always wait with impunity till the coercive evidence shall have arrived? It seems *a priori* improbable that the truth should be so nicely adjusted to our needs and powers as that. In the great boarding-house of nature, the cakes and the butter and the syrup seldom come out so even and leave the plates so clean. Indeed, we should view them with scientific suspicion if they did.

IX

Moral questions immediately present themselves as questions whose solution cannot wait for sensible proof. A moral question is a question not of what sensibly exists, but of what is good, or would be good if it did exist. Science can tell us what exists; but to compare the *worths,* both of what exists and of what does not exist, we must consult not science, but what Pascal calls our heart. Science herself consults her heart when she lays it down that the infinite ascertainment of fact and correction of false belief are the supreme goods for man. Challenge the statement, and science can only repeat it oracularly, or else prove it by showing that such ascertainment and correction bring man all sorts of other goods which man's heart in turn declares. The question of having moral beliefs at all or not having them is decided by our will. Are our moral preferences true or false, or are they only odd biological phenomena, making things good or bad for *us,* but in themselves indifferent? How can your pure intellect decide? If your heart does not *want* a world of moral reality, your head will assuredly never make you believe in one. Mephistophelian scepticism, indeed, will satisfy the head's play-instincts much better than any rigorous idealism can. Some men (even at the student age) are so naturally cool-hearted that the moralistic hypothesis never has for them any pungent life, and in their supercilious presence the hot young moralist always feels strangely ill at ease. The appearance of knowingness is on their side, of *naïveté* and gullibility on his. Yet, in the inarticulate heart of him, he clings to it that he is not a dupe, and that there is a realm in which (as Emerson says) all their wit and intellectual superiority is no better than the cunning of a fox. Moral scepticism can no more be refuted or proved by logic than intellectual scepticism can. When we stick to it that there *is* truth (be it of either kind), we do so with our whole nature, and resolve to stand or fall by the results. The sceptic with his whole nature adopts the doubting attitude; but which of us is the wiser, Omniscience only knows.

Turn now from these wide questions of good to a certain class of questions of fact, questions concerning personal relations, states of mind between one man and another. *Do you like me or not?* — for example. Whether you do or not depends, in countless instances, on whether I meet you half-way, am willing to assume that you must like me, and show you trust and expectation. The previous faith on my part in your liking's existence is in such cases what makes your liking come. But if I stand aloof, and refuse to budge an inch until I have objective evidence, until you shall have done something apt, as the absolutists say, *ad extorquendum assensum meum* [to elicit my sure assent], ten to one your liking never comes. How many women's hearts are vanquished by the mere sanguine insistence of some man that they *must* love him! he will not consent to the hypothesis that they cannot. The desire for a certain kind of truth here brings about that special truth's existence; and so it is in innumerable cases of other sorts. Who gains promotions, boons, appointments, but the man in whose life they are seen to play the part of live hypotheses, who discounts them, sacrifices other things for their sake before they have come, and takes risks for them in advance? His faith acts on the powers above him as a claim, and creates its own verification.

A social organism of any sort whatever, large or small, is what it is because each member proceeds to his own duty with a trust that the other members will simultaneously do theirs. Wherever a desired result is achieved by the co-operation of many independent persons, its existence as a fact is a pure consequence of the precursive faith in one another of those immediately concerned. A government, an army, a commercial system, a ship, a college, an athletic team, all exist on this condition, without which not only is nothing achieved, but nothing is even attempted. A whole train of passengers (individually brave enough) will be looted by a few highwaymen, simply because the latter can count on one another, while each passenger fears that if he makes a movement of resistance, he will be shot before any one else backs him up. If we believed that the whole car-full would rise at once with us, we should each severally rise, and train-robbing would never even be attempted. There are, then, cases where a fact cannot come at all unless a preliminary faith exists in its coming. *And where faith in a fact can help create the fact,* that would be an insane logic which should say that faith running ahead of scientific evidence is the "lowest kind of immorality" into which a thinking being can fall. Yet such is the logic by which our scientific absolutists pretend to regulate our lives!

X

In truths dependent on our personal action, then, faith based on desire is certainly a lawful and possibly an indispensable thing.

But now, it will be said, these are all childish human cases, and have nothing to do with great cosmical matters, like the question of religious faith. Let us then pass on to that. Religions differ so much in their accidents that in discussing the religious question we must make it very generic and broad. What then do we now mean by the religious hypothesis? Science says things are; morality says some things are better than other things; and religion says essentially two things.

First, she says that the best things are the more eternal things, the overlapping things, the things in the universe that throw the last stone, so to speak, and say the final word. "Perfection is eternal," — this phrase of Charles Secrétan seems a good way of putting this first affirmation of religion, an affirmation which obviously cannot yet be verified scientifically at all.

The second affirmation of religion is that we are better off even now if we believe her first affirmation to be true.

Now, let us consider what the logical elements of this situation are *in case the religious hypothesis in both its branches be really true.* (Of course, we must admit that possibility at the outset. If we are to discuss the question at all, it must involve a living option. If for any of you religion be a hypothesis that cannot, by any living possibility be true, then you need go no farther. I speak to the "saving remnant" alone.) So proceeding, we see, first, that religion offers itself as a *momentous* option. We are supposed to gain, even now, by our belief, and to lose by our non-belief, a certain vital good. Secondly, religion is a *forced* option, so far as that good goes. We cannot escape the issue by remaining sceptical and waiting for more light, because, although we do avoid error in that way *if religion be untrue,* we lose the good, *if it be true,* just as certainly as if we positively chose to disbelieve. It is as if a man should hesitate indefinitely to ask a certain woman to marry him because he was not perfectly sure that she would prove an angel after he brought her home. Would he not cut himself off from that particular angel-possibility as decisively as if he went and married some one else? Scepticism, then, is not avoidance of option; it is option of a certain particular kind of risk. *Better risk loss of truth than chance of error,* — that is your faith-vetoer's exact position. He is actively playing his stake as much as the believer is; he is backing the field against the religious hypothesis, just as the believer is backing the religious hypothesis against the field. To preach scepticism to us as a duty until "sufficient evidence" for religion be found, is tantamount therefore to telling us, when in presence of the religious hypothesis, that to yield to our fear of its being error is wiser and better than to yield to our hope that it may be true. It is not intellect against all passions, then; it is only intellect with one passion laying down its law. And by what, forsooth, is the supreme wisdom of this passion warranted? Dupery for dupery, what proof is there that dupery through hope is so much worse than dupery through fear? I, for one, can see no proof; and I simply refuse obedience to the scientist's command to imitate his kind of option, in a case where my own stake is important enough to give me the right to choose my own form of risk. If religion be true and the evidence for it be still insufficient, I do not wish, by putting your extinguisher upon my nature (which feels to me as if it had after all some business in this matter), to forfeit my sole chance in life of getting upon the winning side, — that chance depending, of course, on my willingness to run the risk of acting as if my passional need of taking the world religiously might be prophetic and right.

All this is on the supposition that it really may be prophetic and right, and that, even to us who are discussing the matter, religion is a live hypothesis which may be true. Now, to most of us religion comes in a still further way that makes a veto on our active faith even more illogical. The more perfect and more eternal aspect of the universe is represented in our religions as having personal form. The universe is no longer a mere *It* to us, but a *Thou,* if we are religious; and any relation that may be possible from person to person might be possible here. For instance, although in one sense we are passive portions of the universe, in another we show a curious autonomy, as if we were small active centres on our own account. We feel, too, as if the appeal of religion to us were made to our own active good-will, as if evidence might be forever withheld from us unless we met the hypothesis half-way. To take a trivial illustration: just as a man who in a company of gentlemen made no advances, asked a warrant for every concession, and believed no one's word without proof, would cut himself off by such churlishness from all the social rewards that a more trusting spirit would earn, — so here, one who should shut himself up in snarling logicality and try to make the gods extort his recognition willy-nilly, or not get it at all, might cut himself off forever from his only opportunity of making the gods' acquaintance. This feeling, forced on us we know not whence, that by obstinately believing that there are gods (although not to do so would be so easy both for our logic and our life) we are doing the universe the deepest service we can, seems part of the living essence of the religious hypothesis. If the hypothesis *were* true in all its parts, including this one, then pure intellectualism, with its veto on our making willing advances, would be an absurdity; and some participation of our sympathetic nature would be logically required. I, therefore, for one, cannot see my way to accepting the agnostic rules for truth-seeking, or wilfully agree to keep my willing nature out of the game. I cannot do so for this plain reason, that *a rule of thinking which would absolutely prevent me from acknowledging certain kinds of truth if those kinds of truth were really there, would be an irrational rule.* That for me is the long and short of the formal logic of the situation, no matter what the kinds of truth might materially be.

I confess I do not see how this logic can be escaped. But sad experience makes me fear that some of you may still shrink from radically saying with me, *in abstracto,* that we have the right to believe at our own risk any hypothesis that is live enough to tempt our will. I suspect, however, that if this is so, it is because you have got away from the abstract logical point of view altogether, and are thinking (perhaps without realizing it) of some particular religious hypothesis which for you is dead. The freedom to "believe what we will" you apply to the case of some patent superstition; and the faith you think of is the faith defined by the schoolboy when he said, "Faith is when you believe something that you know ain't true." I can only repeat that this is misapprehension. *In concreto,* the freedom to believe can only cover living options which the intellect of the individual cannot by itself resolve; and living options never seem absurdities to him who has them to consider. When I look at the religious question as it really puts itself to concrete men, and when I think of all the possibilities which both practically and theoretically it involves, then this command that we shall put a stopper on our heart, instincts, and courage, and *wait* — acting of course meanwhile more or less as if religion were *not* true — till doomsday, or till such time as our intellect and senses working together may have raked in evidence enough, — this command, I say, seems to me the queerest idol ever manufactured in the philosophic cave. Were we scholastic absolutists, there might be more excuse. If we had an infallible intellect with its objective certitudes, we might feel ourselves disloyal to such a perfect organ of knowledge in not trusting to it exclusively, in not waiting for its releasing word. But if we are empiricists, if we believe that no bell in us tolls to let us know for certain when truth is in our grasp, then it seems a piece of idle fantasticality to preach so solemnly our duty of waiting for the bell. Indeed we *may* wait if we will, — I hope you do not think that I am denying that, — but if we do so, we do so at our peril as much as if we believed. In either case we *act,* taking our life in our hands. No one of us ought to issue vetoes to the other, nor should we bandy words of abuse. We ought, on the contrary, delicately and profoundly to respect one another's mental freedom: then only shall we bring about the intellectual republic; then only shall we have that spirit of inner tolerance without which all our outer tolerance is soulless, and which is empiricism's glory; then only shall we live and let live, in speculative as well as in practical things.

I began by a reference to Fitz-James Stephen; let me end by a quotation from him. "What do you think of yourself? What do you think of the world? . . . These are questions with which all must deal as it seems good to them. They are riddles of the Sphinx, and in some way or other we must deal with them. . . . In all important transactions of life we have to take a leap in the dark. . . . If we decide to leave the riddles unanswered, that is a choice; if we waver in our answer, that, too, is a choice: but whatever choice we make, we make it at our peril. If a man chooses to turn his back altogether on God and the future, no one can prevent him; no one can show beyond reasonable doubt that he is mistaken. If a man thinks otherwise and acts as he thinks, I do not see that any one can prove that *he* is mistaken. Each must act as he thinks best; and if he is wrong, so much the worse for him. We stand on a mountain pass in the midst of whirling snow and blinding mist, through which we get glimpses now and then of paths which may be deceptive. If we stand still we shall be frozen to death. If we take the wrong road we shall be dashed to pieces. We do not certainly know whether there is any right one. What must we do? 'Be strong and of a good courage.' Act for the best, hope for the best, and take what comes. . . . If death ends all, we cannot meet death better."

MARTIN BUBER

I and Thou

> Martin Buber (1878–1965) emigrated from Germany to Jerusalem, where he became a professor at the Hebrew University. Celebrated as a scholar and translator of the Bible in addition to his work as a philosopher of religion, Buber sought in such works as *I and Thou* to combine the insights of the two fields into a personalistic interpretation of human nature in the light of the mysteries of Creation and Covenant.

NOTHING CAN DOOM MAN but the belief in doom, for this prevents the movement of return.

The belief in doom is a delusion from the start. The scheme of running down is appropriate only for ordering that which is nothing-but-having-become, the severed world-event, objecthood as history. The presence of the You, that which is born of association, is not accessible to this approach, which does not know the actuality of spirit; and this scheme is not valid for spirit. Divination based on objecthood is valid only for those who do not know presentness. Whoever is overpowered by the It-world must consider the dogma of an ineluctable running down as a truth that creates a clearing in the jungle. In truth, this dogma only leads him deeper into the slavery of the It-world. But the world of the You is not locked up. Whoever proceeds toward it, concentrating his whole being, with his power to relate resurrected, beholds his freedom. And to gain freedom from the belief in unfreedom is to gain freedom.

One gains power over an incubus by addressing it by its real name. Similarly, the It-world that but now seemed to dwarf man's small strength with its uncanny power has to yield to anyone who recognizes its true nature: the particularization and alienation of that out of whose abundance, welling up close by, every earthly You emerges to confront us — that which appeared to us at times as great and terrible as the mother goddess, but nevertheless always motherly.

But how can we muster the strength to address the incubus by his right name as long as a ghost lurks inside us — the I that has been robbed of its actuality? How can the buried power to relate be resurrected in a being in which a vigorous ghost appears hourly to stamp down the debris under which this power lies? How is a being to collect itself as long as the mania of his detached I-hood chases it ceaselessly around an empty circle? How is anyone to behold his freedom if caprice is his dwellingplace?

Even as freedom and fate belong together, caprice belongs with doom. But freedom and fate are promised to each other and embrace each other to constitute meaning; caprice and doom, the spook of the soul and the nightmare of the world, get along with each other, living next door and avoiding each other, without connection and friction, at home in meaninglessness — until in one instant eye meets eye, madly, and the confession erupts from both that they are unredeemed. How much intellectual eloquence and artistry is used today to prevent or at least conceal this occurrence!

Free is the man that wills without caprice. He believes in the actual, which is to say: he believes in the real association of the real duality, I and You. He believes in destiny and also that it needs him. It does not lead him, it waits for him. He must proceed toward it without knowing where it waits for him. He must go forth with his whole being: that he knows. It will not turn out the way his resolve intended it; but what wants to come will come only if he resolves to do that which he can will. He must sacrifice his little will, which is unfree and ruled by things and drives, to his great will that moves away from being determined to find destiny. Now he no longer interferes, nor does he merely allow things to happen. He listens to that which grows, to the way of Being in the world, not in order to be carried along by it but rather in order to actualize it in the manner in which it, needing him, wants to be actualized by him — with human spirit and human deed, with human life and human death. He believes, I said; but this implies: he encounters.

The capricious man does not believe and encounter. He does not know association; he only knows the feverish world out there and his feverish desire to use it. We only have to give use an ancient, classical name, and it walks among the gods. When he says You, he means: You,

my ability to use! And what he calls his destiny is merely an embellishment of and a sanction for his ability to use. In truth he has no
destiny but is merely determined by things and drives, feels autocratic,
and is capricious. He has no great will and tries to pass off caprice in
its place. For sacrifice he lacks all capacity, however much he may talk
of it, and you may recognize it by noting that he never becomes
concrete. He constantly interferes, in order "to let it happen." How, he
says to you, could one fail to assist destiny? How could one not employ
all feasible means required for such an end? That is also how he sees
those who are free; he cannot see them differently. But the free man
does not have an end here and then fetch the means from there; he has
only one thing: always only his resolve to proceed toward his destiny.
Having made this resolve, he will renew it at every fork in the road;
and he would sooner believe that he was not really alive than he would
believe that the resolve of the great will was insufficient and required
the support of means. He believes; he encounters. But the unbelieving
marrow of the capricious man cannot perceive anything but unbelief
and caprice, positing ends and devising means. His world is devoid of
sacrifice and grace, encounter and present, but shot through with ends
and means: it could not be different and its name is doom. For all his
autocratic bearing, he is inextricably entangled in unreality; and he
becomes aware of this whenever he recollects his own condition.
Therefore he takes pains to use the best part of his mind to prevent or
at least obscure such recollection.

But if this recollection of one's falling off, of the deactualized and
the actual I, were permitted to reach down to the roots that man calls
despair and from which self-destruction and rebirth grow, this would
be the beginning of the return.

The Brahmana of the hundred paths relates that the gods and the
demons were once engaged in a contest. Then the demons said: "To
whom shall we offer our sacrifices?" They placed all offerings in their
own mouths. But the gods placed the offerings in one another's mouth.
Then Prajapati, the primal spirit, bestowed himself upon the gods.

One can understand how the It-world, left to itself, untouched and
unthawed by the emergence of any You, should become alienated and
turn into an incubus; but how does it happen that, as you say, the I
of man is deactualized? Whether it lives in relation or outside it, the
I remains assured of itself in its self-consciousness, which is a strong
thread of gold on which the changing states are strung. Whether I say,

"I see you" or "I see the tree," seeing may not be equally actual in both cases, but the I is equally actual in both.

Let us examine, let us examine ourselves to see whether this is so. The linguistic form proves nothing. After all, many a spoken You really means an It to which one merely says You from habit, thoughtlessly. And many a spoken It really means a You whose presence one may remember with one's whole being, although one is far away. Similarly, there are innumerable occasions when I is only an indispensable pronoun, only a necessary abbreviation for "This one there who is speaking." But self-consciousness? If one sentence truly intends the You of a relation and the other one the It of an experience, and if the I in both sentences is thus intended in truth, do both sentences issue from the same self-consciousness?

The I of the basic word I-You is different from that of the basic word I-It.

The I of the basic word I-It appears as an ego and becomes conscious of itself as a subject (of experience and use).

The I of the basic word I-You appears as a person and becomes conscious of itself as subjectivity (without any dependent genetive).

Egos appear by setting themselves apart from other egos.

Persons appear by entering into relation to other persons.

One is the spiritual form of natural differentiation, the other that of natural association.

The purpose of setting oneself apart is to experience and use, and the purpose of that is "living" — which means dying one human life long.

The purpose of relation is the relation itself — touching the You. For as soon as we touch a You, we are touched by a breath of eternal life.

Whoever stands in relation, participates in an actuality; that is, in a being that is neither merely a part of him nor merely outside him. All actuality is an activity in which I participate without being able to appropriate it. Where there is no participation, there is no actuality. Where there is self-appropriation, there is no actuality. The more directly the You is touched, the more perfect is the participation.

The I is actual through its participation in actuality. The more perfect the participation is, the more actual the I becomes.

But the I that steps out of the event of the relation into detachment and the self-consciousness accompanying that, does not lose its actuality. Participation remains in it as a living potentiality. To use words that originally refer to the highest relation but may also be applied to all others: the seed remains in him. This is the realm of subjectivity in which the I apprehends simultaneously its association and its detachment. Genuine subjectivity can be understood only dynamically, as the vibration of the I in its lonely truth. This is also the place where the desire for ever higher and more unconditional relation and for perfect participation in being arises and keeps rising. In subjectivity the spiritual substance of the person matures.

The person becomes conscious of himself as participating in being, as being-with, and thus as a being. The ego becomes conscious of himself as being this way and not that. The person says, "I am"; the ego says, "That is how I am." "Know thyself" means to the person: know yourself as being. To the ego it means: know your being-that-way. By setting himself apart from others, the ego moves away from being.

This does not mean that the person "gives up" his being-that-way, his being different; only, this is not the decisive perspective but merely the necessary and meaningful form of being. The ego, on the other hand, wallows in his being-that-way — or rather for the most part in the fiction of his being-that-way — a fiction that he has devised for himself. For at bottom self-knowledge usually means to him the fabrication of an effective apparition of the self that has the power to deceive him ever more thoroughly; and through the contemplation and veneration of this apparition one seeks the semblance of knowledge of one's own being-that-way, while actual knowledge of it would lead one to self-destruction — or rebirth.

The person beholds his self; the ego occupies himself with his My: my manner, my race, my works, my genius.

The ego does not participate in any actuality nor does he gain any. He sets himself apart from everything else and tries to possess as much as possible by means of experience and use. That is *his* dynamics: setting himself apart and taking possession — and the object is always It, that which is not actual. He knows himself as a subject, but this subject can appropriate as much as it wants to, it will never gain any substance: it remains like a point, functional, that which experiences, that which uses, nothing more. All of its extensive and multifarious being-that-way, all of its eager "individuality" cannot help it to gain any substance.

There are not two kinds of human beings, but there are two poles of humanity.

No human being is pure person, and none is pure ego; none is entirely actual, none entirely lacking in actuality. Each lives in a twofold I. But some men are so person-oriented that one may call them persons, while others are so ego-oriented that one may call them egos. Between these and those true history takes place.

The more a human being, the more humanity is dominated by the ego, the more does the I fall prey to inactuality. In such ages the person in the human being and in humanity comes to lead a subterranean, hidden, as it were invalid existence — until it is summoned.

How much of a person a man is depends on how strong the I of the basic world I-You is in the human duality of his I.

The way he says I — what he means when he says I — decides where a man belongs and where he goes. The word "I" is the true shibboleth of humanity.

Listen to it!

How dissonant the I of the ego sounds! When it issues from tragic lips, tense with some self-contradiction that they try to hold back, it can move us to great pity. When it issues from chaotic lips that savagely, heedlessly, unconsciously represent contradiction, it can make us shudder. When the lips are vain and smooth, it sounds embarrassing or disgusting.

Those who pronounce the severed I, wallowing in the capital letter, uncover the shame of the world spirit that has been debased to mere spirituality.

But how beautiful and legitimate the vivid and emphatic I of Socrates sounds! It is the I of infinite conversation, and the air of conversation is present on all its ways, even before his judges, even in the final hour in prison. This I lived in that relation to man which is embodied in conversation. It believed in the actuality of men and went out toward them. Thus it stood together with them in actuality and is never severed from it. Even solitude cannot spell forsakenness, and when th_ human world falls silent for him, he hears his *daimonion* say You.

How beautiful and legitimate the full I of Goethe sounds! It is the I of pure intercourse with nature. Nature yields to it and speaks ceaselessly with it; she reveals her mysteries to it and yet does not betray her mystery. It believes in her and says to the rose: "So it is You" — and at once shares the same actuality with the rose. Hence, when it returns to itself, the spirit of actuality stays with it; the vision of the sun clings to the blessed eye that recalls its own likeness to the sun, and the friendship of the elements accompanies man into the calm of dying and rebirth.

Thus the "adequate, true, and pure" I-saying of the representatives of association, the Socratic and the Goethean persons, resounds through the ages.

And to anticipate and choose an image from the realm of unconditional relation: how powerful, even overpowering, is Jesus' I-saying, and how legitimate to the point of being a matter of course! For it is the I of the unconditional relation in which man calls his You "Father" in such a way that he himself becomes nothing but a son. Whenever he says I, he can only mean the I of the holy basic word that has become unconditional for him. If detachment ever touches him, it is surpassed by association, and it is from this that he speaks to others. In vain you seek to reduce this I to something that derives its power from itself, nor can you limit this You to anything that dwells in us. Both would once again deactualize the actual, the present relation. I and You remain; everyone can speak the You and then becomes I; everyone can say Father and then becomes son; actuality abides.

But what if a man's mission requires him to know only his association with his cause and no real relation to any You, no present encounter with any You, so that everything around him becomes It and subservient to his cause? How about the I-saying of Napoleon? Wasn't that legitimate? Is this phenomenon of experiencing and using no person?

Indeed, this master of the age evidently did not know the dimension of the You. The matter has been put well: all being was for him *valore*. Gently, he compared the followers who denied him after his fall with Peter; but there was nobody whom *he* could have denied, for there was nobody whom he recognized as a being. He was the demonic You for the millions and did not respond; to "You" he responded by saying: It; he responded fictitiously on the personal level — responding only in his own sphere, that of his cause, and only with his deeds. This is the elementary historical barrier at which the basic word of association loses its reality, the character of reciprocity: the demonic You for whom nobody can become a You. This third type, in addition to the person and the ego, to the free and the arbitrary man — not between them — occurs in fateful eminence in fateful times: ardently, everything flames toward him while he himself stands in a cold fire; a thousand relations reach out toward him but none issues from him. He participates in no actuality, but others participate immeasurably in him as in an actuality.

To be sure, he views the beings around him as so many machines capable of different achievements that have to be calculated and used for the cause. But that is also how he views himself (only he can never cease experimenting to determine his own capacities, and yet never experiences their limits). He treats himself, too, as an It.

Thus his I-saying is not vitally emphatic, not full. Much less does it feign these qualities (like the I-saying of the modern ego). He does not even speak of himself, he merely speaks "on his own behalf." The I spoken and written by him is the required subject of the sentences that convey his statements and orders — no more and no less. It lacks subjectivity; neither does it have a self-consciousness that is preoccupied with being-that-way; and least of all does it have any delusions about its own appearance. "I am the clock that exists and does not know itself": thus he himself formulated his fatefulness, the actuality of this phenomenon and the inactuality of this I, after he had been separated from his cause; for it was only then that he could, and had to, think and speak of himself and recollect his I which appeared only then. What appears is not mere subject; neither does it reach subjectivity: the magic spell broken, but unredeemed, it finds expression in the terrible word, as legitimate as it is illegitimate: "The universe contemplates Us!" In the end it sinks back into mystery.

Who, after such a step and such a fall, would dare to claim that this man understood his tremendous, monstrous mission — or that he misunderstood it? What is certain is that the age for which the demonic man who lives without a present has become master and model will misunderstand him. It fails to see that what holds sway here is destiny and accomplishment, not the lust for and delight in power. It goes into ecstasies over the commanding brow and has no inkling of the signs inscribed upon this forehead like digits upon the face of a clock. One tries studiously to imitate the way he looked at others, without any understanding of his need and necessitation, and one mistakes the objective severity of this I for fermenting self-awareness. The word "I" remains the shibboleth of humanity. Napoleon spoke it without the power to relate, but he did speak it as the I of an accomplishment. Those who exert themselves to copy this, merely betray the hopelessness of their own self-contradiction.

KARL BARTH

Faith As Confession

Karl Barth (1886–1968) was a Swiss Reformed pastor when his book *The Epistle to the Romans* issued its summons to Christian theology to pay heed to its roots and its distinct vocation. In his massive *Church Dogmatics,* but also in countless shorter works written for a broader audience, Barth spoke of the meaning of faith with a freshness and power that made him one of the most influential theologians since the Reformation.

CHRISTIAN FAITH is a decision. This is where we have to begin, and wish to begin. Christian faith, to be sure, is an event in the mystery between God and man; the event of the freedom in which God acts towards this man, and of the freedom which God gives this man. But this does not exclude, but actually includes the fact that where there is faith in the sense of the Christian Creed, *history* is taking place, that there something is being undertaken, completed and carried out in time by man. Faith is God's mystery breaking forth; faith is God's freedom and man's freedom in action. Where nothing occurred — in time, of course, that is, occurred visibly and audibly — there would be no faith either. For Christian faith is faith in God, and when the Christian Confession names God the Father, the Son and the Holy Spirit, it is pointing to the fact that in His inner life and nature God is not dead, not passive, not inactive, but that God the Father, the Son and the Holy Spirit exist in an inner relationship and movement, which may very well be described as a story, as an event. God Himself is not suprahistorical, but historical. And this God has in Himself made a decree, an eternal decree, upon which everything rests of which the Confession of Faith speaks. Our fathers called it the decree of creation and of the covenant and of redemption. This decree of God was carried out in time, once

for all, in the work and in the word of Jesus Christ, to which Article
II of the Confession bears concrete testimony, "who suffered under
Pontius Pilate, was crucified, dead and buried. . . ." Faith is man's
answer to this historical existence and nature and action of God. Faith
has to do with the God who is in Himself historical and has fashioned
a decree whose goal is history, and has set this history going and
completed it. Christian faith which was not itself history would not be
Christian faith, not faith in . . . Where there is Christian faith there
arises and grows an historical form, there arises among men, among
contemporaries and non-contemporaries, a *community,* a together-
ness, a brotherhood. But by means of this community, we inevitably
reach, at the point where faith is Christian, a human proclamation and
message as well, to the *world* outside this communion and brotherhood. A light is kindled there, which lightens all them that are in the
house. In other words, where Christian faith exists, there God's
congregation arises and lives in the world for the world; there Israel
gathers apart from the Gentiles of the world; and there the Church
gathers on its own behalf, the communion of saints. Yet not for its own
purposes, but as the manifestation of the Servant of God, whom God
has set there for all men, as the Body of Christ. And this story
happens — now we reach the human work which answers to God's
work and nature in the election of His grace — in the answer of
obedience. Faith is obedience, not just a passive accommodation of
oneself. Where there is obedience, there is also choice on man's part;
faith is chosen instead of its opposite, unbelief, trust instead of distrust, knowledge instead of ignorance. Faith means choosing between
faith and unbelief, wrong belief and superstition. Faith is the act in
which man relates himself to God as is appropriate to God. For this
work takes place in a stepping out of neutrality towards God, out of
any disavowal of obligation towards Him in our existence and attitude,
out of the private sphere, into resoluteness, responsibility and public
life. Faith without this tendency to public life, faith that avoids this
difficulty, has become in itself unbelief, wrong belief, superstition. For
faith that believes in God the Father, the Son and the Holy Spirit
cannot refuse to become public.

"Christian faith is the decision in which men have the freedom . . ."
said the opening sentence. In public responsibility, too, there is a
permission granted to men, an open door, and that means a freedom.
To freedom of trust and freedom of knowledge we must now add
freedom of responsibility. Here one freedom is inseparable from the
other. If you merely want to be free to trust God and think you can

then renounce knowledge, you would not in fact be trusting Him. And if you had all trust and all knowledge and did not have the freedom to answer publicly for your trust and your knowledge, you would have to be told straight that all is not well with your trust and your knowledge! In accordance with what the Christian Church confesses of Him, God Himself is He who did not wish to remain hidden, who did not and does not wish to be God for Himself alone. He is the God who in His royal majesty emerges from the mystery, from the heights of His divine existence and comes down to the humble estate of the universe created by Him. God Himself is He who is revealed as God. He who believes in this God cannot wish to hide this God's gift, this God's love, this God's comfort and light, to hide his trust in His Word and His knowledge. The word and the work of the believer cannot possibly remain a neutral, uncommitted work and word. Where there is faith, God's *doxa, gloria,* His brightness is necessarily made known on earth. And where God's glory did not shine one way or another, however overcast and broken by our ways and our degeneration, there would be no faith; the comfort and the light we receive from God would not be accepted. God's glory is hallowed in the universe, and the Name of the Holy One hallowed on earth, where men may believe, where God's people, God's congregation assembles and goes into action. Where there is faith, man in his complete limitation and helplessness, in his utter abandonment and folly, possesses the freedom, the freedom royal in all humility, to let the light shine of the *doxa,* of the *gloria,* of the glory of God. More is not required of us; but that is required of us. This public responsibility of our trust in God's Word and of our knowledge of the truth of Jesus Christ is the general concept for what in the Christian sense is called confessing and confession.

There is public responsibility in the Church's language, but also in worldly attitudes and also and above all in the corresponding actions and conduct. In these three definitions of the concept of public responsibility, there are, if my diagnosis is correct, three forms of Christian confessing, inseparable from one another, not to be played off against one another, but necessarily to be thought of together; a confessing which, for its part, is an indispensable, basic form of Christian faith. The following expositions are therefore to be regarded as a synthesis.

1. In faith we have the freedom to be publicly responsible *in the language of the Church* for our trust and our knowledge. What does this mean? God's congregation possessed and at all times possesses its own language. Nothing can change this. For it has in history its own special

history, its own special road. It speaks, when it confesses, in relation
to this special history. It stands in the quite special concrete historical
context, which has at all times formed its language and will continue
to form it. Therefore the language of faith, the language of public
responsibility in which as Christians we are bound to speak, will
inevitably be the language of the Bible, the Hebrew and the Greek Bible
and the translations of them, and the language of Christian tradition,
the language in the forms of the thoughts, concepts and ideas, in which
in the course of centuries the Christian Church has gained and upheld
and declared its knowledge. There is a specifically Church language.
That is in order. Let us call it by the familiar name by saying that there
is a "language of Canaan." And when the Christian confesses his faith,
when we have to let the light that is kindled in us shine, no one can
avoid speaking in this language. For this is how it is: if the things of
Christian faith, if our trust in God and His Word is to be expressed
precisely, so to speak in its essence — and time and again it is bitterly
necessary for this to be done, so that things may be made clear — then
it is inevitable that all undaunted the language of Canaan should
sound forth. For certain lights and indications and heartening warnings can be uttered directly in this language alone. To anyone rather
too sensitive in his desires and too tender about dealing with his
soul — "I believe, but my faith is so deep and inward that I cannot
bring myself to utter the words of the Bible, that it is difficult for me
to pronounce God's name, let alone the name of Christ or the blood
of Jesus Christ or the Holy Spirit" — to anyone who should speak in
this strain, I would say: "Dear friend, you may be a very spiritual man,
but see to it that you are deemed worthy to be publicly responsible for
your faith. And is your alleged shyness not shyness about emerging
from your uncommitted private world? Ask yourself!" One thing is
certain, that where the Christian Church does not venture to confess
in its own language, it usually does not confess at all. Then it becomes
the fellowship of the quiet, whereby it is much to be hoped that it does
not become a community of dumb dogs. Where people believe, the
urgent question arises whether they do not speak joyfully and gladly
also, just as the Bible has spoken and as in ancient and more recent
times the Church has spoken and must speak. Where faith in its
freedom and joy is in the field, in this language too God's praise will
be indeed uplifted and sung.

2. But this is not the end of the matter. More than this belongs to
the complete concept of confessing. Let us be fully on our guard
against the idea that confession is a matter of the faith which should

be heard only in the "area of the Church." And that all that is to be done is to make this area visible and perhaps extend it a little into the world. The area of the Church stands in the world, as outwardly the Church stands in the village or in a city, beside the school, the cinema and the railway station. The Church's language cannot aim at being an end in itself. It must be made clear that the Church exists for the sake of the world, that the light is shining in the darkness. As Christ did not come to let Himself be ministered unto, so too it does not become Christians to exist in their faith, as though they existed for themselves. But that means that, in the course of this making public of trust and knowledge, faith necessarily stipulates definite worldly attitudes. Where confession is serious and clear, it must be fundamentally translatable into the speech of Mr. Everyman, the man and woman in the street, into the language of those who are not accustomed to reading Scripture and singing hymns, but who possess a quite different vocabulary and quite different spheres of interest. Such is the world into which Christ sent His disciples and in which all of us exist too. Not one of us is only a Christian; we are all also a bit of the world. And so we are necessarily also concerned with worldly attitudes, with translations of our responsibility into this realm. For the Confession of Faith claims to be fulfilled in its application to the life we all live, to the problems of our actual existence in the theoretical and practical questions of our everyday life. If our faith is real, it must encroach upon our life. The Christian Confession in its original Church form will always be exposed to the misunderstanding that the Christian regards the Creed as a matter of heart and conscience, but that here on earth and in the world other truths hold good. The world lives in this misunderstanding; it regards the whole of Christianity as a friendly "magic," connected with the "realm of religion," which is respected and which ought to be left untampered with; and so we get rid of the matter! But this misunderstanding might even come from within; a Christian might quite well wish to have this realm for himself and to guard faith like a sensitive plant. The relationship between the Church and the world has been widely understood as a question of a fixing of frontiers, whereby each secured itself behind its own frontier, although from time to time it came to a skirmish. From the Church's standpoint, however, such a fixing of frontiers can never exhaust its task. By the very nature of the Christian Church there is only one task, to make the Confession heard in the sphere of the world as well. Not now repeated in the language of Canaan, but in the quite sober, quite unedifying language which is spoken "out there." There must be *translation,* for example, into the language of the newspaper. What we have to do is to say in the common language of the world the same thing as we say in the forms of Church language. The Christian need not be afraid of having to speak "unedifyingly" as well. If a man cannot, let him consider whether he really knows how to speak edifyingly even in the Church. We know this language of the pulpit and the altar, which outside the area of the Church is as effectual as Chinese. Let us beware of remaining stuck where we are and refusing to advance to meet worldly attitudes. For instance, in 1933 in Germany there was plenty of serious, profound and living Christianity and confession — God be praised and thanked! But unfortunately this faith and confession of the German Church remained embedded in the language of the Church, and did not translate what was being excellently said in the language of the Church into the political attitude demanded at the time; in which it would have become clear that the Evangelical Church had to say "No" to National Socialism, "No" from its very roots. The confession of Christianity did not at the time become clear in *this* form. Think what would have happened, had the Evangelical Church at that time expressed its Church knowledge in the form of a worldly, political attitude. It was not capable of that and the results are open to the day. And as a second example there is, even to-day, serious, living Christianity. I am sure that the course of events has aroused in many hunger and thirst for the Word of God, and that a great hour has arrived for the Church. I hope that a space for the Church is not set up again and fortified, and the Christians gather among themselves. Theology must, of course, be pursued in all seriousness. But may we be confronted, and better than twelve years ago, with the fact that what has to happen in the Church must go out into the form of worldly attitudes. An evangelical Church which was to-day, say, prepared to keep silence on the question of guilt with regard to the events from which we have issued, which was unwilling to listen to this question which must be answered honestly for the sake of the future, would *a priori* condemn itself to unfruitfulness. A Church which was not clear on this point of having a duty to this nation in need, and not merely the task of giving Christian instruction in direct form, but which has the task of making this Christian instruction known in words which grapple with the problems of the day — a Church which was not filled with anxiety to discover this word, would *a priori* betake itself to a corner of the graveyard. May every individual Christian be clear that so long as his faith is a snail's shell, in which he feels comfortable, but which does not bother itself with the life of his people, so long, that is, as he lives in dualism, he has not yet really come to believe! This snail's shell is not a desirable residence. It is not good to be here. Man is a whole and can only exist as such a whole.

In conclusion, the last part of the introductory statement ends with "the corresponding actions and attitudes." I have deliberately distinguished this from the second point. What would it avail a man, if he should speak and confess in most powerful language, and had not love? Confession means a living confession. If you believe, you are challenged to pay in person, *payer de sa personne.* That is the crucial point.

CARL JUNG

Modern Man in Search of a Soul

> Carl Gustav Jung (1875–1961), although a colleague of Sigmund Freud, went his own way in psychoanalytic thought, not only in his theory of "the will to live" but also in his more positive treatment of religion. Jung's researches into "archetypes" and his diagnosis of the crisis of modernity, which is reflected in this essay of 1933, led him to emphasize the value of the perennial themes with which religion deals.

THE SPIRITUAL PROBLEM of modern man is one of those questions which belong so intimately to the present in which we are living that we cannot judge of them fully. The modern man is a newly formed human being; a modern problem is a question which has just arisen and whose answer lies in the future. In speaking, therefore, of the spiritual problem of modern man we can at most state a question — and we should perhaps put this statement in different terms if we had but the faintest inkling of the answer. The question, moreover, seems rather vague; but the truth is that it has to do with something so universal that it exceeds the grasp of any single human being. We have reason enough, therefore, to approach such a problem with true moderation and with the greatest caution. I am deeply convinced of this, and wish it stressed the more because it is just such problems which tempt us to use high-sounding words — and because I shall myself be forced to say certain things which may sound immoderate and incautious.

To begin at once with an example of such apparent lack of caution, I must say that the man we call modern, the man who is aware of the immediate present, is by no means the average man. He is rather the man who stands upon a peak, or at the very edge of the world, the abyss of the future before him, above him the heavens, and below him the whole of mankind with a history that disappears in primeval mists. The modern man — or, let us say again, the man of the immediate present — is rarely met with. There are few who live up to the name, for they must be conscious to a superlative degree. Since to be wholly of the present means to be fully conscious of one's existence as a man, it requires the most intensive and extensive consciousness, with a minimum of unconsciousness. It must be clearly understood that the mere fact of living in the present does not make a man modern, for in that case everyone at present alive would be so. He alone is modern who is fully conscious of the present.

The man whom we can with justice call "modern" is solitary. He is so of necessity and at all times, for every step towards a fuller consciousness of the present removes him further from his original *"participation mystique"* with the mass of men — from submersion in a common unconsciousness. Every step forward means an act of tearing himself loose from that all-embracing, pristine unconsciousness which claims the bulk of mankind almost entirely. Even in our civilizations the people who form, psychologically speaking, the lowest stratum, live almost as unconsciously as primitive races. Those of the succeeding stratum manifest a level of consciousness which corresponds to the beginnings of human culture, while those of the highest stratum have a consciousness capable of keeping step with the life of the last few centuries. Only the man who is modern in our meaning of the term really lives in the present; he alone has a present-day consciousness, and he alone finds that the ways of life which correspond to earlier levels pall upon him. The values and strivings of those past worlds no longer interest him save from the historical standpoint. Thus he has become "unhistorical" in the deepest sense and has estranged himself from the mass of men who live entirely within the bounds of tradition. Indeed, he is completely modern only when he has come to the very edge of the world, leaving behind him all that has been discarded and outgrown, and acknowledging that he stands before a void out of which all things may grow.

These words may be thought to be but empty sound, and their meaning reduced to mere banality. Nothing is easier than to affect a consciousness of the present. As a matter of fact, a great horde of worthless people give themselves the air of being modern by overleaping the various stages of development and the tasks of life they represent. They appear suddenly by the side of the truly modern man as uprooted human beings, blood-sucking ghosts, whose emptiness is taken for the unenviable loneliness of the modern man and casts discredit upon him. He and his kind, few in number as they are, are hidden from the undiscerning eyes of mass-men by those clouds of ghosts, the pseudo-moderns. It cannot be helped; the "modern" man is questionable and suspect, and has always been so, even in the past.

An honest profession of modernity means voluntarily declaring bankruptcy, taking the vows of poverty and chastity in a new sense, and — what is still more painful — renouncing the halo which history bestows as a mark of its sanction. To be "unhistorical" is the Promethean sin, and in this sense modern man lives in sin. A higher level of consciousness is like a burden of guilt. But, as I have said, only the man who has outgrown the stages of consciousness belonging to the past and has amply fulfilled the duties appointed for him by his world, can achieve a full consciousness of the present. To do this he must be sound and proficient in the best sense — a man who has achieved as much as other people, and even a little more. It is these qualities which enable him to gain the next highest level of consciousness.

I know that the idea of proficiency is especially repugnant to the pseudo-moderns, for it reminds them unpleasantly of their deceits. This, however, cannot prevent us from taking it as our criterion of the modern man. We are even forced to do so, for unless he is proficient, the man who claims to be modern is nothing but an unscrupulous gambler. He must be proficient in the highest degree, for unless he can atone by creative ability for his break with tradition, he is merely disloyal to the past. It is sheer juggling to look upon a denial of the past as the same thing as consciousness of the present. "Today" stands between "yesterday" and "tomorrow," and forms a link between past and future; it has no other meaning. The present represents a process of transition, and that man may account himself modern who is conscious of it in this sense.

Many people call themselves modern — especially the pseudo-moderns. Therefore the really modern man is often to be found among those who call themselves old-fashioned. He takes this stand for sufficient reasons. On the one hand he emphasizes the past in order to hold the scales against his break with tradition and that effect of guilt of which I have spoken. On the other hand he wishes to avoid being taken for a pseudo-modern.

Every good quality has its bad side, and nothing that is good can come into the world without directly producing a corresponding evil. This is a painful fact. Now there is the danger that consciousness of the present may lead to an elation based upon illusion: the illusion, namely, that we are the culmination of the history of mankind, the fulfilment and the end-product of countless centuries. If we grant this, we should understand that it is no more than the proud acknowledgment of our destitution: we are also the disappointment of the hopes and expectations of the ages. Think of nearly two thousand years of Christian ideals followed, instead of by the return of the Messiah and the heavenly millennium, by the World War among Christian nations and its barbed-wire and poison-gas. What a catastrophe in heaven and on earth!

In the face of such a picture we may well grow humble again. It is true that modern man is a culmination, but tomorrow he will be surpassed; he is indeed the end-product of an age-old development, but he is at the same time the worst conceivable disappointment of the hopes of humankind. The modern man is aware of this. He has seen how beneficent are science, technology and organization, but also how catastrophic they can be. He has likewise seen that well-meaning governments have so thoroughly paved the way for peace on the principle "in time of peace prepare for war," that Europe has nearly gone to rack and ruin. And as for ideals, the Christian church, the brotherhood of man, international social democracy and the "solidarity" of economic interests have all failed to stand the baptism of fire — the test of reality. Today, fifteen years after the war, we observe once more the same optimism, the same organization, the same political aspirations, the same phrases and catch-words at work. How can we but fear that they will inevitably lead to further catastrophes? Agreements to outlaw war leave us sceptical, even while we wish them all possible success. At bottom, behind every such palliative measure, there is a gnawing doubt. On the whole, I believe I am not exaggerating when I say that modern man has suffered an almost fatal shock, psychologically speaking, and as a result has fallen into profound uncertainty.

These statements, I believe, make it clear enough that my being a physician has coloured my views. A doctor always spies out diseases, and I cannot cease to be a doctor. But it is essential to the physician's art that he should not discover diseases where none exists. I will therefore not make the assertion that the white races in general, and occidental nations in particular, are diseased, or that the Western world is on the verge of collapse. I am in no way competent to pass such a judgement.

It is of course only from my own experience with other persons and with myself that I draw my knowledge of the spiritual problem of modern man. I know something of the intimate psychic life of many hundreds of educated persons, both sick and healthy, coming from every quarter of the civilized, white world; and upon this experience I base my statements. No doubt I can draw only a one-sided picture, for the things I have observed are events of psychic life; they lie within us — on the *inner side,* if I may use the expression. I must point out that this is not always true of psychic life; the psyche is not always and everywhere to be found on the inner side. It is to be found on the *outside* in whole races or periods of history which take no account of psychic life as such. As examples we may choose any of the ancient cultures, but especially that of Egypt with its imposing objectivity and its naïve confession of sins that have not been committed. We can no more feel the Pyramids and the Apis tombs of Sakkara to be expressions of personal problems or personal emotions, than we can feel this of the music of Bach.

Whenever there is established an external form, be it ritual or spiritual, by which all the yearnings and hopes of the soul are adequately expressed — as for instance in some living religion — then we may say that the psyche is outside, and no spiritual problem, strictly speaking, exists. In consonance with this truth, the development of psychology falls entirely within the last decades, although long before that man was introspective and intelligent enough to recognize the facts that are the subject-matter of psychology. The same was the case with technical knowledge. The Romans were familiar with all the mechanical principles and physical facts on the basis of which they could have constructed the steam-engine, but all that came of it was the toy made by Hero of Alexandria. There was no urgent necessity to go further. It was the division of labour and specialization in the nineteenth century which gave rise to the need to apply all available knowledge. So also a spiritual need has produced in our time our "discovery" of psychology. There has never, of course, been a time when the psyche did not manifest itself, but formerly it attracted no attention — no one noticed it. People got along without heeding it. But today we can no longer get along unless we give our best attention to the ways of the psyche.

It was men of the medical profession who were the first to notice this; for the priest is concerned only to establish an undisturbed functioning of the psyche within a recognized system of belief. As long as this system gives true expression to life, psychology can be nothing but a technical adjuvant to healthy living, and the psyche cannot be regarded as a problem in itself. While man still lives as a herd-being he has no "things of the spirit" of his own; nor does he need any, save the usual belief in the immortality of the soul. But as soon as he has outgrown whatever local form of religion he was born to — as soon as this religion can no longer embrace his life in all its fulness — then the psyche becomes something in its own right which cannot be dealt with by the measures of the Church alone. It is for this reason that we of today have a psychology founded on experience, and not upon articles of faith or the postulates of any philosophical system. The very fact that we have such a psychology is to me symptomatic of a profound convulsion of spiritual life. Disruption in the spiritual life of an age shows the same pattern as radical change in an individual. As long as all goes well and psychic energy finds its application in adequate and well-regulated ways, we are disturbed by nothing from within. No uncertainty or doubt besets us, and we *cannot* be divided against ourselves. But no sooner are one or two of the channels of psychic activity blocked, than we are reminded of a stream that is dammed up. The current flows backward to its source; the inner man wants something which the visible man does not want, and we are at war with ourselves. Only then, in this distress, do we discover the psyche; or, more precisely, we come upon something which thwarts our will, which is strange and even hostile to us, or which is incompatible with our conscious standpoint. Freud's psychoanalytic labours show this process in the clearest way. The very first thing he discovered was the existence of sexually perverse and criminal fantasies which at their face value are wholly incompatible with the conscious outlook of a civilized man. A person who was activated by them would be nothing less than a mutineer, a criminal or a madman.

We cannot suppose that this aspect of the unconscious or of the hinterland of man's mind is something totally new. Probably it has always been there, in every culture. Each culture gave birth to its destructive opposite, but no culture or civilization before our own was ever forced to take these psychic undercurrents in deadly earnest. Psychic life always found expression in a metaphysical system of some sort. But the conscious, modern man, despite his strenuous and dogged efforts to do so, can no longer refrain from acknowledging the might of psychic forces. This distinguishes our time from all others. We can no longer deny that the dark stirrings of the unconscious are effective powers — that psychic forces exist which cannot, for the present at least, be fitted in with our rational world-order. We have even enlarged our study of these forces to a science — one more proof of the earnest attention we bring to them. Previous centuries could throw them aside unnoticed; for us they are a shirt of Nessus which we cannot strip off.

The revolution in our conscious outlook, brought about by the catastrophic results of the World War, shows itself in our inner life by the shattering of our faith in ourselves and our own worth. We used to regard foreigners — the other side — as political and moral reprobates; but the modern man is forced to recognize that he is politically and morally just like anyone else. Whereas I formerly believed it to be my bounden duty to call other persons to order, I now admit that I need calling to order myself. I admit this the more readily because I realize only too well that I am losing my faith in the possibility of a rational organization of the world, that old dream of the millennium, in which peace and harmony should rule, has grown pale. The modern man's scepticism regarding all such matters has chilled his enthusiasm for politics and world-reform; more than that, it does not favour any smooth application of psychic energies to the outer world. Through his scepticism the modern man is thrown back upon himself; his energies flow towards their source and wash to the surface those psychic contents which are at all times there, but lie hidden in the silt as long as the stream flows smoothly in its course. How totally different did the world appear to mediæval man! For him the earth was eternally fixed and at rest in the centre of the universe, encircled by the course of a sun that solicitously bestowed its warmth. Men were all children of God under the loving care of the Most High, who prepared them for eternal blessedness; and all knew exactly what they should do and how they should conduct themselves in order to rise from a corruptible world to an incorruptible and joyous existence. Such a life no longer seems real to us, even in our dreams. Natural science has long ago torn this lovely veil to shreds. That age lies as far behind as childhood, when one's own father was unquestionably the handsomest and strongest man on earth.

The modern man has lost all the metaphysical certainties of his mediæval brother, and set up in their place the ideals of material security, general welfare and humaneness. But it takes more than an ordinary dose of optimism to make it appear that these ideals are still unshaken. Material security, even, has gone by the board, for the modern man begins to see that every step in material "progress" adds just so much force to the threat of a more stupendous catastrophe. The very picture terrorizes the imagination. What are we to imagine when cities today perfect measures of defence against poison-gas attacks, and practise them in "dress rehearsals"? We cannot but suppose that such attacks have been planned and provided for — again on the principle "in time of peace prepare for war." Let man but accumulate his materials of destruction and the devil within him will soon be unable to resist putting them to their fated use. It is well known that fire-arms go off of themselves if only enough of them are together.

An intimation of the law that governs blind contingency, which Heraclitus called the rule of *enantiodromia* (conversion into the opposite), now steals upon the modern man through the by-ways of his mind, chilling him with fear and paralysing his faith in the lasting effectiveness of social and political measures in the face of these monstrous forces. If he turns away from the terrifying prospect of a blind world in which building and destroying successively tip the scale, and if he then turns his gaze inward upon the recesses of his own mind, he will discover a chaos and a darkness there which he would gladly ignore. Science has destroyed even the refuge of the inner life. What was once a sheltering haven has become a place of terror.

And yet it is almost a relief for us to come upon so much evil in the depths of our own minds. We are able to believe, at least, that we have discovered the root of the evil in mankind. Even though we are shocked and disillusioned at first, we yet feel, because these things are manifestations of our own minds, that we hold them more or less in our own hands and can therefore correct or at least effectively suppress them. We like to assume that, if we succeeded in this, we should have rooted out some fraction of the evil in the world. We like to think that, on the basis of a widespread knowledge of the unconscious and its ways, no one could be deceived by a statesman who was unaware of his own bad motives; the very newspapers would pull him up: "Please have yourself analysed; you are suffering from a repressed father-complex."

I have purposely chosen this grotesque example to show to what absurdities we are led by the illusion that because something is psychic it is under our control. It is, however, true that much of the evil in the world is due to the fact that man in general is hopelessly unconscious, as it is also true that with increasing insight we can combat this evil at its source in ourselves. As science enables us to deal with injuries inflicted from without, so it helps us to treat those arising from within.

The rapid and world-wide growth of a "psychological" interest over the last two decades shows unmistakably that modern man has to some extent turned his attention from material things to his own subjective processes. Should we call this mere curiosity? At any rate, art has a way of anticipating future changes in man's fundamental outlook, and expressionist art has taken this subjective turn well in advance of the more general change.

This "psychological" interest of the present time shows that man expects something from psychic life which he has not received from the outer world: something which our religions, doubtless, ought to contain, but no longer do contain — at least for the modern man. The various forms of religion no longer appear to the modern man to come from within — to be expressions of his own psychic life; for him they are to be classed with the things of the outer world. He is vouchsafed no revelation of a spirit that is not of this world; but he tries on a number of religions and convictions as if they were Sunday attire, only to lay them aside again like worn-out clothes.

Yet he is somehow fascinated by the almost pathological manifestations of the unconscious mind. We must admit the fact, however difficult it is for us to understand, that something which previous ages have discarded should suddenly command our attention. That there is a general interest in these matters is a truth which cannot be denied. Their offence to good taste notwithstanding. I am not thinking merely of the interest taken in psychology as a science, or of the still narrower interest in the psychoanalysis of Freud, but of the widespread interest in all sorts of psychic phenomena as manifested in the growth of spiritualism, astrology, theosophy, and so forth. The world has seen nothing like it since the end of the seventeenth century. We can compare it only to the flowering of Gnostic thought in the first and second centuries after Christ. The spiritual currents of the present have, in fact, a deep affinity with Gnosticism. There is even a Gnostic church in France today, and I know of two schools in Germany which openly declare themselves Gnostic. The modern movement which is numerically most impressive is undoubtedly Theosophy, together with its continental sister, Anthroposophy; these are pure Gnosticism in a Hindu dress. Compared with these movements the interest in scientific psychology is negligible. What is striking about Gnostic systems is that they are based exclusively upon the manifestations of the unconscious, and that their moral teachings do not baulk at the shadow-side of life. Even in the form of its European revival, the Hindu *Kundalini-Yoga* shows this clearly. And as every person informed on the subject of occultism will testify, the statement holds true in this field as well.

The passionate interest in these movements arises undoubtedly from psychic energy which can no longer be invested in obsolete forms of religion. For this reason such movements have a truly religious character, even when they pretend to be scientific. It changes nothing when Rudolf Steiner calls his Anthroposophy "spiritual science," or Mrs. Eddy discovers a "Christian Science." These attempts at concealment merely show that religion has grown suspect — almost as suspect as politics and world-reform.

I do not believe that I am going too far when I say that modern man, in contrast to his nineteenth-century brother, turns his attention to the psyche with very great expectations; and that he does so without reference to any traditional creed, but rather in the Gnostic sense of religious experience. We should be wrong in seeing mere caricature or masquerade when the movements already mentioned try to give themselves scientific airs; their doing so is rather an indication that they are actually pursuing "science" or knowledge instead of the *faith* which is the essence of Western religions. The modern man abhors dogmatic postulates taken on faith and the religions based upon them. He holds them valid only in so far as their knowledge-content seems to accord with his own experience of the deeps of psychic life. He wants to know — to experience for himself. Dean Inge of St. Paul's has called attention to a movement in the Anglican Church with similar objectives.

The age of discovery has only just come to a close in our day when no part of the earth remains unexplored; it began when men would no longer *believe* that the Hyperboreans inhabited the land of eternal sunshine, but wanted to find out and to see with their own eyes what existed beyond the boundaries of the known world. Our age is apparently bent on discovering what exists in the psyche outside of consciousness. The question asked in every spiritualistic circle is: What happens when the medium has lost consciousness? Every Theosophist asks: What shall I experience at higher levels of consciousness? The question which every astrologer puts is this: What are the effective forces and determinants of my fate beyond the reach of my conscious intention? And every psychoanalyst wants to know: What are the unconscious drives behind the neurosis?

Our age wishes to have actual experiences in psychic life. It wants to experience for itself, and not to make assumptions based on the experience of other ages. Yet this does not preclude its trying anything in a hypothetical way — for instance, the recognized religions and the genuine sciences. The European of yesterday will feel a slight shudder run down his spine when he gazes at all deeply into these delvings. Not only does he consider the subject of this research all too obscure and uncanny, but even the methods employed seem to him a shocking misuse of man's finest intellectual attainments. What can we expect an astronomer to say when he is told that at least a thousand horoscopes are drawn today to one three hundred years ago? What will the educator and the advocate of philosophical enlightenment say to the fact that the world has not been freed of one single superstition since Greek antiquity? Freud himself, the founder of psychoanalysis, has thrown a glaring light upon the dirt, darkness and evil of the psychic hinterland, and has presented these things as so much refuse and slag; he has thus taken the utmost pains to discourage people from seeking anything behind them. He did not succeed, and his warning has even brought about the very thing he wished to prevent: it has awakened in many people an admiration for all this filth. We are tempted to call this sheer perversity; and we could hardly explain it save on the ground that it is not a love of dirt, but the fascination of the psyche, which draws these people.

There can be no doubt that from the beginning of the nineteenth century — from the memorable years of the French Revolution onwards — man has given a more and more prominent place to the psyche, his increasing attentiveness to it being the measure of its growing attraction for him. The enthronement of the Goddess of Reason in Nôtre Dame seems to have been a symbolic gesture of great significance to the Western world — rather like the hewing down of Wotan's oak by the Christian missionaries. For then, as at the Revolution, no avenging bolt from heaven struck the blasphemer down.

It is certainly more than an amusing coincidence that just at that time a Frenchman, Anquetil du Perron, was living in India, and, in the early eighteen-hundreds, brought back with him a translation of the *Oupnek'hat* — a collection of fifty *Upanishads* — which gave the Western world its first deep insight into the baffling mind of the East. To the historian this is mere chance without any factors of cause and effect. But in view of my medical experience I cannot take it as accident. It seems to me rather to satisfy a psychological law whose validity in personal life, at least, is complete. For every piece of conscious life that loses its importance and value — so runs the law — there arises a compensation in the unconscious. We may see in this an analogy to the conservation of energy in the physical world, for our psychic processes have a quantitative aspect also. No psychic value can disappear without being replaced by another of equivalent intensity. This is a rule which finds its pragmatic sanction in the daily practice of the psychotherapist; it is repeatedly verified and never fails. Now the doctor in me refuses point blank to consider the life of a people as something that does not conform to psychological law. A people, in the doctor's eyes, presents only a somewhat more complex picture of psychic life than the individual. Moreover, taking it the other way round, has not a poet spoken of the "nations" of his soul? And quite correctly, as it seems to me, for in one of its aspects the psyche is not individual, but is derived from the nation, from collectivity, or from humanity even. In some way or other we are part of an all-embracing psychic life, of a single "greatest" man, to quote Swedenborg.

And so we can draw a parallel: just as in me, a single human being, the darkness calls forth the helpful light, so does it also in the psychic life of a people. In the crowds that poured into Nôtre Dame, bent on destruction, dark and nameless forces were at work that swept the individual off his feet; these forces worked also upon Anquetil du Perron, and provoked an answer which has come down in history. For he brought the Eastern mind to the West, and its influence upon us we cannot as yet measure. Let us beware of underestimating it! So far, indeed, there is little of it to be seen in Europe on the intellectual surface: some orientalists, one or two Buddhist enthusiasts, and a few sombre celebrities like Madame Blavatsky and Annie Besant. These manifestations make us think of tiny, scattered islands in the ocean of mankind; in reality they are like the peaks of submarine mountain-ranges of considerable size. The Philistine believed until recently that astrology had been disposed of long since, and was something that could be safely laughed at. But today, rising out of the social deeps, it knocks at the doors of the universities from which it was banished some three hundred years ago. The same is true of the thought of the East; it takes root in the lower social levels and slowly grows to the surface. Where did the five or six million Swiss francs for the Anthroposophist temple at Dornach come from? Certainly not from one individual. Unfortunately there are no statistics to tell us the exact number of avowed Theosophists today, not to mention the unavowed. But we can be sure that there are several millions of them. To this number we must add a few million Spiritualists of Christian or Theosophic learnings.

Great innovations never come from above; they come invariably from below; just as trees never grow from the sky downward, but upward from the earth, however true it is that their seeds have fallen from above. The upheaval of our world and the upheaval in consciousness is one and the same. Everything becomes relative and therefore doubtful. And while man, hesitant and questioning, contemplates a world that is distracted with treaties of peace and pacts of friendship, democracy and dictatorship, capitalism and Bolshevism, his spirit yearns for an answer that will allay the turmoil of doubt and uncertainty. And it is just people of the lower social levels who follow the unconscious forces of the psyche; it is the much-derided, silent folk of the land — those who are less infected with academic prejudices than great celebrities are wont to be. All these people, looked at from above, present mostly a dreary or laughable comedy; and yet they are as impressively simple as those Galileans who were once called blessed. Is it not touching to see the refuse of man's psyche gathered together in compendia a foot thick? We find recorded in *Anthropophyteia* with scrupulous care the merest babblings, the most absurd actions and the wildest fantasies, while men like Havelock Ellis and Freud have dealt with the like matters in serious treatises which have been accorded all scientific honours. Their reading public is scattered over the breadth of the civilized, white world. How are we to explain this zeal, this almost fanatical worship of repellent things? In this way: the repellent things belong to the psyche, they are of the substance of the psyche and therefore as precious as fragments of manuscript salvaged from ancient ruins. Even the secret and noisome things of the inner life are valuable to modern man because they serve his purpose. But what purpose?

Freud has prefixed to his *Interpretation of Dreams* the citation: *Flectere si nequeo superos Acheronta movebo* — "If I cannot bend the gods on high, I will at least set Acheron in uproar." But to what purpose?

The gods whom *we* are called to dethrone are the idolized values of our conscious world. It is well known that it was the love-scandals of the ancient deities which contributed most to their discredit; and now history is repeating itself. People are laying bare the dubious foundations of our belauded virtues and incomparable ideals, and are calling out to us in triumph: "There are your man-made gods, mere snares and delusions tainted with human baseness — whited sepulchres full of dead men's bones and of all uncleanness." We recognize a familiar strain, and the Gospel words, which we never could make our own, now come to life again.

I am deeply convinced that these are not vague analogies. There are too many persons to whom Freudian psychology is dearer than the Gospels, and to whom the Russian Terror means more than civic virtue. And yet all these people are our brothers, and in each of us there is at least *one* voice which seconds them — for in the end there is a psychic life which embraces us all.

C. S. LEWIS

The Screwtape Letters

Clive Staples Lewis (1898–1963) taught English literature at Oxford and then at Cambridge, and was the author of important scholarly books in that field, notably *The Allegory of Love*. Nevertheless, he achieved his widest readership with his works of Christian apologetics, among which *The Screwtape Letters,* containing the correspondence between a devil on earth and those who were above him (actually below him) in Hell, was the most successful.

My dear wormwood,

So! Your man is in love — and in the worst kind he could possibly have fallen into — and with a girl who does not even appear in the report you sent me. You may be interested to learn that the little misunderstanding with the Secret Police which you tried to raise about some unguarded expressions in one of my letters has been tided over. If you were reckoning on that to secure my good offices, you will find yourself mistaken. You shall pay for that as well as your other blunders. Meanwhile I enclose a little booklet, just issued, on the new House of Correction for Incompetent Tempters. It is profusely illustrated and you will not find a dull page in it.

I have looked up this girl's dossier and am horrified at what I find. Not only a Christian but such a Christian — a vile, sneaking, simpering, demure, monosyllabic, mouse-like, watery, insignificant, virginal, bread-and-butter miss. The little brute. She makes me vomit. She stinks and scalds through the very pages of the dossier. It drives me mad, the way the world has worsened. We'd have had her to the arena in the old days. That's what her sort is made for. Not that she'd do much good there, either. A two-faced little cheat (I know the sort) who looks as if she'd faint at the sight of blood and then dies with a smile. A cheat every way. Looks as if butter wouldn't melt in her mouth and yet has a satirical wit. The sort of creature who'd find *ME* funny! Filthy insipid little prude — and yet ready to fall into this booby's arms like any other breeding animal. Why doesn't the Enemy blast her for it, if He's so moonstruck by virginity — instead of looking on there, grinning?

He's a hedonist at heart. All those fasts and vigils and stakes and crosses are only a façade. Or only like foam on the sea shore. Out at sea, out in His sea, there is pleasure, and more pleasure. He makes no secret of it; at His right hand are "pleasures for evermore." Ugh! I don't think He has the least inkling of that high and austere mystery to which we rise in the Miserific Vision. He's vulgar, Wormwood. He has a bourgeois mind. He has filled His world full of pleasures. There are things for humans to do all day long without His minding in the least — sleeping, washing, eating, drinking, making love, playing, praying, working. Everything has to be *twisted* before it's any use to us. We fight under cruel disadvantages. Nothing is naturally on our side. (Not that that excuses *you*. I'll settle with you presently. You have always hated me and been insolent when you dared.)

Then, of course, he gets to know this woman's family and whole circle. Could you not see that the very house she lives in is one that he ought never to have entered? The whole place reeks of that deadly odour. The very gardener, though he has only been there five years, is beginning to acquire it. Even guests, after a week-end visit, carry some of the smell away with them. The dog and the cat are tainted with it. And a house full of the impenetrable mystery. We are certain (it is a matter of first principles) that each member of the family must in some way be making capital out of the others — but we can't find out how. They guard as jealously as the Enemy Himself the secret of what really lies behind this pretence of disinterested love. The whole house and garden is one vast obscenity. It bears a sickening resemblance to the description one human writer made of Heaven; "the regions where there is only life and therefore all that is not music is silence."

Music and silence — how I detest them both! How thankful we should be that ever since our Father entered Hell — though longer ago than humans, reckoning in light years, could express — no square inch of infernal space and no moment of infernal time has been surrendered to either of those abominable forces, but all has been occupied by Noise — Noise, the grand dynamism, the audible expression of all that is exultant, ruthless, and virile — Noise which alone defends us from silly qualms, despairing scruples, and impossible desires. We will make the whole universe a noise in the end. We have already made great strides in this direction as regards the Earth. The melodies and silences of Heaven will be shouted down in the end. But I admit we are not yet loud enough, or anything like it. Research is in progress. Meanwhile *you,* disgusting little——

[Here the MS. breaks off and is resumed in a different hand.]

In the heat of composition I find that I have inadvertently allowed myself to assume the form of a large centipede. I am accordingly dictating the rest to my secretary. Now that the transformation is complete I recognise it as a periodical phenomenon. Some rumour of it has reached the humans and a distorted account of it appears in the poet Milton, with the ridiculous addition that such changes of shape are a "punishment" imposed on us by the Enemy. A more modern writer — someone with a name like Pshaw — has, however, grasped the truth. Transformation proceeds from within and is a glorious manifestation of that Life Force which Our Father would worship if he worshipped anything but himself. In my present form I feel even more anxious to see you, to unite you to myself in an indissoluble embrace,

(Signed) TOADPIPE

For his Abysmal Sublimity Under Secretary

Screwtape, T.E., B.S., etc.

My dear Wormwood,

Through this girl and her disgusting family the patient is now getting to know more Christians every day, and very intelligent Christians too. For a long time it will be quite impossible to *remove* spirituality from his life. Very well then; we must *corrupt* it. No doubt you have often practised transforming yourself into an angel of light as a parade-ground exercise. Now is the time to do it in the face of the Enemy. The World and the Flesh have failed us; a third Power remains. And success of this third kind is the most glorious of all. A spoiled saint, a Pharisee, an inquisitor, or a magician, makes better sport in Hell than a mere common tyrant or debauchee.

Looking round your patient's new friends I find that the best point of attack would be the border-line between theology and politics. Several of his new friends are very much alive to the social implications of their religion. That, in itself, is a bad thing; but good can be made out of it.

You will find that a good many Christian-political writers think that Christianity began going wrong, and departing from the doctrine of its Founder, at a very early stage. Now this idea must be used by us to encourage once again the conception of a "historical Jesus" to be found by clearing away later "accretions and perversions" and then to be contrasted with the whole Christian tradition. In the last generation we promoted the construction of such a "historical Jesus" on liberal and humanitarian lines; we are now putting forward a new "historical Jesus" on Marxian, catastrophic, and revolutionary lines. The advantages of these constructions, which we intend to change every thirty years or so, are manifold. In the first place they all tend to direct men's devotion to something which does not exist, for each "historical Jesus" is unhistorical. The documents say what they say and cannot be added to; each new "historical Jesus" therefore has to be got out of them by suppression at one point and exaggeration at another, and by that sort of guessing (*brilliant* is the adjective we teach humans to apply to it) on which no one would risk ten shillings in ordinary life, but which is enough to produce a crop of new Napoleons, new Shakespeares, and new Swifts, in every publisher's autumn list. In the second place, all such constructions place the importance of their Historical Jesus in some peculiar theory He is supposed to have promulgated. He has to be a "great man" in the modern sense of the word — one standing at the terminus of some centrifugal and unbalanced line of thought — a crank vending a panacea. We thus distract men's minds from Who He is, and what He did. We first make Him solely a teacher, and then conceal the very substantial agreement between His teachings and those of all other great moral teachers. For humans must not be allowed to notice that all great moralists are sent by the Enemy not to inform men but to remind them, to restate the primeval moral platitudes against our continual concealment of them. We make the Sophists: He raises up a Socrates to answer them. Our third aim is, by these constructions, to destroy the devotional life. For the real presence of the Enemy, otherwise experienced by men in prayer and sacrament, we substitute a merely probable, remote, shadowy, and uncouth figure, one who spoke a strange language and died a long time ago. Such an object cannot in fact be worshipped. Instead of the Creator adored by its creature, you soon have merely a leader acclaimed by a partisan, and finally a distinguished character approved by a judicious historian. And fourthly, besides being unhistorical in the Jesus it depicts, religion of this kind is false to history in another sense. No nation, and few individuals, are really brought into the Enemy's camp by the historical study of the biography of Jesus, simply as biography. Indeed materials for a full biography have been withheld from men. The earliest converts were converted by a single historical fact (the Resurrection) and a single theological doctrine (the Redemption) operating on a sense of sin which they already had — and sin, not against some new fancy-dress law produced as a novelty by a "great man," but against the old, platitudinous, universal moral law which they had been taught by their nurses and mothers. The "Gospels" come later and were written not to make Christians but to edify Christians already made.

The "Historical Jesus" then, however dangerous he may seem to be to us at some particular point, is always to be encouraged. About the general connection between Christianity and politics, our position is more delicate. Certainly we do not want men to allow their Christianity to flow over into their political life, for the establishment of anything like a really just society would be a major disaster. On the other hand we do want, and want very much, to make men treat Christianity as a means; preferably, of course, as a means to their own advancement, but, failing that, as a means to anything — even to social justice. The thing to do is to get a man at first to value social justice as a thing which the Enemy demands, and then work him on to the stage at which he values Christianity because it may produce social justice. For the Enemy will not be used as a convenience. Men or nations who think they can revive the Faith in order to make a good society might just as well think they can use the stairs of Heaven as a short cut to the nearest chemist's shop. Fortunately it is quite easy to coax humans round this little corner. Only today I have found a passage in a Christian writer where he recommends his own version of Christianity on the ground that "only such a faith can outlast the death of old cultures and the birth of new civilisations." You see the little rift? "Believe this, not because it is true, but for some other reason." That's the game,

Your affectionate uncle
SCREWTAPE

RABINDRANATH TAGORE

The Four Stages of Life

> Sir Rabindranath Tagore (1861–1941) was a Bengali poet
> and composer who received the Nobel Prize for literature
> in 1913. In his poems the religious sentiments of the Hindu
> tradition are expressed with beauty and power, and in *The
> Religion of Man*, from which this selection is taken, Tagore
> interpreted the distinctive emphases of Hinduism in a man-
> ner that speaks to the human condition everywhere, at each
> of "the four stages of life."

I HAVE CONCENTRATED my attention upon the subject of religion which
is solely related to man, helping him to train his attitude and behaviour
towards the infinite in its human aspect. At the same time it should
be understood that the tendency of the Indian mind has ever been
towards that transcendentalism which does not hold religion to be
ultimate but rather to be a means to a further end. This end consists
in the perfect liberation of the individual in the universal spirit across
the furthest limits of humanity itself.

Such an extreme form of mysticism may be explained to my Western readers by its analogy in science. For science may truly be described as mysticism in the realm of material knowledge. It helps us
to go beyond appearances and reach the inner reality of things in
principles which are abstractions; it emancipates our mind from the
thraldom of the senses to the freedom of reason.

The common-sense view of the world that is apparent to us has its
vital importance for ourselves. For all our practical purposes the earth
is flat, the sun *does* set behind the western horizon; and whatever may
be the verdict of the great mathematician about the lack of consistency
in time's dealings we should fully trust it in setting our watches right.
In questions relating to the arts and our ordinary daily avocations we

must treat material objects as they seem to be and not as they are in essence. But the revelations of science, even when they go far beyond man's power of direct perception, give him the purest feeling of disinterested delight and a supersensual background to his world. Science offers us the mystic knowledge of matter which very often passes the range of our imagination. We humbly accept it, following those teachers who have trained their reason to free itself from the trammels of appearance or personal preferences. Their mind dwells in an impersonal infinity where there is no distinction between good and bad, high and low, ugly and beautiful, useful and useless, where all things have their one common right of recognition, that of their existence.

The final freedom of spirit which India aspires after has a similar character of realization. It is beyond all limits of personality, divested of all moral or aesthetic distinctions; it is the pure consciousness of Being, the ultimate reality, which has an infinite illumination of bliss. Though science brings our thoughts to the utmost limit of mind's territory it cannot transcend its own creation made of a harmony of logical symbols. In it the chick has come out of its shell, but not out of the definition of its own chickenhood. But in India it has been said by the *yogi* that through an intensive process of concentration and quietude our consciousness *does* reach that infinity where knowledge ceases to be knowledge, subject and object become one — a state of existence that cannot be defined.

We have our personal self. It has its desires which struggle to create a world where they could have their unrestricted activity and satisfaction. While it goes on we discover that our self-realization reaches its perfection in the abnegation of self. This fact has made us aware that the individual finds his meaning in a fundamental reality comprehending all individuals — the reality which is the moral and spiritual basis of the realm of human values. This belongs to our religion. As science is the liberation of our knowledge in the universal reason, which cannot be other than human reason, religion is the liberation of our individual personality in the universal Person who is human all the same.

The ancient explorers in psychology in India who declare that our emancipation can be carried still further into a realm where infinity is not bounded by human limitations, are not content with advancing this as a doctrine; they advocate its pursuit for the attainment of the highest goal of man. And for its sake the path of discipline has been planned which should be opened out across our life through all its stages, helping us to develop our humanity to perfection, so that we may surpass it in a finality of freedom.

Perfection has its two aspects in man, which can to some extent be separated, the perfection in being and perfection in doing. It can be imagined that, through some training or compulsion, good works may possibly be extorted from a man who personally may not be good. Activities that have fatal risks are often undertaken by cowards even though they are conscious of the danger. Such works may be useful and may continue to exist beyond the lifetime of the individual who produced them. And yet, where the question is not that of utility but of moral perfection, we hold it important that the individual should be true in his goodness. His outer good work may continue to produce good results, but the inner perfection of his personality has its own immense value, which for him is spiritual freedom and for humanity is an endless asset though we may not know it. For goodness represents the detachment of our spirit from the exclusiveness of our egoism; in goodness we identify ourselves with the universal humanity. Its value is not merely in some benefit for our fellow beings, but in its truth itself through which we realize within us that man is not merely an animal, bound by his individual passions and appetites, but a spirit that has its unfettered perfection. Goodness is the freedom of our self in the world of man, as is love. We have to be true within, not for worldly duties, but for that spiritual fulfilment, which is in harmony with the Perfect, in union with the Eternal. If this were not true, then mechanical perfection would be considered to be of higher value than the spiritual. In order to realize his unity with the universal, the individual man must live his perfect life which alone gives him the freedom to transcend it.

Doubtless Nature, for its own biological purposes, has created in us a strong faith in life, by keeping us unmindful of death. Nevertheless, not only our physical existence, but also the environment which it builds up around itself, may desert us in the moment of triumph; the greatest prosperity comes to its end, dissolving into emptiness; the mightiest empire is overtaken by stupor amidst the flicker of its festival lights. All this is none the less true because its truism bores us to be reminded of it.

And yet it is equally true that, though all our mortal relationships have their end, we cannot ignore them with impunity while they last. If we behave as if they do not exist, merely because they will not continue for ever, they will all the same exact their dues, with a great deal over by way of penalty. Trying to ignore bonds that are real, albeit temporary, only strengthens and prolongs their bondage. The soul is great, but the self has to be crossed over in order to reach it. We do not attain our goal by destroying our path.

Our teachers in ancient India realized the soul of man as something very great indeed. They saw no end to its dignity, which found its consummation in Brahma himself. Any limited view of man would therefore be an incomplete view. He could not reach his finality as a mere Citizen or Patriot, for neither City nor Country, nor the bubble called the World, could contain his eternal soul.

Bhartrihari, who was once a king, has said: "What if you have secured the fountain-head of all desires; what if you have put your foot on the neck of your enemy, or by your good fortune gathered friends around you? What, even, if you have succeeded in keeping mortal bodies alive for ages — *tatah kim,* what then?"

That is to say, man is greater than all these objects of his desire. He is true in his freedom.

But in the process of attaining freedom one must bind his will in order to save its forces from distraction and wastage, so as to gain for it the velocity which comes from the bondage itself. Those also, who seek liberty in a purely political plane, constantly curtail it and reduce their freedom of thought and action to that narrow limit which is necessary for making political power secure, very often at the cost of liberty of conscience.

India had originally accepted the bonds of her social system in order to transcend society, as the rider puts reins on his horse and stirrups on his own feet in order to ensure greater speed towards his goal.

The Universe cannot be so madly conceived that desire should be an interminable song with no finale. And just as it is painful to stop in the middle of the tune, it should be as pleasant to reach its final cadence.

India has not advised us to come to a sudden stop while work is in full swing. It is true that the unending procession of the world has gone on, through its ups and downs, from the beginning of creation till today; but it is equally obvious that each individual's connection therewith *does* get finished. Must he necessarily quit it without any sense of fulfilment?

So, in the division of man's world-life which we had in India, work came in the middle, and freedom at the end. As the day is divided into morning, noon, afternoon and evening, so India had divided man's life into four parts, following the requirements of his nature. The day has the waxing and waning of its light; so has man the waxing and waning of his bodily powers. Acknowledging this, India gave a connected meaning to his life from start to finish.

First came *brahmacharya,* the period of discipline in education; then *garhasthya,* that of the world's work; then *vanaprasthya,* the retreat for the loosening of bonds; and finally *pravrajya,* the expectant awaiting of freedom across death.

We have come to look upon life as a conflict with death — the intruding enemy, not the natural ending — in impotent quarrel with which we spend every stage of it. When the time comes for youth to depart, we would hold it back by main force. When the fervour of desire slackens, we would revive it with fresh fuel of our own devising. When our sense organs weaken, we urge them to keep up their efforts. Even when our grip has relaxed we are reluctant to give up possession. We are not trained to recognize the inevitable as natural, and so cannot give up gracefully that which has to go, but needs must wait till it is snatched from us. The truth comes as conqueror only because we have lost the art of receiving it as guest.

The stem of the ripening fruit becomes loose, its pulp soft, but its seed hardens with provision for the next life. Our outward losses, due to age, have likewise corresponding inward gains. But, in man's inner life, his will plays a dominant part, so that these gains depend on his own disciplined striving; that is why, in the case of undisciplined man, who has omitted to secure such provision for the next stage, it is so often seen that his hair is grey, his mouth toothless, his muscles slack, and yet his stem-hold on life has refused to let go its grip, so much so that he is anxious to exercise his will in regard to worldly details even after death.

But renounce we must, and through renunciation gain — that is the truth of the inner world.

The flower must shed its petals for the sake of fruition, the fruit must drop off for the re-birth of the tree. The child leaves the refuge of the womb in order to achieve the further growth of body and mind in which consists the whole of the child life; next, the soul has to come out of this self-contained stage into the fuller life, which has varied relations with kinsman and neighbour, together with whom it forms a larger body; lastly comes the decline of the body, the weakening of desire. Enriched with its experiences, the soul now leaves the narrower life for the universal life, to which it dedicates its accumulated wisdom and itself enters into relations with the Life Eternal, so that, when finally the decaying body has come to the very end of its tether, the soul views its breaking away quite simply and without regret, in the expectation of its own entry into the Infinite.

From individual body to community, from community to universe, from universe to Infinity — this is the soul's normal progress.

Our teachers, therefore, keeping in mind the goal of this progress, did not, in life's first stage of education, prescribe merely the learning of books or things, but *brahmacharya,* the living in discipline, whereby both enjoyment and its renunciation would come with equal ease to the strengthened character. Life being a pilgrimage, with liberation in Brahma as its object, the living of it was as a spiritual exercise to be carried through its different stages, reverently and with a vigilant determination. And the pupil, from his very initiation, had this final consummation always kept in his view.

Once the mind refuses to be bound by temperate requirements, there ceases to be any reason why it should cry halt at any particular limit; and so, like trying to extinguish fire with oil, its acquisitions only make its desires blaze up all the fiercer. That is why it is so essential to habituate the mind, from the very beginning, to be conscious of, and desirous of, keeping within the natural limits; to cultivate the spirit of enjoyment which is allied with the spirit of freedom, the readiness for renunciation.

After the period of such training comes the period of world-life — the life of the householder. Manu tells us:

> It is not possible to discipline ourselves so effectively if out of touch with the world, as while pursuing the world-life with wisdom.

That is to say, wisdom does not attain completeness except through the living of life; and discipline divorced from wisdom is not true discipline, but merely the meaningless following of custom, which is only a disguise for stupidity.

Work, especially good work, becomes easy only when desire has learnt to discipline itself. Then alone does the householder's state become a centre of welfare for all the world, and instead of being an obstacle, helps on the final liberation.

The second stage of life having been thus spent, the decline of the bodily powers must be taken as a warning that it is coming to its natural end. This must not be taken dismally as a notice of dismissal to one still eager to stick to his post, but joyfully as maturity may be accepted as the stage of fulfilment.

After the infant leaves the womb, it still has to remain close to its mother for a time, remaining attached in spite of its detachment, until it can adapt itself to its new freedom. Such is the case in the third stage of life, when man though aloof from the world still remains in touch with it while preparing himself for the final stage of complete freedom. He still gives to the world from his store of wisdom and accepts its support; but this interchange is not of the same intimate character as in the stage of the householder, there being a new sense of distance.

Then at last comes a day when even such free relations have their end, and the emancipated soul steps out of all bonds to face the Supreme Soul.

Only in this way can man's world-life be truly lived from one end to the other, without being engaged at every step in trying conclusions with death, not being overcome, when death comes in due course, as by a conquering enemy.

For this fourfold way of life India attunes man to the grand harmony of the universal, leaving no room for untrained desires of a rampant individualism to pursue their destructive career unchecked, but leading them on to their ultimate modulation in the Supreme.

If we really believe this, then we must uphold an ideal of life in which everything else — the display of individual power, the might of nations — must be counted as subordinate and the soul of man must triumph and liberate itself from the bond of personality which keeps it in an ever-revolving circle of limitation.

If that is not to be, *tatah kim,* what then?

But such an ideal of the utter extinction of the individual separateness has not a universal sanction in India. There are many of us whose prayer is for dualism, so that for them the bond of devotion with God may continue for ever. For them religion is a truth which is ultimate and they refuse to envy those who are ready to sail for the further shore of existence across humanity. They know that human imperfection is the cause of our sorrow, but there is a fulfilment in love within the range of our limitation which accepts all sufferings and yet rises above them.

In the Sanskrit language the bird is described as "twice-born" — once in its limited shell and then finally in the freedom of the unbounded sky. Those of our community who believe in the liberation of man's limited self in the freedom of the spirit retain the same epithet for themselves. In all departments of life man shows this dualism — his existence within the range of obvious facts and his transcendence of it in a realm of deeper meaning.

Having this instinct inherent in his mind which ever suggests to him the crossing of the border, he has never accepted what is apparent as final, and his incessant struggle has been to break through the shell of his limitations. In this attempt he often goes against the instincts of his vital nature, and even exults in his defiance of the extreme penal laws of the biological kingdom. The best wealth of his civilization has been achieved by his following the guidance of this instinct in his ceaseless adventure of the Endless Further. His achievement of truth goes far beyond his needs and the realization of his self strives across the frontier of its individual interest. This proves to him his infinity and makes his religion real to him by his own manifestation in truth and goodness. Only for man can there be religion, because his evolution is from efficiency in nature towards the perfection of spirit.

According to some interpretations of the Vedanta doctrine Brahman is the absolute Truth, the impersonal It, in which there can be no distinction of this and that, the good and the evil, the beautiful and its opposite, having no other quality except its ineffable blissfulness in the eternal solitude of its consciousness utterly devoid of all things and all thoughts. But as our religion can only have its significance in this phenomenal world comprehended by our human self, this absolute conception of Brahman is outside the subject of my discussion. What I have tried to bring out in this book is the fact that whatever name may have been given to the divine Reality it has found its highest place in the history of our religion owing to its human character, giving meaning to the idea of sin and sanctity, and offering an eternal background to all the ideals of perfection which have their harmony with man's own nature.

We have the age-long tradition in our country, as I have already stated, that through the process of *yoga* a man can transcend the utmost bounds of his humanity and find himself in a pure state of consciousness of his undivided unity with Parabrahman. There is none who has the right to contradict this belief; for it is a matter of direct experience and not of logic. It is widely known in India that there are individuals who have the power to attain temporarily the state of *Samadhi,* the complete merging of the self in the infinite, a state which is indescribable. While accepting their testimony as true, let us at the same time have faith in the testimony of others who have felt a profound love, which is the intense feeling of union, for a Being who comprehends in himself all things that are human in knowledge, will and action. And he is God, who is not merely a sum total of facts, but the goal that lies immensely beyond all that is comprised in the past and the present.

SEYYED HOSSEIN NASR

The Prophet
and Prophetic Religion

Seyyed Hossein Nasr is one of the leading living proponents of Sufism and in 1981 presented the Gifford Lectures, *Knowledge and the Sacred*. The first incumbent of the Aga Khan Chair of Islamic Studies at the American University of Beirut, he delivered *Ideas and Realities of Islam,* in his own words, at "the meeting place between East and West, between the Islamic world and the Occident, in a land where different branches of Islam are well represented."

THE PROPHET as the founder of Islam and the messenger of God's revelation to mankind is the interpreter *par excellence* of the Book of God; and his Ḥadīth and *Sunnah,* his sayings and actions, are after the Quran, the most important sources of the Islamic tradition. In order to understand the significance of the Prophet it is not sufficient to study, from the outside, historical texts pertaining to his life. One must view him also from within the Islamic point of view and try to discover the position he occupies in the religious consciousness of Muslims. When in any Islamic language one says *the* Prophet, it means Muḥammad — whose name as such is never iterated except that as a courtesy it be followed by the formula *"Ṣall' Allāhu 'alaihī wa sallam,"* that is, "may God's blessing and salutation be upon him."

It is even legitimate to say that, in general, when one says *the* Prophet it means the prophet of Islam; for although in every religion the founder, who is an aspect of the Universal Intellect, becomes the Aspect, the Word, the Incarnation, nevertheless each founder emphasizes a certain aspect of the Truth and even typifies that aspect universally. Although there is belief in incarnation in many religions, when one says *the* Incarnation it refers to Christ who personifies this aspect. And although every prophet and saint has experienced "enlightenment," *the* Enlightenment refers to the experience of the Buddha which is the most outstanding and universal embodiment of this experience. In the same manner the prophet of Islam is the prototype and perfect embodiment of prophecy and so in a profound sense is *the* Prophet. In fact in Islam every form of revelation is envisaged as a prophecy whose complete and total realization is to be seen in Muḥammad — Upon whom be peace. As the Sufi poet Maḥmūd Shabistarī writes in his incomparable *Gulshan-i rāz* (*The Secret Rose Garden*):

> The first appearance of prophethood was in Adam,
> And its perfection was in the "Seal of the Prophets."
>   (Whinfield translation)

It is difficult for a non-Muslim to understand the spiritual significance of the Prophet and his role as the prototype of the religious and spiritual life, especially if one comes from a Christian background. Compared to Christ, or to the Buddha for that matter, the earthly career of the Prophet seems often too human and too engrossed in the vicissitudes of social, economic and political activity to serve as a model for the spiritual life. That is why so many people who write today of the great spiritual guides of humanity are not able to understand and interpret him sympathetically. It is easier to see the spiritual radiance of Christ or even medieval saints, Christian or Muslim, than that of the Prophet, although the Prophet is the supreme saint in Islam without whom there would have been no sanctity whatsoever.

The reason for this difficulty is that the spiritual nature of the Prophet is veiled in his human one and his purely spiritual function is hidden in his duties as the guide of men and the leader of a community. It was the function of the Prophet to be, not only a spiritual guide, but also the organizer of a new social order with all that such a function implies. And it is precisely this aspect of his being that veils his purely spiritual dimension from foreign eyes. Outsiders have understood his political genius, his power of oratory, his great statesmanship, but few have understood how he could be the religious and spiritual guide of men and how his life could be emulated by those who aspire to sanctity. This is particularly true in the modern world in which religion is separated from other domains of life and most modern men can hardly imagine how a spiritual being could also be immersed in the most intense political and social activity.

Actually if the contour of the personality of the Prophet is to be understood he should not be compared to Christ or the Buddha whose message was meant primarily for saintly men and who founded a community based on monastic life which later became the norm of a whole society. Rather, because of his dual function as "king" and "prophet," as the guide of men in his world and the hereafter, the Prophet should be compared to the prophet-kings of the Old Testament, to David and Solomon, and especially to Abraham himself. Or to cite once again an example outside the Abrahamic tradition, the spiritual type of the Prophet should be compared in Hinduism, to Rama and Krishna, who although in a completely different traditional climate, were *avātaras* and at the same time kings and householders who participated in social life with all that such activity implies as recorded in the *Mahabhārata* and the *Ramāyana.*

This type of figure who is at once a spiritual being and a leader of men has always been, relatively speaking, rare in the Christian West, especially in modern times. Political life has become so divorced from spiritual principles that to many people such a function itself appears as an impossibility in proof of which Westerners often point to the purely spiritual life of Christ who said, "My Kingdom is not of this world." And even historically the Occident has not witnessed many figures of this type unless one considers the Templars and in another context such devout kings as Charlemagne and St. Louis. The figure of the Prophet is thus difficult for many Occidentals to understand and this misconception to which often bad intention has been added is responsible for the nearly total ignorance of his spiritual nature in most works written about him in Western languages of which the number is legion. One could in fact say that of the major elements of Islam the real significance of the Prophet is the least understood to non-Muslims and especially to Occidentals.

The Prophet did participate in social life in its fullest sense. He married, had a household, was a father and moreover he was ruler and judge and had also to fight many wars in which he had to undergo painful ordeals. He had to undergo many hardships and experience all the difficulties which human life, especially that of the founder of a new state and society, implies. But within all these activities his heart rested in contentment of the Divine, and he continued inwardly to repose in the Divine Peace. In fact his participation in social and political life was precisely to integrate this domain into a spiritual centre.

The Prophet entertained no political or worldly ambition whatsoever. He was by nature a contemplative. Before being chosen as prophet he did not like to frequent social gatherings and activities. He led a caravan from Mecca to Syria passing through the majestic silence of the desert whose very "infinity" induces man towards contemplation. He often spent long periods in the cave of Ḥirā' in solitude and meditation. He did not believe himself to be by nature a man of the world or one who was naturally inclined to seek political power among the Quraysh or social eminence in Meccan society although he came from the noblest family. It was in fact very painful and difficult for him to accept the burden of prophecy which implied the founding of not only a new religion but also a new social and political order. All the traditional sources, which alone matter in this case, testify to the great hardship the Prophet underwent by being chosen to participate in the active life in its most acute form. Modern studies on the life of the Prophet which depict him as a man who enjoyed fighting wars, are totally untrue and in fact a reversal of the real personality of the Prophet. Immediately after the reception of the first revelation the Prophet confessed to his wife, Khadījah, how difficult it was for him to accept the burden of prophecy and how fearful he was of all that such a mission implied.

Likewise, with the marriages of the Prophet, they are not at all signs of his lenience *vis-à-vis* the flesh. During the period of youth when the passions are most strong the Prophet lived with only one wife who was much older than he and also underwent long periods of abstinence. And as a prophet many of his marriages were political ones which, in the prevalent social structure of Arabia, guaranteed the consolidation of the newly founded Muslim community. Multiple marriage, for him, as is true of Islam in general, was not so much enjoyment as responsibility and a means of integration of the newly founded society. Besides, in Islam the whole problem of sexuality appears in a different light from that in Christianity and should not be judged by the same standards. The multiple marriages of the Prophet, far from pointing to his weakness towards "the flesh," symbolize his patriarchal nature and his function, not as a saint who withdraws from the world, but as one who sanctifies the very life of the world by living in it and accepting it with the aim of integrating it into a higher order of reality.

The Prophet has also often been criticized by modern Western authors for being cruel and for having treated men harshly. Such a charge is again absurd because critics of this kind have forgotten that either a religion leaves the world aside, as Christ did, or integrates the world, in which case it must deal with such questions as war, retribution, justice, etc. When Charlemagne or some other Christian king thrust a sword into the breast of a heathen soldier he was, from the individual point of view, being cruel to that soldier. But on the universal plane this was a necessity for the preservation of a Christian civilization which had to defend its borders or perish. The same holds true for a Buddhist king or ruler, or for that matter any religious authority which seeks to integrate human society.

The Prophet exercised the utmost kindness possible and was harsh only with traitors. Now, a traitor against a newly founded religious community, which God has willed and whose existence is a mercy from heaven for mankind, is a traitor against the Truth itself. The harshness of the Prophet in such cases is an expression of Divine Justice. One cannot accuse God of being cruel because men die, or because there is illness and ugliness in the world. Every construction implies a previous destruction, a clearing of grounds for the appearance of a new form. This holds true not only in case of a physical structure but also in case of a new revelation which must clear the ground if it is to be a new social and political order as well as a purely religious one. What appears to some as the cruelty of the Prophet towards men is precisely this aspect of his function as the instrument of God for the establishment of a new world order whose homeland in Arabia was to be pure of any paganism and polytheism which if present would pollute the very source of this new fountain of life. As to what concerned his own person, the Prophet was always the epitome of kindness and generosity.

Nowhere is the nobility and generosity of the Prophet better exemplified than in his triumphant entry into Mecca, which in a sense highlights his earthly career. There, at a moment when the very people who had caused untold hardships and trials for the Prophet, were completely subdued by him, instead of thinking of vengeance, which was certainly his due, he forgave them. One must study closely the almost unimaginable obstacles placed before the Prophet by these same people, of the immense suffering he had undergone because of them, to realize what degree of generosity this act of the Prophet implies. It is not actually necessary to give an apologetic account of the life of the Prophet, but these matters need to be answered because the false and often malicious accusations of this kind made against the founder of Islam in so many modern studies, make the understanding of him by those who rely upon such studies well nigh impossible.

Also the Prophet was not certainly without love and compassion. Many incidents in his life and sayings recorded in Ḥadīth literature point to his depth of love for God which, in conformity with the general perspective of Islam, was never divorced from the knowledge of Him. For example, in a well known Ḥadīth, he said, "O Lord, grant to me the love of thee. Grant that I love those that love thee. Grant that I may do the deed that wins thy love. Make thy love dear to me more than self, family and wealth." Such sayings clearly demonstrate the fact that although the Prophet was in a sense a king or ruler of a community and a judge and had to deal according to justice in both capacities, he was at the same time one whose being was anchored in the love for God. Otherwise, he could not have been a prophet.

From the Muslim point of view, the Prophet is the symbol of perfection of both the human person and human society. He is the prototype of the human individual and the human collectivity. As such he bears certain characteristics in the eye of traditional Muslims which can only be discovered by studying the traditional accounts of him. The many Western works on the Prophet, with very few exceptions, are useless from this point of view no matter how much historical data they provide for the reader. The same holds true in fact for the new type of biographies of the Prophet written by modernized Muslims who would like at all cost to make the Prophet an ordinary man and neglect systematically any aspect of his being that does not conform to a humanistic and rationalistic framework they have adopted *a priori,* mostly as a result of either influence from or reaction to the modern Western point of view. The profound characteristics of the Prophet which have guided the Islamic community over the centuries and have left an indelible mark on the consciousness of the Muslim cannot be discerned save through the traditional sources and the Ḥadīth, and, of course, the Quran itself which bears the perfume of the soul of the person through whom it was revealed.

The universal characteristics of the Prophet are not the same as his daily actions and day to day life, which can be read in standard biographies of the Prophet, and with which we cannot deal here. They are, rather, characteristics which issue forth from his personality as a particular spiritual prototype. Seen in this light there are essentially three qualities that characterize the Prophet. First of all the Prophet possessed the quality of piety in its most universal sense, that quality which attaches man to God. The Prophet was in that sense pious. He had a profound piety which inwardly attached him to God, that made him place the interest of God before everything else including himself. Secondly he had a quality of combativeness, of always being actively engaged in combat against all that negated the Truth and disrupted harmony. Externally it meant fighting wars, either military, political or social ones, the war which the Prophet named the "little holy war" (al-jihād al-aṣghar). Inwardly this combativeness meant a continuous war against the carnal soul (nafs), against all that in man tends towards the negation of God and His Will, the "great holy war" (al-jihād al-akbar).

It is difficult for modern men to understand the positive symbolism of war thanks to modern technology which has made war total and its instruments the very embodiment of what is ugly and evil. Men therefore think that the role of religion is only in preserving some kind of precarious peace. This, of course, is true, but not in the superficial sense that is usually meant. If religion is to be an integral part of life it must try to establish peace in the most profound sense, namely to establish equilibrium between all the existing forces that surround man and to overcome all the forces that tend to destroy this equilibrium. No religion has sought to establish peace in this sense more than Islam. It is precisely in such a context that war can have a positive meaning as the activity to establish harmony both inwardly and outwardly and it is in this sense that Islam has stressed the positive aspect of combativeness.

The Prophet embodies to an eminent degree this perfection of combative virtue. If one thinks of the Buddha as sitting in a state of contemplation under the Bo-tree, the Prophet can be imagined as a rider sitting on a steed with the sword of justice and discrimination drawn in his hand and galloping at full speed, yet ready to come to an immediate halt before the mountain of Truth. The Prophet was faced from the beginning of his prophetic mission with the task of wielding the sword of Truth, of establishing equilibrium and in this arduous task he had no rest. His rest and repose was in the heart of the holy war (jihād) itself and he represents this aspect of spirituality in which peace comes not in passivity but in true activity. Peace belongs to one who is inwardly at peace with the Will of Heaven and outwardly at war with the forces of disruption and disequilibrium.

Finally, the Prophet possessed the quality of magnanimity in its fullness. His soul displayed a grandeur which every devout Muslim feels. He is for the Muslim nobility and magnanimity personified. This aspect of the Prophet is fully displayed in his treatment of his companions which, in fact, has been the model for later ages and which all generations of Muslims have sought to emulate.

To put it another way, which focuses more sharply the personality of the Prophet, the qualities can be enumerated as strength, nobility and serenity or inner calm. Strength is outwardly manifested in the little holy war and inwardly in the great holy war according to the saying of the Prophet who, returning from one of the early wars, said, "We have returned from the small *jihād* to the great *jihād*." It is this great *jihād* which is of particular spiritual significance as a war against all those tendencies which pull the soul of man away from the Centre and Origin and bar him from the grace of heaven.

The nobility or generosity of the Prophet shows itself most of all in charity towards all men and more generally towards all beings. Of course this virtue is not central as in Christianity which can be called the religion of charity. But it is important on the human level and as it concerns the person of the Prophet. It points to the fact that there was no narrowness or pettiness in the soul of the Prophet, no limitation in giving of himself to others. A spiritual man is one who always gives to those around him and does not receive, according to the saying, "It is more blessed to give than to receive." It was characteristic of the Prophet to have always given till the last moment of his life. He never asked anything for himself and never sought to receive.

The aspect of serenity, which also characterizes all true expressions of Islam, is essentially the love of truth. It is to put the Truth before everything else. It is to be impartial, to be logical on the level of discourse, not to let one's emotions colour and prejudice one's intellectual judgment. It is not to be a rationalist, but to see the truth of things and to love the Truth above all else. To love the Truth is to love God who is the Truth, one of His Names being the Truth (*al-ḥaqq*).

If one were to compare these qualities of the Prophet, namely, strength, nobility and serenity, with those of the founders of the other great religions one would see that they are not necessarily the same because firstly, the Prophet was not himself the Divine Incarnation and secondly, because each religion emphasizes a certain aspect of the Truth. One cannot follow and emulate Christ in the same manner as the Prophet because in Christianity Christ is the God-man, the Divine Incarnation. One can be absorbed into his nature but he cannot be copied as the perfection of the human state. One can neither walk on water nor raise the dead to life. Still, when one thinks of Christianity and Christ another set of characteristics come to mind, such as divinity, incarnation, and on another level love, charity and sacrifice. Or when one thinks of the Buddha and Buddhism it is most of all the ideas of pity for the whole of creation, enlightenment and illumination and extinction in Nirvana that stand out.

In Islam, when one thinks of the Prophet who is to be emulated, it is the image of a strong personality that comes to mind, who is severe

with himself and with the false and the unjust, and charitable towards
the world that surrounds him. On the basis of these two virtues of
strength and sobriety on the one hand and charity and generosity on
the other, he is serene, extinguished in the Truth. He is that warrior
on horseback who halts before the mountain of Truth, passive towards
the Divine Will, active towards the world, hard and sober towards
himself and kind and generous towards the creatures about him.

These qualities characteristic of the Prophet are contained virtually
in the sound of the second *Shahādah, Muḥammadun rasūl Allāh,* that
is, Muḥammad is the Prophet of God, in its Arabic pronunciation, not
in its translation into another language. Here again the symbolism is
inextricably connected to the sounds and forms of the sacred language
and cannot be translated. The very sound of the name Muḥammad
implies force, a sudden breaking forth of a power which is from God
and is not just human. The word *rasūl* with its elongated second
syllable symbolizes this "expansion of the chest" (*inshirāḥ al-ṣadr*),
and a generosity that flows from the being of the Prophet and which
ultimately comes from God. As for Allah it is, of course, the Truth itself
which terminates the formula. The second *Shahādah* thus implies by
its sound the power, generosity and serenity of reposing in the Truth
characteristic of the Prophet. But this repose in the Truth is not based
on a flight from the world but on a penetration into it in order to
integrate and organize it. The spiritual castle in Islam is based on the
firm foundations of harmony within human society and in individual
human life.

In the traditional prayers on the Prophet which all Muslims recite
on certain occasions, God's blessing and salutation are asked for the
Prophet who is God's servant (*'abd*), His messenger (*rasūl*), and the
unlettered Prophet (*al-nabī al-ummī*). For example, one well-known
version of the formula of benediction upon the Prophet is as follows:

> Oh, God, bless our Lord Muḥammad, Thy servant and Thy
> Messenger, the unlettered Prophet, and his family and his
> companions, and salute them.

Here again the three epithets with which his name is qualified symbolize his three basic characteristics which stand out most in the eyes
of devout Muslims. He is first of all an *'abd;* but who is an *'abd* except
one whose will is surrendered to the will of his master, who is himself
poor (*faqīr*) but rich on account of what his master bestows upon him.
As the *'abd* of God the Prophet exemplified in its fullness this spiritual
poverty and sobriety which is so characteristic of Islam. He loved

fasting, vigilance, prayer, all of which have become essential elements in Islamic religious life. As an 'abd the Prophet put everything in the hands of God and realized a poverty which is, in reality, the most perfect and enduring wealth.

The rasūl in this formula again symbolizes his aspect of charity and generosity and metaphysically the rasūl himself is sent because of God's charity for the world and men whom he loves so that he sends his prophets to guide them. That is why the Prophet is "God's mercy to the worlds." For the Muslim the Prophet himself displays mercy and generosity, a generosity which flows from the nobility of character. Islam has always emphasized this quality and sought to inculcate nobility in the souls of men. A good Muslim must have some nobility and generosity which always reflect this aspect of the personality of the Prophet.

As for the nabī al-ummī, it symbolizes extinction before the Truth. The unlettered nature of the Prophet means most of all the extinction of all that is human before the Divine. The soul of the Prophet was a tabula rasa before the Divine Pen and on the human level his quality of "unletteredness" marks that supreme virtue of realizing the Truth through the contemplation of it which marks an "extinction" in the metaphysical sense before the Truth. Only through this extinction (fanā') can one hope to enter into life with God and subsistence in Him (baqā').

To summarize the qualities of the Prophet, it can be said that he is human equilibrium which has become extinct in the Divine Truth. He marks the establishment of harmony and equilibrium between all the tendencies present in man, his sensual, social, economic, political tendencies, which cannot be overcome unless the human state itself is transcended. He displays the integration of these tendencies and forces with the aim of establishing a basis which naturally leads towards contemplation and extinction in the Truth. His spiritual way means to accept the human condition which is normalized and sanctified as the ground for the most lofty spiritual castle. The spirituality of Islam of which the Prophet is the prototype is not the rejection of the world but the transcending of it through its integration into a Centre and the establishment of a harmony upon which the quest for the Absolute is based. The Prophet in these qualities, that he displayed so eminently, is at once the prototype of human and spiritual perfection and a guide towards its realization, for as the Quran states:

Verily in the messenger of Allah ye have a good example. (XXXIII, 21)

Since the Prophet is the prototype of all human perfection to the extent that one of his titles is the "most noble of all creation" (*ashraf al-makhlūqāt*), it may be asked in what way can men emulate him. How can the Prophet become a guide for human life and his life, deeds and thoughts serve as a guide for the Muslim in this terrestrial journey? The answer to this fundamental question, which concerns all the individual and collective life of Muslims of later generations, lies in the sayings which he left behind and are known as *Ḥadīth* and his daily life and practice known as *Sunnah*. The family and companions of the Prophet who had been with him during his life time bore the impressions of his *Sunnah* within their souls with a depth that results from contact with a prophet. When man meets an extraordinary person he carries the impression of this meeting always. Then how permanent must have been the impression made on men by the Prophet, whose encounter is so much outside of ordinary experience today that human beings can hardly imagine it. The first generation of Muslims practiced this *Sunnah* with all the ardour and faith that resulted from their proximity to the source of the revelation and the presence of the *barakah* or grace of the Prophet among them. They in turn were emulated by the next generation and so on to modern times when the faithful still seek to base their lives upon that of the Prophet. This end is achieved through the fresh interpretation that each generation makes of his life (*siyar*), through the litanies and chants (*madā'iḥ*) repeated in his praise and through the celebrations marking his birth (*mawlid*) or other joyous occasions.

GEORGES BERNANOS

The Diary of a Country Priest

Georges Bernanos (1888–1948) was in many ways the Roman Catholic counterpart of his contemporary and French compatriot Albert Camus, for Bernanos was a serious believer who knew that the will to believe is never easy and that both faith and its chief expression, prayer, can be gained and preserved only by constant struggle. His *Diary of a Country Priest* is a fictional documentation of that struggle in one simple — and complicated—soul.

Yes, I PRAY BADLY and not enough. Almost every day after mass I have to interrupt my act of thanksgiving to see some parishioner — usually ailing and asking for medicine. Fabregarques, my classmate at the junior seminary, now a chemist somewhere near Montreuil, often sends me samples of patent cures. It appears this competition annoys the headmaster who alone used to perform these small services.

How hard it is to avoid offending somebody! And however hard you try, people seem less inclined to use goodwill to their advantage, than unconsciously eager to set one goodwill against another. Inconceivable sterility of souls — what is the cause of it?

Truly, man is always at enmity with himself — a secret sly kind of hostility. Tares, scattered no matter where, will almost certainly take root. Whereas the smallest seed of good needs more than ordinary good fortune, prodigious luck, not to be stifled.

*   *   *   *   *

Another horrible night, sleep interspersed with evil dreams. It was raining so hard that I couldn't venture into church. Never have I made such efforts to pray, at first calmly and steadily, then with a kind of savage, concentrated violence, till at last, having struggled back into calm with a huge effort, I persisted, almost desperately (desperately! How horrible it sounds!) in a sheer transport of will which set me shuddering with anguish. Yet — nothing.

I know, of course, that the wish to pray is a prayer in itself, that God can ask no more than that of us. But this was no duty which I discharged. At that moment I needed prayer as much as I needed air to draw my breath or oxygen to fill my blood. What lay behind me was no longer any normal, familiar life, that everyday life out of which the impulse to pray raises us, with still at the back of our minds the certainty that whensoever we wish we can return. A void was behind me. And in front a wall, a wall of darkness.

The usual notion of prayer is so absurd. How can those who know nothing about it, who pray little or not at all, dare speak so frivolously of prayer? A Carthusian, a Trappist will work for years to make of himself a man of prayer, and then any fool who comes along sets himself up as judge of this lifelong effort. If it were really what they suppose, a kind of chatter, the dialogue of a madman with his shadow, or even less — a vain and superstitious sort of petition to be given the good things of this world, how could innumerable people find until their dying day, I won't even say such great "comfort" — since they put no faith in the solace of the senses — but sheer, robust, vigorous, abundant joy in prayer? Oh, of course "suggestion," say the scientists. Certainly they can never have known old monks, wise, shrewd, unerring in judgement, and yet aglow with passionate insight, so very tender in their humanity. What miracle enables these semi-lunatics, these prisoners of their own dreams, these sleepwalkers, apparently to enter more deeply each day into the pain of others? An odd sort of dream, an unusual opiate which, far from turning him back into himself and isolating him from his fellows, unites the individual with mankind in the spirit of universal charity!

This seems a very daring comparison. I apologize for having advanced it, yet perhaps it might satisfy many people who find it hard to think for themselves, unless the thought has first been jolted by some unexpected, surprising image. Could a sane man set himself up as a judge of music because he has sometimes touched a keyboard with the tips of his fingers? And surely if a Bach fugue, a Beethoven symphony leave him cold, if he has to content himself with watching on the face of another listener the reflected pleasure of supreme, inaccessible delight, such a man has only himself to blame.

But alas! We take the psychiatrists' word for it. The unanimous testimony of saints is held as of little or no account. They may all affirm that this kind of deepening of the spirit is unlike any other experience, that instead of showing us more and more of our own complexity it ends in sudden total illumination, opening out upon azure light — they can be dismissed with a few shrugs. Yet when has any man of prayer told us that prayer had failed him?

Literally I can scarcely stand up this morning. Those hours which seemed to me so long have left me with no precise recollection — nothing but the sensation of a blow, directed from nowhere, its force striking me full in the chest, leaving me mercifully half stunned, so that I can still not gauge its seriousness.

We never pray alone. Doubtless my sorrow was too great. I wanted to have God to myself. He did not come to me.

I read these lines again on awaking this morning. Since then —

Can it only have been an illusion? . . . Or perhaps — The saints experienced those hours of failure and loss. But most certainly never this dull revolt, this spiteful silence of the spirit which almost brings to hate . . .

One o'clock: the last lamp is out in the village. Wind and rain.

The same solitude, the same silence. And no hope this time of forcing or turning away the obstacle. Besides, there isn't any obstacle. Nothing. God! I breathe, I inhale the night, the night is entering into me by some inconceivable, unimaginable gap in my soul. I, myself, am the night.

*   *   *   *   *

No, I have not lost my faith. The expression "to lose one's faith," as one might a purse or a ring of keys, has always seemed to me rather foolish. It must be one of those sayings of *bourgeois* piety, a legacy of those wretched priests of the eighteenth century who talked so much.

Faith is not a thing which one "loses," we merely cease to shape our lives by it. That is why old-fashioned confessors are not far wrong in showing a certain amount of scepticism when dealing with "intellectual crises," doubtless far more rare than people imagine. An educated man may come by degrees to tuck away his faith in some back corner of his brain, where he can find it again on reflection, by an effort of memory; yet even if he feels a tender regret for what no longer exists and might have been, the term "faith" would nevertheless be inapplicable to such an abstraction, no more like real faith, to use a very well-worn simile, than the constellation of Cygnus is like a swan.

No, I have not lost my faith. The cruelty of this test, its devastation, like a thunderbolt, and so inexplicable, may have shattered my reason and my nerves, may have withered suddenly within me the joy of prayer — perhaps for ever, who can tell? — may have filled me to the very brim with a dark, more terrible resignation than the worst convulsions of despair in its cataclysmic fall; but my faith is still whole, for I can feel it. I cannot reach it now; I can find it neither in my poor mind, unable to link two ideas correctly, working only on half delirious images, nor in my sensibility, nor yet in my conscience. Sometimes I feel that my faith has withdrawn and still persists where certainly I should never have thought of seeking it, in my flesh, my wretched flesh, in my flesh and blood, my perishable flesh which yet was baptized.

*   *   *   *   *

For weeks I had not prayed, had not been able to pray. Unable? Who knows? That supreme grace has got to be earned like any other, and I no doubt had ceased to merit it. And so at last God had withdrawn Himself from me — of this at any rate I am sure. From that instant I was as nothing, and yet I kept it to myself! Worse still: I gloried in my secrecy. I thought of it as fine, heroic. I *did* try to see the Curé de Torcy. But I should have gone to my superior, the Dean of Blangermont, and confessed. I ought to have said: "I am no longer fit to guide a parish. I have neither prudence, nor judgement, nor common sense, nor real humility. God has punished me. Send me back to my seminary, I am a danger to souls. . . ."

Of course I am "praying better." But I no longer recognize my prayer. Once it had an obstinate, imploring quality, and even when, for instance, my whole mind was riveted on a passage in the breviary, deep in myself I still could feel my soul in touch with God, sometimes imploring, then insistent, imperious even — yes, I would have liked to snatch His graces from Him, to storm His tenderness. Now it is hard really to desire anything. My prayer, like the village, has no more weight to it, flies away. . . . Is that a good or a bad thing? I don't know.

*   *   *   *   *

I went into an old church — I don't know its name. It was too crowded for me. That is childish too, but I would like to have been able to kneel freely on the stone floor, or lie down rather, lie with my face to the ground. Never have I known such sheer physical revolt against prayer — and it was so real that I felt no remorse. My will was powerless. I would never have believed that prayer, which is commonly called a mere recreation, could have assumed this tearing, crumbling quality. For I was not struggling against fear, but against a number of fears which seemed infinite: a fear for each fibre of my being, myriad fears. And when I shut my eyes to concentrate, I seemed to hear the rustling voices of this huge invisible crowd lurking in the depths of my anguish, as in the deepest night.

Perspiration was on my forehead and my hands. In the end I went out. The cold outside caught me in the face. I began to walk quickly. Had I been aware of any suffering, I think I might have taken pity on myself, cried over myself, over my loss. But I felt only an incredible lightness. My stupor, as I was caught up by the noisy crowd, was like the shock of joy. It gave me wings.

III THE GRANDEUR OF GOD

As "the experience of the Holy," religion speaks in a multitude of ways about a grandeur that transcends — and at the same time transforms — the ordinary experiences of life. When Immanuel Kant identified "the starred heaven above" and "the moral law within" as the two realities that continued to fill him with awe even when the usual "proofs" for religious doctrines had lost their cogency, he was speaking for believers in every age and in every religion and setting the religious agenda for much of the modern era. For it is one of the most universal and abiding intuitions of religious faith that somehow these two realities, the inner order of the self in alignment with the Holy and the outer order of the universe as the visible image of the Holy, must finally be congruent.

A failure to recognize the presence of that intuition also in the sacramental observances of simple faith is what has sometimes blinded modern observers to the authentic religious component in practices and beliefs that they so easily dismiss as superstition. Our present-day use of the term *magic* almost exclusively to speak about prestidigitation as a form of popular entertainment may conceal from us the way many cultures have acknowledged even the manipulative aspects of magic as keys to what is ultimately and profoundly true. In the ancient Near East, what we call astronomy and what we call astrology were identical, and both of them were seen as revelatory of the deepest mysteries of the universe. The continuing hold that astrology has on large portions of the population in many so-called modern and secular societies — most newspapers in the United States feel obliged to publish a daily horoscope — suggests that such ideas were not confined to the ancient Near East.

Nevertheless it is astronomy far more than astrology that discloses to moderns the meaning of the grandeur of God, and physics has become for many of them the chief path to metaphysics. If there ever was a time in the history of science when the observers and students of nature looked askance at that sense of grandeur — and it is doubtful that there ever was — that is certainly not true of science in the twentieth century. As the physical and biological sciences have simultaneously moved to the contemplation of the vastness of the universe and to the examination of the minuteness of the particle and the cell, they have certainly found some popular conceptions of God unacceptable. But that is only because such a conception of God lacks the grandeur that they have found in the cosmos itself. And so from Newton to Einstein, some of the most moving credos affirmed in this modern era have come from scientists. Yet Einstein himself affirmed that in the modern era, as in every era, it has been the poets and the musicians — to mention only two examples among many, Wolfgang Amadeus Mozart and Johann Wolfgang von Goethe — who have been the most effective in articulating the human response to divine grandeur.

GERARD MANLEY HOPKINS

God's Grandeur

Gerard Manley Hopkins (1844–1899), although born a member of the Church of England and educated at Oxford, became a Roman Catholic as a young man and eventually joined the Society of Jesus. He was a student of the Greek classics, and a poet whose celebration of God the Creator in this and in his other works expressed, in extremely complicated but profoundly beautiful verse, the deepest intuitions of faith.

THE WORLD is charged with the grandeur of God.
    It will flame out, like shining from shook foil;
    It gathers to a greatness, like the ooze of oil
Crushed. Why do men then now not reck his rod?
Generations have trod, have trod, have trod;
    And all is seared with trade; bleared, smeared with toil;
    And wears man's smudge and shares man's smell: the soil
Is bare now, nor can foot feel, being shod.

And for all this, nature is never spent;
    There lives the dearest freshness deep down things;
And though the last lights off the black West went
    Oh, morning, at the brown brink eastward, springs —
Because the Holy Ghost over the bent
    World broods with warm breast and with ah! bright wings.

IMMANUEL KANT

The Starred Heaven Above and the Moral Law Within

> Immanuel Kant (1724–1804) taught at Königsberg in Prussia. In his *Critique of Pure Reason,* Kant examined, more thoroughly than anyone else ever had in the history of philosophy, the nature and presuppositions of human knowledge, including the knowledge of God, free will, and immortality. Here in the conclusion to his *Critique of Practical Reason* of 1788 he stated his own conviction about the two things that even after that examination "fill the mind with ever new and increasing awe and admiration."

Two things fill the mind with ever new and increasing awe and admiration the more frequently and continuously reflection is occupied with them; the starred heaven above me and the moral law within me. I ought not to seek either outside my field of vision, as though they were either shrouded in obscurity or were visionary. I see them confronting me and link them immediately with the consciousness of my existence. The first begins with the place I occupy in the external world of sense, and expands the connection in which I find myself into the incalculable vastness of worlds upon worlds, of systems within systems, over endless ages of their periodic motion, their beginnings and perpetuation. The second starts from my invisible self, from my personality, and depicts me as in a world possessing true infinitude which can be sensed only by the intellect. With this I recognize myself to be in a necessary and general connection, not just accidentally as appears to be the case with the external world. Through this recognition I also see myself linked with all visible worlds. The first view of a numberless quantity of worlds destroys my importance, so to speak, since I am an *animal-like being* who must return its matter from whence it came to the planet (a mere speck in the universe), after having been endowed with vital energy for a short time, one does not know how. The second view raises my value infinitely, as an *intelligence,* through my personality; for in this personality the moral law reveals a life independent of animality and even of the entire world of sense. This is true at least as far as one can infer from the purposeful determination of my existence according to this law. This is not restricted to the conditions and limits of this life, but radiates into the infinite.

Admiration and respect may stimulate further inquiry, but they cannot provide a substitute for the lack of either. Then what can be done in order to pursue such inquiry in a useful way appropriate to the sublime quality of the topic? Examples may serve as a warning, but they may also inspire imitation. The observation of nature began with the most marvelous spectacle that human senses could present and our intellect could bear to trace to its full extent, but it ended in — astrology. Morals started with the noblest quality of human nature whose development and cultivation suggests infinite advantage, but it ended in — idle speculation or superstition. This is what happens to all clumsy attempts in which the use of reason plays the most important part. Such use does not, like the use of one's feet, happen by itself as a result of frequent employment. This is especially true where much use concerns qualities which cannot be presented immediately in common experience. Then, though late, the maxim came into fashion to consider carefully all steps that reason has to take and not to allow reason to proceed except in the tracks of a method carefully thought-out beforehand. After that the judgment concerning the structure of the world took a very different direction and at the same time arrived at a much happier result. The fall of a stone when analyzed into its elements, the forces which manifested themselves were then treated mathematically and eventually produced the clear insight into the structure of the world which will remain unchanged in the future and which allows the hope that progressive observation will ever extend it, and never have to fear retrogression.

To follow the same road in dealing with the moral qualities of our nature is suggested by that example which offers hope for a similar good result. We have at hand many examples of reason judging morally. To analyze these judgments [and break them down] into their elementary concepts, to employ, in repeated experiments with ordinary common sense, a method similar to that of *chemistry,* (as *mathematics* is not available for the purpose of *separating* the empirical from the rational which may be found in such judgments), should make known *purely* and with certainty both the empirical and the rational and ought to show what each can accomplish by itself. If true, such a procedure ought to be able to forestall the errors of a *coarse,* unskilled judging, as well as *pretensions of genius* which is even more necessary. For imaginary treasures are promised on these pretensions without any methodical inquiry or knowledge of nature, while real treasures are squandered, as happens with the adepts of the stone of wisdom. In a word, scientific knowledge, critically explored and systematically introduced, is the narrow gateway which leads to *wisdom,* if by such wisdom is understood not merely what one ought to *do,* but what ought to serve as a guide for *teachers,* in order to find well and clearly the paths to wisdom on which every man ought to tread, and to preserve others from dead alleys. This is true knowledge, of which philosophy must remain the guardian at all times. In its sophisticated analysis the general public cannot share, but they do share in the doctrines which clearly convince them after such an analysis.

JANE ELLEN HARRISON

Prolegomena to the Study of Greek Religion

> Jane Ellen Harrison (1850–1928), who studied and taught at Cambridge University, brought to the study of Greek religious practice and thought the insights of anthropology and comparative religion into the centrality of ritual and myth. In *Prolegomena to the Study of Greek Religion*, from whose opening chapter this excerpt is taken, she proposed a fundamental reinterpretation based on those insights.

IN CHARACTERIZING THE GENIUS of the Greeks Mr. Ruskin says: "*There is no dread in their hearts; pensiveness, amazement, often deepest grief and desolation, but terror never. Everlasting calm in the presence of all Fate, and joy such as they might win, not indeed from perfect beauty, but from beauty at perfect rest.*" The lovely words are spoken of course mainly with reference to art, but they are meant also to characterize the Greek in his attitude towards the invisible, in his religion — meant to show that the Greek, the favoured child of fortune yet ever unspoilt, was exempt from the discipline to which the rest of mankind has been subject, never needed to learn the lesson that in the Fear of the Lord is the beginning of Wisdom.

At first sight it seems as though the statement were broadly true. Greek writers of the fifth century B.C. have a way of speaking of, an attitude towards, religion, as though it were wholly a thing of joyful confidence, a friendly fellowship with the gods, whose service is but a high festival for man. In Homer sacrifice is but, as it were, the signal for a banquet of abundant roast flesh and sweet wine; we hear nothing of fasting, of cleansing, and atonement. This we might perhaps explain as part of the general splendid unreality of the heroic saga, but sober historians of the fifth century B.C. express the same spirit. Thucydides is assuredly by nature no reveller, yet religion is to him in the main "a rest from toil." He makes Pericles say: "Moreover we have provided for our spirit very many opportunities of recreation, by the celebration of games and sacrifices throughout the year."

Much the same external, quasi-political, and always cheerful attitude towards religion is taken by the "Old Oligarch" [described in a treatise attributed to Xenophon]. He is of course thoroughly orthodox and even pious, yet to him the main gist of religion appears to be a decorous social enjoyment. In easy aristocratic fashion he rejoices that religious ceremonials exist to provide for the less well-to-do citizens suitable amusements that they would otherwise lack. "As to sacrifices and sanctuaries and festivals and precincts, the People, knowing that it is impossible for each poor man individually to sacrifice and feast and have sanctuaries and a beautiful and ample city, has discovered by what means he may enjoy these privileges. The whole state accordingly at the common cost sacrifices many victims, while it is the People who feast on them and divide them among themselves by lot"; and again, as part of the splendour of Athens, he notes that "she celebrates twice as many religious holidays as any other city." The very language used by this typical Athenian gentleman speaks for itself. Burnt-sacrifice [*thysia*], feasting, agonistic games, stately temples are to him the essence of religion; the word sacrifice brings to his mind not renunciation but a social banquet; the temple is not to him so much the awful dwelling-place of a divinity as an integral part of a "beautiful and ample city."

Thucydides and Xenophon need and attempt no searching analysis of religion. Socrates of course sought a definition, a definition that left him himself sad and dissatisfied, but that adequately embodied popular sentiment and is of importance for our enquiry. The end of the *Euthyphron* is the most disappointing thing in Plato; Socrates extracts from Euthyphron what he thinks religion is; what Socrates thought he cannot or will not tell.

Socrates in his enquiry uses not one abstract term for religion — the Greeks have in fact no one word that covers the whole field — he uses two, piety and holiness. Euthyphron of course begins with cheerful confidence: he and all other respectable men know quite well what piety and holiness are. He willingly admits that "holiness is a part of justice," that part of justice that appertains to the gods; it is giving the gods their due. He also allows, not quite seeing to what the argument is tending, that piety and holiness are "a sort of tendance [*therapeia*] of the gods." This "tendance," Socrates presses on, "must be of the nature of service or ministration," and Euthyphron adds that it is the sort of service that servants show their masters. Socrates wants to know in what particular work and operation the gods need help and ministration. Euthyphron answers with some impatience that, to put it plainly and cut the matter short, holiness consists in "a man understanding how to do what is pleasing to the gods in word and deed," i.e. by prayer and sacrifice. Socrates eagerly seizes his advantage and asks: "You mean then that holiness is a sort of art of praying and sacrificing?" "Further," he adds, "sacrifice is giving to the gods, prayer is asking of them, holiness then is an art of asking and giving." If we give to the gods they must want something of us, they must want to "do business with us." "Holiness is then an art in which gods and men do business with each other." So Socrates triumphantly concludes, to the manifest discomfort of Euthyphron, who however can urge no tenable objection. He feels as a pious man that the essence of the service or tendance he owes to the gods is of the nature of a freewill tribute of honour, but he cannot deny that the gods demand this as a *quid pro quo.*

Socrates, obviously unfair though he is, puts his finger on the weak spot of Greek religion as orthodoxly conceived in the fifth century B.C. Its formula is *do ut des* [I give that you may give]. It is, as Socrates says, a "business transaction" and one in which, because god is greater than man, man gets on the whole the best of it. The argument of the *Euthyphron* is of importance to us because it clearly defines one, and a prominent, factor in Greek religion, that of *service* [*therapeia*]; and in this service, this kindly "tendance," there is no element of fear. If man does his part in the friendly transaction, the gods will do theirs. None of the deeper problems of what we moderns call religion are even touched: there is no question of sin, repentance, sacrificial atonement, purification, no fear of judgment to come, no longing after a future complete beatitude. Man offers what seems to him in his ignorance a reasonable service to gods conceived of as human and rational. There is no trace of scepticism; the gods certainly exist, otherwise as Sextus Empiricus quaintly argues "you could not serve them": and they have human natures. "You do not serve Hippocentauri, because Hippocentauri are non-existent."

To the average orthodox Greek, the word [*therapeia*], service, tendance, covered a large, perhaps the largest, area of his conception of religion. It was a word expressing, not indeed in the Christian sense a religion whose mainspring was love, but at least a religion based on a rational and quite cheerful mutual confidence. The Greeks have however another word expressive of religion, which embodies a quite other attitude of mind, the word *deisidaimonia, fear of spirits;* fear, not tendance, fear not of gods but of spirit-things, or, to put it abstractly, of the supernatural.

It is certainly characteristic of the Greek mind that the word *deisidaimonia* and its cognates early began to be used in a bad sense, and this to some extent bears out Mr. Ruskin's assertion. By the time of Theophrastos *ho deisidaimōn* is frankly in our sense "the superstitious man," and superstition Theophrastos defines as not just and proper reverence but simply "cowardice in regard to the supernatural." Professor Jebb has pointed out that already in Aristotle the word *deisidaimon* has about it a suspicion of its weaker side. An absolute ruler, Aristotle says, will be the more powerful "if his subjects believe that he fears the spiritual beings" but he adds significantly "he must show himself such *without fatuity.*"

Plutarch has left us an instructive treatise on "the fear of the supernatural." He saw in this fear, this superstition, the great element of danger and weakness in the religion that he loved so well. His intellect steeped in Platonism revolted from its unmeaning folly, and his gentle gracious temperament shrank from its cruelty. He sees in superstition not only an error, a wrong judgment of the mind, but that worse thing a "wrong judgment inflamed by passion." Atheism is a cold error, a mere dislocation of the mind: superstition is a "dislocation complicated, inflamed, by a bruise." "Atheism is an apathy towards the divine which fails to perceive the good: superstition is an excess of passion which suspects the good to be evil; the superstitious are afraid of the gods yet fly to them for refuge, flatter and yet revile them, invoke them and yet heap blame upon them."

Superstition grieved Plutarch in two ways. He saw that it terrified men and made them miserable, and he wanted all men to be as cheerful and kindly as himself; it also made men think evil of the gods, fear them as harsh and cruel. He knew that the canonical religion of the poets was an adequate basis for superstitious fear, but he had made for himself a way out of the difficulty, a way he explains in his treatise on "How the poets ought to be taken." "If Ares be evil spoken of we must imagine it to be said of War, if Hephaistos of Fire, if Zeus of Fate, but if anything honourable it is said of the real gods." Plutarch was too gentle to say sharply and frankly:

> If gods do aught that's shameful, they are no gods,

but he shifted the element of evil, of fear and hate, from his theological ideals to the natural and purely human phenomena from which they had emerged. He wants to treat the gods and regard them as he himself would be treated and regarded, as kindly civilized men. "What!" he says, "is he who thinks there are no gods an impious man, while he who describes them as the superstitious man does, does he not hold views much more impious? Well anyhow I for my part would rather people would say of me there never was or is any such a man as Plutarch, than that they should say Plutarch is an unstable, changeable fellow, irritable, vindictive, and touchy about trifles; if you invite friends to dinner and leave out Plutarch, or if you are busy and omit to call on him, or if you do not stop to speak to him, he will fasten on you and bite you, or he will catch your child and beat him, or turn his beast loose into your crops and spoil your harvest."

But though he is concerned for the reputation of the gods, his chief care and pity are for man. Atheism shuts out a man, he says, from the pleasant things of life. "These most pleasant things," he adds in characteristic fashion, "are festivals and feastings in connection with sacred things, and initiations and orgiastic festivals, and invocations and adorations of the gods. At these most pleasant things the atheist can but laugh his sardonic laugh, but the superstitious man would fain rejoice and cannot, his soul is like the city of Thebes:

> It brims with incense and burnt sacrifice
> And brims with paeans and with lamentations.

A garland is on his head and pallor on his face, he offers sacrifice and is afraid, he prays and yet his tongue falters, he offers incense and his hand trembles, he turns the saying of Pythagoras into foolishness: 'Then we become best when we approach the gods, for those who fear spirits when they approach the shrines and dwellings of the gods make as though they came to the dens of bears and the holes of snakes and the lairs of sea-monsters.' " In his protest against the religion of fear Plutarch rises to a real eloquence. "He that dreads the gods dreads all things, earth and sea, air and heaven, darkness and light, a voice, a silence, a dream. Slaves forget their masters in sleep, sleep looses their fetters, salves their gangrened sores, but for the superstitious man his reason is always adreaming but his fear always awake."

Plutarch is by temperament, and perhaps also by the decadent time in which he lived, unable to see the good side of the religion of fear, unable to realize that in it was implicit a real truth, the consciousness that all is not well with the world, that there is such a thing as evil. Tinged with Orphism as he was, he took it by its gentle side and never realized that it was this religion of fear, of consciousness of evil and sin and the need of purification, of which Orphism took hold and which it transformed to new issues. The cheerful religion of "tendance" had in it no seeds of spiritual development; by Plutarch's time, though he failed to see this, it had done its work for civilization.

Still less could Plutarch realize that what in his mind was a degradation, superstition in our sense, had been to his predecessors a vital reality, the real gist of their only possible religion. He deprecates the attitude of the superstitious man who enters the presence of his gods as though he were approaching the hole of a snake, and forgets that the hole of a snake had been to his ancestors, and indeed was still to many of his contemporaries, literally and actually the sanctuary of a god. He has explained and mysticized away all the primitive realities of his own beloved religion. It can, I think, be shown that what Plutarch regards as superstition was in the sixth and even the fifth century before the Christian era the *real* religion of the main bulk of the people, a religion not of cheerful tendance but of fear and deprecation. The formula of that religion was not *do ut des* "I give that you may give," but *do ut abeas* "I give that you may go, and keep away." The beings worshipped were not rational, human, law-abiding *gods*, but vague, irrational, mainly malevolent *daimones*, spirit-things, ghosts and bogeys and the like, not yet formulated and enclosed into god-head. The word *deisidaimonia* tells its own tale, but the thing itself was born long before it was baptized.

DOROTHY L. SAYERS

The Image of God

Dorothy Leigh Sayers (1893–1957) is associated in the minds of most readers with Lord Peter Wimsey, the detective whom she created, or with Dante Alighieri, whose writings she translated and interpreted, or with *The Mind of the Maker,* an analysis of the creative process in God as Maker and in the poet as maker (the etymology of "poet" in Greek). This chapter from that book shows how she held all three of these preoccupations together.

In the beginning God created. He made this and He made that and He saw that it was good. And He created man in His own image; in the image of God created He him; male and female created He them.

Thus far the author of *Genesis.* The expression "in His own image" has occasioned a good deal of controversy. Only the most simple-minded people of any age or nation have supposed the image to be a physical one. The innumerable pictures which display the Creator as a hirsute old gentleman in flowing robes seated on a bank of cloud are recognized to be purely symbolic. The "image," whatever the author may have meant by it, is something shared by male and female alike; the aggressive masculinity of the pictorial Jehovah represents power, rationality or what you will: it has no relation to the text I have quoted. Christian doctrine and tradition, indeed, by language and picture, sets its face against all sexual symbolism for the divine fertility. Its Trinity is wholly masculine, as all language relating to Man as a species is masculine.

The Jews, keenly alive to the perils of pictorial metaphor, forbade the representation of the Person of God in graven images. Nevertheless, human nature and the nature of human language defeated them. No legislation could prevent the making of verbal pictures: God walks in the garden, He stretches out His arm, His voice shakes the cedars, His eyelids try the children of men. To forbid the making of pictures about God would be to forbid thinking about God at all, for man is so made that he has no way to think except in pictures. But continually, throughout the history of the Jewish-Christian Church, the voice of warning has been raised against the power of the picture-makers: "God is a spirit," "without body, parts or passions"; He is pure being, "I AM THAT I AM."

Man, very obviously, is not a being of this kind; his body, parts and passions are only too conspicuous in his make-up. How then can he be said to resemble God? Is it his immortal soul, his rationality, his self-consciousness, his free will, or what, that gives him a claim to this rather startling distinction? A case may be argued for all these elements in the complex nature of man. But had the author of *Genesis* anything particular in his mind when he wrote? It is observable that in the passage leading up to the statement about man, he has given no detailed information about God. Looking at man, he sees in him something essentially divine, but when we turn back to see what he says about the original upon which the "image" of God was modeled, we find only the single assertion, "God created." The characteristic common to God and man is apparently that: the desire and the ability to make things.

This, we may say, is a metaphor like other statements about God. So it is, but it is none the worse for that. All language about God must, as St. Thomas Aquinas pointed out, necessarily be analogical. We need not be surprised at this, still less suppose that because it is analogical it is therefore valueless or without any relation to the truth. The fact is, that all language about everything is analogical; we think in a series of metaphors. We can explain nothing in terms of itself, but only in terms of other things. Even mathematics can express itself in terms of itself only so long as it deals with an ideal system of pure numbers; the moment it begins to deal with numbers of *things* it is forced back into the language of analogy. In particular, when we speak about something of which we have no direct experience, we must think by analogy or refrain from thought. It may be perilous, as it must be inadequate, to interpret God by analogy with ourselves, but we are compelled to do so; we have no other means of interpreting anything. Skeptics frequently complain that man has made God in his own image; they should in reason go further (as many of them do) and acknowledge that man has made all existence in his own image. If the tendency to anthropomorphism is a good reason for refusing to think about God, it is an equally good reason for refusing to think about light, or oysters, or battleships. It may quite well be perilous, as it must be inadequate, to interpret the mind of our pet dog by analogy with ourselves; we can by no means enter directly into the nature of a dog; behind the appealing eyes and the wagging tail lies a mystery as inscrutable as the mystery of the Trinity. But that does not prevent us from ascribing to the dog feelings and ideas based on analogy with our own experience; and our behavior to the dog, controlled by this kind of experimental guesswork, produces practical results which are reasonably satisfactory. Similarly the physicist, struggling to interpret the alien structure of the atom, finds himself obliged to consider it sometimes as a "wave" and sometimes as a "particle." He knows very well that both these terms are analogical — they are metaphors, "picture-thinking," and, as pictures, they are incompatible and mutually contradictory. But he need not on that account refrain from using them for what they are worth. If he were to wait till he could have immediate experience of the atom, he would have to wait until he was set free from the framework of the universe. In the meantime, so long as he remembers that language and observation are human functions, partaking at every point of the limitations of humanity, he can get along quite well with them and carry out fruitful researches. To complain that man measures God by his own experience is a waste of time; man measures everything by his own experience; he has no other yardstick.

We have, then, various analogies by which we seek to interpret to ourselves the nature of God as it is known to us by experience. Sometimes we speak of Him as a king, and use metaphors drawn from that analogy. We talk, for instance, of His kingdom, laws, dominion, service and soldiers. Still more frequently, we speak of Him as a father, and think it quite legitimate to argue from the analogy of human fatherhood to the "fatherhood" of God. This particular "picture-thought" is one of which Christ was very fond, and it has stamped itself indelibly on the language of Christian worship and doctrine: "God the Father Almighty," "like as a father pitieth his own children," "your Father in Heaven careth for you," "the children of God," "the Son of God," "as many as are led by the spirit of God are sons of God," "I will arise and go to my father," "Our Father which art in Heaven." In books and sermons we express the relation between God and mankind in terms of human parenthood; we say that, just as a father is kind, careful, unselfish and forgiving in his dealings with his children, so is God in his dealings with men; that there is a true likeness of nature between God and man as between a father and his sons; and that because we are sons of one Father, we should look on all men as our brothers.

When we use these expressions, we know perfectly well that they are metaphors and analogies; what is more, we know perfectly well where the metaphor begins and ends. We do not suppose for one moment that God procreates children in the same manner as a human father and we are quite well aware that preachers who use the "father" metaphor intend and expect no such perverse interpretation of their language. Nor (unless we are very stupid indeed) do we go on to deduce from the analogy that we are to imagine God as being a cruel, careless or injudicious father such as we may see from time to time in daily life; still less, that *all* the activities of a human father may be attributed to God, such as earning money for the support of the family or demanding the first use of the bathroom in the morning. Our own common sense assures us that the metaphor is intended to be drawn from the best kind of father acting within a certain limited sphere of behavior, and is to be applied only to a well-defined number of the divine attributes.

I have put down these very elementary notes on the limitations of metaphor, because this book is an examination of metaphors about God, and because it is well to remind ourselves before we begin of the way in which metaphorical language — that is to say, all language — is properly used. It is an expression of experience and of the relation of one experience to the other. Further, its meaning is realized only in experience. We frequently say, "Until I had that experience, I never knew what the word fear (or love, or anger, or whatever it is) *meant.*" The language, which had been merely pictorial, is transmuted into experience and we then have immediate knowledge of the reality behind the picture.

The words of creeds come before our eyes and ears as pictures; we do not apprehend them as statements of experience; it is only when our own experience is brought into relation with the experience of the men who framed the creeds that we are able to say: "I recognize that for a statement of experience; I know now what the words mean."

The analogical statements of experience which I want to examine are those used by the Christian creeds about God the Creator.

And first of all, is the phrase "God the Creator" metaphorical in the same sense that "God the Father" is clearly metaphorical? At first sight, it does not appear to be so. We know what a human father is, but what is a human creator? We are very well aware that man cannot create in the absolute sense in which we understand the word when we apply it to God. We say that "He made the world out of nothing," but we cannot ourselves make anything out of nothing. We can only rearrange the unalterable and indestructible units of matter in the universe and build them up into new forms. We might reasonably say that in the "father" metaphor we are arguing from the known to the unknown; whereas, in the "creator" metaphor, we are arguing from the unknown to the unknowable.

But to say this is to overlook the metaphorical nature of all language. We use the word "create" to convey an extension and amplification of something that we do know, and we limit the application of the metaphor precisely as we limit the application of the metaphor of fatherhood. We know a father and picture to ourselves an ideal Father; similarly, we know a human "maker" and picture to ourselves an ideal "Maker." If the word "Maker" does not mean something related to our human experience of making, then it has no meaning at all. We extend it to the concept of a Maker who can make something out of nothing; we limit it to exclude the concept of employing material tools. It is analogical language simply because it is human language, and it is related to human experience for the same reason.

This particular metaphor has been much less studied than the metaphor of "the Father." This is partly because the image of divine Fatherhood has been particularly consecrated by Christ's use of it; partly because most of us have a very narrow experience of the act of creation. It is true that everybody is a "maker" in the simplest meaning of the term. We spend our lives putting matter together in new patterns and so "creating" forms which were not there before. This is so intimate and universal a function of nature that we scarcely ever think about it. In a sense, even this kind of creation is "creation out of nothing." Though we cannot create matter, we continually, by rearrangement, create new and unique entities. A million buttons, stamped out by machine, though they may be exactly alike, are not the *same* button; with each separate act of making, an entity has appeared in the world that was not there before. Nevertheless, we perceive that this is only a very poor and restricted kind of creation. We acknowledge a richer experience in the making of an individual and original work. By a metaphor vulgar but corresponding to a genuine experience, we speak of a model hat or gown as a "creation": it is unique, not merely by its entity but by its individuality. Again, by another natural metaphor, we may call a perfectly prepared beefsteak pudding, "a work of art"; and in these words we acknowledge an analogy with what we instinctively feel to be a still more satisfying kind of "creation."

It is the artist who, more than other men, is able to create something out of nothing. A whole artistic work is immeasurably more than the sum of its parts.

> But here is the will of God, a flash of the will that can,
>   Existent behind all laws, that made them, and lo,
>   they are!
> And I know not if, save in this, such gift be allowed to man,
>   That out of three sounds he frame, not a fourth sound, but
>   a star.

> Consider it well: each tone of our scale in itself is nought,
>   It is everywhere in the world — loud, soft, and all is said:
> Give it to me to use! I mix it with two in my thought:
>   And there! Ye have heard and seen: consider and bow the
>   head!

"I mix it with two *in my thought*"; this is the statement of the fact of universal experience that the work of art has real existence apart from its translation into material form. Without the thought, though the material parts already exist, the form does not and cannot. The "creation" is not a product of the matter, and is not simply a rearrangement of the matter. The amount of matter in the universe is limited, and its possible rearrangements, though the sum of them would amount to astronomical figures, is also limited. But no such limitation of numbers applies to the creation of works of art. The poet is not obliged, as it were, to destroy the material of a Hamlet in order to create a Falstaff, as a carpenter must destroy a tree-form to create a table-form. The components of the material world are fixed; those of the world of imagination increase by a continuous and irreversible process, without any destruction or rearrangement of what went before. This represents the nearest approach we experience to "creation out of nothing," and we conceive of the act of absolute creation as being an act analogous to that of the creative artist. Thus Berdyaev is able to say: "God created the world by imagination."

This experience of the creative imagination in the common man or woman and in the artist is the only thing we have to go upon in entertaining and formulating the concept of creation. Outside our own experience of procreation and creation we can form no notion of how anything comes into being. The expressions "God the Father" and

"God the Creator" are thus seen to belong to the same category — that is, of analogies based on human experience, and limited or extended by a similar mental process in either case.

If all this is true, then it is to the creative artists that we should naturally turn for an exposition of what is *meant* by those credal formulae which deal with the nature of the Creative Mind. Actually, we seldom seem to consult them in the matter. Poets have, indeed, often communicated in their own mode of expression truths identical with the theologians' truths; but just because of the difference in the modes of expression, we often fail to see the identity of the statements. The artist does not recognize that the phrases of the creeds purport to be observations of fact about the creative mind *as such,* including his own; while the theologian, limiting the application of the phrases to the divine Maker, neglects to inquire of the artist what light he can throw upon them from his own immediate apprehension of truth. The confusion is as though two men were to argue fiercely whether there was a river in a certain district or whether, on the contrary, there was a measurable volume of H_2O moving in a particular direction with an ascertainable velocity; neither having any suspicion that they were describing the same phenomenon.

Our minds are not infinite; and as the volume of the world's knowledge increases, we tend more and more to confine ourselves, each to his special sphere of interest and to the specialized metaphor belonging to it. The analytic bias of the last three centuries has immensely encouraged this tendency, and it is now very difficult for the artist to speak the language of the theologian or the scientist the language of either. But the attempt must be made; and there are signs everywhere that the human mind is once more beginning to move towards a synthesis of experience.

JAMES FRAZER

Sacraments of Africa

Sir James George Frazer (1854–1941) was born in Scotland but taught in England. He published *The Golden Bough,* which eventually grew to twelve volumes, over a twenty-five-year period, coordinating a vast amount of information about the myths, rituals, and beliefs of "high" as well as of "primitive" religion in a way that had an abiding effect on both anthropology and theology even after his specific theories had been surrendered. His grasp of the religions of Africa has been especially influential.

PRIMITIVE PEOPLES often partake of the new corn and the new fruits sacramentally, because they suppose them to be instinct with a divine spirit or life. At a later age, when the fruits of the earth are conceived as created rather than as animated by a divinity, the new fruits are no longer partaken of sacramentally as the body and blood of a god; but a portion of them is offered to the divine beings who are believed to have produced them. Originally, perhaps, offerings of first-fruits were supposed to be necessary for the subsistence of the divinities, who without them must have died of hunger; but in after times they seem to be looked on rather in the light of a tribute or mark of homage rendered by man to the gods for the good gifts they have bestowed on him. Sometimes the first-fruits are presented to the king, perhaps in his character of a god; very often they are made over to the spirits of the human dead, who are sometimes thought to have it in their power to give or withhold the crops. Till the first-fruits have been offered to the deity, the dead, or the king, people are not at liberty to eat of the new crops. But, as it is not always possible to draw a sharp line between the sacrament and the sacrifice of first-fruits, it may be well to round off this part of the subject by giving some examples of the latter.

The Ovambo or Ovakuanjama of South-West Africa stand in great fear of the spirits of the dead, who are believed to exercise a powerful influence over the living; in particular the spirits of dead chiefs can give or withhold rain, a matter of vital importance in the parched region of Ovamboland. Accordingly the people pay great respect to the spirits of the departed, and they hold a thanksgiving festival in their honour at the close of the harvest. When the new corn has been reaped and ground, a portion of it is made into porridge and carried to the quarters of the principal wife. Here all the inhabitants of the kraal assemble; the head of the family takes some of the porridge, dips it in melted fat, and throws it to the east, saying, "Take it, ye spirits of the East!" Then he does the same towards the west, saying, "Take it, ye spirits of the West!" This is regarded as a thank-offering presented to the spirits of the dead for not visiting the people with sickness while they were cultivating the fields, and especially for sending the rain.

Among the Basutos, when the corn has been threshed and win-nowed, it is left in a heap on the threshing-floor. Before it can be touched a religious ceremony must be performed. The persons to whom the corn belongs bring a new vessel to the spot, in which they boil some of the grain. When it is boiled they throw a few handfuls of it on the heap of corn, saying, "Thank you, gods; give us bread to-morrow also!" When this is done the rest is eaten, and the provision for the year is considered pure and fit to eat. Here the sacrifice of the first-fruits to the gods is the prominent idea, which comes out again in the custom of leaving in the threshing-floor a little hollow filled with grain, as a thank-offering to these powerful beings. Still the Basutos retain a lively sense of the sanctity of the corn in itself; for, so long as it is exposed to view, all defiled persons are carefully kept from it. If it is necessary to employ a defiled person in carrying home the harvest, he remains at some distance while the sacks are being filled, and only approaches to place them upon the draught oxen. As soon as the load is deposited at the dwelling he retires, and under no pretext may he help to pour the corn into the baskets in which it is kept. The Makalaka worship a god called Shumpaoli, whose image is to be found in the enclosure outside of their huts. The image consists of the head of an axe, a stone from the river, and a twig or long stalk of grass planted between them in the ground. About this god they scatter the first-fruits of their harvest, and when they brew beer they pour some of it on him. Of the Bantu tribes of South Africa in general we are told that they might not eat of the new crops till the chief gave them leave to do so. When the millet was ripe he appointed a general assembly of the people at his residence, which was known as the Great Place; he then performed certain rites, and in particular he offered a small quantity of the fresh grain to the spirits of his ancestors, either by laying it on their graves or by casting it into a stream. After that he granted the people permission to gather and eat the new corn.

Among the Maraves or Zimbas, a tribe of the Upper Zambesi, bordering on the Portuguese territory, it is the custom that first-fruits of all produce must be offered to the spirits of the dead (*muzimos*), to whom they attribute all the good and ill that befall them. Every year at harvest-time the offerings are brought to these mighty beings. Small portions of all kinds of fruits, together with cooked fowls and *pombe* (the native intoxicant), are carried in procession, with songs, dances, and the beating of drums, to the burial-ground, which is always situated in a grove or a wilderness and is esteemed a sacred place; no tree may be felled and no animal killed on the holy ground, for the natives believe that a spirit of the dead is present in everything within the precincts. Among the Yaos of British Central Africa "offerings are made to the spirit world or to *mulungu* as the great agency in the affairs of human life. Outside the village, or beside the head-man's hut, may often be seen a rough shed. In this are placed the first-fruits of the new crop, green maize, beans, pumpkins, peas, etc., as a thank-offering from the villagers for their harvest. This is described as *kulomba mulungu*, to worship *mulungu*." By *mulungu* the Yaos mean primarily and strictly the soul of a dead person, which is believed to influence the lives and fortunes of the survivors, and therefore needs to be honoured and propitiated; but they employ the word in an extended sense to signify the aggregate of the spirits of all the dead, and missionaries have adopted it as the nearest equivalent for the word God. Among the Winamwanga, a tribe of north-eastern Rhodesia, between Lake Nyassa and Lake Tanganyika, it is customary to offer the first beer and the first flour made from the new harvest of millet to the spirits of the dead. The head of the family pours out some beer and a small quantity of the new flour in a heap on the floor of his own house, after which he prays to the spirits of his forefathers, thanks them for the harvest, and invites them to come and partake of it with the family. The priest performs the same ceremony at the shrine for the whole village. The householder or the priest speaks to the spirits as if they were sitting around him. Thus he may say, "O ye great spirits, fathers in the spirit world, mothers in the spirit world, and all ye others, bless us now. Here is the food, and here is the offering, call ye all of you each other." Then after summoning the dead by their names he may go on: "Come all of you and partake of this offering. Ye great spirits, all things of this earth were known to you while yet ye were here. Take care of this your family, and of all these your children. May we ever go in our ways in prosperity. Oh! ye great spirits, give to us food and all the produce of the land. Drive ye away all illnesses from your family, ye great spirits; every evil spirit put far away from us, and whatever might seek to hurt us may it fly away on the wind. Cause ye us to abide in peace." Among the Yombe of Northern Rhodesia, to the west of Lake Tanganyika, no one is allowed to partake of the new fruits until certain ceremonies have been performed. Escorted by a band of drummers, his medicine-men, and the village elders, the chief ascends the Kalanga Mountain until he reaches the hollow fastness which in former days his forefathers held against the marauding Angoni. Here the grandfather of the present chief lies buried. Before his tomb a bull is slain, and pots of freshly-brewed beer and porridge made from the first-fruits are deposited before the shrine. The ground is then carefully cleaned of weeds, and the blood of the bull is sprinkled on the freshly-turned-up soil and on the rafters of the little hut. After offering the customary prayers in thanksgiving for the harvest, and beseeching the spirits to partake with them of the first-fruits, the procession retires. On their return to the village, the carcase of the bull is divided, all partake of the fresh porridge and beer awaiting them, and the day closes with beer-drinking and dancing.

The A-Kamba of British East Africa offer first-fruits to the spirits of their dead before anybody may eat of the new crop. Sometimes these offerings are piled on the graves of chiefs and left there along with the meat of a goat which has been sacrificed. Sometimes the offerings are made in a cleared place under the sacred wild fig tree (*mumbo*) of the village; for the A-Kamba think that the spirits of the dead (*aiimu*) dwell in wild fig trees, and they build miniature huts at the foot of the trees for the accommodation of the ghosts. The clearing under the wild fig tree of the village is called the Place of Prayer (*ithembo*). When any crop is ripe, all the inhabitants of the district assemble, and a very old man and woman, chosen for the purpose, leave the crowd and go to the Place of Prayer, where they call aloud to the spirits of the dead and ask leave to eat the crop. The people then dance, and during the dance one of the women is sure to be seized with a fit of shaking and to cry aloud, which is deemed the answer of the spirits to the people's prayer. Amongst the Baganda a man used to offer the first-fruits of a new garden to his god, imploring the blessing of the deity on the future crops. Among the Dinka of the White Nile no member of a family may eat the new fruits until the father or mother has scattered some of them over the courtyard of the house in order to ensure the blessing of God. When the millet is ripe, the Nubas of Jebel-Nuba, a range of mountains in the eastern Sudan, observe the following ceremony. Every group of villages is presided over by a sacred pontiff called a *cogiour* or *codjour,* who is believed to act under the inspiration of a spirit named Laro. So when it is known that the grain is ready to be cut, a drum is beaten, the pontiff mounts his horse and, attended by all the elderly men and women, repairs to his fields, while the rest of the people betake themselves to their own farms. There the people whose eldest child is a boy break five ears of corn, and those whose eldest child is a girl break four. But young unmarried people break five or four ears according as they desire to have a boy or a girl for their first-born. All then return to the village and place the ears they have gathered on the hedge which serves as an enclosure. When the beat of the drum and multitudinous cries of joy announce the return of the pontiff, the people take the gathered ears and advance to meet him. He rides at the head of a cavalcade composed of all the men who have horses. After that, attended by the elders, he retires to his house, while the rest of the people deposit the ears of corn in the cave of Laro, the being who inspires the holy pontiff. Feasting, drinking, and horse-races conclude the ceremony. At the races the young folk amuse themselves by flinging stalks of millet before the horses to make them shy and throw their riders.

The Igbiras, a pagan tribe at the confluence of the Niger and the Benue, bury their dead in their houses and have great faith in the power of the ghosts, whose guidance and protection they seek to ensure by periodical offerings of goats and cocks. Also they offer the first-fruits of their crops to the dead, hanging bunches of the new grain over the burial-places in their huts. The Igbiras also celebrate the festival of the new yams with great pomp. It is their New Year's Day. Sacrifices of fowls and goats are offered, and wine and oil are freely poured out. The king takes a prominent part in the feast. Among the Cross River natives, in the lower valley of the Niger, the eating of the new yams is an occasion of great rejoicing, but no one may partake of them until a portion has been ceremonially offered to the deities. The festival is not held simultaneously but separately for each village according to the state of the crops. High and low, old and young, men, women, and children dance to music on these joyful occasions. The Matse tribe of Ewe negroes in Togoland worship the Earth at the times when they dig the ripe yams in September, when they reap the ripe maize in November, and when they burn the grass in February. The place where they offer sacrifices to the Earth goddess is called "the Wood of our Mother." In the month of November the hunters, led by the Chief Huntsman and the High Priest, repair to the maize-fields, where they gather cobs of the ripe grain. Some of these they deposit, with prayers, in the sacrificial place in the wood, but they keep the finest cobs for themselves. After this sacrifice of the new corn to the Earth goddess everybody is free to get in his maize. Amongst the Hos, another Ewe tribe of Togoland, when a man is about to dig up his yam crop, he first of all digs up two yams which he had planted for the goddess Mawu Sodza. These he holds up to her and prays, saying, "O Mawu Sodza, thou ship full of yams, give to me, and I will give to you; pass me over, and I will pass you over. Here are thy yams, which I have dug for thee. When I dig mine, grant that I may have plenty." Thereupon he begins to dig the crop. Among the Bassari, another tribe of Togoland, no man may eat of the new yams until the people have paid a tribute of the first-fruits to the king. At such times long files of men, women, and children may be seen wending their way to the capital to render to the king his dues. But the king himself may not partake of the new yams until he has offered a portion of them, along with ten white fowls, to the fetish. Before the Adeli of the Slave Coast may eat of the new yams, the owner of each farm must bring the first yams of his field to the fetish priest, who offers them to the fetish, after which he declares that the harvest may take place. The festival, accompanied by shooting and dancing, lasts several days; it generally falls in August.

Among the Betsileo of Madagascar the king used to receive first-fruits of all the crops, such as rice, maize, manioc, beans, and sweet potatoes: indeed this tribute of first-fruits formed a large part of his revenue. The Hovas of Madagascar present the first sheaves of the new grain to the sovereign. The sheaves are carried in procession to the palace from time to time as the grain ripens. So in Burma, when the *pangati* fruits ripen, some of them used to be taken to the king's palace that he might eat of them; no one might partake of them before the king. It has been suggested that the modern system of taxation may be directly derived from the ancient obligation of paying first-fruits to a sacred pontiff or king.

*   *   *   *   *

While many savages thus fear to eat the flesh of slow-footed animals lest they should themselves become slow-footed, the Bushmen of South Africa purposely ate the flesh of such creatures, and the reason which they gave for doing so exhibits a curious refinement of savage philosophy. They imagined that the game which they pursued would be influenced sympathetically by the food in the body of the hunter, so that if he had eaten of swift-footed animals, the quarry would be swift-footed also and would escape him; whereas if he had eaten of slow-footed animals, the quarry would also be slow-footed, and he would be able to overtake and kill it. For that reason hunters of gemsbok particularly avoided eating the flesh of the swift and agile springbok; indeed they would not even touch it with their hands, because they believed the springbok to be a very lively creature which did not go to sleep at night, and they thought that if they ate springbok, the gemsbok which they hunted would likewise not be willing to go to sleep, even at night. How, then, could they catch it?

Certain tribes on the Upper Zambesi believe in transmigration, and every man in his lifetime chooses the kind of animal whose body he wishes at death to enter. He then performs an initiatory rite, which consists in swallowing the maggots bred in the putrid carcase of the animal of his choice; thenceforth he partakes of that animal's nature. And on the occasion of a calamity, while the women are giving themselves up to lamentation, you will see one man writhing on the ground like a boa constrictor or a crocodile, another howling and leaping like a panther, a third baying like a jackal, roaring like a lion, or grunting like a hippopotamus, all of them imitating the characters of the various animals to perfection. Clearly these people imagine that the soul or vital essence of the animal is manifested in the maggots bred in its decaying carcase; hence they imagine that by swallowing the maggots they imbue themselves with the very life and spirit of the creature which they desire to become. The Namaquas abstain from eating the flesh of hares, because they think it would make them faint-hearted as a hare. But they eat the flesh of the lion, or drink the blood of the leopard or lion, to get the courage and strength of these beasts. The Bushmen will not give their children a jackal's heart to eat, lest it should make them timid like the jackal; but they give them a leopard's heart to eat to make them brave like the leopard. When a Wagogo man of German East Africa kills a lion, he eats the heart in order to become brave like a lion; but he thinks that to eat the heart of a hen would make him timid. Among the Ja-luo, a tribe of Nilotic negroes, young men eat the flesh of leopards in order to make themselves fierce in war. The flesh of the lion and also that of the spotted leopard are sometimes cooked and eaten by native warriors in South-Eastern Africa, who hope thereby to become as brave as lions. When a Zulu army assembles to go forth to battle, the warriors eat slices of meat which is smeared with a powder made of the dried flesh of various animals, such as the leopard, lion, elephant, snakes, and so on; for thus it is thought that the soldiers will acquire the bravery and other warlike qualities of these animals. Sometimes if a Zulu has killed a wild beast, for instance a leopard, he will give his children the blood to drink, and will roast the heart for them to eat, expecting that they will thus grow up brave and daring men. But others say that this is dangerous, because it is apt to produce courage without prudence, and to make a man rush heedlessly on his death. Among the Wabondei of Eastern Africa the heart of a lion or leopard is eaten with the intention of making the eater strong and brave. In British Central Africa aspirants after courage consume the flesh and especially the hearts of lions, while lecherous persons eat the testicles of goats. Among the Suk of British East Africa the fat and heart of a lion are sometimes given to children to eat in order that they may become strong; but they are not allowed to know what they are eating. Arab women in North Africa give their male children a piece of a lion's heart to eat to make them fearless. The flesh of an elephant is thought by the Ewe-speaking peoples of West Africa to make the eater strong. Before they go forth to fight, Wajagga warriors drink a magical potion, which often consists of shavings of the horn and hide of a rhinoceros mixed with beer; this is supposed to impart to them the strength and force of the animal. When a serious disease has attacked a Zulu kraal, the medicine-man takes the bone of a very old dog, or the bone of an old cow, bull, or other very old animal, and administers it to the healthy as well as to the sick people, in order that they may live to be as old as the animal of whose bone they have partaken. So to restore the aged Aeson to youth, the witch Medea infused into his veins a decoction of the liver of the long-lived deer and the head of a crow that had outlived nine generations of men. In antiquity the flesh of deer and crows was eaten for other purposes than that of prolonging life. As deer were supposed not to suffer from fever, some women used to taste venison every morning, and it is said that in consequence they lived to a great age without ever being attacked by a fever; only the venison lost all its virtue if the animal had been killed by more blows than one. Again, ancient diviners sought to imbue themselves with the spirit of prophecy by swallowing vital portions of birds and beasts of omen; for example, they thought that by eating the hearts of crows or moles or hawks they took into their bodies, along with the flesh, the prophetic soul of the creature.

ALBERT EINSTEIN

Strange Is Our Situation Here upon Earth

> Albert Einstein (1879–1955) enunciated the special and the general theories of relativity in 1905 and 1916, receiving the Nobel Prize for physics in 1921. The unmistakable reverence with which he approached both the universe itself and his own study of it lent special interest to his views about God, in which, as this selection from *Living Philosophies* shows, he diverged from traditional theism but did so in an authentically religious manner.

STRANGE IS OUR SITUATION here upon earth. Each of us comes for a short visit, not knowing why, yet sometimes seeming to divine a purpose.

From the standpoint of daily life, however, there is one thing we do know: that man is here for the sake of other men — above all for those upon whose smile and well-being our own happiness depends, and also for the countless unknown souls with whose fate we are connected by a bond of sympathy. Many times a day I realize how much my own outer and inner life is built upon the labors of my fellow-men, both living and dead, and how earnestly I must exert myself in order to give in return as much as I have received. My peace of mind is often troubled by the depressing sense that I have borrowed too heavily from the work of other men.

I do not believe we can have any freedom at all in the philosophical sense, for we act not only under external compulsion but also by inner necessity. Schopenhauer's saying — "A man can surely do what he wills to do, but he cannot determine what he wills" — impressed itself upon me in youth and has always consoled me when I have witnessed or suffered life's hardships. This conviction is a perpetual breeder of tolerance, for it does not allow us to take ourselves or others too seriously; it makes rather for a sense of humor.

To ponder interminably over the reason for one's own existence or the meaning of life in general seems to me, from an objective point of view, to be sheer folly. And yet everyone holds certain ideals by which he guides his aspiration and his judgment. The ideals which have always shone before me and filled me with the joy of living are goodness, beauty, and truth. To make a goal of comfort or happiness has never appealed to me; a system of ethics built on this basis would be sufficient only for a herd of cattle.

Without the sense of collaborating with like-minded beings in the pursuit of the ever unattainable in art and scientific research, my life would have been empty. Ever since childhood I have scorned the commonplace limits so often set upon human ambition. Possessions, outward success, publicity, luxury — to me these have always been contemptible. I believe that a simple and unassuming manner of life is best for everyone, best both for the body and the mind.

My passionate interest in social justice and social responsibility has always stood in curious contrast to a marked lack of desire for direct association with men and women. I am a horse for single harness, not cut out for tandem or team work. I have never belonged wholeheartedly to country or state, to my circle of friends, or even to my own family. These ties have always been accompanied by a vague aloofness and the wish to withdraw into myself increases with the years.

Such isolation is sometimes bitter, but I do not regret being cut off from the understanding and sympathy of other men. I lose something by it, to be sure, but I am compensated for it in being rendered independent of the customs, opinions, and prejudices of others, and am not tempted to rest my peace of mind upon such shifting foundations.

My political ideal is democracy. Everyone should be respected as an individual, but no one idolized. It is an irony of fate that I should have been showered with so much uncalled-for and unmerited admiration and esteem. Perhaps this adulation springs from the unfulfilled wish of the multitude to comprehend the few ideas which I, with my weak powers, have advanced.

Full well do I know that in order to attain any definite goal it is imperative that *one* person should do the thinking and commanding and carry most of the responsibility. But those who are led should not be driven, and they should be allowed to choose their leader. It seems to me that the distinctions separating the social classes are false; in the last analysis they rest on force. I am convinced that degeneracy follows every autocratic system of violence, for violence inevitably attracts moral inferiors. Time has proved that illustrious tyrants are succeeded by scoundrels.

For this reason I have always been passionately opposed to such régimes as exist in Russia and Italy to-day. The thing which has discredited the European forms of democracy is not the basic theory of democracy itself, which some say is at fault, but the instability of our political leadership, as well as the impersonal character of party alignments.

I believe that those in the United States have hit upon the right idea. A President is chosen for a reasonable length of time and enough power is given him to acquit himself properly of his responsibilities. In the German Government, on the other hand, I like the state's more extensive care of the individual when he is ill or unemployed. What is truly valuable in our bustle of life is not the nation, I should say, but the creative and impressionable individuality, the personality — he who produces the noble and sublime while the common herd remains dull in thought and insensible in feeling.

This subject brings me to that vilest offspring of the herd mind — the odious militia. The man who enjoys marching in line and file to the strains of music falls below my contempt; he received his great brain by mistake — the spinal cord would have been amply sufficient. This heroism at command, this senseless violence, this accursed bombast of patriotism — how intensely I despise them! War is low and despicable, and I had rather be smitten to shreds than participate in such doings.

Such a stain on humanity should be erased without delay. I think well enough of human nature to believe that it would have been wiped out long ago had not the common sense of nations been systematically corrupted through school and press for business and political reasons.

The most beautiful thing we can experience is the mysterious. It is the source of all true art and science. He to whom this emotion is a stranger, who can no longer pause to wonder and stand rapt in awe, is as good as dead: his eyes are closed. This insight into the mystery of life, coupled though it be with fear, has also given rise to religion. To know that what is impenetrable to us really exists, manifesting itself as the highest wisdom and the most radiant beauty which our dull faculties can comprehend only in their most primitive forms — this knowledge, this feeling, is at the center of true religiousness. In this sense, and in this sense only, I belong in the ranks of devoutly religious men.

I cannot imagine a God who rewards and punishes the objects of his creation, whose purposes are modeled after our own — a God, in short, who is but a reflection of human frailty. Neither can I believe that the individual survives the death of his body, although feeble souls harbor such thoughts through fear or ridiculous egotism. It is enough for me to contemplate the mystery of conscious life perpetuating itself through all eternity, to reflect upon the marvelous structure of the universe which we can dimly perceive, and to try humbly to comprehend even an infinitesimal part of the intelligence manifested in nature.

ALFRED NORTH WHITEHEAD

The New Reformation

Alfred North Whitehead (1861–1947) had made his mark on the intellectual world as a mathematician and logician and as a professor of mechanics. Then, at an age when his contemporaries were contemplating retirement, he became professor of philosophy at Harvard; his Gifford Lectures were called *Process and Reality*, and here in a chapter from his *Adventures of Ideas* he articulated his guiding vision of a God who works by persuasion rather than coercion.

SECTION I. The theme of this chapter can be introduced by directing attention to a contrast. Protestant Christianity, so far as concerns the institutional and dogmatic forms in which it flourished for three hundred years as derived from Luther, Calvin, and the Anglican Settlement, is shewing all the signs of a steady decay. Its dogmas no longer dominate: its divisions no longer interest: its institutions no longer direct the patterns of life. That is one side of the contrast.

The other side is that the religious spirit as an effective element in the affairs of men has just obtained one of its most signal triumphs. In India the forces of violence and strife, between rulers and people, between races, between religions, between social grades, — forces threatening to overwhelm with violence hundreds of millions of mankind — these forces have for the moment been halted by two men acting with the moral authority of religious conviction, the Mahatma Gandhi and the Viceroy of India.

They may fail. More than two thousand years ago, the wisest of men proclaimed that the divine persuasion is the foundation of the order of the world, but that it could only produce such a measure of harmony as amid brute forces it was possible to accomplish. This, I suggest, is a plain anticipation by Plato of a doctrine of Grace, seven hundred years before the age of Pelagius and Augustine.

But the dramatic halt effected by Gandhi and the Viceroy, requiring as it does an effective response from uncounted millions in India, in England, in Europe, and America, witnesses that the religious motive, I mean the response to the divine persuasion, still holds its old power, even more than its old power, over the minds and the consciences of men. In this response the protestant populations of the British Empire, and importantly, though more remotely, that of the United States, have sustained their part. We stand at a moment when the course of history depends upon the calm reasonableness arising from a religious public opinion. An initial triumph has already been gained.

There is the contrast, decay and survival. We have to estimate what has decayed, and what has survived. My thesis is that a new Reformation is in full progress. It is a *re*-formation; but whether its issue be fortunate or unfortunate depends largely on the actions of comparatively few men, and notably upon the leaders of the protestant clergy.

I do not hold it to be possible, or even desirable, that identity of detailed belief can be attained. But it is possible that amid diversities of belief, arising from differences of stress exhibited in metaphysical insight and from differences of sympathetic intuition respecting historical events, — that it is possible, amid these differences, to reach a general agreement as to those elements, in intimate human experience and in general history, which we select to exemplify that ultimate theme of the divine immanence, as a completion required by our cosmological outlook. In other words, we may agree as to the qualitative aspects of religious facts, and as to their general way of coördination in metaphysical theory, while disagreeing in various explanatory formulations.

The problem, however, is not nearly so simple as this exordium suggests. We are dealing with a topic, complex and many-sided. It comprises the deliverances of the understanding as it harmonizes our deepest intuitions. It comprises emotional responses to formulations of thought and to modes of behaviour. It comprises the direction of purposes and the modifications of behaviour. It cuts into every aspect of human existence. So far as concerns religious problems, simple solutions are bogus solutions. It is written, that he who runs, may read. But it is not said, that he provides the writing.

For religion is concerned with our reactions of purpose and emotion due to our personal measure of intuition into the ultimate mystery of the universe. We must not postulate simplicity. The witness of history and of common sense tells us that systematic formulations are potent engines of emphasis, of purification, and of stability. Christianity would long ago have sunk into a noxious superstition, apart from the Levantine and European intellectual movement, sustained from the very beginning until now. This movement is the effort of Reason to provide an accurate system of theology. Indeed, in outlying districts where this effort at rationalization died away, the religion has in fact sunk into the decrepitude of failure.

SECTION II. Thus the attack of the liberal clergy and laymen, during the eighteenth and nineteenth centuries, upon systematic theology was entirely misconceived. They were throwing away the chief safeguard against the wild emotions of superstition. A civilized religion should aim at the training of such emotions as naturally arise from a civilized rational criticism of the metaphysical intuitions powerfully influential in great epochs of human history. The appeal to history is the appeal to summits of attainment beyond any immediate clarity in our own individual existence. It is an appeal to authority. The appeal to reason is the appeal to that ultimate judge, universal and yet individual to each, to which all authority must bow. History has authority so far, and exactly so far, as it admits of some measure of rational interpretation.

Thus an attack upon systematic thought is treason to civilization. Yet the great minds who laid the foundations of our modern mentality — John Locke, for example — had reason for their dissatisfaction with the traditional dogmatic theology, though they partially misconceived the grounds upon which they should base their attitude. Their true enemy was the doctrine of dogmatic finality, a doctrine which flourished and is flourishing with equal vigour throughout Theology, Science, and Metaphysics. The methodology of rational thought from the Greeks to our own times has been vitiated by this fundamental misconception. These errors are not confined to religious thought. They have infected all departments. Their total effect has been to introduce in each age a dogmatic sense of finality. The emphasis of certainty has been wrongly placed, and with equal error dogmatic rejection.

From the very beginning of critical thought, we find the distinction between topics susceptible of certain knowledge, and topics about which only uncertain opinions are available. The dawn of this distinction, explicitly entertained, is the dawn of modern mentality. It introduces criticism. Such a notion hardly enters into any book of the Bible, either in the mind of Jehovah, or of any of his worshippers. The first effect of this new distinction was very unfortunate. For it was much too simple-minded, and the area of certainty was misconceived. For example, we find Plato in his old age advocating religious persecution and justifying himself by the importance of the topic and the certainty of his own demonstrations.

I suggest that the development of systematic theology should be accompanied by a critical understanding of the relation of linguistic expression to our deepest and most persistent intuitions. Language was developed in response to the excitements of practical actions. It is concerned with the prominent facts. Such facts are those seized upon by consciousness for detailed examination, with the view of emotional response leading to immediate purposeful action. These prominent facts are the variable facts, — the appearance of a tiger, of a clap of thunder, or of a spasm of pain. They are the facts entering into experience by the medium of our sense-organs. Hence the sensationalist doctrine concerning the data which are the origin of experience.

But the prominent facts are the superficial facts. They vary because they are superficial; and they enter into conscious discrimination because they vary. There are other elements in our experience, on the fringe of consciousness, and yet massively qualifying our experience. In regard to these other facts, it is our consciousness that flickers, and not the facts themselves. They are always securely there, barely discriminated, and yet inescapable. For example, consider our derivation from our immediate past of a quarter of a second ago. We are continuous with it, we are the same as it, prolonging its effective tone, enjoying its data. And yet we are modifying it, deflecting it, changing its purposes, altering its tone, re-conditioning its data with new elements.

We reduce this past to a perspective, and yet retain it as the basis of our present moment of realization. We are different from it, and yet we retain our individual identity with it. This is the mystery of personal identity, the mystery of the immanence of the past in the present, the mystery of transience. All our science, all our explanations require concepts originating in this experience of derivation. In respect to such intuitions, language is peculiarly inadequate. Our powers of analysis, and of expression, flicker with our consciousness. It is not true that there is a definite area of human consciousness, within which there is clear discrimination and beyond which mere darkness. Nor is it true that elements of experience are important in proportion to their clarity in consciousness.

The appeal to history gains its importance by reason of this complex character of human experience. Metaphysics and theology alike require it. The requisite evidence cannot be gained by mere acts of direct introspection conducted at one epoch by a few clear-sighted individuals. If a flood of oblivion should overwhelm human memory, we could in this way of introspection recover the multiplication table. But not much else. In each age of the world, the actions of men and their interpretations of feelings, motives, and purposes, throw light upon the recesses of their experience. In this elucidation of what it means to live, to act, and feel, age differs from age. In the discrimination of this historical evidence, there is required a criticism founded upon taste, and a criticism founded upon logical analysis and inductive probability.

The two grounds of criticism, æsthetic and logical, are welded together in the final judgment of reason as to the comparison of historical periods, one with the other. Each age deposits its message as to the secret character of the nature of things. Civilizations can only be understood by those who are civilized. And they have this property, that the appropriation of them in the understanding unveils truths concerning our own natures. It has been said that the great dramatic tragedies in their representations before audiences act as a purification of the passions. In the same way, the great periods of history act as an enlightenment. They reveal ourselves to ourselves.

SECTION III. Christianity bases itself upon an intensive study of the significance of certain historical occasions scattered irregularly within a period of about twelve hundred years, from the earlier Hebrew prophets and historians to the stabilization of western theology by Augustine. The story wanders around the shores of the Eastern Mediterranean, from the Palestine of the prophets to the Athens of Plato: it culminates in Galilee and Jerusalem: the main interest then fluctuates uncertainly backwards and forwards between Antioch, Ephesus, Egypt, Rome, Constantinople and Africa. When Augustine died at Hippo in the year 430, the religion of the European races was in its main outlines settled. All its capacities of variant forms were already inherent in it. The Papal Church, the Eastern Church, Wycliffe and Huss, Luther and Calvin, Archbishop Cranmer, Jonathan Edwards and John Wesley, Erasmus, Ignatius Loyola, the Socinians, George Fox, and the Vatican Council could with equal right appeal to history. The conclusion to be drawn from the appeal entirely depends upon the value-judgments guiding your selection, and upon the metaphysical presuppositions dictating your notions of a coherent theology. The appeal is to the actions, thoughts, emotions, and institutions, which

great persons and great occasions had made effective on the shores of
the Mediterranean within that earlier period of time.

In this appeal to history we must remember the gaps in time
between the extant written Gospels, and the events which they relate:
the discordances in accounts, the translations of tradition from language to language, the suspicious passages: also the seeming indifference to direct historical evidence, notably in the case of St. Paul,
who retired to Arabia when we should have expected him to have
recourse to the disciples who had seen his Lord. I mention these latter
points, upon which whole libraries have been written, merely to draw
the unquestioned conclusion that any modern re-formation of the
religion must first concentrate upon the moral and metaphysical
intuitions scattered throughout the whole epoch. This conclusion is
a commonplace of modern thought.

I suggest, with the diffidence due to my entire lack of expertness in
the literature of this immense stretch of history, that even now there
is room for a new appeal to the lesson to be derived from it. In this
chapter I shall deal wholly in general principles. My personal conclusions as to the details of reconstruction have none of the importance to be ascribed to scholarship. Also to speak with complete
candour, I cannot place any of the events within that period as out of
scale in type of happenings with analogous occurrences elsewhere. I
do hold, however, the culminating points of the period embody the
greatest advances in the expression of moral and intellectual intuitions
which mark the growth of recent civilization.

The period as a whole begins in barbarism and ends in failure. The
failure consisted in the fact that barbaric elements and the defects in
intellectual comprehension had not been discarded, but remained as
essential elements in the various formulations of Christian theology,
orthodox and heretical alike. Also the later Protestant Reformation
was, in this respect, an even more complete failure, in no way improving Catholic theology. The Quakers perhaps form a minor exception to this statement. But George Fox lived a hundred years after
the age of Luther. The issue of these failures is the tragic history of
Christianity.

Section IV. I suggest that in the whole period there are three
culminating phases which, in theological language, constitute its
threefold revelation. The first and the last phases were primarily
intellectual with a sufficient background of moral insight. The middle
phase, which forms the driving power of the religion, is primarily an
exhibition in life of moral intuition, with a sufficiency of intellectual

insight to give an articulate expression of singular beauty. The three phases are bound together as intellectual discovery, — then exemplification, — finally metaphysical interpretation. The discovery and the exemplification are historically independent.

The first phase is constituted by Plato's publication of his final conviction, towards the end of his life, that the divine element in the world is to be conceived as a persuasive agency and not as a coercive agency. This doctrine should be looked upon as one of the greatest intellectual discoveries in the history of religion. It is plainly enunciated by Plato, though he failed to coördinate it systematically with the rest of his metaphysical theory. Indeed, Plato always failed in his attempts at systematization, and always succeeded in displaying depth of metaphysical intuition — the greatest metaphysician, the poorest systematic thinker. The alternative doctrine, prevalent then and now, sees either in the many gods or in the one God, the final coercive forces wielding the thunder. By a metaphysical sublimation of this doctrine of God as the supreme agency of compulsion, he is transformed into the one supreme reality, omnipotently disposing a wholly derivative world. Plato wavered inconsistently between these diverse conceptions. But he does finally enunciate without qualification the doctrine of the divine persuasion, by reason of which ideals are effective in the world and forms of order evolve.

The second phase is the supreme moment in religious history, according to the Christian religion. The essence of Christianity is the appeal to the life of Christ as a revelation of the nature of God and of his agency in the world. The record is fragmentary, inconsistent, and uncertain. It is not necessary for me to express any opinion as to the proper reconstruction of the most likely tale of historic fact. Such a procedure would be useless, without value, and entirely out of place in this book. But there can be no doubt as to what elements in the record have evoked a response from all that is best in human nature. The Mother, the Child, and the bare manger: the lowly man, homeless and self-forgetful, with his message of peace, love, and sympathy: the suffering, the agony, the tender words as life ebbed, the final despair: and the whole with the authority of supreme victory.

I need not elaborate. Can there be any doubt that the power of Christianity lies in its revelation in act, of that which Plato divined in theory?

The third phase is again intellectual. It is the first period in the formation of Christian theology by the schools of thought mainly associated with Alexandria and Antioch. The originality and value of

their contribution to the thought of the world has been greatly underestimated. This is partly their own fault. For they persisted in
declaring that they were only stating the faith once delivered to the
saints; whereas in fact they were groping after the solution of a
fundamental metaphysical problem, although presented to them in a
highly special form.

These Christian theologians have the distinction of being the only
thinkers who in a fundamental metaphysical doctrine have improved
upon Plato. It is true that this period of Christian theology was
Platonic. But it is also true that Plato is the originator of the heresies
and of the feeblest side of Christian Theology. When Plato is faced
with the problem of expressing the relationship of God to the World,
and of the relation to the World of those Ideas which it is in God's
nature to contemplate, Plato's answer is invariably framed in terms of
mere dramatic imitation. When Plato turns to the World, after considering God as giving life and motion to the ideas by the inclusion of
them in the divine nature, he can find only second-rate substitutes and
never the originals. For Plato there is a derivative second-rate God of
the World, who is a mere Icon, that is to say an image. Also when he
looks for the ideas, he can only find, in the World, imitations. Thus
the World, for Plato, includes only the image of God, and imitations
of his ideas, and never God and his ideas.

Plato has definite reasons for this gap between the transient world
and the eternal nature of God. He is avoiding difficulties, although he
only achieves the feeblest of solutions. What metaphysics requires is
a solution exhibiting the plurality of individuals as consistent with the
unity of the Universe, and a solution which exhibits the World as
requiring its union with God, and God as requiring his union with the
World. Sound doctrine also requires an understanding how the Ideals
in God's nature, by reason of their status in his nature, are thereby
persuasive elements in the creative advance. Plato grounded these
derivations from God upon his will; whereas metaphysics requires
that the relationships of God to the World should lie beyond the
accidents of will, and that they be founded upon the necessities of the
nature of God and the nature of the World.

These problems came before the Christian theologians in highly
special forms. They had to consider the nature of God. On this topic,
there can be no doubt that the Arian solution, involving a derivative
Image, is orthodox Platonism, though it be heterodox Christianity.
The accepted solution of a multiplicity in the nature of God, each
component being unqualifiedly Divine, involves a doctrine of mutual

immanence in the divine nature. I am not in any way venturing upon a decision upon the correctness of the original assumption of this multiplicity. The point is the recourse to a doctrine of mutual immanence.

Again, the theologians had also to construct a doctrine of the person of Christ. And again they rejected the doctrine of an association of the human individual with a divine individual, involving responsive imitations in the human person. They decided for the direct immanence of God in the one person of Christ. They also decided for some sort of direct immanence of God in the World generally. This was their doctrine of the third person of the Trinity. I am not making any judgment about the details of their theology, for example, about the Trinitarian doctrine. My point is that in the place of Plato's solution of secondary images and imitations they demanded a direct doctrine of immanence. It is in this respect that they made a metaphysical discovery. They pointed out the way in which Platonic metaphysics should develop, if it was to give a rational account of the rôle of the persuasive agency of God.

Unfortunately, the theologians never made this advance into general metaphysics. The reason for this check was another unfortunate presupposition. The nature of God was exempted from all the metaphysical categories which applied to the individual things in this temporal world. The concept of him was a sublimation from its barbaric origin. He stood in the same relation to the whole World as early Egyptian or Mesopotamian kings stood to their subject populations. Also the moral characters were very analogous. In the final metaphysical sublimation, he became the one absolute, omnipotent, omniscient source of all being, for his own existence requiring no relations to anything beyond himself. He was internally complete. Such a conception fitted on very well to the Platonic doctrine of subordinate derivations. The final insistence, after much wavering, on the immanence of God was therefore all the more a fine effort of metaphysical imagination on the part of the theologians of the early Christian ages. But their general concept of the Deity stopped all further generalization. They made no effort to conceive the World in terms of the metaphysical categories by means of which they interpreted God, and they made no effort to conceive God in terms of the metaphysical categories which they applied to the World. For them, God was eminently real, and the World was derivatively real. God was necessary to the World, but the World was not necessary to God. There was a gulf between them.

The worst of a gulf is, that it is very difficult to know what is happening on the further side of it. This has been the fate of the God of traditional theology. It is only by drawing the long bow of mysticism that evidences for his existence can be collected from our temporal World. Also the worst of unqualified omnipotence is that it is accompanied by responsibility for every detail of every happening. This whole topic is discussed by Hume in his famous Dialogues.

SECTION V. I am suggesting that Protestant theology should develop as its foundation an interpretation of the Universe which grasps its unity amid its many diversities. The interpretation to be achieved is a reconciliation of seeming incompatibilities. But these incompatibilities are not hypothetical. They are there on the stage of history, undoubted and claiming interpretation. There stand in the public view the persuasiveness of the eternal ideals, the same today as when realized in the Founder of Christianity, and the compulsoriness of physical nature, which passes and yet remains, and the compulsoriness of that realized urge toward social union, such as the Roman Empire, which was then, and is now as it were a dream. Nature changes and yet remains. The ideals declare themselves as timeless; and yet they pass on, as it were the flicker of a brightness.

It is the business of philosophical theology to provide a rational understanding of the rise of civilization, and of the tendernesses of mere life itself, in a world which superficially is founded upon the clashings of senseless compulsion. I am not disguising my belief that in this task, theology has largely failed. The notion of the absolute despot has stood in the way. The doctrine of Grace has been degraded, and the doctrines of the Atonement are mostly crude. The defect of the liberal theology of the last two hundred years is that it has confined itself to the suggestion of minor, vapid reasons why people should continue to go to church in the traditional fashion.

The last book in the Bible illustrates the barbaric elements which have been retained to the undoing of Christian intuition. In itself and apart from its bearing upon religious sentiment, it is one of the finest examples of imaginative literature as it stands translated in King James's Bible. Also, as an historical document, whether its origin be Christian or Jewish, it is of priceless value for the understanding of strains of thought prevalent when the Christian religion was in process of formation. Finally, the book only states, more pointedly and more vividly, ideas spread throughout the Old Testament and the New Testament, even in the Gospels themselves. Yet it is shocking to think that this book has been retained for the formation of religious sentiment, while the speech of Pericles, descriptive of the Athenian ideal of civilization, has remained neglected in this connection. What I am advocating can be symbolized by this shift in the final book of the authoritative collection of religious literature, namely, the replacement of the book of the Revelation of St. John the Divine by the imaginative account given by Thucydides of the Speech of Pericles to the Athenians. Neither of them is history: St. John never received just that revelation, nor did Pericles ever make just that speech.

SECTION VI. There remains for discussion one final question. I wish to emphasize the importance that, amid many divergencies of interpretation, the leaders of religious thought should today concentrate upon the Christian tradition and more particularly upon its historical origins. In the case of the more conservative schools of thought such advice is, of course, unnecessary, and indeed impertinent. But it is a question for discussion why the more radical schools should not cut entirely free from any appeal to the past, and concentrate entirely upon the contemporary world and contemporary examples. The summary answer is that in so far as such an appeal to tradition can be made with complete honesty, without any shadow of evasion, there is an enormous gain in popular effectiveness.

Civilization is constituted out of four elements, (1) Patterns of Behaviour, (2) Patterns of Emotion, (3) Patterns of Belief, and (4) Technologies. We can at once dismiss Technologies as beyond our topic, though all four constitutive elements interact upon each other. Also patterns of behaviour are in the long run sustained or modified by patterns of emotion and patterns of belief. It is the primary business of religion to concentrate upon emotion and belief.

Now, so far as concerns beliefs of a general character, it is much easier for them to destroy emotion than to generate it. In any survey of the adventure of ideas nothing is more surprising than the ineffectiveness of novel general ideas to acquire for themselves an appropriate emotional pattern of any intensity. Profound flashes of insight remain ineffective for centuries, not because they are unknown, but by reason of dominant interests which inhibit reaction to that type of generality. The history of religion is the history of the countless generations required for interest to attach itself to profound ideas. For this reason religions are so often more barbarous than the civilizations in which they flourish.

This faintness of impress of general ideas upon the human mind has another effect. It is difficult even for acute thinkers to understand the analogies between ideas expressed in diverse phraseologies and illustrated by different sorts of examples. Desperate intellectual battles have been fought by philosophers who have expressed the same idea in different ways. For both these reasons, if you want to make a new start in religion, based upon ideas of profound generality, you must be content to wait a thousand years. Religions are like species of animals: they do not originate from special creations.

Finally, if there be any truth in the contention that dogmatic finality of verbal expression is a mistaken notion, there is an enormous advantage in keeping together, with common modes of procedure, religious opinions of analogous types. They can learn from each other, borrow from each other, and individuals can make imperceptible transitions. Above all, they can learn to understand each other and to love.

Must "religion" always remain as a synonym for "hatred"? The great social ideal for religion is that it should be the common basis for the unity of civilization. In that way it justifies its insight beyond the transient clash of brute forces.

This discussion has concentrated upon three culminating phases, the thought of Plato, the life of Christ, and the first formative period of Christian theology. But this whole period of twelve centuries, with its legendary antecedents and its modern successors, is required to complete the tale of the Christian religion. The story is wholly concerned with the interplay of ideas belonging to different levels of insight. The religious spirit is always in process of being explained away, distorted, buried. Yet, since the travel of mankind toward civilization, it is always there.

The task of Theology is to show how the World is founded on something beyond mere transient fact, and how it issues in something beyond the perishing of occasions. The temporal World is the stage of finite accomplishment. We ask of Theology to express that element in perishing lives which is undying by reason of its expression of perfections proper to our finite natures. In this way we shall understand how life includes a mode of satisfaction deeper than joy or sorrow.

ETIENNE GILSON

The Intelligence in the
Service of Christ

Etienne Henry Gilson (1884–1978) taught the history of philosophy, especially of medieval philosophy, at the Sorbonne, at the Collège de France, and in Toronto. In *The Spirit of Medieval Philosophy*, his Gifford Lectures, he summarized the major themes of religious philosophy in the Middle Ages, and in this essay from a book entitled *Christianity and Philosophy* he explains the religious foundations of his philosophical and scholarly work.

"Love not the world, nor the things which are in the world. If any man love the world, the charity of the Father is not in him. For all that is in the world is the concupiscence of the flesh, and the concupiscence of the eyes, and the pride of life; which is not of the Father, but is of the world. And the world passeth away, and the concupiscence thereof: but he that doth the will of God abideth forever." Bossuet recalls these words of the first Epistle of John at the end of his *Treatise on Concupiscence*, and he adds to them this brief but pithy commentary: "The last words of this Apostle show us that the world, of which he is here speaking, is those who prefer visible and transient things to those invisible and everlasting." Allow me to add simply in my turn that, if we attain to an understanding of the meaning of this definition, the mighty problem we have to examine together will resolve itself.

We are in the world; whether we like it or not, it is a fact, and to be there or not to be there does not depend on us; but we ought not to be of the world. How is it possible to be in the world without being of it? That is the problem which has haunted the Christian conscience since the foundation of the Church, and which looms particularly large with regard to our intelligence. For it is quite true that the

Christian life offers us a radical solution of this difficulty: to leave the world, to renounce it completely by taking refuge in the monastic life. But in the first place, states of perfection will always remain the portion of an elite; but more important still, the perfect themselves flee from the world in order to save it by saving themselves, and it is a remarkable fact that the world doesn't always even permit them to save it. There will always be among us souls desirous of fleeing from the world, but it is by no means certain that the world will always permit them to flee from it; for not only does the world affirm itself, it does not even want to admit that some renounce it. That is the cruelest injury that can be inflicted on it. Now, the Christian use of the intelligence is an injury of the same sort, and perhaps, among all, that which wounds it most profoundly; for the more it takes account of the fact that the intelligence is the highest thing in man, the more it longs to arrogate its homage and subject it to itself alone. To deny it this homage is the first intellectual duty of the Christian. Why and how? That is what we have to find out.

The everlasting protest of the world against Christians is that they scorn it, and that by scorning it they misunderstand what constitutes the proper value of its nature: its goodness, its beauty, and its intelligibility. That explains the ceaseless reproaches directed against us, in the name of philosophy, of history, and of science: Christianity refuses to take the whole man, and, under the pretext of making him better, it mutilates him, forcing him to close his eyes to things that constitute the excellence of nature and life, to misunderstand the progress of society throughout history, and to hold suspect science which progressively discloses the laws of nature and those of societies. These reproaches, repeatedly flung at us, are so familiar as to cease to interest us; nevertheless, it is our duty never to cease replying to them, and above all never to lose sight ourselves of what is the reply to them. Yes, Christianity is a radical condemnation of the world, but it is at the same time an unreserved approbation of nature; for the world is not nature, it is nature shaping its course without God.

What is true of nature is eminently true of the intelligence, the crown of nature. In the evening of creation, God looked at His work and He judged, says the Scripture, that all that was very good. But what was best in His work was man, created to His image and likeness; and if we seek the basis of this divine likeness, we find it, says St. Augustine, *in mente*: in thought. Let us go further, still following the same doctor: we find that this likeness is in that part of thought which is, so to speak, the summit, that by which, in contact with the divine light of which it is a sort of reflection, it conceives truth. To seize truth here below by the intelligence, be it in an obscure and partial manner, while waiting to see it in its complete splendor — such is man's destiny according to Christianity. Indeed far from scorning knowledge, it cherishes it: *intellectum valde ama* [love the intelligence intensely].

Unless, therefore, a person pretends to know better than St. Augustine what Christianity is, he cannot reproach us with betraying it or accommodating it to the needs of the cause by following the advice of this saint: love intelligence, and love it very much. The truth is that if we love the intelligence as much as our adversaries, and sometimes even more, we do not love it in the same way. There is a love of the intelligence which consists in turning it toward visible and transient things: that belongs to the world; but there is another which consists in turning it toward the invisible and eternal: that belongs to Christians. It is, therefore, ours; and if we prefer it to the first, it is because it does not deny us anything the first would give us, and yet it overwhelms us with everything which the other is incapable of giving us.

That there is something in Christianity which its adversaries do not succeed in grasping is clearly seen in the contradictory character of the objections that they address to it, but it is also a consolation for us to note that their objections rest on such misunderstandings. For they reproach it with putting man at the center of everything, but also with underestimating his greatness; and I am willing to admit that we may be mistaken in saying one thing or the other, but not in saying them both at the same time. And what is true of man in general is true of the intelligence in particular. I could let a person reproach St. Thomas Aquinas with having betrayed the spirit of Christianity by unduly exalting the rights of the intelligence, or reproach him for having betrayed the spirit of philosophy by unduly exalting the rights of faith, but I cannot understand how he could do both at the same time. What mystery, therefore, must be hidden in the depths of the Christian man, that his most spontaneous and unvaried steps seem so mysterious to those who observe them from without!

This mystery, for it is really a mystery, is the mystery of Jesus Christ. It is enough to be informed, no matter how vaguely, as to what Christianity is, in order to know in what this mystery consists. By the Incarnation, God became man; that is to say, the two natures, divine and human, are found united in the person of Christ. What is less well known to those who adhere to this mystery by faith is the astonishing transformation which He introduced into all nature and consequently into the manner in which we must henceforth conceive it. One ought rather to say the astonishing transformations, for this mystery includes in it so many others that one would never have done considering the consequences of it.

Let us be content here with examining one of them: that which leads us directly to the heart of our subject. From the moment human nature was assumed by the divine nature in the person of Christ, God no longer dominates and governs nature solely as God, but also as man. If among all men there is one who truly merits the title of Man-God, how could such a one not be also the chief and the sovereign of all the others, in short, their king? That is why Christ is not only the spiritual sovereign of the world, but also its temporal sovereign. But we know, on the other hand, that the Church is the mystical body of Christ: that its faithful are the members of this mystical body, that is to say, according to the doctrine of St. Paul: the members of Christ; all the faithful are, therefore, in so far as they are members of Christ, priests and kings: *"Et quod est amplius,"* says St. Thomas, *"omnes Christi fideles, in quantum sunt membra ejus, reges et sacerdotes dicuntur"* [And what is more, all believers in Christ, inasmuch as they are his members, are called kings and priests]. There is, then, henceforth, in every Christian, as an image, and even as a participation of this supreme mystery, humanity divinized by grace, reclothed, in its very misery, by a dignity at once sacerdotal and royal, which makes up the mystery of the Christian man.

Of this prodigious transformation of nature by the Incarnation we have an interpretation of incomparable profundity in Pascal, for that is what gives to his work the plenitude of its meaning. That we know God only through the person of Christ, Who was God Himself living, speaking, and acting among us, God showing Himself as man to men in order to be known by them, is too evident; but the great discovery, or rediscovery, of Pascal is to have understood that the Incarnation, by profoundly changing the nature of man, has become the only means that there is for us to understand man. Such a truth gives a new meaning to our nature, to our birth, to our end. "Not only," wrote Pascal, "do we understand God only through Jesus Christ, but we understand ourselves only through Jesus Christ. We understand life and death only through Jesus Christ. Outside Jesus Christ we do not know what life is, nor death, nor God, nor ourselves."

Let us apply these principles to the exercise of our intelligence; we shall immediately see that that of the Christian, as opposed to one which knows not Jesus Christ, knows itself to be fallen and restored, incapable consequently of yielding its full return without grace, and, in this sense, just as the royalty of Christ dominates the order of nature and the order of society, so also it dominates the order of the intelligence. Perhaps we Catholics have forgotten it too much; perhaps we have never even truly understood it, and if ever there was a time that needed to understand it, it is indeed our own.

What, in fact, does this mystery teach us in regard to the ends and the nature of the intelligence?

Like the nature which it crowns, the intelligence is good; but it is only so if, by it and in it, the whole nature turns toward its end, which is to conform itself to God. But, by taking itself as its own end, the intelligence has turned away from God, turning nature with it, and grace alone can aid both of them in returning to what is really their end, since it is their origin. The "world" is just this refusal to participate in grace which separates nature from God, and the intelligence itself is of the world in so far as it joins with it in rejecting grace. The intelligence which accepts grace is that of the Christian. And it is in the abandonment of precisely this Christian state of the intelligence that the world, because of its hate for it, ever urges us to accompany it.

That is what constitutes the real danger for us. We have no doubts concerning the truth of Christianity; we are firmly resolved to think as Christians; but do we know what must be done in order to accomplish that? Do we even know exactly in what Christianity consists? The first Christians knew it, because Christianity then was very near its beginnings, and the adversary against which it fought could not be unknown or misconceived by anyone; it was paganism, that is to say, ignorance at once of sin which damns and the grace of Jesus Christ which saves. That is why the Church, not only then but throughout the ages, has especially recalled to men the corruption of nature by sin, the weakness of reason without Revelation, the impotence of the will to do good when it is not aided by grace. When St. Augustine battled against Pelagius, who called himself Christian and thought himself Christian, it was against an attempt of paganism to restore the ancient naturalism and introduce it into the very heart of Christianity, that the great doctor fought. The naturalism of the Renaissance was another attempt of the same kind and we are still, today, in a world which believes itself naturally healthy, just, and good, because, having forgotten sin and grace, it takes its corruption for the rule of nature itself.

There is nothing in all that which the Christian may not and even ought not to expect. We know that the battle of good against evil will end only with the world itself. What is more serious is that paganism may ceaselessly try to penetrate within Christianity itself, as in the time of Pelagius, and may succeed in the attempt. That is a never-ending danger for us and one which we can avoid only with great difficulty. To live as Christians, to feel as Christians, to think as Christians in a society which is not Christian, when we see, hear, and read almost nothing which does not offend or contradict Christianity; when especially life places an obligation on us, and charity often gives us the duty of not making a visible break with the ideas and customs that we reprove, all that is difficult and hardly possible. That is also the reason why we are continually tempted to diminish or adapt our truth, in order to lessen the distance which separates our ways of thinking from those of the world, or indeed, and sometimes in all sincerity, in the hope of rendering Christianity more acceptable to the world and of seconding its work of salvation.

Hence the errors, the looseness of thought, and the compromises against which, at all times, the zeal of certain reformers has rebelled. The restoration of Christianity to the purity of its essence was in fact the first intention of Luther and Calvin; such is still today that of the illustrious Calvinistic theologian, Karl Barth, who employs all his powers to purify liberal Protestantism from naturalism, and to restore the Reform itself to the unconditional respect of the word of God. We all know how energetically he pursues that aim. God speaks, says K. Barth; man listens and repeats what God has said. Unfortunately, as is inevitable from the moment that a man sets himself up as His interpreter: God speaks, the Barthian listens and repeats what Barth has said. That is why, if we believe this new gospel of his, God would be reputed as having said that, ever since the first sin, nature is so totally corrupted that nothing of it remains but its very corruption, a mass of perdition which grace can indeed still pardon, but which nothing henceforth could ever heal. Thus, then, in order the better to fight against paganism and Pelagianism, this doctrine invites us to despair of nature, to renounce all effort to save reason and rechristianize it.

It is these two perils which ceaselessly plague us, and which, lest our thought be free from all attack, sometimes reduce us to a state of uncertainty as to what is or is not Christian. We forget the golden rule which decides all issues and dissipates every confusion, and one which we ought to have ever present to thought as the light which no obscurity can resist. It is that Catholicism teaches before everything the restoration of wounded nature by the grace of Jesus Christ. The restoration of nature: so there must be a nature, and of what value, since it is the work of a God Who created it and recreated it by repurchasing it at the price of His own blood! Thus grace presupposes nature, and the excellence of nature which it comes to heal and transfigure. As opposed to Calvinism and Lutheranism, the Church refuses to despair of nature, as if sin had totally corrupted it, but she tenderly bends over it, to heal its sores and save it. The God of our Church is not only a judge Who pardons, He is a judge Who can pardon only because He is first a doctor Who heals. But if she doesn't despair of nature, neither does the Church hope that it can heal itself. Just as she opposes the despair of Calvinism, so too she opposes the foolish hope of naturalism, which seeks in the malady itself the principle of its cure. The truth of Catholicism is not a mean between two errors, which would participate in both the one and the other, but a real truth, that is to say a peak, from which it is possible to discover both what the errors are and what makes them to be so. For the Calvinist, a Catholic is so respectful of nature that he is in nothing distinguished from a pagan, save by an additional blindness which makes him degrade even Christianity itself into paganism. But the Catholic well knows that there is nothing in that, and that it is the Calvinist who, confounding nature with the world, can no longer love nature under the world which clothes it, that is to say, love the work of God while hating sin which deforms it. For the pagan, the Christian saint is an enemy of nature, who rushes furiously in a foolish rage to torture it and even to mutilate it; but the Catholic knows well that he chastises nature only out of love for it: the evil which he fights against has entered too deeply into it to be able to be plucked out of it without making it suffer. Just as Calvinism despairs of nature while believing to despair only of its corruption, so naturalism puts its hope only in corruption when it thinks it is putting it in nature. Catholicism alone knows exactly what is nature, and what is the world, and what is grace, but it knows it only because it keeps its eyes fixed on the concrete union of nature and of grace in the Redeemer of nature, the person of Jesus Christ.

To imitate the Church ought to be our rule, if we wish to put our intelligence at the service of Christ the King. For, to serve Him, is to unite our efforts to His; to make ourselves, according to the word of St. Paul, His co-operators, that is to say, work with Him, or permit Him to work in us and through us for the salvation of the intelligence blinded by sin. But to work thus, it will be necessary for us to follow the example He Himself gives us: to free the nature which the world hides from us, to make that use of the intelligence to which God destined it when creating it.

It is here, it seems to me, that we have to make a return on ourselves, to ask ourselves if we are doing our duty and especially if we are doing it well. We have all met, either in history or indeed round about us, Christians who believe they are rendering homage to God by affecting, in regard to science, philosophy, and art, an indifference which sometimes approaches contempt. But this contempt may express either supreme greatness or supreme littleness. I like to be told that all philosophy is not worth an hour of trouble, when he who tells me so is called Pascal, that is to say a man who is at once one of the greatest philosophers, one of the greatest scientists, and one of the greatest artists of all time. A person always has the right to disdain what he surpasses, especially if what he disdains is not so much the thing loved as the excessive attachment which enslaves us to it. Pascal despised neither science nor philosophy, but he never pardoned them for having once hidden from him the most profound mystery of charity. Let us be careful, therefore, we who are not Pascal, of despising what perhaps surpasses us, for science is one of the highest praises of God: the understanding of what God has made.

That is not all. No matter how high science may be, it is only too clear that Jesus Christ did not come to save men by science or philosophy; He came to save all men, *even* philosophers and scientists; and though these human activities are not indispensable to salvation, yet even they have need of being saved as does this whole order of nature which grace has come to repurchase. But it is necessary to be careful not to save them by an indiscreet zeal, which, under the pretense of purifying them more completely, would only result in corrupting their essences. There is reason to fear that this fault is committed quite often, and this with the best intentions in the world, in view of what certain defenders of the faith call the apologetical use of science. An excellent formula, no doubt, yet only when one knows not only what science is, but also what apologetics is.

To be an efficacious apologist, it is necessary first to be a theologian; I will even say, an excellent theologian. That is rarer than we might think, which will be a scandal to those who speak of theology only by hearsay, or are content with reciting its formulas without having taken time to plumb their significance. But if one wishes to make an apologetic from science, it is not even sufficient that he be an excellent theologian; he must also be an excellent savant. I say savant advisedly, and not merely an intelligent and cultivated man more or less anointed by science. If one wishes to practice science for God, the first condition is to practice science for itself, or as if one practiced it for itself, since that is the only way of acquiring it. The same holds for philosophy. It is self-delusion to think to serve God by taking a certain number of formulas which bespeak what one knows ought to be said, without understanding why what they say is true. It is not even serving Him to denounce errors, however false they may be, while showing that one does not even understand in what they are false. At least we can say that it is not serving Him as a savant or as a philosopher, which is all we are for the moment concerned in showing. And I will add that the same thing holds for art, for it is necessary to possess it before pretending to put it at the service of God. We are told that it is faith which constructed the cathedrals of the middle ages. Without doubt, but faith would have constructed nothing at all if there had not also been architects; and if it is true that the façade of Notre Dame of Paris is a yearning of the soul toward God, that does not prevent its being also a geometrical work. It is necessary to know geometry in order to construct a façade which may be an act of love.

Catholics, who confess the eminent value of nature because it is a work of God, let us therefore show our respect for it by positing as the first rule of our action, that *piety never dispenses with technique*. For technique is that without which even the most lively piety is incapable of using nature for God. No one, nor anything, obliges the Christian to busy himself with science, art, or philosophy, for other ways of serving God are not wanting; but *if that is the way of serving God that he has chosen*, the end itself, which he proposes for himself in studying them, binds him to excellence. He is bound, by the very intention which guides him, to become a good savant, a good philosopher, or a good artist. That is for him the only way of becoming a good servant.

Such is, after all, the teaching of the Church and the example she has transmitted to us. Did not St. Paul say that "the invisible perfections of God, His eternal power and dignity are, since the creation of the world, rendered visible to the intelligence by means of His works?" That is why so many doctors, who were at the same time savants, lovingly bent over the work of creation. For them, to study it is to study God in His works; never did a St. Albert the Great think to know enough about nature, because the better he knew it, the better also he knew God. But there are not two ways of knowing it: a person possesses science or he doesn't possess it, he studies things scientifically or is resigned to never knowing anything about them. St. Albert the Great became, therefore, first of all a savant, in the proper sense of the term. Of those who are astonished or scandalized, he says that, brute beasts, they blaspheme what they do not know. He knows what he is doing: he does not wait until the care of repairing an evil already committed obliges him to busy himself in his turn with science in order to remedy it. He does not believe in the policy of letting the adversaries do everything with the intention of later joining their school in order to learn laboriously the use of the weapons that will be turned against them. Albert studied the sciences against no one, but for God. When you find a man of that sort, he does not waste his time proving that the teaching of science does not contradict that of the Church: he suppresses the question by his example, showing the world that a man can be a man of science, because he is a man of God. Such is also the attitude the Church recommends to us. By making St. Albert the Great the patron of Catholic schools, she reminds us permanently that these schools ought never be afraid of placing the level of their teaching and of their scientific exigencies too high. Everything is worth the trouble of being well done that is worth the trouble of being done for God.

Still we must never forget that it is for Him that it is being done, and to forget that is the second danger which threatens us. To serve God by science or art, it is necessary to begin by practicing them *as if* these disciplines were in themselves their own ends; and it is difficult to make such an effort without being taken in. So much the more difficult is it when we are surrounded by savants and artists who treat them effectively as ends. Their attitude is a spontaneous expression of naturalism or, to give its old name, which is its name for all time, of paganism, into which society ceaselessly tends to fall back because it has never completely left it. It is important, however, to free ourselves from it. It is impossible to place the intelligence at the service of God without respecting integrally the rights of the intelligence: otherwise it would not be the intelligence that is put at His service; but still more is it impossible to do so without respecting the rights of God: otherwise it is no longer at His service that the intelligence is placed. What has to be done in order to observe this second condition?

Here, with due apology, I am going to be obliged to play the thankless role of one who denounces errors, not only among his adversaries, but among his friends. To excuse such a one, it is necessary to remember that he who accuses his friends accuses himself in the first place. The ardor of his criticisms expresses above all the consciousness of the fault which he himself has committed and into which he always feels in danger of falling again. I believe, therefore, that I ought to say, first of all, that one of the gravest evils from which Catholicism suffers today is that Catholics are no longer proud enough of their faith. This lack of pride is unfortunately not incompatible with a certain satisfaction in what Catholics do or say, nor with an optimistic air more proper in a party than in a Church. What I regret is that instead of confessing in all simplicity what we owe to our Church and to our faith, instead of showing what they bring to us and what we would not have without them, we believe it good politics or good tactics, in the interests of the Church itself, to act as if, after all, we distinguish ourselves in no way from others. What is the greatest praise that many among us may hope for? The greatest that the world can give them: he is a Catholic, but he is really very nice, you would never think he was one.

Ought not the very contrary be desired? Not indeed Catholics who would wear their faith as a feather in their hat, but Catholics who would make Catholicism so enter into their everyday lives and work that the unbelieving would come to wonder what secret force animated that work and that life, and that, having discovered it, they would say to themselves, on the contrary: he is a very good man, and now I know why: it is because he is a Catholic.

In order that we may be thus thought of, it is necessary that we ourselves believe in the efficacy of the divine work in transforming and redeeming nature. Let us believe in it, and let us say so on occasion, or at least let us not deny it when we are asked about it. That is not what we always do. If there is one principle that our doctors have transmitted to us and insistently recommended, it is that philosophy is the handmaid of theology. Not a single one of the great theologians has not said so; not one of our great popes has failed to recall it to us. And yet it is hardly the fashion to speak of it today, even among Catholics. Men endeavor rather to show that the formula does not really mean what it appears to mean. They think it clever to present the Christian who philosophizes as a good philosopher, because he philosophizes as if he were not a Christian. In short, just as he is a very good man, he is a very good philosopher: it isn't noticeable that he is a Catholic. What would be interesting, on the contrary, would be a philosopher who, like St. Thomas or Duns Scotus, would take the lead in the philosophical movement of his time, precisely because he was Catholic.

It seems to be thought sometimes that a philosophy which confessed itself Catholic would be discredited in advance, and that, in order to make truth accepted, the cleverest way is to present it as if it had nothing to do with Catholicism. I am afraid that that is even a tactical error. If our traditional philosophy doesn't find today the audience we would wish for it, it is not at all because it is suspected of being sustained by a faith, it is indeed rather because, being so, it pretends not to be so, and because no one wishes to take seriously a doctrine which begins by denying the most evident of its sources. Run through the history of French philosophy in these latter years; you will see that Catholic thinkers have been taken seriously by the unbelieving in the exact measure in which they have put in the first place what, for them, is really first: the person of Jesus Christ and His grace. Let a Pascal or a Malebranche be born to us tomorrow, I promise them that no one will reproach them for being Catholics, for everybody will know that their Catholicism itself is the source of their greatness. They will wonder: whence comes this greatness to them, and perhaps will desire the faith which has given it to them.

It doesn't depend on us that we be a Pascal, a Malebranche or a Maine de Biran, but we can prepare the ground which will favor the action of their successors when they do come. We can so act that it may become easy for their successors to surpass these great minds, by clearing the ground of difficulties which, avoidable in themselves, might otherwise retard their action. We shall do so only by restoring in their fullness the Christian values; that is to say, above all by fully reestablishing the primacy of theology.

Here, as before, and with perhaps even greater emphasis, I will say that the great danger consists in thinking that, for the intelligence which wishes to refer itself to God, piety dispenses with technique. One might be tempted to address the contrary reproach to those who lean in that direction, and tell them that they act as if technique took the place of piety for them, but I do not think that that is what happens. Such men have not only acquired a faultless mastery of their science or art and are at times the admiration of their equals; they have also kept the most integral faith joined to the most lively piety. What they lack is that they do not know that, in order to link together the science they have acquired with the faith which they have preserved, a technique of faith is necessary along with that of science. What I see in them — rather let us say what we perceive fundamentally in ourselves — as an ever-present difficulty, is the inability of getting reason to guide itself by faith, because, for such a collaboration, faith no longer suffices; what is wanting is that sacred science which is the keystone of the edifice in which all the others ought to take their place; namely, theology. The most ardent theologian, animated by good intentions, we have said, will do as much harm as good if he pretends to "utilize" the sciences without having mastered them; but the savant, the philosopher, the artist, animated by the most ardent piety, run into the worst misfortunes if they pretend to refer their science to God without having, if not mastered, at least practiced the science of divine things. Practiced, I say, for, like the others, this science is learned only by practicing it. It alone can teach us what is the last end of nature and of intelligence, putting before our eyes these truths which God Himself has revealed to us and which enrich with such profound perspectives those truths which science teaches. As a converse, therefore, of what I said of an apologist, I will say here that it is possible to be a savant, a philosopher, and an artist without having studied theology, but it is impossible without it to become a Christian savant, philosopher, or artist. Without it, we can indeed be, on the one hand, Christians, and on the other hand savants, philosophers, or artists, but never without it will our Christianity descend into our science, into our philosophy, into our art, to reform them from within and vivify them. For that, the best will in the world would not suffice. It is necessary to know how to do it, in order to be able to do it; and, like the rest, it cannot be known without being learned.

If, therefore, we owe to our Catholicism our respect for nature, for the intelligence and the technique by which the intelligence scrutinizes nature, to it also we owe the knowledge of how to direct this science toward God, Who is its Author: *Deus scientiarum dominus* [God is the Lord of all forms of knowledge]. And just as I permitted myself to recommend the practice of the scientific disciplines or artistic disciplines *to those whose vocation it is to serve God in these domains*, so also I permit myself to recommend with all my power the teaching and practicing of theology to all those who, having mastered these techniques, seriously want to refer them to God.

We must not conceal from ourselves that, in the one case as in the other, it is a question here of undertaking a long effort. Nothing less will be necessary than the collaboration of all good wills qualified to succeed therein. We are here facing a new problem, which demands a new solution. In the middle ages, the sciences were the privilege of the clerics; that is to say, of those who possessed by their very state the science of theology. The problem, therefore, did not arise for them. Today, owing to an evolution, the investigation of which is not within our present scope, those who know theology are not those who make science, and those who make science, even when they do not despise theology, do not see the least inconvenience in not knowing it. There could be nothing more natural on the part of those who are not

Catholics, but nothing more abnormal on the part of those who make profession of Catholicism. For even if they experience the most sincere desire of putting their intelligence at the service of their faith, they will never succeed in doing so, because the science of faith is wanting to them. In order for them to succeed in that, it is necessary that they be taught, not how to make it (it is for them to find it), but what this sacred truth is with which their intelligence longs to be inspired.

It is important, therefore, to understand that we are living in a time when theology can no longer be the privilege of some specialists devoted to its study by the religious state which they have embraced. Doubtless the clerics ought to consider it as their proper science and retain the mastery in it, for it belongs to them in full right; and not merely retain it but exercise it in all its fullness, for it is a question of life or death for the future of the Christian life, in souls as well as in society. As soon as theology surrenders the exercise of its rights, it is the word of God which gives up making itself heard, nature which turns away from grace, and paganism which reclaims the rights that it has never surrendered. But, inversely, if it be desired that the word of God make itself heard, hearers are necessary to receive it. It is necessary that those who wish to work as Christians in the great work of science, philosophy, or art, themselves know how to hear His voice, and not only be instructed in His principles, but also and above all be imbued with them.

Here, less than anywhere else, it is neither the number nor the extent of the knowledges which is important; it will be sufficient to choose a very small number of fundamental principles, provided that the thought of those who receive them be impregnated with them, and that they inform it from within to the point of becoming one with it, of living in it and through it, as a grafted limb, which draws to itself all the sap from the tree in order to make it bear its fruit. To choose these principles, organize the teaching of them, give it to those she judges worthy of it, is the work of the teaching Church, not of the Church taught. But if the latter can in no case pretend to the mastery, it can at least present its demands and make known its needs. That is all I have wished to do, by demanding that the truth of faith be taught in its fullness and that the magisterial function of theology recover its full authority.

I would be nourishing the most naïve illusions if I thought I were now setting forth popular opinions. They are not so among the unbelieving, who are going to accuse me (some have already done so) of wishing to rekindle the funeral piles of the Inquisition and entrust the control of science to the Court of Inquisition. They are not so even among certain Catholics who, knowing that such ideas lead to such retorts, do not judge it expedient, in the interests of religion itself, to expose themselves to them. To reply to them, however, it is not necessary to reopen the discussion of what were the Inquisition and the affair of Galileo. Whatever happened in former times, the official and constant doctrine of the Church is that science is free in its own domains. No one pretends that philosophy and physics can or ought to be deduced from theology; St. Thomas even taught the exact opposite against certain of his contemporaries who were making of what we call today positive science a particular case of Revelation. To demand that science and philosophy regulate themselves under theology is first of all to ask of them to agree to recognize their limits, to be content to be a science or a philosophy, without pretending to transform themselves, as they are constantly doing, into a theology. It is also to ask of them to take into consideration certain truths taught by the Church regarding the origin and the end of nature and of man, not always with the intention of transforming them into so many scientific truths and to teach them as such (for they may be objects of pure faith) but to avoid in their researches aimless adventures, which are ultimately much more prejudicial to science itself than they can be to Revelation. The greater the authority of faith, the more those who are qualified to speak in its name ought to use prudence and wisdom before committing themselves, but the more exacting and rigorous the scientific disciplines in the matter of proofs, the more scrupulous ought they to be in putting on an equal footing all that they teach: the observed fact, the hypothesis controlled by experience, and the theory which, withdrawn from all experimental control properly so called, will be replaced tomorrow by another, although today it is imposed to all intent and purpose as a dogma. A visit to the cemetery of scientific doctrines that were irreconcilable with Revelation would take us by a great many graves. In our own lifetime, in the name of how many doctrines, abandoned since by their very authors, have we been summoned to renounce the teaching of the Church? How many false steps from which historians and savants would have been saved if they had listened to the voice of the Church when she warned them that they were exceeding the limits of their competence; that is to say, those of science itself? We ask of them nothing else: to renounce those costly and sterile experiments, and to recognize, in this sense, the primacy of theology, is precisely to renounce them.

Thus, therefore, to restore in their fullness the theological values, to do so in such a way that they descend into the thought of the savant who calculates or who experiments, into the reason of the philosopher who meditates, into the inspiration of the artist who creates, is truly to place the intelligence in the service of Christ the King, since it is to promote the coming of His reign, by aiding nature to be born again under the fruitful action of His grace and in the light of His truth. Such is the end, such also the means, and there is no other, for the only service that Christ demands from us is to aid Him in saving the world; but it is His word alone that saves. In order to co-operate with Him, let us therefore first of all listen to His word, repeat it as does the Church, and not hesitate to make it publicly when necessary. It does not depend on us that it be believed, but we can do very much toward making it respected; and if it happen that those among us who are not ashamed of the Gospel fail to get others to follow us, those who are ashamed of it can be sure not even to get others to respect them.

IV REVERENCE FOR LIFE

During the nineteenth and twentieth centuries no development has had more far-reaching consequences for religious faith than the discovery of the profound affinities between human life and all the rest of life. In many respects, of course, the "discovery" was in fact a rediscovery, for such affinities with all living beings have long been a central element in the world religions, over the full range from primitive religion to high religion (even if one accepts this highly suspect system of classification). It was, in the light of the long history of religion, only a brief episode when, particularly during the Enlightenment, an artificial distinction between "nature" and "culture" expelled such affinities from the vocabulary of worship and theology.

The rediscovery, however, came in considerable measure from an unexpected source: the Darwinian theory of evolution. Because of the emphasis placed, especially in various Western religions, upon a literal interpretation of the authoritative traditional accounts of the special origin of the human race, Darwin's assertion in his *Descent of Man* that there was a biological continuum between man and the lower forms of life seemed to be a threat to the idea of a special creation "in the image of God." But after the initial shock had worn off, there were many who began instead to see in this biological continuum the confirmation of a perennial religious insight. The English poet Samuel Taylor Coleridge was manifesting his affinity with the expressions of that insight in Eastern as well as Western religious thought when he wrote:

He prayeth best, who loveth best
All things both great and small;
For the dear God who loveth us,
He made and loveth all.

"Reverence for life" has become a way of affirming that continuum, especially as the ravages of the human pollution of the world have come to be seen as a sin of desecration.

Because this reverence for life was a lesson that those creeds laying claim to an exclusive revelation had to learn (or relearn) especially from faiths that had always been more inclusive in their view of religious truth, a new sense of continuity between the religions seemed to be connected with such a rediscovery of the biological continuum. Divine revelation had to be continuous, or it had not been authentic in the first place. For the gap between the Infinite "god above god" and all our finite efforts to speak about the Infinite is so much greater than any differences between one such effort and another that it ill behooves the adherents of any particular system to despise or ridicule other believers. The very principle that had seemed to be at stake in the controversies over evolution, the doctrine of the image of God, also seemed to imply this obligation to show respect for others as part of a due reverence for God the Creator and for all of God's creatures.

ALBERT SCHWEITZER

Reverence for Life

Albert Schweitzer (1875–1965), born in Alsace, was an internationally renowned New Testament scholar, a major figure in the reinterpretation of the music of Johann Sebastian Bach, and the recipient of the Nobel Prize for peace in 1952. Yet he will perhaps best be remembered for his ministry as a medical missionary at Lambaréné in French equatorial Africa and for his doctrine of "reverence for life," as stated in this sermon from February 16, 1919.

And one of the scribes came, and having heard them reasoning together, and perceiving that he had answered them well, asked him, Which is the first commandment of all? And Jesus answered him, The first of all the commandments is, Hear, O Israel; The Lord our God is one Lord: And thou shalt love the Lord thy God with all thy heart, and with all thy soul, and with all thy mind, and with all thy strength: this is the first commandment. And the second is like, namely this, Thou shalt love thy neighbour as thyself. There is none other commandment greater than these. And the scribe said unto him, Well, Master, thou hast said the truth: for there is one God; and there is none other but he: And to love him with all the heart, and with all the understanding, and with all the soul, and with all the strength, and to love his neighbour as himself, is more than all whole burnt offerings and sacrifices. And when Jesus saw that he answered discreetly, he said unto him, Thou art not far from the kingdom of God. And no man after that durst ask him any question.
MARK 12:28–34

THE SCRIBE WHO ASKS JESUS which commandment is the greatest is in search of knowledge. He wants information about a matter that concerns him, as it does many of his compatriots. In St. Matthew's Gospel, Chapter 22, the scribes pose this question to Jesus in order to tempt him. But the evangelist Mark surely has a better memory when he describes the sympathetic scene in which Jesus and the scribe for one moment have mutual understanding and look into one another's hearts, and then to go their separate ways.

In those days Israelite thinkers used to discuss the possibility of tracing all the commandments, both great and small, back to a single basic law. We, too, have a similar need. What is intrinsic good? I have read to you the eternal sayings of our Lord about forgiveness, mercy, love, and all the other characteristics that we as his disciples should act upon in the world. But we all seem to feel that these are only separate colors broken down from the whitelight of a basic ethical attitude which he requires from us.

Let me ponder this question with you now: What exactly is this basic ethical attitude? Later I will devote several meditations to questions on Christian ethics about which I have been thinking in far-off lands, in the loneliness of the jungle, always with these services here at St. Nicolai's in mind and in the confident hope that someday I might be permitted to speak to you about them.

The question of the basic ethical attitude is uppermost in our minds nowadays. We are forced to a recognition that previous generations and even we ourselves until recently refused to accept. Now we cannot escape it if we would be truthful: the Christian ethic has never become a power in the world. It has not sunk deep into the minds of men. It has been accepted only superficially, acknowledged in theory more than put into practice. Mankind behaves as if the teaching of Jesus did not exist, as if Christian behavior had no ethical principles at all.

Therefore, constantly repeating the ethical teaching of Jesus is of no use, nor is expounding it as though it were bound to win universal acceptance in the end. It is like trying to paint a wet wall with pretty colors. We first have to create a foundation for the understanding of the teaching and guide our world to a frame of mind in which the teachings of Jesus have meaning. It is by no means easy to interpret Jesus' teachings so as to make them practical to daily life. Let us take as an example the sayings about the greatest of the commandments. What does it mean to love God with all our heart and to do good only out of love for him? Follow up this train of thought and a whole world of new ideas will open. When in life have you chosen to do good out of love for God when you might otherwise have chosen to do evil?

Or take the other commandment: "Love thy neighbour as thyself." Truly, it is wonderful. I could give you the most alluring illustrations to prove it. But can it be done? Suppose you make a resolution to obey it literally, starting tomorrow. What would be the result in a few days?

This is the greatest riddle in Christian ethics. We cannot apply Jesus' teachings directly to our lives, however holy our desire to serve him. Our frustration then leads us to the great danger of making a reverent bow toward Jesus' words, praising them as the "ideal," but in reality leaving them unheeded.

Still another misunderstanding endangers the realization of Christian morality. A certain ethical attitude can easily make us arrogant. If we forgive our enemies, we think we are being virtuous. If we help a man who needs our assistance, we consider ourselves very noble indeed. We perform small acts of goodness possibly in the name of Christ, considering our deeds somehow different and better than those of other men. Thus we acquire a superior and complacent attitude which actually makes us more unethical than those who do not acknowledge the commandments of Jesus or try to live up to them. The demands of Jesus are difficult just because they require us to do something extraordinary. At the same time he asks us to regard these as something usual, ordinary. While the unusual is exactly what he demands of us. For he says that we should regard ourselves as unprofitable servants, however much we may have accomplished.

So there you have it. Now you know why we must think together about the intrinsic good. We want to learn to understand how the exalted demands of Jesus can be carried out in daily life. We wish to take them as the natural duty of man although they are so exalted in fact.

We want to grasp the underlying principle of all ethics and use that principle as the supreme law from which all ethical actions can be derived. Yes, but can morality be grasped at all? Is it not a matter of the heart? Does it not rest upon love? This we have been told again and again for two thousand years. And what is the result?

Let us study men around us both collectively and individually. Why are they so often unstable? Why are even the most devout among them, and often the pious in particular, capable of being swept by prejudice and passions of nationalism into judgments and courses of action entirely void of ethical truth? Because they lack an ethic based on reason and rooted in logic. Because they do not regard ethics as a natural endowment or as part of their faculty of reason.

Reason and heart must act together if a true morality is to be established. Herein lies the real problem for abstract ethics as well as for practical decisions of daily life.

The reason of which I speak penetrates the heart of the matter and embraces the whole of reality, including the realm of the will.

We experience a strange duality when we seek self-understanding in the light of the ethical will within us. On the one hand, we notice its connection with reason. On the other hand, we are forced into decisions that are not rational in ordinary terms but are expressions of demands that would normally be considered extravagant. In this duality, in this strange tension, lies the essence of ethics. We need not fear that an ethic based on reason is geared too low, that it may be too detached and heartless. For when reason really reaches the core of the matter it ceases to be cold reason, whether it wants to or not, and begins to speak with the melody of the heart. And the heart, when it tries to fathom itself, discovers that its realm overlaps the realm of reason. It has to pass through the land of reason to reach the furthest boundary of its own superfluous sphere. How can that be?

Let us explore the basic principle of goodness both from the heart's point of view and then from reason's point of view, and see where both meet.

The heart maintains that ethics is based on love. Let us explore this word. "Love" means harmony of being, community of being. Originally it applied to groups or persons who in some way belonged to one another, who had an inner reciprocal relationship, such as children and parents, married couples, or intimate friends. Morality requires that people we don't know should not be considered as strangers. That applies equally to those who are worse than strangers to us, because we feel an aversion toward them or because they have shown hostility to us. Even such people we must treat as our friends. In the last analysis the commandment of love means this: no one is a stranger to you; every man's welfare is your concern. We so often take for granted that some people are our immediate concern while others are a matter of indifference to us. Clearly this natural feeling is not permitted by ethical standards. Jesus rules out behaving toward one another as strangers when he says. "The other man must mean as much to you as your own self. You must feel his welfare as your own direct concern."

Further, let the heart explain the first commandment: "Thou shalt love thy God with all thy heart and with all thy mind and with all thy strength." To love God — this remote, unfathomable being! Here it is plain that the word "love," used ethically, is meant in a figurative sense. Should God, who has no need of us, be loved as though he were a creature we meet in daily life? In a human context, love means, for example, sharing an experience, showing compassion, and helping one another. But our love of God is akin to reverent love. God is infinite life. Thus the most elementary ethical principle, when un-

derstood by the heart, means that out of reverence for the unfathomable, infinite, and living Reality we call God, we must never consider
ourselves strangers toward any human being. Rather, we must bind
ourselves to the task of sharing his experiences and try being of help
to him.

That, then, is what the heart says when it tries to give meaning to
the command of love toward God and neighbor.

But now let reason speak. Let us pretend that we have learned
nothing about ethics from the past, and see how far we can get by
pondering the forces that influence our actions. Can reason, too, make
us step outside ourselves?

People often say that only egotism can be justified by reason. What
can I do to have it easy? That is their reason's wisdom, nothing else.
At most it can teach us a certain integrity and justice, and these things
are more or less the recognized key to happiness. Reason is the desire
for knowledge and the desire for happiness, and both are mysteriously
connected with one another, in an inward way.

Desire for wisdom! Explore everything around you, penetrate to the
furthest limits of human knowledge, and always you will come up
against something inexplicable in the end. It is called life. It is a
mystery so inexplicable that the knowledge of the educated and the
ignorant is purely relative when contemplating it.

But what is the difference between the scientist who observes in his
microscope the most minute and unexpected signs of life; and the old
farmer who by contrast can barely read or write, who stands in
springtime in his garden and contemplates the buds opening on the
branches of his trees? Both are confronted with the riddle of life. One
may be able to describe life in greater detail, but for both it remains
equally inscrutable. All knowledge is, in the final analysis, the knowledge of life. All realization is amazement at this riddle of life — a
reverence for life in its infinite and yet ever-fresh manifestations. How
amazing this coming into being, living, and dying! How fantastic that
in other existences something comes into being, passes away again,
comes into being once more, and so forth from eternity to eternity!
How can it be? We can do all things, and we can do nothing. For in
all our wisdom we cannot create life. What we create is dead.

Life means strength, will, arising from the abyss, dissolving into the
abyss again. Life is feeling, experience, suffering. If you study life
deeply, looking with perceptive eyes into the vast animated chaos of
this creation, its profundity will seize you suddenly with dizziness. In
everything you recognize yourself. The tiny beetle that lies dead in

your path — it was a living creature, struggling for existence like yourself, rejoicing in the sun like you, knowing fear and pain like you. And now it is no more than decaying matter — which is what you will be sooner or later, too.

You walk outside and it is snowing. You carelessly shake the snow from your sleeves. It attracts your attention: a lacy snowflake glistens in your hand. You can't help looking at it. See how it sparkles in a wonderfully intricate pattern. Then it quivers, and the delicate needles of which it consists contract. It melts and lies dead in your hand. It is no more. The snowflake which fluttered down from infinite space upon your hand, where it sparkled and quivered and died — that is yourself. Wherever you see life — that is yourself!

What is this recognition, this knowledge within the reach of the most scientific and the most childlike? It is reverence for life, reverence for the unfathomable mystery we confront in our universe, an existence different in its outward appearance and yet inwardly of the same character as our own, terribly similar, awesomely related. The strangeness between us and other creatures is here removed.

Reverence for the infinity of life means removal of the alienation, restoration of empathy, compassion, sympathy. And so the final result of knowledge is the same as that required of us by the commandment of love. Heart and reason agree together when we desire and dare to be men who seek to fathom the depths of the universe.

Reason discovers the bridge between love for God and love for men — love for all creatures, reverence for all being, compassion with all life, however dissimilar to our own.

I cannot but have reverence for all that is called life. I cannot avoid compassion for everything that is called life. That is the beginning and foundation of morality. Once a man has experienced it and continues to do so — and he who has once experienced it will continue to do so — he is ethical. He carries his morality within him and can never lose it, for it continues to develop within him. He who has never experienced this has only a set of superficial principles. These theories have no root in him, they do not belong to him, and they fall off him. The worst is that the whole of our generation had only such a set of superficial principles. Then the time came to put the ethical code to the test, and it evaporated. For centuries the human race had been educated with only a set of superficial principles. We were brutal, ignorant, and heartless without being aware of it. We had no scale of values, for we had no reverence for life.

It is our duty to share and maintain life. Reverence concerning all life is the greatest commandment in its most elementary form. Or expressed in negative terms: "Thou shalt not kill." We take this prohibition so lightly, thoughtlessly plucking a flower, thoughtlessly stepping on a poor insect, thoughtlessly, in terrible blindness because everything takes its revenge, disregarding the suffering and lives of our fellow men, sacrificing them to trivial earthly goals.

Much talk is heard in our times about building a new human race. How are we to build a new humanity? Only by leading men toward a true, inalienable ethic of our own, which is capable of further development. But this goal cannot be reached unless countless individuals will transform themselves from blind men into seeing ones and begin to spell out the great commandment which is: Reverence for Life. Existence depends more on reverence for life than the law and the prophets. Reverence for life comprises the whole ethic of love in its deepest and highest sense. It is the source of constant renewal for the individual and for mankind.

RALPH WALDO EMERSON

Divinity School Address

Ralph Waldo Emerson (1803–1882) had been a Unitarian
minister in Boston, but resigned from the ministry to devote himself to lecturing (Phi Beta Kappa Address on "The
American Scholar") and writing (*Nature, Representative
Men,* and other books). When the graduating class of the
Harvard Divinity School invited him to address them in
1838, he delivered the following "Address," whose radical
repercussions shocked the entire American Protestant
community.

IN THIS REFULGENT summer it has been a luxury to draw the breath of
life. The grass grows, the buds burst, the meadow is spotted with
fire and gold in the tint of flowers. The air is full of birds, and sweet
with the breath of the pine, the balm-of-Gilead, and the new hay.
Night brings no gloom to the heart with its welcome shade.
Through the transparent darkness the stars pour their almost
spiritual rays. Man under them seems a young child, and his huge
globe a toy. The cool night bathes the world as with a river, and
prepares his eyes again for the crimson dawn. The mystery of
nature was never displayed more happily. The corn and the wine
have been freely dealt to all creatures, and the never-broken silence
with which the old bounty goes forward, has not yielded yet one
word of explanation. One is constrained to respect the perfection of
this world, in which our senses converse. How wide; how rich;
what invitation from every property it gives to every faculty of man!
In its fruitful soils; in its navigable sea; in its mountains of metal
and stone; in its forests of all woods; in its animals; in its chemical
ingredients; in the powers and path of light, heat, attraction, and
life, it is well worth the pith and heart of great men to subdue and
enjoy it. The planters, the mechanics, the inventors, the astron-

omers, the builders of cities, and the captains, history delights to honor.

But the moment the mind opens, and reveals the laws which traverse the universe, and make things what they are, then shrinks the great world at once into a mere illustration and fable of this mind. What am I? and What is? asks the human spirit with a curiosity new-kindled, but never to be quenched. Behold these outrunning laws, which our imperfect apprehension can see tend this way and that, but not come full circle. Behold these infinite relations, so like, so unlike; many, yet one. I would study, I would know, I would admire forever. These works of thought have been the entertainments of the human spirit in all ages.

A more secret, sweet, and overpowering beauty appears to man when his heart and mind open to the sentiment of virtue. Then instantly he is instructed in what is above him. He learns that his being is without bound; that, to the good, to the perfect, he is born, low as he now lies in evil and weakness. That which he venerates is still his own, though he has not realized it yet. *He ought.* He knows the sense of that grand word, though his analysis fails entirely to render account of it. When in innocency, or when by intellectual perception, he attains to say, — "I love the Right; Truth is beautiful within and without, forevermore. Virtue, I am thine: save me: use me: thee will I serve, day and night, in great, in small, that I may be not virtuous, but virtue"; — then is the end of the creation answered, and God is well pleased.

The sentiment of virtue is a reverence and delight in the presence of certain divine laws. It perceives that this homely game of life we play, covers, under what seem foolish details, principles that astonish. The child amidst his baubles, is learning the action of light, motion, gravity, muscular force; and in the game of human life, love, fear, justice, appetite, man, and God, interact. These laws refuse to be adequately stated. They will not by us or for us be written out on paper, or spoken by the tongue. They elude, evade our persevering thought, and yet we read them hourly in each other's faces, in each other's actions, in our own remorse. The moral traits which are all globed into every virtuous act and thought, — in speech, we must sever, and describe or suggest by painful enumeration of many particulars. Yet, as this sentiment is the essence of all religion, let me guide your eye to the precise objects of the sentiment, by an enumeration of some of those classes of facts in which this element is conspicuous.

The intuition of the moral sentiment is an insight of the perfection of the laws of the soul. These laws execute themselves. They are out of time, out of space, and not subject to circumstance. Thus; in the soul of man there is a justice whose retributions are instant and entire. He who does a good deed, is instantly ennobled himself. He who does a mean deed, is by the action itself contracted. He who puts off impurity, thereby puts on purity. If a man is at heart just, then in so far is he God; the safety of God, the immortality of God, the majesty of God do enter into that man with justice. If a man dissemble, deceive, he deceives himself, and goes out of acquaintance with his own being. A man in the view of absolute goodness, adores, with total humility. Every step so downward, is a step upward. The man who renounces himself, comes to himself by so doing.

See how this rapid intrinsic energy worketh everywhere, righting wrongs, correcting appearances. and bringing up facts to a harmony with thoughts. Its operation in life, though slow to the senses, is, at last, as sure as in the soul. By it, a man is made the Providence to himself, dispensing good to his goodness, and evil to his sin. Character is always known. Thefts never enrich; alms never impoverish; murder will speak out of stone walls. The least admixture of a lie, — for example, the smallest mixture of vanity, the least attempt to make a good impression, a favorable appearance, — will instantly vitiate the effect. But speak the truth, and all nature and all spirits help you with unexpected furtherance. Speak the truth, and all things alive or brute are vouchers, and the very roots of the grass underground there, do seem to stir and move to bear you witness. See again the perfection of the Law as it applies itself to the affections, and becomes the law of society. As we are, so we associate. The good, by affinity, seek the good; the vile, by affinity, the vile. Thus of their own volition, souls proceed into heaven, into hell.

These facts have always suggested to man the sublime creed, that the world is not the product of manifold power, but of one will, of one mind; and that one mind is everywhere active, in each ray of the star, in each wavelet of the pool; and whatever opposes that will, is every-where baulked and baffled, because things are made so, and not otherwise. Good is positive. Evil is merely privative, not absolute. It is like cold, which is the privation of heat. All evil is so much death or nonentity. Benevolence is absolute and real. So much benevolence as a man hath, so much life hath he. For all things proceed out of this same spirit, which is differently named love, justice, temperance, in its different applications, just as the ocean receives different names on the several shores which it washes. All things proceed out of the same spirit, and all things conspire with it. Whilst a man seeks good ends, he is strong by the whole strength of nature. In so far as he roves from these ends, he bereaves himself of power, of auxiliaries; his being shrinks out of all remote channels, he becomes less and less, a mote, a point, until absolute badness is absolute death.

The perception of this law of laws always awakens in the mind a sentiment which we call the religious sentiment, and which makes our highest happiness. Wonderful is its power to charm and to command. It is a mountain air. It is the embalmer of the world. It is myrrh and storax, and chlorine and rosemary. It makes the sky and the hills sublime, and the silent song of the stars is it. By it, is the universe made safe and habitable, not by science or power. Thought may work cold and intransitive in things, and find no end or unity. But the dawn of the sentiment of virtue on the heart, gives and is the assurance that Law is sovereign over all natures; and the worlds, time, space, eternity, do seem to break out into joy.

This sentiment is divine and deifying. It is the beatitude of man. It makes him illimitable. Through it, the soul first knows itself. It corrects the capital mistake of the infant man, who seeks to be great by following the great, and hopes to derive advantages *from another*, — by showing the fountain of all good to be in himself, and that he, equally with every man, is an inlet into the deeps of Reason. When he says, "I ought"; when love warms him; when he chooses, warned from on high, the good and great deed; then, deep melodies wander through his soul from Supreme Wisdom. Then he can worship, and be enlarged by his worship; for he can never go behind this sentiment. In the sublimest flights of the soul, rectitude is never surmounted, love is never outgrown.

This sentiment lies at the foundation of society, and successively creates all forms of worship. The principle of veneration never dies out. Man fallen into superstition, into sensuality, is never wholly without the visions of the moral sentiment. In like manner, all the expressions of this sentiment are sacred and permanent in proportion to their purity. The expressions of this sentiment affect us deeper, greatlier, than all other compositions. The sentences of the oldest time, which ejaculate this piety, are still fresh and fragrant. This thought dwelled always deepest in the minds of men in the devout and contemplative East; not alone in Palestine, where it reached its purest expression, but in Egypt, in Persia, in India, in China. Europe has always owed to oriental genius, its divine impulses. What these holy bards said, all sane men found agreeable and true. And the unique impression of Jesus upon mankind, whose name is not so much written as ploughed into the history of this world, is proof of the subtle virtue of this infusion.

Meantime, whilst the doors of the temple stand open, night and day, before every man, and the oracles of this truth cease never, it is guarded by one stern condition; this, namely; It is an intuition. It cannot be received at second hand. Truly speaking, it is not instruction, but provocation, that I can receive from another soul. What he announces, I must find true in me, or wholly reject; and on his word, or as his second, be he who he may, I can accept nothing. On the contrary, the absence of this primary faith is the presence of degradation. As is the flood so is the ebb. Let this faith depart, and the very words it spake, and the things it made, become false and hurtful. Then falls the church, the state, art, letters, life. The doctrine of the divine nature being forgotten, a sickness infects and dwarfs the constitution. Once man was all; now he is an appendage, a nuisance. And because the indwelling Supreme Spirit cannot wholly be got rid of, the doctrine of it suffers this perversion, that the divine nature is attributed to one or two persons, and denied to all the rest, and denied with fury. The doctrine of inspiration is lost; the base doctrine of the majority of voices, usurps the place of the doctrine of the soul. Miracles, prophecy, poetry, the ideal life, the holy life, exist as ancient history merely; they are not in the belief, nor in the aspiration of society; but, when suggested, seem ridiculous. Life is comic or pitiful, as soon as the high ends of being fade out of sight, and man becomes near-sighted, and can only attend to what addresses the senses.

These general views, which, whilst they are general, none will contest, find abundant illustration in the history of religion, and especially in the history of the Christian church. In that, all of us have had our birth and nurture. The truth contained in that, you, my young friends, are now setting forth to teach. As the Cultus, or established worship of the civilized world, it has great historical interest for us. Of its blessed words, which have been the consolation of humanity, you need not that I should speak. I shall endeavor to discharge my duty to you, on this occasion, by pointing out two errors in its administration, which daily appear more gross from the point of view we have just now taken.

Jesus Christ belonged to the true race of prophets. He saw with open eye the mystery of the soul. Drawn by its severe harmony, ravished with its beauty, he lived in it, and had his being there. Alone in all history, he estimated the greatness of man. One man was true to what is in you and me. He saw that God incarnates himself in man, and evermore goes forth anew to take possession of his world. He said, in this jubilee of sublime emotion, "I am divine. Through me, God acts; through me, speaks. Would you see God, see me; or, see thee, when thou also thinkest as I now think." But what a distortion did his doctrine and memory suffer in the same, in the next, and the following ages! There is no doctrine of the Reason which will bear to be taught by the Understanding. The understanding caught this high chant from the poet's lips, and said, in the next age, "This was Jehovah come down out of heaven. I will kill you, if you say he was a man." The idioms of his language, and the figures of his rhetoric, have usurped the place of his truth; and churches are not built on his principles, but on his tropes. Christianity became a Mythus, as the poetic teaching of Greece and of Egypt, before. He spoke of miracles; for he felt that man's life was a miracle, and all that man doth, and he knew that this daily miracle shines, as the man is diviner. But the very word Miracle, as pronounced by Christian churches, gives a false impression; it is Monster. It is not one with the blowing clover and the falling rain.

He felt respect for Moses and the prophets; but no unfit tenderness at postponing their initial revelations, to the hour and the man that now is; to the eternal revelation in the heart. Thus was he a true man. Having seen that the law in us is commanding, he would not suffer it to be commanded. Boldly, with hand, and heart, and life, he declared it was God. Thus was he a true man. Thus is he, as I think, the only soul in history who has appreciated the worth of a man.

1. In thus contemplating Jesus, we become very sensible of the first defect of historical Christianity. Historical Christianity has fallen into the error that corrupts all attempts to communicate religion. As it appears to us, and as it has appeared for ages, it is not the doctrine of the soul, but an exaggeration of the personal, the positive, the ritual. It has dwelt, it dwells, with noxious exaggeration about the *person* of Jesus. The soul knows no persons. It invites every man to expand to the full circle of the universe, and will have no preferences but those of spontaneous love. But by this eastern monarchy of a Christianity, which indolence and fear have built, the friend of man is made the injurer of man. The manner in which his name is surrounded with expressions, which were once sallies of admiration and love, but are now petrified into official titles, kills all generous sympathy and liking. All who hear me, feel, that the language that describes Christ to Europe and America, is not the style of friendship and enthusiasm to a good and noble heart, but is appropriated and formal, — paints a demigod,

as the Orientals or the Greeks would describe Osiris or Apollo. Accept the injurious impositions of our early catechetical instruction, and even honesty and self-denial were but splendid sins, if they did not wear the Christian name. One would rather be

A pagan suckled in a creed outworn,

than to be defrauded of his manly right in coming into nature, and finding not names and places, not land and professions, but even virtue and truth foreclosed and monopolized. You shall not be a man even. You shall not own the world; you shall not dare, and live after the infinite Law that is in you, and in company with the infinite Beauty which heaven and earth reflect to you in all lovely forms; but you must subordinate your nature to Christ's nature; you must accept our interpretations; and take his portrait as the vulgar draw it.

That is always best which gives me to myself. The sublime is excited in me by the great stoical doctrine, Obey thyself. That which shows God in me, fortifies me. That which shows God out of me, makes me a wart and a wen. There is no longer a necessary reason for my being. Already the long shadows of untimely oblivion creep over me, and I shall decease forever.

The divine bards are the friends of my virtue, of my intellect, of my strength. They admonish me, that the gleams which flash across my mind, are not mine, but God's; that they had the like, and were not disobedient to the heavenly vision. So I love them. Noble provocations go out from them, inviting me also to emancipate myself; to resist evil; to subdue the world; and to Be. And thus by his holy thoughts, Jesus serves us, and thus only. To aim to convert a man by miracles, is a profanation of the soul. A true conversion, a true Christ, is now, as always, to be made, by the reception of beautiful sentiments. It is true that a great and rich soul, like his, falling among the simple, does so preponderate, that, as his did, it names the world. The world seems to them to exist for him, and they have not yet drunk so deeply of his sense, as to see that only by coming again to themselves, or to God in themselves, can they grow forevermore. It is a low benefit to give me something; it is a high benefit to enable me to do somewhat of myself. The time is coming when all men will see, that the gift of God to the soul is not a vaunting, overpowering, excluding sanctity, but a sweet, natural goodness, a goodness like thine and mine, and that so invites thine and mine to be and to grow.

The injustice of the vulgar tone of preaching is not less flagrant to Jesus, than it is to the souls which it profanes. The preachers do not see that they make his gospel not glad, and shear him of the locks of beauty and the attributes of heaven. When I see a majestic Epaminondas, or Washington; when I see among my contemporaries, a true orator, an upright judge, a dear friend; when I vibrate to the melody and fancy of a poem; I see beauty that is to be desired. And so lovely, and with yet more entire consent of my human being, sounds in my ear the severe music of the bards that have sung of the true God in all ages. Now do not degrade the life and dialogues of Christ out of the circle of this charm, by insulation and peculiarity. Let them lie as they befel, alive and warm, part of human life, and of the landscape, and of the cheerful day.

2. The second defect of the traditionary and limited way of using the mind of Christ is a consequence of the first; this, namely; that the Moral Nature, that Law of laws, whose revelations introduce greatness, — yea, God himself, into the open soul, is not explored as the fountain of the established teaching in society. Men have come to speak of the revelation as somewhat long ago given and done, as if God were dead. The injury to faith throttles the preacher; and the goodliest of institutions becomes an uncertain and inarticulate voice.

It is very certain that it is the effect of conversation with the beauty of the soul, to beget a desire and need to impart to others the same knowledge and love. If utterance is denied, the thought lies like a burden on the man. Always the seer is a sayer. Somehow his dream is told. Somehow he publishes it with solemn joy. Sometimes with pencil on canvas; sometimes with chisel on stone; sometimes in towers and aisles of granite, his soul's worship is builded; sometimes in anthems of indefinite music; but clearest and most permanent, in words.

The man enamored of this excellency, becomes its priest or poet. The office is coeval with the world. But observe the condition, the spiritual limitation of the office. The spirit only can teach. Not any profane man, not any sensual, not any liar, not any slave can teach, but only he can give, who has; he only can create, who is. The man on whom the soul descends, through whom the soul speaks, alone can teach. Courage, piety, love, wisdom, can teach; and every man can open his door to these angels, and they shall bring him the gift of tongues. But the man who aims to speak as books enable, as synods use, as the fashion guides, and as interest commands, babbles. Let him hush.

To this holy office, you propose to devote yourselves. I wish you may feel your call in throbs of desire and hope. The office is the first in the world. It is of that reality, that it cannot suffer the deduction of any falsehood. And it is my duty to say to you, that the need was never greater of new revelation than now. From the views I have already expressed, you will infer the sad conviction, which I share, I believe, with numbers, of the universal decay and now almost death of faith in society. The soul is not preached. The Church seems to totter to its fall, almost all life extinct. On this occasion, any complaisance, would be criminal, which told you, whose hope and commission it is to preach the faith of Christ, that the faith of Christ is preached.

It is time that this ill-suppressed murmur of all thoughtful men against the famine of our churches; this moaning of the heart because it is bereaved of the consolation, the hope, the grandeur, that come alone out of the culture of the moral nature; should be heard through the sleep of indolence, and over the din of routine. This great and perpetual office of the preacher is not discharged. Preaching is the expression of the moral sentiment in application to the duties of life. In how many churches, by how many prophets, tell me, is man made sensible that he is an infinite Soul; that the earth and heavens are passing into his mind; that he is drinking forever the soul of God? Where now sounds the persuasion, that by its very melody imparadises my heart, and so affirms its own origin in heaven? Where shall I hear words such as in elder ages drew men to leave all and follow, — father and mother, house and land, wife and child? Where shall I hear these august laws of moral being so pronounced, as to fill my ear, and I feel ennobled by the offer of my uttermost action and passion? The test of the true faith, certainly, should be its power to charm and command the soul, as the laws of nature control the activity of the hands, — so commanding that we find pleasure and honor in obeying. The faith should blend with the light of rising and of setting suns, with the flying cloud, the singing bird, and the breath of flowers. But now the priest's Sabbath has lost the splendor of nature; it is unlovely; we are glad when it is done; we can make, we do make, even sitting in our pews, a far better, holier, sweeter, for ourselves.

Whenever the pulpit is usurped by a formalist, then is the worshipper defrauded and disconsolate. We shrink as soon as the prayers begin, which do not uplift, but smite and offend us. We are fain to wrap our cloaks about us, and secure, as best we can, a solitude that hears not. I once heard a preacher who sorely tempted me to say, I would go to church no more. Men go, thought I, where they are wont to go, else had no soul entered the temple in the afternoon. A snowstorm was falling around us. The snowstorm was real; the preacher merely spectral; and the eye felt the sad contrast in looking at him, and then out of the window behind him, into the beautiful meteor of the snow. He had lived in vain. He had no one word intimating that he had laughed or wept, was married or in love, had been commended, or cheated, or chagrined. If he had ever lived and acted, we were none the wiser for it. The capital secret of his profession, namely, to convert life into truth, he had not learned. Not one fact in all his experience, had he yet imported into his doctrine. This man had ploughed, and planted, and talked, and bought, and sold; he had read books; he had eaten and drunken; his head aches; his heart throbs; he smiles and suffers; yet was there not a surmise, a hint, in all the discourse, that he had ever lived at all. Not a line did he draw out of real history. The true preacher can always be known by this, that he deals out to the people his life, — life passed through the fire of thought. But of the bad preacher, it could not be told from his sermon, what age of the world he fell in; whether he had a father or a child; whether he was a free-holder or a pauper; whether he was a citizen or a countryman; or any other fact of his biography.

It seemed strange that the people should come to church. It seemed as if their houses were very unentertaining, that they should prefer this thoughtless clamor. It shows that there is a commanding attraction in the moral sentiment, that can lend a faint tint of light to dulness and ignorance, coming in its name and place. The good hearer is sure he has been touched sometimes; is sure there is somewhat to be reached, and some word that can reach it. When he listens to these vain words, he comforts himself by their relation to his remembrance of better hours, and so they clatter and echo unchallenged.

I am not ignorant that when we preach unworthily, it is not always quite in vain. There is a good ear, in some men, that draws supplies to virtue out of very indifferent nutriment. There is poetic truth concealed in all the common-places of prayer and of sermons, and though foolishly spoken, they may be wisely heard; for, each is some select expression that broke out in a moment of piety from some stricken or jubilant soul, and its excellency made it remembered. The prayers and even the dogmas of our church, are like the zodiac of Denderah, and the astronomical monuments of the Hindoos, wholly insulated from anything now extant in the life and business of the people. They mark the height to which the waters once rose. But this docility is a check upon the mischief from the good and devout. In a large portion of the community, the religious service gives rise to quite other thoughts and emotions. We need not chide the negligent servant. We are struck with pity, rather, at the swift retribution of his sloth. Alas for the unhappy man that is called to stand in the pulpit, and *not* give bread of life. Everything that befals, accuses him. Would he ask contributions for the missions, foreign or domestic? Instantly his face is suffused with shame, to propose to his parish, that they should send money a hundred or a thousand miles, to furnish such poor fare as they have at home, and would do well to go the hundred or the thousand miles, to escape. Would he urge people to a godly way of living; — and can he ask a fellow creature to come to Sabbath meetings, when he and they all know what is the poor uttermost they can hope for therein? Will he invite them privately to the Lord's Supper? He dares not. If no heart warm this rite, the hollow, dry, creaking formality is too plain, than that he can face a man of wit and energy, and put the invitation without terror. In the street, what has he to say to the bold village blasphemer? The village blasphemer sees fear in the face, form, and gait of the minister.

Let me not taint the sincerity of this plea by any oversight of the claims of good men. I know and honor the purity and strict conscience of numbers of the clergy. What life the public worship retains, it owes to the scattered company of pious men, who minister here and there in the churches, and who, sometimes accepting with too great tenderness the tenet of the elders, have not accepted from others, but from their own heart, the genuine impulses of virtue, and so still command our love and awe, to the sanctity of character. Moreover, the exceptions are not so much to be found in a few eminent preachers, as in the better hours, the truer inspirations of all, — nay, in the sincere moments of every man. But with whatever exception, it is still true, that tradition characterizes the preaching of this country; that it comes out of the memory, and not out of the soul; that it aims at what is usual, and not at what is necessary and eternal; that thus, historical Christianity destroys the power of preaching, by withdrawing it from the exploration of the moral nature of man, where the sublime is, where are the resources of astonishment and power. What a cruel injustice it is to that Law, the joy of the whole earth, which alone can make thought dear and rich; that Law whose fatal sureness the astronomical orbits poorly emulate, that it is travestied and depreciated, that it is behooted and behowled, and not a trait, not a word of it articulated. The pulpit in losing sight of this Law, loses all its inspiration, and gropes after it knows not what. And for want of this culture, the soul of the community is sick and faithless. It wants nothing so much as a stern, high, stoical, Christian discipline, to make it know itself and the divinity that speaks through it. Now man is ashamed of himself; he skulks and sneaks through the world, to be tolerated, to be pitied, and scarcely in a thousand years does any man dare to be wise and good, and so draw after him the tears and blessings of his kind.

Certainly there have been periods when, from the inactivity of the intellect on certain truths, a greater faith was possible in names and persons. The Puritans in England and America, found in the Christ of the Catholic Church, and in the dogmas inherited from Rome, scope for their austere piety, and their longings for civil freedom. But their creed is passing away, and none arises in its room. I think no man can go with his thoughts about him, into one of our churches, without feeling that what hold the public worship had on men, is gone or going. It has lost its grasp on the affection of the good, and the fear of the bad. In the country, — neighborhoods, half parishes are *signing off*, — to use the local term. It is already beginning to indicate character and religion to withdraw from the religious meetings. I have heard a devout person, who prized the Sabbath, say in bitterness of heart, "On Sundays, it seems wicked to go to church." And the motive, that holds the best there, is now only a hope and a waiting. What was once a mere circumstance, that the best and the worst men in the parish, the poor and the rich, the learned and the ignorant, young and old, should meet one day as fellows in one house, in sign of an equal right in the soul, — has come to be a paramount motive for going thither.

My friends, in these two errors, I think, I find the causes of that calamity of a decaying church and a wasting unbelief, which are casting malignant influences around us, and making the hearts of good men sad. And what greater calamity can fall upon a nation, than the loss of worship? Then all things go to decay. Genius leaves the temple, to haunt the senate, or the market. Literature becomes frivolous. Science is cold. The eye of youth is not lighted by the hope of other worlds, and age is without honor. Society lives to trifles, and when men die, we do not mention them.

And now, my brothers, you will ask, What in these desponding days can be done by us? The remedy is already declared in the ground of our complaint of the Church. We have contrasted the Church with the Soul. In the soul, then, let the redemption be sought. In one soul, in your soul, there are resources for the world. Wherever a man comes, there comes revolution. The old is for slaves. When a man comes, all books are legible, all things transparent, all religions are forms. He is religious. Man is the wonderworker. He is seen amid miracles. All men bless and curse. He saith yea and nay, only. The stationariness of religion; the assumption that the age of inspiration is past, that the Bible is closed; the fear of degrading the character of Jesus by representing him as a man; indicate with sufficient clearness the falsehood of our theology. It is the office of a true teacher to show us that God is, not was; that He speaketh, not spake. The true Christianity, — a faith like Christ's in the infinitude of man, — is lost. None believeth in the soul of man, but only in some man or person old and departed. Ah me! no man goeth alone. All men go in flocks to this saint or that poet, avoiding the God who seeth in secret. They cannot see in secret; they love to be blind in public. They think society wiser than their soul, and know not that one soul, and their soul, is wiser than the whole world. See how nations and races flit by on the sea of time, and leave no ripple to tell where they floated or sunk, and one good soul shall make the name of Moses, or of Zeno, or of Zoroaster, reverend forever. None assayeth the stern ambition to be the Self of the nation, and of nature, but each would be an easy secondary to some Christian scheme, or sectarian connexion, or some eminent man. Once leave your own knowledge of God, your own sentiment, and take secondary knowledge, as St. Paul's, or George Fox's, or Swedenborg's, and you get wide from God with every year this secondary form lasts, and if, as now, for centuries — the chasm yawns to that breadth, that men can scarcely be convinced there is in them anything divine.

Let me admonish you, first of all, to go alone; to refuse the good models, even those most sacred in the imagination of men, and dare to love God without mediator or veil. Friends enough you shall find who will hold up to your emulation Wesleys and Oberlins, Saints and Prophets. Thank God for these good men, but say, "I also am a man." Imitation cannot go above its model. The imitator dooms himself to hopeless mediocrity. The inventor did it, because it was natural to him, and so in him it has a charm. In the imitator, something else is natural, and he bereaves himself of his own beauty, to come short of another man's.

Yourself a newborn bard of the Holy Ghost, — cast behind you all conformity, and acquaint men at first hand with Deity. Be to them a man. Look to it first and only, that you are such; that fashion, custom, authority, pleasure, and money are nothing to you, — are not bandages over your eyes, that you cannot see, — but live with the privilege of the immeasurable mind. Not too anxious to visit periodically all families and each family in your parish connexion, — when you meet one of these men or women, be to them a divine man; be to them thought and virtue; let their timid aspirations find in you a friend; let their trampled instincts be genially tempted out in your atmosphere; let their doubts know that you have doubted, and their wonder feel that you have wondered. By trusting your own soul, you shall gain a greater confidence in other men. For all our penny-wisdom, for all our soul-destroying slavery to habit, it is not to be doubted, that all men have sublime thoughts; that all men do value the few real hours of life; they love to be heard; they love to be caught up into the vision of principles. We mark with light in the memory the few interviews we have had in the dreary years of routine and of sin, with souls that made our souls wiser; that spoke what we thought; that told us what we knew; that gave us leave to be what we inly were. Discharge to men the priestly office, and, present or absent, you shall be followed with their love as by an angel.

And, to this end, let us not aim at common degrees of merit. Can we not leave, to such as love it, the virtue that glitters for the commendation of society, and ourselves pierce the deep solitudes of absolute ability and worth? We easily come up to the standard of goodness in society. Society's praise can be cheaply secured, and almost all men are content with those easy merits; but the instant effect of conversing with God, will be, to put them away. There are sublime merits; persons who are not actors, not speakers, but influences; persons too great for fame, for display; who disdain eloquence; to whom all we call art and artist, seems too nearly allied to show and by-ends, to the exaggeration of the finite and selfish, and loss of the universal. The orators, the poets, the commanders encroach on us only as fair women do, by our allowance and homage. Slight them by preoccupation of mind, slight them, as you can well afford to do, by high and universal aims, and they instantly feel that you have right, and that it is in lower places that they must shine. They also feel your right; for they with you are open to the influx of the all-knowing Spirit, which annihilates before its broad noon the little shades and gradations of intelligence in the compositions we call wiser and wisest.

In such high communion, let us study the grand strokes of rectitude: a bold benevolence, an independence of friends, so that not the unjust wishes of those who love us, shall impair our freedom, but we shall resist for truth's sake the freest flow of kindness, and appeal to sympathies far in advance; and, — what is the highest form in which we know this beautiful element, — a certain solidity of merit, that has nothing to do with opinion, and which is so essentially and manifestly virtue, that it is taken for granted, that the right, the brave, the generous step will be taken by it, and nobody thinks of commending it. You would compliment a coxcomb doing a good act, but you would not praise an angel. The silence that accepts merit as the most natural thing in the world, is the highest applause. Such souls, when they appear, are the Imperial Guard of Virtue, the perpetual reserve, the dictators of fortune. One needs not praise their courage, — they are the heart and soul of nature. O my friends, there are resources in us on which we have not drawn. There are men who rise refreshed on hearing a threat; men to whom a crisis which intimidates and paralyzes the majority — demanding not the faculties of prudence and thrift, but comprehension, immovableness, the readiness of sacrifice, — comes graceful and beloved as a bride. Napoleon said of Massena, that he was not himself until the battle began to go against him; then, when the dead began to fall in ranks around him, awoke his powers of combination, and he put on terror and victory as a robe. So it is in rugged crises, in unweariable endurance, and in aims which put sympathy out of question, that the angel is shown. But these are heights that we can scarce remember and look up to, without contrition and shame. Let us thank God that such things exist.

And now let us do what we can to rekindle the smouldering, nigh quenched fire on the altar. The evils of the church that now is, are manifest. The question returns, What shall we do? I confess, all attempts to project and establish a Cultus with new rites and forms, seem to me vain. Faith makes us, and not we it, and faith makes its own forms. All attempts to contrive a system, are as cold as the new worship introduced by the French to the goddess of Reason, — today, pasteboard and fillagree, and ending to-morrow in madness and murder. Rather let the breath of new life be breathed by you through the forms already existing. For, if once you are alive, you shall find they shall become plastic and new. The remedy to their deformity is, first, soul, and second, soul, and evermore, soul. A whole popedom of forms, one pulsation of virtue can uplift and vivify. Two inestimable advantages Christianity has given us; first; the Sabbath, the jubilee of the whole world; whose light dawns welcome alike into the closet of the philosopher, into the garret of toil, and into prison cells, and everywhere suggests, even to the vile, a thought of the dignity of spiritual being. Let it stand forevermore, a temple, which new love, new faith, new sight shall restore to more than its first splendor to mankind. And secondly, the institution of preaching, — the speech of man to men, — essentially the most flexible of all organs, of all forms. What hinders that now, everywhere, in pulpits, in lecture-rooms, in houses, in fields, wherever the invitation of men or your own occasions lead you, you speak the very truth, as your life and conscience teach it, and cheer the waiting, fainting hearts of men with new hope and new revelation?

I look for the hour when that supreme Beauty, which ravished the souls of those Eastern men, and chiefly of those Hebrews, and through their lips spoke oracles to all time, shall speak in the West also. The Hebrew and Greek Scriptures contain immortal sentences, that have been bread of life to millions. But they have no epical integrity; are fragmentary; are not shown in their order to the intellect. I look for the new Teacher, that shall follow so far those shining laws, that he shall see them come full circle; shall see their rounding complete grace; shall see the world to be the mirror of the soul; shall see the identity of the law of gravitation with purity of heart; and shall show that the Ought, that Duty, is one thing with Science, with Beauty, and with Joy.

FAZLUR RAHMAN

The Qur'ān

> Fazlur Rahman, teaching at the University of Karachi in
> Pakistan and at one of the major centers of Islamic studies
> in the English-speaking world, McGill University in Mon-
> treal, wrote his book *Islam*, as he says in the preface,
> "equally for Western and Muslim readers." But the chapter
> entitled "The Qur'ān," from which this excerpt is taken,
> together with the one on the Prophet, was especially in-
> tended for this dual readership.

IF WE ARE TO DEAL WITH FACTS of Islamic history, the factual statements
of the Qur'ān about itself call for some treatment. In the following brief
outline an attempt is made to do justice both to historical and Islamic
demands. We have explicitly stated in the preceding chapter that the
basic *élan* of the Qur'ān is moral, whence flows its emphasis on
monotheism as well as on social justice. The moral law is immutable:
it is God's "Command," Man cannot make or unmake the Moral Law:
he must submit himself to it, this submission to it being called *islām*
and its implementation in life being called *'ibāda* or "service to God."
It is because of the Qur'ān's paramount emphasis on the Moral Law
that the Qur'ānic God has seemed to many people to be primarily the
God of justice. But the Moral Law and spiritual values, in order to be
implemented, must be known. Now, in their power of cognitive
perception men obviously differ to an indefinite degree. Further,
moral and religious perception is also very different from a *purely*
intellectual perception, for an intrinsic quality of the former is that
along with perception it brings an extraordinary sense of "gravity" and
leaves the subject significantly transformed. Perception, also moral
perception, then has degrees. The variation is not only between
different individuals, but the inner life of a given individual varies at

different times from this point of view. We are not here talking of an intrinsic moral and intellectual development and evolution, where variation is most obvious. But even in a good, mature person whose average intellectual and moral character and calibre, are, in a sense, fixed, these variations occur.

Now a Prophet is a person whose average, overall character, the sum total of his actual conduct, is far superior to those of humanity in general. He is a man who is *ab initio* impatient with men and even with most of their ideals, and wishes to re-create history. Muslim orthodoxy, therefore, drew the logically correct conclusion that Prophets must be regarded as immune from serious errors (the doctrine of *'isma*). Muhammad was such a person, in fact the only such person really known to history. That is why his overall behaviour is regarded by the Muslims as Sunna or the "perfect model." But, with all this, there were moments when he, as it were, "transcends himself" and his moral cognitive perception becomes so acute and so keen that his consciousness becomes identical with the moral law itself. "Thus did we inspire you with a Spirit of Our Command: You did not know what the Book was. But We have made it a light" (XLII, 52). But the moral law and religious values are God's Command, and although they are not identical with God entirely, they are part of Him. The Qur'ān is, therefore, purely divine. Further, even with regard to ordinary consciousness, it is a mistaken notion that ideas and feelings float about in it and can be mechanically "clothed" in words. There exists, indeed, an organic relationship between feelings, ideas and words. In inspiration, even in poetic inspiration, this relationship is so complete that feeling-idea-word is a total complex with a life of its own. When Muhammad's moral intuitive perception rose to the highest point and became identified with the moral law itself (indeed, in these moments his own conduct at points came under Qur'ānic criticism, as is shown by our account in the second section of the preceding chapter and as is evident from the pages of the Qur'ān), the Word was given with the inspiration itself. The Qur'ān is thus pure Divine Word, but, of course, it is equally intimately related to the inmost personality of the Prophet Muhammad whose relationship to it cannot be mechanically conceived like that of a record. The Divine Word flowed through the Prophet's heart.

But if Muhammad, in his Qur'ānic moments, became one with the moral law, he may not be absolutely identified either with God or even with a part of Him. The Qur'ān categorically forbids this, Muhammad insistently avoided this and all Muslims worthy of the name have condemned as the gravest error associating (*shirk*) a creature with God. The reason is that no man may say, "I am the Moral Law." Man's duty is carefully to formulate this Law and to submit to it with all his physical, mental and spiritual faculties. Besides this, Islam knows of no way of assigning any meaning to the sentence, "So-and-so is Divine."

The Qur'ānic Teaching

In the foregoing we have repeatedly emphasized that the basic *élan* of the Qur'ān is moral and we have pointed to the ideas of social and economic justice that immediately followed from it in the Qur'ān. This is absolutely true so far as man and his destiny are concerned. As the Qur'ān gradually worked out its world-view more fully, the moral order for men comes to assume a central point of divine interest in a full picture of a cosmic order which is not only charged with a high religious sensitivity but exhibits an amazing degree of coherence and consistency. A concept of God, the absolute author of the universe, is developed where the attributes of creativity, order, and mercy are not merely conjoined or added to one another but interpenetrate completely. To Him belong creativity and "ordering" or "commanding" (VII, 54). "My mercy encompasses everything" (VII, 156). Indeed, the "Merciful" (Raḥmān) is the only adjectival name of God that is very frequently used in the Qur'ān as a substantive name of God besides Allāh. It is of course, true, as modern research has revealed, that Raḥmān was used as name for the Deity in South Arabia before Islam, but this fact of historical transportation from the South is obviously irrelevant from our point of view. If we leave out man, for the time being, i.e. his specific spiritual-moral constitution, and consider the rest of the entire created universe, the interpretation of these three ultimate attributes is that God creates everything, and that in the very act of this creation order or "command" is ingrained in things whereby they cohere and fall into a pattern, and rather than "go astray" from the ordained path, evolve into a cosmos; that, finally, all this is nothing but the sheer mercy of God for, after all, existence is not the absolute desert of anything, and in the place of existence there could just as well be pure, empty nothingness.

Indeed, the most intense impression that the Qur'ān as a whole leaves upon a reader is not of a watchful, frowning and punishing God, as the Christians have generally made it out to be, nor of a chief judge as the Muslim legalists have tended to think, but of a unitary and purposive will creative of order in the universe: the qualities of power or majesty, of watchfulness or justice and of wisdom attributed to God in the Qur'ān with unmistakable emphasis are, in fact, immediate inferences from the creative orderliness of the cosmos. Of all the Qur'ānic terms, perhaps the most basic, comprehensive and revelatory at once of divine nature of the universe is the term *amr* which we have translated above as order, orderliness or command. To everything that is created is *ipso facto* communicated its *amr* which is its own law of being but which is also a law whereby it is integrated into a system. This *amr*, i.e. order or command of God, is ceaseless. The term used to indicate the communication of *amr* to all things, including man, is *wahy* . . . "inspiration." With reference to inorganic things it should be translated as "ingraining." This is because with reference to man, who constitutes a special case, it is not just *amr* that is sent down from high, but a "spirit-from-*amr*" (*rūh min al-amr*), as the Qur'ān repeatedly tells us.

With reference to man (and possibly also to the *jinn*, an invisible order of creation, parallel to man but said to be created of a fiery substance, a kind of duplicate of man which is, in general, more prone to evil, and from whom the devil is also said to have sprung), both the nature and the content of *amr* are transformed, because *amr* really becomes here the moral command: it is not that which actually is an order but that which actually is a disorder wherein an order *is to be* brought about. The actual moral disorder is the result of a deep-seated moral fact to remedy which God and man must collaborate. This fact is that coeval with man is the devil (*shaytān*) who beguiles him unceasingly.

The Qur'ān portrays the moral dualism in man's character which gives rise to the moral struggle, and the potentialities man and man alone possesses, by two strikingly effective stories. According to one, when God intended to create man as his vicegerent, the angels protested to Him saying that man would be prone to evil, "corrupt the earth and shed blood," while they were utterly obedient to the Divine Will, whereupon God replied, "I have knowledge of that which you do not know" (II, 30). The other story tells us that when God offered "The Trust" to the Heavens and the Earth, the entire Creation refused to accept it, until man came forward and bore it, adding with a sympathetic rebuke, "Man is so ignorant and foolhardy!" (XXXIII, 72). There can be hardly a more penetrating and effective characterization of the human situation and man's frail and faltering nature, yet his innate boldness and the will to transcend the actual towards the ideal constitutes his uniqueness and greatness. This fact of the devil creates an entirely new dimension in the case of man. God "has ingrained in it (i.e. the human soul) a discernment of good and evil" (XCI, 8); but so artful and powerful is the devil's seduction that men normally fail even to decipher properly this eternal inscription of God on the human heart, while some who can decipher it fail to be moved and impelled by it sufficiently strongly. At times of such crisis God finds and selects some human to whom he sends the angel "the spirit of the Command" that is "with Him." The Command that is with Him is so sure, so definite in what it affirms and denies that it is, indeed, the "Invisible Book" written on a "Preserved Tablet," the "Mother of (all) Books" (LVI, 78; LXXXV, 21–22; XIII, 39). Men charged with these fateful messages to humanity are the Prophets. The Qur'ān "sent" to Muḥammad is the Book that reveals the Command: Muḥammad is the final Prophet and the Qur'ān the last Book that has been so revealed.

With this background, therefore, the Qur'ān emerges as a document that from the first to the last seeks to emphasize all those moral tensions that are necessary for creative human action. Indeed, at bottom the centre of the Qur'ān's interest is man and his betterment. For this it is essential that men operate within the framework of certain tensions which, indeed, have been created by God in him. First and foremost, man may not jump to the suicidal conclusion that he can make and unmake moral law according to his "heart's desire" from the obvious fact that this law is there *for him.* Hence the absolute supremacy and the majesty of God are most strikingly emphasized by the Qur'ān. On the other hand among all creation, man has been given the most immense potentialities and is endowed with the "Trust" which entire creation shrank back in fear from accepting. Again, the idea of justice flows directly from that of the supremacy of the moral law, an idea equally emphasized by the Qur'ān. But with the same insistence the Qur'ān condemns hopelessness and lack of trust in the mercy of God, which it declares to be a cardinal infidelity. The same is true of the whole range of moral tensions, including human power and weakness, knowledge and ignorance, sufferance and retaliation, etc. While the potentialities of man are immense, equally immense, therefore, are the penalties which man must face as a result of his failure.

In pursuance of this picture, belief in one God stands at the apex of the Muslim system of belief derived from the Qur'ān. From this belief is held to follow belief in angels (spirits of the Command) as transmitters of the Divine message to man, in the Prophets, the human repositories of the Divine revelation (the last in the series being

Muḥammad), in the genuineness of the messages of the Prophets, the "Book," and in the Day of Reckoning.

The Qur'ān emphasizes prayer because "it prevents from evil" and helps man to conquer difficulties, especially when combined with "patience." The *five* daily prayers are not all mentioned in the Qur'ān, but must be taken to represent the later usage of the Prophet himself, since it would be historically impossible to support the view that the Muslims themselves added two new prayers to the three mentioned in the Qur'ān. In the Qur'ān itself the two morning and the evening prayers are mentioned, and later on at Medina the "middle" prayer at noon was added. But it appears that during the later part of the Prophet's life the prayer "from the declension of the sun unto the thick darkness of the night" (XVII, 78) was split into two and similarly the noon prayer and thus the number five was reached.

The fact, however, that the prayers were fundamentally three is evidenced by the fact that the Prophet is reported to have combined these four prayers into two, even without there being any reason. It was in the post-Prophetic period that the number of prayers was inexorably fixed without any alternative at five, and the fact of the fundamental three prayers was submerged under the rising tide of the Ḥadīth which was put into circulation to support the idea that prayers were five.

One month's fast, a considerably strenuous total abstention from eating and drinking from dawn till sunset, is prescribed by the Qur'ān (II, 183 ff.). Those who may be sick (or experiencing difficulties) on a journey may postpone the fast until a more favourable time. The Qur'ān is believed to have been first revealed in the month of Ramaḍān.

So long as the small Muslim Community remained in Mecca, alms-giving, even though very recurrently emphasized, remained a voluntary donation towards the welfare of the poorer section of the Community. In Medina, however, the *zakāt*, or welfare tax, was duly ordained for the welfare of the Community and tax-collectors were appointed. So strong is the emphasis of the Qur'ān on this point that even prayer is seldom mentioned without being accompanied by *zakāt*. The ban on usury, the moral condemnation of which also started in Mecca, came in a series of pronouncements — one threatening war from God and His Prophet against those who practised usury — on the ground that it rendered the debt "several-fold" of the original capital and was opposed to fair commerce (*bay'*).

Pilgrimage to Mecca was made obligatory for every Muslim once in a lifetime for "Those who can afford it," i.e. who can not only pay their way to Mecca and back but can also provide for their families during their absence. The institution of pilgrimage has been a very potent vehicle of furthering Islamic brotherhood and a pan-Islamic sentiment among Muslims of diverse races and cultures.

The Qur'ān calls upon believers to undertake *jihād*, which is to surrender "your properties and yourselves in the path of Allāh"; the purpose of which in turn is to "establish prayer, give *zakāt*, command good and forbid evil" — i.e. to establish the Islamic socio-moral order. So long as the Muslims were a small, persecuted minority in Mecca, *jihād* as a positive organized thrust of the Islamic movement was unthinkable. In Medina, however, the situation changed and henceforth there is hardly anything, with the possible exception of prayer and *zakāt*, that receives greater emphasis than *jihād*. Among the later Muslim legal schools, however, it is only the fanatic Khārijites who have declared *jihād* to be one of the "pillars of the Faith." Other schools have played it down for the obvious reason that the expansion of Islam had already occurred much too swiftly in proportion to the internal consolidation of the Community in the Faith. Every virile and expansive ideology has, at a stage, to ask itself the question as to what are its terms of co-existence, if any, with other systems, and how far it may employ methods of direct expansion. In our own age, Communism, in its Russian and Chinese versions, is faced with the same problems and choices. The most unacceptable on historical grounds, however, is the stand of those modern Muslim apologists who have tried to explain the *jihād* of the early Community in purely defensive terms.

The Qur'ān Legislation

The Qur'ān is primarily a book of religious and moral principles and exhortations, and is not a legal document. But it does embody some important legal enunciations issued during the community-state building process at Medina. . . .The ban on consumption of alcohol affords an interesting example of the Qur'ānic method of legislation and throws light on the attitude of the Qur'ān to the nature and function of legislation itself. The use of alcohol was apparently unreservedly permitted in the early years. Then offering prayers while under the influence of alcohol was prohibited. Later it is said, "They ask you about alcohol and gambling. Say: in these there is great harm and also profits for people but their harm far outweighs their profits" (II, 219). Finally a total ban was proclaimed (V, 90–91) on the ground that both alcohol and gambling "are works of the devil. . . . The devil wants to sow enmity and rancour among you." This shows the slow *experimental* legal tackling of problems *as they arise.*

But the most important legal enactments and general reform pronouncements of the Qur'ān have been on the subjects of women and slavery. The Qur'ān immensely improved the status of the woman in several directions but the most basic is the fact that the woman was given a fully-pledged personality. The spouses are declared to be each other's "garments": the woman has been granted the same rights over man as man has over his wife, except that man, being the earning partner, is a degree higher. Unlimited polygamy was strictly regulated and the number of wives was limited to four, with the rider that if a husband feared that he could not do justice among several wives, he must marry only one wife. To all this was added a general principle that "you shall never be able to do justice among wives no matter how desirous you are (to do so)" (IV, 3, 128). The overall logical consequence of these pronouncements is a banning of polygamy under normal circumstances. Yet as an already existing institution polygamy was accepted on a legal plane, with the obvious guiding lines that when gradually social circumstances became more favourable, monogamy might be introduced. This is because no reformer who means to be effective can neglect the real situation and simply issue visionary statements. But the later Muslims did not watch the guiding lines of the Qur'ān and, in fact, thwarted its intentions.

The case of the Qur'ānic treatment of the institution of slavery runs parallel to that of the family. As an immediate solution, the Qur'ān accepts the institution of slavery on the legal plane. No alternative was possible since slavery was ingrained in the structure of society, and its overnight wholesale liquidation would have created problems which it would have been absolutely impossible to solve, and only a dreamer could have issued such a visionary statement. But at the same time every legal and moral effort was made to free the slaves and to create a *milieu* where slavery ought to disappear. "Liberating the neck" (*fakk raqaba*) is not only praised as a virtue but is declared, along with feeding the poor and orphans, to be that "uphill path" which is absolutely essential for man to tread (XC, 10–16). Indeed, the Qur'ān has categorically told the Muslims that if a slave wants to purchase his or her freedom by paying off in instalments a sum that may be decided upon according to the situation of the slave, then the owner of the slave must allow such a contract for freedom and may not reject it: "And those of your slaves who wish to enter into freedom-purchasing contracts, accept their proposals if you think they are any good and give to them of the wealth that God has given you. And do not compel your slave-girls to resort to a foul life when they want to be chaste, seeking thereby petty gains of life; but if they act under sheer compulsion, God is forgiving and merciful" (XXIV, 33). Here again we are confronted by a situation where the clear logic of the Qur'ānic attitude was not worked out in actual history by Muslims. The words of the Qur'ān "If you think they are any good" when properly understood, only mean that if a slave cannot show any earning capacity, then he cannot be expected to stand on his own feet even if freed and therefore it may be better for him to enjoy at least the protection of his master.

These examples, therefore, make it abundantly clear that whereas the spirit of the Qur'ānic legislation exhibits an obvious direction towards the progressive embodiment of the fundamental human values of freedom and responsibility in fresh legislation, nevertheless the actual legislation of the Qur'ān had partly to accept the then existing society as a term of reference. This clearly means that the actual legislation of the Qur'ān cannot have been meant to be literally eternal by the Qur'ān itself. This fact has no reference to the doctrine of the eternity of the Qur'ān or to the allied doctrine of the verbal revelation of the Qur'ān. Very soon, however, the Muslim lawyers and dogmaticians began to confuse the issue and the strictly legal injunctions of the Qur'ān were thought to apply to any society, no matter what its conditions, what its structure and what its inner dynamics. One clear proof that, as time passed, Muslim legists became more and more literalists is reflected in the fact that sometime during the 2nd/8th century the Muslim legal doctrine began to draw a very sharp distinction between the clear wording (naṣṣ), the text and what was deducible therefrom. There is a good deal of evidence to believe that in the very early period the Muslims interpreted the Qur'ān pretty freely. But after a period of juristic development during the late 1st/7th and throughout the 2nd/8th century (the prominent features of which were the rise of the Tradition and the development of technical, analogical reasoning), the lawyers neatly tied themselves and the Community down to the "text " of the Holy Book until the content of Muslim law and theology became buried under the weight of literalism.

Throughout the centuries, Muslims have not only written innumerable commentaries on the Qur'ān from different points of view and with different, indeed, conflicting tendencies, but have evolved a science of Qur'ānic exegesis ('ilm al-tafsīr), with its auxiliary branches of learning, including Arabic grammar, lexicography, the Prophetic tradition, the circumstantial background of the verses of the Qur'ān, etc. Indeed, it is claimed by Muslim scholars with a good deal of justice that all the sciences in Islam which are not absolutely secular owe their origin to the Qur'ān. The Qur'ān has also exerted an incalculable influence on the growth of Arabic literature and literary style, and continues to exert it up to this day. The doctrine of the "inimitability" (*i'jāz*) of the Qur'ān, not only in content but even in literary form, is common to almost all Muslim schools, and has attained a cardinal status and found expression in various treatises specially devoted to this topic. Muslim orthodoxy had strenuously resisted any attempt to produce a translation of the Book in any language without the Arabic text. This has contributed not a little to the unity of Muslims who, throughout the world, recite the Qur'ān in their prayers five times a day in Arabic. Only recently in Kemalist Turkey the Qur'ān was translated and produced in Turkish without the original Arabic, although the Arabic text continued to be used in prayers. But even in Turkey, there has been a return to the Arabic text even for ordinary reading. For the purpose of understanding the text, accompanying translations in local languages are allowed.

Commentaries on the Qur'ān

During the lifetime of the Prophet the Qur'ān had been committed to memory by many people and recited in prayers. It was also written down on leaves, bones, parchments and such other material as was available. The entire Book was collected together by the first Caliph Abū Bakr. The commonly accepted text, however, the Vulgate edition, dates from the time of the third Caliph, 'Uthmān, who, on the recommendation of a committee appointed for the purpose and headed by Zayd ibn Thābit, the faithful servant of the Prophet, also effected the present arrangement of the Qur'ān, which, as opposed to the chronological order, is based more or less on the length of the Sūras.

Whereas there is some evidence that in the earliest generation after the Prophet people were shy of, and even opposed to, any interpretation of the Qur'ān, this attitude soon gave way to all books of interpretations which were more or less coloured by the faiths and old ideas of the new converts. Such interpretations, which probably sometimes diverged markedly from the obvious meaning of the text and had an arbitrary character, were severely attacked as "interpretation of arbitrary opinion (*tafsīr bi'l-ra'y*)." . . .

The need was thus felt to develop some scientific instruments whereby to control the progress of the science of Qur'ānic commentary ('ilm al-tafsīr). First of all, therefore, the principle was recognized that a knowledge not only of the Arabic language but also of the Arabic idiom of the times of the Prophet was requisite for a proper understanding of the Qur'ān. Hence Arabic grammar, lexicography and Arabic literature were intensively cultivated. Next, the backgrounds of the Qur'ānic revelations called the "occasions of revelation" were recorded as a necessary aid for fixing the correct meaning of the Word of God. Thirdly, historical tradition containing reports about how those among whom the Qur'ān first appeared understood its injunctions and statements was given great weight. After these requirements were fulfilled came the scope for a free play of human reason. A monument of traditional commentary, based on reports from earlier generations, was compiled by al-Ṭabarī (d.310/922) in his extensive work. In course of time, as various schools of thought and converts of intellectual and spiritual life developed in Islam, commentaries came into existence. Indeed, it is quite true to say that whatever views Muslims have wanted to project and advocate have taken the form of Qur'ānic commentaries.

The language and the style of the Qur'ān have also exerted a most powerful influence on the growth and development of Arabic literature. The Muslims early developed the doctrine of the literary and artistic "unsurpassability" of the Qur'ān, but even for the non-Muslim Arab it remains an ideal of literary production even to this day. The Qur'ān strenuously rejected the epithet "poet" flung at Muḥammad by his opponents and never allowed that it be called poetry. Yet in its depth of feeling, in its telling expressiveness and in its effective rhythm the Qur'ān is not less than poetry of the highest order. Indeed, Muslims have developed a special art of its recitation (called tajwīd), and when the Qur'ān is chanted in this way it does not fail to affect even a hearer who does not know Arabic. In translation, of course, it is impossible to keep its artistic beauty and grandeur. We quote below three passages from different dates, not because they will convey to the reader its artistic excellence but to illustrate the development of its content stage by stage. The first passage, belonging to an early Meccan Sūra, reads:

> As for man, whenever his Lord trieth him by honouring him
> and is gracious unto him, he saith "My Lord honoureth me."
> But whenever He trieth him by straitening his means of life,
> he says "My Lord despiseth me." Nay, but (this is because) ye

honour not the orphan. And urge (others) not on the feeding of the poor; and ye devour heritages with devouring greed and are attached to wealth with excessive attachment. Nay, but when the earth is ground to atoms, grinding, grinding and thy Lord shall come with angels, rank and rank (LXXXIX, 15–22).

The following verses belong to the later Meccan period:

Successful, indeed, are the believers who are humble in their prayers; and who shun vain conversation; and who pay up the welfare tax; and who guard their modesty — save their wives or the (slaves) that their right hands possess (for them they are not blameworthy) — but whoso craveth beyond that, such are transgressors; and who guard their pledge and fulfil their covenant; and who pay heed to their prayers. These are the heirs who will inherit Heaven. There they will abide (XXIII, 1–11).

This passage is from a Medinese Sūra:

(Here is) a Sūra We have revealed and enjoined and wherein We have revealed plain tokens, that haply ye may take heed. The adulterer and the adulteress strike ye each one of them with a hundred stripes. And let not pity for them withhold you from obedience to Allāh, if ye believe in Allāh and the Last Day. And let a party of believers witness their punishment. The adulterer shall not marry save an adulteress or an idol-atress, and the adulteress none shall marry save an adulterer or an idolater. All that is forbidden unto believers. And those who accuse honourable women (of unchastity) but bring not four witnesses, strike them with eighty stripes and never accept their testimony — they, indeed, are evil-doers — except those who afterward repent and make amends (XXIV, 1–5).

NATHAN SÖDERBLOM

Continued Revelation

Nathan Söderblom (1866–1931) was a professor of the history of religions at Uppsala and at Leipzig, and then became archbishop of Uppsala and primate of the Church of Sweden, receiving the Nobel Prize for peace in 1930. He was a major figure in the development of Christian ecumenism, but as he makes clear in the following excerpt from his Gifford Lectures, *The Living God,* his ecumenism reached far beyond the borders of Christendom.

Does God continue to reveal himself to mankind?

A little boy is reading his lesson in Bible history. "And God said unto Moses." His critical younger brother, who has not yet begun to go to school: "What a stupid you are! God can't speak in that way to a man." "Shut up, he could in those days." Does not theology reason much in the same way?

In certain later writings of the Old Testament and in Judaism piety no longer discerns the action of God in the present history and its personalities — with less difficulty, it is true, in his wise and great works in nature — but, as regards history, only in the ancient wonders of revelation. Through the position of Christ in the communion of Christians with God Christianity finds itself in another situation in regard to its belief in revelation. But a certain likeness exists, *mutatis mutandis,* between this Judaism, which was able to keep its certainty of a revelation apparent mainly in times long past, and the average Protestant conception, according to which the revelation of God was completed in ancient times and completely written in the sacred book.

Some Christians say: "God did reveal himself once. We have it all written down. He is in the Holy Scriptures." This contains part of the essential truth. God did reveal himself once for all in Jesus Christ, and that Revelation needs no repeating or improving. Jesus says about the Holy Ghost: "He shall take of mine, and shall declare it unto you." Christ who suffered under Pontius Pilate, the Christ of history and of faith, suffices for all time. The history related in the Bible is God's Revelation in a fuller, richer, weightier sense than in any other history. The uniqueness of God's Revelation in the history recorded in the Bible seems impossible and unlikely to reasoning *a priori,* but still it is a fact which comparative religion will make more and more evident. One can prove that a thing is impossible, and yet it really happens in history and in the moral life.

For history has not been laid down according to the laws of logic. What is to be found there might be very absurd; one would say in advance that it is unthinkable. But still it has happened. It is a material for research, which here as elsewhere, in order to reach real results, has to put itself in subordination to its subject, listening, receiving, explaining, not above its subject in lordly wise. In the history of religion a supernatural life is revealed, but not in a way which seems just and right to human thought. The real aspect of the history of religion corresponds to St. Paul's words of a universal revelation, inside which we can discern the special revelation. Or, to use an expression without metaphysical meaning, in the religion of mankind phenomena appear, which, as Hermann Usener saw, in a specific way deserve the name of "religion of revelation."

But that it is absurd to look upon God's Revelation as finished with Christ or the Bible, is clearly shown by another question. Our question: "Does God continue to reveal himself to mankind?" gives rise to another question. "Did God ever reveal himself to mankind?" I am anxious to emphasize this question, which lurks behind our topic. It makes evident how impossible it is to realize and to maintain the conviction of a real Revelation of God without applying it also to the present time. Take somebody who does not believe in any working of God; take a man for whom the Living God does not exist; how are you to convince him of the existence of a God who has once revealed himself to mankind, if God does not reveal himself to that man as living and working his salvation? But there are pious people who believe in God, not only as a law and principle, or as a great all-pervading mystery, but as a Will, as Love, that has made itself known and perceptible to man, yet who consider that the Revelation in a proper sense was finished with Christ or with the Bible.

*   *   *   *   *

God continues to reveal himself in *genius*. Genius proves that the real essence of existence is creation, not merely necessity. In other words, the inherent necessity which works behind that which our eyes see and our ears hear, is a necessary striving after, creating, producing, saving, vivifying, bringing forth new things out of the hidden treasures of existence. It is not a mechanical necessity that merely combines things already existing. For in genius breaks forth a mighty flood of creative power. No doubt, the origin of genius is determined by certain laws. Innumerable generations are behind the child in whose embryo the wonderful treasure lies dormant. Dangerous heritages, good heritages, weak heritages, subdivided in a thousand different ways, have produced diverse results in his forefathers. A combination and a mutual influence takes place from the natural gifts of his father and mother respectively, but also from earlier heritages which the parents, in a mysterious way and perhaps without either winning any advantages from them or suffering under them personally, transfer from preceding generations to the individual or individuals who, after them, are to inherit possibility of good or evil thus obscurely prepared. Then the gift of genius bursts forth apparently as suddenly and unexpectedly as those phenomena which De Vries has called mutation, thus showing that the thing remains unexplained. Concerning lower organisms, from the vegetable kingdom and the lower species of the animal kingdom, exceedingly acute analyses of the laws of heredity have been made. Of course, there are hidden laws of heredity which in part may be discovered by science. In preceding generations there are innumerable facts and details which must be explained in the appearance of genius, to us sudden and mysterious. No mere process of addition of great and fine qualities can give such a result. The riddle of heredity and generation is, of course, very much more subtle than any process of addition. We shall never be able to analyse perfectly the causes and elements of creative genius. We shall never be able to predict it. But we know that there exists no element of chance, nothing accidental — although the absolute determinism of classical physics has been abandoned for ever by the new physics. The human eye cannot penetrate the sequence of causes and effects. Our Christian faith and our constructive outlook on life and history know something more. They know that God works in the complicated course of generations, and that the right man is there to do his work, when he is wanted.

The very fact that creative genius exists proves as clearly as one can wish, that life is essentially a continued creation, not merely the regulation of things created. For the manner in which genius works, with whatever material — with human hearts, states, armies, tones, colours, words — language, with instinctive precision, has chosen the word "creation." Certainly there is something original, something new in every human being. Erik Gustaf Geijer says: "There is no man who cannot do *one* thing better than everybody else" — one of the most comforting sentences ever pronounced. But in the extraordinary outfit of creative genius the original and peculiar appears more clearly.

Poet, *poiētēs*, means maker, creator; poem, *poiēma*, creation. The poet is a collaborator with the Creator in two respects. He is an interpreter of creation. And he is continuing the creation. The artist is helping us to understand it, whether it be the painter who reproduces a sunset or the poet who describes man's life. And the characteristic of the poet is that he is able to give life to his figures. They are taken out of reality and still they are creations of his spirit. They are living and possess in thoughts and shape something of the inexhaustibleness and the riches which characterize creation.

We are using, every one of us, words as coins in our everyday life, in the barter between men, and once in a while we put up a temporary hut or store for our thought and feeling. But the artist knows how to erect a building with language as material, which he is polishing and selecting and treating and arranging; a building, built in a severe style, created by imagination and order, not only serving for the occasion, but offering a home, a refuge, an expression even to our more or less homeless and wandering feelings and thoughts.

In genius new things appear, things which have never before existed. It is not always easy to say wherein the originality lies. But the quality of creating something which may be called new is the distinction between genius and mere talent. This peculiarity stands out the more clearly if we consider the fact that mere talent, be it ever so great, can be attained by rules and patterns. But genius itself in its turn gives rise to new rules, which are afterwards established by analysis. First comes *creation* — revelation, beauty of character, the building up of society, a work of art. Then comes *theory* — theology, ethics, political science, theory of art. It is just the same as in God's created world — first, the flower, then botany. Genius appears as a part of the Almighty's continuous creation. And so in working, genius is conscious of being part of a miracle. Plato already knew that such as are inspired say things the whole import of which they themselves are unable to grasp. Harald Hjärne wrote: "Not all seers are able to interpret their visions." History confirms this observation. God alone knows the import of what genius says. Coming generations do not tire of going deep into the works of genius in order to gather new knowledge and new enlightenment from them. And to the learned professors there lies a wholesome warning in my paradox, that the Great are always right, even if they contradict each other.

But in what we have said above, the whole importance of the creative activity of genius has not even been hinted at. This activity has another side, perhaps even more noteworthy, which has seldom had attention paid to it. I shall call it the organic connexion between God's entire continued creative work and the work of genius. Let me first elucidate this phenomenon with an observation from the way in which science works.

The scientific method can fit men for all works. It gives a general view, the power of distinguishing essentials and non-essentials.

Another point is the secrecy of investigation, or rather the secrecy of the investigator. Here there is no question of obscure mysticism. Nobody can be more sternly intellectual, more averse from cheap methods, than the investigator. But as the investigation issues from, and works on the presumption that there is a connexion, the investigator also learns that he himself is involved in a mysterious association. I do not mean merely that he has predecessors, fellow-workers, and successors and that there is a certain continuity in the work of research. But an unfathomable association is to be discerned between knowing and doing, between clearness and effectiveness. A sheer desire of knowledge, a genuine bent for research shows itself in its results to be much more important for life than any activity however practically directed. Can anything be more practical than medicine? Nevertheless, it attains its best observations through a plainly theoretical method. Practice is wonderfully served and made efficient by the purely theoretical worker.

Can anything be more practical than technique? But it has made its greatest progress through pure disinterested science, i.e. research into the nature and the spirit of the subjects in question. Therefore the investigator gets the sensation of being led up to what he does not know, if only he is obedient to his method. He is the servant of an association which he cannot survey.

* * * * *

Great men of genius when serving God consciously and with all their hearts belong to the saints. The doctrine of saints lost its importance in Evangelic theology when the cult of the saints was abolished in the name of the Gospel. In this matter I agree with the Roman Church and its theology in so far as the saints are Christian men and women who specially reveal the power of God. But divine power ought not to be assigned in a primitive way to extraordinary cases of suggestion. It ought not to be defined as a miracle, but be regarded in accordance with a Christian conception of God.

A place of honour is due to those saints of religion who have put their whole soul into serving and apprehending God's will in *history*. It is on purpose that I put "serving" first and then "apprehending." For in God's kingdom and in the realm of the Spirit and of moral truth, man can see nothing, so long as he is standing as a mere spectator; only those who serve God fully and self-sacrificingly can perceive God's will. In other things one usually wants to look ahead and to understand before undertaking anything. But in God's kingdom it is the reverse. Here we enter on the second way in which God continues to reveal himself, *history*. We have already in previous lectures studied those who were the first to see a real revelation of God in history, Zarathushtra and the prophets in the Old Testament, and, under their influence, Christianity and Islam.

How alien the thought of a revelation in history was to the Graeco-Roman antiquity can be seen in Cicero. In *De natura Deorum* [On the Nature of the Gods] Cicero classifies the expressions of divine providence with his customary particularity and orderliness, but he never even touches on the idea of the appearance of God in the events and associations of history. For Mosaism the marvels of history were of fundamental importance. God brought his oppressed people out of Egypt. History told of his righteousness and his grace. What is it that distinguishes the prophets and spirits akin to them from other saints and great men of religion? Characteristic of all saints it is that they have deeply experienced God's mind and revealed it for the benefit of many. But other great men of religion have sought and experienced God by flying from history into a timeless intercourse with God, as Yajnavalkya and his followers in India and several mystics in Western civilization and in the Church. The prophets communicate with God in history. Their inner experience grows stronger, clearer, and richer when expanded by God's work in history. There they hear God's voice. They hear also other voices; they hear the voices of a frivolous, unrepentant, and self-sufficient people; they see ignorance and darkness, so that sometimes everything grows dark to them; the wrecks of kingdoms falling to pieces and the self-satisfied nationalism of their fellow countrymen threaten to fill their eyes with dust. But they know that God lives and, in spite of all, holds the threads in his hands. The characteristic of prophetic piety through all times is this: God speaks to me, to us, in history, in my little history, in the great history.

We need not go back to the Old Testament to find this. The greatest witness of God's revelation in history is Christ himself. How very much did the prophets and the psalmists contribute to the work of his spirit! He builds on what they have thought and suffered from God's way of dealing with them. Jesus does not live in the mystic's peaceful corner, but he is a combatant in the midst of the confusion of battle. Jesus does not stand aloof on a hill as a spectator; he is in the very throng of the people — although he sometimes had to go "up into a mountain apart to pray." His value for every age and for every soul Jesus attained, not by abstracting himself from his own time and standing aloof from its struggles, but on the contrary by thrusting himself into that which was a matter of life and death to his people in the very epoch in which he lived. No people has more intensely lived its history than Israel. No personality is deeper rooted in history than Jesus. How he fought for this people: "Let the tree alone this year also." How he struggled with this people for its soul: "How often would I have gathered thy children together." If history be not the revelation of God, Jesus' striving becomes incomprehensible. If you admit Christ, then you must admit history. For he stands in it with full responsibility and in violent, dramatic tension.

*   *   *   *   *

And indeed, to-day, after the miserable and gigantic breakdown of our Western Commonwealth and European politics, courage is needed to maintain, *quand même*, in spite of the bankruptcy of European statesmanship and the general unrest and actual or menacing economic disorder and distress, the confidence that history is in God's hands and that it has a goal, surpassing human understanding.

God's Revelation is not finished — it continues. Here a most essential distinction must be made. Heaven was not shut up after the manifestation of God recorded in the Bible. We see it open over the Bible and in the Bible as nowhere else, and go to it in order to see the Eternal Light shine through the grey mist of existence. God is ever revealing himself. God's continued revelation is history. Of course, I hold that the Church is God's work and God's instrument. The religious value of the Church is sometimes overrated, but often also underrated. God has entrusted the Church with the divine privilege and the tremendous duty of giving to the world in word and deed and sacrament the Grace of God. Our belief in God's continued revelation in history makes us consider, more diligently and more reverently than before, the value of men, means, and institutions, which God has given to the Church in the course of history. But God's revelation is not confined to the Church, although the Church has, in the Scriptures and in its experience, the means of interpreting God's continued revelation. The Church ought to open its eyes, more than it does, to see how God is perpetually revealing himself. The Evangelic statement that God has revealed himself once for all in the Bible is true and must be maintained in its true sense about the divine action recorded in the Scriptures. But we often fail to learn the lesson of the Bible, that our God is a living, a still living God, who has not become older and less active than in earlier days.

Roman Catholic opinion finds the Protestant appeal to "the Bible and the Bible only" narrow-minded, and says: "God is in his Church. He is speaking through the ecclesiastical authority" — and at the same time this very authority is cutting off its connexions with real history and is burying itself in a mausoleum of antiquated thoughts and ideas. Against the Roman theory we thus raise two objections: (1) It makes the continuous revelation of God leave the ground of history and enter an institution. (2) It makes the continuous revelation of God leave the area of life and enter a theological system, that venerable and comprehensive Thomism, which used once to be alive, but is now a venerable memorial from the past.

God reveals himself in history, outside the Church as well as in it. Cyrus, the Persian king, is called Messiah by the prophet.

God reveals himself as much in the vicissitudes of nations as in the institutions of religion. If one stands on the Acropolis and allows one's gaze to fall on the waters of the Saronic Gulf along the bold coast-line from Cape Sunium to the Bay of Eleusis behind Salamis, one may ask oneself, which meant more for the history of God's dominion and the spiritual profit of mankind — Marathon and Salamis, where the Athenians fought for their state, or Eleusis, lying far within the quiet bay, where they sought consolation against the fleeting destiny of man? It may be that statesmen in certain historical situations have greater importance for God's kingdom than thousands of sermons.

It may be that some despised Utopians, dreaming and working, do more for God's plan than a most perfect and stately hierarchy or a well-balanced piety, which call them crazy. It may be that political changes and social movements mean a mightier revelation of God than the undertakings of the Church. The voice of God can speak to mankind even by lips that deny his existence. These statements are in no wise paradoxes, but are meant quite literally. In the complicated course of events the will of God may be dimly conceived by one who is fighting in the battle. No one must say to us, Lo, here is God or there. But each one must struggle at his post in the ranks. Suddenly, maybe, the mist will lift, and he will be permitted to see what God is doing.

There are courses of events in which the watchful eye of a Christian cannot but recognize the work of God. What weight have, in fact, our Churches and our religious associations with the men who now are working with heads and hearts? What does God think about it? Surely we and our Christianity stand denounced before him.

Are the Christianity and theology of to-day equal to the emergency? Does it live, does it think, does it act in the presence of the Living God, or is it confined within the insipid self-complacency of a clique, and in a kind of esoteric scholasticism? In what does our Christianity consist? In the revelation of God to us and within us, or in forms, training, mental suggestion?

The certainty of God's creation cannot be given to men and preserved in men, when they need it, by any inference from or reflections upon civilization or history, but only by God first taking men out of civilization and history to be alone with him, revealing himself to them and continuing his revelation in their lives. The distress of the soul and the mercy of God must force us out of all the strongholds of the world, that we may be able to see in the world the workings of God. We must ourselves possess a hidden life with God in order to discern clearly for ourselves and believe thoroughly in his continued Revelation in history.

Thus from creative genius and from history we pass on to the third sphere of God's revelation, *the regeneration of the individual*. What is implied, strictly speaking, by a man's being or becoming a Christian? In this connexion we, to begin with, give two answers: (1) that a creation takes place in him, that something original appears in him in a way analogous to genius in its manifestation; and (2) that he consciously enters into the history of Revelation.

1. God creates something new in the individual. We have discerned God's continued, mysterious creation in genius. In plain men and women also something can take place, analogous to what we said about genius. The resemblance, of course, need not consist in any peculiar intuitive or ecstatic working of the mind. Such resemblance is not essential. The resemblance lies in the result; something relatively new and original arises. This is done by the new liberty, gained through perfect submission under the will of God. Moral independence, the moral personality, the "new man," is no more made after a recipe than the works of genius come into existence by a ready-made rule; but in a "new man" there appears a life raised above nature, a life which has its principle in itself. When a man simply and bravely does what his conscience bids him in opposition to calculation and enticement, when he in repentance and contrition turns from sin, when a soul sincerely and unconditionally throws itself upon God's judging and saving mercy, when it concentrates itself on a whole-hearted prayer, when in the midst of confusion and temptation light is won triumphantly, whenever, in fact, a personality vindicates its liberty, then, in that sacred hour, God creates. In conversion, in the birth to a new life, when inward truthfulness is put in practice sincerely and bravely: then, at the summit of moral life and communion with God, the soul is by the power of God raised to a state resembling in originality that of genius.

I like to quote the words of Kierkegaard, that life is a poem that we are to write ourselves; but a Christian lets God write his life's poem.

How essential moral independence is to Christianity is made evident by, amongst other things, its recognized relation to the most sincere and infallible religious characteristic of Christian piety, the prayer of the heart.

The test of real answer to prayer is that the presence of God is proved, not only or not at all by fervent emotions, but by a new-born power against sin and difficulties. The moral criterion of the answer to prayer is not only more life under favourable circumstances, rest in weariness, concentration in the midst of uneasiness and anxiety. Does prayer give you peace of mind to work in spite of violent attacks, bitter misunderstandings, and heavy afflictions? Can prayer create confidence under spiritual and bodily visitations and derive from suffering its spiritual gain? Do you, during your daily toil and in your troubles, walk with God, and speak with God? Without spiritual independence there is no true Christianity. No truth has in our time been more precisely formulated than this.

Kant is in this respect the authentic interpreter of the Gospel. And we are quite right in considering — whether approving or disapproving — Kant's teaching of the majesty and absoluteness of the moral demands as an effect or a fulfilment of the metaphysical faith which is the foundation of Christian morality. The paltry religion of Kant, "Religion within the bounds of bare reason," at one point grows deep and wonderful. In face of the majesty of moral obligation he prostrates himself in the dust and worships. There he feels absolute reverence and willing obedience. He takes man as far as the claims of conscience. Herrmann takes him one step farther, up to Christ. And that is right. For the nature of the claim when unconditioned is purely formal. In Christ the claim has a concrete substance, which judges man and puts him to death, as long as he is self-dependent, but which works a divine creation in him, namely, confidence in the mercy of God, when he lets God create in him.

In placing side by side, from a certain point of view, the moral emancipation of the individual and the existence of the genius, we mean no lack of appreciation of the special position of morality in comparison with a form of humanity which is merely natural or merely determined by civilization or merely defined by the special nature of the endowments of genius. As a matter of fact between an individual life, which is animated from within by a spiritual and moral revival, and a human existence without any starting-point, thus raised above mere nature, there is the most essential difference which we are able to discern in the grades of existence, accessible to us. None the less, moral life, when it has raised itself above mere legality and customary ethics into personal independence, exhibits striking analogies to the creation of genius.

(a) In both cases, in the moral character as well as in the genius, there is a standard, but not in the form of an external rule, not a scheme lying ready to hand or a model to imitate, but as an internal principle, the result of which cannot be determined beforehand, but which in every function forms its own rule and, when the action has been completed, reveals a consistency and a beauty in accordance with the peculiar nature of life. To let the standard mean merely a model after which something is shaped is to misjudge the nature both of creative work of genius and of individual life itself.

(b) The internal principle — for the work of art or for the moral personality — expresses itself in both cases as unconditioned, as something compulsory, but not, like the compulsion of emotional life, or the compulsion imposed from without, a compulsion that enslaves, debases, and finally breaks up and renders impossible the true unity that characterizes the morally responsible man. Rather it is something unconditioned, which, when it is obeyed in the burning zeal of creative capacity or in the travails and decisions of the life of the conscience, attains, enhances, and strengthens liberty and internal unity.

(c) This unconditioned compulsion arising from an inner principle reveals the nature of life as being in both cases a continued creation, which brings forth something new. Even in the primitive stage of religion initiation into the mysteries of the tribe often take the form of the youth being regarded as dying and then being reborn into a new and higher life so that, in very fact, he is "twice born." The infinitely varying symbolism, found in the rites of the mysteries and in the world of religious expression with regard to dying and revival to a higher state of existence, obtains a new content, more definite and more remarkable, when it is applied to moral renewal. "The new man" is more than a mode of speaking: it is a revelation of a process of creation which aspires upwards.

2. Secondly, what does it mean that the soul meets Christ? The great Revelation of God turns into God's transaction with me. History becomes my history. "It was done for me." "Given for you, shed for you." The most important event of my life will be Jesus Christ. At the same time the individual is brought into the history of Revelation. God's creation is continued in him. That which takes place in the petty history of a man's soul receives a new significance, it becomes God's way of dealing with his child. The drama of the world takes hold of the individual soul. He finds that his own history means a choice between God and the Devil. Shall God create or shall the Devil destroy in him? God's struggle against evil, lethargy, and death is manifested throughout history. Every human being must take part in that grand and perilous fight between Life and Death, between God's revealing miracle and darkness.

The difference between religious research in general and Christian theology in particular consists in the fact that the belief in revelation is an essential part of the latter. For Christian theology the history of religions is a divine self-communication. The comparative study of religions in general leaves the question about revelation open. He who practises it may be inspired by the conviction that a supernatural reality is lying behind the phenomena of religion. Or he may deny the belief in the spiritual which is fundamental for religion. Or he may remain inquiring and uncertain about the revelation, certain only of the impossibility of knowing anything about it. Or he may lack interest in the question about the truth of religion. Different views as regards the idea of revelation may of course not influence the method of research and the historical and psychological investigations in such a way that these are displaced in one direction or another by dogmatism. The remedy against such mistakes (faults) is not to forbid the investigator to have a certain conviction, but solely to carry out the investigation rightly, conscientiously, and seriously, and to submit readily to perceived truths.

DOROTHY DAY

The Sacredness of Life

Dorothy Day (1897–1980) was the founder of *The Catholic Worker*, whose pages became one of the principal voices for Roman Catholic social thought in America. Her own evolution from Socialism (though never quite beyond Socialism) to Roman Catholicism was the subject of her remarkable autobiography, *The Long Loneliness*, from which the following chapter (originally entitled "Confession") is taken.

WHEN YOU GO to confession on a Saturday night, you go into a warm, dimly lit vastness, with the smell of wax and incense in the air, the smell of burning candles, and if it is a hot summer night there is the sound of a great electric fan, and the noise of the streets coming in to emphasize the stillness. There is another sound too, besides that of the quiet movements of the people from pew to confession to altar rail; there is the sliding of the shutters of the little window between you and the priest in his "box."

Some confessionals are large and roomy — plenty of space for the knees, and breathing space in the thick darkness that seems to pulse with your own heart. In some poor churches, many of the ledges are narrow and worn, so your knees almost slip off the kneeling bench, and your feet protrude outside the curtain which shields you from the others who are waiting. Some churches have netting, or screens, between you and priest and you can see the outline of his face inclined toward you, quiet, impersonal, patient. Some have a piece of material covering the screen, so you can see nothing. Some priests leave their lights on in their boxes so they can read their breviaries between confessions. The light does not bother you if that piece of material is there so you cannot see or be seen, but if it is only a grating so that he can see your face, it is embarrassing and you do not go back to that priest again.

Going to confession is hard — hard when you have sins to confess, hard when you haven't, and you rack your brain for even the beginnings of sins against charity, chastity, sins of detraction, sloth or gluttony. You do not want to make too much of your constant imperfections and venial sins, but you want to drag them out to the light of day as the first step in getting rid of them. The just man falls seven times daily.

"Bless me, Father, for I have sinned," is the way you begin. "I made my last confession a week ago, and since then . . ."

Properly, one should say the *Confiteor*, but the priest has no time for that, what with the long lines of penitents on a Saturday night, so you are supposed to say it outside the confessional as you kneel in a pew, or as you stand in line with others.

"I have sinned. These are my sins." That is all you are supposed to tell; not the sins of others, or your own virtues, but only your ugly, gray, drab, monotonous sins.

When one writes the story of his life and the work he has been engaged in, it is a confession too, in a way. When I wrote the story of my conversion twelve years ago, I left out all my sins but told of all the things which had brought me to God, all the beautiful things, all the remembrances of God that had haunted me, pursued me over the years so that when my daughter was born, in grateful joy I turned to God and became a Catholic. I could worship, adore, praise and thank Him in the company of others. It is difficult to do that without a ritual, without a body with which to love and move, love and praise. I found faith. I became a member of the Mystical Body of Christ.

Going to confession is hard. Writing a book is hard, because you are "giving yourself away." But if you love, you want to give yourself. You write as you are impelled to write, about man and his problems, his relation to God and his fellows. You write about yourself because in the long run all man's problems are the same, his human needs of sustenance and love. "What is man that Thou art mindful of him?" the Psalmist asks, and he indicates man's immense dignity when he says, "Thou hast made him a little less than the angels." He is made in the image and likeness of God, he is a temple of the Holy Spirit. He is of tremendous importance. What is man, where is he going, what is his destiny? It is a mystery. We are sons of God, and "it is a terrible thing to fall into the hands of the living God."

I can write only of myself, what I know of myself, and I pray with St. Augustine, "Lord, that I may know myself, in order to know Thee." I could write long chapters about my daughter, about my early associates, about the men and women I have been working with these last eighteen years. Probably I have been unfair not to have written more about them, but if I started to tell about all the saints and sinners among us and the fascinating account of their lives, I would never end. Moreover, I feel hesitant to go too deeply in writing of other lives. It is hard enough to write about my own. I do feel, however, that I have a right to give an account of myself, a reason for the faith that is in me. But I have not that right to discuss others. Just the same, if I have slighted anyone, if I have failed to give credit where credit is due, if I have neglected some aspects of the work in stressing others, I beg pardon of my readers. I am a journalist, not a biographer, not a *book* writer. The sustained effort of writing, of putting pen to paper so many hours a day when there are human beings around who need me, when there is sickness, and hunger, and sorrow, is a harrowingly painful job. I feel that I have done nothing well. But I have done what I could.

I have not always felt the richness of life, its sacredness. I do not see how people can, without a religious faith. Children have a sense of joy in life but that soon wears away. One hears adolescents say, "I did not ask to be born." Rebellion has started.

My life has been divided into two parts. The first twenty-five years were floundering, years of joy and sorrow, it is true, but certainly with a sense of that insecurity one hears so much about these days. I did not know in what I believed, though I tried to serve a cause. Five years after I became a Catholic I met Peter Maurin and his story must play a great part in this work because he was my master and I was his disciple; he gave me "a way of life and instruction," and to explain what has come to be known as "The Catholic Worker Movement" in the Church throughout the world, I must write of him.

But I will begin with my own story. "All my life I have been haunted by God," as Kiriloff said in *The Possessed*. This must indeed be so, as former friends and comrades have said this of me. Not long ago when I was visiting a patient at Bellevue, I again met someone whom I had known casually at the University of Illinois and in Chicago in the early days of the Communist party there.

"I remember you," she said, "because Fred Ellis' mother-in-law did a painting of you which they still have." Fred is a *Daily Worker* cartoonist. "The last time I saw you, years ago, you were talking to me of God."

A Cleveland Communist said once, "Dorothy was never a Communist. She was too religious."

How much did I hear of religion as a child? Very little, and yet my heart leaped when I heard the name of God. I do believe every soul has a tendency toward God. "As soon as man recalls the Godhead, a certain sweet movement fills his heart. . . . Our understanding has never such great joy as when thinking of God," St. Francis de Sales writes.

MIGUEL DE UNAMUNO

The Tragic Sense of Life

> Miguel de Unamuno y Jugo (1864–1936), a professor at the University of Salamanca, Spain, for most of his life except for several years as an exile, was the author of many essays and poems. In *The Tragic Sense of Life* he expounded an existentialist philosophy of life, and in that context, as the following exposition makes eloquently clear, he gave his own highly individual answers to the religious questions of traditional philosophy and theology.

To AFFIRM that the religious sense is a sense of divinity and that it is impossible without some abuse of the ordinary usages of human language to speak of an atheistic religion, is not, I think, to do violence to the truth; although it is clear that everything will depend upon the concept that we form of God, a concept which in its turn depends upon the concept of divinity.

Our proper procedure, in effect, will be to begin with this sense of divinity, before prefixing to the concept of this quality the definite article and the capital letter and so converting it into "the Divinity" — that is, into God. For man has not deduced the divine from God, but rather he has reached God through the divine.

In the course of these somewhat wandering but at the same time urgent reflections upon the tragic sense of life, I have already alluded to the *timor fecit deos* of Statius with the object of limiting and correcting it. It is not my intention to trace yet once again the historical processes by which peoples have arrived at the consciousness and concept of a personal God like the God of Christianity. And I say peoples and not isolated individuals, for if there is any feeling or concept that is truly collective and social it is the feeling and concept of God, although the individual subsequently individualizes it. Philosophy may, and in fact does, possess an individual origin; theology is necessarily collective.

Schleiermacher's theory, which attributes the origin, or rather the essence, of the religious sense to the immediate and simple feeling of dependency, appears to be the most profound and exact explanation. Primitive man, living in society, feels himself to be dependent upon the mysterious forces invisibly environing him; he feels himself to be in social communion, not only with beings like himself, his fellow-men, but with the whole of Nature, animate and inanimate, which simply means, in other words, that he personalizes everything. Not only does he possess a consciousness of the world, but he imagines that the world, like himself, possesses consciousness also. Just as a child talks to his doll or his dog as if it understood what he was saying, so the savage believes that his fetich hears him when he speaks to it, and that the angry storm-cloud is aware of him and deliberately pursues him. For the newly born mind of the primitive natural man has not yet wholly severed itself from the cords which still bind it to the womb of Nature, neither has it clearly marked out the boundary that separates dreaming from waking, imagination from reality.

The divine, therefore, was not originally something objective, but was rather the subjectivity of consciousness projected exteriorly, the personalization of the world. The concept of divinity arose out of the feeling of divinity, and the feeling of divinity is simply the dim and nascent feeling of personality vented upon the outside world. And strictly speaking it is not possible to speak of outside and inside, objective and subjective, when no such distinction was actually felt; indeed it is precisely from this lack of distinction that the feeling and concept of divinity proceed. The clearer our consciousness of the distinction between the objective and the subjective, the more obscure is the feeling of divinity in us.

It has been said, and very justly so it would appear, that Hellenic paganism was not so much polytheistic as pantheistic. I do not know that the belief in a multitude of gods, taking the concept of God in the sense in which we understand it to-day, has ever really existed in any human mind. And if by pantheism is understood the doctrine, not that everything and each individual thing is God — a proposition which I find unthinkable — but that everything is divine, then it may be said without any great abuse of language that paganism was pantheistic. Its gods not only mixed among men but intermixed with them; they begat gods upon mortal women and upon goddesses mortal men begat demi-gods. And if demi-gods, that is, demi-men, were believed to exist, it was because the divine and the human were viewed as different aspects of the same reality. The divinization of everything was simply its humanization. To say that the sun was a god was equivalent to saying that it was a man, a human consciousness, more or less, aggrandized and sublimated. And this is true of all beliefs from fetichism to Hellenic paganism.

The real distinction between gods and men consisted in the fact that the former were immortal. A god came to be identical with an immortal man and a man was deified, reputed as a god, when it was deemed that at his death he had not really died. Of certain heroes it was believed that they were alive in the kingdom of the dead. And this is a point of great importance in estimating the value of the concept of the divine.

In those republics of gods there was always some predominating god, some real monarch. It was through the agency of this divine monarchy that primitive peoples were led from monocultism to monotheism. Hence monarchy and monotheism are twin brethren. Zeus, Jupiter, was in process of being converted into an only god, just as Jahwé, originally one god among many others, came to be converted into an only god, first the god of the people of Israel, then the god of humanity, and finally the god of the whole universe.

Like monarchy, monotheism had a martial origin. "It is only on the march and in time of war," says Robertson Smith in *The Prophets of Israel,* "that a nomad people feels any urgent need of a central authority, and so it came about that in the first beginnings of national organization, centring in the sanctuary of the ark, Israel was thought of mainly as the host of Jehovah. The very name of Israel is martial, and means "God (*El*) fighteth," and Jehovah in the Old Testament is Iahwè Çebãôth — the Jehovah of the armies of Israel. It was on the battlefield that Jehovah's presence was most clearly realized; but in primitive nations the leader in time of war is also the natural judge in time of peace."

God, the only God, issued, therefore, from man's sense of divinity as a warlike, monarchical and social God. He revealed himself to the people as a whole, not to the individual. He was the God of a people and he jealously exacted that worship should be rendered to him alone. The transition from this monocultism to monotheism was effected largely by the individual action, more philosophical perhaps than theological, of the prophets. It was, in fact, the individual activity of the prophets that individualized the divinity. And above all by making the divinity ethical.

Subsequently reason — that is, philosophy — took possession of this God who had arisen in the human consciousness as a consequence of the sense of divinity in man, and tended to define him and convert him into an idea. For to define a thing is to idealize it, a process which necessitates the abstraction from it of its incommensurable or irrational element, its vital essence. Thus the God of feeling, the divinity felt as a unique person and consciousness external to us, although at the same time enveloping and sustaining us, was converted into the idea of God.

The logical, rational God, the *ens summum*, the *primum movens*, the Supreme Being of theological philosophy, the God who is reached by the three famous ways of negation, eminence and causality, *viæ negationis, eminentiæ, causalitatis*, is nothing but an idea of God, a dead thing. The traditional and much debated proofs of his existence are, at bottom, merely a vain attempt to determine his essence; for as Vinet has very well observed, existence is deduced from essence; and to say that God exists, without saying what God is and how he is, is equivalent to saying nothing at all.

And this God, arrived at by the methods of eminence and negation or abstraction of finite qualities, ends by becoming an unthinkable God, a pure idea, a God of whom, by the very fact of his ideal excellence, we can say that he is nothing, as indeed he has been defined by Scotus Erigena: *Deus propter excellentiam non inmerito nihil vocatur*. Or in the words of the pseudo-Dionysius the Areopagite, in his fifth Epistle, "The divine darkness is the inaccessible light in which God is said to dwell." The anthropomorphic God, the God who is felt, in being purified of human, and as such finite, relative and temporal, attributes, evaporates into the God of deism or of pantheism.

The traditional so-called proofs of the existence of God all refer to this God-Idea, to this logical God, the God by abstraction, and hence they really prove nothing, or rather, they prove nothing more than the existence of this idea of God.

In my early youth, when first I began to be puzzled by these eternal problems, I read in a book, the author of which I have no wish to recall, this sentence: "God is the great X placed over the ultimate barrier of human knowledge; in the measure in which science advances, the barrier recedes." And I wrote in the margin, "On this side of the barrier, everything is explained without Him; on the further side, nothing is explained, either with Him or without Him; God therefore is superfluous." And so far as concerns the God-Idea, the God of the proofs, I continue to be of the same opinion. Laplace is said to have stated that he had not found the hypothesis of God necessary in order to construct his scheme of the origin of the Universe, and it is very true. In no way whatever does the idea of God help us to understand better the existence, the essence and the finality of the Universe.

That there is a Supreme Being, infinite, absolute and eternal, whose existence is unknown to us, and who has created the Universe, is not more conceivable than that the material basis of the Universe itself, its matter, is eternal and infinite and absolute. We do not understand the existence of the world one whit the better by telling ourselves that God created it. It is a begging of the question, or a merely verbal solution, intended to cover up our ignorance. In strict truth, we deduce the existence of the Creator from the fact that the thing created exists, a process which does not justify rationally His existence. You cannot deduce a necessity from a fact, or else everything were necessary.

And if from the nature of the Universe we pass to what is called its order, which is supposed to necessitate an Ordainer, we may say that order is what there is, and we do not conceive of any other. This deduction of God's existence from the order of the Universe implies a transition from the ideal to the real order, an outward projection of our mind, a supposition that the rational explanation of a thing produces the thing itself. Human art, instructed by Nature, possesses a conscious creative faculty, by means of which it apprehends the process of creation, and we proceed to transfer this conscious and artistic creative faculty to the consciousness of an artist-creator, but from what nature he in his turn learnt his art we cannot tell.

The traditional analogy of the watch and the watchmaker is inapplicable to a Being absolute, infinite and eternal. It is, moreover, only another way of explaining nothing. For to say that the world is as it is and not otherwise because God made it so, while at the same time we do not know for what reason He made it so, is to say nothing. And if we knew for what reason God made it so, then God is superfluous and the reason itself suffices. If everything were mathematics, if there were no irrational element, we should not have had recourse to this explanatory theory of a Supreme Ordainer, who is nothing but the reason of the irrational, and so merely another cloak for our ignorance. And let us not discuss here that absurd proposition that, if all the type in a printing-press were printed at random, the result could not possibly be the composition of *Don Quixote*. Something would be composed which would be as good as *Don Quixote* for those who would have to be content with it and would grow in it and would form part of it.

In effect, this traditional supposed proof of God's existence resolves itself fundamentally into hypostatizing or substantivating the explanation or reason of a phenomenon; it amounts to saying that Mechanics is the cause of movement, Biology of life, Philology of language, Chemistry of bodies, by simply adding the capital letter to the science and converting it into a force distinct from the phenomena from which we derive it and distinct from our mind which effects the derivation. But the God who is the result of this process, a God who is nothing but reason hypostatized and projected towards the infinite, cannot possibly be felt as something living and real, nor yet be conceived of save as a mere idea which will die with us.

The question arises, on the other hand, whether a thing the idea of which has been conceived but which has no real existence, does not exist because God wills that it should not exist, or whether God does not will it to exist because, in fact, it does not exist; and, with regard to the impossible, whether a thing is impossible because God wills it so, or whether God wills it so because, in itself and by the very fact of its own inherent absurdity, it is impossible. God has to submit to the logical law of contradiction, and He cannot, according to the theologians, cause two and two to make either more or less than four. Either the law of necessity is above Him or He Himself is the law of necessity. And in the moral order the question arises whether falsehood, or homicide, or adultery, are wrong because He has so decreed it, or whether He has so decreed it because they are wrong. If the former, then God is a capricious and unreasonable God, who decrees one law when He might equally well have decreed another, or, if the latter, He obeys an intrinsic nature and essence which exists in things themselves independently of Him — that is to say, independently of His sovereign will; and if this is the case, if He obeys the innate reason of things, this reason, if we could but know it, would suffice us without any further need of God, and since we do not know it, God explains nothing. This reason would be above God. Neither is it of any avail to say that this reason is God Himself, the supreme reason of things. A reason of this kind, a necessary reason, is not a personal something. It is will that gives personality. And it is because of this problem of the relations between God's reason, necessarily necessary, and His will, necessarily free, that the logical and Aristotelian God will always be a contradictory God.

The scholastic theologians never succeeded in disentangling themselves from the difficulties in which they found themselves involved when they attempted to reconcile human liberty with divine prescience and with the knowledge that God possesses of the free and contingent future; and that is strictly the reason why the rational God is wholly inapplicable to the contingent, for the notion of contingency is fundamentally the same as the notion of irrationality. The rational God is necessarily necessary in His being and in His working; in every single case He cannot do other than the best, and a number of different things cannot all equally be the best, for among infinite possibilities there is only one that is best accommodated to its end, just as among the infinite number of lines that can be drawn from one point to another, there is only one straight line. And the rational God, the God of reason, cannot but follow in each case the straight line, the line that leads most directly to the end proposed, a necessary end, just as the only straight line that leads to it is a necessary line. And thus for the divinity of God is substituted His necessity. And in the necessity of God, His free will — that is to say, His conscious personality — perishes. The God of our heart's desire, the God who shall save our soul from nothingness, must needs be an arbitrary God.

Not because He thinks can God be God, but because He works, because He creates; He is not a contemplative but an active God. A God-Reason, a theoretical or contemplative God, such as is this God of theological rationalism, is a God that is diluted in His own contemplation. With this God corresponds, as we shall see, the beatific vision, understood as the supreme expression of human felicity. A quietist God, in short, as reason, by its very essence, is quietist.

There remains the other famous proof of God's existence, that of the supposed unanimous consent in a belief in Him among all peoples. But this proof is not strictly rational, neither is it an argument in favour of the rational God who explains the Universe, but of the God of the heart, who makes us live. We should be justified in calling it a rational proof only on the supposition that we believed that reason was identical with a more or less unanimous agreement among all peoples, that it corresponded with the verdict of a universal suffrage, only on the supposition that we held that *vox populi*, which is said to be *vox Dei*, was actually the voice of reason.

Such was, indeed, the belief of Lamennais, that tragic and ardent spirit, who affirmed that life and truth were essentially one and the same thing — would that they were! — and that reason was one, universal, everlasting and holy. He invoked the *aut omnibus credendum est aut nemini* of Lactantius — we must believe all or none — and the saying of Heraclitus that every individual opinion is fallible, and that of Aristotle that the strongest proof consists in the general agreement of mankind, and above all that of Pliny, to the effect that one man cannot deceive all men or be deceived by all — *nemo omnes, neminem omnes fefellerunt.* Would that it were so! And so he concludes with the dictum of Cicero, that we must believe the tradition of our ancestors even though they fail to render us a reason — *maioribus autem nostris, etìam nulla ratione reddita credere.*

Let us suppose that this belief of the ancients in the divine inter-penetration of the whole of Nature is universal and constant, and that it is, as Aristotle calls it, an ancestral dogma; this would prove only that there is a motive impelling peoples and individuals — that is to say, all or almost all or a majority of them — to believe in a God. But may it not be that there are illusions and fallacies rooted in human nature itself? Do not all peoples begin by believing that the sun turns round the earth? And do we not all naturally incline to believe that which satisfies our desires? Shall we say with Hermann that, "if there is a God, He has not left us without some indication of Himself, and it is His will that we should find Him."

A pious desire, no doubt, but we cannot strictly call it a reason, unless we apply to it the Augustinian sentence, but which again is not a reason, "Since thou seekest Me, it must be that thou hast found Me," believing that God is the cause of our seeking Him.

This famous argument from the supposed unanimity of mankind's belief in God, the argument which with a sure instinct was seized upon by the ancients, is in its essence identical with the so-called moral proof which Kant employed in his *Critique of Practical Reason,* trans-posing its application from mankind collectively to the individual, the proof which he derives from our conscience, or rather from our feeling of divinity. It is not a proof strictly or specifically rational, but vital, it cannot be applied to the logical God, the *ens summum,* the essentially simple and abstract Being, the immobile and impassible prime mover, the God-Reason, in a word, but to the biotic God, to the Being essentially complex and concrete, to the suffering God who suffers and desires in us and with us, to the Father of Christ who is only to be approached through Man, through His Son (John xiv. 6), and whose revelation is historical, or if you like, anecdotical, but not philosoph-ical or categorical.

The unanimous consent of mankind (let us suppose the unanimity) or, in other words, this universal longing of all human souls who have arrived at the consciousness of their humanity, which desires to be the end and meaning of the Universe, this longing, which is nothing but that very essence of the soul which consists in its effort to persist eternally and without a break in the continuity of consciousness, leads us to the human, anthropomorphic God, the projection of our consciousness to the Consciousness of the Universe; it leads us to the God who confers human meaning and finality upon the Universe and who is not the *ens summum*, the *primum movens*, nor the Creator of the Universe, nor merely the Idea-God. It leads us to the living, subjective God, for He is simply subjectivity objectified or personality universalized — He is more than a mere idea, and He is will rather than reason. God is Love — that is, Will. Reason, the Word, derives from Him, but He, the Father, is, above all, Will.

"There can be no doubt whatever," Ritschl says, "that a very imperfect view was taken of God's spiritual personality in the older theology, when the functions of knowing and willing alone were employed to illustrate it. Religious thought plainly ascribes to God affections of feeling as well. The older theology, however, laboured under the impression that feeling and emotion were characteristic only of limited and created personality; it transformed, e.g., the religious idea of the Divine blessedness into eternal self-knowledge, and that of the Divine wrath into a fixed purpose to punish sin." Yes, this logical God, arrived at by the *via negationis*, was a God who, strictly speaking, neither loved nor hated, because He neither enjoyed nor suffered, an inhuman God, and His justice was a rational or mathematical justice — that is, an injustice.

The attributes of the living God, of the Father of Christ, must be deduced from His historical revelation in the Gospel and in the conscience of every Christian believer, and not from metaphysical reasonings which lead only to the Nothing-God of Scotus Erigena, to the rational or pantheistic God, to the atheist God — in short, to the de-personalized Divinity.

Not by the way of reason, but only by the way of love and of suffering, do we come to the living God, the human God. Reason rather separates us from Him. We cannot first know Him in order that afterwards we may love Him; we must begin by loving Him, longing for Him, hungering after Him, before knowing Him. The knowledge of God proceeds from the love of God, and this knowledge has little or nothing of the rational in it. For God is indefinable. To seek to define Him is to seek to confine Him within the limits of our mind — that is to say, to kill Him. In so far as we attempt to define Him, there rises up before us — Nothingness.

The idea of God, formulated by a theodicy that claims to be rational, is simply an hypothesis, like the hypothesis of ether, for example.

Ether is, in effect, a merely hypothetical entity, valuable only in so far as it explains that which by means of it we endeavour to explain — light, electricity or universal gravitation — and only in so far as these facts cannot be explained in any other way. In like manner the idea of God is also an hypothesis, valuable only in so far as it enables us to explain that which by means of it we endeavour to explain — the essence and existence of the Universe — and only so long as these cannot be explained in any other way. And since in reality we explain the Universe neither better nor worse with this idea than without it, the idea of God, the supreme *petitio principii*, is valueless.

But if ether is nothing but an hypothesis explanatory of light, air, on the other hand, is a thing that is directly felt; and even though it did not enable us to explain the phenomenon of sound, we should nevertheless always be directly aware of it, and above all, of the lack of it in moments of suffocation or air-hunger. And in the same way God Himself, not the idea of God, may become a reality that is immediately felt; and even though the idea of Him does not enable us to explain either the existence or the essence of the Universe, we have at times the direct feeling of God, above all in moments of spiritual suffocation. And this feeling — mark it well, for all that is tragic in it and the whole tragic sense of life is founded upon this — this feeling is a feeling of hunger for God, of the lack of God. To believe in God is, in the first instance, as we shall see, to wish that there may be a God, to be unable to live without Him.

So long as I pilgrimaged through the fields of reason in search of God, I could not find Him, for I was not deluded by the idea of God, neither could I take an idea for God, and it was then, as I wandered among the wastes of rationalism, that I told myself that we ought to seek no other consolation than the truth, meaning thereby reason, and yet for all that I was not comforted. But as I sank deeper and deeper into rational scepticism on the one hand and into heart's despair on the other, the hunger for God awoke within me, and the suffocation of spirit made me feel the want of God, and with the want of Him, His reality. And I wished that there might be a God, that God might exist. And God does not exist, but rather super-exists, and He is sustaining our existence, existing us (*existiéndonos*).

God, who is Love, the Father of Love, is the son of love in us. There are men of a facile and external habit of mind, slaves of reason, that reason which externalizes us, who think it a shrewd comment to say that so far from God having made man in His image and likeness, it is rather man who has made his gods or his God in his own image and likeness, and so superficial are they that they do not pause to consider that if the second of these propositions be true, as in fact it is, it is owing to the fact that the first is not less true. God and man, in effect, mutually create one another; God creates or reveals Himself in man and man creates himself in God. God is His own maker, *Deus ipse se facit*, said Lactantius, and we may say that He is making Himself continually both in man and by man. And if each of us, impelled by his love, by his hunger for divinity, creates for himself an image of God according to his own desire, and if according to His desire God creates Himself for each of us, then there is a collective, social, human God, the resultant of all the human imaginations that imagine Him. For God is and reveals Himself in collectivity. And God is the richest and most personal of human conceptions.

The Master of divinity has bidden us be perfect as our Father who is in heaven is perfect (Matt. v. 48), and in the sphere of thought and feeling our perfection consists in the zeal with which we endeavour to equate our imagination with the total imagination of the humanity of which in God we form a part.

The logical theory of the opposition between the extension and the comprehension of a concept, the one increasing in the ratio in which the other diminishes, is well known. The concept that is most extensive and at the same time least comprehensive is that of being or of thing, which embraces everything that exists and possesses no other distinguishing quality than that of being; while the concept that is most comprehensive and least extensive is that of the Universe, which is only applicable to itself and comprehends all existing qualities. And the logical or rational God, the God obtained by way of negation, the absolute entity, merges, like reality itself, into nothingness; for, as Hegel pointed out, pure being and pure nothingness are identical. And the God of the heart, the God who is felt, the God of living men, is the Universe itself conceived as personality, is the consciousness of the Universe. A God universal and personal, altogether different from the individual God of a rigid metaphysical monotheism.

PAUL TILLICH

The God above God

Paulus Johannes Tillich (1886–1965) was a professor of theology and then of philosophy in Germany, and upon coming to Union Theological Seminary in New York he became professor of philosophical theology. The task of mediation suggested by that career shaped his thought and his books, including his three-volume *Systematic Theology* and what was to be perhaps his best-known book, *The Courage to Be*, from which this essay is taken.

T HE COURAGE to be in all its forms has, by itself, revelatory character. It shows the nature of being, it shows that the self-affirmation of being is an affirmation that overcomes negation. In a metaphorical statement (and every assertion about being-itself is either metaphorical or symbolic) one could say that being includes nonbeing but nonbeing does not prevail against it. "Including" is a spatial metaphor which indicates that being embraces itself and that which is opposed to it, nonbeing. Nonbeing belongs to being, it cannot be separated from it. We could not even think "being" without a double negation: being must be thought as the negation of the negation of being. This is why we describe being best by the metaphor "power of being." Power is the possibility a being has to actualize itself against the resistance of other beings. If we speak of the power of being-itself we indicate that being affirms itself against nonbeing. In our discussion of courage and life we have mentioned the dynamic understanding of reality by the philosophers of life. Such an understanding is possible only if one accepts the view that nonbeing belongs to being, that being could not be the ground of life without nonbeing. The self-affirmation of being without nonbeing would not even be self-affirmation but an immovable self-identity. Nothing would be manifest, nothing expressed, nothing revealed. But nonbeing drives being out of its seclusion, it forces it to affirm itself dynamically. Philosophy has dealt with the dynamic self-affirmation of being-itself wherever it spoke dialectically, notably in Neoplatonism, Hegel, and the philosophers of life and process. Theology has done the same whenever it took the idea of the living God seriously, most obviously in the trinitarian symbolization of the inner life of God. Spinoza, in spite of his static definition of substance (which is his name for the ultimate power of being), unites philosophical and mystical tendencies when he speaks of the love and knowledge with which God loves and knows himself through the love and knowledge of finite beings. Nonbeing (that in God which makes his self-affirmation dynamic) opens up the divine self-seclusion and reveals him as power and love. Nonbeing makes God a living God. Without the No he has to overcome in himself and in his creature, the divine Yes to himself would be lifeless. There would be no revelation of the ground of being, there would be no life.

But where there is nonbeing there is finitude and anxiety. If we say that nonbeing belongs to being-itself, we say that finitude and anxiety belong to being-itself. Wherever philosophers or theologians have spoken of the divine blessedness they have implicitly (and sometimes explicitly) spoken of the anxiety of finitude which is eternally taken into the blessedness of the divine infinity. The infinite embraces itself and the finite, the Yes includes itself and the No which it takes into itself, blessedness comprises itself and the anxiety of which it is the conquest. All this is implied if one says that being includes nonbeing and that through nonbeing it reveals itself. It is a highly symbolic language which must be used at this point. But its symbolic character does not diminish its truth; on the contrary, it is a condition of its truth. To speak unsymbolically about being-itself is untrue.

The divine self-affirmation is the power that makes the self-affirmation of the finite being, the courage to be, possible. Only because being-itself has the character of self-affirmation in spite of nonbeing is courage possible. Courage participates in the self-affirmation of being-itself, it participates in the power of being which prevails against nonbeing. He who receives this power in an act of mystical or personal or absolute faith is aware of the source of his courage to be.

Man is not necessarily aware of this source. In situations of cynicism and indifference he is not aware of it. But it works in him as long as he maintains the courage to take his anxiety upon himself. In the act of the courage to be the power of being is effective in us, whether we recognize it or not. Every act of courage is a manifestation of the ground of being, however questionable the content of the act may be. The content may hide or distort true being, the courage in it reveals true being. Not arguments but the courage to be reveals the true nature of being-itself. By affirming our being we participate in the self-affirmation of being-itself. There are no valid arguments for the "existence" of God, but there are acts of courage in which we affirm the power of being, whether we know it or not. If we know it, we accept acceptance consciously. If we do not know it, we nevertheless accept it and participate in it. And in our acceptance of that which we do not know the power of being is manifest to us. Courage has revealing power, the courage to be is the key to being-itself.

Theism Transcended

The courage to take meaninglessness into itself presupposes a relation to the ground of being which we have called "absolute faith." It is without a *special* content, yet it is not without content. The content of absolute faith is the "God above God." Absolute faith and its consequence, the courage that takes the radical doubt, the doubt about God, into itself, transcends the theistic idea of God.

Theism can mean the unspecified affirmation of God. Theism in this sense does not say what it means if it uses the name of God. Because of the traditional and psychological connotations of the word God such an empty theism can produce a reverent mood if it speaks of God. Politicians, dictators, and other people who wish to use rhetoric to make an impression on their audience like to use the word God in this sense. It produces the feeling in their listeners that the speaker is serious and morally trustworthy. This is especially successful if they can brand their foes as atheistic. On a higher level people without a definite religious commitment like to call themselves theistic, not for special purposes but because they cannot stand a world without God, whatever this God may be. They need some of the connotations of the word God and they are afraid of what they call atheism. On the highest level of this kind of theism the name of God is used as a poetic or practical symbol, expressing a profound emotional state or the highest ethical idea. It is a theism which stands on the boundary line between the second type of theism and what we call "theism transcended." But it is still too indefinite to cross this boundary line. The atheistic negation of this whole type of theism is as vague as the theism itself. It may produce an irreverent mood and angry reaction of those who take their theistic affirmation seriously. It may even be felt as justified against the rhetorical-political abuse of the name God, but it is ultimately as irrelevant as the theism which it negates. It cannot reach the state of despair any more than the theism against which it fights can reach the state of faith.

Theism can have another meaning, quite contrary to the first one: it can be the name of what we have called the divine-human encounter. In this case it points to those elements in the Jewish-Christian tradition which emphasize the person-to-person relationship with God. Theism in this sense emphasizes the personalistic passages in the Bible and the Protestant creeds, the personalistic image of God, the word as the tool of creation and revelation, the ethical and social character of the kingdom of God, the personal nature of human faith and divine forgiveness, the historical vision of the universe, the idea of a divine purpose, the infinite distance between creator and creature, the absolute separation between God and the world, the conflict between holy God and sinful man, the person-to-person character of prayer and practical devotion. Theism in this sense is the nonmystical side of biblical religion and historical Christianity. Atheism from the point of view of this theism is the human attempt to escape the divine-human encounter. It is an existential — not a theoretical — problem.

Theism has a third meaning, a strictly theological one. Theological theism is, like every theology, dependent on the religious substance which it conceptualizes. It is dependent on theism in the first sense insofar as it tries to prove the necessity of affirming God in some way; it usually develops the so-called arguments for the "existence" of God. But it is more dependent on theism in the second sense insofar as it tries to establish a doctrine of God which transforms the person-to-person encounter with God into a doctrine about two persons who may or may not meet but who have a reality independent of each other.

Now theism in the first sense must be transcended because it is irrelevant, and theism in the second sense must be transcended because it is one-sided. But theism in the third sense must be transcended because it is wrong. It is bad theology. This can be shown by a more penetrating analysis. The God of theological theism is a being beside others and as such a part of the whole of reality. He certainly is considered its most important part, but as a part and therefore as subjected to the structure of the whole. He is supposed to be beyond the ontological elements and categories which constitute reality. But every statement subjects him to them. He is seen as a self which has a world, as an ego which is related to a thou, as a cause which is separated from its effect, as having a definite space and an endless time.

He is a being, not being-itself. As such he is bound to the subject-object structure of reality, he is an object for us as subjects. At the same time we are objects for him as a subject. And this is decisive for the necessity of transcending theological theism. For God as a subject makes me into an object which is nothing more than an object. He deprives me of my subjectivity because he is all-powerful and all-knowing. I revolt and try to make *him* into an object, but the revolt fails and becomes desperate. God appears as the invincible tyrant, the being in contrast with whom all other beings are without freedom and subjectivity. He is equated with the recent tyrants who with the help of terror try to transform everything into a mere object, a thing among things, a cog in the machine they control. He becomes the model of everything against which Existentialism revolted. This is the God Nietzsche said had to be killed because nobody can tolerate being made into a mere object of absolute knowledge and absolute control. This is the deepest root of atheism. It is an atheism which is justified as the reaction against theological theism and its disturbing implications. It is also the deepest root of the Existentialist despair and the widespread anxiety of meaninglessness in our period.

Theism in all its forms is transcended in the experience we have called absolute faith. It is the accepting of the acceptance without somebody or something that accepts. It is the power of being-itself that accepts and gives the courage to be. This is the highest point to which our analysis has brought us. It cannot be described in the way the God of all forms of theism can be described. It cannot be described in mystical terms either. It transcends both mysticism and personal encounter, as it transcends both the courage to be as a part and the courage to be as oneself.

The God above God and the Courage to Be

The ultimate source of the courage to be is the "God above God"; this is the result of our demand to transcend theism. Only if the God of theism is transcended can the anxiety of doubt and meaninglessness be taken into the courage to be. The God above God is the object of all mystical longing, but mysticism also must be transcended in order to reach him. Mysticism does not take seriously the concrete and the doubt concerning the concrete. It plunges directly into the ground of being and meaning, and leaves the concrete, the world of finite values and meanings, behind. Therefore it does not solve the problem of meaninglessness. In terms of the present religious situation this means that Eastern mysticism is not the solution of the problems of Western

Existentialism, although many people attempt this solution. The God above the God of theism is not the devaluation of the meanings which doubt has thrown into the abyss of meaninglessness; he is their potential restitution. Nevertheless absolute faith agrees with the faith implied in mysticism in that both transcend the theistic objectivation of a God who is a being. For mysticism such a God is not more real than any finite being, for the courage to be such a God has disappeared in the abyss of meaninglessness with every other value and meaning.

The God above the God of theism is present, although hidden, in every divine-human encounter. Biblical religion as well as Protestant theology are aware of the paradoxical character of this encounter. They are aware that if God encounters man God is neither object nor subject and is therefore above the scheme into which theism has forced him. They are aware that personalism with respect to God is balanced by a transpersonal presence of the divine. They are aware that forgiveness can be accepted only if the power of acceptance is effective in man — biblically speaking, if the power of grace is effective in man. They are aware of the paradoxical character of every prayer, of speaking to somebody to whom you cannot speak because he is not "somebody," of asking somebody of whom you cannot ask anything because he gives or gives not before you ask, of saying "thou" to somebody who is nearer to the I than the I is to itself. Each of these paradoxes drives the religious consciousness toward a God above the God of theism.

The courage to be which is rooted in the experience of the God above the God of theism unites and transcends the courage to be as a part and the courage to be as oneself. It avoids both the loss of oneself by participation and the loss of one's world by individualization. The acceptance of the God above the God of theism makes us a part of that which is not also a part but is the ground of the whole. Therefore our self is not lost in a larger whole, which submerges it in the life of a limited group. If the self participates in the power of being-itself it receives itself back. For the power of being acts through the power of the individual selves. It does not swallow them as every limited whole, every collectivism, and every conformism does. This is why the Church, which stands for the power of being-itself or for the God who transcends the God of the religions, claims to be the mediator of the courage to be. A church which is based on the authority of the God of theism cannot make such a claim. It inescapably develops into a collectivist or semicollectivist system itself.

But a church which raises itself in its message and its devotion to the God above the God of theism without sacrificing its concrete symbols can mediate a courage which takes doubt and meaninglessness into itself. It is the Church under the Cross which alone can do this, the Church which preaches the Crucified who cried to God who remained his God after the God of confidence had left him in the darkness of doubt and meaninglessness. To be as a part in such a church is to receive a courage to be in which one cannot lose one's self and in which one receives one's world.

Absolute faith, or the state of being grasped by the God beyond God, is not a state which appears beside other states of the mind. It never is something separated and definite, an event which could be isolated and described. It is always a movement in, with, and under other states of the mind. It is the situation on the boundary of man's possibilities. It *is* this boundary. Therefore it is both the courage of despair and the courage in and above every courage. It is not a place where one can live, it is without the safety of words and concepts, it is without a name, a church, a cult, a theology. But it is moving in the depth of all of them. It is the power of being, in which they participate and of which they are fragmentary expressions.

One can become aware of it in the anxiety of fate and death when the traditional symbols, which enable men to stand the vicissitudes of fate and the horror of death have lost their power. When "providence" has become a superstition and "immortality" something imaginary that which once was the power in these symbols can still be present and create the courage to be in spite of the experience of a chaotic world and a finite existence. The Stoic courage returns but not as the faith in universal reason. It returns as the absolute faith which says Yes to being without seeing anything concrete which could conquer the nonbeing in fate and death.

And one can become aware of the God above the God of theism in the anxiety of guilt and condemnation when the traditional symbols that enable men to withstand the anxiety of guilt and condemnation have lost their power. When "divine judgment" is interpreted as a psychological complex and forgiveness as a remnant of the "father-image," what once was the power in those symbols can still be present and create the courage to be in spite of the experience of an infinite gap between what we are and what we ought to be. The Lutheran courage returns but not supported by the faith in a judging and forgiving God. It returns in terms of the absolute faith which says Yes although there is no special power that conquers guilt. The courage to take the anxiety of meaninglessness upon oneself is the boundary line up to which the courage to be can go. Beyond it is mere non-being. Within it all forms of courage are re-established in the power of the God above the God of theism. *The courage to be is rooted in the God who appears when God has disappeared in the anxiety of doubt.*

FRIEDRICH HEILER

The Essence of Prayer

Friedrich Heiler (1892–1967) was professor of the comparative history of religions at Marburg and, as a Roman Catholic who became a high church Lutheran, a leader of the liturgical movement in all the churches. That blending of liturgical interest with scholarship in the history of religions made him uniquely qualified to write his book *Prayer,* which ranges through all the religions to find "the essence of prayer."

PRAYER APPEARS in history in an astonishing multiplicity of forms; as the calm collectedness of a devout individual soul, and as the ceremonial liturgy of a great congregation; as an original creation of a religious genius, and as an imitation on the part of a simple, average religious person; as the spontaneous expression of upspringing religious experiences, and as the mechanical recitation of an incomprehensible formula; as bliss and ecstasy of heart, and as painful fulfilment of the law; as the involuntary discharge of an overwhelming emotion, and as the voluntary concentration on a religious object; as loud shouting and crying, and as still, silent absorption; as artistic poetry, and as stammering speech; as the flight of the spirit to the supreme Light, and as a cry out of the deep distress of the heart; as joyous thanksgiving and ecstatic praise, and as humble supplication for forgiveness and compassion; as a childlike entreaty for life, health, and happiness, and as an earnest desire for power in the moral struggle of existence; as a simple petition for daily bread, and as an all-consuming yearning for God Himself; as a selfish wish, and as an unselfish solicitude for a brother; as wild cursing and vengeful thirst, and as heroic intercession for personal enemies and persecutors; as a stormy clamour and demand, and as joyful renunciation and holy serenity; as a desire to change God's will and make it chime with our petty wishes, and as a self-forgetting vision of and surrender to the Highest Good; as the timid entreaty of the sinner before a stern judge, and as the trustful talk of a child with a kind father; as swelling phrases of politeness and flattery before an unapproachable King, and as a free outpouring in the presence of a friend who cares; as the humble petition of a servant to a powerful master, and as the ecstatic converse of the bride with the heavenly Bridegroom.

In considering these varied contrasts and in the survey of the different leading types of prayer, the problem emerges: what is common to all these diverse kinds of prayer, what underlies all these phenomenal forms, in a word, what is the essence of prayer? The answer to this question is not easy. There is the danger of fundamentally misinterpreting prayer by making its essence an empty abstraction. If we would understand the essence of prayer we must look attentively at those types in which we see it as the naïve, spontaneous utterance of the soul; we must, therefore, separate the primary types from the secondary. This separation is easily effected. The primary types which cannot be confounded with the others are these: — the naïve prayer of primitive man, the devotional life of men of religious genius, the prayers of great men, the common prayer of public worship in so far as it has not hardened into a stiff, sacrosanct institution. In all these instances prayer appears as a purely psychical fact, the immediate expression of an original and profound experience of the soul. It bursts forth with innate energy. Very different are the secondary types. They are no longer an original, personal experience, but an imitation or a congealment of such a living experience. The personal prayer of the average religious man is a more or less true reflection of the original experience of another; it remains inferior to the ideal model in power, depth, and vitality. The philosophical idea of prayer is a cold abstraction built up in harmony with metaphysical and ethical standards; by it living prayer is subjected to an alien law, to the principles of philosophy, and is transformed and revised in accordance with this law. The product of this amendment is no longer real prayer, but its shadow, an artificial, dead simulacrum of it. The ritual forms of prayer, the cultural hymn, liturgical common prayer as an institution of the cultus, all these types are phenomena of congelation in which the upspringing personal life has been transmuted into objective, impersonal forms and rules. The penetration into their inner meaning may indeed give rise in devout, susceptible souls to new experiences of prayer, their recitation in public or private worship may take place in a devotional mood, but they themselves are not the direct expression of a personal experience. The essential features of prayer are never visible in these disintegrated, dead, secondary forms, but only in unadulterated, simple prayer as it lives in unsophisticated, primitive human beings and in outstanding men of creative genius. In determining the essence of prayer, therefore, we must fix our attention exclusively on prayer in its primitive simplicity. Only then can we take into consideration the secondary types and inquire how far the essence of prayer is expressed by them.

To answer our question, we must first of all discover the essential motive of prayer, its common psychological root. What moves men to pray? What do men seek when they pray? Da Costa Guimaraens, a French psychologist, defined it thus: "To pray means to satisfy a psychical need." The definition is superficial and is, moreover, insipidly formulated, but it is on the track of a correct psychological motivation. Prayer is the expression of a primitive impulsion to a higher, richer, intenser life. Whatever may be the burden of the prayer, to whatever realm of values it may belong, whether to the eudaemonistic, the ethical, or the purely religious realm — it is always a great longing for life, for a more potent, a purer, a more blessed life. "When I seek Thee, my God," prays Augustine, "I seek a blessed life." His words uncover the psychical root of all prayer. The hungry pygmy who begs for food, the entranced mystic, absorbed in the greatness and beauty of the infinite God, the guilt-oppressed Christian who prays for forgiveness of sins and assurance of salvation — all are seeking life; they seek a confirmation and an enrichment of their realization of life. Even the Buddhist beggar-monk, who by meditation works himself up into a state of perfect indifference, seeks in the denial of life to attain a higher and purer life.

The effort to fortify, to reinforce, to enhance one's life is the motive of all prayer. But the discovery of the deepest root of prayer does not disclose its peculiar essence. In order to get to the bottom of this, we should not ask for the psychological motive of prayer; we must rather make clear the religious ideas of him who prays in simplicity, we must grasp his inner attitude and spiritual aim, the intellectual presuppositions which underlie prayer as a psychical experience. What does the simple, devout person, undisturbed by reflection, think when he prays? He believes that he speaks with a God, immediately present and personal, has intercourse with Him, that there is between them a vital and spiritual commerce. There are three elements which form the inner structure of the prayer experience: faith in a living personal God, faith in His real, immediate presence, and a realistic fellowship into which man enters with a God conceived as present.

Every prayer is a turning of man to another Being to whom he inwardly opens his heart; it is the speech of an "I" to a "Thou." This "Thou," this other with whom the devout person comes into relation, in whose presence he stands as he prays, is no human being but a supersensuous, superhuman Being on whom he feels himself dependent, yet a being who plainly wears the features of a human personality, with thought, will, feeling, self-consciousness. "Prayer," says Tylor, "is the address of a personal spirit to a personal spirit." Belief in the personality of God is the necessary presupposition, the fundamental condition of all prayer. The anthropomorphism which is always found in primitive prayer and which often appears in the prayer of outstanding religious personalities, the prophets among them, is a coarsening and materialising of this belief in God's personality; it does not, however, belong to the essence of prayer as faith does. But wherever the vital conception of the divine personality grows dim, where, as in the philosophical ideal or in pantheistic mysticism, it passes over into the "One and All," genuine prayer dissolves and becomes purely contemplative absorption and adoration.

The man who prays feels himself very close to this personal God. Primitive man believes that God dwells in a visible place; to this place he hastens when he would pray, or he turns his eyes and hands towards it. The religious genius experiences the divine presence in the stillness of his own heart, in the deepest recesses of his soul. But it is always the reverential and trustful consciousness of the living presence of God, which is the keynote of the genuine prayer-experience. It is true that the God to whom the worshipper cries transcends all material things — and yet the pious man feels His nearness with an assurance as undoubted as though a living man stood before him.

Belief in God's personality and the assurance of His presence are the two presuppositions of prayer. But prayer itself is no mere belief in the reality of a personal God — such a belief underlies even a theistic metaphysic; — nor is it a mere experience of His presence — for this is the accompaniment of the entire life and thought of the great men of religion. Prayer is rather a living relation of man to God, a direct and inner contact, a refuge, a mutual intercourse, a conversation, spiritual commerce, an association, a fellowship, a communion, a converse, a one-ness, a union of an "I" and a "Thou." Only an accumulation of these synonyms which human speech employs to make clear the innermost relations of man to man, can give an appropriate picture of the realistic power and vitality of that relation into which the praying man enters with God. Since prayer displays a communion, a conversation between an "I" and a "Thou," it is a social phenomenon. The relation to God of him who prays always reflects an earthly social relation: that of servant or child or friend or bride. In the praying of primitive man, as in the devoutness of creative religious personalities, the religious bond is conceived after the analogy of human society. It is just this earthly social element that lends to natural prayer its dramatic vivacity. Wherever, as with many mystics, the religious relation no longer exhibits an analogy to social relations, prayer passes over from a real relation of communion to mere contemplation and adoration.

As anthropomorphism is only a crude form of belief in the personality of God, so belief in the real influence of prayer on the divine will, in the winning over of God to our side as it appears most clearly in primitive and prophetic prayer, is only a crude form of immediate, vital, and dynamic intercourse with God. It does not belong to the essence of prayer. The miracle of prayer does not lie in the accomplishment of the prayer, in the influence of man on God, but in the mysterious contact which comes to pass between the finite and the infinite Spirit. It is by this very fact that prayer is a genuine fellowship of man with God, that it is something not merely psychological, but transcendental and metaphysical, or as Tholuck has expressed it, "no mere earthly power but a power which reaches to the heavens." In the words of Söderblom: "in the depths of our inner life we have not a mere echo of our own voice, of our own being, resounding from the dark depths of personality, but a reality higher and greater than our own, which we can adore and in which we can trust."

Prayer is, therefore, a living communion of the religious man with God, conceived as personal and present in experience, a communion which reflects the forms of the social relations of humanity. This is prayer in essence. It is only imperfectly realised in the subordinate types of prayer. In ritual prayer, cultural hymn, in liturgical prayer, as in prayer regulated by law and deemed a thing in itself meritorious, the experience of the Divine presence is, for the most part, weak and shadowy. Here we have prayer as a more or less external action, not as an inner contact of the heart with God. But also in the philosophical ideal of prayer and in certain forms of mystical communion, we can discern but faintly the essence of prayer. If we are to distinguish clearly between the religious experiences and states of mind related to prayer, which play an important part in the religion of philosophers and mystics, and prayer itself considered simply from the point of view which makes it to be prayer, some elucidation of what we mean by "adoration" and "devotion" is necessary.

Adoration (or reverent contemplation) and devotion are absolutely necessary elements in religious experience. Both terms stand for conceptions much wider than that of prayer; both denote religious experiences and states, the nature of which is obviously different from that of prayer; nay, we may go further and say that they comprehend psychical events and experiences which belong to the "secular," not to the strictly religious realm, or are on the borderland of both.

Adoration is the solemn contemplation of the "Holy One" as the highest Good, unreserved surrender to Him, a mingling of one's being with His. We see this even in the religious life of primitive peoples. The awe which primitive man evinces by speech and gesture as he stands in the presence of a "holy object," that is, an object filled with supernatural and magical power, is "adoration," although in a crude and imperfect fashion. The "holy" object has for him ideal worth: yes, even supreme value in the moment when, overcome by awe and wonder, he sinks in the dust before it. But it is in the personal experience of the poet and the mystic that we find adoration in its absolute purity and perfection. It is the soul-satisfying contemplation of the highest good, the very climax of mystical prayer: it is the unreserved losing of one's self in the glory of Nature as seen in the sacred poetry of ancient peoples and in the aesthetic mysticism of modern poets. Compared with it primitive ceremonial adoration is but a preliminary form. Now, a personal God can be the object of this adoration, just as He is the object of prayer. The God whom primitive man worships is an anthropomorphic being; the *summum bonum* of a mysticism centering in a personal God shows the traits of a spiritual personality. But the note of personality is by no means essential to the object of adoration. Primitive cults knew not only spiritual beings made after man's image, but also lifeless objects which being "holy," that is, as *mana* and *tabu,* lay claim to worship. Moreover, the object in which the poetic spirit sinks in an ecstasy of adoration, is not personal: it is the life-giving sun, creative and nurturing Mother Nature, the Alone and the Infinite as revealed in the beautiful. There is, nevertheless, something that is beyond experience, something which shines through Nature as through a translucent medium. Just as the God whom the worshipper invokes, is felt to be palpably near and immediately present, so also the object of adoration which the pious spirit regards with awe is felt to be equally near and present. The relation to God into which he who prays enters, resembles in its intimacy the relation which subsists between the adoring person and the object of his adoration.

Subsidiary to religious adoration is the "secular." Ordinarily we indicate by the word "adoration" the state of being laid hold of by a supreme good, the complete surrender to it, whether this good be religious (*numinous*) or "secular," natural or supernatural, earthly or heavenly. Everything which man experiences as a supreme good, whatever is the object of "love" — a person, an association of persons, an abstract idea — can also in the wider sense of the word be an object of adoration. The young lover adores his beloved, the patriotic citizen his fatherland, the loyal working man his class, the creative artist his muse, the high-minded philosopher the idea of the true and the good. If love means the belief of a man in his supreme good, adoration is this belief at its highest point of intensity, the culmination of love. The adoring person steadily contemplates his ideal object; he is filled with inspiration, admiration, rapture, yearning; all other thoughts and wishes have vanished; he belongs only to the one object, loses himself in it, and in it dissolves away. *Adoration is the contemplative surrender to a supreme good.*

Devotion (*Andacht*) is a necessary presupposition and foundation alike of prayer and adoration. The praying man who converses with God, the adoring man who is absorbed in his highest ideal — both are devout, self-collected, concentrated. But the state of a soul in contemplation can just as well dispense with every reference to God or a supreme good. Devotion is, to begin with, concentration of the mind on a definite point, a wide-awake state of consciousness whose field is greatly circumscribed. But the mathematician who solves a geometrical problem also experiences this state of concentration, or the designer who constructs a model. Devotion, as distinct from mere mental concentration, from intensity of attention, is a solemn, still, exalted, consecrated mood of the soul. The philosopher experiences devotion when the mystery of the human spirit rises up before him in its autonomy and freedom: the scholar when he deciphers ancient documents and recalls to life long-forgotten men and peoples; the lover of nature when he stands before some lofty mountain peak or when he delights in the contemplation of some modest wild flower; the artist when suddenly a new idea forces itself upon him; the lover of art when he admires Raphael's Madonna or listens to a Symphony of Beethoven; the man engaged in a moral struggle when he searches his conscience, judges himself, and sets before himself lofty aims and tasks; the pious man when he participates in a holy act of worship or ponders on a religious mystery; even the irreligious man when he enters into the still dimness of a majestic cathedral or witnesses the solemn high mass in a Roman Catholic church. Devotion may rise into complete absorption; the field of consciousness is narrowed, the intensity of the experience grows; the concrete perceptions and ideas which aroused the experience of devotion wave themselves in a mood that is at once deep and agreeable. The states of absorption appear in the religious as in the "secular" experience. They meet us just as much in the mystical devotional life as in scientific investigation and artistic creation. In absorption the mystic experiences perfect stillness and serenity, holy joy and equanimity — all of them experiences which may be clearly distinguished from contemplative adoration. Yet in them there lives in some manner the thought of an ultimate and highest state, though not so vividly as in adoration. Even in Buddhist absorption the idea of an ultimate and a highest — Nirvana — is operative.

Devotion is, therefore, the quiet, solemn mood of the soul which is caused by the contemplation of ethical and intellectual, but especially of aesthetic and religious values, whether of external objects or of imaginative conceptions dominated by feeling. Whilst adoration is concerned inwardly with an ideal object and holds it fast with con-vulsive energy, the objective presupposition of the experience of devotion acts purely as a stimulus. Devotion itself tends to depart from its objective presupposition, and to become wholly subjective, con-centrated, and absorbed. In short, adoration has an objective, devotion a subjective character.

The analysis of adoration and devotion enables us to set the essence of prayer in the clearest light. Prayer is no mere feeling of exaltation, no mere hallowed mood, no mere prostration before a supreme good. It is rather a real intercourse of God with man, a living fellowship of the finite spirit with the Infinite. And just because the modern has no correct conception of the immediacy and tenderness of the relation effected by prayer in which the simple and devout soul stands to God, he is constantly confusing with genuine prayer these more general religious phenomena — adoration and devotion — which have their analogies even outside the religious sphere. Because the man of to-day, entangled in the prejudices of a rationalistic philosophy, struggles against the primitive realism of frank and free prayer, he is inclined to see the ideal and essence of prayer in a vague, devotional mood and in aesthetic contemplation. But the essence of prayer is revealed with unquestionable clearness to penetrating psychological study, and it may be put thus: *to pray means to speak to and have intercourse with God,* as suppliant with judge, servant with master, child with father, bride with bridegroom. The severely non-rational character of religion nowhere makes so overwhelming an impression as in prayer. For modern thought, dominated by Copernicus and Kant, prayer is as great a stone of stumbling as it was for the enlightened philosophy of the Greeks. But a compromise between unsophisticated piety and a rational world-view obliterates the essential features of prayer, and the most living manifestation of religion withers into a lifeless abstraction. There are only two possibilities: either decisively to affirm prayer "in its entirely non-rational character and with all its difficulties," as Ménégoz says, or to surrender genuine prayer and substitute for it adoration and devotion which resemble prayer. Every attempt to mingle the two conceptions violates psychological veracity.

Religious persons and students of religion agree in testifying that prayer is the centre of religion, the soul of all piety. The definition of the essence of prayer explains this testimony; prayer is a living communion of man with God. Prayer brings man into direct touch with God, into a personal relation with Him. Without prayer faith remains a theoretical conviction; worship is only an external and formal act; moral action is without spiritual depth; man remains at a distance from God; an abyss yawns between the finite and the Infinite. "God is in heaven and thou art on the earth." "We cannot come to God," says Luther, "except through prayer alone, for He is too high above us." In prayer man rises to heaven, heaven sinks to earth, the veil between the visible and the invisible is torn asunder, man comes before God to speak with Him about his soul's welfare and salvation. "Prayer," says Mechthild of Magdeburg, "draws the great God down into a small heart; it drives the hungry soul up to God in His fulness." Similarly Johann Arndt says: "In prayer the highest and the lowest come together, the lowliest heart and the most exalted God."

As the mysterious linking of man with the Eternal, prayer is an incomprehensible wonder, a miracle of miracles which is daily brought to pass in the devout soul. The historian and psychologist of religion can only be a spectator and interpreter of that deep and powerful life which is unveiled in prayer: only the religious man can penetrate the mystery. But in the final analysis scientific inquiry stands under the same overwhelming impression as living religion. It is compelled to agree with the confession of Chrysostom: "There is nothing more powerful than prayer and there is nothing to be compared with it."

V THE RECONSTRUCTION OF TRADITION

"Tradition," according to Gilbert Chesterton's definition, is "democracy extended through time." "Tradition," he continued, "means giving votes to the most obscure of all classes, our ancestors. It is the democracy of the dead." But modernity has frequently defined itself, in the formula quoted earlier from Kant, as "the exodus of humanity from its self-imposed tutelage," and thus as the overthrow of tradition in the name of emancipation and enlightenment.

That superficial dichotomy between the traditional and the modern has repeatedly been transcended during the nineteenth and twentieth centuries by a phenomenon that we are calling here — in a term borrowed from Islam (Muhammad Iqbal), from Neo-Confucian thought (Carsun Chang), and from Judaism (Mordecai Kaplan) — the "reconstruction" of religious tradition. Contemporary movements in various of the world religions that the mass media often loosely call "fundamentalism" could be described far more accurately as the reconstruction of tradition. It is probably safe to say that such a recovery has been taking place in every one of the world's religious faiths. To be sure, any reinterpretation of a tradition is a highly selective process: what is discarded and what is kept (or revived) from earlier centuries often appears to depend primarily on the caprice of the individual — which is, of course, the very antithesis of tradition. The recovery of the idea of tradition in our modern age is, moreover, frequently tinged with a romanticism about some golden age long ago, when sainthood was in flower and the faithful were supposedly not as lax as they are today in their observance of the prescribed rules of conduct. But the selections that follow are proof that the reconstruction of tradition can also be based on a vigorous and clear-eyed understanding both of the past and of the present.

It is characteristic of the restatements of tradition reprinted here that they have all been shaped in a decisive manner by the modern historical study of religion. Having begun in many cases as the critical examination of the received understanding of a sacred past and therefore as a "debunking" of tradition, historical research, after doing that job very well, has sometimes felt both qualified and obliged to go on to a more constructive appraisal of those elements of continuity in the tradition that can and should be reclaimed even in the modern era. The scholarly editing of the great collections of source material from all the world religions has helped in that process, but so has the recognition of how much is surrendered when the next generation is deprived of the stability and the collective memory that only tradition provides. And while every one of the traditions seems to contain more than enough of the sins against charity for which piety has become so notorious, they also all contain resources for a deeper and a larger faith, in which both particularity and universality can be affirmed.

MUHAMMAD IQBAL

The Reconstruction of Tradition

Sir Muhammad Iqbal (1877–1938) was a Muslim philosopher and Persian poet in India who worked for a separate Muslim state, which after partition eventually came to be known as Pakistan. His book, *The Reconstruction of Religious Thought in Islam,* has been called, among contemporary expositions of Islamic thought, "one of the few works that would qualify as philosophy of religion."

BROADLY SPEAKING religious life may be divided into three periods. These may be described as the periods of "Faith," "Thought," and "Discovery." In the first period religious life appears as a form of discipline which the individual or a whole people must accept as an unconditional command without any rational understanding of the ultimate meaning and purpose of that command. This attitude may be of great consequence in the social and political history of a people, but is not of much consequence in so far as the individual's inner growth and expansion are concerned. Perfect submission to discipline is followed by a rational understanding of the discipline and the ultimate source of its authority. In this period religious life seeks its foundation in a kind of metaphysics — a logically consistent view of the world with God as a part of that view. In the third period metaphysics is displaced by psychology, and religious life develops the ambition to come into direct contact with the ultimate Reality. It is here that religion becomes a matter of personal assimilation of life and power; and the individual achieves a free personality, not by releasing himself from the fetters of the law, but by discovering the ultimate source of the law within the depths of his own consciousness. As in the words of a Muslim Sufi — "no understanding of the Holy Book is possible until it is actually revealed to the believer just as it was revealed to the Prophet." It is, then, in the sense of this last phase in the development of religious life that I use the word religion in the question that I now propose to raise. Religion in this sense is known by the unfortunate name of Mysticism, which is supposed to be a life-denying, act-avoiding attitude of mind directly opposed to the radically empirical outlook of our times. Yet higher religion, which is only a search for a larger life, is essentially experience and recognized the necessity of experience as its foundation long before science learnt to do so. It is a genuine effort to clarify human consciousness, and is, as such, as critical of its level of experience as Naturalism is of its own level.

As we all know, it was Kant who first raised the question: "Is metaphysics possible?" He answered this question in the negative; and his argument applies with equal force to the realities in which religion is especially interested. The manifold of sense, according to him, must fulfil certain formal conditions in order to constitute knowledge. The thing in itself is only a limiting idea. Its function is merely regulative. If there *is* some actuality corresponding to the idea it falls outside the boundaries of experience, and consequently its existence cannot be rationally demonstrated. This verdict of Kant cannot be easily accepted. It may fairly be argued that in view of the more recent developments of science, such as the nature of matter as "bottled-up light waves," the idea of the universe as an act of thought, finiteness of space and time and Heisenberg's principle of indeterminacy in nature, the case for a system of rational theology is not so bad as Kant was led to think. But for our present purposes it is unnecessary to consider this point in detail. As to the thing in itself, which is inaccessible to pure reason because of its falling beyond the boundaries of experience, Kant's verdict can be accepted only if we start with the assumption that all experience other than the normal level of experience is impossible. The only question, therefore, is whether the normal level is the only level of knowledge-yielding experience. Kant's view of the thing in itself and the thing as it appears to us very much determined the character of his question regarding the possibility of metaphysics. But what if the position, as understood by him, is reversed? The great Muslim Sufi philosopher, Muhyuddin Ibnul Arabi of Spain, has made the acute observation that God is a percept; the world is a concept. Another Muslim Sufi thinker and poet, Iraqi, insists on the plurality of space-orders and time-orders and speaks of a Divine Time and a Divine Space. It may be that what we call the external world is only an intellectual construction, and that there are other levels of human experience capable of being systematized by other orders of space and time — levels in which concept and analysis do not play the same role as they do in the case of our normal experience. It may, however, be said that the level of experience to which concepts are inapplicable cannot yield any knowledge of a universal character; for concepts alone are capable of being socialized. The standpoint of the man who relies on religious experience for capturing Reality must always remain individual and incommunicable. This objection has some force if it is meant to insinuate that the mystic is wholly ruled by his traditional ways, attitudes, and expectations. Conservatism is as bad in religion as in any other department of human activity. It destroys the ego's creative freedom and closes up the paths of fresh spiritual enterprise. This is the main reason why our medieval mystic techniques can no longer produce original discoverers of ancient Truth. The fact, however, that religious experience is incommunicable does not mean that the religious man's pursuit is futile. Indeed, the incommunicability of religious experience gives us a clue to the ultimate nature of the ego. In our daily social intercourse we live and move in seclusion, as it were. We do not care to reach the inmost individuality of men. We treat them as mere functions, and approach them from those aspects of their identity which are capable of conceptual treatment. The climax of religious life, however, is the discovery of the ego as an individual deeper than his conceptually describable habitual self-hood. It is in contact with the Most Real that the ego discovers its uniqueness, its metaphysical status, and the possibility of improvement in that status. Strictly speaking, the experience which leads to this discovery is not a conceptually manageable intellectual fact; it is a vital fact, an attitude consequent on an inner biological transformation which cannot be captured in the net of logical categories. It can embody itself only in a world-making or world-shaking act; and in this form alone the content of this timeless experience can diffuse itself in the time-movement, and make itself effectively visible to the eye of history. It seems that the method of dealing with Reality by means of concepts is not at all a serious way of dealing with it. Science does not care whether its electron is a real entity or not. It may be a mere symbol, a mere convention. Religion, which is essentially a mode of actual living, is the only serious way of handling Reality. As a form of higher experience it is corrective of our concepts of philosophical theology or at least makes us suspicious of the purely rational process which forms these concepts. Science can afford to ignore metaphysics altogether, and may even believe it to be "a justified form of poetry," as Lange defined it, or "a legitimate play of grown-ups," as Nietzsche described it. But the religious expert who seeks to discover his personal status in the constitution of things cannot, in view of the final aim of his struggle, be satisfied with what science may regard as a vital lie, a mere "as-if" to regulate thought and conduct. In so far as the ultimate nature of Reality is concerned nothing is at stake in the venture of science; in the religious venture the whole career of the ego as an assimilative personal centre of life and experience is at stake. Conduct which involves a decision of the ultimate fate of the agent cannot be based on illusions. A wrong concept misleads the understanding; a wrong deed degrades the whole man, and may eventually demolish the structure of the human ego. The mere concept affects life only partially; the deed is dynamically related to reality and issues from a generally constant attitude of the whole man towards reality. No doubt the deed, i.e. the control of psychological and physiological processes with a view to tune up the ego for an immediate contact with the ultimate Reality is, and cannot but be, individual in form and content; yet the deed, too, is liable to be socialized when others begin to live through it with a view to discover for themselves its effectiveness as a method of approaching the Real. The evidence of religious experts in all ages and countries is that there are potential types of consciousness lying close to our normal consciousness. If these types of consciousness open up possibilities of life-giving and knowledge-yielding experience the question of the possibility of religion as a form of higher experience is a perfectly legitimate one and demands our serious attention.

But, apart from the legitimacy of the question, there are important reasons why it should be raised at the present moment of the history of modern culture. In the first place, the scientific interest of the question. It seems that every culture has a form of Naturalism peculiar to its own world-feeling; and it further appears that every form of Naturalism ends in some sort of Atomism. We have Indian Atomism, Greek Atomism, Muslim Atomism, and Modern Atomism. Modern Atomism is, however, unique. Its amazing mathematics which sees the universe as an elaborate differential equation; and its physics which, following its own methods, has been led to smash some of the old gods of its own temple, have already brought us to the point of asking the question whether the causality-bound aspect of nature is the whole truth about it? Is not the ultimate Reality invading our consciousness from some other direction as well? Is the purely intellectual method of overcoming nature the only method? "We have acknowledged," says Professor Eddington, "that the entities of physics can from their very nature form only a partial aspect of the reality. How are we to deal with the other part? It cannot be said that that other part concerns us less than the physical entities. Feelings, purpose, values, make up our consciousness as much as sense-impressions. We follow up the sense-impressions and find that they lead into an external world discussed by science; we follow up the other elements of our being and find that they lead — not into a world of space and time, but surely somewhere."

In the second place we have to look to the great practical importance of the question. The modern man with his philosophies of criticism and scientific specialism finds himself in a strange predicament. His Naturalism has given him an unprecedented control over the forces of nature, but has robbed him of faith in his own future. It is strange how the same idea affects different cultures differently. The formulation of the theory of evolution in the world of Islam brought into being Rumi's tremendous enthusiasm for the biological future of man. No cultured Muslim can read such passages as the following without a thrill of joy:

> Low in the earth
> I lived in realms of ore and stone;
> And then I smiled in many-tinted flowers;
> Then roving with the wild and wandering hours,
> O'er earth and air and ocean's zone,
> In a new birth,
> I dived and flew,
> And crept and ran,
> And all the secret of my essence drew
> Within a form that brought them all to view —
> And lo, a Man!
> And then my goal,
> Beyond the clouds, beyond the sky,
> In realms where none may change or die —
> In angel form; and then away
> Beyond the bounds of night and day,
> And Life and Death, unseen or seen,
> Where all that is hath ever been,
> As One and Whole.
> (*Rumi*: Thadani's Translation.)

On the other hand, the formulation of the same view of evolution with far greater precision in Europe has led to the belief that "there now appears to be no scientific basis for the idea that the present rich complexity of human endowment will ever be materially exceeded." That is how the modern man's secret despair hides itself behind the screen of scientific terminology. Nietzsche, although he thought that the idea of evolution did not justify the belief that man was unsurpassable, cannot be regarded as an exception in this respect. His enthusiasm for the future of man ended in the doctrine of eternal recurrence — perhaps the most hopeless idea of immortality ever formed by man. This eternal repetition is not eternal "becoming"; it is the same old idea of "being" masquerading as "becoming."

Thus, wholly overshadowed by the results of his intellectual activity, the modern man has ceased to live soulfully, i.e. from within. In the domain of thought he is living in open conflict with himself; and in the domain of economic and political life he is living in open conflict with others. He finds himself unable to control his ruthless egoism and his infinite gold-hunger which is gradually killing all higher striving in him and bringing him nothing but life-weariness. Absorbed in the "fact," that is to say, the optically present source of sensation, he is entirely cut off from the unplumbed depths of his own being. In the wake of his systematic materialism has at last come that paralysis of energy which Huxley apprehended and deplored. The condition of things in the East is no better. The technique of medieval mysticism by which religious life, in its higher manifestations, developed itself both in the East and in the West has now practically failed. And in the Muslim East it has, perhaps, done far greater havoc than anywhere else. Far from reintegrating the forces of the average man's inner life, and thus preparing him for participation in the march of history, it has taught him a false renunciation and made him perfectly contented with his ignorance and spiritual thraldom. No wonder then that the modern Muslim in Turkey, Egypt, and Persia is led to seek fresh sources of energy in the creation of new loyalties, such as patriotism and nationalism which Nietzsche described as "sickness and unreason," and "the strongest force against culture." Disappointed of a purely religious method of spiritual renewal which alone brings us into touch with the everlasting fountain of life and power by expanding our thought and emotion, the modern Muslim fondly hopes to unlock fresh sources of energy by narrowing down his thought and emotion. Modern atheistic socialism, which possesses all the fervour of a new religion, has a broader outlook; but having received its philosophical basis from the Hegelians of the left wing, it rises in revolt against the very source which could have given it strength and purpose. Both nationalism and atheistic socialism, at least in the present state of human adjustments, must draw upon the psychological forces of hate, suspicion, and resentment which tend to impoverish the soul of man and close up his hidden sources of spiritual energy. Neither the technique of medieval mysticism nor nationalism nor atheistic socialism can cure the ills of a despairing humanity. Surely the present moment is one of great crisis in the history of modern culture. The modern world stands in need of biological renewal. And religion, which in its higher manifestations is neither dogma, nor priesthood, nor ritual, can alone ethically prepare the modern man for the burden of the great responsibility which the advancement of modern science necessarily involves, and restore to him that attitude of faith which makes him capable of winning a personality here and retaining it hereafter. It is only by rising to a fresh vision of his origin and future, his whence and whither, that man will eventually triumph over a society motivated by an inhuman competition, and a civilization which has lost its spiritual unity by its inner conflict of religious and political values.

As I have indicated before, religion as a deliberate enterprise to seize the ultimate principle of value and thereby to reintegrate the forces of one's own personality, is a fact which cannot be denied. The whole religious literature of the world, including the records of specialists' personal experiences, though perhaps expressed in the thought-forms of an out-of-date psychology, is a standing testimony to it. These experiences are perfectly natural, like our normal experiences. The evidence is that they possess a cognitive value for the recipient, and, what is much more important, a capacity to centralize the forces of the ego and thereby to endow him with a new personality. The view that such experiences are neurotic or mystical will not finally settle the question of their meaning or value. If an outlook beyond physics is possible, we must courageously face the possibility, even though it may disturb or tend to modify our normal ways of life and thought. The interests of truth require that we must abandon our present attitude. It does not matter in the least if the religious attitude is originally determined by some kind of physiological disorder. George Fox may be a neurotic; but who can deny his purifying power in England's religious life of his day? Mohammed, we are told, was a psycopath. Well, if a psycopath has the power to give a fresh direction to the course of human history, it is a point of the highest psychological interest to search his original experience which has turned slaves into leaders of men, and has inspired the conduct and shaped the career of whole races of mankind. Judging from the various types of activity that emanated from the movement initiated by the Prophet of Islam, his spiritual tension and the kind of behaviour which issued from it, cannot be regarded as a response to a mere fantasy inside his brain. It is impossible to understand it except as a response to an objective situation generative of new enthusiasms, new organizations, new starting-points. It we look at the matter from the standpoint of anthropology it appears that a psycopath is an important factor in the economy of humanity's social organization. His way is not to classify facts and discover causes: he thinks in terms of life and movement with a view to create new patterns of behaviour for mankind. No doubt he has his pitfalls and illusions just as the scientist who relies on sense-experience has his pitfalls and illusions. A careful study of his method, however, shows that he is not less alert than the scientist in the matter of eliminating the alloy of illusion from his experience.

The question for us outsiders is to find out an effective method of inquiry into the nature and significance of this extraordinary experience. The Arab historian Ibn Khaldun, who laid the foundations of modern scientific history, was the first to seriously approach this side of human psychology and reached what we now call the idea of the subliminal self. Later, Sir William Hamilton in England and Leibnitz in Germany, interested themselves in some of the more unknown phenomena of the mind. Jung, however, is probably right in thinking that the essential nature of religion is beyond the province of analytic psychology. In his discussion of the relation of analytic psychology to poetic art he tells us that the process of artistic *form* alone can be the object of psychology. The essential nature of art, according to him, cannot be the object of a psychological method of approach. "A similar distinction," says Jung, "must also be made in the realm of religion; there also a psychological consideration is permissible only in respect of the emotional and symbolical phenomena of a religion, wherein the essential nature of religion is in no way involved, as indeed it cannot be. For were this possible, not religion alone, but art also could be treated as a mere sub-division of psychology." Yet Jung has violated his own principle more than once in his writings. The result of this procedure is that instead of giving us a real insight into the essential nature of religion and its meaning for human personality, our modern psychology has given us quite a plethora of new theories which proceed on a complete misunderstanding of the nature of religion as revealed in its higher manifestations, and carry us in an entirely hopeless direction. The implication of these theories, on the whole, is that religion does not relate the human ego to any objective reality beyond himself; it is merely a kind of well-meaning biological device calculated to build barriers of an ethical nature round human society in order to protect the social fabric against the otherwise unrestrainable instincts of the ego. That is why, according to this newer psychology, Christianity has already fulfilled its biological mission, and it is impossible for the modern man to understand its original significance. Jung concludes:

> Most certainly we should still understand it, had our customs even a breath of ancient brutality, for we can hardly realize in this day the whirlwinds of the unchained libido which roared through the ancient Rome of the Caesars. The civilized man of the present day seems very far removed from that. He has become merely neurotic. So for us the necessities which brought forth Christianity have actually been lost, since we no longer understand their meaning. We do not know against what it had to protect us. For enlightened people the so-called religiousness has already approached very close to a neurosis. In the past two thousand years Christianity has done its work and has erected barriers of repression which protect us from the sight of our own sinfulness.

This is missing the whole point of higher religious life. Sexual self-restraint is only a preliminary stage in the ego's evolution. The ultimate purpose of religious life is to make this evolution move in a direction far more important to the destiny of the ego than the moral health of the social fabric which forms his present environment. The basic perception from which religious life moves forward is the present slender unity of the ego, his liability to dissolution, his amenability to re-formation and his capacity for an ampler freedom to create new situations in known and unknown environments. In view of this fundamental perception higher religious life fixes its gaze on experiences symbolic of those subtle movements of reality which seriously affect the destiny of the ego as a possibly permanent element in the constitution of reality. If we look at the matter from this point of view modern psychology has not yet touched even the outer fringe of religious life, and is still far from the richness and variety of what is called religious experience. In order to give you an idea of its richness and variety I quote here the substance of a passage from a great religious genius of the seventeenth century — Sheikh Ahmad of Sarhand — whose fearless analytical criticism of contemporary Sufiism resulted in the development of a new technique. All the various systems of Sufi technique in India came from Central Asia and Arabia; his is the only technique which crossed the Indian border and is still a living force in the Punjab, Afghanistan, and Asiatic Russia. I am afraid it is not possible for me to expound the real meaning of this passage in the language of modern psychology; for such language does not yet exist. Since, however, my object is simply to give you an idea of the infinite wealth of experience which the ego in his Divine quest has to sift and pass through, I do hope you will excuse me for the apparently outlandish terminology which possesses a real substance of meaning, but which was formed under the inspiration of a religious psychology developed in the atmosphere of a different culture. Coming now to the passage. The experience of one Abdul Momin was described to the Sheikh as follows:

> Heavens and Earth and God's throne and Hell and Paradise have all ceased to exist for me. When I look round I find them nowhere. When I stand in the presence of somebody I see nobody before me: nay even my own being is lost to me. God is infinite. Nobody can encompass Him; and this is the extreme limit of spiritual experience. No saint has been able to go beyond this.

On this the Sheikh replied:

> The experience which is described has its origin in the ever-varying life of the *qalb;* and it appears to me that the recipient of it has not yet passed even one-fourth of the innumerable "Stations" of the "Qalb." The remaining three-fourths must be passed through in order to finish the experiences of this first "Station" of spiritual life. Beyond this "Station" there are other "Stations" known as *Ruh, Sirr-i-Khafi,* and *Sirr-i-Akhfa,* each of these "Stations" which together constitute what is technically called *Alam-i-Amr* has its own characteristic states and experiences. After having passed through these "Stations" the seeker of truth gradually receives the illuminations of "Divine Names" and "Divine Attributes" and finally the illuminations of the Divine Essence.

Whatever may be the psychological ground of the distinctions made in this passage it gives us at least some idea of a whole universe of inner experience as seen by a great reformer of Islamic Sufiism. According to him this *Alam-i-Amr*, i.e. "the world of directive energy" must be passed through before one reaches that unique experience which symbolizes the purely objective. This is the reason why I say that modern psychology has not yet touched even the outer fringe of the subject. Personally, I do not at all feel hopeful of the present state of things in either biology or psychology. Mere analytical criticism with some understanding of the organic conditions of the imagery in which religious life has sometimes manifested itself is not likely to carry us to the living roots of human personality. Assuming that sex-imagery has played a role in the history of religion, or that religion has furnished imaginative means of escape from, or adjustment to, an unpleasant reality, these ways of looking at the matter cannot, in the least, affect the ultimate aim of religious life, that is to say, the reconstruction of the finite ego by bringing him into contact with an eternal life-process, and thus giving him a metaphysical status of which we can have only a partial understanding in the half-choking atmosphere of our present environment. If, therefore, the science of psychology is ever likely to possess a real significance for the life of mankind it must develop an independent method calculated to discover a new technique better suited to the temper of our times. Perhaps a psycopath endowed with a great intellect — the combination is not an impossibility — may give us a clue to such a technique. In modern Europe Nietzsche, whose life and activity form, at least to us Easterns, an exceedingly interesting problem in religious psychology, was endowed with some sort of a constitutional equipment for such an undertaking. His mental history is not without a parallel in the history of Eastern Sufiism. That a really "imperative" vision of the Divine in man did come to him cannot be denied. I call his vision "imperative" because it appears to have given him a kind of prophetic mentality which, by some kind of technique, aims at turning its visions into permanent life-forces. Yet Nietzsche was a failure; and his failure was mainly due to his intellectual progenitors such as Schopenhauer, Darwin, and Lange whose influence completely blinded him to the real significance of his vision. Instead of looking for a spiritual rule which would develop the Divine even in a plebeian and thus open up before him an infinite future, Nietzsche was driven to seek the realization of his vision in such schemes as aristocratic radicalism. As I have said of him elsewhere:

The "I am" which he seeketh,
Lieth beyond philosophy, beyond knowledge.
The plant that groweth only from the invisible soil of the
   heart of man,
Groweth not from a mere heap of clay!

Thus failed a genius whose vision was solely determined by his internal forces, and remained unproductive for want of expert external guidance in his spiritual life. And the irony of fate is that this man, who appeared to his friends "as if he had come from a country where no man lived," was fully conscious of his great spiritual need. "I confront alone," he says, "an immense problem: it is as if I am lost in a forest, a primeval one. I need help. I need disciples: I need a *master*. It would be so sweet to obey." And again: "Why do I not find among the living men who see higher than I do and have to look down on me? Is it only that I have made a poor search? And I have so great a longing for such."

The truth is that the religious and the scientific processes, though involving different methods, are identical in their final aim. Both aim at reaching the most real. In fact, religion, for reasons which I have mentioned before, is far more anxious to reach the ultimately real than science. And to both the way to pure objectivity lies through what may be called the purification of experience. In order to understand this we must make a distinction between experience as a natural fact, significant of the normally observable behaviour of reality, and experience as significant of the inner nature of reality. As a natural fact it is explained in the light of its antecedents, psychological and physiological; as significant of the inner nature of reality we shall have to apply criteria of a different kind to clarify its meaning. In the domain of science we try to understand its meaning in reference to the external *behaviour* of reality; in the domain of religion we take it as representative of some kind of reality and try to discover its meanings in reference mainly to the inner *nature* of that reality. The scientific and the religious processes are in a sense parallel to each other. Both are really descriptions of the same world with this difference only that in the scientific process the ego's standpoint is necessarily exclusive, whereas in the religious process the ego integrates its competing tendencies and develops a single inclusive attitude resulting in a kind of synthetic transfiguration of his experiences. A careful study of the nature and purpose of these really complementary processes shows that both of them are directed to the purification of experience in their respective spheres. An illustration will make my meaning clear.

Hume's criticism of our notion of cause must be considered as a chapter in the history of science rather than that of philosophy. True to the spirit of scientific empiricism we are not entitled to work with any concepts of a subjective nature. The point of Hume's criticism is to emancipate empirical science from the concept of force which, as he urges, has no foundation in sense-experience. This was the first attempt of the modern mind to purify the scientific process.

Einstein's mathematical view of the universe completes the process of purification started by Hume, and, true to the spirit of Hume's criticism, dispenses with the concept of force altogether. The passage I have quoted from the great Indian saint shows that the practical student of religious psychology has a similar purification in view. His sense of objectivity is as keen as that of the scientist in his own sphere of objectivity. He passes from experience to experience, not as a mere spectator, but as a critical sifter of experience who by the rules of a peculiar technique, suited to his sphere of inquiry, endeavours to eliminate all subjective elements, psychological or physiological, in the content of his experience with a view finally to reach what is absolutely objective. This final experience is the revelation of a new life-process — original, essential, spontaneous. The eternal secret of the ego is that the moment he reaches this final revelation he recognizes it as the ultimate root of his being without the slightest hesitation. Yet in the experience itself there is no mystery. Nor is there anything emotional in it. Indeed with a view to secure a wholly non-emotional experience the technique of Islamic Sufiism at least takes good care to forbid the use of music in worship, and to emphasize the necessity of daily congregational prayers in order to counteract the possible anti-social effects of solitary contemplation. Thus the experience reached is a perfectly natural experience and possesses a biological significance of the highest importance to the ego. It is the human ego rising higher than mere reflection, and mending its transiency by appropriating the eternal. The only danger to which the ego is exposed in this Divine quest is the possible relaxation of his activity caused by his enjoyment of and absorption in the experiences that precede the final experience. The history of Eastern Sufiism shows that this is a real danger. This was the whole point of the reform movement initiated by the great Indian saint from whose writings I have already quoted a passage. And the reason is obvious. The ultimate aim of the ego is not to *see* something, but to *be* something. It is in the ego's effort to *be* something that he discovers his final opportunity to sharpen his objectivity and acquire a more fundamental "I am" which finds evidence of its reality not in the Cartesian "I think" but in the Kantian "I can." The end of the ego's quest is not emancipation from the limitations of individuality; it is, on the other hand, a more precise definition of it. The final act is not an intellectual act, but a vital act which deepens the whole being of the ego, and sharpens his will with the creative assurance that the world is not something to be merely seen or known through concepts, but something to be made and re-made by continuous action. It is a moment of supreme bliss and also a moment of the greatest trial for the ego:

> Art thou in the stage of "life," "death," or "death-in-life"?
> Invoke the aid of three witnesses to verify thy "Station."
> The first witness is thine own consciousness —
> See thyself, then, with thine own light.
> The second witness is the consciousness of another ego —
> See thyself, then, with the light of an ego other than thee.
> The third witness is God's consciousness —
> See thyself, then, with God's light.
> If thou standest unshaken in front of this light,
> Consider thyself as living and eternal as He!
> That man alone is real who dares —
> Dares to see God face to face!
> What is "Ascension"? Only a search for a witness
> Who may finally confirm thy reality —
> A witness whose confirmation alone makes thee eternal.
> No one can stand unshaken in His Presence;
> And he who can, verily, he is pure gold.
> Art thou a mere particle of dust?
> Tighten the knot of thy ego;
> And hold fast to thy tiny being!
> How glorious to burnish one's ego
> And to test its lustre in the presence of the Sun!
> Re-chisel, then, thine ancient frame;
> And build up a new being.
> Such being is real being;
> Or else thy ego is a mere ring of smoke!
>
>   *Fawīd Nāma.*

MIRCEA ELIADE

In the Beginning

Mircea Eliade (1907–1986) was born and educated in Romania, but became a major influence in religious thought after his moves to France and then to the United States, where he was a professor at the University of Chicago until his death. Eliade paid special attention to the recurrence, in various religious traditions, of myths about what had happened "in the beginning" and to the interpretation of these myths for modern readers.

1. *Orientatio*. Tools to Make Tools. The "Domestication" of Fire

Despite its importance for an understanding of the religious phenomenon, we shall not here discuss the problem of "hominization." It is sufficient to recall that the vertical posture already marks a transcending of the condition typical of the primates. Uprightness cannot be maintained except in a state of wakefulness. It is because of man's vertical posture that space is organized in a structure inaccessible to the prehominians: in four horizontal directions radiating from an "up"-"down" central axis. In other words, space can be organized around the human body as extending forward, backward, to right, to left, upward, and downward. It is from this original and originating experience — feeling oneself "thrown" into the middle of an apparently limitless, unknown, and threatening extension — that the different methods of *orientatio* are developed; for it is impossible to survive for any length of time in the vertigo brought on by disorientation. This experience of space oriented around a "center" explains the importance of the paradigmatic divisions and distributions of territories, agglomerations, and habitations and their cosmological symbolism.

An equally decisive difference from the mode of existence of the primates is clearly shown by the use of tools. The Paleanthropians not only use tools, they are also able to manufacture them. It is true that certain monkeys use objects as if they were tools, and are even known to make them in certain cases. But the Paleanthropians also produce tools to make tools. In addition, their use of tools is much more complex; they keep them accessible, ready for use in the future. In short, their use of tools is not confined to a particular situation or a specific moment, as is the case with monkeys. It is also important to note that tools do not serve as extensions of the human body, for the earliest-known worked stones were shaped to perform a function not prefigured in the body's structure, namely, the function of cutting (an action completely different from tearing with the teeth or scratching with the nails). The very slow progress made in technology does not imply a similar development of intelligence. We know that the extraordinary upsurge in technology during the past two centuries has not found expression in a comparable development of Western man's intelligence. Besides, as has been said, "every innovation brought with it the danger of collective death" (André Varagnac). Their technical immobility insured the survival of the Paleanthropians.

The domestication of fire — that is, the possibility of producing, preserving, and transporting it — marks, we might say, the definitive separation of the Paleanthropians from their zoological predecessors. The most ancient "document" for the use of fire dates from Choukoutien (about 600,000 B.C.), but its domestication probably took place much earlier and in several places.

These few well-known facts needed to be repeated so that the reader of the following analyses will bear in mind that prehistoric man already behaved in the manner of a being endowed with intelligence and imagination. As for the activity of the unconscious — dreams, fantasies, visions, fabulization, and so on — it is presumed not to have differed in intensity and scope from what is found among our contemporaries. But the terms "intensity" and "scope" must be understood in their strongest and most dramatic sense. For man is the final product of a decision made "at the beginnings of Time": the decision to kill in order to live. In short, the hominians succeeded in outstripping their ancestors by becoming flesh-eaters. For some two million years, the Paleanthropians lived by hunting; fruits, roots, mollusks, and so on, gathered by the women and children, did not suffice to insure the survival of the species. Hunting determined the division of labor in accordance with sex, thus reinforcing "hominization"; for among the carnivora, and in the entire animal world, no such difference exists.

But the ceaseless pursuit and killing of game ended by creating a unique system of relationships between the hunter and the slain animals. We shall return to this problem. For the moment, we merely state that the "mystical solidarity" between the hunter and his victims is revealed by the mere act of killing: the shed blood is similar in every respect to human blood. In the last analysis, this "mystical solidarity" with the game reveals the kinship between human societies and the animal world. To kill the hunted beast or, later, the domestic animal is equivalent to a "sacrifice" in which the victims are interchangeable. We must add that all these concepts came into existence during the last phases of the process of hominization. They are still active — altered, revalorized, camouflaged — millennia after the disappearance of the Paleolithic civilizations.

2. The "Opaqueness" of Prehistoric Documents

If the Paleanthropians are regarded as complete men, it follows that they also possessed a certain number of beliefs and practiced certain rites. For, as we stated before, the experience of the sacred constitutes an element in the structure of consciousness. In other words, if the question of the religiosity or nonreligiosity of prehistoric men is raised, it falls to the defenders of nonreligiosity to adduce proofs in support of their hypothesis. Probably the theory of the nonreligiosity of the Paleanthropians was conceived and generally accepted during the heyday of evolutionism, when similarities to the primates had just been discovered. But a misconception is involved here, for what matters is not the anatomico-osteological structure of the Paleanthropians (which is similar, to be sure, to that of the primates) but their *works;* and these demonstrate the activity of an intelligence that cannot be defined otherwise than as "human."

But if today there is agreement on the fact that the Paleanthropians had a religion, in practice it is difficult, if not impossible, to determine what its content was. The investigators, however, have not cried defeat; for there remain a certain number of testimonial "documents" for the life of the Paleanthropians, and it is hoped that their religious meaning will one day be deciphered. In other words, it is hoped that these "documents" can constitute a "language," just as, thanks to the genius of Freud, the creations of the unconscious, which until his time were regarded as absurd or meaningless — dreams, waking dreams, phantasms, and so on — have revealed the existence of a language that is extremely precious for a knowledge of man.

These documents are, in fact, comparatively numerous, but they are "opaque" and not very various: human bones, especially skulls, stone tools, pigments (most abundantly red ocher, hematite), various objects found in burials. It is only from the late Paleolithic that we have rock paintings and engravings, painted pebbles, and bone and stone statuettes. In certain cases (burials, works of art) and within the limits that we shall examine, there is at least the certainty of a religious intention, but the majority of the documents from before the Aurignacian (30,000 B.C.) — that is, tools — reveal nothing beyond their utilitarian value.

Yet it is inconceivable that tools were not charged with a certain sacrality and did not inspire numerous mythological episodes. The first technological discoveries — the transformation of stone into instruments for attack and defense, the mastery over fire — not only insured the survival and development of the human species; they also produced a universe of mythico-religious values and inspired and fed the creative imagination. It is enough to examine the role of tools in the religious life and mythology of the primitives who still remain at the hunting and fishing stage. The magico-religious value of a weapon — be it made of wood or stone or metal — still survives among the rural populations of Europe, and not only in their folklore. We shall not here consider the kratophanies and hierophanies of stone, of rocks, of pebbles. . . .

It is, above all, mastery over distance, gained by the projectile weapon, which gave rise to countless beliefs, myths, and legends. We need only think of the mythologies built up around lances that pierce the vault of the sky and thus make an ascent to heaven possible, of arrows that fly through clouds, transfix demons, or form a chain reaching to heaven, and so on. It is necessary to cite at least some of the beliefs and mythologies that surround tools and implements — and especially weapons — in order better to estimate all that the worked stones of the Paleanthropians *can no longer communicate to us*. The semantic opaqueness of these prehistoric documents is not peculiar to them. Every document, even of our own time, is spiritually opaque as long as it has not been successfully deciphered by being integrated into a system of meanings. A tool, be it prehistoric or contemporary, can reveal only its technological intention; all that its producer or its owners thought, felt, dreamed, hoped in relation to it escapes us. But we must at least try to imagine the nonmaterial values of prehistoric tools. Otherwise, this semantic opaqueness may well force us to entertain a completely erroneous conception of the history of culture. We are in danger, for example, of confusing the appearance of a belief with the date at which it is clearly documented for the first time. When, in the age of metals, certain traditions refer to craft secrets in respect to mining, metallurgy, and the making of weapons, it would be rash to believe that we are in the presence of an unprecedented invention, for these traditions continue, at least in part, an inheritance from the Stone Age.

For some two million years, the Paleanthropians lived chiefly by hunting, fishing, and gathering. But the first archeological indications in respect to the religious universe of the Paleolithic hunter go back only to Franco-Cantabrian rock art (30,000 B.C.). What is more, if we examine the religious beliefs and behavior of contemporary hunting peoples, we realize the almost complete impossibility of *proving the existence or the absence* of similar beliefs among the Paleanthropians. Primitive hunters regard animals as similar to men but endowed with supernatural powers; they believe that a man can change into an animal and vice versa; that the souls of the dead can enter animals; finally, that mysterious relations exist between a certain person and a certain animal (this used to be termed "nagualism"). As for the supernatural beings documented in the religions of hunting peoples, we find that they are of various kinds: theriomorphic companions or guardian spirits — divinities of the type Supreme Being–Lord of Wild Beasts — which protect both the game and the hunters; spirits of the bush; and spirits of the different species of animals.

In addition, certain patterns of religious behavior are peculiar to hunting civilizations. For example, killing the animal constitutes a ritual, which implies the belief that the Lord of Wild Beasts takes care that the hunter kills only what he needs as food and that food is not wasted. Then, too, the bones, especially the skull, have a marked ritual value (probably because of the belief that they contain the "soul" or the "life" of the animal and that it is from the skeleton that the Lord of Wild Beasts will cause a new flesh to grow); this is why the skull and the long bones are exposed on branches or on high places. Finally, among certain peoples the soul of the slain animal is sent to its spiritual home (cf. the "bear festival" among the Ainus and the Giliaks); the custom of offering the Supreme Beings a piece of each slain animal (Pygmies, Philippine Negritos, and others) or the skull and the long bones (Samoyeds and others) also exists; and among certain Sudanese peoples the young man, after bringing down his first game animal, smears the walls of a cave with its blood.

How many of these beliefs and ceremonies can be identified in the archeological documents in our possession? At most, the offerings of skulls and long bones. The richness and complexity of the religious ideology of hunting peoples must never be underestimated — and likewise the almost complete impossibility of proving or denying its existence among the Paleanthropians. As has often been said: beliefs and ideas cannot be fossilized. Hence certain scholars have preferred to say nothing about the ideas and beliefs of the Paleanthropians, instead of reconstructing them by the help of comparisons with the hunting civilizations. This radical methodological position is not without its dangers. To leave an immense part of the history of the human mind a blank runs the risk of encouraging the idea that during all those millennia the activity of the mind was confined to the preservation and transmission of technology. Such an opinion is not only erroneous, it is fatal to a knowledge of man. *Homo faber* was at the same time *Homo ludens, sapiens,* and *religiosus.* Since we cannot reconstruct his religious beliefs and practices, we must at least point out certain analogies that can illuminate them, if only indirectly.

3. Symbolic Meanings of Burials

The earliest and most numerous "documents" are, obviously, bones. From the Mousterian (70,000–50,000 B.C.), we can speak with certainty of burials. But skulls and lower mandibles have been found at much earlier sites, for example at Choukoutien (at a level datable at 400,000–300,000 B.C.), and their presence has raised problems. Since there is no question of burials here, the preservation of these skulls could be explained as due to religious reasons. The Abbé Breuil and Wilhelm Schmidt have referred to the custom, documented among the Australians and other primitive peoples, of preserving the skulls of dead relatives and carrying them along when the tribe travels. Though credible, the hypothesis has not been accepted by most scholars. The same facts have also been interpreted as proof of cannibalism, whether ritual or profane. It is in this way that A. C. Blane has explained the mutilation of a Neanderthal skull found in a cave at Monte Circeo: the man would have been killed by a blow that broke his right eye-socket and the hole would later have been enlarged so that the brain could be extracted through it and eaten ritually. But this explanation has not been unanimously accepted either.

Belief in a survival after death seems to be demonstrated, from the earliest times, by the use of red ocher as a ritual substitute for blood, hence as a symbol of life. The custom of dusting corpses with ocher is universally disseminated in both time and space, from Choukoutien to the western shores of Europe, in Africa as far as the Cape of Good

Hope, in Australia, in Tasmania, in America as far as Tierra del Fuego. As to the religious meaning of burials, it has been the subject of vigorous controversy. There can be no doubt that the burial of the dead *should* have a justification — but which one? To begin with, it must not be forgotten that "pure and simple abandonment of the corpse in some thicket, dismemberment, leaving it to be devoured by birds, instant flight from the habitation, leaving the corpse inside it, did not signify the absence of ideas of survival." A fortiori, belief in survival is confirmed by burials; otherwise there would be no understanding the effort expended in interring the body. This survival could be purely spiritual, that is, conceived as a postexistence of the soul, a belief corroborated by the appearance of the dead in dreams. But certain burials can equally well be interpreted as a precaution against the possible return of the deceased; in these cases the corpses were bent and perhaps tied. On the other hand, nothing makes it impossible that the bent position of the dead body, far from expressing fear of "living corpses" (a fear documented among certain peoples), on the contrary signifies the hope of a rebirth; for we know of a number of cases of intentional burial in the fetal position.

Among the best examples of burials with a magico-religious signification we will mention the one at Teshik Tash, in Uzbekistan (a child surrounded by an arrangement of ibex horns); the one at La Chapelle-aux-Saints, in Corrèze (several flint tools and some pieces of red ocher were found in the excavation in which the body lay); and the one at Farrassie, in Dordogne (several grave mounds, with deposits of flint tools). The cemetery in a cave on Mount Carmel, with ten burials, should be added. The authenticity and the meaning of food offerings or objects placed in graves are still the subject of discussion; the most familiar example is that of the woman's skull at Mas-d'Azil, fitted with artificial eyes and placed on the lower jaw and antler of a reindeer.

During the Upper Paleolithic, the practice of inhumation appears to have become general. Corpses sprinkled with red ocher are buried in graves in which a certain number of objects intended for personal adornment (shells, pendants, necklaces) have been found. It is probable that the animal skulls and bones discovered near graves are the remains of ritual feasts, if not of offerings. Leroi-Gourhan holds that "funerary chattels," that is, the personal objects of the deceased, are "very questionable." The problem is important, for the presence of such objects implies not only belief in a personal survival but also the certainty that the deceased will continue his particular activity in the other world. Similar ideas are abundantly documented, and on various levels of culture. In any case, Leroi-Gourhan recognizes the authenticity of an Aurignacian grave in Liguria, where the skeleton is accompanied by four of those mysterious objects called *bâtons de commandement*. Hence at least certain graves undoubtedly indicate belief in a postmortem continuation of a particular activity.

To sum up, we may conclude that the burials confirm the belief in survival (already indicated by the use of red ocher) and furnish some additional details: burials oriented toward the East, showing an intention to connect the fate of the soul with the course of the sun, hence the hope of a rebirth, that is, of a postexistence in another world; belief in the continuation of a specific activity; certain funeral rites, indicated by offerings of objects of personal adornment and by the remains of meals.

But an examination of burial as practiced by an archaic people of our own time is enough to demonstrate the richness and depth of the religious symbolism implied in a ceremony that appears to be so simple. Reichel-Dolmatoff has given a detailed description of a contemporary (1966) burial of a girl among the Kogi Indians, a tribe speaking the Chibcha language and inhabiting the Sierra Nevada de Santa Maria in Colombia. After choosing the site for the grave, the shaman (*máma*) performs a series of ritual gestures and declares: "Here is the village of Death; here is the ceremonial house of Death; here is the womb. I will open the house. The house is shut, and I will open it." After this he announces, "The house is open," shows the men the place where they are to dig the grave, and withdraws. The dead girl is wrapped in white cloth, and her father sews the shroud. During all this time her mother and grandmother chant a slow, almost wordless song. Small green stones, shells of shellfish, and the shell of a gastropod are placed in the bottom of the grave. Then the shaman tries to lift the body, giving the impression that it is too heavy; he does not succeed until the ninth attempt. The body is laid with its head toward the East, and "the house is closed," that is, the excavation is filled up. Other ritual movements around the grave follow, and finally all withdraw. The ceremony has continued for two hours.

As Reichel-Dolmatoff observes, a future archeologist, excavating the grave, will find only a skeleton with its head toward the East and some stones and shells. The rites, and especially the implied religious ideology, are no longer recoverable on the basis of these remains. In addition, the symbolism will remain inaccessible even to a contemporary observer who does not know the religion of the Kogi. For, as Reichel-Dolmatoff writes, what is involved is verbalization of the cemetery as "village of Death" and "ceremonial house of Death," and verbalization of the grave as "house" and "womb" (which explains the fetal position of the corpse, laid on its left side), followed by verbalization of the offerings as "food for Death," and by the ritual of the "opening" and "closing" of the "house-womb." A final purification by a ritual circumvallation completes the ceremony.

On the other hand, the Kogi identify the world — womb of the Universal Mother — with each village, each cult house, each habitation, and each grave. When the shaman lifts the corpse nine times, he indicates the return of the body to the fetal state by going through the nine months of gestation in reverse order. And since the grave is assimilated to the world, the funerary offerings acquire a cosmic meaning. In addition, the offerings, "food for Death," also have a sexual meaning (in the myths, dreams, and marriage regulations of the Kogi the act of eating symbolizes the sexual act) and consequently constitute a "semen" that fertilizes the Mother. The shellfish shells carry a quite complex symbolism, which is not only sexual: they represent the living members of the family. On the other hand, the gastropod shell symbolizes the dead girl's "husband," for if it is not present in the grave, the girl, as soon as she reaches the other world, "will demand a husband," and this will cause the death of a young man of the tribe.

Here we end our analysis of the religious symbolism contained in a Kogi burial. But it is important to emphasize that, *approached solely on the archeological level,* this symbolism is as inaccessible to us as that of a Paleolithic interment. It is the particular modality of archeological documents that limits and impoverishes the "messages" that they can transmit. This fact must always be kept in mind when we are confronted by the poverty and opaqueness of our sources.

MORDECAI KAPLAN

What Is Traditional Judaism?

Mordecai Menahem Kaplan (1881–1983), for much of his long life a professor at the Jewish Theological Seminary of America, was the principal founder of Reconstructionist Judaism. His effort, in *Judaism As a Civilization* and other works, to affirm a Judaism without supernaturalism gave him a unique outlook also on the meaning of the tradition, articulated in this excerpt from his *The Greater Judaism in the Making*.

THE OVERWHELMING majority of Jews have become modernized, or westernized, as a result of their integration into the body politic of the various European and American nations of which they are citizens, and of their self-adjustment to the cultural climate of their surroundings. This process of westernization began during the latter part of the eighteenth century almost simultaneously among the Jews in France, Prussia, and Austria. Western mankind was then undergoing a transformation which heralded changes that were certain to take place in the world outlook and in the social structure of Jewish life.

Individual Jews had begun to be westernized intellectually some decades before they were westernized politically and socially. Wherever Jews lived in considerable numbers, the more ambitious among them undertook to help their fellow-Jews to be integrated culturally into the general body politic. They would first westernize their own lives, and then seek to influence their fellow-Jews to follow their example. The process of westernization would usually begin, as it did in Prussia under the leadership of Moses Mendelssohn and his followers, with the effort to have the Jews exchange their own Yiddish dialect — or as they then termed it "Jüdisch-Deutsch" — for the native vernacular, and to take up secular studies which were the hallmark of culture.

Thus arose *Haskalah,* or the militant Jewish Enlightenment movement. From Prussia of the end of the eighteenth century the movement
passed within less than a generation to Austria and, soon after, to
Poland and Russia. Despite the long time that has elapsed since the
beginnings of the westernizing process among Jews and the numerous
catastrophic changes and vast migrations since then, there are still
islands in Jewry in all parts of the world which have remained immune
to modern cultural influences. Sooner or later even these islands are
bound to disappear. Their places will be taken by various Jewish
groups which identify themselves with one or another of the existing
trends in modern Judaism.

Each modern trend in Judaism represents a specific version, or
interpretation, of pre-modern Judaism. The Reform version, which is
the first to have been formulated, emerged during the forties of the
nineteenth century. The Conservative version, known at first as "Positive Historical Judaism," and the Orthodox version likewise arose
then as counter-movements to Reform at about the same time. Orthodoxy and Conservatism treat Traditional Judaism as normative for
all time. Orthodoxy strongly deprecates all deviation from Traditional
Judaism. Conservatism, however, is prepared to sanction innovations,
provided they can be kept within the framework of traditional law.
Even the Reform version, which avowedly departs both in belief and
practice from Traditional Judaism, maintains, as a rule, that its devi-
ations are only from the letter, and not from the spirit, of Jewish
tradition. Whatever in that tradition it rejects Reform treats as only
incidental to the inner spirit of ancient Judaism, and as generally the
product of abnormal conditions of life during the pre-modern centuries which a hostile world imposed on the Jews.

In evaluating the trends in contemporary Judaism, we need to know
as accurately as possible what pre-modern Judaism had to say concerning God, the Jewish People, the Torah, and the destiny of human
life. We have to recapture as much of its original spirit as possible. All
too often tradition is invoked to validate as authentic whatever derives
its authoritative character from its connection with the past. It is then
that appeal to tradition is popular, intended to lead us into believing
that nothing really catastrophic has happened to sever that connection. We are lured into assuming that we can go about our business
as of old, without having to resort to any drastic measures to set things
right. That is why we should be on our guard against forming a
distorted picture of Traditional Judaism. Such a distorted picture
would minimize the effort which has to be exerted in rendering

Traditional Judaism relevant to the spiritual needs of Jews of today.

The findings of an *objective* study of Traditional Judaism, summarized in the first part of this book, unmistakably point to the following conclusion: *The conceptions of God, Israel, Torah, human nature, sin, repentance, messianic redemption and the world to come in pre-modern or Traditional Judaism belong to a radically different universe of thought, or world outlook, from that of the average westernized Jew.* This means that every one of the modern trends in Judaism, insofar as it is articulated by Jews who have come under the influence of modern thought, cannot possibly be the original Judaism of tradition. It can only be an adaptation of it to the spirit of the times, whether that fact is recognized or not. The scholars and theologians who sponsor these trends are generally tempted to force the tradition into a mold that will resemble their own adaptation of the tradition to the contemporaneous needs of Jewish life. Consequently, their histories of the Jewish People and of its religion are more often idealizations than a recording of facts.

Rabbinic Judaism

Traditional Judaism is the religious culture, or civilization, of the Jews, as they lived it before they felt the impact of Western thought through the medium of Arabic culture in the Middle East during the tenth to the twelfth centuries of the common era. The salient character of Traditional Judaism was the pervasive awareness on the part of every Jew that his People had been covenanted to God, or committed to the task of making Him and His will known to the rest of mankind. The account of the enactment of the covenant and the duties that it imposed on the Jews were to be found in the Torah which God had revealed or dictated to Moses. Those duties, however, were spelled out with great detail in the patterns, ideals, institutions and norms of conduct formulated by the Sages of the Talmud.

"The Sages of the Talmud" is a term used to denote the *Tannaim* and the *Amoraim*. The *Tannaim,* all of whom were Palestinian Jews, were the authors of the various laws included in the *Mishnah,* which was adopted as an authoritative code by Rabbi Judah the Prince at the end of the second century. The *Amoraim,* some of whom were Palestinian and others Babylonian Jews, were the scholars whose interpretations of the *Mishnah* and the Bible, both legalistic and homiletic, are contained in the *Gemara* and the *Midrashim.* They flourished from about the beginning of the third century to the end of the fifth century, C.E.

That pattern of Traditional Judaism was maintained essentially intact until the invasion of Jewish life by modernism. The finality of Talmudic law formulated by the *Amoraim* was never questioned. "Rav Ashi and Ravina," we are told, "represent the consummation of authoritative teaching." That implies that no one has any right to change that teaching, "whether in substance or in form."

The sharply discerning eye of the scholar may perceive slightly different shades of belief and practice in the Rabbinic pattern, slight changes in emphasis under the influence of varying conditions. But by and large that pattern remained unchanged during the seventeen centuries that elapsed between R. Yohanan ben Zakkai and Moses Mendelssohn. The slight changes in outlook and in social structure of Jewish life which took place in the course of those centuries were so gradual as to be imperceptible. They certainly were not deliberate. To the ancient mind any deliberate change was considered subversive of tradition as a whole, and therefore dangerous.

To the generations of Jews whose mode of life was regulated by the Talmud, all the teachings of the Sages appeared inherently consistent. A considerable portion of the post-Talmudic writings is devoted to the reconciliation of contradictory statements in the tradition itself. Very seldom was a traditional text interpreted in the light of either literary or historical context. Whenever new conditions arose, it was tacitly assumed that they had been provided for in the tradition, since the tradition was assumed to have been revealed by God to Moses simultaneously with the written Torah. That is the assumption on which the entire Rabbinic literature is based. The discussions recorded in the Talmud were carried on in the Rabbinic academies of Palestine and Babylonia over a period of about five centuries. Their purpose was a twofold one; first, to arrive at an inherently consistent interpretation of the tradition as it had come down from the *Tannaim,* and as recorded in the *Mishnah, Tosefta* and other sources; and secondly, to relate that interpretation to the written Torah.

Except for the large-scale revolt against Rabbinic Judaism known as Karaism which flourished for a long time during the ninth to the twelfth century in the Middle East, and the extreme antinomian wing of the Shabbatean sect which arose in Smyrna in 1665, the Talmudic tradition was universally regarded as the norm of Jewish life. "The positive influence of this way of life (the Mosaic and Rabbinic Law) over the Jewish mind had been so great," writes G. G. Scholem, "that for centuries no movement, least of all an organized movement, had rebelled against the values linked up with the practical fulfillment of the Law."

During the three centuries between the tenth and twelfth inclusive, the rising tide of rationalism, which derived from Greek culture, had invaded the Moslem countries where most of the Jews then lived. It also seeped into Jewish life, and for a time jeopardized not only the authority of the Talmudic tradition but the very existence of Judaism, especially among the intellectual elite and the well-to-do. But before long, that threat was offset by a succession of writings which countered successfully the challenge of rationalist thought. Those writings were of two types, philosophic and mystic. Of the two, the mystic writings were by far the more potent in fortifying the Talmudic tradition. The mystic writings kept growing in scope and influence, while the philosophic writings remained limited in both. By the time Traditional Judaism began to feel the impact of modernism, there were but few extant copies of Maimonides' *Guide for the Perplexed,* and the interest in Medieval Jewish philosophy was at its lowest ebb, whereas the study of the *Zohar* received a new impetus with the rise of the Hasidic movement during the middle of the eighteenth century.

Another remarkable fact is that, in the pre-modern era, faith in Traditional Judaism was shared alike by all classes, regardless of their general educational background. Due to the fact that, with few exceptions, neither the philosophic nor the mystic writings seemed to challenge Traditional Judaism, there was little discrepancy in world outlook between the masses and the learned among the Jews. A Jewish woman like Glueckel of Hameln, though more literate than the majority of her kind, was nevertheless typical. Through the medium of the Judeo-German version of Rabbinic teachings she acquired a world outlook that contained virtually all the fundamental concepts and values articulated by the ancient Jewish Sages.

What Judaism as a whole meant to the Jews in the pre-modern era of Jewish history may be inferred from what the term "Torah" meant to them. There is, indeed, no Hebrew term for "Judaism" in the entire literature of that period. *Yahadut,* by which Judaism is designated in modern Hebrew, always meant in the past "Jewishness" or Jewish practice. The term used throughout that period as summing up the entire substance and import of Jewish life is "Torah." For the Jews before modern times *the* Torah consisted essentially of the Pentateuch as interpreted by the oral tradition, *Torah she-be-al-peh.* The authorship of the Pentateuch and of the traditional interpretations of its text was ascribed, in all literalness, to God. Unlike the other parts of the

Bible, which were regarded as having been written under the inspiration of the Divine Spirit, but which also reflect the thought and personality of those who wrote them, the text of the Pentateuch was regarded as free from any human admixture. This assumption was so self-evident to the Sages that they did not hesitate to use a Pentateuchal text as source of verification or refutation, in the same way as we would use a logical or mathematical axiom.

The following passage from *Sifrē,* a collection of Tannaitic interpretations of Numbers and Deuteronomy, is a typical illustration of that sort of reasoning: *"I, even I am He, and there is no God beside Me."* This verse is an answer to those who say, *"There is no Power in heaven,"* or to those who say, *"There are two Powers in heaven."* "One can imagine," C. G. Montefiore and H. Loewe comment, "that this verse might be used against those who say that there are two powers, because such persons might also acknowledge the divine authority of Scriptures. But it is exceedingly curious that the Rabbis, who are not wanting in great acuteness when it comes to making legal distinctions or indeed to anything juristic, should not have seen that for those who deny that there is any God at all . . . the verse is valueless, as such people would obviously deny any authority to the book from which the verse comes."

Another example of how literally they took the tradition that the precepts in the Torah were authored by God is the following: Yehudah Halevi in his *Al-Khazari* has the Rabbi say to the Khazar king: "What is now your opinion of a select community which has merited the appellation 'people of God' and also a special name called 'the inheritance of God,' and of seasons fixed by Him, not merely agreed upon or settled by astronomical calculations, and therefore styled 'feasts of the Lord?' The rules regarding purity and worship, prayers and performances, are fixed by God, and therefore called 'work of God' and 'service of the Lord.' " It is not easy for a modern person to recapture that complete sense of acceptance of whatever was stated in the Torah as absolute truth. Such acceptance was possible only so long as Jews had implicit faith in the divine authorship of its contents.

Throughout the centuries of Traditional Judaism, the doctrine, or dogma, that the Torah had been dictated directly by God to Moses during Israel's sojourn at Sinai, was the cardinal principle to which every Jew had to give assent, or else he was read out of the fold. "He who says that the Torah is not from heaven forfeits his share in the world to come," that is, he is deprived of salvation. When the Sages said of the Torah that it was "from heaven," they were not speaking in metaphors. Heaven was to them a place actually above the earth. Just as literally as they believed in the existence of waters in the upper regions, so literally did they believe that the Torah emanated from the upper regions, that is, from God who dwelt in the heavens above.

Moses' relation to the Torah was nothing more than that of an amanuensis, according to Rabbi Meir, who used as an illustration the instance of Jeremiah's dictating his prophecies to Baruch. "Whoever says that Moses himself wrote even one word of the Torah, of him it is said that he holds God's word in contempt. He forfeits his share in the world to come." The only question was whether God dictated the contents of the entire Torah at one time, or in sections at different times. Some Rabbis maintain that it is forbidden to write the Pentateuch on the same scroll with the rest of the Scriptures, because of the superior sanctity of the former. For the same reason it is not permitted to place a scroll containing the writings of the Prophets and the Hagiographa upon one containing the Pentateuch.

If it were not for Israel's sins, we are told, only the Pentateuch and the parts of Joshua which indicate the boundary lines of Eretz Yisrael would have constituted the Sacred Scriptures. The benediction, *"Blessed art Thou . . . for having given us Thy Torah"* may not be recited before reading any section of the Scriptures outside the Pentateuch, though it may be recited before a passage from the *Mishnah.* In the future, according to R. Yohanan, when Israel's sins have been eliminated, the Pentateuch alone will continue to be studied, to the exclusion of the Prophetic writings and the Hagiographa.

The importance which Traditional Judaism attaches to the Oral Law may be gathered from the fact that it views the Oral Law not merely as coordinate with the Written Law, but as related to it organically. The Sage whose function it is to transmit the Oral Law is deferred to more implicitly than the Prophet. That is why the Oral Law is more authoritative than the Prophetic writings. The relation of the Oral Law to the Written Law is indicated in the story of Hillel and the would-be proselyte. The latter at first refused to accept the Oral Law. Hillel, however, convinced him by means of a lesson in the Hebrew alphabet that the Oral Law was as indispensable to the Written Law as was the tradition concerning the name and pronunciation of each letter of the alphabet to the letters themselves.

The Palestinian *Amoraim* of the third and fourth centuries advance the opinion that the Oral Law is that element of Torah which renders it the unique possession of Israel. This Amoraic conception of the Oral Law is, no doubt, intended to offset the claim of Christianity to the effect that, in adopting the Jewish Scriptures, including the Torah, as part of its sacred writings, it embraces all the revealed truth of which Judaism claims to be the sole possessor. The inclusion by non-Jews of the Pentateuch among their sacred scriptures was resented by the *Tannaim,* as is evident from the following passage in a Tannaitic *Midrash:* "The Torah is betrothed to Israel, and cannot therefore be espoused by any other people."

The Twofold Function of Traditional Judaism

The Torah, in the sense of the Oral and the Written teaching and legislation, performed a twofold function in the life of the Jews: It served as an instrument of national and of individual salvation. The verse in Deuteronomy which reads: "That your days may be multiplied and the days of your children, as the days of the heavens above the earth" is commented upon in *Sifrē,* as follows: " 'That your days may be multiplied,' in this world; 'and the days of your children,' in the Messianic era; 'as the days of the heavens upon the earth,' in the world to come." Among the various petitions which the Jew has been wont to recite at the end of the prayer of thanksgiving after a meal is one which reads: "May the All-merciful make us worthy of the days of the Messiah and of the life of the world to come." This petition sums up in succinct fashion the two goals which Traditional Judaism sought to help the Jew attain. "The days of the Messiah" refers to national redemption, to freedom from oppression at the hands of other nations, and to the return of the Jews to Eretz Yisrael, their ancestral land. "The life of the world to come" refers to the life of bliss which awaits the individual Jew who, while in this world, lives in conformity with the will of God as expressed in the Torah.

The Torah, or Traditional Judaism, must therefore be understood as having made of the Jews both a nation (ummah) *and an ecclesia* (K'nesset Yisrael). As a nation, the Jews developed all those institutions which were essential to the conduct of everyday affairs in men's relations to one another and in their relations as a group *vis-a-vis* other groups. A nation is a political group. Before the modern era the Jews were a political group insofar as they always enjoyed a measure of autonomy. On the other hand, they were also an ecclesia or *K'nesset.* "Ecclesia" is a distinctly religious concept, religious in the *traditional* sense of being based upon some supernatural revelation of divinity. An ecclesia is a *corpus mysticum.* Its members are united by the common bond of allegiance to some specific instrument of a supernatural character. That instrument may be a sacred text, or it may be a sacred personality.

By means of that instrument, it is assumed, men learn what God would have them do in order to achieve salvation.

Of the two functions of the Torah, that of maintaining the solidarity of the Jews as a People was expected to lead to the advent of the Messiah. The other function, that of uniting them into a holy nation, or ecclesia, designated as *K'nesset Yisrael* was expected to enable them, as individuals, to achieve salvation, or a share in the world to come. Those two functions were not inherently integral to each other, though, before Rabbinic Judaism became crystallized, they gradually fused into the one eschatological hope of a miraculously bright future for the entire People.

However, the belief in the hereafter, or in the world to come, because of its reference to the destiny of the individual, was bound to play a greater role in the Jewish consciousness during the centuries of exile than the Messianic expectation, which had to do with the destiny of the nation. This is apparent from the tendency of the Sages to reinterpret scriptural passages which unmistakenly refer to the future destiny of the nation as referring to the world to come. Thus the teaching of the Mishnah that "All who are of Israel have a share in the world to come" is based upon the statement in Isaiah which reads: *"Thy people are all righteous; they will inherit the land* (eretz) *forever."* Even if *eretz* means "the earth," it could mean that only in the same sense as in Psalm 37:11, where the poet wishes to affirm his faith in the ultimate survival of the meek and humble instead of the aggressive and violent ones. In any event, the Prophet is concerned with the destiny of the entire People and not merely with that of the individual. Moreover, the *Chapters of the Fathers,* which have as their central theme the importance of Torah study, and the reading of which is preceded by the foregoing *Mishnah* about the world to come, do not treat that study as a means to national redemption but to a share of the individual Jew in the world to come.

If we call to mind the difference between the origin of the belief in the advent of the Messiah and of the belief in the world to come, we sense the difference in the connotations of those beliefs. The belief in the Messiah stems directly from Biblical sources. It is indigenously Jewish. On the other hand, the belief in the world to come, with its concomitant belief in bodily resurrection, is an importation mainly from Zoroastrian civilization.

In the Bible, the People of Israel, after having undergone divine chastisement, is assured of its return to its land and of the attainment of bliss. Every such assurance became part of the pattern of hope in which the central figure was a scion of David, known as the Messiah. The prophecies of Balaam, the concluding verses in the farewell song of Moses, the prophecy in Isaiah and Micah concerning "the latter days," the description of the Messiah given in *Isaiah,* Chapter 11, the entire collection of consolatory prophecies in the second part of Isaiah, those in all the other prophetic books from Jeremiah through Malachi, the allusions in the book of Psalms, and the concluding chapter in Daniel — all were uniformly interpreted as referring to the Messianic era which awaited the Jewish nation.

On the other hand, the belief in bodily resurrection and the belief in the world to come stem from non-Jewish sources. It was accepted by the Jews to meet a spiritual expectation which had arisen during the period of the Second Commonwealth. That expectation was to find some correspondence between the merit and the lot of the individual. Experience seemed to refute the principle of reward and punishment stressed in the Torah. The Jews therefore had recourse to the same solution as all other religions which stressed the salvation of the individual. That solution posited another world wherein the inequities of this one were righted. Thus the belief in the world to come is essentially motivated by the desire to vindicate the principle of individual retribution. Both the Messianic hope and the expectation of bliss in the world to come are voiced in the traditional liturgy, as in the following: "May it be Thy will that we keep Thy statutes in this world, and be worthy to live to witness and inherit happiness and blessing in the days of the Messiah and in the life of the world to come."

JOSEPH MITSUO KITAGAWA

Buddhism in the Modern World

Joseph Mitsuo Kitagawa is a native of Japan whose research
and teaching have been carried on in the United States. That
experience has allowed him to interpret the various traditions of the religions of the East (the title of the book from
which this excerpt is taken), and especially that of Japanese
Buddhism, to Western readers with a special sensitivity to
the distinctive elements of both religious cultures.

It HAS BEEN our purpose to understand the dual character of Buddhism,
its Indianness and its Pan-Asianness, for as Snellgrove states: "Buddhism is not just the word of one master, promulgated and fixed for
all time. It was part of India's religious experience, changing, adapting,
developing through the centuries, yet at the same time retaining a
certain continuity and independence in its traditions." Buddhism
continued to grow in India's immediate neighbors and also in other
areas where indigenous religions and cultures had been established.
In both cases the genius of Buddhism enabled it to maintain and
express its *Lebensgefühl,* which is distinct and unmistakable. Eventually, Buddhism developed into a Pan-Asian religion, closely identified with various cultures of Asia.

Some general characterization of Asian cultures may be useful at
this point. It has often been said that while the ethos of Europe may
be described as a conscious and unconscious desire for unity of diverse
elements, the ethos of Asia may be described in terms of "juxtaposition
and identity," to use Haas's phrase. For example, two great Asian
cultures, the Indian and the Chinese, developed independently with
very little sense of mutual dependence or interpenetration. They stand
side by side in juxtaposition and have developed in relative insularity.

In this situation, Buddhism alone developed and maintained cross-cultural regional ties.

Haas is of the opinion that the ideological differences between the East and the West can be seen most clearly in their understanding of the concept of the "natural." The East takes it for granted that social and political institutions are rooted in the "natural," which is identified with the "original." This view may be contrasted to the Hebraic-Christian notion of the Fall of man, which implies that the "natural" is a corruption of the "original." "The East admits no reason, or logos, in opposition and superior to the natural. The natural possesses, so to speak, its own reason. And it is the part of human wisdom to recognize and submit to it." What distinguishes Buddhism from other Asian religions is that while accepting the necessity of transcendental wisdom, it refused to accept the empirical sociopolitical system as a path to the realization of the "original." Instead, Buddha created a separate community of the faithful (Samgha), which alone was integrally related to the Dharma. However, the early Buddhist concept of the Buddhist Community, consisting of the monastics and the laity alike, was soon overshadowed by the monastic emphasis of Theravāda Buddhism, and eventually the secularization of the monastic institutions closely involved them in the sociopolitical systems of Asia. Also, this nontheistic religion began to embrace local spirit-worship in Southeast Asia and to create its own pantheon in the Far East.

The historical development of Buddhism in Asia shows its intimate connections with the ruling classes. To be sure, there were sincere Buddhists in all walks of life, who tried to follow the footsteps of their master, seeking not worldly success or prosperity but sanctification and liberation. And yet the growth of the Buddhist institutions was marked by a passionate attachment to this-worldly values and to monarchic, hierarchic sociopolitical systems. This phenomenon may be explained, at least in part, by the fact that the early concept of the Buddhist Community was not taken seriously. Consequently, while Buddhism developed on the local level something analogous to the Western pattern of the parish, with temples and lay adherents, it never developed on a national or regional level a sense of solidarity of all the faithful. Instead, Buddhists remember the reign of Asoka as the golden age of Buddhism, implying that the ideal of Buddhism is the establishment of a Buddhist state. Because of this aspiration, the ecclesiastical hierarchy often became for all practical purposes servants of the state, with the result that Buddhism reflected the ethos of powers that were far greater than it ever acknowledged. There is a saying that

Buddhism did not convert China but China converted Buddhism, and this was often true in other Asian countries as well. In short, Buddhism came to share the strength and weaknesses of Asian cultures over a long period of time.

During the eighteenth and nineteenth centuries, traditional Asian cultures were disintegrating from within, and this process coincided with the advance of European colonial powers in Asia. To put it another way, "it was not their own stagnancy which delivered the Eastern peoples into the hands of the West," but "it was a stagnation that developed inversely as a result of their contact with the West" that resulted in the decline of the East. The driving force behind the expansion of the Western nations was "modernity," which was destined to remain in Asia even after the end of the Western colonialism. Initially, of course, the impact of modernity was most directly felt in the areas that were taken over by European nations, such as Ceylon, Burma, and Indo-China, but it also precipitated social and political revolutions in Japan, China, and Thailand.

This is not the place to discuss the complex problem of colonialism in the Asian scene, nor was everything introduced by the Western administration necessarily bad, as some emotional nationalists insinuate. In fact, by eliminating some of the worst features of traditional autocratic and irrational political systems, the Western colonial administration prepared the way for more modern national governments. At the same time, the Western administrations disrupted the traditional ways of life in Asia. For example, Margaret Mead points out that the traditional government of Burma was based on a dual system: the king had customary powers over local hereditary headmen, who in turn governed people mainly by means of arbitration and not by coercion. In this situation, law and order were based on an accepted pattern of living and were not dependent on external authority. The Western administration, by making these hereditary headmen government officials, changed personal authority to bureaucratic authority, and transformed the organic relationships among the people into new territorial entities based on space. "When the organic unity of the village was shattered, when external authority with penal sanctions was substituted for the authority inherent in a traditional way of life, the traditional guiding principle of social conduct was destroyed and there was nothing to take its place."

The most far-reaching effect of modernity was felt in the field of education, which divided Asians into two classes, a minority of young intellectuals with Westernized education and the mass of people without it. This is what Coomaraswamy called the separation of literacy from culture. The modern elite in Asia were uprooted from their ancestral ways of life, leaving indigenous religions and cultures to those who were less sensitive to the challenge of industrialized modern civilization. During the nineteenth and the early part of the twentieth century, modern education provided an avenue for upward social mobility in Asia. The colonial administrators were not totally unaware of the possible repercussions of this trend. The Administration Report of Ceylon (1877) stated, "Whether the spread of . . . English education . . . is an unmixed benefit or not, there can be no doubt that one of its results is to create a large and daily increasing class of men who reject all means of livelihood which savor at all of manual labor." And this is precisely what happened. Everywhere in Asia there developed a new social group of native intelligentsia, and it was this group which later provided leadership in nationalist movements.

During the first two decades of our century, however, the young intellectuals — whether they were nationalists, socialists, or communists — failed to capture the masses. In the meantime, traditional religious leaders gained prestige among the masses as spokesmen of the old ways of life, against the advance of the West, against Christian missionary work, and against the culturally uprooted native intellectuals. Gradually the traditional religions, which at first served only as rallying points of the illiterate peasantry, gained strength among the lower middle class. In the 1930's, many Asian intellectuals who had Westernized educations suddenly recognized the strength of their ancestral religions and cultures which they had hitherto spurned. Recognizing the need of relating themselves to their own peoples, some young Asian intellectuals and leaders became converts to the traditional religions, and this explains why some of them talk at one moment like radical revolutionaries and at the next moment like dreamy mystics.

Early in the 1940's, Western colonialism in Asia came to a sudden end with the Japanese invasion. Japan, be it noted, was an Asian nation where modern civilization and education had been taken over and utilized by the traditional culture. As soon as Japan occupied Southeast Asia, it eliminated the Western and pro-Western elements from government positions in the occupied area, and made every effort to eradicate the myth of Western supremacy. The Japanese occupation authorities also offered administrative positions to those natives who had been denied such advancement under Western rule, and gave large-scale military training to the natives for the first time. Furthermore, the Japanese were not idle in courting religious and political spokesmen in the countries they occupied. Although the period of Japanese occupation was very brief, it nevertheless accelerated the growing nationalist movements in Southeast Asia, and this trend could not be easily reversed after the defeat of the Japanese.

After World War II, many Southeast Asian nations gained political independence. In this situation, what happened in Burma was repeated in many other countries. In the words of U Kyaw Thet: "Painfully aware that their national pride — even their continued existence — was manifestly debatable, the Burmese had to produce something tangible and traditional to justify their future as a separate entity. They found what they needed in Buddhism."

Many books and articles have been written on the resurgence of Buddhism since World War II. Even the most casual traveler passing through the Far East and Southeast Asia cannot help being impressed by the vitality of Buddhism. Like any other vital contemporary movement, the resurgence of Buddhism has many facets, and no sweeping statements can be made because the situations vary according to different areas of Asia. Here we will discuss two major aspects of the resurgence of Buddhism. The first is the relationship between Buddhism and the nation-states, and the second is the problem of the supernational solidarity of the Buddhist Community.

The problem of the relationship between Buddhism and the nation-state is acutely felt by many Asian leaders, both political and religious, who are shouldering the responsibility of guiding their nations in this difficult period of history. In recent decades, Asian leaders were struggling for independence; they fought against foreign rule by resistance movements and revolutionary actions. During that time, the problem was simple: politics meant struggle against imperialism, and religion stood for the indigenous values and ways of life which were suppressed by the alien rulers. Now that the native leaders are in power, they have to re-examine the relationship between Buddhism and the nation-state in the light of the contemporary situations in various countries. For example, Burma envisages the establishment of a "Buddhist Welfare State," based on dual roots of Buddhism and a planned economy. The problem that confronts Buddhist Burma is stated succinctly by U Kyaw Thet: "Are these two concepts really compatible? Are they self-defeating? Can a convinced Buddhist, who knows that things of this world are insubstantial and worthless, bring to the hard and tedious task of developing a still backward and badly war-ravaged country the energy and perseverance the job will require?" Similar searching questions are being asked by thoughtful people throughout the Buddhist world. On the one hand, they want to preserve the Buddhist tradition, and on the other hand, they have to develop a new sociopolitical order.

Admittedly, Buddhism, which was closely interwoven with the premodern cultures of Asia, cannot be emancipated from the past overnight. In many areas of life Buddhism still represents the ultra-conservative elements in society. For example, Bryce Ryan, in his interviews with eighty-six monks and priests in Ceylon on the question of family-planning, found that the views of the scholarly monks were overwhelmingly favorable but that the responses of uneducated village priests were uniformly negative to the idea of family-planning. The latter's views conform to those of the village laity, and this is where the actual strength of Buddhism is found today. Despite Ryan's optimistic conclusion that with careful public relations "the Sangha [Samgha] through its intellectual leaders would be a far more positive force than it would be negative," it may not be so easy to counteract the deep-rooted religious and social conservatism of the village priests and laity. The author of *The Revolt in the Temple* is impatient with those who loosely and naïvely talk about Buddhism as the only remedy for all the political isms, or a new way of life to the world. "Have those who use these slogans ever thought what kind of Buddhism they mean to offer to a distracted world? If by 'Buddhism' they mean the kind of Buddhism that is practiced in everyday Ceylon and dosed out to the people from the temples, loud-speakers, and the Broadcasting Service, we think there is little likelihood of that Buddhism taking root in the West, or anywhere else." This type of self-criticism is going on in various parts of Asia regarding the actual situations of empirical Buddhism.

One of the important features of contemporary Buddhism is a serious effort on the part of some scholars to re-examine the historical Buddhist doctrines in the light of modern philosophical and social thought. For example, Wijesekera tries to portray Buddha as a rationalist and empiricist, who held an evolutionary view of the world and society. There are others who also attempt to reinterpret Buddha as a social prophet, and Dharma as an ideology for the new age. Such attempts are not welcomed by conservative Buddhists, who resent any kind of change, doctrinal or practical. The modernist wing, however, advocates a new birth of Buddhism, emancipated from social and religious medievalism. "The sponsors of this revitalized religion, the Sangha [Samgha], would pursue not a will-o'-the-wisp Nirvāna secluded in the cells of their monasteries, but a Nirvāna attained here and now by a life of self-forgetful activity. Theirs will not be a selfish existence, pursuing their own salvation whilst living on the charity of others, but an existence full of service and self-sacrifice. To bring about this transformation the Sangha [Samgha] must be reorganized and the *bhikkhus* trained not only in Buddhist theory but also in some form of social service."

There is no doubt that Buddhism can develop a dynamic social consciousness, a social philosophy, and social action, as well evidenced by the example of B. R. Ambedkar (d. 1956), the spokesman of the scheduled class of India, and a crusader for the rights of the oppressed. He launched a movement for abolishing untouchability in India by turning toward Buddhism. Although his Buddhist movement among the scheduled class has not been taken too seriously by the Hindu majority thus far, it is creating a significant minority of dedicated Buddhists in India. Ambedkar was a visionary who knew how to translate his vision into concrete social, educational, and political programs, and by his own example he demonstrated that Buddhism can inspire people to fight for the cause of justice and freedom, even defying the existing order of things, without any encouragement from the government or outside groups.

However, Ambedkar's was an unusual case. In general, most Buddhists today depend heavily on the leadership and assistance of their Governments. Historically Buddhism has been closely related to the state, and there is little effort on either side to alter this. While many Asian nations affirm in theory the freedom of conscience as well as the practice and propagation of all religions, in practice they accord special consideration to Buddhism. Conversely, many sincere Buddhists are convinced that teaching and preaching Buddhist doctrine and ethics is not enough, and that the political structure must be made consonant with the Law of Buddha. "The task which the Buddha left to his followers was to create on earth a polity ordered in accordance with his teaching." U Win, onetime Minister for Home and Religious Affairs in Burma, is more explicit on this point. He says: "Our religion has been in a neglected state for the sixty years since the overthrow [by the British] of King Thebaw, Promoter of the Faith. The prosperity of a religion . . . depends on the presence of a ruler who is genuinely inclined to promote it. . . . Now the circumstances have changed.

Independence is once more restored and the Government is duly elected according to the constitution. It is but inevitable that the Government become the Promoter of the Faith, on behalf of the people who elect it." In accordance with this principle, the Government of Burma passed in 1950 the Pali University and Dhammacarya Act to promote Buddhist study and to train priests. The Government also established the Buddhist Sasana Council of the Union of Burma to promote the cause of Buddhism, including the restoration of temples, encouragement of Buddhist study and meditation, and the propagation of Buddhism within and without Burma.

Today, the vitality of the resurgence of Buddhism is expressed in its missionary and "ecumenical" concerns, which are, of course, inseparably interrelated. The missionary outreach was not a particular concern of modern Buddhists until after World War II. Of course, there were exceptions. For example, in the 1930's Abbot T'ai-hsu and the leaders of the Chinese Buddhist Association sought the cooperation of Buddhists in other lands for a world-wide evangelism. It was T'ai-hsu's conviction that "Buddhist doctrine is fully capable of uniting all the existing forms of civilization, and should spread throughout the world so that it may become a compass, as it were, for the human mind." With this far-reaching objective in mind, he suggested the establishment of an international Buddhist university for the training of learned monks, as well as the publication of Buddhist literature and a training program for laymen and laywomen. Similar objectives were advocated by the Maha-Bodhi Society in India. However, organized Buddhist missionary work was not undertaken on a big scale until the Burmese inaugurated the work among their animistic peoples in 1946. Today there are several missionary societies that are dedicated to the cause of the Buddhist missions in Asia, Europe, and America.

The Buddhist counterpart of the Christian "ecumenical" movement is bringing together the Theravāda, Mahāyāna and Mantrayāna traditions for the first time in Buddhism's long history. The World Fellowship of Buddhists, which by the way elected an able layman, G. P. Malalasekera, as its president, has had conferences in Ceylon (1950), Japan (1952), Burma (1954), and Nepal (1956), and provided valuable ecumenical experience to the delegates from various parts of Asia and the West. Also, celebrating the twenty-five hundredth anniversary of the Buddhist era, the Buddha Jayanti was held recently in many countries, which contributed greatly to the cause of Buddhist unity. Probably the most ambitious and dramatic undertaking of contemporary Buddhism was the Sixth Great Buddhist Council held in Burma, 1954–1956. This council, known officially as the Chattha Sangayana, was made possible by the combined efforts of the Government and the people of Burma under the leadership of the then prime minister, U Nu. The council, among other accomplishments, re-edited the sacred scriptures of Buddhism, which were recited and formally adopted as the canonical texts. Based on these experiences, Malalasekera is quite optimistic about the future of Buddhist unity. "The Buddhist flag now flies in every country as the emblem of World Buddhism, Mahāyāna monks are entering monasteries in Theravāda lands and vice versa to learn each other's language and canonical texts. They are co-operating in Ceylon's Buddha Jayanti project of an encyclopedia of Buddhism."

Thus, in less than two decades, Buddhism has made notable advances toward the twofold goal of missionary outreach and Buddhist unity. To be sure, the Buddhist Community is still divided by different traditions, cultural heritages, and national interests, and the Buddhist nations are haunted by almost insurmountable problems concerning industrialization, communism, and social and economic welfare. Besides, whether the spokesmen of Buddhism admit it or not, Buddhism is not yet a live option in the religious life of people outside Asia. Despite all these problems which confront them today, Buddhists are beginning to see "in faith" the possibility of relating their holy Community to the totality of the human community. This is another way of saying that today Buddhists are seeing a glimpse of the Samgha Universal in the midst of the brokenness of the empirical Buddhist Community.

CARSUN CHANG, TANG CHUN-I, MOU TSUNG-SAN, HSU FO-KUAN

A Neo-Confucian Manifesto

Carsun Chang (1886–1969), the author of a definitive two-volume work, *The Development of Neo-Confucian Thought*, joined with several colleagues in 1957 to prepare "A Manifesto for a Reappraisal of Sinology and Reconstruction of Chinese Culture," which was published on New Year's Day 1958. It was, in the words of its authors, "primarily intended as an aid to Western intellectuals in appreciating Chinese culture," but it spoke to Chinese concerns as well.

Introduction

In this declaration we propose to discuss our basic understanding of the past and present developments of Chinese culture, its outlook, and what we deem to be the correct approach to its study. We will also deal with what we expect of world civilization.

These problems have been under our close attention, as well as that of numerous other scholars and statesmen, for scores of years it is true; yet, we would not have penetrated them as we have were it not for the fact that several years ago China suffered from an unprecedented catastrophe which forced us into exile, and under such forlorn circumstances we were prompted to ponder upon many fundamental problems. Genuine wisdom is born of afflictions; only through suffering can our spirit transcend set patterns of life and beliefs to examine thoroughly all the aspects of each problem. Scholars of other nationalities, like the Chinese scholars of old, have not had similar experiences and consequently are liable to numerous misunderstandings due to their limited points of view and may therefore not see what we have been able to discover.

We must promulgate our views because we sincerely believe that the problems of Chinese culture have their universal significance. Even setting aside the fact that China is one of the very few nations whose cultural history has not been disrupted for thousands of years or that the Chinese culture had elicited ample admiration in pre-eighteenth century Europe, in addition to its considerable contributions to mankind, there is still the problem of her immense population, which comprises one-fourth of that of the world. China's problem has long since become a world problem; and if the conscience of mankind will not permit the annihilation of the nearly six hundred million of her people, then it has to assume the unending burden of their destiny. We sincerely believe that the solution hinges on a genuine understanding of her culture, in both its actualities and its potentialities.

*   *   *   *   *

What the West Can Learn from Oriental Thought

The development of Western civilization is outlined by innumerous flashes of brilliancy as well as many crises. Such crises have their origin in man's inability to control his cultural products and inventions. Thus, perhaps the highest achievement of modern scientific technology is nuclear fission, and yet the biggest world problem now is precisely due to the fact that Western civilization is unable to control this nuclear fission. We cannot, of course, assert that oriental cultures can surmount such difficulties, but it is clear that the formation of a world civilization is contingent upon co-operation on a high plane among the various cultures of the world. What the Orient, in particular China, needs in preparation for this has been delineated. What, in our opinion, the West should learn from the East will now be set forth.

In the first place, the West needs the spirit and capacity of sensing the presence of what *is* at every particular moment, (*Tang-hsia-chi-shih*) and of giving up everything that can be had (*I-ch'ieh-fang-hsia*). The strength of the West's cultural spirit lies in its ability to push ahead indefinitely. However, there is no secure foundation underlying this feverish pursuit of progress. Along with this pursuit of progress there is a feeling of discontentment and of emptiness. In order to fill this emptiness, the individual and the nation constantly find new ways for progress and expansion. At the same time external obstructions and an internal exhaustion of energy cause the collapse of the individual and the nation. This is why the most powerful ancient Western nations collapsed and never did recover from their downfall. Chinese culture traces all values to "hsin-hsin," and in so doing achieves the capacity to "accept what is self-sufficient at the moment." Chinese thought has always regarded "retreat" as more fundamental than "advance." Complementing the characteristically Western push for progress, this will provide a solid and secure foundation for Western civilization.

Moreover, as the West builds its culture on the activities of the intellect it is principally concerned with the formation of concepts. In thus attributing the essence of life to intellectual processes, it tends unwittingly to value human life in proportion to its conceptual content. Such a criterion is not without merit, but it overlooks the fact that concepts as such are separate and distinct from life. When human life is committed to certain clear-cut concepts, it can no longer enjoy and adapt itself. This is the prime cause of the West's difficulty in achieving communion with the East. Authentic communication is possible only if the participant parties present an "empty mind" ready to identify with one another. While concepts can be a means of communicating between those mutually sympathetic, they can also be the most obstinate obstacle to genuine communication. As such, they — consisting of premeditated plans and objectives, abstract ideals of human relations and values, forming our prejudices, passions, habitual notions, etc. — must all be suppressed. In Indian thought this is known as the "wisdom of emptiness" or "wisdom of liberation from worldliness." In Taoism it is called the wisdom of the "void" or "nothingness"; and in Chinese Buddhism it is known as the wisdom of "emptiness," "freedom from pre-conceptions, pre-determinations, obstinacy, or egoism," and "broad-mindedness." With such wisdom, everything is seen through as if transparent, so that though one still possesses concepts and ideals of thought one can readily disentangle oneself from them and not be limited and confined by them.

The second element the West can learn from the East is all-round and all-embracing understanding or wisdom. This Chuang-tzu called "spiritual understanding" or "meeting the object with the spirit." In Western science or philosophy, principles and universals are attained by intellect and are sharply enunciated and defined. They are abstract and cannot be applied to what is concrete, because the characteristics which are peculiar to each class, and which are inexhaustible, have been eliminated. Wisdom is needed to comprehend and to deal with all the unprecedented changes of life. This wisdom does not operate by adhering to universals, but by submerging universals in order to observe the changing conditions and peculiarities. To a large extent universals are determined by particular classes of objects. Universals which are related to these objects can be stored in the mind and called upon to function when the case applies. On the other hand one needs to submerge universals in order to rise to a higher plane of comprehension. In this way one's mind and wisdom which are all embracing achieve what Chuang-tzu calls "spiritual understanding." Meng-tzu said: "What has passed is merged; what has been preserved goes to the spirit and revolves with the universe." The term "spiritual" in Chinese means "stretchability." In applying universals to the physical world, certain universals correspond to certain physical objects. In the event that there is no correspondence between universals and objects the mind feels frustrated. Should one possess an all-embracing wisdom, he would not feel thwarted.

This wisdom is similar to the dialectical method and to Bergson's "intuition." The dialectical method employs a new kind of universal to explain a concrete reality, e.g., Hegel's philosophy of history. Nonetheless, the method is limited in its scope. The characteristic of the all-embracing wisdom of the Chinese, on the other hand, is a comprehensive understanding of reality. Bergson's "intuition" is similar to this, but his "intuition" is merely a fundamental tenet of his philosophical theory and does not penetrate his entire outlook on reality. In the Chinese view of life this wisdom goes into its literature, art, philosophy, Ch'an Buddhism, and the dialogues of the Sung Confucianists; it also shapes the attitudes of the scholars in their daily lives. This is why the Chinese can feel a unity with the universe. They can adapt themselves to different changes without feeling frustration. The Western world is in great need of this wisdom if she intends to understand the nature of the different cultures and to have an authentic communication with them. In addition to their knowledge, technology, ideals, and God, they must above all search deeper for the source of life, the depth of personality and the common origin of human culture in order to arrive at a true unity with mankind.

The third point that the West can learn from the East is a feeling of mildness and compassion. The Westerner's loyalty to ideals, his spirit of social services, and his warmth and love for others are indeed precious virtues, to which oriental counterparts cannot measure up. However, the highest affection between men is not zeal or love, for with these emotions is often mingled the will to power and its acquisitive instinct. To forestall such an adulteration, Western civilization principally relies on its religious emphasis on personal humility and on all merits ultimately coming from God. However, the name of

God can be borrowed as a back-prop in the conviction that one's actions bear His sanction; or else one may even selfishly wish to possess Him, such as during a war to pray for victory. It is for this reason that Christianity also teaches forgiveness. But extreme forgiveness tends to become complete renunciation of the world. To avoid such a fault zeal and love must again be emphasized, thus forming a logical circle and leaving the intermingling of love and the will to dominate or to possess still an unresolved difficulty. The resolution lies in eradicating this will to dominate or possess, and this is possible only if love is accompanied by respect. In that case, if I feel that the source of my love for others is God's infinite love, then my respect for others is likewise boundless. As the Chinese put it, the good man "serves his parents like Heaven" and "employment of people is as important as the sacrificial services." Genuine respect for others is possible only if man is without qualifications considered as an end in himself; but with such a respect love expresses itself through *li* (etiquette), thereby becoming courteous and mild. In this way love is transformed into compassion. This is precisely the Buddhist doctrine of "the great compassion." Its difference from ordinary love lies in the fact that in ordinary love the lover's spiritual feeling flows towards others in the manner of "regarding others as oneself," and this may frequently be mingled with the desire to possess others. Compassion, on the other hand, is the sympathetic consonance between the life-spirit of one's own and another's authentic being. Here, there is also natural interflowing of true sympathy, which is partly directed outwards and partly inwards. The emotional flowback makes it possible to purge any desire to dominate or possess. In other words, to effect such a transformation of Western love, God must be identified with man's heart of hearts, manifesting Himself through our bodies as the direct communication between the life-spirits of all authentic being, not merely as a transcendental being, the object of man's prayers.

Fourthly, the West can obtain from the East the wisdom of how to perpetuate its culture. Contemporary Western culture is, it is true, at its height of brilliance, yet many observers have been concerned with its future, whether it will perish like ancient Greece and Rome. Culture is the expression of a people's spiritual life, and by the laws of nature all expression drains the energy of life. If this energy is exhausted, perishing is inevitable. To preserve his spiritual life, man needs a depth formed by an historical awareness which reaches both into the past and into the future and this depth connects with the life-giving source of the cosmos. In the West, this life-giving source is called God. In their religious life, Westerners could have more or less come into contact with the source were it not that they relied on prayer and faith. As it is, God is an external transcendental being and man can only reflect on His eternity. Besides, through prayer and faith what approaches God is man's spirit in adoration, not his authentic being. Painstaking labor is needed to make possible an authentic being's contact with the life-giving source. Man must begin by seeing to it that all his external acts do not merely follow a natural course, but rather go against this natural course to return to the cosmic life-giving source, and only then to fulfill nature. By such exertions against the natural course, energy is diverted into communication with the cosmic life-giving source. From this point of view, the West's chief concern with speed and efficiency constitutes a great problem. While the former easy-going attitude of the Chinese is not a suitable remedy in many respects, yet the maximum rate of progress with which the West leads the world is not conducive to durability. There will come the day when the West will realize that without lasting history and culture, though there be an eternal God, man cannot live peacefully. The West needs to develop an historical awareness with which to tap the life-giving source. It will then come to appreciate the value of conservation of life-energy and the meaning of filial piety, and learn to fulfill the ancestral will in order to preserve and prolong its culture.

The fifth point the West can learn from the East is the attitude that "the whole world is like one family." Though there are many nations now, mankind will eventually become one and undivided. Chinese thought has emphasized this attitude. Thus Motians advocate all-embracing love; Taoists urge forgetting the differences; Buddhists advise commiseration and love for all things; and Confucians teach universal kindness (*jen*). The Christian doctrine of love has much in common with the Confucian doctrine of universal kindness. However, Christianity insists that man is tainted by original sin and that salvation comes from God, from above. Confucians, on the other hand, generally believe that human nature is good and that man can attain sagehood and thence harmony in virtue with Heaven by his own efforts. We think it better to rely on both rather than just Christianity in working towards world union. This is because Christianity is an organized religion, with numerous sects which are difficult to harmonize. Furthermore, it has its doctrines of heaven and hell, so that Christian love really comes with a proviso, namely that "you accept my religion." The Confucian view, however, is that all men can achieve sagehood. It has no organization, and does not require worship of Confucius since any man can potentially become like him. Consequently, Confucianism does not conflict with any religion. It has a concept of Heaven and Earth, but has no hell for those of differing views. If indeed the world is to be united, the Confucian spirit certainly deserves emulation. The same attitude can be found in Buddhism and Brahmanism, which also deserve close study.

Our list is, of course, by no means exhaustive. What we have pointed out is that the West must also learn from the East if it is to carry out its task as the world's cultural leader. These things are certainly not entirely alien to Western culture. However, we would like to see their seeds bloom into full blossom.

What We Expect from World Thought

While the West can certainly learn from the East, we have also a few remarks to make concerning the intellectual development of China and of the world.

1. The expansion of Western civilization has brought the peoples into close contact and unfortunately has also produced much friction. What needs to be done now is for each nation critically to re-examine and re-evaluate its own culture, taking into consideration the future of mankind as a whole. In order to achieve co-existence of the various cultures and world peace, one must first, through a transcendental feeling that goes beyond philosophical and scientific research, attain an attitude of respect and sympathy towards other cultures, and thereby acquire genuine compassion and commiseration towards mankind in adversity. Without this feeling, one could not regard culture as the expression of the spiritual life or endeavor, in the spirit of "reviving the perished state and restoring the broken family," to preserve and develop what is of value in these cultures.

2. In cultivating this feeling, it is evident that objective and scientific learning is inadequate. Man needs a different kind of learning, one that treats himself as a conscious, existential being. It is not theology; it cannot be the merely phenomenological study of ethics or mental hygiene. Rather it is a learning that applies understanding to conduct, by which one may transcend existence to attain spiritual enlightenment; it is what the Confucianists call the doctrine of "hsin-hsin." Its essence is, of course, not exclusive to China. India has it in the practice of yoga; European existentialism has also grasped it, especially in Kierkegaard's emphasis on becoming and being a Christian as against the externalia of church attendance and other acts of religiosity. Yet,

because Western civilization was moulded by rationalistic Hellenism, legalistic Hebraism, and jurisprudential Romanism, such a learning has not been made its core. Without this capability to transcend existence and to attain spiritual enlightenment man cannot really espouse God, so that his religious faith cannot be shaken. Similarly he cannot support the metaphysical and the scientific worlds of his own creation, or the oppression of the individual by the social, political, and judicial institutions of his own invention. That this should be the case is because man has sought only objective knowledge of the universe, from which he derives his ideals; and these ideals he in turn objectivizes in the natural and the social world. The external culture thus accumulated consequently becomes alienated from man and his control. On the other hand, this new learning, which can change the universe, makes possible authentic control over man's own existence. This is what in China is called "Establishing Man as the Ultimate." Only after this can man have unshakable faith, and control and utilize his production.

3. The human existence as formed by "establishing Man as the Ultimate" is that of a moral being which, at the same time, attains a higher spiritual enlightenment; for this reason, it can truly embrace God, thereby attaining "harmony in virtue with Heaven." Hence, this human existence is simultaneously moral and religious existence. Such a man is, in politics, the genuine citizen of democracy, in epistemology one who stands over and above the physical world. Not being bound by his concepts, his intellectual knowledge does not contradict his spiritual apprehension.

Such should be the direction of the new movement. When this conception will be realized, we do not know. In any case, for China, the pressing problem is to consummate, in fulfillment of the propensity of her culture, her work of democratic, scientific and industrial reconstruction. For the West, there is the problem of self-examination as the leader of the world, in the spirit of "reviving the perished and restoring the broken," of the various cultures. The time has come for the world to co-operate in bearing the burden of human suffering, and to open a new road for humanity.

JOHN HENRY NEWMAN

Apologia pro Vita Sua

> John Henry Newman (1801–1890) was a leader of the
> Oxford Movement in the Church of England until his
> conversion to Roman Catholicism in 1845. That event was
> closely associated with his growing sense that the principle
> of authority in religion required a theory of the develop-
> ment of doctrine as its counterpart, and with his need to
> explain, in this intellectual and religious autobiography,
> what he called "the position of my mind since 1845." He
> was created cardinal in 1879.

STARTING then with the being of a God, (which, as I have said, is as
certain to me as the certainty of my own existence, though when I try
to put the grounds of that certainty into logical shape I find a difficulty
in doing so in mood and figure to my satisfaction,) I look out of myself
into the world of men, and there I see a sight which fills me with
unspeakable distress. The world seems simply to give the lie to that
great truth, of which my whole being is so full; and the effect upon me
is, in consequence, as a matter of necessity, as confusing as if it denied
that I am in existence myself. If I looked into a mirror, and did not see
my face, I should have the sort of feeling which actually comes upon
me, when I look into this living busy world, and see no reflexion of
its Creator. This is, to me, one of those great difficulties of this absolute
primary truth, to which I referred just now. Were it not for this voice,
speaking so clearly in my conscience and my heart, I should be an
atheist, or a pantheist, or a polytheist when I looked into the world.
I am speaking for myself only; and I am far from denying the real force
of the arguments in proof of a God, drawn from the general facts of
human society and the course of history, but these do not warm me
or enlighten me; they do not take away the winter of my desolation,
or make the buds unfold and the leaves grow within me, and my moral

being rejoice. The sight of the world is nothing else than the prophet's scroll, full of "lamentations, and mourning, and woe."

To consider the world in its length and breadth, its various history, the many races of man, their starts, their fortunes, their mutual alienation, their conflicts; and then their ways, habits, governments, forms of worship; their enterprises, their aimless courses, their random achievements and acquirements, the impotent conclusion of long-standing facts, the tokens so faint and broken of a superintending design, the blind evolution of what turn out to be great powers or truths, the progress of things, as if from unreasoning elements, not towards final causes, the greatness and littleness of man, his far-reaching aims, his short duration, the curtain hung over his futurity, the disappointments of life, the defeat of good, the success of evil, physical pain, mental anguish, the prevalence and intensity of sin, the pervading idolatries, the corruptions, the dreary hopeless irreligion, that condition of the whole race, so fearfully yet exactly described in the Apostle's words, "having no hope and without God in the world," — all this is a vision to dizzy and appal; and inflicts upon the mind the sense of a profound mystery, which is absolutely beyond human solution.

What shall be said to this heart-piercing, reason-bewildering fact? I can only answer, that either there is no Creator, or this living society of men is in a true sense discarded from His presence. Did I see a boy of good make and mind, with the tokens on him of a refined nature, cast upon the world without provision, unable to say whence he came, his birth-place or his family connexions, I should conclude that there was some mystery connected with his history, and that he was one, of whom, from one cause or other, his parents were ashamed. Thus only should I be able to account for the contrast between the promise and the condition of his being. And so I argue about the world; — *if* there be a God, *since* there is a God, the human race is implicated in some terrible aboriginal calamity. It is out of joint with the purposes of its Creator. This is a fact, a fact as true as the fact of its existence; and thus the doctrine of what is theologically called original sin becomes to me almost as certain as that the world exists, and as the existence of God.

And now, supposing it were the blessed and loving will of the Creator to interfere in this anarchical condition of things, what are we to suppose would be the methods which might be necessarily or naturally involved in His purpose of mercy? Since the world is in so abnormal a state, surely it would be no surprise to me, if the interposition were of necessity equally extraordinary — or what is called miraculous. But that subject does not directly come into the scope of my present remarks. Miracles as evidence, involve a process of reason, or an argument; and of course I am thinking of some mode of interference which does not immediately run into argument. I am rather asking what must be the face-to-face antagonist, by which to withstand and baffle the fierce energy of passion and the all-corroding, all-dissolving scepticism of the intellect in religious inquiries? I have no intention at all of denying, that truth is the real object of our reason, and that, if it does not attain to truth, either the premiss or the process is in fault; but I am not speaking here of right reason, but of reason as it acts in fact and concretely in fallen man. I know that even the unaided reason, when correctly exercised, leads to a belief in God, in the immortality of the soul, and in a future retribution; but I am considering the faculty of reason actually and historically; and in this point of view, I do not think I am wrong in saying that its tendency is towards a simple unbelief in matters of religion. No truth, however sacred, can stand against it, in the long run; and hence it is that in the pagan world, when our Lord came, the last traces of the religious knowledge of former times were all but disappearing from those portions of the world in which the intellect had been active and had had a career.

And in these latter days, in like manner, outside the Catholic Church things are tending, — with far greater rapidity than in that old time from the circumstance of the age, — to atheism in one shape or other. What a scene, what a prospect, does the whole of Europe present at this day! and not only Europe, but every government and every civilization through the world, which is under the influence of the European mind! Especially, for it most concerns us, how sorrowful, in the view of religion, even taken in its most elementary, most attenuated form, is the spectacle presented to us by the educated intellect of England, France, and Germany! Lovers of their country and of their race, religious men, external to the Catholic Church, have attempted various expedients to arrest fierce wilful human nature in its onward course, and to bring it into subjection. The necessity of some form of religion for the interests of humanity, has been generally acknowledged: but where was the concrete representative of things invisible, which would have the force and the toughness necessary to be a breakwater against the deluge? Three centuries ago the establishment of religion, material, legal, and social, was generally adopted as the best expedient for the purpose, in those countries which separated from the Catholic Church; and for a long time it was successful; but now the crevices of those establishments are admitting the enemy. Thirty years ago, education was relied upon: ten years ago there was a hope that wars would cease for ever, under the influence of commercial enterprise and the reign of the useful and fine arts; but will any one venture to say that there is any thing any where on this earth, which will afford a fulcrum for us, whereby to keep the earth from moving onwards?

The judgment, which experience passes whether on establishments or on education, as a means of maintaining religious truth in this anarchical world, must be extended even to Scripture, though Scripture be divine. Experience proves surely that the Bible does not answer a purpose for which it was never intended. It may be accidentally the means of the conversion of individuals; but a book, after all, cannot make a stand against the wild living intellect of man, and in this day it begins to testify, as regards its own structure and contents, to the power of that universal solvent, which is so successfully acting upon religious establishments.

Supposing then it to be the Will of the Creator to interfere in human affairs, and to make provisions for retaining in the world a knowledge of Himself, so definite and distinct as to be proof against the energy of human scepticism, in such a case, — I am far from saying that there was no other way, — but there is nothing to surprise the mind, if He should think fit to introduce a power into the world, invested with the prerogative of infallibility in religious matters. Such a provision would be a direct, immediate, active, and prompt means of withstanding the difficulty; it would be an instrument suited to the need; and, when I find that this is the very claim of the Catholic Church, not only do I feel no difficulty in admitting the idea, but there is a fitness in it, which recommends it to my mind. And thus I am brought to speak of the Church's infallibility, as a provision, adapted by the mercy of the Creator, to preserve religion in the world, and to restrain that freedom of thought, which of course in itself is one of the greatest of our natural gifts, and to rescue it from its own suicidal excesses. And let it be observed that, neither here nor in what follows, shall I have occasion to speak directly of Revelation in its subject-matter, but in reference to the sanction which it gives to truths which may be known independently of it, — as it bears upon the defence of natural religion. I say, that a power, possessed of infallibility in religious teaching, is happily adapted to be a working instrument, in the course of human affairs, for smiting hard and throwing back the immense energy of the aggressive, capricious, untrustworthy intellect: — and in saying this, as in the other things that I have to say, it must still be recollected that I am all along bearing in mind my main purpose, which is a defence of myself.

I am defending myself here from a plausible charge brought against Catholics, as will be seen better as I proceed. The charge is this: — that I, as a Catholic, not only make profession to hold doctrines which I cannot possibly believe in my heart, but that I also believe in the existence of a power on earth, which at its own will imposes upon men any new set of *credenda* [articles of faith], when it pleases, by a claim to infallibility; in consequence, that my own thoughts are not my own property; that I cannot tell that to-morrow I may not have to give up what I hold to-day, and that the necessary effect of such a condition of mind must be a degrading bondage, or a bitter inward rebellion relieving itself in secret infidelity, or the necessity of ignoring the whole subject of religion in a sort of disgust, and of mechanically saying every thing that the Church says, and leaving to others the defence of it. As then I have above spoken of the relation of my mind towards the Catholic Creed, so now I shall speak of the attitude which it takes up in the view of the Church's infallibility.

And first, the initial doctrine of the infallible teacher must be an emphatic protest against the existing state of mankind. Man had rebelled against his Maker. It was this that caused the divine inter-position: and to proclaim it must be the first act of the divinely-accredited messenger. The Church must denounce rebellion as of all possible evils the greatest. She must have no terms with it; if she would be true to her Master, she must ban and anathematize it. This is the meaning of a statement of mine which has furnished matter for one of those special accusations to which I am at present replying: I have, however, no fault at all to confess in regard to it; I have nothing to withdraw, and in consequence I here deliberately repeat it. I said, "The Catholic Church holds it better for the sun and moon to drop from heaven, for the earth to fail, and for all the many millions on it to die of starvation in extremest agony, as far as temporal affliction goes, than that one soul, I will not say, should be lost, but should commit one single venial sin, should tell one wilful untruth, or should steal one poor farthing without excuse." I think the principle here enunciated to be the mere preamble in the formal credentials of the Catholic Church, as an Act of Parliament might begin with a "Whereas." It is because of the intensity of the evil which has possession of mankind, that a suitable antagonist has been provided against it; and the initial act of that divinely-commissioned power is of course to deliver her challenge and to defy the enemy. Such a preamble then gives a meaning to her position in the world, and an interpretation to her whole course of teaching and action.

In like manner she has ever put forth, with most energetic distinctness, those other great elementary truths, which either are an explanation of her mission or give a character to her work. She does not teach that human nature is irreclaimable, else wherefore should she be sent? not, that it is to be shattered and reversed, but to be extricated, purified, and restored; not, that it is a mere mass of hopeless evil, but that it has the promise upon it of great things, and even now, in its present state of disorder and excess, has a virtue and a praise proper to itself. But in the next place she knows and she preaches that such a restoration, as she aims at effecting in it, must be brought about, not simply through certain outward provisions of preaching and teaching, even though they be her own, but from an inward spiritual power or grace imparted directly from above, and of which she is the channel. She has it in charge to rescue human nature from its misery, but not simply by restoring it on its own level, but by lifting it up to a higher level than its own. She recognizes in it real moral excellence though degraded, but she cannot set it free from earth except by exalting it towards heaven. It was for this end that a renovating grace was put into her hands; and therefore from the nature of the gift, as well as from the reasonableness of the case, she goes on, as a further point, to insist, that all true conversion must begin with the first springs of thought, and to teach that each individual man must be in his own person one whole and perfect temple of God, while he is also one of the living stones which build up a visible religious community. And thus the distinctions between nature and grace, and between outward and inward religion, become two further articles in what I have called the preamble of her divine commission.

Such truths as these she vigorously reiterates, and pertinaciously inflicts upon mankind; as to such she observes no half-measures, no economical reserve, no delicacy or prudence. "Ye must be born again," is the simple, direct form of words which she uses after her Divine Master: "your whole nature must be re-born; your passions, and your affections, and your aims, and your conscience, and your will, must all be bathed in a new element, and reconsecrated to your Maker, — and, the last not the least, your intellect." It was for repeating these points of her teaching in my own way, that certain passages of one of my Volumes have been brought into the general accusation which has been made against my religious opinions. The writer has said that I was demented if I believed, and unprincipled if I did not believe, in my own statement, that a lazy, ragged, filthy, story-telling beggar-woman, if chaste, sober, cheerful, and religious, had a prospect of heaven, such as was absolutely closed to an accomplished statesman, or lawyer, or noble, be he ever so just, upright, generous, honourable, and conscientious, unless he had also some portion of the divine Christian graces; — yet I should have thought myself defended from criticism by the words which our Lord used to the chief priests, "The publicans and harlots go into the kingdom of God before you." And I was subjected again to the same alternative of imputations, for having ventured to say that consent to an unchaste wish was indefinitely more heinous than any lie viewed apart from its causes, its motives, and its consequences: though a lie, viewed under the limitation of these conditions, is a random utterance, an almost outward act, not directly from the heart, however disgraceful and despicable it may be, however prejudicial to the social contract, however deserving of public reprobation; whereas we have the express words of our Lord to the doctrine that "whoso looketh on a woman to lust after her, hath committed adultery with her already in his heart." On the strength of these texts, I have surely as much right to believe in these doctrines which have caused so much surprise, as to believe in original sin, or that there is a supernatural revelation, or that a Divine Person suffered, or that punishment is eternal.

Passing now from what I have called the preamble of that grant of power, which is made to the Church, to that power itself, Infallibility, I premise two brief remarks: — 1. on the one hand, I am not here determining any thing about the essential seat of that power, because that is a question doctrinal, not historical and practical; 2. nor, on the other hand, am I extending the direct subject-matter, over which that power of Infallibility has jurisdiction, beyond religious opinion: — and now as to the power itself.

This power, viewed in its fulness, is as tremendous as the giant evil which has called for it. It claims, when brought into exercise but in the legitimate manner, for otherwise of course it is but quiescent, to know for certain the very meaning of every portion of that Divine Message in detail, which was committed by our Lord to His Apostles. It claims to know its own limits, and to decide what it can determine absolutely and what it cannot. It claims, moreover, to have a hold upon statements not directly religious, so far as this, — to determine whether they indirectly relate to religion, and, according to its own definitive judgment, to pronounce whether or not, in a particular case, they are simply consistent with revealed truth. It claims to decide magisterially, whether as within its own province or not, that such and such statements are or are not prejudicial to the *Depositum* of faith, in their spirit or in their consequences, and to allow them, or condemn and forbid them, accordingly. It claims to impose silence at will on any matters, or controversies, of doctrine, which on its own *ipse dixit,* it pronounces to be dangerous, or inexpedient, or inopportune. It claims that, whatever may be the judgment of Catholics upon such acts, these acts should be received by them with those outward marks of reverence, submission, and loyalty, which Englishmen, for instance, pay to the presence of their sovereign, without expressing any criticism on them on the ground that in their matter they are inexpedient, or in their manner violent or harsh. And lastly, it claims to have the right of inflicting spiritual punishment, of cutting off from the ordinary channels of the divine life, and of simply excommunicating, those who refuse to submit themselves to its formal declarations. Such is the infallibility lodged in the Catholic Church, viewed in the concrete, as clothed and surrounded by the appendages of its high sovereignty: it is, to repeat what I said above, a supereminent prodigious power sent upon earth to encounter and master a giant evil.

And now, having thus described it, I profess my own absolute submission to its claim. I believe the whole revealed dogma as taught by the Apostles, as committed by the Apostles to the Church, and as declared by the Church to me. I receive it, as it is infallibly interpreted by the authority to whom it is thus committed, and (implicitly) as it shall be, in like manner, further interpreted by that same authority till the end of time. I submit, moreover, to the universally received traditions of the Church, in which lies the matter of those new dogmatic definitions which are from time to time made, and which in all times are the clothing and the illustration of the Catholic dogma as already defined. And I submit myself to those other decisions of the Holy See, theological or not, through the organs which it has itself appointed, which, waiving the question of their infallibility, on the lowest ground come to me with a claim to be accepted and obeyed. Also, I consider that, gradually and in the course of ages, Catholic inquiry has taken certain definite shapes, and has thrown itself into the form of a science, with a method and a phraseology of its own, under the intellectual handling of great minds, such as St. Athanasius, St. Augustine, and St. Thomas; and I feel no temptation at all to break in pieces the great legacy of thought thus committed to us for these latter days.

All this being considered as the profession which I make *ex animo,* as for myself, so also on the part of the Catholic body, as far as I know it, it will at first sight be said that the restless intellect of our common humanity is utterly weighed down, to the repression of all independent effort and action whatever, so that, if this is to be the mode of bringing it into order, it is brought into order only to be destroyed. But this is far from the result, far from what I conceive to be the intention of that high Providence who has provided a great remedy for a great evil, — far from borne out by the history of the conflict between Infallibility and Reason in the past, and the prospect of it in the future. The energy of the human intellect "does from opposition grow"; it thrives and is joyous, with a tough elastic strength, under the terrible blows of the divinely-fashioned weapon, and is never so much itself as when it has lately been overthrown. It is the custom with Protestant writers to consider that, whereas there are two great principles in action in the history of religion, Authority and Private Judgment, they have all the Private Judgment to themselves, and we have the full inheritance and the superincumbent oppression of Authority. But this is not so; it is the vast Catholic body itself, and it only, which affords an arena for both combatants in that awful, never-dying duel. It is necessary for the very life of religion, viewed in its large operations and its history, that the warfare should be incessantly carried on. Every exercise of Infallibility is brought out into act by an intense and varied operation of the Reason, both as its ally and as its opponent, and provokes again, when it has done its work, a re-action of Reason against it; and, as in a civil polity the State exists and endures by means of the rivalry and collision, the encroachments and defeats of its constituent parts, so in like manner Catholic Christendom is no simple exhibition of religious absolutism, but presents a continuous picture of Authority and Private Judgment alternately advancing and retreating as the ebb and flow of the tide; — it is a vast assemblage of human beings with wilful intellects and wild passions, brought together into one by the beauty and the Majesty of a Superhuman Power, — into what may be called a large reformatory or training-school, not as if into a hospital or into a prison, not in order to be sent to bed, not to be buried alive, but (if I may change my metaphor) brought together as if into some moral factory, for the melting, refining, and moulding, by an incessant, noisy process, of the raw material of human nature, so excellent, so dangerous, so capable of divine purposes.

ADOLF VON HARNACK

The Essence of Christianity

Adolf von Harnack (1851–1930), after serving as professor
of church history at several German universities, came to
the University of Berlin for the major part of his academic
career. Having studied and edited most of the sources of
early Christian history and having traced the development
of doctrine in his *History of Dogma,* he undertook in a series
of public lectures to define what was, beyond the dogma,
the abiding "essence of Christianity."

THE GREAT ENGLISH PHILOSOPHER, John Stuart Mill, has somewhere
observed that mankind cannot be too often reminded that there was
once a man of the name of Socrates. That is true; but still more
important is it to remind mankind again and again that a man of the
name of Jesus Christ once stood in their midst. The fact, of course, has
been brought home to us from our youth up; but unhappily it cannot
be said that public instruction in our time is calculated to keep the
image of Jesus Christ before us in any impressive way, and make it an
inalienable possession after our school-days are over and for our
whole life. And although no one who has once absorbed a ray of
Christ's light can ever again become as though he had never heard of
him; although at the bottom of every soul that has been once touched
an impression remains, a confused recollection of this kind, which is
often only a "superstitio," is not enough to give strength and life. But
where the demand for further and more trustworthy knowledge about
him arises, and a man wants positive information as to who Jesus
Christ was, and as to the real purport of his message, he no sooner asks
for it than he finds himself, if he consults the literature of the day,
surrounded by a clatter of contradictory voices. He hears some people
maintaining that primitive Christianity was closely akin to Buddhism,

and he is accordingly told that it is in fleeing the world and in pessimism that the sublime character of this religion and its profound meaning are revealed. Others, on the contrary, assure him that Christianity is an optimistic religion, and that it must be thought of simply and solely as a higher phase of Judaism; and these people also suppose that in saying this they have said something very profound. Others, again, maintain the opposite; they assert that the Gospel did away with Judaism, but itself originated under Greek influences of mysterious operation; and that it is to be understood as a blossom on the tree of Hellenism. Religious philosophers come forward and declare that the metaphysical system which, as they say, was developed out of the Gospel is its real kernel and the revelation of its secret; but others reply that the Gospel has nothing to do with philosophy, that it was meant for feeling and suffering humanity, and that philosophy has only been forced upon it. Finally, the latest critics that have come into the field assure us that the whole history of religion, morality, and philosophy, is nothing but wrapping and ornament; that what at all times underlies them, as the only real motive power, is the history of economics; that, accordingly, Christianity, too, was in its origin nothing more than a social movement and Christ a social deliverer, the deliverer of the oppressed lower classes.

There is something touching in the anxiety which everyone shows to rediscover himself, together with his own point of view and his own circle of interest, in this Jesus Christ, or at least to get a share in him. It is the perennial repetition of the spectacle which was seen in the "Gnostic" movement even as early as the second century, and which takes the form of a struggle, on the part of every conceivable tendency of thought, for the possession of Jesus Christ. Why, quite recently, not only, I think, Tolstoi's ideas, but even Nietzsche's, have been exhibited in their special affinity with the Gospel; and there is perhaps more to be said even upon this subject that is worth attention than upon the connexion between a good deal of "theological" and "philosophical" speculation and Christ's teaching.

But nevertheless, when taken together, the impression which these contradictory opinions convey is disheartening: the confusion seems hopeless. How can we take it amiss of anyone, if, after trying to find out how the question stands, he gives it up? Perhaps he goes further, and declares that after all the question does not matter. How are we concerned with events that happened, or with a person who lived, nineteen hundred years ago? We must look for our ideals and our strength to the present; to evolve them laboriously out of old manuscripts is a fantastic proceeding that can lead nowhere. The man who so speaks is not wrong; but neither is he right. What we are and what we possess, in any high sense, we possess from the past and by the past — only so much of it, of course, as has had results and makes its influence felt up to the present day. To acquire a sound knowledge of the past is the business and the duty not only of the historian but also of every one who wishes to make the wealth and the strength so gained his own. But that the Gospel is a part of this past which nothing else can replace has been affirmed again and again by the greatest minds. "Let intellectual and spiritual culture progress, and the human mind expand, as much as it will; beyond the grandeur and the moral elevation of Christianity, as it sparkles and shines in the Gospels, the human mind will not advance." In these words Goethe, after making many experiments and labouring indefatigably at himself, summed up the result to which his moral and historical insight had led him. Even though we were to feel no desire on our own part, it would still be worth while, because of this man's testimony, to devote our serious attention to what he came to regard as so precious; and if, contrary to his declaration, louder and more confident voices are heard to-day, proclaiming that the Christian religion has outlived itself, let us accept that as an invitation to make a closer acquaintance with this religion whose certificate of death people suppose that they can already exhibit.

But in truth this religion and the efforts which it evokes are more active to-day then they used to be. We may say to the credit of our age that it takes an eager interest in the problem of the nature and value of Christianity, and that there is more search and inquiry in regard to this subject now than was the case thirty years ago. Even in the experiments that are made in and about it, the strange and abstruse replies that are given to questions, the way in which it is caricatured, the chaotic confusion which it exhibits, nay even in the hatred that it excites, a real life and an earnest endeavour may be traced. Only do not let us suppose that there is anything exemplary in this endeavour, and that we are the first who, after shaking off an authoritative religion, are struggling after one that shall really make us free and be of independent growth — a struggle which must of necessity give rise to much confusion and half-truth. Sixty-two years ago Carlyle wrote: — "In these distracted times, when the Religious Principle, driven out of most Churches, either lies unseen in the hearts of good men, looking and longing and silently working there towards some new Revelation; or else wanders homeless over the world, like a disembodied soul seeking its terrestrial organisation, — into how many strange shapes, of Superstition and Fanaticism, does it not tentatively and errantly cast itself! The higher Enthusiasm of man's nature is for the while without Exponent; yet does it continue indestructible, unweariedly active, and work blindly in the great chaotic deep: thus Sect after Sect, and Church after Church, bodies itself forth, and melts again into new metamorphosis."

No one who understands the times in which we live can deny that these words sound as if they had been written to-day. But it is not with "the religious principle" and the ways in which it has developed that we are going to concern ourselves in these lectures. We shall try to answer the more modest but not less pressing question, What is Christianity? What was it? What has it become? The answer to this question may, we hope, also throw light by the way on the more comprehensive one, What is Religion, and what ought it to be to us? In dealing with religion, is it not after all with the Christian religion alone that we have to do? Other religions no longer stir the depths of our hearts.

What is Christianity? It is solely in its historical sense that we shall try to answer this question here; that is to say, we shall employ the methods of historical science, and the experience of life gained by studying the actual course of history. This excludes the view of the question taken by the apologist and the religious philosopher. On this point permit me to say a few words.

Apologetics holds a necessary place in religious knowledge, and to demonstrate the validity of the Christian religion and exhibit its importance for the moral and intellectual life is a great and a worthy undertaking. But this undertaking must be kept quite separate from the purely historical question as to the nature of that religion, or else historical research will be brought into complete discredit. Moreover, in the kind of apologetics that is now required no really high standard has yet been attained. Apart from a few steps that have been taken in the direction of improvement, apologetics as a subject of study is in a deplorable state: it is not clear as to the positions to be defended, and it is uncertain as to the means to be employed. It is also not infrequently pursued in an undignified and obtrusive fashion. Apologists imagine that they are doing a great work by crying up religion as though it were a job-lot at a sale, or a universal remedy for all social ills. They are perpetually snatching, too, at all sorts of baubles, so as to deck out religion in fine clothes. In their endeavour to present it as a glorious necessity, they deprive it of its earnest character, and at the best only prove that it is something which may be safely accepted because it can do no harm. Finally, they cannot refrain from slipping in some church programme of yesterday and "demonstrating" its claims as well. The structure of their ideas is so loose that an idea or two more makes no difference. The mischief that has been thereby done already and is still being done is indescribable. No! the Christian religion is something simple and sublime; it means one thing and one thing only: Eternal life in the midst of time, by the strength and under the eyes of God. It is no ethical or social *arcanum* for the preservation or improvement of things generally. To make what it has done for civilisation and human progress the main question, and to determine its value by the answer, is to do it violence at the start. Goethe once said, "Mankind is always advancing, and man always remains the same." It is to *man* that religion pertains, to man, as one who in the midst of all change and progress himself never changes. Christian apologetics must recognise, then, that it is with religion in its simple nature and its simple strength that it has to do. Religion, truly, does not exist for itself alone, but lives in an inner fellowship with all the activities of the mind and with moral and economical conditions as well. But it is emphatically not a mere function or an exponent of them; it is a mighty power that sets to work of itself, hindering or furthering, destroying or making fruitful. The main thing is to learn what religion is and in what its essential character consists; no matter what position the individual who examines it may take up in regard to it, or whether in his own life he values it or not.

*   *   *   *   *

Where are we to look for our materials? The answer seems to be simple and at the same time exhaustive: Jesus Christ and his Gospel. But however little doubt there may be that this must form not only our point of departure but also the matter with which our investigations will mainly deal, it is equally certain that we must not be content to exhibit the mere image of Jesus Christ and the main features of his Gospel. We must not be content to stop there, because every great and powerful personality reveals a part of what it is only when seen in those whom it influences. Nay, it may be said that the more powerful the personality which a man possesses, and the more he takes hold of the inner life of others, the less can the sum-total of what he is be known only by what he himself says and does. We must look at the reflection and the effects which he produced in those whose leader and master he became. That is why a complete answer to the question, What is Christianity, is impossible so long as we are restricted to Jesus Christ's teaching alone. We must include the first generation of his disciples as well — those who ate and drank with him — and we must listen to what they tell us of the effect which he had upon their lives.

But even this does not exhaust our materials. If Christianity is an example of a great power valid not for one particular epoch alone; if in and through it, not only once, but again and again, great forces have been disengaged, we must include all the later products of its spirit. It is not a question of a "doctrine" being handed down by uniform repetition or arbitrarily distorted; it is a question of a *life,* again and again kindled afresh, and now burning with a flame of its own. We may also add that Christ himself and the apostles were convinced that the religion which they were planting would in the ages to come have a greater destiny and a deeper meaning than it possessed at the time of its institution; they trusted to its spirit leading from one point of light to another and developing higher forces. Just as we cannot obtain a complete knowledge of a tree without regarding not only its root and its stem but also its bark, its branches, and the way in which it blooms, so we cannot form any right estimate of the Christian religion unless we take our stand upon a comprehensive induction that shall cover all the facts of its history. It is true that Christianity has had its classical epoch; nay more, it had a founder who himself was what he taught — to steep ourselves in him is still the chief matter; but to restrict ourselves to him means to take a point of view too low for his significance. Individual religious life was what he wanted to kindle and what he did kindle; it is, as we shall see, his peculiar greatness to have led men to God, so that they may thenceforth live their own life with Him. How, then, can we be silent about the history of the Gospel if we wish to know what he was?

*　　*　　*　　*　　*

From these circumstances it follows that the historian, whose business and highest duty it is to determine what is of permanent value, is of necessity required not to cleave to words but to find out what is essential. The "whole" Christ, the "whole" Gospel, if we mean by this motto the external image taken in all its details and set up for imitation, is just as bad and deceptive a shibboleth as the "whole" Luther, and the like. It is bad because it enslaves us, and it is deceptive because the people who proclaim it do not think of taking it seriously, and could not do so if they tried. They cannot do so because they cannot cease to feel, understand and judge as children of their age.

There are only two possibilities here: either the Gospel is in all respects identical with its earliest form, in which case it came with its time and has departed with it; or else it contains something which, under differing historical forms, is of permanent validity. The latter is the true view. The history of the Church shows us in its very commencement that "primitive Christianity" had to disappear in order that "Christianity" might remain; and in the same way in later ages one metamorphosis followed upon another. From the beginning it was a question of getting rid of formulas, correcting expectations, altering ways of feeling, and this is a process to which there is no end. But by the very fact that our survey embraces the whole course as well as the inception we enhance our standard of what is essential and of real value.

We enhance our standard, but we need not wait to take it from the history of those later ages. The thing itself reveals it. We shall see that the Gospel in the Gospel is something so simple, something that speaks to us with so much power, that it cannot easily be mistaken. No far-reaching directions as to method, no general introductions, are necessary to enable us to find the way to it. No one who possesses a fresh eye for what is alive, and a true feeling for what is really great, can fail to see it and distinguish it from its contemporary integument. And even though there may be many individual aspects of it where the task of distinguishing what is permanent from what is fleeting, what is rudimentary from what is merely historical, is not quite easy, we must not be like the child who, wanting to get at the kernel of a bulb, went on picking off the leaves until there was nothing left, and then could not help seeing that it was just the leaves that made the bulb. Endeavours of this kind are not unknown in the history of the Christian religion, but they fade before those other endeavours which seek to convince us that there is no such thing as either kernel or husk, growth or decay, but that everything is of equal value and alike permanent.

GILBERT KEITH CHESTERTON

Orthodoxy

> Gilbert Keith Chesterton (1874–1936) was not a scholar or a theologian but a journalist and the author of the popular Father Brown detective stories. Nevertheless, in books on Francis of Assisi and Thomas Aquinas and in two inter-connected works entitled *Heretics* and *Orthodoxy,* he defended the integrity of the theological tradition with a vigor that many professional theologians and scholars could (and did) envy.

IT IS COMMONLY the loose and latitudinarian Christians who pay quite indefensible compliments to Christianity. They talk as if there had never been any piety or pity until Christianity came, a point on which any mediæval would have been eager to correct them. They represent that the remarkable thing about Christianity was that it was the first to preach simplicity or self-restraint, or inwardness and sincerity. They will think me very narrow (whatever that means) if I say that the remarkable thing about Christianity was that it was the first to preach Christianity. Its peculiarity was that it was peculiar, and simplicity and sincerity are not peculiar, but obvious ideals for all mankind. Christianity was the answer to a riddle, not the last truism uttered after a long talk. Only the other day I saw in an excellent weekly paper of Puritan tone this remark, that Christianity when stripped of its armour of dogma (as who should speak of a man stripped of his armour of bones), turned out to be nothing but the Quaker doctrine of the Inner Light. Now, if I were to say that Christianity came into the world specially to destroy the doctrine of the Inner Light, that would be an exaggeration. But it would be very much nearer to the truth. The last Stoics, like Marcus Aurelius, were exactly the people who did believe in the Inner Light. Their dignity, their weariness, their sad external care for others, their incurable internal care for themselves, were all due to the Inner Light, and existed only by that dismal illumination. Notice that Marcus Aurelius insists, as such introspective moralists always do, upon small things done or undone; it is because he has not hate or love enough to make a moral revolution. He gets up early in the morning, just as our own aristocrats living the Simple Life get up early in the morning; because such altruism is much easier than stopping the games of the amphitheatre or giving the English people back their land. Marcus Aurelius is the most intolerable of human types. He is an unselfish egoist. An unselfish egoist is a man who has pride without the excuse of passion. Of all conceivable forms of enlightenment the worst is what these people call the Inner Light. Of all horrible religions the most horrible is the worship of the god within. Any one who knows any body knows how it would work; any one who knows any one from the Higher Thought Centre knows how it does work. That Jones shall worship the god within him turns out ultimately to mean that Jones shall worship Jones. Let Jones worship the sun or moon, anything rather than the Inner Light; let Jones worship cats or crocodiles, if he can find any in his street, but not the god within. Christianity came into the world firstly in order to assert with violence that a man had not only to look inwards, but to look outwards, to behold with astonishment and enthusiasm a divine company and a divine captain. The only fun of being a Christian was that a man was not left alone with the Inner Light, but definitely recognized an outer light, fair as the sun, clear as the moon, terrible as an army with banners.

All the same, it will be as well if Jones does not worship the sun and moon. If he does, there is a tendency for him to imitate them; to say, that because the sun burns insects alive, he may burn insects alive. He thinks that because the sun gives people sun-stroke, he may give his neighbour measles. He thinks that because the moon is said to drive men mad, he may drive his wife mad. This ugly side of mere external optimism had also shown itself in the ancient world. About the time when the Stoic idealism had begun to show the weaknesses of pessimism, the old nature worship of the ancients had begun to show the enormous weaknesses of optimism. Nature worship is natural enough while the society is young, or, in other words, Pantheism is all right as long as it is the worship of Pan. But Nature has another side which experience and sin are not slow in finding out, and it is no flippancy to say of the god Pan that he soon showed the cloven hoof. The only objection to Natural Religion is that somehow it always becomes unnatural. A man loves Nature in the morning for her innocence and amiability, and at nightfall, if he is loving her still, it is for her darkness and her cruelty. He washes at dawn in clear water as did the Wise Man of the Stoics, yet, somehow at the dark end of the day, he is bathing in hot bull's blood, as did Julian the Apostate. The mere pursuit of health always leads to something unhealthy. Physical nature must not be made the direct object of obedience; it must be enjoyed, not worshipped. Stars and mountains must not be taken seriously. If they are, we end where the pagan nature worship ended. Because the earth is kind, we can imitate all her cruelties. Because sexuality is sane, we can all go mad about sexuality. Mere optimism had reached its insane and appropriate termination. The theory that everything was good had become an orgy of everything that was bad.

On the other side our idealist pessimists were represented by the old remnant of the Stoics. Marcus Aurelius and his friends had really given up the idea of any god in the universe and looked only to the god within. They had no hope of any virtue in nature, and hardly any hope of any virtue in society. They had not enough interest in the outer world really to wreck or revolutionise it. They did not love the city enough to set fire to it. Thus the ancient world was exactly in our own desolate dilemma. The only people who really enjoyed this world were busy breaking it up; and the virtuous people did not care enough about them to knock them down. In this dilemma (the same as ours) Christianity suddenly stepped in and offered a singular answer, which the world eventually accepted as *the* answer. It was the answer then, and I think it is the answer now.

This answer was like the slash of a sword; it sundered; it did not in any sense sentimentally unite. Briefly, it divided God from the cosmos. That transcendence and distinctness of the deity which some Christians now want to remove from Christianity, was really the only reason why any one wanted to be a Christian. It was the whole point of the Christian answer to the unhappy pessimist and the still more unhappy optimist. As I am here only concerned with their particular problem, I shall indicate only briefly this great metaphysical suggestion. All descriptions of the creating or sustaining principle in things must be metaphorical, because they must be verbal. Thus the pantheist is forced to speak of God *in* all things as if he were in a box. Thus the evolutionist has, in his very name, the idea of being unrolled like a carpet. All terms, religious and irreligious, are open to this charge. The only question is whether all terms are useless, or whether one can, with such a phrase, cover a distinct *idea* about the origin of things. I think one can, and so evidently does the evolutionist, or he would not talk about evolution. And the root phrase for all Christian theism was this, that God was a creator, as an artist is a creator. A poet is so separate from his poem that he himself speaks of it as a little thing he has "thrown off." Even in giving it forth he has flung it away. This principle that all creation and procreation is a breaking off is at least as consistent through the cosmos as the evolutionary principle that all growth is a branching out. A woman loses a child even in having a child. All creation is separation. Birth is as solemn a parting as death.

It was the prime philosophic principle of Christianity that this divorce in the divine act of making (such as severs the poet from the poem or the mother from the new-born child) was the true description of the act whereby the absolute energy made the world. According to most philosophers, God in making the world enslaved it. According to Christianity, in making it, He set it free. God had written, not so much a poem, but rather a play; a play he had planned as perfect, but which had necessarily been left to human actors and stage-managers, who had since made a great mess of it. I will discuss the truth of this theorem later. Here I have only to point out with what a startling smoothness it passed the dilemma we have discussed in this chapter. In this way at least one could be both happy and indignant without degrading one's self to be either a pessimist or an optimist. On this system one could fight all the forces of existence without deserting the flag of existence. One could be at peace with the universe and yet be at war with the world. St. George could still fight the dragon, however big the monster bulked in the cosmos, though he were bigger than the mighty cities or bigger than the everlasting hills. If he were as big as the world he could yet be killed in the name of the world. St. George had not to consider any obvious odds or proportions in the scale of things, but only the original secret of their design. He can shake his sword at the dragon, even if it is everything; even if the empty heavens over his head are only the huge arch of its open jaws.

And then followed an experience impossible to describe. It was as if I had been blundering about since my birth with two huge and unmanageable machines, of different shapes and without apparent connection — the world and the Christian tradition. I had found this hole in the world: the fact that one must somehow find a way of loving the world without trusting it; somehow one must love the world without being worldly. I found this projecting feature of Christian theology, like a sort of hard spike, the dogmatic insistence that God was personal, and had made a world separate from Himself. The spike of dogma fitted exactly into the hole in the world — it had evidently been meant to go there — and then the strange thing began to happen. When once these two parts of the two machines had come together, one after another, all the other parts fitted and fell in with an eerie exactitude. I could hear bolt after bolt over all the machinery falling into its place with a kind of click of relief. Having got one part right, all the other parts were repeating that rectitude, as clock after clock strikes noon. Instinct after instinct was answered by doctrine after doctrine. Or, to vary the metaphor, I was like one who had advanced into a hostile country to take one high fortress. And when that fort had fallen the whole country surrendered and turned solid behind me. The whole land was lit up, as it were, back to the first fields of my childhood. All those blind fancies of boyhood which in the fourth chapter I have tried in vain to trace on the darkness, became suddenly transparent and sane. I was right when I felt that roses were red by some sort of choice: it was the divine choice. I was right when I felt that I would almost rather say that grass was the wrong colour than say it must by necessity have been that colour: it might verily have been any other. My sense that happiness hung on the crazy thread of a condition did mean something when all was said: it meant the whole doctrine of the Fall. Even those dim and shapeless monsters of notions which I have not been able to describe, much less defend, stepped quietly into their places like colossal caryatides of the creed. The fancy that the cosmos was not vast and void, but small and cosy, had a fulfilled significance now, for anything that is a work of art must be small in the sight of the artist; to God the stars might be only small and dear, like diamonds. And my haunting instinct that somehow good was not merely a tool to be used, but a relic to be guarded, like the goods from Crusoe's ship — even that had been the wild whisper of something originally wise, for, according to Christianity, we were indeed the survivors of a wreck, the crew of a golden ship that had gone down before the beginning of the world.

But the important matter was this, that it entirely reversed the reason for optimism. And the instant the reversal was made it felt like the abrupt ease when a bone is put back in the socket. I had often called myself an optimist, to avoid the too evident blasphemy of pessimism. But all the optimism of the age had been false and disheartening for this reason, that it had always been trying to prove that we fit in to the world. The Christian optimism is based on the fact that we do *not* fit in to the world. I had tried to be happy by telling myself that man is an animal, like any other which sought its meat from God. But now

I really was happy, for I had learnt that man is a monstrosity. I had been right in feeling all things as odd, for I myself was at once worse and better than all things. The optimist's pleasure was prosaic, for it dwelt on the naturalness of everything; the Christian pleasure was poetic, for it dwelt on the unnaturalness of everything in the light of the supernatural. The modern philosopher had told me again and again that I was in the right place, and I had still felt depressed even in acquiescence. But I had heard that I was in the *wrong* place, and my soul sang for joy, like a bird in spring. The knowledge found out and illuminated forgotten chambers in the dark house of infancy. I knew now why grass had always seemed to me as queer as the green beard of a giant, and why I could feel homesick at home.

VI LOVE ABIDES

Nowhere are the world religions closer together in the abstract — but also, nowhere are they further apart in the concrete — than in their "study of good," as Nishida Kitarō has called it. The irony of that contradiction pervades modern religious thought, as well as the modern criticisms of religion in every culture, and it continues to be a source of hope and yet of despair.

At one level, therefore, it has repeatedly seemed possible in the modern era to bring together the adherents of the historic religious denominations of the human race on the basis of some shared principles of ethics (sometimes facetiously called a "least common interdenominator"). The Columbian Exposition of 1892–1893 in Chicago was the occasion for a World Parliament of Religions, at which a serious attempt was made to discover and formulate such common principles. Particularly since the Second World War there have been several conferences between Eastern and Western religious leaders at which the international moral crisis of the twentieth century has been the occasion for an exploration of the spiritual resources in the teachings of all the traditions. The frequently demonstrated inability even of nations with the same theological background (e.g., Muslim, Buddhist, or Christian) to achieve peace and understanding does not augur well for the success of such efforts that cut across the boundaries of the historic differences, but there have been just enough individual achievements to continue to provide some encouragement for the efforts.

It would seem that the principal obstacles to this search for common ground do not lie in the area of religious thought itself, but, as the religious thought of every tradition has pointed out, in the all but universal lack of good will. For whatever the differences in ethical and theological vocabulary may be, love of God and love of neighbor may indeed be said to constitute the "great commandments" in most traditions. The quest for perfection described in Annemarie Schimmel's essay on Islamic moral theology, "Man and His Perfection," runs through all of them, as does a recognition of "the part of imagination in the moral life," as set forth by the twentieth-century Russian Orthodox philosopher Nikolay Aleksandrovich Berdyaev. But the importance of this emphasis on the abiding power of love goes even beyond the themes of imagination and perfection. There is throughout modern religious thought a hope that because "doctrine divides but love unites," those who join in common tasks of service to humanity may find in that service the unity that has eluded them when they have discussed metaphysical differences. "Now abide faith, hope, and love, but the greatest of these is love": this affirmation is one on which believers can unite; and, once they have been united in love, they may pray together for a unity in hope and perhaps even for a unity in faith.

SØREN KIERKEGAARD

Love Abides

> Soren Aabye Kierkegaard (1813–1855), had he written in a world language, would have altered the development of philosophy during the second half of the nineteenth century as thoroughly as he has twentieth-century thought, but it was only when he was translated from Danish into German and English that the world recognized his major contribution to aesthetics and to the philosophy of religion, where he is now seen as the founder of Existentialism.

"Love never faileth" — it abides.

When a child has been away all day among strangers and now considers that it ought to go home, but is afraid to go alone, and yet really wants to stay as long as possible, it says to the older children, who perhaps wished to leave earlier, "Wait for me"; and so the older ones do as the child asks. When of two equals one is more advanced than the other, the latter says to the first, "Wait for me"; and so the second does what the first asks. When two have planned and taken pleasure in the thought of a trip together, but one of them is taken sick, the sick man owes another man money and cannot pay, then he says, "Wait on me," and so the other man grants his request. When the maiden in love sees that there will be great and perhaps complicated difficulties in the way of her union with the beloved, she says to him, "Wait for me," and so the beloved does as he is asked. And all this is very excellent and commendable, to wait thus on another man. But whether it is love which thus waits, we have not yet seen. Perhaps the interval of waiting is too short really to show how far that which determines the one thus to wait, deserves in a decisive sense to be called love. Alas! perhaps the interval of waiting was so long that the older children said to the child, "No, we can't wait any longer for you."

Perhaps the time of waiting went so slowly that the one more advanced said, "No, I can't wait for you any longer without retarding myself too much." Perhaps the sickness dragged out so long that the friend said, "No, I can't wait any longer for you, I shall have to go alone." Perhaps the time dragged out so long for the man who could not pay his debt, that the other said, "No, I can't wait any longer on you. I must have my money now." Perhaps the prospect of marriage with the young girl became so remote that the lover said, "No, I can't wait any longer for you; I owe it to myself and my life not to put it off in this way any longer, hoping year after year for that which is uncertain." — But love *abides*.

The fact of love abiding, or, perhaps more correctly, the question of whether it really abides in this or that case, or whether it ceases: is something which occupies the thoughts of men in such manifold ways, is so frequently the subject of their conversation, and very frequently the principal content of all their poets' works. It is regarded as praiseworthy that love abides, but as unworthy that it does not last, that it ceases, that it changes. Only the first is love; the other seems, because of the change, not to be love — and consequently not to have been love. The facts are these, one cannot cease to be loving; if one is in truth loving, one remains so; if one ceases to *be* loving, then one *was* not loving. Ceasing to love has therefore, in relation to love, a retroactive power. Moreover, I can never weary of saying this and of demonstrating it: wherever there is love, there is something infinitely profound. For instance, a man may have had money, and when he no longer has it, it still remains entirely true that he *had had* money. But when one ceases to be loving, he *has never been* loving. What is still so gentle as love, and what so strict, so jealous for itself, so chastening as love!

Furthermore! If then love ceases, if in the love, the friendship, in short, in the affectionate relation between two, something comes between them so love ceases; then there takes place, as we say, a breach between these two. Love was the connection, was in good understanding; love displaced, it ceases, the connection between them is broken, and the breach effects a separation between them. Consequently there is a breach. Christianity, however, does not know this manner of speaking, does not understand it, does not wish to understand it. If one speaks about there being a breach, this is because one believes that love is a relation only between two, instead of its being a relation between three, as was shown. This talk about there being a breach between the two is much too thoughtless; it gives the impression of the love-relationship being merely a matter between these two, as if there were no third party whom it concerned. If then the two are agreed about breaking with each other, there would consequently be no one to object to it. Again, because these two break with each other, it does not follow that these same two might not have affection for others; hence they retain their loving attributes, but their love now applies only in relation to others. Again, the one guilty of causing the breach would have the upper hand, and the innocent one would be defenseless. Still it would be pitiful for an innocent person to be the weaker; it certainly is this way in this world, but eternally understood it can never be this way. Therefore, what does Christianity do? Its earnestness immediately fixes the attention of eternity upon the individual, upon each of the two. Just as the two clung to each other in love, each one especially clings in himself to "*love.*" Now that does not simply go out with the breach. Before it comes to the breach, before one came to break his love-relationship with the other, he must first have fallen away from "love." This is the important thing; therefore Christianity does not speak of the breach between the two, but always only about what the individual can do who falls away from "*love.*" A breach between two smacks too much of business in the temporal existence, as if then the matter were not so dangerous; but to fall away from "*love,*" this expression has the seriousness of eternity. Lo, now everything is in order; now eternity can maintain discipline and order; now will the innocent sufferer in and through the breach, yet become the stronger, if he, too, does not fall away from "*love.*" If love were solely a relationship between two, then the one would constantly be in the other's power, insofar as the other were an unprincipled man who wished to dissolve the relationship. When a relationship is only between two, then one constantly dominates the relationship through being able to break it; for as soon as one has broken it, the *relationship* is broken. But when there are three, then one alone cannot do it. The third, as we said, is "*love*" itself, to whom in the breach the innocent sufferer can cling, so that the breach has no power over him. . . .

But the true lover never falls away from "*love*"; therefore for him there can never come a breach; for love abides. Still in a relationship between two, can one prevent the breach if the other breaks it? It must indeed seem that one of the two is sufficient to break the relationship, and if it is broken, then there is a breach. In a certain sense this is indeed true, but if the lover still does not fall away from "*love,*" he can prevent the breach, he can effect the miraculous; for if he abides, the breach can never really be brought about. Through abiding (and in this abiding the lover is in a covenant with the eternal) he retains superiority over the past, so he transforms what in the past and through it, is a breach, into a possible future relationship. If viewed in connection with the past, the breach becomes with every day and with every year clearer and clearer; but the lover who abides, belongs, through abiding, to the future, to the eternal, and from the viewpoint of the future the breach is not a breach; on the contrary, it is a possibility. But to that the forces of eternity belong; and therefore the lover who abides, must abide in "*love,*" otherwise the past, nevertheless, gradually acquires power, and then gradually the breach becomes evident. Oh, and to this, belong the powers of eternity, in the decisive moment, immediately to transform the past into the future! Yet it has this power of abiding.

How shall I now describe this work of love? Oh, that I might be inexhaustible in describing what is so indescribably joyous, and so edifying to consider!

*   *   *   *   *

That a certain natural, good disposition, a certain benevolent sympathy and helpfulness, which we gratefully appreciate, still has to spend some time in affectionately waiting — that it becomes weary in the course of time, or when it progresses so slowly and consequently over a long period of time: is only too certain. The long process of time is certainly the exigency which causes most people to liquidate their estates. In the commercial world it generally happens that a house fails because suddenly there is all at once a great run on it; but in the spiritual world it is the long time which makes away with so many. Men have spiritual strength enough for a moment, but in the long run, on the contrary, they become irresponsible. Yet love abides. Oh, how well do not the poet and the novelist know how to describe the mutability of everything, to show the power of time over all things which existed in time, over the greatest, the mightiest, the most glorious achievements, over the wonders of the world, which in time became almost unrecognizable ruins; over the most immortal names, which in time ended in the vagueness of legends!

But cannot something happen to love now while it abides, so that although it abides it is transformed in time, but yet in such a way that this transformation is not its fault but is something suffered? Consequently the relationship would be: love abides, no circumstance alters it or forces it to give itself up, yet it is transformed in a change which we call *decrepitude,* and that although we may say about this same love, that it never failed.

*   *   *   *   *

But love abides — it never fails. For in spiritual love itself is the spring which wells up in eternal life. That this lover, too, grows old in years and dies sometime in time, proves nothing, for his love remains eternally young. In his love he does not lay hold on the temporal existence as does earthly love, dependent on the temporal existence; for his love eternity is the true season. When he dies he has simply reached the goal; when he dies it simply shows that he had not waited in vain. Alas, when the young maiden died, we simply said: "Unfortunately it seems that she waited in vain." And how could the love which abides become infirm? Can then immortality become infirm? But what is it which gives a man immortality, what except the love which abides? For earthly love is of the temporal existence the most beautiful of temporal things, but yet the frail invention of the temporal existence. Therefore there is here a more profound contradiction. There was no fault in the maiden; she was and remained true to her love. Yet her love changed somewhat through the years. This change lies in the nature of the earthly love. The contradiction is then this: that one with the most honest intentions, willing to be sacrificed, cannot in the deepest sense be absolutely steadfast, or abide in what does not itself abide eternally — and earthly love does not do this. Perhaps the girl herself did not understand this connection; but this persistence of the self-contradiction was what made her death sad. That she is sacrificed has not the solemnity of the eternal, and, hence, neither its inspiration nor its elevation, but it has the sadness of the temporal existence, and so it inspires the poet.

The young maiden wasted away. Even if "he" had come, consequently had come before her death, it would still have been too late. She remained; but time had weakened her desire, the desire for which she lived, while at the same time the desire consumed her. In the most profound sense, on the contrary, the lover who abides, does not become infirm; his love does not consume away. If the one who misunderstood him, the one who became cold to him, the one who hated him, returns, he finds him unchanged, unchanged in his same longing for the eternal, and with the same quiet calmness in the temporal. His love is eternal, he lays hold on the eternal, he rests in the eternal; therefore he expects *each moment* the same as he expects *eternally,* and therefore he is without disquietude, for in eternity there is time enough. . . .

What faithfulness in the love which abides! It is far from our intention to wish to disparage the loving maiden, as if it were a kind of disloyalty in her (alas, a disloyalty — to a faithless lover!) that she weakened through the years and faded away, so that her earthly love became changed in the change which is the change of love itself through the years. And yet, yet — aye, it is a strange intercrossing of the self-contradictory thought, but it cannot now be otherwise with even the highest form of faithfulness in earthly love, than that it almost seems to be disloyalty, because the earthly love is not the eternal. The contradiction does not lie in the girl, she remained faithful; the contradiction, which the girl herself suffered, lies in the fact that the earthly love is not the eternal, and consequently in the fact that it is impossible with *eternal* loyalty to lay hold on that which *is not* in itself the *eternal.* What faithfulness of love, on the other hand, to abide completely unchanged, without the slightest weakening, the same at every moment — whenever, at whatever time or hour, the misunderstanding, the enemy, the hater wishes to return to this lover! That he who abides never becomes infirm, is indeed to him an eternal gain; but it is in addition, and thus we here regard it, and thus he himself regards it, a work of love in faithfulness to those he loves. . . .

Such is the lover. That the most beautiful of everything, that the moment of reconciliation, should become a fruitless effort, a vain attempt, because by that time he had changed: he *prevents* that; for he abides, and never becomes worn out. And that the transition of forgiveness may be as easy as the meeting with one whom one has not seen for a long time; that the conversation of love may immediately be as natural as it is with one with whom one carries on a conversation; that the rambling pace may be as swift in measure as it is between two who for the *first* time begin a new life — in short, that there may be nothing, simply no halting, which might repel, not a second, not a split second: the lover *effects* this, for he abides and never becomes infirm.

LIN YUTANG

The Importance of Living

Lin Yutang (1895–1976) was born in China of Christian
parents, but spent most of his adult life in the United States
as a writer in both English and Chinese, becoming ever
more staunchly Chinese in his philosophical and religious
outlook. This excerpt from *The Importance of Living*, entitled "Relationship to God," presents his defense of that
"pagan" outlook against Christian and generally Western
truth claims.

I. The Restoration of Religion

So many people presume to know God and what God approves and
God disapproves that it is impossible to take up this subject without
opening oneself to attack as sacrilegious by some and as a prophet by
others. We human creatures who individually are less than a billionth
part of the earth's crust, which is less than a billionth part of the great
universe, presume to know God!

Yet no philosophy of life is complete, no conception of man's
spiritual life is adequate, unless we bring ourselves into a satisfactory
and harmonious relation with the life of the universe around us. Man
is important enough; he is the most important topic of our studies: that
is the essence of humanism. Yet man lives in a magnificent universe,
quite as wonderful as the man himself, and he who ignores the greater
world around him, its origin and its destiny, cannot be said to have a
truly satisfying life.

The trouble with orthodox religion is that, in its process of historical
development, it got mixed up with a number of things, strictly outside
religion's moral realm — physics, geology, astronomy, criminology,
the conception of sex and woman. If it had confined itself to the realm

of the moral conscience, the work of re-orientation would not be so enormous to-day. It is easier to destroy a pet notion of "Heaven" and "Hell" than to destroy the notion of God.

On the other hand, science opens up to the modern Christian a newer and deeper sense of the mystery of the universe and a new conception of matter as a convertible term with energy, and as for God Himself, in the words of Sir James Jeans, "The universe seems to be nearer to a great thought than to a great machine." Mathematical calculation itself proves the existence of the mathematically incalculable. Religion will have to retreat and instead of saying so many things in the realm of natural sciences as it used to do, simply acknowledge that they are none of religion's business; much less should it allow the validity of spiritual experience to depend on totally irrelevant topics, like whether the age of man is 4,000-odd years or a million, or whether the earth is flat, or round, or shaped like a collapsible tea-table, or borne aloft by Hindu elephants or Chinese turtles. Religion should, and will, confine itself to the moral realm, the realm of the moral conscience, which has a dignity of its own comparable in every sense to the study of flowers, the fishes and the stars. St. Paul performed the first surgical operation upon Judaism and, by separating cuisine (eating hoofed animals) from religion, immensely benefited it. Religion stands to gain immensely by being separated not only from cuisine but also from geology and comparative anatomy. Religion must cease to be a dabbler in astronomy and geology and a preserver of ancient folkways. Let religion respectfully keep its mouth shut when teachers of biology are talking, and it will seem infinitely less silly and gain immeasurably in the respect of mankind.

Such religion as there can be in modern life, every individual will have to salvage from the churches for himself. There is always a possibility of surrendering ourselves to the Great Spirit in an atmosphere of ritual and worship as one kneels praying without words and looking at the stained-glass windows, in spite of all that one may think of the theological dogmas. In this sense, worship becomes a true æsthetic experience, an æsthetic experience that is one's own, very similar, in fact, to the experience of viewing a sun setting behind an outline of trees on hills. For that man, religion is a final fact of consciousness, for it will be an æsthetic experience very much akin to poetry.

But what contempt he must have for the churches, as they are at present! For the God that he worships will not be one that can be beseeched for daily small presents. He will not command the wind to blow north when he sails north, and command the wind to blow south when he sails south. To thank God for a good wind is sheer impudence, and selfishness also, for it implies that God does not love the people sailing south when HE, the important individual, is sailing north. It will be a communion of spirits without one party trying to beg a favour of the other. He will not be able to comprehend the meaning of the churches as they are. He will wonder at the strange metamorphosis that religion has gone through. He will be puzzled when he tries to define religions in their present forms. Is religion a glorification of the *status quo* with mystic emotion? Or is it certain moral truths so mystified and decorated and camouflaged as to make it possible for a priestcraft to make a living? Doesn't revelation stand in the same relation to religion as "a secret patented process" stands in relation to certain advertised nostrums? Or is religion a juggling with the invisible and the unknowable because the invisible and the unknowable lend themselves so conveniently to juggling? Is faith to be based on knowledge, or does faith only begin where knowledge ends? Or is religion a baseball that Sister Aimée McPherson can hit with a baseball bat right into an audience — something that Joe can catch and "get" in the way that he catches a baseball? Or is religion the preservation of Aryan, Nordic blood, or is it merely opposition to divorce and birth control and calling every social reformer a "Red" and a "Communist"? Did Christ really have to receive Tolstoy in His arms in a blazing snowstorm after he was excommunicated from the Greek Orthodox Church? Or is Jesus going to stand outside Bishop Manning's cathedral window and beckon to the rich men's children in their pews and repeat His gentle request, "Suffer little children to come unto me"?

So we are left with the uncomfortable and yet, for me, strangely satisfying feeling that what religion is left in our lives will be a very much more simplified feeling of reverence for the beauty and grandeur and mystery of life, with its responsibilities, but will be deprived of the good old, glad certainties and accretions which theology has accumulated and laid over its surface. Religion in this form is simple and, for many modern men, sufficient. The spiritual theocracy of the Middle Ages is definitely receding and as for personal immortality, which is the second greatest reason for the appeal of religion, many men to-day are quite content to be just dead when they die.

Our preoccupation with immortality has something pathological about it. That man desires immortality is understandable, but were it not for the influence of the Christian religion, it should never have

assumed such a disproportionately large share of our attention. Instead of being a fine reflection, a noble fancy, lying in the poetic realm
between fiction and fact, it has become a deadly earnest matter, and
in the case of monks, the thought of death, or life after it, has become
the main occupation of this life. As a matter of fact, most people on
the other side of fifty, whether pagans or Christians, are not afraid of
death, which is the reason why they can't be scared by, and are
thinking less of, Heaven and Hell. We find them very often chattering
glibly about their epitaphs and tomb designs and the comparative
merits of cremation. By that I do not mean only those who are sure that
they are going to heaven, but also many who take the realistic view of
the situation that when they die, life is extinguished like light from a
candle. Many of the finest minds of to-day have expressed their
disbelief in personal immortality and are quite unconcerned about
it — H. G. Wells, Albert Einstein, Sir Arthur Keith and a host of
others — but I do not think it requires first-rate minds to conquer this
fear of death.

Many people have substituted for this personal immortality, immortality of other kinds, much more convincing — the immortality of
the race, and the immortality of work and influence. It is sufficient that
when we die, the work we leave behind us continues to influence
others and play a part, however small, in the life of the community in
which we live. We can pluck the flower and throw its petals to the
ground, and yet its subtle fragrance remains in the air. It is a better,
more reasonable and more unselfish kind of immortality. In this very
real sense, we may say that Louis Pasteur, Luther Burbank and Thomas
Edison are still living among us. What if their bodies are dead, since
"body" is nothing but an abstract generalization for a constantly
changing combination of chemical constituents! Man begins to see his
own life as a drop in an ever-flowing river and is glad to contribute his
part to the great stream of life. If he were only a little less selfish, he
should be quite contented with that.

II. Why I Am a Pagan

Religion is always an individual, personal thing. Every person must
work out his own views of religion, and if he is sincere, God will not
blame him, however it turns out. Every man's religious experience is
valid for himself, for, as I have said, it is not something that can be
argued about. But the story of an honest soul struggling with religious
problems, told in a sincere manner, will always be of benefit to other

people. That is why, in speaking about religion, I must get away from generalities and tell my personal story.

I am a pagan. The statement may be taken to imply a revolt against Christianity; and yet "revolt" seems a harsh word and does not correctly describe the state of mind of a man who has passed through a very gradual evolution, step by step, away from Christianity, during which he clung desperately, with love and piety, to a series of tenets which, against his will, were slipping away from him. Because there was never any hatred, therefore it is impossible to speak of a rebellion.

As I was born in a pastor's family and at one time prepared for the Christian ministry, my natural emotions were on the side of religion during the entire struggle rather than against it. In this conflict of emotions and understanding, I gradually arrived at a position where I had, for instance, definitely renounced the doctrine of redemption, a position which could most simply be described as that of a pagan. It was, and still is, a condition of belief concerning life and the universe in which I feel natural and at ease, without having to be at war with myself. The process came as naturally as the weaning of a child or the dropping of a ripe apple on the ground; and when the time came for the apple to drop, I would not interfere with its dropping. In Taoistic phraseology, this is but to live in the Tao, and in Western phraseology it is but being sincere with oneself and with the universe, according to one's lights. I believe no one can be natural and happy unless he is intellectually sincere with himself, and to be natural is to be in heaven. To me, being a pagan is just being natural.

"To be a pagan" is no more than a phrase, like "to be a Christian." It is no more than a negative statement, for, to the average reader, to be a pagan means only that one is not a Christian; and, since "being a Christian" is a very broad and ambiguous term, the meaning of "not being a Christian" is equally ill-defined. It is all the worse when one defines a pagan as one who does not believe in religion or in God, for we have yet to define what is meant by "God" or by the "religious attitude toward life." Great pagans have always had a deeply reverent attitude toward nature. We shall therefore have to take the word in its conventional sense and mean by it simply a man who does not go to church (except for an æsthetic inspiration, of which I am still capable), does not belong to the Christian fold, and does not accept its usual, orthodox tenets.

On the positive side, a Chinese pagan, the only kind of which I can speak with any feeling of intimacy, is one who starts out with this earthly life as all we can or need to bother about, wishes to live intently and happily as long as his life lasts, often has a sense of the poignant sadness of this life and faces it cheerily, has a keen appreciation of the beautiful and the good in human life wherever he finds them, and regards doing good as its own satisfactory reward. I admit, however, he feels a slight pity or contempt for the "religious" man, who does good in order to get to heaven and who, by implication, would not do good if he were not lured by heaven or threatened with hell. If this statement is correct, I believe there are a great many more pagans in this country than are themselves aware of it. The modern liberal Christian and the pagan are really close, differing only when they start out to *talk* about God.

I think I know the depths of religious experience, for I believe one can have this experience without being a great theologian like Cardinal Newman — otherwise Christianity would not be worth having or must already have been horribly misinterpreted. As I look at it at present, the difference in spiritual life between a Christian believer and a pagan is simply this: the Christian believer lives in a world governed and watched over by God, to whom he has a constant personal relationship, and therefore in a world presided over by a kindly father; his conduct is also often uplifted to a level consonant with this consciousness of being a child of God, no doubt a level which is difficult for a human mortal to maintain consistently at all periods of his life or of the week or even of the day; his actual life varies between living on the human and the truly religious levels.

On the other hand, the pagan lives in this world like an orphan, without the benefit of that consoling feeling that there is always someone in heaven who cares and who will, when that spiritual relationship called prayer is established, attend to his private personal welfare. It is no doubt a less cheery world; but there is the benefit and dignity of being an orphan who by necessity has learned to be independent, to take care of himself, and to be more mature, as all orphans are. It was this feeling rather than any intellectual belief — this feeling of dropping into a world without the love of God — that really scared me till the very last moment of my conversion to paganism; I felt, like many born Christians, that if a personal God did not exist the bottom would be knocked out of this universe.

And yet a pagan can come to the point where he looks on that perhaps warmer and cheerier world as at the same time a more childish, I am tempted to say a more adolescent, world; useful and workable, if one keep the illusion unspoiled, but no more and no less justifiable than a truly Buddhist way of life; also a more beautifully coloured world but consequently less solidly true and therefore of less worth. For me personally, the suspicion that anything is coloured or not solidly true is fatal. There is a price one must be willing to pay for truth; whatever the consequences, let us have it. This position is comparable to and psychologically the same as that of a murderer: if one has committed a murder, the best thing he can do next is to confess it. That is why I say it takes a little courage to become a pagan. But, after one has accepted the worst, one is also without fear. Peace of mind is that mental condition in which you have accepted the worst. (Here I see for myself the influence of Buddhist or Taoist thought.)

Or I might put the difference between a Christian and a pagan world like this: the pagan in me renounced Christianity out of both pride and humility, emotional pride and intellectual humility, but perhaps on the whole less out of pride than of humility. Out of emotional pride because I hated the idea that there should be any other reason for our behaving as nice, decent men and women than the simple fact that we are human beings; theoretically and if you want to go in for classifications, classify this as a typically humanist thought. But more out of humility, of intellectual humility, simply because I can no longer, with our astronomical knowledge, believe that an individual human being is so terribly important in the eyes of that Great Creator, living as the individual does, an infinitesimal speck on this earth, which is an infinitesimal speck of the solar system, which is again an infinitesimal speck of the universe of solar systems. The audacity of man and his presumptuous arrogance are what stagger me. What right have we to conceive of the character of a Supreme Being, of whose work we can see only a millionth part, and to postulate about His attributes?

The importance of the human individual is undoubtedly one of the basic tenets of Christianity. But let us see what ridiculous arrogance that leads to in the usual practice of Christian daily life.

Four days before my mother's funeral there was a pouring rain, and if it continued, as was usual in July in Changchow, the city would be flooded, and there could be no funeral. As most of us came from Shanghai, the delay would have meant some inconvenience. One of my relatives — a rather extreme but not an unusual example of a Christian believer in China — told me that she had faith in God, Who would always provide for His children. She prayed, and the rain stopped, apparently in order that a tiny family of Christians might have their funeral without delay. But the implied idea that, but for us, God would willingly subject the tens of thousands of Changchow inhabitants to a devastating flood, as was often the case, or that He did not stop the rain because of them but because of us who wanted to have a conveniently dry funeral, struck me as an unbelievable type of selfishness. I cannot imagine God providing for such selfish children.

There was also a Christian pastor who wrote the story of his life, attesting to many evidences of the hand of God in his life, for the purpose of glorifying God. One of the evidences adduced was that, when he had got together 600 silver dollars to buy his passage to America, God lowered the rate of exchange on the day this so very important individual was to buy his passage. The difference in the rate of exchange for 600 silver dollars could have been at most ten or twenty dollars, and God was willing to rock the bourses in Paris, London, and New York in order that this curious child of His might save ten or twenty dollars. Let us remind ourselves that this way of glorifying God is not at all unusual in any part of Christendom.

Oh, the impudence and conceit of man, whose span of life is but three-score and ten! Mankind as an aggregate may have a significant history, but man as an individual, in the words of Su Tungp'o, is no more than a grain of millet in an ocean or an insect *fuyu* born in the morning and dying at eve, as compared with the universe. The Christian will not be humble. He will not be satisfied with the aggregate immortality of his great stream of life, of which he is already a part, flowing on to eternity, like a mighty stream which empties into the great sea and changes and yet does not change. The clay vessel will ask of the potter, "Why hast thou cast me into this shape and why hast thou made me so brittle?" The clay vessel is not satisfied that it can leave little vessels of its own kind when it cracks up. Man is not satisfied that he has received this marvellous body, this almost divine body. He wants to live for ever! And he will not let God alone. He must say his prayers and he must pray daily for small personal gifts from the Source of All Things. Why can't he let God alone?

There was once a Chinese scholar who did not believe in Buddhism, and his mother who did. She was devout and would acquire merit for herself by mumbling, "*Namu omitabha!*" a thousand times day and night. But every time she started to call Buddha's name, her son would call, "Mamma!" The mother became annoyed. "Well," said the son, "don't you think Buddha would be equally annoyed, if he could hear you?"

My father and mother were devout Christians. To hear my father conduct the evening family prayers was enough. And I was a sensitively religious child. As a pastor's son I received the facilities of missionary education, profited from its benefits, and suffered from its weaknesses. For its benefits I was always grateful and its weaknesses I turned into my strength. For according to Chinese philosophy there are no such things in life as good and bad luck.

I was forbidden to attend Chinese theatres, never allowed to listen to Chinese minstrel singers, and entirely cut apart from the great Chinese folk tradition and mythology. When I entered a missionary college, the little foundation in classical Chinese given me by my father was completely neglected. Perhaps it was just as well — so that later, after a completely Westernized education, I could go back to it with the freshness and vigorous delight of a child of the West in an Eastern wonderland. The complete substitution of the fountain pen for the writing brush during my college and adolescent period was the greatest luck I ever had and preserved for me the freshness of the Oriental mental world unspoiled, until I should become ready for it. If Vesuvius had not covered up Pompeii, Pompeii would not be so well preserved, and the imprints of carriage-wheels on her stone pavements would not be so clearly marked to-day. The missionary college education was my Vesuvius.

Thinking was always dangerous. More than that, thinking was always allied with the devil. The conflict during the collegiate-adolescent period, which, as usual, was my most religious period, between a heart which felt the beauty of the Christian life and a head which had a tendency to reason everything away, was taking place. Curiously enough, I can remember no moments of torment or despair, of the kind that drove Tolstoy almost to suicide. At every stage I felt myself a unified Christian, harmonious in my belief, only a little more liberal than the last, and accepting some fewer Christian doctrines. Anyway, I could always go back to the Sermon on the Mount. The poetry of a saying like "Consider the lilies of the field" was too good to be untrue. It was that and the consciousness of the inner Christian life that gave me strength.

But the doctrines were slipping away terribly. Superficial things first began to annoy me. The "resurrection of the flesh," long disproved when the expected second coming of Christ in the first century did not come off and the Apostles did not rise bodily from their graves, was still there in the Apostles' Creed. This was one of those things.

Then, enrolling in a theological class and initiated into the holy of holies, I learned that another article in the creed, the virgin birth, was open to question, different deans in American theological seminaries holding different views. It enraged me that Chinese believers should be required to believe categorically in this article before they could be baptized, while the theologians of the same church regarded it as an open question. It did not seem sincere and somehow it did not seem right.

Further schooling in meaningless commentary scholarship as to the whereabouts of the "water gate" and such minutiæ completely relieved me of responsibility to take such theological studies seriously, and I made a poor showing in my grades. My professors considered that I was not cut out for the Christian ministry, and the bishop thought I might as well leave. They would not waste their instruction on me. Again this seems to me now a blessing in disguise. I doubt, if I had gone on with it and put on the clerical garb, whether it would have been so easy for me to be honest with myself later on. But this feeling of rebellion against the discrepancy of the beliefs required of the theologian and of the average convert was the nearest kind of feeling to what I may call a "revolt."

By this time I had already arrived at the position that the Christian theologians were the greatest enemies of the Christian religion. I could never get over two great contradictions. The first was that the theologians had made the entire structure of the Christian belief hang upon the existence of an apple. If Adam had not eaten an apple, there would be no original sin, and if there were no original sin, there would be no need of redemption. That was plain to me, whatever the symbolic value of the apple might be. This seemed to me preposterously unfair to the teachings of Christ, who never said a word about the original sin or the redemption. Anyway, from pursuing literary studies, I feel, like all modern Americans, no consciousness of sin and simply do not believe in it. All I know is that if God loves me only half as much as my mother does, He will not send me to Hell. That is a final fact of my inner consciousness, and for no religion could I deny its truth.

Still more preposterous another proposition seemed to me. This was the argument that, when Adam and Eve ate an apple during their honeymoon, God was so angry that He condemned their posterity to suffer from generation to generation for that little offence but that, when the same posterity murdered the same God's only Son, God was so delighted that He forgave them all. No matter how people explain and argue, I cannot get over this simple untruth. This was the last of the things that troubled me.

Still, even after my graduation, I was a zealous Christian and voluntarily conducted a Sunday school at Tsing Hua, a non-Christian college at Peking, to the dismay of many faculty members. The Christmas meeting of the Sunday school was a torture to me, for here

I was passing on to the Chinese children the tale of herald angels singing upon a midnight clear when I did not believe it myself. Everything had been reasoned away, and only love and fear remained: a kind of clinging love for an all-wise God which made me feel happy and peaceful and suspect that I should not have been so happy and peaceful without that reassuring love — and fear of entering into a world of orphans.

Finally my salvation came. "Why," I reasoned with a colleague, "if there were no God, people would not do good and the world would go topsy-turvy."

"Why?" replied my Confucian colleague. "We should lead a decent human life simply because we are decent human beings," he said.

This appeal to the dignity of human life cut off my last tie to Christianity, and from then on I was a pagan.

It is all so clear to me now. The world of pagan belief is a simpler belief. It postulates nothing, and is obliged to postulate nothing. It seems to make the good life more immediately appealing by appealing to the good life alone. It better justifies doing good by making it unnecessary for doing good to justify itself. It does not encourage men to do, for instance, a simple act of charity by dragging in a series of hypothetical postulates — sin, redemption, the cross, laying up treasure in heaven, mutual obligation among men on account of a third-party relationship in heaven — all so unnecessarily complicated and roundabout, and none capable of direct proof. If one accepts the statement that doing good is its own justification, one cannot help regarding all theological baits to right living as redundant and tending to cloud the lustre of a moral truth. Love among men should be a final, absolute fact. We should be able just to look at each other and love each other without being reminded of a third party in heaven. Christianity seems to me to make morality appear unnecessarily difficult and complicated and sin appear tempting, natural, and desirable. Paganism, on the other hand, seems alone to be able to rescue religion from theology and restore it to its beautiful simplicity of belief and dignity of feeling.

In fact, I seem to be able to see how many theological complications arose in the first, second, and third centuries and turned the simple truths of the Sermon on the Mount into a rigid, self-contained structure to support a priestcraft as an endowed institution. The reason was contained in the word *revelation* — the revelation of a special mystery or divine scheme given to a prophet and kept by all apostolic succession, which was found necessary in all religions, from Mohammedanism and Mormonism to the Living Buddha's Lamaism and Mrs. Eddy's Christian Science, in order for each of them to handle exclusively a special, patented monopoly of salvation. All priestcraft lives on the common staple food of revelation. The simple truths of Christ's teaching on the Mount must be adorned, and the lily He so marvelled at must be gilded. Hence we have the "first Adam" and the "second Adam," and so on and so forth.

But Pauline logic, which seemed so convincing and unanswerable in the early days of the Christian era, seems weak and unconvincing to the more subtle modern critical consciousness; and in this discrepancy between the rigorous Asiatic deductive logic and the more pliable, more subtle appreciation of truth of the modern man, lies the weakness of the appeal to the Christian revelation or any revelation for the modern man. Therefore, only by a return to paganism and renouncing the revelation can one return to primitive (and for me more satisfying) Christianity.

It is wrong, therefore, to speak of a pagan as an irreligious man: irreligious he is only as one who refuses to believe in any special variety of revelation. A pagan always believes in God but would not like to say so, for fear of being misunderstood. All Chinese pagans believe in God, the most commonly met with designation in Chinese literature being the term *chaowu,* or the Creator of Things. The only difference is that the Chinese pagan is honest enough to leave the Creator of Things in a halo of mystery, toward whom he feels a kind of awed piety and reverence. What is more, that feeling suffices for him. Of the beauty of this universe, the clever artistry of the myriad things of this creation, the mystery of the stars, the grandeur of heaven, and the dignity of the human soul he is equally aware. But that again suffices for him. He accepts death as he accepts pain and suffering and weighs them against the gift of life and the fresh country breeze and the clear mountain moon and he does not complain. He regards bending to the will of Heaven as the truly religious and pious attitude and calls it "living in the Tao." If the Creator of Things wants him to die at seventy, he gladly dies at seventy. He also believes that "heaven's way always goes round" and that there is no permanent injustice in this world. He does not ask for more.

ANDERS NYGREN

Agape and Eros in Augustine

Anders Nygren (1890–1978) was a professor in the University of Lund, Sweden, and later the bishop of Lund. His special scholarly interest lay in the question of philosophical-theological method in relation to the nineteenth-century systems of Kant and Schleiermacher, but his most widely discussed work was his history of the Christian idea of love, *Agape and Eros,* from which this chapter is taken.

1. The Eros Motif in Augustine's Religious Development

LOVE IS UNQUESTIONABLY CENTRAL in Augustinian Christianity; but it is not easy to say what kind of love it is, whether its features are mainly those of Eros or those of Agape. At first sight Eros seems to predominate, and this impression is confirmed by a glance at Augustine's development as described by himself in the *Confessions.*

Plato describes progress on the path of Eros as follows: "The right way of Eros, whether one goes alone or is led by another, is to begin with the beautiful things that are here and ascend ever upwards aiming at the beauty that is above, climbing, as it were, on a ladder from one beautiful body to two, and from two to all the others, and from beautiful bodies to beautiful actions and from beauty of actions to beautiful forms of knowledge, till at length from these one reaches that knowledge which is the knowledge of nothing other than Beauty itself." This, in brief, is the Platonic Way of salvation; it is the *ordo salutis* [sequence of the events of salvation] of Eros doctrine.

Although Augustine means to take a Christian view of his development in the *Confessions,* he provides in fact a singularly clear example of what Plato calls "the right way of Eros." Augustine's earlier development is particularly dramatic; he passionately embraces a doctrine and as abruptly abandons it. Yet, running through these apparently aimless veerings from one point of view to another, there is a remarkably strong continuity. There is something permanent amid the change; something virtually unaltered accompanies him through all his different phases: it is the Eros point of view. It was not Neoplatonism that introduced him to it; he had it from the beginning, and it dominates him equally as a Manichæan, as a Neoplatonist and as a Christian. His spiritual life from first to last bears in a high degree the stamp of Eros.

Augustine dates the beginning of greater stability in his spiritual life from his acquaintance with Cicero's *Hortensius*. Through the study of this book he was gripped by the philosophic Eros, which in later retrospect he identifies with Christian love to God. "With an incredible fervour of heart," he writes, "I yearned for the immortal wisdom, and I began to arise in order to return to Thee. . . . How did I burn, O my God, how did I burn with desire to soar from earth to Thee, and I knew not what Thou wouldest do with me. For with Thee is wisdom. But love of wisdom is in Greek called philosophy, and with this that book inflamed me." Afterwards he made Neoplatonic Eros, love for the Divine, so deeply and inwardly his own that it became, so to speak, the very core of his being.

That is how Augustine began, and so he continued. That crisis which is usually called his conversion produced no essential change. It falls entirely within the framework created by Eros piety, and Augustine himself describes it as the second act of what happened to him when he was gripped by the philosophic Eros. What he then wanted but could not achieve — namely, to contemn things earthly, to turn his longing wholly to the supersensible, and to rise on the wings of the soul to the sphere of the Divine — this became a reality at his conversion. True to the Neoplatonic scheme of salvation as this change is, Neoplatonism had been unable to effect it; for although it adequately showed him what ought to be the object of his love, that object was too abstract and remote to hold him permanently. Neoplatonism had kindled in him love to God, but that love was rather a fleeting mood than a permanent disposition. Augustine himself describes it as follows: "I was amazed that I already loved Thee and not a phantasm instead of Thee. Yet I did not persist to enjoy my God, but now I was drawn to Thee by Thy beauty, now borne away from Thee by my own weight." On the Eros ladder which Neoplatonism showed him, he could ascend from the beauty of the corporeal world, through the world of the soul and reason, to the eternal and immutable Being, and in a moment of trembling vision glimpse the Divine itself. Augustine never doubts that Christian love to God is the same as Platonic Eros and that the Way of Eros leads ultimately to the same God as Christianity proclaims — only as yet he lacks staying power. "I lacked strength to hold my gaze fixed on Thee, and in my weakness was struck back and returned to my accustomed ways." Then comes the *conversion, and its primary significance is that the inconstant Eros mood is elevated to a stable and permanent Eros disposition.*

What is true of the beginnings of Augustine's religious life and of the maturity it reaches in his "conversion" is equally true of the heights it attains later. There too the Eros motif is the main factor. We may recall the conversation Augustine had with his mother, a few days before her death, about the kingdom of heaven. The whole spiritual attitude it expresses has its prototype in the ascent to the Divine of the soul that is fired with Eros. Step by step the way leads through the various spheres of the material world up to the human spirit; then beyond that, to a still higher sphere, to the great silence where there is unmediated apprehension of God Himself. True, in certain respects this differs from the Neoplatonic tradition, and in particular the ecstatic absorption in God is lacking; yet it is impossible to doubt that the entire scheme of this ascent is determined by the Eros motif.

2. The Agape Motif As a Basic Factor in Augustine's Outlook

It would however be quite unjust to Augustine to conclude from the above that he is exclusively a representative of Eros piety for whom the Agape motif plays but little part. He has a multitude of ideas and opinions which are undoubtedly to be traced back to the Agape motif. He, more than any of the Fathers of the Early Church, has given a central place to Christian love in the sense of Agape.

His doctrine of *Grace* and *Predestination,* above all, shows this to be so. He speaks much of Divine grace as "præveniens" and "gratis data"; and what is that but a proclamation of God's Agape? The Augustinian doctrine of Predestination also, from one point of view, is the most emphatic confession of the unmotivated and spontaneous nature of Divine love. Augustine has taken seriously the idea: "You have not chosen me, but I have chosen you." In spontaneous love God has chosen us before we turned in faith and love to Him. "This," says Augustine, "is that ineffable grace. For what were we, when we had not yet chosen Christ and, consequently, did not love Him? . . . What else but unrighteous and lost?" Paul's word: "God commendeth his own love toward us in that, while we were yet sinners, Christ died for us" (Rom. v. 8), has by no means escaped Augustine. For him, too, God's love is paradoxical and "incomprehensibilis."

When Augustine speaks of God's love, he appears at times to break away from the Eros-scheme. According to Eros theory it is, strictly speaking, impossible to talk of God's love at all, for Eros-love always presupposes imperfection, a need as yet unfulfilled. It looks, indeed, like a conscious attack on Eros theory when Augustine, in order to show the precise nature of Divine love, distinguishes between two sorts of love, a love that is due to the dryness of need and longing (*indigentiæ siccitate*) and a love that springs out of the fulness of goodness and benevolence (*beneficentiæ ubertate*), or, otherwise expressed, *amor ex miseria* and *amor ex misericordia*. What is the difference between these two, if not that between Eros and Agape? Augustine seems to be well aware that God's love to us must be distinguished from Eros-love. *God's love is a love of mercy and of the fulness of goodwill.* Eros-love ascends and seeks the satisfaction of its needs; Agape-love descends in order to help and to give. Just because of its unmotivated and spontaneous character — or, in Augustine's own words, because God loves "ultro" — God's love has so much more power to kindle the response of love in man. Man can make no claim to God's love. If it is given to him, that rests upon a Divine miracle. God, the highest Judge, condescends to sinful man. This line of thought is rather isolated in Augustine, but it is remarkable that it occurs at all in so definite a form. In view of such statements, especially if we also recall the central importance of the idea of Grace and Predestination, we can no longer doubt that Agape is a basic factor in the religious life and thought of Augustine.

A further proof, and one of the strongest, of Augustine's interest in Agape is his energetic affirmation of *the idea of Incarnation.* In all ages, this idea has always been a safeguard of the Agape motif. By the Incarnation of the Son, God Himself has come down to us in the world of transience and sin. This formed the permanent centre of Augustine's Christian thought. The prominence of the idea of Incarnation in the writings immediately following his "conversion" is striking — the more so since these writings are otherwise so definitely Neoplatonic in character, and there is scarcely any idea for which Neoplatonism has less room than that of Incarnation. If Augustine's conversion meant, as we saw above, the full emergence of the idea of Eros, we can now state that it also meant, in a measure, the emergence of the idea of Agape. That love which descends in order to help and to give, which is spontaneous and unmotivated, was not alien to Augustine. Yet he never knew Agape in its Christian fulness.

We now come to the great and fatal contradiction in Augustine's view of love. He wanted to maintain both Eros and Agape at once. He was unaware that they are diametrically opposed to each other and that the relation between them must be an Either — Or; instead, he tried to make it a Both — And. But this was not done without tension and conflict.

3. The Settlement of the Issue between Eros and Agape

In the seventh book of the *Confessions* we can read between the lines how Augustine settled the issue between Eros and Agape. He describes here what he found and did not find in Neoplatonism. He found God and the eternal world, and was fired with Eros for the Divine. But he is himself too weak, and God is too remote for him to attain. "When I first knew Thee, Thou didst draw me up to Thee . . . but my weak sight was beaten back when Thou didst powerfully shed Thy rays upon me, and I trembled with love and awe and found myself to be far off from Thee." *Neoplatonism had been able to show him the object for his love and longing, but not the way to gain it.* Between God and man is a gulf which man cannot bridge. In Eros man is bound to God but cannot reach Him. The wings of yearning are not strong enough to bear him up to the Eternal. Augustine has no doubt that Eros is the way to God, but he has begun to doubt whether we, as we actually are, can gain access to Him by that way. If we are to find God, He must Himself come to meet us — but of that Neoplatonism knew nothing. Of God and His nature, of man's Eros for Him, indeed, of the Word of God which in the beginning was with God — of all these he could read in the writings of the Neoplatonists. "But that the Word became flesh, and dwelt among us, I read not there," says Augustine. These writings might tell him that the Son was in the form of God, but that He emptied Himself and took the form of a servant, that He humbled Himself and became obedient unto death, that God spared not His own Son but delivered Him up for us all — "those books do not contain." *In Neoplatonism he finds human Eros which tries to take heaven by storm, but he misses God's Agape which descends, and without which Eros cannot attain to God.*

The strange thing is that Augustine never sees that Christian Agape is the direct opposite of Neoplatonic Eros, and these two motifs agree no better than fire and water. He seeks a compromise which will do justice to both. Even when he has become aware of God's Agape, he still lives with his whole soul in the realm of Eros. Agape is simply added as a new element to what he already possessed, and the validity of the latter is never questioned; Agape is fitted into the framework of Eros. Agape is a necessary corrective, without which Eros cannot reach its goal.

What, then, is the fault in Eros, which must be corrected? It is, in a word, the *superbia* that is always bound up with Eros. The soul's ascent to the higher world easily produces a feeling of self-sufficiency and pride — as Augustine knew by experience. Neoplatonism had taught him to know God and had kindled his love to God, but it had also called forth his pride. When the soul in the rapture of Eros leaves the earthly and transient far below and ascends ever higher, it is seized with a "*Hochgefühl*" which is nearly akin to superbia. It begins to feel it has already attained, becomes self-sufficient and forgets the distance between itself and the Divine. But such dreams are a cause of its never reaching the goal.

In the light of Christianity, Augustine finds Neoplatonic Eros subject to a peculiar contradiction: *Eros is man's longing to get beyond all that is transient and even beyond himself, up to the Divine; but the ascent provokes superbia and self-sufficiency, with the result that man remains after all within himself and never reaches the Divine.* Looking back on what Neoplatonism had taught him, Augustine will not deny that it showed him the right goal, but he asks: "Where was that love which builds on the foundation of humility, which is Christ Jesus? Or when should these books teach me it?" When he came from this to the Holy Scriptures (or, as he puts it, "When I had been tamed by Thy books"), he found that there is a fundamental opposition between the Neoplatonic and the Christian spirit: on the one side there is *superbia* [pride], on the other *humilitas* [humility].

The only real cure for this superbia which prevents Eros reaching its goal is God's Agape, His love in sending His Son, who humbled Himself even to the death of the Cross. In this context, Augustine can perceive the "unmotivated" character, the paradox of God's love. It was not strictly fitting that He who was God should take the form of a servant and suffer death upon the Cross; the Incarnation is a condescension on God's part which is incomprehensible to us. Yet it was necessary, "that there might be a way for man to man's God through the God-man." Nothing less than God's Agape could break man's superbia. Augustine's keen interest in the Incarnation is connected with the fact that it is for him an evidence of God's Agape, but he is interested in Agape chiefly as *exemplum humilitatis* [the example of humility]. Nothing can reveal and overcome man's superbia like God's humilitas, nothing shows how far man had strayed from God so much as the fact that he could only be restored through an incarnate God. "To cure man's superbia God's Son descended and became humble. Why are thou proud, O man? God has for thy sake become humble. Thou wouldst perchance be ashamed to imitate a humble man; imitate at least the humble God." God's Agape, or as Augustine prefers to say, God's humilitas, is the antidote to man's superbia.

According to Augustine, the relation between Agape and Eros is therefore as follows. Eros, left to itself, can see God and feel itself drawn to Him. But it sees God only at a remote distance; between Him and the soul lies an immense ocean, and when the soul imagines it has reached Him it has simply entered, in self-sufficiency and pride, into the harbour of itself. But for pride, Eros would be able to bring the soul to God. Here Agape must come to its assistance: God's humilitas must vanquish man's superbia. For even if all other ties that bind the soul to things earthly and transient are broken, its ascent will not succeed so long as it is infected with superbia. By superbia the soul is chained to itself and cannot ascend to what is above itself. *It is the task of Agape to sever this last link of the soul with things finite.* When a man has been freed from himself under the influence of God's humilitas, then the ascent succeeds. There is no longer anything to drag the soul down. The humility of Christ, the Cross of Christ, bears it over the ocean to its fatherland.

To sum up, we may quote Augustine's own words from his exposition of the first chapter of the Fourth Gospel: "These things, too [that all things were made by the Word], are found in the books of the philosophers: and that God has an only-begotten Son, through whom are all things. They could see that which is, but they saw it from afar: they would not hold the humilitas of Christ, in which ship they could have arrived safely at that which they were able to see from afar; and they despised the Cross of Christ. The sea has to be crossed, and dost thou despise the Wood? O, proud wisdom! thou laughest at the crucified Christ; it is He whom thou sawest from afar: 'In the beginning was the Word, and the Word was with God.' But why was He crucified? Because the Wood of His humiliation was necessary for thee. For thou wast puffed up with pride, and hadst been cast out far from that fatherland; and by the waves of this world the way has been cut off, and there is no means of crossing to the fatherland, unless thou be carried by the Wood. Ungrateful one! thou mockest Him who has come to thee that thou mayest return. He has become the way, and that through the sea. . . . Believe in the Crucified, and thou shalt be able to arrive thither. For thy sake He was crucified, to teach thee humilitas."

NIKOLAY ALEKSANDROVICH BERDYAEV

The Part of Imagination in the Moral Life

Nikolay Aleksandrovich Berdyaev (1874–1948) was born in Czarist Russia, but became part of the Russian exile community in Paris after the Revolution. In his own intellectual development he followed an odyssey from scepticism and Marxism to religious faith, and in a series of books, among them *The Destiny of Man* (from which this excerpt comes), he reinterpreted traditional religion and philosophy to address the needs of post-Enlightenment thought.

THE ETHICS of creativeness presupposes that the task which confronts man is infinite and that the world is not completed. But the tragedy is that the realization of every infinite task is finite. Creative imagination is of fundamental importance to the ethics of creativeness. Without imagination there can be no creative activity. Creativeness means, in the first instance, imagining something different, better, and higher. Imagination calls up before us something better than the reality around us. Creativeness always rises above reality. Imagination plays this part not only in art and in myth making but also in scientific discoveries, technical inventions, and moral life, creating a better type of relation between human beings. There is such a thing as moral imagination, which creates the image of a better life; it is absent only from legalistic ethics. No imagination is needed for automatically carrying out a law or norm. In moral life the power of creative imagination plays the part of talent. By the side of the self-contained moral world of laws and rules, to which nothing can be added, man builds, in imagination, a higher world, a free and beautiful world, lying beyond ordinary good and evil. And this is what gives beauty to life.

As a matter of fact, life can never be determined solely by law; men always imagine for themselves a different and better life, freer and more beautiful, and they realize those images. The Kingdom of God is the image of a full, perfect, beautiful, free, and divine life. Only law has nothing to do with imagination, or rather, it is limited to imagining compliance with, or violation of, its behests. But the most perfect fulfillment of the law is not the same as the perfect life.

Imagination may also be a source of evil; there may be bad imagination and phantasms. Evil thoughts are an instance of bad imagination. Crimes are conceived in imagination. But imagination also brings about a better life. A man devoid of imagination is incapable of creative moral activity and of building a better life. They very conception of a better life, towards which we ought to strive, is the result of creative imagination. Those who have no imagination think that there is no better life and that there ought not to be. All that exists for them is the unalterable order of existence in which unalterable law ought to be realized. Jacob Boehme ascribed enormous importance to imagination. The world is created by God through imagination, through images which arise in God in eternity and are both ideal and real. Modern psychologists also ascribe great importance to imagination, both good and bad. They have discovered that imagination plays an infinitely greater part in people's lives than has been hitherto thought. Diseases and psychoses arise through imagination and can also be cured by it. The ethics of law forbids man to imagine a better world and a better life, it fetters him to the world as given and to the socially organized herd life, laying down taboos and prohibitions everywhere. But the ethics of creativeness breaks with the herd existence and refuses to recognize legalistic prohibitions. To the "law" of the present life it opposes "the image" of a higher one.

The ethics of creativeness is the ethics of energy. Quantitative and qualitative increase in life's intensity and creative energy is one of the criteria of moral valuation. The good is like radium in spiritual life and its essential quality is radioactivity, inexhaustible radiation. The conceptions of energy and of norm come into conflict in ethics. The morality of law and the morality of creative energy are perpetually at war. If the good is understood as a real force, it cannot be conceived as the purpose of life. A perfect and absolute realization of the good would make it unnecessary and lead us completely to forget moral distinctions and valuations. The nature of the good and of moral life presuppose dualism and struggle, i.e., a painful and difficult path. Complete victory over the dualism and the struggle leads to the disappearance of what, on the way, we had called good and moral. To realize the good is to cancel it out. The good is not at all the final end of life and of being. It is only a way, only a struggle on the way. The good must be conceived in terms of energy and not of purpose. The thing that matters most is the realization of creative energy, not the ideal normative end. Man realizes the good, not because he has set himself the purpose of doing so, but because he is good or virtuous, i.e., because he has in himself the creative energy of goodness. The source is important, not the goal. A man fights for a good cause, not because it is his conscious purpose to do so, but because he has combative energy and the energy of goodness. Goodness and moral life are a path on which the starting point and the goal coincide: the emanation of creative energy.

But from the ontological and cosmological point of view, the final end of being must be thought of as beauty and not as goodness. Plato defined beauty as the magnificence of the good. Complete, perfect, and harmonious being is beauty. Teleological ethics is normative and legalistic. It regards the good as the purpose of life, i.e., as a norm or a law which must be fulfilled. Teleological ethics always implies absence of moral imagination, for it conceives the end as a norm and not as an image, not as a product of the creative energy of life. Moral life must be determined not by a purpose or a norm but by imagery and the exercise of creative activity. Beauty is the image of creative energy radiating over the whole world and transforming it. Teleological ethics based upon the idea of the good as an absolute purpose is hostile to freedom, but creative ethics is based upon freedom. Beauty means a transfigured creation, the good means creation fettered by the law which denounces sin. The paradox is that the law fetters the energy of the good; it does not want the good to be interpreted as a force, for in that case the world would escape from the power of law. To transcend the morality of law means to put infinite creative energy in the place of commands, prohibitions, and taboos.

Instinct plays a twofold part in man's moral life: it dates back to ancient, primitive times, and ancient terror, slavishness, superstition, animalism, and cruelty find expression in it; but at the same time it is reminiscent of Paradise, of primitive freedom and power, of man's ancient bond with the cosmos and the primeval force of life. Hence the attitude of the ethics of creativeness toward instincts is complex: it liberates instincts repressed by the moral law and at the same time struggles with them for the sake of a higher life. Instincts are repressed by the moral law, but since they have their origin in the social life of primitive clans, they themselves tend to become a law and to fetter the creative energy of life. Thus, for instance, the instinct of vengeance is, as has already been said, a heritage of the social life of antiquity, and is connected with law. The ethics of creativeness liberates not all instincts but only creative ones, i.e., man's creative energy hampered by the prohibitions of the law. It also struggles against instincts and strives to sublimate them.

Teleological ethics, which is identical with the ethics of law, metaphysically presupposes the power of time in the bad sense of the word. Time is determined either by the idea of purpose which has to be realized in the future or by the idea of creativeness which is to be carried on in the future. In the first case, man is in the power of the purpose and of the time created by it; in the second, he is the master of time, for he realizes in it his creative energy. The problem of time is bound up with the ethics of creativeness. Time and freedom are the fundamental, and the most painful, of metaphysical problems. Heidegger, in his *Sein und Zeit,* formulates it in a new way, but he connects time with care and not with creativeness. There can be no doubt, however, that creativeness is connected with time. It is usually said that creativeness needs the perspective of the future and presupposes changes that take place in time. In truth, it would be more correct to say that movement, change, creativeness, give rise to time. Thus we see that time has a double nature. It is the source both of hope and of pain and torture. The charm of the future is connected with the fact that the future may be changed and to some extent depends upon ourselves. But to the past we can do nothing, we can only remember it — with reverence and gratitude, or with remorse and indignation. The future may bring with it the realization of our desires, hopes, and dreams. But it also inspires us with terror. We are tortured with anxiety about the unknown future. Thus the part of time which we call the future and regard as dependent upon our own activity may be determined in two ways. It may be determined by duty, by painful anxiety and a command to realize a set purpose, or by our creative energy, by a constructive vital impulse through which new values are created. In the first case, time oppresses us, we are in its power. The loftiest purpose projected into the future enslaves us, becomes external to us, and makes us anxious. Anxiety is called forth not only by the lower material needs but also by the higher ideal ends. In the second case, when we are determined by free creative energy, by our free vital force, we regard the future as immanent in us and are its masters. In time everything appears as already determined and necessary, and in our feeling of the future we anticipate this determinateness; events to come sometimes appear to us as an impending fate. But a free creative act is not dominated by time, for it is not determined in any way: it springs from the depths of being, which are not subject to time, and belongs to a different order of existence. It is only later that everything comes to appear as determined in time. The task of the ethics of creativeness is to make the perspective of life independent of the fatal march of time, of the future which terrifies and torments us. The creative act is an escape from time; it is performed in the realm of freedom, not of necessity. It is, by its very nature, opposed to anxiety, which makes time so terrible. And if the whole of human life could be one continuous creative act, there would be no more time; there would be no future as a part of time; there would be movement out of time, in nontemporal reality. There would be no determination, no necessity, no binding laws. There would be the life of the spirit. In Heidegger, reality subject to time is a fallen reality, though he does not make clear what was its state before the Fall. It is the realm of the "herd man." It is connected with care for the future and anxiety. But Christ teaches us not to care about the future. "Enough for the day is the evil thereof." This is an escape from the power of time, from the nightmare of the future born of anxiety.

The future may or may not bring with it disappointment, suffering, and misfortune. But certainly, and to everyone, it brings death. And fear of the future, natural to everyone, is, in the first place, fear of impending death. Death is determined for everyone in this world; it is our fate. But man's free and creative spirit rises against this slavery to death and fate. It has another view of life, springing from freedom and creativeness. In and through Christ, the fate of death is canceled, although empirically every man dies. Our attitude to the future, which ends for us in death, is false because, being divided in ourselves, we analyze it and think of it as determined. But the future is unknowable and cannot be subjected to analysis. Only prophecy is possible with regard to it, and the mystery of prophecy lies precisely in the fact that it has nothing to do with determinations and is not knowledge within the categories of necessity. For a free creative act there exist no fate and no predetermined future. At the moment when a free creative act takes place there is no thought of the future, of the inevitable death, of future suffering; it is an escape from time and from all determinateness. In creative imagination the future is not determined. The creative image is outside the process of time, it is in eternity. Time is the child of sin, of sinful slavery, of sinful anxiety. It will stop and

disappear when the world is transfigured. But the transfiguration of
the world is taking place already in all true creativeness. We possess
a force by means of which we escape from them. That creative force
is full of grace and saves us from the power of the law. The greatest
moral task is to build a life free from determinateness and anxiety
about the future and out of the perspective of time. The moral freedom
to do so is given us, but we make poor use of it.

Freedom requires struggle and resistance. We are therefore confronted with the necessarily determined everyday world in which
processes are taking place in time and the future appears as fated. Man
is fettered and weighed down. He both longs for freedom and fears it.
The paradox of liberation is that in order to preserve freedom and to
struggle for it one must, in a sense, be already free, have freedom
within oneself. Those who are slaves to the very core of their being do
not know the name of freedom and cannot struggle for it. Ancient
taboos surround man on all sides and fetter his moral life. In order to
free himself from their power man must first be conscious of himself
as inwardly free; only then can he struggle for freedom outwardly. The
inner conquest of slavery is the fundamental task of moral life. Every
kind of slavery is meant here — slavery to the power of the past and
of the future; slavery to the external world and to oneself, to one's
lower self. The awakening of creative energy is inner liberation and is
accompanied by a sense of freedom. Creativeness is the way of liberation. Liberation cannot result in inner emptiness — it is not merely
liberation *from* something but also liberation *for the sake of* something.
And this "for the sake of" is creativeness. Creativeness cannot be
aimless and objectless. It is an ascent and therefore presupposes
heights, and that means that creativeness rises from the world to God.
It does not move along a flat surface in endless time but ascends toward
eternity. The products of creativeness remain in time, but the creative
act itself, the creative flight, communes with eternity. Every creative
act which we perform in relation to other people — an act of love, of
pity, of help, of peacemaking — not only has a future but is eternal.

Victory over the categories of master and slave in moral life is a great
achievement. A man must not be the slave of other men, nor must he
be their master, for then other people will be slaves. To achieve this
is one of the tasks of the ethics of creativeness, which knows nothing
of mastery and slavery. A creator is neither a slave nor a master, he is
one who gives, and gives abundantly. All dependence of one man upon
another is morally degrading. It is incomprehensible how the slavish
doctrine that a free and independent mind is forsaken by divine grace

could ever have arisen. Where the Spirit of God is, there is liberty. Where there is liberty, there is the Spirit of God, the grace. Grace acts upon liberty and cannot act upon anything else. A slavish mind cannot receive grace and grace cannot affect it. But slavish theories which distort Christianity build their conception of it not upon grace and liberty but upon mastery and slavery, upon the tyranny of society, of the family, and of the state. They generally recognize free will, but only for the sake of urging it to obedience. Free will cannot, however, be called in merely to be threatened. The "freedom of will" which has frequently led to man's enslavement must itself be liberated, i.e., imbued with gracious force. Creativeness is the gracious force which makes free will really free, free from fear, from the law, from inner dividedness.

The paradox of good and evil — the fundamental paradox of ethics — is that the good presupposes the existence of evil and requires that it should be tolerated. This is what the Creator does in allowing the existence of evil. Hence absolute perfection, absolute order and rationality, may prove to be an evil, a greater evil than the imperfect, unorganized, irrational life which admits of a certain freedom of evil. Absolute good which is incompatible with the existence of evil is possible only in the Kingdom of God, when there will be a new heaven and a new earth, and God will be all in all. But outside the Divine Kingdom of grace, freedom, and love, absolute good which does not allow the existence of evil is always a tyranny, the kingdom of the Grand Inquisitor and the Antichrist. Ethics must recognize this once and for all. So long as there exists a distinction between good and evil, there must inevitably be a struggle, a conflict between opposing principles, and resistance, i.e., exercise of human freedom. Absolute good and perfection outside the Kingdom of God turns man into an automaton of virtue, i.e., really abolishes moral life, since moral life is impossible without spiritual freedom.

Hence our attitude to evil must be twofold: we must be tolerant of it as the Creator is tolerant, and we must mercilessly struggle against it. There is no escaping from this paradox, for it is rooted in freedom and in the very fact of a distinction between good and evil. Ethics is bound to be paradoxical because it has its source in the Fall. The good must be realized, but it has a bad origin. The only thing that is really fine about it is the recollection of the beauty of Paradise. Is the struggle waged in the name of the good in this world an expression of the true life, the "first life"? And how can "first life," life in itself, be attained? We may say with certainty that *love* is life in itself, and so is *creativeness,* and so is the *contemplation* of the spiritual world. But this life in itself is absent from a considerable part of our legalistic morality, from physiological processes, from politics, and from civilization. "First life," or life in itself, is to be found only in firsthand, free moral acts and judgments. It is absent from moral acts which are determined by social environment, heredity, public opinion, party doctrines — i.e., it is absent from a great part of our moral life. True life is only to be found in moral acts in so far as they are creative. Automatic fulfillment of the moral law is not life. Life is always an expansion, a gain. It is present in firsthand aesthetic perceptions and judgments and in a creatively artistic attitude to the world, but not in aesthetic snobbishness.

Nietzsche thought that morality was dangerous because it hindered the realization of the higher type of man. This is true of legalistic morality, which does not allow the human personality to express itself as a whole. In Christianity itself, legalistic elements are unfavorable to the creative manifestation of the higher type of man. The morality of chivalry, of knightly honor and loyalty, was creative and could not be subsumed under the ethics of law or the ethics of redemption. And in spite of the relative, transitory, and even bad characteristics which chivalry has had as a matter of historical fact, it contained elements of permanent value and was a manifestation of the eternal principles of the human personality. Chivalry would have been impossible without Christianity.

Nietzsche opposes to the distinction between good and evil, which he regards as a sign of decadence, the distinction between the noble and the low. The noble, the fine, is a higher type of life — aristocratic, strong, beautiful, well-bred. The conception of "fineness" is ontological, while that of goodness is moralistic. This leads not to amoralism, which is a misleading conception, but to the subordination of moral categories to the ontological. It means that the important thing is not to fulfill the moral law but to perfect one's nature, i.e., to attain transfiguration and enlightenment. From this point of view, the saint must be described as "fine," not as "good," for he has a lofty, beautiful nature penetrated by the divine light through and through. But all Nietzsche knew of Christianity was the moral law, and he rebelled against it. He had quite a mistaken idea about the spirit and spiritual life. He thought that a bad conscience was born of the conflict between the instincts and the behests of society — just as Freud, Adler, and Jung suppose. The instinct turns inward and becomes spirit. Spirit is the repressed, inward-driven instinct, and therefore really an epiphenomenon. For Nietzsche, the true, rich, unrepressed life is not spirit, and indeed is opposed to it. Nietzsche is clearly the victim of reaction against degenerate legalistic Christianity and against the bad spirituality which, in truth, has always meant suppression of the spirit. Nietzsche mistook it for the true spirituality. He rejected God because he thought God was incompatible with creativeness and the creative heroism to which his philosophy was a call. God was, for him, the symbol not of man's ascent to the heights but of his remaining on a flat surface below. Nietzsche was fighting not against God but against a false conception of God, which certainly ought to be combated. The idea, so widespread in theology, that the existence of God is incompatible with man's creativeness, is a source of atheism. And Nietzsche waged an agonizing struggle against God. He went further, and asserted that spirit is incompatible with creativeness, while in truth spirit is the only source of creativeness. In this connection, too, Nietzsche's attitude was inspired by a feeling of protest. Theology systematically demanded that man should bury his talents in the ground. It failed to see that the Gospel required creativeness of man and confined its attention to commands and laws; it failed to grasp the meaning of parables and of the call to freedom; it sought to know only the revealed and not the hidden. Theologians have not sufficiently understood that freedom should not be forced, repressed, and burdened with commands and prohibitions. Rather, it ought to be enlightened, transfigured, and strengthened through the power of grace.

PIERRE TEILHARD DE CHARDIN

The Phenomenon of Man

Pierre Teilhard de Chardin (1881–1955) was a paleontologist with a special concentration on prehistoric human life. He was also a member of the Society of Jesus and a theologian who combined his paleontological interest in the distant past with a vision of the distant future, where human evolution would attain its divinely destined goal, the "Omega point" of a "Christified" cosmos, and where, as the New Testament promised, God would become "all in all."

1. The Convergence of the Person and the Omega Point

A. THE PERSONAL UNIVERSE

Unlike the primitives who gave a face to every moving thing, or the early Greeks who defined all the aspects and forces of nature, modern man is obsessed by the need to depersonalise (or impersonalise) all that he most admires. There are two reasons for this tendency, The first is *analysis,* that marvellous instrument of scientific research to which we owe all our advances but which, breaking down synthesis after synthesis, allows one soul after another to escape, leaving us confronted with a pile of dismantled machinery, and evanescent particles. The second reason lies in the discovery of the sidereal world, so vast that it seems to do away with all proportion between our own being and the dimensions of the cosmos around us. Only one reality seems to survive and be capable of succeeding and spanning the infinitesimal and the immense: energy — that floating, universal entity from which all emerges and into which all falls back as into an ocean; energy, the new spirit; the new god. So, at the world's Omega, as at its Alpha, lies the Impersonal.

Under the influence of such impressions as these, it looks as though we have lost both respect for the person and understanding of his true nature. We end up by admitting that to be pivoted on oneself, to be able to say "I," is the privilege (or rather the blemish) of the element in the measure to which the latter closes the door on all the rest and succeeds in setting himself up at the antipodes of the All. In the opposite direction we conceive the "ego" to be diminishing and eliminating itself, with the trend to what is most real and most lasting in the world, namely the Collective and the Universal. Personality is seen as a specifically corpuscular and ephemeral property; a prison from which we must try to escape.

Intellectually, that is more or less where we stand today.

Yet if we try, as I have done in this essay, to pursue the logic and coherence of facts to the very end, we seem to be led to the precisely opposite view by the notions of space-time and evolution.

We have seen and admitted that evolution is an ascent towards consciousness. That is no longer contested even by the most materialistic, or at all events by the most agnostic of humanitarians. Therefore it should culminate forwards in some sort of supreme consciousness. But must not that consciousness, if it is to be supreme, contain in the highest degree what is the perfection of our consciousness — the illuminating involution of the being upon itself? It would manifestly be an error to extend the curve of hominisation in the direction of a state of diffusion. It is only in the direction of hyper-reflection — that is to say, hyper-personalisation — that thought can extrapolate itself. Otherwise how could it garner our conquests which are all made in the field of what is reflected? At first sight we are disconcerted by the association of an Ego with what is the All. The utter disproportion of the two terms seems flagrant, almost laughable. That is because we have not sufficiently meditated upon the three-fold property possessed by every consciousness: (i) of centring *everything* partially upon itself; (ii) of being able to centre itself upon itself *constantly*; and (iii) of being brought *more* by this very super-centration *into association with all the other centres* surrounding it. Are we not at every instant living the experience of a universe whose immensity, by the play of our senses and our reason, is gathered up more and more simply in each one of us? And in the establishment now proceeding through science and the philosophies of a collective human *Weltanschauung* in which every one of us co-operates and participates, are we not experiencing the first symptoms of an aggregation of a still higher order, the birth of some single centre from the convergent beams of millions of elementary centres dispersed over the surface of the thinking earth?

All our difficulties and repulsions as regards the opposition between the All and the Person would be dissipated if only we understood that, by structure, the noosphere (and more generally the world) represent a whole that is not only closed but also *centred.* Because it contains and engenders consciousness, space-time is necessarily *of a convergent nature.* Accordingly its enormous layers, followed in the right direction, must somewhere ahead become involuted to a point which we might call *Omega,* which fuses and consumes them integrally in itself. However immense the sphere of the world may be, it only exists and is finally perceptible in the directions in which its radii meet — even if this were beyond time and space altogether. Better still: the more immense this sphere, the richer and deeper and hence the more conscious is the point at which the "volume of being" that it embraces is concentrated; because the mind, seen from our side, is essentially the power of synthesis and organisation.

Seen from this point of view, the universe, without losing any of its immensity and thus without suffering any anthropomorphism, begins to take shape: since to think it, undergo it and make it act, it is *beyond* our souls that we must look, *not the other way round.* In the perspective of a noogenesis, time and space become truly humanised — or rather super-humanised. Far from being mutually exclusive, the Universal and Personal (that is to say, the "centred") grow in the same direction and culminate simultaneously in each other.

It is therefore a mistake to look for the extension of our being or of the noosphere in the Impersonal. The Future-Universal could not be anything else but the Hyper-Personal — at the Omega Point.

B. THE PERSONALISING UNIVERSE

Personalisation. It is by this internal deepening of consciousness upon itself that we have characterised the particular destiny of the element that has become fully itself by crossing the threshold of reflection — and there, as regards the fate of individual human beings — we brought our inquiry to a provisional halt. *Personalisation:* the same type of progress reappears here, but this time it defines the collective future of totalised grains of thought. There is an identical function for the element as for the sum of the elements brought together in a synthesis. How can we conceive and foresee that the two movements harmonise? How, without being impeded or deformed, can the innumerable particular curves be inscribed or even prolonged in their common envelope?

The time has come to tackle this problem, and, for that purpose, to analyse still further the nature of the personal centre of convergence upon whose existence hangs the evolutionary equilibrium of the noosphere. What should this higher pole of evolution be, in order to fulfil its role?

It is by definition in Omega that — in its flower and its integrity — the hoard of consciousness liberated little by little on earth by noo-genesis adds itself together and concentrates. So much has already been accepted. But what exactly do we mean, what is implied, when we use the apparently simple phrase "addition of consciousness"?

When we listen to the disciples of Marx, we might think it was enough for mankind (for its growth and to justify the sacrifices imposed on us) to gather together the successive acquisitions we bequeath to it in dying — our ideas, our discoveries, our works of art, our example. Surely this imperishable treasure is the best part of our being.

Let us reflect a moment, and we shall soon see that for a universe which, by hypothesis, we admitted to be a "collector and custodian of consciousness," the mere hoarding of these remains would be nothing but a colossal wastage. What passes from each of us into the mass of humanity by means of invention, education and diffusion of all sorts is admittedly of vital importance. I have sufficiently tried to stress its phyletic value and no one can accuse me of belittling it. But with that accepted, I am bound to admit that, in these contributions to the collectivity, far from transmitting the most precious, we are bequeath-ing, at the utmost, only the shadow of ourselves. Our works? But even in the interest of life in general, what is the work of works for man if not to establish, in and by each one of us, an absolutely original centre in which the universe reflects itself in a unique and inimitable way? And those centres are our very selves and personalities. The very centre of our consciousness, deeper than all its radii; that is the essence which Omega, if it is to be truly Omega, must reclaim. And this essence is obviously not something of which we can dispossess ourselves for the benefit of others as we might give away a coat or pass on a torch. For we are the very flame of that torch. To communicate itself, my ego must subsist through abandoning itself or the gift will fade away. The conclusion is inevitable that the concentration of a conscious universe would be unthinkable if it did not reassemble in itself *all conscious-nesses* as well as all *the conscious;* each particular consciousness remaining conscious of itself at the end of the operation, and even (this must absolutely be understood) each particular consciousness becoming still more itself and thus more clearly distinct from others the closer it gets to them in Omega.

The exaltation, not merely the conservation, of elements by convergence: what, after all, could be more simple, and more thoroughly in keeping with all we know?

In any domain — whether it be the cells of a body, the members of a society or the elements of a spiritual synthesis — *union differentiates*. In every organised whole, the parts perfect themselves and fulfil themselves. Through neglect of this universal rule many a system of pantheism has led us astray to the cult of a great All in which individuals were supposed to be merged like a drop in the ocean or like a dissolving grain of salt. Applied to the case of the summation of consciousnesses, the law of union rids us of this perilous and recurrent illusion. No, following the confluent orbits of their centres, the grains of consciousness do not tend to lose their outlines and blend, but, on the contrary, to accentuate the depth and incommunicability of their *egos*. The more "other" they become in conjunction, the more they find themselves as "self." How could it be otherwise since they are steeped in Omega? Could a centre dissolve? Or rather, would not its particular way of dissolving be to supercentralise itself?

Thus, under the influence of these two factors — the essential immiscibility of consciousnesses, and the natural mechanism of all unification — the only fashion in which we could correctly express the final state of a world undergoing psychical concentration would be as a system whose unity coincides with a paroxysm of harmonised complexity. Thus it would be mistaken to represent Omega to ourselves simply as a centre born of the fusion of elements which it collects, or annihilating them in itself. By its structure Omega, in its ultimate principle, can only be a *distinct Centre radiating at the core of a system of centres;* a grouping in which personalisation of the All and personalisations of the elements reach their maximum, simultaneously and without merging, under the influence of a supremely autonomous focus of union. That is the only picture which emerges when we try to apply the notion of collectivity with remorseless logic to a granular whole of thoughts.

And at this point we begin to see the motives for the fervour and the impotence which accompany every egoistic solution of life. Egoism, whether personal or racial, is quite rightly excited by the idea of the element ascending through faithfulness to life, to the extremes of the incommunicable and the exclusive that it holds within it. It *feels* right. Its only mistake, but a fatal one, is *to confuse individuality with personality*. In trying to separate itself as much as possible from others, the element individualises itself; but in doing so it becomes retrograde and seeks to drag the world backwards towards plurality and into matter. In fact it diminishes itself and loses itself. To be fully ourselves it is in the opposite direction, in the direction of convergence with all the rest, that we must advance — towards the "other." The peak of ourselves, the acme of our originality, is not our individuality but our person; and according to the evolutionary structure of the world, we can only find our person by uniting together. There is no mind without synthesis. The same law holds good from top to bottom. The true ego grows in inverse proportion to "egoism." Like the Omega which attracts it, the element only becomes personal when it universalises itself.

There is, however, an obvious and essential proviso to be made. For the human particles to become really personalised under the creative influence of union — according to the preceding analysis — not every kind of union will do. Since it is a question of achieving a synthesis of centres, it is centre to centre that they must make contact and *not otherwise*. Thus, amongst the various forms of psychic inter-activity animating the noosphere, the energies we must identify, harness and develop before all others are those of an "intercentric" nature, if we want to give effective help to the progress of evolution in ourselves.

Which brings us to the problem of love.

2. Love As Energy

We are accustomed to consider (and with what a refinement of analysis!) only the sentimental face of love, the joy and miseries it causes us. It is in its natural dynamism and its evolutionary significance that I shall be dealing with it here, with a view to determining the ultimate phases of the phenomenon of man.

Considered in its full biological reality, love — that is to say, the affinity of being with being — is not peculiar to man. It is a general property of all life and as such it embraces, in its varieties and degrees, all the forms successively adopted by organised matter. In the mammals, so close to ourselves, it is easily recognised in its different modalities: sexual passion, parental instinct, social solidarity, etc. Farther off, that is to say lower down on the tree of life, analogies are more obscure until they become so faint as to be imperceptible. But this is the place to repeat what I said earlier when we were discussing

the "*within* of things." If there were no real internal propensity to unite,
even at a prodigiously rudimentary level — indeed in the molecule
itself — it would be physically impossible for love to appear higher up,
with us, in "hominised" form. By rights, to be certain of its presence
in ourselves, we should assume its presence, at least in an inchoate
form, in everything that is. And in fact if we look around us at the
confluent ascent of consciousnesses, we see it is not lacking anywhere.
Plato felt this and has immortalised the idea in his *Dialogues*. Later,
with thinkers like Nicolas of Cusa, medieval philosophy returned
technically to the same notion. Driven by the forces of love, the
fragments of the world seek each other so that the world may come
to being. This is no metaphor; and it is much more than poetry.
Whether as a force or a curvature, the universal gravity of bodies, so
striking to us, is merely the reverse or shadow of that which really
moves nature. To perceive cosmic energy "at the fount" we must, if
there is a *within* of things, go down into the internal or radial zone of
spiritual attractions.

Love in all its subtleties is nothing more, and nothing less, than the
more or less direct trace marked on the heart of the element by the
psychical convergence of the universe upon itself.

This, if I am not mistaken, is the ray of light which will help us to
see more clearly around us.

We are distressed and pained when we see modern attempts at
human collectivisation ending up, contrary to our expectations and
theoretical predictions, in a lowering and an enslavement of consciousnesses. But so far how have we gone about the business of
unification? A material situation to be defended; a new industrial field
to be opened up, better conditions for a social class or less favoured
nations — those are the only and very mediocre grounds on which we
have so far tried to get together. There is no cause to be surprised if,
in the footsteps of animal societies, we become mechanised in the very
play of association. Even in the supremely intellectual activity of
science (at any rate as long as it remains purely speculative and
abstract) the impact of our souls only operates obliquely and indirectly. Contact is still superficial, involving the danger of yet another
servitude. Love alone is capable of uniting living beings in such a way
as to complete and fulfil them, for it alone takes them and joins them
by what is deepest in themselves. This is a fact of daily experience. At
what moment do lovers come into the most complete possession of
themselves if not when they say they are lost in each other? In truth,
does not love every instant achieve all around us, in the couple or the

team, the magic feat, the feat reputed to be contradictory, of "personalising" by totalising? And if that is what it can achieve daily on a small scale, why should it not repeat this one day on world-wide dimensions?

Mankind, the spirit of the earth, the synthesis of individuals and peoples, the paradoxical conciliation of the element with the whole, and of unity with multitude — all these are called Utopian and yet they are biologically necessary. And for them to be incarnated in the world all we may well need is to imagine our power of loving developing until it embraces the total of men and of the earth.

It may be said that this is the precise point at which we are invoking the impossible. Man's capacity, it may seem, is confined to giving his affection to one human being or to very few. Beyond that radius the heart does not carry, and there is only room for cold justice and cold reason. To love all and everyone is a contradictory and false gesture which only leads in the end to loving no-one.

To that I would answer that if, as you claim, a universal love is impossible, how can we account for that irresistible instinct in our hearts which leads us towards unity whenever and in whatever direction our passions are stirred? A sense of the universe, a sense of the *all*, the nostalgia which seizes us when confronted by nature, beauty, music — these seem to be an expectation and awareness of a Great Presence. The "mystics" and their commentators apart, how has psychology been able so consistently to ignore this fundamental vibration whose ring can be heard by every practised ear at the basis, or rather at the summit, of every great emotion? Resonance to the All — the keynote of pure poetry and pure religion. Once again: what does this phenomenon, which is born with thought and grows with it, reveal if not a deep accord between two realities which seek each other; the severed particle which trembles at the approach of "the rest"?

We are often inclined to think that we have exhausted the various natural forms of love with a man's love for his wife, his children, his friends and to a certain extent for his country. Yet precisely the most fundamental form of passion is missing from this list, the one which, under the pressure of an involuting universe, precipitates the elements one upon the other in the Whole — cosmic affinity and hence cosmic sense. A universal love is not only psychologically possible; it is the only complete and final way in which we are able to love.

But, with this point made, how are we to explain the appearance all around us of mounting repulsion and hatred? If such a strong potentiality is besieging us from within and urging us to union, what is it waiting for to pass from potentiality to action? Just this, no doubt: that we should overcome the "anti-personalist" complex which paralyses us, and make up our minds to accept the possibility, indeed the reality, of some *source* of love and *object* of love at the summit of the world above our heads. So long as it absorbs or appears to absorb the person, collectivity kills the love that is trying to come to birth. As such collectivity is essentially unlovable. That is where philanthropic systems break down. Common sense is right. It is impossible to give oneself to an anonymous number. But if the universe ahead of us assumes a face and a heart, and so to speak personifies itself, then in the atmosphere created by this focus the elemental attraction will immediately blossom. Then, no doubt, under the heightened pressure of an infolding world, the formidable energies of attraction, still dormant between human molecules, will burst forth.

The discoveries of the last hundred years, with their unitary perspectives, have brought a new and decisive impetus to our sense of the world, to our sense of the earth, and to our human sense. Hence the rise of modern pantheism. But this impetus will only end by plunging us back into super-matter unless it leads us towards someone.

For the failure that threatens us to be turned into success, for the concurrence of human monads to come about, it is necessary and sufficient for us that we should extend our science to its farthest limits and recognise and accept (as being necessary to close and balance space-time) not only some vague future existence, but also, as I must now stress, the radiation *as a present reality* of that mysterious centre of our centres which I have called Omega.

3. The Attributes of the Omega Point

After allowing itself to be captivated in excess by the charms of analysis to the extent of falling into illusion, modern thought is at last getting used once more to the idea of the creative value of synthesis in evolution. It is beginning to see that there is definitely *more* in the molecule than in the atom, *more* in the cell than in the molecule, *more* in society than in the individual, and *more* in mathematical construction than in calculations and theorems. We are now inclined to admit that at each further degree of combination *something* which is irreducible to isolated elements *emerges* in a new order. And with this admission, consciousness, life and thought are on the threshold of acquiring a right to existence in terms of science. But science is nevertheless still far from recognising that this *something* has a particular value of independence and solidity. For, born of an incredible concourse of chances on a precariously assembled edifice, and failing to create any measurable increase of energy by their advent, are not these "creatures of synthesis," from the experimental point of view, the most beautiful as well as the most fragile of things? How could they anticipate or survive the ephemeral union of particles on which their souls have alighted? So in the end, in spite of a half-hearted conversion to spiritual views, it is still on the *elementary* side — that is, towards matter infinitely diluted — that physics and biology look to find the eternal and the Great Stability.

In conformity with this state of mind the idea that some Soul of souls should be developing at the summit of the world is not as strange as might be thought from the present-day views of human reason. After all, is there any other way in which our thought can generalise the Principle of Emergence? At the same time, as this Soul coincides with a supremely improbable coincidence of the totality of elements and causes, it remains understood or implied that it could not form itself save at an extremely distant future and in a total dependence on the reversible laws of energy.

Yet it is precisely from these two restrictions (fragility and distance), both incompatible to my mind with the nature and function of Omega, that we want to rid ourselves — and this for two positive reasons, one of love, the other of survival.

First of all the *reason of Love*. Expressed in terms of internal energy, the cosmic function of Omega consists in initiating and maintaining within its radius the unanimity of the world's "reflective" particles. But how could it exercise this action were it not in some sort loving and lovable *at this very moment*? Love, I said, dies in contact with the impersonal and the anonymous. With equal infallibility it becomes impoverished with remoteness in space — and still more, much more, with difference in time. For love to be possible there must be co-existence. Accordingly, however marvellous its foreseen figure, Omega could never even so much as equilibrate the play of human attractions and repulsions if it did not act with equal force, that is to say with the same stuff of proximity. With love, as with every other sort of energy, it is within the existing datum that the lines of force must at every instant come together. Neither an ideal centre, nor a potential centre could possibly suffice. A present and real noosphere goes with a real and present centre. To be supremely attractive, Omega must be supremely present.

In addition, the *reason of survival*. To ward off the threat of disap-pearance, incompatible with the mechanism of reflective activity, man tries to bring together in an ever vaster and more permanent subject the collective principle of his acquisitions — civilisation, humanity, the spirit of the earth. Associated in these enormous entities, with their incredibly slow rhythm of evolution, he has the impression of having escaped from the destructive action of time.

But by doing this he has only pushed back the problem. For after all, however large the radius traced within time and space, does the circle ever embrace anything but the perishable? So long as our constructions rest with all their weight on the earth, they will vanish with the earth. The radical defect in all forms of belief in progress, as they are expressed in positivist credos, is that they do not definitely eliminate death. What is the use of detecting a focus of any sort in the van of evolution if that focus can and must one day disintegrate? To satisfy the ultimate requirements of our action, Omega must be independent of the collapse of the forces with which evolution is woven.

Actuality, irreversibility. There is only one way in which our minds can integrate into a coherent picture of noogenesis these two essential properties of the autonomous centre of all centres, and that is to resume and complement our Principle of Emergence. In the light of our experience it is abundantly clear that emergence *in the course of evolution* can only happen successively and with mechanical dependence on what precedes it. First the grouping of the elements; then the manifestation of "soul" whose operation only betrays, from the point of view of energy, a more and more complex and sublimated involution of the powers transmitted by the chains of elements. The radial function of the tangential: a pyramid whose apex is supported from below: that is what we see during the course of the process. And it is in the very same way that Omega itself is discovered to us at the end of the whole processus, inasmuch as in it the movement of synthesis culminates. Yet we must be careful to note that under this evolutive facet Omega still only reveals *half of itself*. While being the last term of its series, it is also *outside all series*. Not only does it crown, but it closes. Otherwise the sum would fall short of itself, in organic contradiction with the whole operation. When, going beyond the elements, we come to speak of the conscious Pole of the world, it is not enough to say that it *emerges* from the rise of consciousnesses: we must add that from this genesis it has already *emerged;* without which it could neither subjugate into love nor fix in incorruptibility. If by its very nature it did not escape from the time and space which it gathers together, it would not be Omega.

Autonomy, actuality, irreversibility, and thus finally transcendence are the four attributes of Omega. In this way we round off without difficulty the scheme left incomplete at the end of our second chapter, where we sought to enclose the energy-complex of our universe.

In Omega we have in the first place the principle we needed to explain both the persistent march of things towards greater consciousness, and the paradoxical solidity of what is most fragile. Contrary to the appearances still admitted by physics, the Great Stability is not at the bottom in the infra-elementary sphere, but at the top in the ultra-synthetic sphere. It is thus entirely by its tangential envelope that the world goes on dissipating itself in a chance way into matter. By its radial nucleus it finds its shape and its natural consistency in gravitating against the tide of probability towards a divine focus of mind which draws it onward.

Thus something in the cosmos escapes from entropy, and does so more and more.

During immense periods in the course of evolution, the radial, obscurely stirred up by the action of the *Prime Mover ahead,* was only able to express itself, in diffuse aggregates, in animal consciousness. And at that stage, not being able, above them, to attach themselves to a support whose order of simplicity was greater than their own, the nuclei were hardly formed before they began to disaggregate. But as soon as, through reflection, a type of unity appeared no longer closed or even centred, but punctiform, the sublime physics of centres came into play. When they became centres, and therefore persons, the elements could at last begin to react, directly as such, to the personalising action of the centre of centres. When consciousness broke through the critical surface of hominisation, it really passed from divergence to convergence and changed, so to speak, both hemisphere and pole. Below that critical "equator" lay the relapse into multiplicity; above it, the plunge into growing and irreversible unification. Once formed, a reflective centre can no longer change except by involution upon itself. To outward appearance, admittedly, man disintegrated just like any animal. But here and there we find an inverse function of the phenomenon. By death, in the animal, the radial is reabsorbed into the tangential, while in man it escapes and is liberated from it. It escapes from entropy by turning back to Omega: the *hominisation* of death itself.

Thus from the grains of thought forming the veritable and indestructible atoms of its stuff, the universe — a well-defined universe in the outcome — goes on building itself above our heads in the inverse direction of matter which vanishes. The universe is a collector and conservator, not of mechanical energy, as we supposed, but of persons. All round us, one by one, like a continual exhalation, "souls" break away, carrying upwards their incommunicable load of consciousness. One by one, yet not in isolation. Since, for each of them, by the very nature of Omega, there can only be one possible point of definitive emersion — that point at which, under the synthesising action of personalising union, the noosphere (furling its elements upon themselves as it too furls upon itself) will reach collectively its point of convergence — at the "end of the world."

ANNEMARIE SCHIMMEL

Man and His Perfection in Islam

Annemarie Schimmel has translated into German a collection of Muslim prayers, and she has also translated the philosophical-theological writings of Muhammad Iqbal. Thus she is especially qualified to see the link of the Islamic piety and liturgy of the Koran with Islamic scholarship and speculation, as these are related to both morality and eschatology in the distinctively Muslim view of human "perfection."

THE POSITION of man in Islam, and especially in Sufism, has been a subject of controversy among Western scholars. Some of them have held that man, as "slave of God," has no importance whatsoever before the Almighty God; he almost disappears, loses his personality, and is nothing but an instrument of eternal fate. The concept of "humanism" of which European culture is so proud is, according to these scholars, basically alien to Islamic thought. Others have sensed in the development of later Sufism an inherent danger that might result in an absolute subjectivism, because the human personality is, so to speak, "inflated" to such an extent that it is considered the microcosm, the perfect mirror of God. The doctrine of the Perfect Man seemed, to some orientalists, extremely dangerous for Islamic anthropology — no less dangerous than the allegedly humiliating role of man as "slave of God."

It is, in fact, not easy to give an account of mystical anthropology in Islam, since it is as many-sided as Islam itself; the differences between the earliest and the later mystical currents are considerable. It is possible, therefore, to point to only a few facets of the problem that seem important for the understanding of "man" in Sufism, without even attempting to sketch most of the lines in the picture.

According to the Koran, man was created "by God's hands" (Sūra 38:75), an idea that the tradition elaborated: God kneaded Adam's clay forty days before He gave him life and spirit by breathing into him with His own breath (Sūra 15:29; 38:72). "That means, His Presence was operative 40,000 years upon him" (B 545), as Baqlī interprets this tradition. And he continues: "The form of Adam is the mirror of both worlds. Whatever has been put into these two kingdoms, was made visible in human form. 'And we will show them Our signs in the horizons and in themselves' " (Sūra 41:53; B 437).

This creation myth assigns an extremely high position to man: he is in every respect God's perfect work, living through His breath, and is, thus, almost a mirror reflecting God's qualities. As the tradition says, "He created Adam in His image" (ʿalā ṣūratihi). Adam, seen from this angle, is the prototype of the Perfect Man; he was blessed with the special grace of knowledge: "He taught Adam the names," says the Koran (Sūra 2:31). To know a thing's name means to be able to rule it, to use it for one's self: by virtue of his knowledge of the names, Adam became master over all created things. Yet the simple Koranic statement was sometimes explained to imply that God had granted Adam the knowledge of the divine names reflected in creation, which he might "use" in his prayers. Adam became, thus, the ʿallamaʾ l-asmāʾ-bēg, as Rūmī says, with a remarkable combination of Arabic and Turkish components (M 1:1234), "the prince of He taught the names." God made Adam his khalīfa, his vicegerent, on earth and ordered the angels to prostrate themselves before him — man is superior to the angels (cf. H 239), who have not been given the secret of the names and who do nothing but worship God in perfect obedience, whereas man enjoys — or suffers from — the choice between obedience and rebellion (though this choice may be limited by predestination). Man was entrusted with the amāna, the "trust" (Sūra 33:72) that Heaven and earth refused to carry — a trust that has been differently interpreted: as responsibility, free will, love, or the power of individuation. Yet the Sufis often longed for their true home, for the time and place of their lofty primeval state:

> We were in heaven, we were the companions of angels —
> when will we return there again?
>
> (D 463)

This remembrance of the paradisiacal days accompanies them in this vale of tears and leads them back from their worldly exile. In man, creation reaches its final point. One Bektashi poet wrote:

> This universe is a tree — man became its fruit.
> That which was intended is the fruit — do not think it
>   is the tree!
>
> (BO 118)

Later tradition ascribed to God the words *kuntu kanzan makhfiyan,* "I was a hidden treasure, and I wanted to be known, so I created the world." God, in His eternal loneliness, wanted to be known, so he created a world in which man is the highest manifestation. Man is the microcosm and is created — again according to a *hadīth qudsī* — for God's sake, who in turn created everything for man's sake.

The Koran has, indeed, assigned a very high place to man, without entering into detailed discussion. The Sufis, however, dwelt intently upon the different aspects of man. The operations of divine omnipotence are carried out on man; he is, as Rūmī says in a poignant image, "the astrolabe of the qualities of highness" (M 6:3138–43). The mystics have found numerous allusions in the Koran to prove man's lofty rank. One of their favorite verses in this respect is: "And we shall show you our signs on the horizons and in yourselves — do you not see?" (Sūra 41:53), a verse that they interpreted as God's order to look into their own hearts to find the source of knowledge and, eventually, the divine beloved, who is "closer than the jugular vein" (Sūra 50:16).

From this feeling the *hadīth* "*man ᶜarafa nafsahu faqad ᶜarafa rab-bahu,*" "who knows himself knows his Lord," must have developed; it may originally have been an adaptation of the Delphic *gnothi seauton,* "know yourself." The mystical theorists have relied heavily upon this tradition: to know one's innermost heart means to discover the point at which the divine is found as the *dulcis hospes animae,* the meeting point of the human and the divine. The *hadīth* has been interpreted differently. One of the finest allegories ever written is by Rūmī, who tells the story of Ayāz, Maḥmūd of Ghazna's favorite slave, who looked every morning at the outworn shoes and shabby clothes he wore before Maḥmūd elected him for himself; it was necessary for him to remember his former lowly state so that he could appreciate the bounty that his lord had bestowed upon him (M 5:2113). Thus, concludes Rūmī, man should likewise remember how weak he was created, and then he will recognize his nothingness before God, who gives him everything out of grace.

Most mystics, however, would interpret the *hadīth* as a condensation of the basic experience of the mystical path as a way inward, an interiorization of experience, a journey into one's own heart (CL 93).

This has been beautifully described by 'Aṭṭār in the *Muṣībatnāma,* where the hero eventually finds his peace in the ocean of the soul.

That God resides in the loving heart is expressed by another favorite tradition: "Heaven and earth contain Me not, but the heart of my faithful servant contains Me." The heart is the dwelling place of God; or it is, in other terminology, the mirror in which God reflects Himself. But this mirror has to be polished by constant asceticism and by permanent acts of loving obedience until all dust and rust have disappeared and it can reflect the primordial divine light.

Another image often used to show how man has to prepare for this state of "finding" is that of "breaking." One *ḥadīth qudsī* attests: "I am with those whose hearts are broken for My sake." The theme of breaking for the sake of construction is in full accord with ascetic practices as a preparatory stage. Junayd's statement that "God is affirmed more by Not-being than by Being" (P 1:45) led Massignon to the conclusion that the general tendency of Islamic theology is "to affirm God rather through destruction than through construction" (P 2:631). The *nafs* has to be broken, the body has to be broken, and the heart, too, has to be broken and everything in it naughted so that God can build a new mansion for Himself in it. For the ruined house contains treasures — such treasures can only be found by digging up the foundation (as the story of Khiḍr in Sūra 18 tells).

> Wherever there is a ruin, there is hope for a treasure —
> why do you not seek the treasure of God in the wasted
>   heart?
>
>   (D 141)

ᶜAṭṭār often spoke of "breaking" as a means of attaining peace and unity — be it the broken millstone, which no longer turns in endless restlessness (U 149), or the puppet-player in the *Ushturnāme,* who breaks all the figures he has used and puts them back into the box of unity (V 137). In later Sufi poetry, mainly in the Indo-Persian style around 1700 — when all the leading poets were under the influence of the Naqshbandiyya *ṭarīqa* — the word *shikast,* "broken," became a favorite term. Perhaps, in a period in which Muslim India broke down completely, they hoped to find some consolation in the idea that breaking is necessary for a new beginning.

The mystic may find the figure of the friend who dwells within the heart emptied of everything, may find in its ruin the hidden treasure and discover, in a jubilant experience, "What I have never found, I found in man!" (Y 79). The utterances of a number of enthusiastic mystics who had reached this state have often opened the way to a boundless feeling of all-embracing unity, which, along with the theories of Ibn ʿArabī, could easily lead to a state in which the boundary between man and God seemed forgotten. However, the Lord remains Lord, the slave, slave — this is the generally accepted viewpoint of moderate Sufism.

Sufi psychology, like everything else in Sufism, is based on Koranic ideas — the ideas on the *nafs,* the lowest principle of man, have already been mentioned. Higher than the *nafs* is the *qalb,* "heart," and the *rūḥ,* "spirit." This tripartition forms the foundation of later, more complicated systems; it is found as early as the Koranic commentary by Jaʿfar aṣ-Ṣādiq. He holds that the *nafs* is peculiar to the *ẓālim,* "tyrant," the *qalb* to the *muqtaṣid,* "moderate," and the *rūḥ* to the *sābiq,* "preceding one, winner"; the *ẓālim* loves God for his own sake, the *muqtaṣid* loves Him for Himself, and the *sābiq* annihilates his own will in God's will (W 17). Bāyezīd Bisṭāmī, al-Ḥakīm at-Tirmidhī, and Junayd have followed this tripartition. Kharrāz, however, inserts between *nafs* and *qalb* the element *ṭabʿ,* "nature," the natural functions of man (W 240–42).

At almost the same time in history, Nūrī saw in man four different aspects of the heart, which he derived in an ingenious way from the Koran:

Ṣadr, "breast," is connected with Islam (Sūra 39:23);
qalb, "heart," is the seat of *īmān,* "faith" (Sūra 49:7; 16:106);
fuʾād, "heart," is connected with *maʿrifa,* "gnosis" (Sūra 53:11); and
lubb, "innermost heart," is the seat of *tauḥīd* (Sūra 3:190) (W 321).

The Sufis often add the element of *sirr,* the innermost part of the heart in which the divine revelation is experienced. Jaʿfar introduced, in an interesting comparison, reason, *ʿaql,* as the barrier between *nafs* and *qalb* — "the barrier which they both cannot transcend" (Sūra 55:20), so that the dark lower instincts cannot jeopardize the heart's purity (W 163).

Each of these spiritual centers has its own functions, and ʿAmr al-Makkī has summed up some of the early Sufi ideas in a lovely myth:

> God created the hearts seven thousand years before the bodies
> and kept them in the station of proximity to Himself and He
> created the spirits seven thousand years before the hearts and
> kept them in the garden of intimate fellowship (*uns*) with

Himself, and the consciences — the innermost part — He
created seven thousand years before the spirits and kept them
in the degree of union (*wasl*) with Himself. Then he impris-
oned the conscience in the spirit and the spirit in the heart and
the heart in the body. Then He tested them and sent prophets,
and then each began to seek its own station. The body occupied itself with prayer, the heart attained to love, the spirit
arrived at proximity to its Lord, and the innermost part found
rest in union with Him.

Later Sufis have elaborated these comparatively simple teachings into
a minute system of correspondences in which every spiritual experience is connected with its respective recipient part.

In the same way, the different kinds of revelations (*kashf*) that are
granted to the Sufis have been classified on the basis of the different
levels of consciousness on which they occur and whether they lead to
intellectual or intuitive knowledge of the divine. A late mystic, relying
upon the traditional terminology, classifies the revelations as follows:

a) *Kashf kaunī*, revelation on the plane of the created things, is a result
   of pious actions and purifications of the lower soul; it becomes
   manifest in dreams and clairvoyance.
b) *Kashf ilāhī*, divine revelation, is a fruit of constant worship and
   polishing of the heart; it results in the knowledge of the world of
   spirits and in cardiognosy ["soul-reading"] so that the mystic sees
   the hidden things and reads the hidden thoughts.
c) *Kashf ʿaqlī*, revelation by reason, is essentially the lowest grade of
   intuitive knowledge; it can be attained by polishing the moral
   faculties, and can be experienced by the philosophers as well.
d) *Kashf īmānī*, revelation through faith, is the fruit of perfect faith
   after man has acquired proximity to the perfections of prophet-
   hood; then he will be blessed by direct divine addresses; he talks
   with the angels, meets the spirits of the prophets, sees the Night
   of Might and the blessings of the month of Ramaḍan in human
   form in the ʿālam al-mithāl. (IK 443–44).

On the whole, these last specifications belong to a later development
of Sufism; however, the different degrees of nonrational revelation of
supernatural realities have been accepted by all the mystics from early
times. They clearly distinguished the *ilm ladunnī* (cf. Sūra 18:65), the
"wisdom that is with and from God" and is granted to the gnostic by

an act of divine grace, from normal knowledge. They "tasted" (*dhauq*) in this experience new levels of revealed wisdom that were not to be attained by a scientific approach or by theological reasoning.

Good and Evil: The Role of Satan

One of the most fascinating aspects of mystical psychology in Islam is the way in which the Sufis have dealt with Satan, the power of evil. Satan, according to the Koran either a fallen angel or a jinn created from fire, plays a dominant role in the story of creation as told in the Koran (Sūra 2:28–34). According to some mystics, he was the teacher of the angels and in this role was even made the subject of a Bengali Muslim poem of the early seventeenth century, the *Iblīsnāme* by Sayyid Sulṭān. The author says that the angels were ordered to honor Iblis even after God had cursed him, since he had been their teacher — the same applies to the disciple who has to honor and obey his sheikh, even if the sheikh is a veritable satan.

A well-known tradition says that Satan sits in the blood of Adam's children (cf. S 471), and thus he could be equated with the *nafs*, the lower principle, the "flesh." But never in the history of Islam has Satan been given absolute power over men: he can tell them lies and seduce them as he did with Adam, but they have the possibility to resist his insinuations (Iqbal's Satan sadly complains that it is much too easy for him to seduce people). Iblis never becomes "evil as such"; he always remains a creature of God and, thus, a necessary instrument in His hands.

In some mystical circles something like a rehabilitation of Satan was attempted. It seems that this idea was first formulated by Ḥallāj: Satan boasts of having served God for thousands of years before Adam's creation, and his pride in being created from fire makes him refuse God's order to prostrate himself before Adam, newly created from clay. Ḥallāj recognizes only two true monotheists in the world, Muhammad and Satan — but Muhammad is the treasurer of divine grace, whereas Iblis has become the treasurer of divine wrath. In Ḥallāj's theory, Satan becomes "more monotheist than God Himself" (R 538). For God's eternal will is that no one should be worshiped except Him, and Satan refuses to fall down before a created being, notwithstanding God's explicit order. As Ḥallāj translates his outcry in a famous quatrain: "My rebellion means to declare Thee Holy!" Iblis was kept between will and order, and

> He was thrown in the water, his hands tied to his back,
> and He said to him: "Beware lest you become wet."

This tragic situation of Satan has inspired a number of poets to express their sympathies with him whose predicament, in a certain sense, foreshadowed the difficulties man would have to undergo in this world. The most beautiful poem in this respect is that by Sanā'ī (SD 871) — a first great "Lament of Satan," in which the fallen angel, whose "heart was the nest for the Sīmurgh of love," complains of God's ruse: He had intended from eternity to condemn him and made Adam the outward cause for his fall:

> He put the hidden snare into my way —
> Adam was the corn in the ring of this snare.
> He wanted to give me the mark of curse —
> He did what He wanted — the earthen Adam was but an
> excuse.

To be sure, Satan had read on the Well-preserved Tablet that one creature would be cursed by God — but how could he, with his thousands of treasures of obedience, expect that it would be he himself? There are few poems that show the tragic greatness of Iblis better than this little-known *ghazal* by the master of Ghazna.

Sanā'ī may have been influenced in his thought by his elder contemporary Aḥmad Ghazzālī (d. 1126), the classical representative of Satan's rehabilitation, who dared to say: "Who does not learn *tauḥīd* from Satan, is an infidel" — a remark that infuriated the orthodox but found an echo in many later Sufi writings. ʿAṭṭār follows him in his approach — he too sees in Iblis the perfect monotheist and lover, who, once cursed by God, accepts this curse as a robe of honor; for (in the true Ḥallājian tradition), "to be cursed by Thee, is a thousand times dearer to me than to turn my head away from Thee to anything else" (cf. MT 217). Iblis becomes here the model of the perfect lover, who obeys every wish of the beloved and prefers eternal separation willed by the beloved to the union for which he longs. Centuries later Sarmad, the Jewish convert to Sufism (executed 1661) in Mogul India, shocked the orthodox with a quatrain in which he called men to imitate Satan:

> Go, learn the method of servantship from Satan:
> Choose one *qibla* and do not prostrate yourself before
> anything else.
>
> (AP 238)

Even the poetry of the eighteenth-century mystic Shāh ʿAbduʾl-Laṭīf in the remote province of Sind calls the reader to admire Iblis as the one true lover and to follow his example — a verse that has caused considerable puzzlement to the commentators.

Other mystics, however, have seen in Iblis's refusal to fall down before Adam not only an act of disobedience — the prototype of all disobedience in the world — but an act resulting from lack of love. Iblis was, as Rūmī has repeatedly asserted, one-eyed: He saw only Adam's form, made of dust, and therefore boasted, "I am better than he," fire being superior to clay. But he overlooked the decisive fact that God had breathed His breath into man and formed him according to His image (M 4:1617). He is, thus, a representative of one-eyed intellectualism, lacking in that divine love that is Adam's heritage, as Rūmī (M 4:1402) and, following him, Iqbal have shown.

Satan becomes a tragic figure, lost, hopeless, and lonely, sometimes visualized by the mystics in a sad attire or playing melancholy songs of separation. The manifold aspects of Satan developed throughout the centuries by the Sufis have been echoed, in our day, in the work of Muhammad Iqbal, whose multicolored picture of Satan is quite unusual. He sees in him the lover as well as the intellectual, the monotheist and the spirit of evil who longs to be overcome by the perfect man (faithful to the Prophetic tradition, "My shaytān has become Muslim") and to be broken in order to find salvation. Thus, he will eventually prostrate himself before man, who proves stronger than he. On the other hand, Iqbal has also employed the more common image of Satan the seducer, the materialist, and the destroyer.

The problems of Satanology are closely connected with those of good and evil and, thus, with predestination and free will. These problems constituted the subject of the first theological discussions in early Islamic thought and have never ceased to puzzle the minds of the pious. For if there is no agent but God, what is the role of man? To what extent can his deeds and actions be attributed to him? What is the derivation of evil? To what extent is man caught, like the mythical Satan, between divine will and divine order?

"Predestination (qadar) is the secret of God with which neither a close angel nor a sent messenger is acquainted." It is, as Rūzbihān Baqlī says, quoting this alleged hadīth, "the divine mystery from the time before creation, which nothing created in time can ever hope to solve" (B 175). The mystics knew well that an unquestioned acceptance of all-embracing predestination could produce dangerous consequences for human activities and faith. The early ascetics, though, were never certain about their fate. In spite of their supererogative prayers, vigils, and fasts, they constantly dreaded the Day of Judgment that might lead them to Hell, according to God's eternal decree: "These to Hell, and I do not care, and those to Paradise, and I do not care" — this *ḥadīth* is quoted even by Ghazzālī to point to the inscrutability of the divine will.

Later mystics tried to solve the problem by the introduction of the principle of love: the will of someone who has reached annihilation through asceticism, suffering, and love persists in God's will. Then man no longer attributes any actions to himself but lives and works, so to speak, out of the divine will, thus experiencing the *jabr maḥmūd*, "agreeable constraint."

More outspoken than other Sufis, Rūmī pondered the incompatibility of piety and the acceptance of a blind predestination. He charmingly told the story of a man who climbed a tree and ate the fruit, assuring the gardener that "this is God's garden, and I am eating from God's fruit given by Him." The gardener, thereupon, nicely thrashed him "with the stick of God" until the thief had to acknowledge that the transgression was done by his own will, not by God's order (M 5:3077–100).

In the same line of thought, Rūmī refuses to believe in the generally accepted explanation of the *ḥadīth* "*qad jaffa'l-qalam*," "the pen has dried up," which means that nothing once decreed and written on the Well-preserved Tablet can ever be changed. This *ḥadīth*, he thinks, says that God has ordered once and for all that the good deeds of the faithful shall never be lost, but not that good and evil actions are of equal value (M 5:3131–53).

> Dress in that material which you yourself have woven,
> and drink the product of what you have planted.
>
> (M 5:3181)

This *ḥadīth* is not an invitation to laziness but rather a charge to work harder and to act in perfect sincerity so that one's service becomes purer and thus more acceptable (M 5:3113). For,

> One beats a cow when it refuses to carry the yoke,
> but not because it does not put on wings!
>
> (M 5:3110)

One may also argue that man's acting in accordance with his God-given nature constitutes, in itself, an identification with the divine purpose in creation: whatever God brings into existence and allows to be done must be useful for some good end, even though man may not be able to see the final goal of his own action. Man is, as the tradition says, "between the two fingers of the Merciful." That means that each action has two faces, each state of constraint has in itself an extension, just as in the very act of breathing extension and compression are united. In the same way, God manifests Himself through His different and contradictory attributes and names, and the manifestation of the attribute of majesty is as necessary as that of kindness for the maintenance of the current of creation. Man sees only the outward phenomena and takes them at face value but rarely thinks of the hidden power that brings them into existence. He sees — to use Rūmī's favorite comparison — the dust but not the wind; he looks at the foam but not at the bottom of the sea. The divine is the *coincidentia oppositorum,* but in order to become known it has to show itself in contrasting forms and colors, for the absolute light is too strong to be perceived and must be broken through material media. Through the opposite of light one recognizes the light (M 1:1133). Thus, the mystic can understand that God's wrath is mercy in disguise, and that the pain and punishment that He inflicts upon those who love Him are necessary for their spiritual growth — just as bitter medicine is necessary for the sick. How often is man misled by the delusion of outward appearances:

> How many enmities were friendship,
> how many destructions were renovation!
> (M 5:186)

For God hides His grace in wrath and His wrath in grace. And everything created shows this double face:

> The cold wind became a murderer for the people of ʿĀd,
> but for Solomon it served as a porter.
>
> (M 6:2660)

Poison is the life element for the serpent, but it carries death to others (M 5:3295). The figure of Khiḍr, whose seemingly illogical actions had a deep meaning, can be understood from this viewpoint.

On the other hand, the Sufi should not only accept good and evil as coming from God and therefore equally welcome, he should also be careful that no ruse be hidden in grace. Constant watchfulness is required to keep the soul safe.

The great theosophists of later centuries have devoted detailed studies to the will and knowledge of God, discussing minutely the relation of the human to the divine will. A good example is Jīlī's thought, as explained so excellently by Reynold A. Nicholson. But even the most learned systems could not eliminate the painful dilemma of predestination and free will; for this problem cannot be solved by intellect but only, if at all, by love. Ḥallāj, Rūmī, and their followers understood that the *jabr maḥmūd,* the "higher predestination," as Iqbal calls it, can be achieved not simply by accepting a given situation but by actively conforming with God's will through love and prayer. Once such a change of human will is achieved by absolute and loving surrender, the mystic can hope for new doors to open before him on his spiritual path into the depths of God —

> And if He closes before you all the ways and passes,
> He will show a hidden way which nobody knows.
>
> (D 765)

NISHIDA KITARŌ

A Study of Good

Nishida Kitarō (1875–1945) taught at Kanazawa Higher School and at the University of Kyoto. His book *A Study of Good* is, as the Japanese National Committee for UNESCO declared, "one of the most monumental works by a modern Japanese author" and is still regarded in Japan as indispensable to students of philosophy; yet despite his acquaintance with Western thought, "Nishida belongs to the East," as his lifelong friend Suzuki once said.

WE CALL THE FOUNDATION of this universe God. I do not view God as a transcendent creator outside the universe, but I think He is directly the foundation of this reality. The relationship between God and the universe is not a relationship such as that between an artist and his work, but is the relationship between essence and phenomenon, and the universe is not a thing created by God, but is a "manifestation" of God. From the movement of the sun, moon and constellations to the inner workings of the human soul, among all there is nothing which is not a manifestation of God; at the foundation of these things, through each one we are able to worship the spiritual light of God.

Just as Newton and Kepler in seeing the order of the movement of the heavens were struck with the idea of devotion, the more we study natural phenomena the more we are able to know that one unifying power behind them is in control. The advance of learning is nothing more than the unity of this kind of knowledge. In this way, just as we recognize without, in the foundation of nature, the control of one unifying force, so too must we recognize within, in the foundation of the human soul as well, the control of one unifying force. Even though the human heart appears in a thousand forms and ten thousand states and appears to be almost without a fixed law, when we contemplate it, it seems that both in the past and the present, throughout East and West, a tremendous unifying force is in control. When, advancing further, we consider the matter, we see that nature and spirit are not things which are utterly without communication but that one has an intimate relationship with the other. We are unable not to think of the unity of these two, i.e., that there must be an even greater single unifying force at the foundation of these two. In both philosophy and science there is no one who does not recognize this unity. And this unity is precisely God. Of course, if as materialists and most scientists say, matter is the only reality and the manifold things merely follow the laws of material force, we probably are unable to think that there is such a thing as God. But is the true aspect of reality after all this kind of thing?

As I have discussed previously concerning reality, we are unable to know even matter separately as an independent reality apart from our phenomena of consciousness. The facts of direct experience which are given to us are only these phenomena of consciousness. Space, time, and material force are all nothing more than concepts established on behalf of unifying and explaining these facts. Such a thing as pure matter which has excluded the nature of all of us individuals, such as physicists speak of, is an abstract concept most distant from concrete fact. The more one approaches concrete facts, the more they become individual. The most concrete fact is that which is most individual. For this reason, primitive explanations, as in mythology, were all person-ificatory, but as pure knowledge advanced, they became increasingly general and abstract, and finally we arrived at creating a concept such as that of pure matter. While this kind of explanation is extremely external and shallow, however, we must not forget that in back of it also there is concealed a thing which is our subjective unity. The most basic explanation necessarily comes to return to the self. The secret key of explaining the universe lies in this self. We must say that to attempt to explain spirit according to matter is to have inverted cause and effect.

Also that which Newton and Kepler observed and considered as the order of natural phenomena actually is nothing more than the order of our phenomena of consciousness. Consciousness is all established according to unity. And this unity, from the smallest, the unity within the daily consciousness of each individual, arrives at the largest, the universal unity of consciousness which combines the consciousness of all men. (To limit the unity of consciousness within individual consciousness is nothing more than a dogmatism added to pure experience.) The natural world is one system of consciousness composed according to this kind of trans-individual unity. We unify the experience of the self according to individual subjectivity and we further proceed to unify the experience of each individual according to the trans-individual subjectivity, and the natural world is born as the object of this trans-individual subjectivity. Royce too stated that the existence of nature is combined with the faith in the existence of our fellow man. Thus it comes about that we say that even the unity of the natural world is ultimately nothing more than a kind of unity of consciousness. It is not that originally there are two kinds of reality, spirit and nature; the distinction of these two arises from the difference of the way of looking at an identical reality. In the facts of direct experience there is not the opposition of subject and object, there is not the distinction of spirit and matter; matter equals spirit, spirit equals matter, and there is only one actuality. However, the conflict of the systems of this kind of reality, i.e., if seen from one side, the opposition of subject and object from their development, comes to appear. In other words, in the continuation of intellectual perception there is not the distinction of subject and object; however, this opposition comes to arise by means of reflection. At the time of conflict of systems of reality the aspect of their unifying function is thought of as spirit, and the aspect which opposes as its object is thought of as nature. So-called objective nature too, however, actually cannot exist apart from subjective unity, and in subjective unity as well it cannot be expected that there exists unity without the object of unity, namely, content. Both together are the same kind of reality, and merely differ in the form of their unity. Moreover, each of these which leans to one side is an abstract, incomplete reality. This kind of reality in the union of the two first becomes perfect, concrete reality. That which is the unity of spirit and nature does not unify two kinds of systems; originally they are under the identical unity.

If in this kind of reality there is not the distinction between spirit and nature and consequently there are not two kinds of unities, and only the facts of the identical direct experience themselves create various distinctions according to the way of looking at the matter, the God who is the foundation of the reality I mentioned previously must be the foundation of the facts of this direct experience, i.e., of our phenomena of consciousness. However, all of our phenomena of consciousness are things which constitute a system. Even the so-called natural phenomena which are formed according to the trans-individual unity cannot depart from this form. The self-development of a certain unifying thing is the form of all reality, and God is the unifier of this kind of reality. The relationship of the universe and God is the relationship of our phenomena of consciousness with their unity. Even as in both thought and the will mental images are unified by means of one object concept, and all are considered as expressions of this unifying concept, God is the unifier of the universe, and the universe is the expression of God. This comparison is not merely metaphoric, it is fact. God is the greatest and ultimate unifier of our consciousness; nay, our consciousness is a part of the consciousness of God, and its unity comes from the unity of God. From the smallest, our single joy and single sorrow, to the largest, the movement of the sun, moon, and constellations — in all there is nothing which is not based on this unity. Newton and Kepler too were struck by the unity of this tremendous universal consciousness.

If this be so, what kind of a thing is God who in this sense is the unifier of the universe and the foundation of reality? That which controls spirit must be the laws of spirit. Such a thing as matter, as I have said above, is nothing more than a most shallow, abstract concept established on behalf of explanation. Spiritual phenomena are the function of so-called intelligence, emotion, and will, and that which controls them must also be the laws of intelligence, emotion, and will. And spirit is not merely the combination of these functions, but behind it there is one unifying force, and these phenomena are its expression. If we now call this unifying force personality, we must say that God is one great personality who is the foundation of the universe. From the phenomena of nature to the historical development of mankind, in each great thought there is nothing which does not have the form of a great will, and the universe we come to call the personality expression of God. However, even speaking in this way, I cannot think, as people of a certain school think, that God transcends the universe and is something like our subjective spirit possessing separately a particular thought and will apart from the advance of the universe. In God intelligence equals action and action equals intelligence; reality must be directly the thought and the will of God. Such things as our subjective thought and will are imperfect, abstract realities arising from the conflict of various systems. We are unable to compare these kinds of things with God directly. Illingworth, in his book entitled *The Personality of God and Man,* gives three things as the elements of personality: self-awareness, freedom of the will, and love. Before one considers these three things as elements of personality, however, one must make clear what kind of facts these functions mean in practice. Self-awareness is a phenomenon which accompanies the circumstance wherein a partial system of consciousness is unified in the center of the entire consciousness. Self-awareness emerges according to reflection, and reflection of the self is the function which seeks the center of this kind of consciousness. The self does not exist outside of the unifying function of consciousness, and if this unity is changed the self too changes; apart from this such a thing as the basic substance of the self is nothing more than an empty term. We think that turning inwardly we acquire the consciousness of a kind of special self, but as the psychologists say, this is nothing more than an emotion which accompanies this unity. It is not that if there is this kind of consciousness, this unity takes place, but if there is this unity, this kind of consciousness is born. This unity itself cannot become the object of knowledge; we can become this thing and operate but we cannot know it. True self-awareness resides rather in the activity of the will and not in intellectual reflection. If there is self-awareness in the personality of God, the unity of the phenomena of this universe must be those self-awarenesses one-by-one. For example that the sum of all the angles of a triangle equals two right angles must be thought of in this way by everyone in every era. This too is one self-awareness of God. It is probably correct to say that all the ideas of universal unity which control our spirit are the self-same consciousness of God. The myriad things are established according to the unity of God, in God everything is actuality, and God is always active. In God there is neither past nor future; time and space are born according to the universal unity of consciousness, and in God everything is the present. As Augustine has said, because time was created by God and God transcends time, God resides in the eternal now. Therefore, in God there is no reflection, there is no memory, there is no hope, and consequently there is no consciousness of a special self. Since everything is the self and apart from the self there is nothing, there is no consciousness of the self.

Next, even in the freedom of the will there are various meanings, but true freedom must be in the sense of so-called necessary freedom which operates from the internal characteristics of the self. Not only is such a thing as a will wholly without cause indeed irrational, but this kind of a thing is an utterly accidental event in the self too, and the free behavior of the self probably cannot be felt. Since God is the basis of the myriad existences and apart from Him there is not anything which is, and the myriad things all emerge from the internal characteristics of God, He is free, and in this sense God truly is absolute freedom. If we speak in this way, perhaps it seems as if God is restricted by the characteristics of the self and loses his omnipotence, but to operate contrary to the characteristics of the self means the imperfection or the contradiction of the characteristics of the self. I think that the perfection and omniscience of God cannot stand together with His variable free will. Augustine too has stated that the will of God is unchanging and is not such a thing as one wherein at times He desires and at times He does not desire; still less is it one wherein after a previous decision He cancels it. Such a thing as a selective will must accompany rather the conscious states of us imperfect men, and it is not something which we attribute to God. For example, in things wherein we have become sufficiently proficient there is not the slightest space into which the selective will can enter, and the selective will becomes necessary in circumstances of doubt, contradiction, and conflict. Of course, as everyone says, within knowing already the fact of freedom is included; intelligence means precisely potentiality. It is not, however, that this potentiality must necessarily mean variable potentiality. Intelligence must not be used only in the case of reflection, for intuition too is intelligence. Intuition rather is true intelligence. The more intelligence becomes perfect, on the contrary, the more variable potentiality ceases. Since in this kind of God there is no variable will, i.e., voluntariness, the love of God too is not an illiberal love such as one wherein God loves a certain person and hates another person, wherein He causes a certain person to prosper and another to die. With God as the foundation of all reality, His love must be equal and universal; moreover, its self-development itself must be directly infinite love for us. Apart from the development of the myriad things of nature, there is no love of God. Originally love is the emotion which seeks unity, and the demand for self-unity is self-love, and the demand for unity of the self and another is altruism. Since the unifying function of God is directly the unifying function of all things, as Eckhardt has said, God's altruism must be precisely His self-love. Just as we love our own hands and feet so too does God love all things. Eckhardt has also stated that God's loving man is not a voluntary activity but must be that way.

As I have discussed above, even the statement that God is personal cannot be viewed directly as identical with our subjective spirit; rather it must be compared to the state of pure experience wherein there is no separation between subject and object and there is no distinction between the thing and the self. This state is truly the beginning and the end of our spirit and at the same time it is also the true aspect of reality. Even as Christ has said that the pure in heart shall see God, and also that he who is as a little child shall enter the kingdom of heaven, at such times our heart is closest to God. Pure experience too does not merely mean perceptive consciousness. At the rear of the reflective consciousness too there is unity, and the reflective consciousness is established according to it, i.e., this too is also a kind of pure experience. At the foundation of our consciousness in every kind of circumstance there is the unity of pure experience, and we cannot jump outside of this. We can view God in this sense as one great intellectual intuition at the foundation of the universe, and we can view Him as the unifier of pure experience which embraces the universe. In this way we can understand Augustine's statement that God intuits all things with an unchanging intuition and that God, while still, is in motion and while in motion, is still, and we are also able to perceive the meaning of such words as Eckhardt's *"Gottheit"* and Boehme's *"Stille ohne Wesen."* All unity of consciousness transcends change and must be clearly unchanging; and change comes to arise from this, i.e., it is that which moves and does not move. Moreover, the unity of consciousness cannot become the object of knowledge, and transcends all categories; we are unable to give it any fixed form, and all things are established according to it. Thus that which we call the spirit of God, seen from one side, is extremely inscrutable, but seen from another, on the contrary, is infinitely connected with our spirit. In this foundation of the unity of consciousness we are able directly to touch the visage of God. Therefore, Boehme too said that heaven is everywhere, where you stand and where you go are all heaven, and one arrives at God through the deepest internal life.

Certain people may say when I have discussed the matter as I have above that God becomes identical with the essence of matter, and that even if He is spiritual there is no distinction whatever between Him and reason or conscience and that He loses His living, individual personality. Individuality is able to emerge only from negative free will. (This is the point of argument wherein previously in medieval philosophy Scotus opposed Thomas.) Towards this kind of God we are certainly unable to arouse religious emotion. In religion, sin is not merely breaking the law, it is going against personality, and repentance is not merely moral, but it is an earnest act for having hurt a parent or having gone against a benefactor. Erskine of Linlathen stated that religion and morality are divided according to whether or not one recognizes personality at the rear of conscience. As such men as Hegel have said, however, true individuality does not exist apart from generality, and that which is limited by generality ("*bestimmte Allgemeinheit*") becomes individuality. That which is general is the spirit of that which is concrete. Individuality is not that which is added as a certain other thing to generality from without, but that which has developed from generality becomes individuality. In something which is merely an accidental combination of various characteristics without the least internal unity, there is nothing which must be called individuality. The freedom of the will which is an element of individual personality means that that which is general limits itself ("self-determination"). Just as the concept of a triangle can be divided into various triangles, that a certain general thing is aware of the potentiality of various limits included within it is the feeling of freedom. From absolute free will wholly without foundation, on the contrary, individual self-awareness probably does not arise. Although there is the expression "in individuality there is no reason" ("*ratio singularitatis frustra quaeritur*"), this kind of individuality must truly be identical with a nothingness wholly without content. However, it is only that concrete individuality cannot be known by abstract concepts. Even individuality which cannot be expressed by abstract concepts can be expressed clearly by the brush of an artist or a novelist.

In saying that God is the unity of the universe, I do not mean merely a unity of an abstract concept, for God is a concrete unity like our individual self, i.e., one living spirit. Just as we are able to say that our spirit, in the sense which I have stated above, is individual, we are probably able to say that God too is individual. Reason and conscience may be a part of the unifying function of God, but they are not His living spirit itself. The existence of this kind of divine spirit is not merely a philosophical discussion but is a fact of spiritual experience in actuality. At the bottom of our consciousness, in everyone this kind of spirit is working. (Reason and conscience are its voice.) However, when we are hindered by our small self, we are unable to know it. For example, such a man as the poet Tennyson too had the following kind of experience. When he intoned his own name softly from the great depths of his own individual consciousness, the individuality of the self dissolved and became infinite reality, and it was certainly not that consciousness was vague but that it was most clear and certain. He stated that at that time death was a laughable impossibility and that the death of the individual was felt as true life. He says that from childhood on occasions of lonely solitude he often had this kind of experience. Also such a man as the literary figure J. A. Symonds has stated that while our ordinary consciousness gradually becomes dim, the original consciousness at its base becomes strong, and finally only one pure, absolute, abstract self remains. In addition, if one were to present the religious mystics' experience of this kind, there would be no limit. Perhaps one may consider all of these kinds of phenomena as morbid, but whether they are morbid or not comes to be decided according to whether they are rational or not. As I have stated previously, if one considers that reality is spiritual and our spirit is nothing more than a small part of it, then there is not the slightest reason to be astounded that when we break the small consciousness of the self we become aware of one great spirit. Perhaps our clinging fast to the limits of our small consciousness is instead error. I think that in great men, of necessity, there must be, as above, a far deeper spiritual experience than in ordinary men.

DIETRICH BONHOEFFER

Letters from Prison

Dietrich Bonhoeffer (1906–1945) is best remembered for having become a victim of the Nazi Gestapo, who hanged him for his part in a plot to assassinate Adolf Hitler. For him, his political action was of a piece with his Christian faith, which he voiced in his *Letters from Prison* with great courage and with a radical conviction that existing forms of religious belief and practice were no longer adequate to a secularized "world come of age."

TEN YEARS is a long time in anyone's life. As time is the most valuable thing that we have, because it is the most irrevocable, the thought of any lost time troubles us whenever we look back. Time lost is time in which we have failed to live a full human life, gain experience, learn, create, enjoy, and suffer; it is time that has not been filled up, but left empty. These last years have certainly not been like that. Our losses have been great and immeasurable, but time has not been lost. It is true that the knowledge and experience that were gained, and of which one did not become conscious till later, are only abstractions of reality, of life actually lived. "But just as the capacity to forget is a gift of grace, so memory, the recalling of lessons we have learnt, is also part of responsible living." In the following pages I should like to try to give some account of what we have experienced and learnt in common during these years — not personal experiences, or anything systematically arranged, or arguments and theories, but conclusions reached more or less in common by a circle of like-minded people, and related to the business of human life, put down one after the other, the only connection between them being that of concrete experience. There is nothing new about them, for they were known long before; but it has been given to us to reach them anew by first-hand experience. One cannot write about these things without a constant sense of gratitude for the fellowship of spirit and community of life that have been proved and preserved throughout these years.

No Ground under Our Feet

One may ask whether there have ever before in human history been people with so little ground under their feet — people to whom every available alternative seemed equally intolerable, repugnant, and futile, who looked beyond all these existing alternatives for the source of their strength so entirely in the past or in the future, and who yet, without being dreamers, were able to await the success of their cause so quietly and confidently. Or perhaps one should rather ask whether the responsible thinking people of any generation that stood at a turning-point in history did not feel much as we do, simply because something new was emerging that could not be seen in the existing alternatives.

Who Stands Fast?

The great masquerade of evil has played havoc with all our ethical concepts. For evil to appear disguised as light, charity, historical necessity, or social justice is quite bewildering to anyone brought up on our traditional ethical concepts, while for the Christian who bases his life on the Bible it merely confirms the fundamental wickedness of evil.

The *reasonable* people's failure is obvious. With the best intentions and a naïve lack of realism, they think that with a little reason they can bend back into position the framework that has got out of joint. In their lack of vision they want to do justice to all sides, and so the conflicting forces wear them down with nothing achieved. Disappointed by the world's unreasonableness, they step aside in resignation or collapse before the stronger party.

Still more pitiable is the total collapse of moral *fanaticism*. The fanatic thinks that his single-minded principles qualify him to do battle with the powers of evil; but like a bull he rushes at the red cloak instead of at the person who is holding it; he exhausts himself and is beaten. He gets entangled in non-essentials and falls into the trap set by cleverer people.

Then there is the man with a *conscience,* who fights single-handed against heavy odds in situations that call for a decision. But the scale of the conflicts in which he has to choose — with no advice or support except from his own conscience — tears him to pieces. Evil approaches him in so many respectable and seductive disguises that his conscience becomes nervous and vacillating, till at last he contents himself with a salved instead of a clear conscience, so that he lies to his own conscience in order to avoid despair; for a man whose only support is his conscience can never realize that a bad conscience may be stronger and more wholesome than a deluded one.

From the perplexingly large number of possible decisions, the way of *duty* seems to be the sure way out. Here, what is commanded is accepted as what is most certain, and the responsibility for it rests on the commander, not on the person commanded. But no one who confines himself to the limits of duty ever goes so far as to venture, on his sole responsibility, to act in the only way that makes it possible to score a direct hit on evil and defeat it. The man of duty will in the end have to do his duty by the devil too.

As to the man who asserts his complete *freedom* to stand four-square to the world, who values the necessary deed more highly than an unspoilt conscience or reputation, who is ready to sacrifice a barren principle for a fruitful compromise, or the barren wisdom of a middle course for a fruitful radicalism — let him beware lest his freedom should bring him down. He will assent to what is bad so as to ward off something worse, and in doing so he will no longer be able to realize that the worse, which he wants to avoid, might be the better. Here we have the raw material of tragedy.

Here and there people flee from public altercation into the sanctuary of private *virtuousness*. But anyone who does this must shut his mouth and his eyes to the injustice around him. Only at the cost of self-deception can he keep himself pure from the contamination arising from responsible action. In spite of all that he does, what he leaves undone will rob him of his peace of mind. He will either go to pieces because of this disquiet, or become the most hypocritical of Pharisees.

Who stands fast? Only the man whose final standard is not his reason, his principles, his conscience, his freedom, or his virtue, but who is ready to sacrifice all this when he is called to obedient and responsible action in faith and in exclusive allegiance to God — the responsible man, who tries to make his whole life an answer to the question and call of God. Where are these responsible people?

Civil Courage?

What lies behind the complaint about the dearth of civil courage? In recent years we have seen a great deal of bravery and self-sacrifice, but civil courage hardly anywhere, even among ourselves. To attribute this simply to personal cowardice would be too facile a psychology; its background is quite different. In a long history, we Germans have had to learn the need for and the strength of obedience. In the subordination of all personal wishes and ideas to the tasks to which we have been called, we have seen the meaning and the greatness of our lives. We have looked upwards, not in servile fear, but in free trust, seeing in our tasks a call, and in our call a vocation. This readiness to follow a command from "above" rather than our own private opinions and wishes was a sign of legitimate self-distrust. Who would deny that in obedience, in their task and calling, the Germans have again and again shown the utmost bravery and self-sacrifice? But the German has kept his freedom — and what nation has talked more passionately of freedom than the Germans, from Luther to the idealist philosophers? — by seeking deliverance from self-will through service to the community. Calling and freedom were to him two sides of the same thing. But in this he misjudged the world; he did not realize that his submissiveness and self-sacrifice could be exploited for evil ends. When that happened, the exercise of the calling itself became questionable, and all the moral principles of the German were bound to totter. The fact could not be escaped that the German still lacked something fundamental: he could not see the need for free and responsible action, even in opposition to his task and his calling; in its place there appeared on the one hand an irresponsible lack of scruple, and on the other a self-tormenting punctiliousness that never led to action. Civil courage, in fact, can grow only out of the free responsibility of free men. Only now are the Germans beginning to discover the meaning of free responsibility. It depends on a God who demands responsible action in a bold venture of faith, and who promises forgiveness and consolation to the man who becomes a sinner in that venture.

Of Success

Although it is certainly not true that success justifies an evil deed and shady means, it is impossible to regard success as something that is ethically quite neutral. The fact is that historical success creates a basis for the continuance of life, and it is still a moot point whether it is ethically more responsible to take the field like a Don Quixote against a new age, or to admit one's defeat, accept the new age, and agree to serve it. In the last resort success makes history; and the ruler of history repeatedly brings good out of evil over the heads of the history-makers. Simply to ignore the ethical significance of success is a short-circuit created by dogmatists who think unhistorically and irresponsibly; and it is good for us sometimes to be compelled to grapple seriously with the ethical problem of success. As long as goodness is successful, we can afford the luxury of regarding it as having no ethical significance; it is when success is achieved by evil means that the problem arises. In the face of such a situation we find that it cannot be adequately dealt with, either by theoretical dogmatic arm-chair criticism, which means a refusal to face the facts, or by opportunism, which means giving up the struggle and surrendering to success. We will not and must not be either outraged critics or opportunists, but must take our share of responsibility for the moulding of history in every situation and at every moment, whether we are the victors or the vanquished. One who will not allow any occurrence whatever to deprive him of his responsibility for the course of history — because he knows that it has been laid on him by God — will thereafter achieve a more fruitful relation to the events of history than that of barren criticism and equally barren opportunism. To talk of going down fighting like heroes in the face of certain defeat is not really heroic at all, but merely a refusal to face the future. The ultimate question for a responsible man to ask is not how he is to extricate himself heroically from the affair, but how the coming generation is to live. It is only from this question, with its responsibility towards history, that fruitful solutions can come, even if for the time being they are very humiliating. In short, it is much easier to see a thing through from the point of view of abstract principle than from that of concrete responsibility. The rising generation will always instinctively discern which of these we make the basis of our actions, for it is their own future that is at stake.

Of Folly

Folly is a more dangerous enemy to the good than evil. One can protest against evil; it can be unmasked and, if need be, prevented by force. Evil always carries the seeds of its own destruction, as it makes people, at the least, uncomfortable. Against folly we have no defence. Neither protests nor force can touch it; reasoning is no use; facts that contradict personal prejudices can simply be disbelieved — indeed, the fool can counter by criticizing them, and if they are undeniable, they can just be pushed aside as trivial exceptions. So the fool, as distinct from the scoundrel, is completely self-satisfied; in fact, he can easily become dangerous, as it does not take much to make him aggressive. A fool must therefore be treated more cautiously than a scoundrel; we shall never again try to convince a fool by reason, for it is both useless and dangerous.

If we are to deal adequately with folly, we must try to understand its nature. This much is certain, that it is a moral rather than an intellectual defect. There are people who are mentally agile but foolish, and people who are mentally slow but very far from foolish — a discovery that we make to our surprise as a result of particular situations. We thus get the impression that folly is likely to be, not a congenital defect, but one that is acquired in certain circumstances where people *make* fools of themselves or allow others to make fools of them. We notice further that this defect is less common in the unsociable and solitary than in individuals or groups that are inclined or condemned to sociability. It seems, then, that folly is a sociological rather than a psychological problem, and that it is a special form of the operation of historical circumstances on people, a psychological by-product of definite external factors. If we look more closely, we see that any violent display of power, whether political or religious, produces an outburst of folly in a large part of mankind; indeed, this seems actually to be a psychological and sociological law: the power of some needs the folly of the others. It is not that certain human capacities, intellectual capacities for instance, become stunted or destroyed, but rather that the upsurge of power makes such an overwhelming impression that men are deprived of their independent judgment, and — more or less unconsciously — give up trying to assess the new state of affairs for themselves. The fact that the fool is often stubborn must not mislead us into thinking that he is independent. One feels in fact, when talking to him, that one is dealing, not with the man himself, but with slogans, catchwords, and the like, which have taken hold of him. He is under a spell, he is blinded, his very nature is being misused and exploited. Having thus become a passive instrument, the fool will be capable of any evil and at the same time incapable of seeing that it is evil. Here lies the danger of a diabolical exploitation that can do irreparable damage to human beings.

But at this point it is quite clear, too, that folly can be overcome, not by instruction, but only by an act of liberation; and so we have to come to terms with the fact that in the great majority of cases inward liberation must be preceded by outward liberation, and that until that has taken place, we may as well abandon all attempts to convince the fool. In this state of affairs we have to realize why it is no use our trying to find out what "the people" really think, and why the question is so

superfluous for the man who thinks and acts responsibly — but
always given these particular circumstances. The Bible's words that
"the fear of the Lord is the beginning of wisdom" (Ps. 111.10) tell us
that a person's inward liberation to live a responsible life before God
is the only real cure for folly.

But there is some consolation in these thoughts on folly: they in no
way justify us in thinking that most people are fools in all circumstances. What will really matter is whether those in power expect more
from people's folly than from their wisdom and independence of mind.

Contempt for Humanity?

There is a very real danger of our drifting into an attitude of contempt
for humanity. We know quite well that we have no right to do so, and
that it would lead us into the most sterile relation to our fellow-men.
The following thoughts may keep us from such a temptation. It means
that we at once fall into the worst blunders of our opponents. The man
who despises another will never be able to make anything of him.
Nothing that we despise in the other man is entirely absent from
ourselves. We often expect from others more than we are willing to
do ourselves. Why have we hitherto thought so intemperately about
man and his frailty and temptability? We must learn to regard people
less in the light of what they do or omit to do, and more in the light
of what they suffer. The only profitable relationship to others — and
especially to our weaker brethren — is one of love, and that means the
will to hold fellowship with them. God himself did not despise
humanity, but became man for men's sake.

Immanent Righteousness

It is one of the most surprising experiences, but at the same time one
of the most incontrovertible, that evil — often in a surprisingly short
time — proves its own folly and defeats its own object. That does not
mean that punishment follows hard on the heels of every evil action;
but it does mean that deliberate transgression of the divine law in the
supposed interests of worldly self-preservation has exactly the opposite effect. We learn this from our own experience, and we can
interpret it in various ways. At least it seems possible to infer with
certainty that in social life there are laws more powerful than anything
that may claim to dominate them, and that it is therefore not only
wrong but unwise to disregard them. We can understand from this
why Aristotelian-Thomist ethics made wisdom one of the cardinal
virtues. Wisdom and folly are not ethically indifferent, as Neo-

protestant motive-ethics would have it. In the fulness of the concrete situation and the possibilities which it offers, the wise man at the same time recognizes the impassable limits that are set to all action by the permanent laws of human social life; and in this knowledge the wise man acts well and the good man wisely.

It is true that all historically important action is constantly overstepping the limits set by these laws. But it makes all the difference whether such overstepping of the appointed limits is regarded in principle as the superseding of them, and is therefore given out to be a law of a special kind, or whether the overstepping is deliberately regarded as a fault which is perhaps unavoidable, justified only if the law and the limit are re-established and respected as soon as possible. It is not necessarily hypocrisy if the declared aim of political action is the restoration of the law, and not mere self-preservation. The world is, in fact, so ordered that a basic respect for ultimate laws and human life is also the best means of self-preservation, and that these laws may be broken only on the odd occasion in case of brief necessity, whereas anyone who turns necessity into a principle, and in so doing establishes a law of his own alongside them, is inevitably bound, sooner or later, to suffer retribution. The immanent righteousness of history rewards and punishes only men's deeds, but the eternal righteousness of God tries and judges their hearts.

A Few Articles of Faith on the Sovereignty of God in History

I believe that God can and will bring good out of evil, even out of the greatest evil. For that purpose he needs men who make the best use of everything. I believe that God will give us all the strength we need to help us to resist in all time of distress. But he never gives it in advance, lest we should rely on ourselves and not on him alone. A faith such as this should allay all our fears for the future. I believe that even our mistakes and shortcomings are turned to good account, and that it is no harder for God to deal with them than with our supposedly good deeds. I believe that God is no timeless fate, but that he waits for and answers sincere prayers and responsible actions.

Confidence

There is hardly one of us who has not known what it is to be betrayed. The figure of Judas, which we used to find so difficult to understand, is now fairly familiar to us. The air that we breathe is so polluted by mistrust that it almost chokes us. But where we have broken through the layer of mistrust, we have been able to discover a confidence hitherto undreamed of. Where we trust, we have learnt to put our very lives into the hands of others; in the face of all the different interpretations that have been put on our lives and actions, we have learnt to trust unreservedly. We now know that only such confidence, which is always a venture, though a glad and positive venture, enables us really to live and work. We know that it is most reprehensible to sow and encourage mistrust, and that our duty is rather to foster and strengthen confidence wherever we can. Trust will always be one of the greatest, rarest, and happiest blessings of our life in community, though it can emerge only on the dark background of a necessary mistrust. We have learnt never to trust a scoundrel an inch, but to give ourselves to the trustworthy without reserve.

The Sense of Quality

Unless we have the courage to fight for a revival of wholesome reserve between man and man, we shall perish in an anarchy of human values. The impudent contempt for such reserve is the mark of the rabble, just as inward uncertainty, haggling and cringing for the favour of insolent people, and lowering oneself to the level of the rabble are the way of becoming no better than the rabble oneself. When we forget what is due to ourselves and to others, when the feeling for human quality and the power to exercise reserve cease to exist, chaos is at the door. When we tolerate impudence for the sake of material comforts, then we abandon our self-respect, the flood-gates are opened, chaos bursts the dam that we were to defend; and we are responsible for it all. In other times it may have been the business of Christianity to champion the equality of all men; its business today will be to defend passionately human dignity and reserve. The misinterpretation that we are acting for our own interests, and the cheap insinuation that our attitude is anti-social, we shall simply have to put up with; they are the invariable protests of the rabble against decency and order. Anyone who is pliant and uncertain in this matter does not realize what is at stake, and indeed in his case the reproaches may well be justified. We are witnessing the levelling down of all ranks of society, and at the same time the birth of a new sense of nobility, which is binding together a circle of men from all former social classes. Nobility arises from and exists by sacrifice, courage, and a clear sense of duty to oneself and society, by expecting due regard for itself as a matter of course; and it shows an equally natural regard for others, whether they are of higher or of lower degree. We need all along the line to recover the lost sense of quality and a social order based on quality. Quality is the greatest enemy of any kind of mass-levelling. Socially it means the renunciation of all place-hunting, a break with the cult of the "star," an open eye both upwards and downwards, especially in the choice of one's more intimate friends, and pleasure in private life as well as courage to enter public life. Culturally it means a return from the newspaper and the radio to the book, from feverish activity to un-hurried leisure, from dispersion to concentration, from sensational-ism to reflection, from virtuosity to art, from snobbery to modesty, from extravagance to moderation. Quantities are competitive, quali-ties are complementary.

Sympathy

We must allow for the fact that most people learn wisdom only by personal experience. This explains, first, why so few people are ca-pable of taking precautions in advance — they always fancy that they will somehow or other avoid the danger, till it is too late. Secondly, it explains their insensibility to the sufferings of others; sympathy grows in proportion to the fear of approaching disaster. There is a good deal of excuse on ethical grounds for this attitude. No one wants to meet fate head-on; inward calling and strength for action are acquired only in the actual emergency. No one is responsible for all the injustice and suffering in the world, and no one wants to set himself up as the judge of the world. Psychologically, our lack of imagination, of sen-sitivity, and of mental alertness is balanced by a steady composure, an ability to go on working, and a great capacity for suffering. But from a Christian point of view, none of these excuses can obscure the fact that the most important factor, large-heartedness, is lacking. Christ kept himself from suffering till his hour had come, but when it did come he met it as a free man, seized it, and mastered it. Christ, so the Scriptures tell us, bore the sufferings of all humanity in his own body as if they were his own — a thought beyond our comprehension — accepting them of his own free will. We are certainly not Christ; we are not called on to redeem the world by our own deeds and sufferings, and we need not try to assume such an impossible burden. We are not lords, but instruments in the hand of the Lord of history; and we can share in other people's sufferings only in a very limited degree. We are not Christ, but if we want to be Christians, we must have some share in Christ's large-heartedness by acting with responsibility and in freedom when the hour of danger comes, and by showing a real sympathy that springs, not from fear, but from the liberating and redeeming love of Christ for all who suffer. Mere waiting and looking on is not Christian behaviour. The Christian is called to sympathy and action, not in the first place by his own sufferings, but by the sufferings of his brethren, for whose sake Christ suffered.

Of Suffering

It is infinitely easier to suffer in obedience to a human command than in the freedom of one's own responsibility. It is infinitely easier to suffer with others than to suffer alone. It is infinitely easier to suffer publicly and honourably than apart and ignominiously. It is infinitely easier to suffer through staking one's life than to suffer spiritually. Christ suffered as a free man alone, apart and in ignominy, in body and spirit; and since then many Christians have suffered with him.

Present and Future

We used to think that one of the inalienable rights of man was that he should be able to plan both his professional and his private life. That is a thing of the past. The force of circumstances has brought us into a situation where we have to give up being "anxious about tomorrow" (Matt. 6.34). But it makes all the difference whether we accept this willingly and in faith (as the Sermon on the Mount intends), or under continual constraint. For most people, the compulsory abandonment of planning for the future means that they are forced back into living just for the moment, irresponsibly, frivolously, or resignedly; some few dream longingly of better times to come, and try to forget the present. We find both these courses equally impossible, and there remains for us only the very narrow way, often extremely difficult to find, of living every day as if it were our last, and yet living in faith and responsibility as though there were to be a great future: "Houses and fields and vineyards shall again be bought in this land" proclaims Jeremiah (32.15), in paradoxical contrast to his prophecies of woe, just before the destruction of the holy city. It is a sign from God and a pledge of a fresh start and a great future, just when all seems black. Thinking and acting for the sake of the coming generation, but being ready to go any day without fear or anxiety — that, in practice, is the spirit in which we are forced to live. It is not easy to be brave and keep that spirit alive, but it is imperative.

Optimism

It is wiser to be pessimistic; it is a way of avoiding disappointment and ridicule, and so wise people condemn optimism. The essence of optimism is not its view of the present, but the fact that it is the inspiration of life, and hope when others give in; it enables a man to hold his head high when everything seems to be going wrong; it gives him strength to sustain reverses and yet to claim the future for himself instead of abandoning it to his opponent. It is true that there is a silly, cowardly kind of optimism, which we must condemn. But the optimism that is will for the future should never be despised, even if it is proved wrong a hundred times; it is health and vitality, and the sick man has no business to impugn it. There are people who regard it as frivolous, and some Christians think it impious for anyone to hope and prepare for a better earthly future. They think that the meaning of present events is chaos, disorder, and catastrophe; and in resignation or pious escapism they surrender all responsibility for reconstruction and for future generations. It may be that the day of judgment will dawn tomorrow; and in that case, though not before, we shall gladly stop working for a better future.

Insecurity and Death

In recent years we have become increasingly familiar with the thought of death. We surprise ourselves by the calmness with which we hear of the death of one of our contemporaries. We cannot hate it as we used to, for we have discovered some good in it, and have almost come to terms with it. Fundamentally we feel that we really belong to death already, and that every new day is a miracle. It would probably not be true to say that we welcome death (although we all know that weariness which we ought to avoid like the plague); we are too inquisitive for that — or, to put it more seriously, we should like to see something more of the meaning of our life's broken fragments. Nor do we try to romanticize death, for life is too great and too precious. Still less do we suppose that danger is the meaning of life — we are not desperate enough for that, and we know too much about the good things that life has to offer, though on the other hand we are only too familiar with life's anxieties and with all the other destructive effects of prolonged personal insecurity. We still love life, but I do not think that death can take us by surprise now. After what we have been through during the war, we hardly dare admit that we should like death to come to us, not accidentally and suddenly through some trivial cause, but in the fulness of life and with everything at stake. It is we ourselves, and not outward circumstances, who make death what it can be, a death freely and voluntarily accepted.

Are We Still of Any Use?

We have been silent witnesses of evil deeds; we have been drenched by many storms; we have learnt the arts of equivocation and pretence; experience has made us suspicious of others and kept us from being truthful and open; intolerable conflicts have worn us down and even made us cynical. Are we still of any use? What we shall need is not geniuses, or cynics, or misanthropes, or clever tacticians, but plain, honest, straightforward men. Will our inward power of resistance be strong enough, and our honesty with ourselves remorseless enough, for us to find our way back to simplicity and straightforwardness?

VII VISIONS OF THE OTHER WORLD

Among the many aspects of religion — institutional, cultic, doctrinal, ethical — none is more difficult to define or even to describe than the mystical experience. It is not to be identified with religious experience as such, since there are many religious people, some would even say entire religious traditions, that do not know it. Nor is it, on the other hand, to be regarded as an alien element in any religion, for even the most austerely transcendent creeds such as Judaism and Islam (as the Hasidic and the Sufi schools of thought show) have been known to manifest mystical tendencies in their history. Wherever mysticism has appeared, moreover, it has contained so many similar elements that scholars have felt justified in speaking about it as a phenomenon that cannot be understood within the framework merely of this religion or of that one, but that must be interpreted as an authentic universal.

To speak of mystical experience as a "vision of the other world," as we have done here on the basis of the remarkable outpourings of ecstatic insight recorded in *Black Elk Speaks,* is to interpret it as a heightening of the general religious awareness that this imperfect world of sin and sorrow cannot be the only world there is. But whereas most believers, even most prophets, have had to content themselves with speaking only in general and metaphorical language about that awareness and about the yearning it arouses, it has been given to the mystical seers to catch a detailed glimpse of the other world and to find ways of speaking about it as though they were travelers returning from a far country.

So overpowering can the mystical experience be for an individual that the other dimensions of the religious life, and above all the moral dimension, can seem to disappear in the incandescent light of heaven. Most of the great mystics, regardless of their particular religious tradition, have strongly objected to this as a distortion of authentic vision. Sarvepalli Radhakrishnan's essay "Mysticism and Ethics in Hindu Thought," while based on the distinctive insight and discipline of the Indian tradition, presents a defense against the allegation of moral indifference that can, with due allowance for the differences, be applied to other species of mysticism as well.

At the same time, no characteristic emphasis of mystical thought has been as troubling, and yet as penetrating, as its cultivation of "negative theology," the recognition that any language about the Ultimate is perforce negative: God is neither a rock nor a pool of water nor a father, neither mighty nor ancient nor even real after the manner of any creature; but we must use all such terms in the awareness that they are not a literal description but an indication of what God is *not,* so that we may adore the mystery. In that adoration, the mystics of every tradition have their special contribution to make.

BLACK ELK

Visions of the Other World

Black Elk (1863–1950) was, as the subtitle of the book *Black Elk Speaks* calls him, "a holy man of the Oglala Sioux." The book, including this moving chapter, entitled "Visions of the Other World," came out of discourses he delivered in 1930 and 1931 "through" John J. Neihardt (Flaming Rainbow), a poet and journalist, who claimed, despite various criticisms, that he was faithfully reproducing what the ancient seer had said.

So I DRESSED MYSELF in a sacred manner, and before the dance began next morning I went among the people who were standing around the withered tree. Good Thunder, who was a relative of my father and later married my mother, put his arms around me and took me to the sacred tree that had not bloomed, and there he offered up a prayer for me. He said: "Father, Great Spirit, behold this boy! Your ways he shall see!" Then he began to cry.

I thought of my father and my brother and sister who had left us, and I could not keep the tears from running out of my eyes. I raised my face up to keep them back, but they came out just the same. I cried with my whole heart, and while I cried I thought of my people in despair. I thought of my vision, and how it was promised me that my people should have a place in this earth where they could be happy every day. I thought of them on the wrong road now, but maybe they could be brought back into the hoop again and to the good road.

Under the tree that never bloomed I stood and cried because it had withered away. With tears on my face I asked the Great Spirit to give it life and leaves and singing birds, as in my vision.

Then there came a strong shivering all over my body, and I knew that the power was in me.

Good Thunder now took one of my arms, Kicking Bear the other, and we began to dance. The song we sang was like this:

Who do you think he is that comes?
It is one who seeks his mother!

It was what the dead would sing when entering the other world and looking for their relatives who had gone there before them.

As I danced, with Good Thunder and Kicking Bear holding my arms between them, I had the queer feeling that I knew and I seemed to be lifted clear off the ground. I did not have a vision all that first day. That night I thought about the other world and that the Wanekia himself was with my people there and maybe the holy tree of my vision was really blooming yonder right then, and that it was there my vision had already come true. From the center of the earth I had been shown all good and beautiful things in a great circle of peace, and maybe this land of my vision was where all my people were going, and there they would live and prosper where no Wasichus were or could ever be.

Before we started dancing next day, Kicking Bear offered a prayer, saying: "Father, Great Spirit, behold these people! They shall go forth to-day to see their relatives, and yonder they shall be happy, day after day, and their happiness will not end."

Then we began dancing, and most of the people wailed and cried as they danced, holding hands in a circle; but some of them laughed with happiness. Now and then some one would fall down like dead, and others would go staggering around and panting before they would fall. While they were lying there like dead they were having visions, and we kept on dancing and singing, and many were crying for the old way of living and that the old religion might be with them again.

After awhile I began to feel very queer. First, my legs seemed to be full of ants. I was dancing with my eyes closed, as the others did. Suddenly it seemed that I was swinging off the ground and not touching it any longer. The queer feeling came up from my legs and was in my heart now. It seemed I would glide forward like a swing, and then glide back again in longer and longer swoops. There was no fear with this, just a growing happiness.

I must have fallen down, but I felt as though I had fallen off a swing when it was going forward, and I was floating head first through the air. My arms were stretched out, and all I saw at first was a single eagle feather right in front of me. Then the feather was a spotted eagle dancing on ahead of me with his wings fluttering, and he was making the shrill whistle that is his. My body did not move at all, but I looked ahead and floated fast toward where I looked.

There was a ridge right in front of me, and I thought I was going to run into it, but I went right over it. On the other side of the ridge I could see a beautiful land where many, many people were camping in a great circle. I could see that they were happy and had plenty. Everywhere there were drying racks full of meat. The air was clear and beautiful with a living light that was everywhere. All around the circle, feeding on the green, green grass, were fat and happy horses; and animals of all kinds were scattered all over the green hills, and singing hunters were returning with their meat.

I floated over the tepees and began to come down feet first at the center of the hoop where I could see a beautiful tree all green and full of flowers. When I touched the ground, two men were coming toward me, and they wore holy shirts made and painted in a certain way. They came to me and said: "It is not yet time to see your father, who is happy. You have work to do. We will give you something that you shall carry back to your people, and with it they shall come to see their loved ones."

I knew it was the way their holy shirts were made that they wanted me to take back. They told me to return at once, and then I was out in the air again, floating fast as before. When I came right over the dancing place, the people were still dancing, but it seemed they were not making any sound. I had hoped to see the withered tree in bloom, but it was dead.

Then I fell back into my body, and as I did this I heard voices all around and above me, and I was sitting on the ground. Many were crowding around, asking me what vision I had seen. I told them just what I had seen, and what I brought back was the memory of the holy shirts the two men wore.

That evening some of us got together at Big Road's tepee and decided to use the ghost shirts I had seen. So the next day I made ghost shirts all day long and painted them in the sacred manner of my vision. As I made these shirts, I thought how in my vision everything was like old times and the tree was flowering, but when I came back the tree was dead. And I thought that if this world would do as the vision teaches, the tree could bloom here too.

I made the first shirt for Afraid-of-Hawk and the second for the son of Big Road.

In the evening I made a sacred stick like that I had seen in my first vision and painted it red with the sacred paint of the Wanekia. On the top of it I tied one eagle feather, and this I carried in the dance after that, wearing the holy shirt as I had seen it.

Because of my vision and the power they knew I had, I was asked to lead the dance next morning. We all stood in a straight line, facing the west, and I prayed: "Father, Great Spirit, behold me! The nation that I have is in despair. The new earth you promised you have shown me. Let my nation also behold it."

After the prayer we stood with our right hands raised to the west, and we all began to weep, and right there, as they wept, some of them fainted before the dance began.

As we were dancing I had the same queer feeling I had before, as though my feet were off the earth and swinging. Kicking Bear and Good Thunder were holding my arms. Afterwhile it seemed they let go of me, and once more I floated head first, face down, with arms extended, and the spotted eagle was dancing there ahead of me again, and I could hear his shrill whistle and his scream.

I saw the ridge again, and as I neared it there was a deep, rumbling sound, and out of it there leaped a flame. But I glided right over it. There were six villages ahead of me in the beautiful land that was all clear and green in living light. Over these in turn I glided, coming down on the south side of the sixth village. And as I touched the ground, twelve men were coming towards me, and they said: "Our Father, the two-legged chief, you shall see!"

Then they led me to the center of the circle where once more I saw the holy tree all full of leaves and blooming.

But that was not all I saw. Against the tree there was a man standing with arms held wide in front of him. I looked hard at him, and I could not tell what people he came from. He was not a Wasichu and he was not an Indian. His hair was long and hanging loose, and on the left side of his head he wore an eagle feather. His body was strong and good to see, and it was painted red. I tried to recognize him, but I could not make him out. He was a very fine-looking man. While I was staring hard at him, his body began to change and became very beautiful with all colors of light, and around him there was light. He spoke like singing: "My life is such that all earthly beings and growing things belong to me. Your father, the Great Spirit, has said this. You too must say this."

Then he went out like a light in a wind.

The twelve men who were there spoke: "Behold them! Your nation's life shall be such!"

I saw again how beautiful the day was — the sky all blue and full of yellow light above the greening earth. And I saw that all the people were beautiful and young. There were no old ones there, nor children either — just people of about one age, and beautiful.

Then there were twelve women who stood in front of me and spoke: "Behold them! Their way of life you shall take back to earth." When they had spoken, I heard singing in the west, and I learned the song I heard.

Then one of the twelve men took two sticks, one painted white and one red, and, thrusting them in the ground, he said: "Take these! You shall depend upon them. Make haste!"

I started to walk, and it seemed as though a strong wind went under me and picked me up. I was in the air, with outstretched arms, and floating fast. There was a fearful dark river that I had to go over, and I was afraid. It rushed and roared and was full of angry foam. Then I looked down and saw many men and women who were trying to cross the dark and fearful river, but they could not. Weeping, they looked up to me and cried: "Help us!" But I could not stop gliding, for it was as though a great wind were under me.

Then I saw my earthly people again at the dancing place, and fell back into my body lying there. And I was sitting up, and people were crowding around me to ask what vision I had seen.

I told my vision through songs, and the older men explained them to the others. I sang a song, the words of which were those the Wanekia spoke under the flowering tree, and the air of it was that which I heard in the West after the twelve women had spoken. I sang it four times, and the fourth time all the people began to weep together because the Wasichus had taken the beautiful world away from us.

I thought and thought about this vision. The six villages seemed to represent the Six Grandfathers that I had seen long ago in the Flaming Rainbow Tepee, and I had gone to the sixth village, which was for the Sixth Grandfather, the Spirit of the Earth, because I was to stand for him in the world. I wondered if the Wanekia might be the red man of my great vision, who turned into a bison, and then into the four-rayed herb, the daybreak-star herb of understanding. I thought the twelve men and twelve women were for the moons of the year.

SIMONE WEIL

Waiting for God

> Simone Weil (1909–1943) was a political activist and sup-
> porter of radical social causes in her native France and
> elsewhere, but in the final years of her short life she in-
> creasingly turned to spirituality. Out of that came mystical
> writings of abiding beauty, together with a continually
> unsatisfied openness to divine leading, expressed in the
> title and the content of her autobiography, *Waiting for God,*
> which included a poignant letter to a priest, a major portion
> of which is reprinted here.

P.S. To Be Read First.

This letter is fearfully long — but as there is no question of an
answer — especially as I shall doubtless have gone before it reaches
you — you have years ahead of you in which to read it if you care to.
Read it all the same, one day or another.

From Marseilles, about May 15

Father,

Before leaving I want to speak to you again, it may be the last time
perhaps, for over there I shall probably send you only my news from
time to time just so as to have yours.

I told you that I owed you an enormous debt. I want to try to tell
you exactly what it consists of. I think that if you could really
understand what my spiritual state is you would not be at all sorry that
you did not lead me to baptism. But I do not know if it is possible for
you to understand this.

You neither brought me the Christian inspiration nor did you bring
me to Christ; for when I met you there was no longer any need; it had
been done without the intervention of any human being. If it had been
otherwise, if I had not already been won, not only implicitly but
consciously, you would have given me nothing, because I should have

received nothing from you. My friendship for you would have been a reason for me to refuse your message, for I should have been afraid of the possibilities of error and illusion which human influence in the divine order is likely to involve.

I may say that never at any moment in my life have I "sought for God." For this reason, which is probably too subjective, I do not like this expression and it strikes me as false. As soon as I reached adolescence, I saw the problem of God as a problem the data of which could not be obtained here below, and I decided that the only way of being sure not to reach a wrong solution, which seemed to me the greatest possible evil, was to leave it alone. So I left it alone. I neither affirmed nor denied anything. It seemed to me useless to solve the problem, for I thought that, being in this world, our business was to adopt the best attitude with regard to the problems of this world, and that such an attitude did not depend upon the solution of the problem of God.

This held good as far as I was concerned at any rate, for I never hesitated in my choice of an attitude; I always adopted the Christian attitude as the only possible one. I might say that I was born, I grew up, and I always remained within the Christian inspiration. While the very name of God had no part in my thoughts, with regard to the problems of this world and this life I shared the Christian conception in an explicit and rigorous manner, with the most specific notions it involves. Some of these notions have been part of my outlook for as far back as I can remember. With others I know the time and manner of their coming and the form under which they imposed themselves upon me.

For instance I never allowed myself to think of a future state, but I always believed that the instant of death is the center and object of life. I used to think that, for those who live as they should, it is the instant when, for an infinitesimal fraction of time, pure truth, naked, certain, and eternal enters the soul. I may say that I never desired any other good for myself. I thought that the life leading to this good is not only defined by a code of morals common to all, but that for each one it consists of a succession of acts and events strictly personal to him, and so essential that he who leaves them on one side never reaches the goal. The notion of vocation was like this for me. I saw that the carrying out of a vocation differed from the actions dictated by reason or inclination in that it was due to an impulse of an essentially and manifestly different order; and not to follow such an impulse when it made itself felt, even if it demanded impossibilities, seemed to me the greatest of all ills. Hence my conception of obedience; and I put this conception to the test when I entered the factory and stayed on there, even when I was in that state of intense and uninterrupted misery about which I recently told you. The most beautiful life possible has always seemed to me to be one where everything is determined, either by the pressure of circumstances or by impulses such as I have just mentioned and where there is never any room for choice.

At fourteen I fell into one of those fits of bottomless despair that come with adolescence, and I seriously thought of dying because of the mediocrity of my natural faculties. The exceptional gifts of my brother, who had a childhood and youth comparable to those of Pascal, brought my own inferiority home to me. I did not mind having no visible successes, but what did grieve me was the idea of being excluded from that transcendent kingdom to which only the truly great have access and wherein truth abides. I preferred to die rather than live without that truth. After months of inward darkness, I suddenly had the everlasting conviction that any human being, even though practically devoid of natural faculties, can penetrate to the kingdom of truth reserved for genius, if only he longs for truth and perpetually concentrates all his attention upon its attainment. He thus becomes a genius too, even though for lack of talent his genius cannot be visible from outside. Later on, when the strain of headaches caused the feeble faculties I possess to be invaded by a paralysis, which I was quick to imagine as probably incurable, the same conviction led me to persevere for ten years in an effort of concentrated attention that was practically unsupported by any hope of results.

Under the name of truth I also included beauty, virtue, and every kind of goodness, so that for me it was a question of a conception of the relationship between grace and desire. The conviction that had come to me was that when one hungers for bread one does not receive stones. But at that time I had not read the Gospel.

Just as I was certain that desire has in itself an efficacy in the realm of spiritual goodness whatever its form, I thought it was also possible that it might not be effective in any other realm.

As for the spirit of poverty, I do not remember any moment when it was not in me, although only to that unhappily small extent compatible with my imperfection. I fell in love with Saint Francis of Assisi as soon as I came to know about him. I always believed and hoped that one day Fate would force upon me the condition of a vagabond and a beggar which he embraced freely. Actually I felt the same way about prison.

From my earliest childhood I always had also the Christian idea of love for one's neighbor, to which I gave the name of justice — a name it bears in many passages of the Gospel and which is so beautiful. You know that on this point I have failed seriously several times.

The duty of acceptance in all that concerns the will of God, whatever it may be, was impressed upon my mind as the first and most necessary of all duties from the time when I found it set down in Marcus Aurelius under the form of the *amor fati* [love of fate] of the Stoics. I saw it as a duty we cannot fail in without dishonoring ourselves.

The idea of purity, with all that this word can imply for a Christian, took possession of me at the age of sixteen, after a period of several months during which I had been going through the emotional unrest natural in adolescence. This idea came to me when I was contemplating a mountain landscape and little by little it was imposed upon me in an irresistible manner.

Of course I knew quite well that my conception of life was Christian. That is why it never occurred to me that I could enter the Christian community. I had the idea that I was born inside. But to add dogma to this conception of life, without being forced to do so by indisputable evidence, would have seemed to me like a lack of honesty. I should even have thought I was lacking in honesty had I considered the question of the truth of dogma as a problem for myself or even had I simply desired to reach a conclusion on this subject. I have an extremely severe standard for intellectual honesty, so severe that I never met anyone who did not seem to fall short of it in more than one respect; and I am always afraid of failing in it myself.

Keeping away from dogma in this way, I was prevented by a sort of shame from going into churches, though all the same I like being in them. Nevertheless, I had three contacts with Catholicism that really counted.

After my year in the factory, before going back to teaching, I had been taken by my parents to Portugal, and while there I left them to go alone to a little village. I was, as it were, in pieces, soul and body. That contact with affliction had killed my youth. Until then I had not had any experience of affliction, unless we count my own, which, as it was my own, seemed to me to have little importance, and which moreover was only a partial affliction, being biological and not social. I knew quite well that there was a great deal of affliction in the world, I was obsessed with the idea, but I had not had prolonged and first-hand experience of it. As I worked in the factory, indistinguishable to all eyes, including my own, from the anonymous mass, the affliction of others entered into my flesh and my soul. Nothing separated me from it, for I had really forgotten my past and I looked forward to no future, finding it difficult to imagine the possibility of surviving all the fatigue. What I went through there marked me in so lasting a manner that still today when any human being, whoever he may be and in whatever circumstances, speaks to me without brutality, I cannot help having the impression that there must be a mistake and that unfortunately the mistake will in all probability disappear. There I received forever the mark of a slave, like the branding of the red-hot iron the Romans put on the foreheads of their most despised slaves. Since then I have always regarded myself as a slave.

In this state of mind then, and in a wretched condition physically, I entered the little Portuguese village, which, alas, was very wretched too, on the very day of the festival of its patron saint. I was alone. It was the evening and there was a full moon over the sea. The wives of the fishermen were, in procession, making a tour of all the ships, carrying candles and singing what must certainly be very ancient hymns of a heart-rending sadness. Nothing can give any idea of it. I have never heard anything so poignant unless it were the song of the boatmen on the Volga. There the conviction was suddenly borne in upon me that Christianity is pre-eminently the religion of slaves, that slaves cannot help belonging to it, and I among others.

In 1937 I had two marvelous days at Assisi. There, alone in the little twelfth-century Romanesque chapel of Santa Maria degli Angeli, an incomparable marvel of purity where Saint Francis often used to pray, something stronger than I was compelled me for the first time in my life to go down on my knees.

In 1938 I spent ten days at Solesmes, from Palm Sunday to Easter Tuesday, following all the liturgical services. I was suffering from splitting headaches; each sound hurt me like a blow; by an extreme effort of concentration I was able to rise above this wretched flesh, to leave it to suffer by itself, heaped up in a corner, and to find a pure and perfect joy in the unimaginable beauty of the chanting and the words. This experience enabled me by analogy to get a better understanding of the possibility of loving divine love in the midst of affliction. It goes without saying that in the course of these services the thought of the Passion of Christ entered into my being once and for all.

There was a young English Catholic there from whom I gained my first idea of the supernatural power of the sacraments because of the truly angelic radiance with which he seemed to be clothed after going to communion. Chance — for I always prefer saying chance rather than Providence — made of him a messenger to me. For he told me of the existence of those English poets of the seventeenth century who are named metaphysical. In reading them later on, I discovered the poem of which I read you what is unfortunately a very inadequate translation. It is called "Love." I learned it by heart. Often, at the culminating point of a violent headache, I make myself say it over, concentrating all my attention upon it and clinging with all my soul to the tenderness it enshrines. I used to think I was merely reciting it as a beautiful poem, but without my knowing it the recitation had the virtue of a prayer. It was during one of these recitations that, as I told you, Christ himself came down and took possession of me.

In my arguments about the insolubility of the problem of God I had never foreseen the possibility of that, of a real contact, person to person, here below, between a human being and God. I had vaguely heard tell of things of this kind, but I had never believed in them. In the *Fioretti* the accounts of apparitions rather put me off if anything, like the miracles in the Gospel. Moreover, in this sudden possession of me by Christ, neither my sense nor my imagination had any part; I only felt in the midst of my suffering the presence of a love, like that which one can read in the smile on a beloved face.

I had never read any mystical works because I had never felt any call to read them. In reading as in other things I have always striven to practice obedience. There is nothing more favorable to intellectual progress, for as far as possible I only read what I am hungry for at the moment when I have an appetite for it, and then I do not read, I *eat.* God in his mercy had prevented me from reading the mystics, so that it should be evident to me that I had not invented this absolutely unexpected contact.

Yet I still half refused, not my love but my intelligence. For it seemed to me certain, and I still think so today, that one can never wrestle enough with God if one does so out of pure regard for the truth. Christ likes us to prefer truth to him because, before being Christ, he is truth. If one turns aside from him to go toward the truth, one will not go far before falling into his arms.

After this I came to feel that Plato was a mystic, that all the *Iliad* is bathed in Christian light, and that Dionysus and Osiris are in a certain sense Christ himself; and my love was thereby redoubled.

I never wondered whether Jesus was or was not the Incarnation of God; but in fact I was incapable of thinking of him without thinking of him as God.

In the spring of 1940 I read the *Bhagavad-Gita.* Strange to say it was in reading those marvelous words, words with such a Christian sound, put into the mouth of an incarnation of God, that I came to feel strongly that we owe an allegiance to religious truth which is quite different from the admiration we accord to a beautiful poem; it is something far more categorical.

Yet I did not believe it to be possible for me to consider the question of baptism. I felt that I could not honestly give up my opinions concerning the non-Christian religions and concerning Israel — and as a matter of fact time and meditation have only served to strengthen them — and I thought that this constituted an absolute obstacle. I did not imagine it as possible that a priest could even dream of granting me baptism. If I had not met you, I should never have considered the problem of baptism as a practical problem.

During all this time of spiritual progress I had never prayed. I was afraid of the power of suggestion that is in prayer — the very power for which Pascal recommends it. Pascal's method seems to me one of the worst for attaining faith.

Contact with you was not able to persuade me to pray. On the contrary I thought the danger was all the greater, since I also had to beware of the power of suggestion in my friendship with you. At the same time I found it very difficult not to pray and not to tell you so. Moreover I knew I could not tell you without completely misleading you about myself. At that time I should not have been able to make you understand.

Until last September I had never once prayed in all my life, at least not in the literal sense of the word. I had never said any words to God, either out loud or mentally. I had never pronounced a liturgical prayer. I had occasionally recited the *Salve Regina,* but only as a beautiful poem.

Last summer, doing Greek with T——, I went through the Our Father word for word in Greek. We promised each other to learn it by heart. I do not think he ever did so, but some weeks later, as I was turning over the pages of the Gospel, I said to myself that since I had promised to do this thing and it was good, I ought to do it. I did it. The infinite sweetness of this Greek text so took hold of me that for several days I could not stop myself from saying it over all the time. A week afterward I began the vine harvest. I recited the Our Father in Greek every day before work, and I repeated it very often in the vineyard.

Since that time I have made a practice of saying it through once each morning with absolute attention. If during the recitation my attention wanders or goes to sleep, in the minutest degree, I begin again until

I have once succeeded in going through it with absolutely pure attention. Sometimes it comes about that I say it again out of sheer pleasure, but I only do it if I really feel the impulse.

The effect of this practice is extraordinary and surprises me every time, for, although I experience it each day, it exceeds my expectation at each repetition.

At times the very first words tear my thoughts from my body and transport it to a place outside space where there is neither perspective nor point of view. The infinity of the ordinary expanses of perception is replaced by an infinity to the second or sometimes the third degree. At the same time, filling every part of this infinity of infinity, there is silence, a silence which is not an absence of sound but which is the object of a positive sensation, more positive than that of sound. Noises, if there are any, only reach me after crossing this silence.

Sometimes, also, during this recitation or at other moments, Christ is present with me in person, but his presence is infinitely more real, more moving, more clear than on that first occasion when he took possession of me.

I should never have been able to take it upon myself to tell you all this had it not been for the fact that I am going away. And as I am going more or less with the idea of probable death, I do not believe that I have the right to keep it to myself. For after all, the whole of this matter is not a question concerning me myself. It concerns God. I am really nothing in it all. If one could imagine any possibility of error in God, I should think that it had all happened to me by mistake. But perhaps God likes to use castaway objects, waste, rejects. After all, should the bread of the host be moldy, it would become the Body of Christ just the same after the priest had consecrated it. Only it cannot refuse, while we can disobey. It sometimes seems to me that when I am treated in so merciful a way, every sin on my part must be a mortal sin. And I am constantly committing them.

I have told you that you are like a father and brother at the same time to me. But these words only express an analogy. Perhaps at bottom they only correspond to a feeling of affection, of gratitude and admiration. For as to the spiritual direction of my soul, I think that God himself has taken it in hand from the start and still looks after it.

SARVEPALLI RADHAKRISHNAN

Mysticism and Ethics in Hindu Thought

> Sarvepalli Radhakrishnan (1888–1975), born in India, was for almost two decades a professor at Oxford, where he compared and contrasted the two traditions represented in the title of the book from which this chapter is taken, *Eastern Religions and Western Thought.* Then he returned to his native land, first as a professor and chancellor at Benares and at Delhi and eventually as the president of an independent India.

ANY ETHICAL THEORY must be grounded in metaphysics, in a philosophical conception of the relation between human conduct and ultimate reality. As we think ultimate reality to be, so we behave. Vision and action go together. If we believe absurdities, we shall commit atrocities. A self-sufficient humanism has its own metaphysical presuppositions. It requires us to confine our attention to the immediate world of space and time and argues that moral duty consists in conforming to nature and modelling our behaviour in accordance with the principles of her working. It attempts to perfect the causes of human life by purely natural means. The subject of ethics is treated as a branch of sociology or a department of psychology. Scientific materialism and mystical nationalism are two types of humanist ethics, interpreted in a narrow sense. They look upon man as a purely natural phenomenon whose outlook is rigorously confined by space and time. They encourage a cynical subservience to nature and historical process and an acquiescence in the merely practicable. Renunciation, self-sacrifice, disinterested service of humanity are not stimulated by the workings of natural law.

An abundance of material things will not help to make life more interesting. The rich of the world are among those who find life stale, flat, and unprofitable. Even the social conscience that urges us to extend the benefits of a material civilization cannot be accounted for by the principles of scientific naturalism. The material basis, while essential, is still too narrow for real living. The collective myths of Nazism, Fascism, and Communism propose to make life seem rich and significant by asking us to banish all considerations of reason and humanity and to worship the State. Man is not merely an emotional being. The Nation-State falls short of the human and the universal and constitutes a deadly menace to the growth of the universal in man which is postulated with increasing force by the advance of science and which the well-being of human society demands.

The question has its centre in the nature of man. Is he only a body which can be fed, clothed, and housed, or is he also a spirit that can aspire? The feeling of frustration experienced even by those who are provided with all the comforts and conveniences which a material civilization can supply indicates that man does not live by bread or emotional excitement alone. Besides, progress is not its own end. If it is the ultimate reality, it cannot ever be completed. We can draw nearer and nearer the goal, but cannot reach it. Its process has neither a beginning nor an end. It starts nowhere and leads nowhere. It has no issue, no goal. Senseless cycles of repetition cannot give meaning to life. It may be argued that, although the universe may have no purpose, items in the universe such as nations and individuals may have their purposes. The rise and fall of nations, the growth and crash of individuals may be quite interesting, and the universe may be viewed as an infinite succession of finite purposes. This cannot be regarded as a satisfactory goal of ethics. Does not the humanist hope to build a terrestrial paradise inhabited by a perfect race of artists and thinkers? What is the good of telling us that though our sun, moon, and stars will share in the destruction of earthly life, other suns, moons, and stars will arise? We long for a good which is never left behind and never superseded. Man's incapacity to be satisfied with what is merely relative and remain permanently within the boundaries of the finite and empirical reality cannot be denied. Man stands before the shrine of his own mystery. He enters it the moment he becomes aware of his own eternity. Apart from eternity there is nothing that can, strictly speaking, be called human. A meaningful ethical ideal must be transcendent to the immediate flow of events.

Again, in view of the enigmatic character of the actual, is moral life possible? There are some thinkers who exhort us to do what is right even though we may not know whether it can be realized or not. Moral enthusiasm is possible only if our motive includes the expectation of being able to contribute to the achievement of moral ideals. If we are not certain that active service of the ideals will further their actualization, we cannot be sure of their worthwhileness.

We cannot help asking ourselves whether our ideals are mere private dreams of our own or bonds created by society, or even aspirations characteristic of the human species. Only a philosophy which affirms that they are rooted in the universal nature of things can give depth and fervour to moral life, courage and confidence in moral difficulties. We need to be fortified by the conviction that the service of the ideals is what the cosmic scheme demands of us, that our loyalty or disloyalty to them is a matter of the deepest moment not only to ourselves or to society, or even to the human species, but to the nature of things. If ethical thought is profound, it will give a cosmic motive to morality. Moral consciousness must include a conviction of the reality of ideals. If the latter is religion, then ethical humanism is acted religion. When man realizes his essential unity with the whole of being, he expresses this unity in his life. Mysticism and ethics, otherworldliness and worldly work go together. In the primitive religions we have this combination. Otherworldliness appears as *māna,* which the savage derives from an innate sense of some mysterious power within the phenomena and behind the events of the visible world, and morality appears as taboo, and the sense of sacredness in things and persons, which with its inhibitions controls the whole range of his conduct. In the higher religions of mankind, belief in the transcendent and work in the natural have grown together in close intimacy and interaction. Religion is the soul's attitude, response, and adjustment in the presence of the supreme realities of the transcendent order; ethics deal with the right adjustment of life on earth, especially in human society. Both are motived by a desire to live in the light of ideals. If we are satisfied with what exists, there is no meaning in "ought"; if we are a species of passing phenomena, there is no meaning in religion. Religion springs from the conviction that there is another world beyond the visible and the temporal with which man has dealings, and ethics require us to act in this world with the compelling vision of another. With our minds anchored in the beyond we are to strive to make the actual more nearly like what it ought to be. Religion alone can give assurance and wider reference to ethics and a new meaning to human life. We make moral judgements about individual lives and societies simply because we are spiritual beings, not merely social animals.

If there is one doctrine more than another which is characteristic of Hindu thought, it is the belief that there is an interior depth to the human soul, which, in its essence, is uncreated and deathless and absolutely real. The spirit in man is different from the individual ego; it is that which animates and exercises the individual, the vast background of his being in which all individuals lie. It is the core of all being, the inner thread by being strung on which the world exists. In the soul of man are conflicting tendencies: the attraction of the infinite, which abides for ever, changeless, unqualified, untouched by the world; and the fascination of the finite, that which like the wind-beaten surface of the waters is never for a moment the same. Every human being is a potential spirit and represents, as has been well said, a hope of God and is not a mere fortuitous concourse of episodes like the changing forms of clouds or the patterns of a kaleidoscope. If the feeling for God were not in man, we could not implant it any more than we could squeeze blood from a stone. The heart of religion is that man truly belongs to another order, and the meaning of man's life is to be found not in this world but in more than historical reality. His highest aim is release from the historical succession denoted by birth and death. So long as he is lost in the historical process without a realization of the super-historical goal, he is only "once born" and is liable to sorrow. God and not the world of history is the true environment of our souls. If we overlook this important fact, and make ethics or world affirmation independent of religion or world negation, our life and thought become condescending, though this condescension may take the form of social service or philanthropy. But it is essentially a form of self-assertion and not real concern for the well-being of others. If goodwill, pure love, and disinterestedness are our ideals, then our ethics must be rooted in other-worldliness. This is the great classical tradition of spiritual wisdom. The mystery cults of Greece had for their central doctrine that man's soul is of divine origin and is akin to the spirit of God. The influence of these mystery cults on Socrates and Plato is unmistakable. When Jesus tells Nicodemus that until a man is begotten from above he cannot see or enter the Kingdom of God, when Paul declares that "he that soweth to the flesh shall of the flesh reap corruption; but he that soweth to the spirit shall of the spirit reap everlasting life," they are implying that our natural life is mortal and it is invaded by sin and death, and that the life of spirit is immortal. St. John in the First Epistle says: "the world passeth away, and the lust thereof: but he that doeth the will of God abideth for ever." We are amphibious beings, according to Plotinus. We live on earth and in a world of spirit.

Although the view about the coexistence of the human and the divine in close intimacy and interpenetration may be true, does not Hindu thought declare that life is empty and unreal, and that it has no purpose or meaning? Schweitzer tells us that for the Upaniṣads "the world of the senses is a magic play staged by the universal soul for itself. The individual soul is brought into this magic play under a spell. By reflection about itself it must become capable of seeing through the deception. Thereupon it gives up taking part in the play. It waits quietly and enjoys its identity with the universal soul until, at death, the magic play for it ceases to be." "Man cannot engage in ethical activity in a world with no meaning." 'For any believer in the māyā doctrine ethics can have only a quite relative importance." This account is by no means a fair representation of the position of the Upaniṣads. The long theistic tradition interprets the doctrine of the Upaniṣads in a way directly opposed to this account. Śaṁkara adopts the doctrine of māyā, and it is doubtful whether Schweitzer's view is adequate to Śaṁkara's thought. Religious experience, by its affirmation that the basic fact in the universe is spiritual, implies that the world of sound and sense is not final. All existence finds its source and support in a supreme reality whose nature is spirit. The visible world is the symbol of a more real world. It is the reflection of a spiritual universe which gives to it its life and significance.

What is the relation of absolute being to historical becoming, of eternity to time? Is succession, history, progress, real and sufficient in its own right, or does man's deep instinct for the unchanging point to an eternal perfection which alone gives the world meaning and worth? Is the inescapable flux all, or is there anything which abides? Religious consciousness bears testimony to the reality of something behind the visible, a haunting beyond, which both attracts and disturbs, in the light of which the world of change is said to be unreal. The Hebrews contrasted the abidingness of God with the swift flow of human generations. "Before the mountains were brought forth or ever Thou hadst formed the earth and the world even from everlasting to everlasting, Thou art God." The Psalmist cries to his God: "They [i.e. heaven and earth] shall be changed: but Thou art the same, and Thy years shall have no end." The Christian exclaims: "The things which are seen are temporal; but the things which are not seen are eternal." The mutability of things which is part of the connotation of the word *māyā* is a well-known theme in the world's literature. The saying that "time and chance happeneth to them all" of Ecclesiastes is the refrain we hear often.

Gauḍapāda argues that "whatever is non-existent at the beginning and in the end is non-existent in the middle also." In other words, the things of the world are not eternal. The world is *māyā,* i.e. passes away, but God is eternal. Change, causality, activity are finite categories and the Eternal is lifted above them. God is not a mere means to explain the universe or improve human society.

Śaṁkara, who is rightly credited with the systematic formulation of the doctrine of *māyā*, tells us that the highest reality is unchangeable, and therefore that changing existence such as human history has not ultimate reality (*pāramārthika sattā*). He warns us, however, against the temptation to regard what is not completely real as utterly illusory. The world has empirical being (*vyāvahārika sattā*) which is quite different from illusory existence (*prātibhāsika sattā*). Human experience is neither ultimately real nor completely illusory. Simply because the world of experience is not the perfect form of reality, it does not follow that it is a delusion, without any significance. The world is not a phantom, though it is not real. Brahman is said to be the real of the real, *satyasyasatyam*. In all objective consciousness, we are in a sense aware of the real.

Similarly, all knowledge presupposes the knower who is constant, while the known is unsteady. When Plato tells us that we bring universal ideas with us from the world in which we lived before our birth, he is referring to the non-phenomenal, time-transcending power in us which belongs to a different world from the observed phenomena. The "nous" which organizes the facts of experience and interprets them is not itself a fact of experience. It must have had its origin in and belong to another world. It beholds by virtue of its own nature eternal realities. This presence in us is an assurance that we are in touch with reality. Spirit is real being and the rest its limited activity. The spirit is pure existence, self-aware, timeless, spaceless, unconditioned, not dependent for its being on its sense of objects, not dependent for its delight on the gross or subtle touches of outward things. It is not divided in the multitude of beings. Śaṁkara's *advaita* or non-duality has for its central thesis the non-difference between the individual self and Brahman. As for difference or multiplicity (*nānātva*), it is not real. Its self-discrepant character shows that it is only an appearance of the real. All schools of *advaita* are agreed on these two propositions. Differences arise when the nature of the actuality of the manifold world as distinct from the reality is described. Śaṁkara accepts the empirical reality of the world, which is negated only when perfect insight or intuition of the oneness of all is attained. Until then it has empirical validity or pragmatic justification. There are *advaitins* who argue that the world of difference has not even empirical validity. Śaṁkara, however, tells us that so long as we are in the world of *māyā* and occupy a dualistic standpoint, the world is there, standing over against us, determining our perceptions and conduct.

Besides, the world we see and touch is not independent and self-sufficing. It carries no explanation of itself. It is a world reflecting the condition of our minds, a partial construction made from insufficient data under the stress of self-conscious individuality with its cravings and desires. What is perceived and shaped into meaning depends on the powers of apprehension we employ and the interests we possess. Our passion-limited apprehension gives us the world of common sense. Take the apparent facts of the universe. Matter is not primal. It is a thing made, not self-existent. It is not unreal but being as it forms itself to sense. It is not a baseless fiction but at the lowest a misrepresentation of truth; at the highest an imperfect representation or translation of the truth into a lower plane. Even as our knowledge implies the presence of a constant consciousness, the object of our knowledge implies the reality of pure being. Our conceptions of the universe answer to our degrees of consciousness. As our consciousness increases in its scope, we see more clearly. We now see partly as an animal and partly as a human being. Sometimes the world is viewed as one of self-satisfaction, at other times as an object of curiosity and contemplation. To see it in truth, one has to free oneself from sense addiction and concentrate the whole energy of one's consciousness on the nature of reality. It is the only way by which we can attain a clear consciousness of reality as it is and get a true picture of the world instead of partial sketches. Knowledge which we now obtain through senses and reason cannot be regarded as complete or perfect. It is flawed with antinomies and contradictions. Through the force of *avidyā* (not knowing) we impose on the reality of the one the multiplicity of the world. Being which is one only appears to the soul as manifoldness, and the soul beholds itself as entangled in the world of *saṁsāra,* in the chain of birth and death. This *avidyā* is natural (*naisargika*) to the human mind, and the world is organically connected with it. It is not therefore mere waking dream.

Māyā is not solipsism. It does not say that suns and universes are the invention of the solitary mind. Śaṁkara proclaims his opposition to *Vijñānavāda* or mentalism. He argues that waking experiences are distinct from dreamstates, though neither can be regarded as real metaphysically. Our world of waking experience is not the ultimate reality, but neither is it a shadow-show. We are surrounded by something other than ourselves, which cannot be reduced to states of our own consciousness. Though the world is always changing, it has a unity and a meaning. These are revealed by the reality present all through it. This reality lies not in the facts but in the principle which makes them into a whole. We are able to know that the world is imperfect, finite, and changing, because we have a consciousness of the eternal and the perfect. It is by the light of this consciousness that we criticize ourselves or condemn the world. Even as the human individual is a complex of the eternal and the temporal, the world which confronts him contains both. It is for Śaṁkara a mixture of truth and illusion. It partakes of the characteristics of being and non-being (*sadasadātmaka*). Although, therefore, it has a lower form of reality than pure spirit, it is not non-existent. While Śaṁkara refuses to acquiesce in the seeming reality of the actual, he does not dismiss it as an unreal phantasmagoria. It is not determinable either as real or as unreal. Its truth is in being, reality, truth (*sat*); its multiplicity and division, its dispersal in space and time is untrue (*an-ṛtam*). In the world itself we have change. Śaṁkara does not tell us that the process of the world is perpetual recurrence, in which events of past cycles are repeated in all their details. If everything is recurrent, perpetually rotating, and governed by a law of cyclic motion, there is nothing new, no meaning in history. But there is an historical fulfilment and destiny for the cosmic process. Mankind is engaged in a pursuit that tends towards a definite goal. Truth will be victorious on earth, and it is the nature of the cosmic process that the finite individual is called upon to work through the exercise of his freedom for that goal through ages of struggle and effort. The soul has risen from the sleep of matter, through plant and animal life, to the human level, and is battling with ignorance and imperfection to take possession of its infinite kingdom. It is absolute not in its actual empirical condition but in its potentiality, in its capacity to appropriate the Absolute. The historical process is not a mere external chain of events, but offers a succession of spiritual opportunities. Man has to attain a mastery over it and reveal the higher world operating in it. The world is not therefore an empty dream or an eternal delirium.

FRIEDRICH VON HÜGEL

The Three Elements
of Religion

Baron Friedrich von Hügel (1852–1925) was a German
nobleman who was born in Florence and lived most of his
life in England. In *The Mystical Element of Religion As Studied in St. Catherine of Genoa and Her Friends* he attempted a
systematization of mystical theology on the basis of its history, noting its affinities as well as its differences with the
institutional and the intellectual expressions of religion.

Introductory

WE HAVE FOUND THEN that all life and all truth are, for all their unity,
deeply complex, for us men at all events; indeed that they are both in
exact proportion to their reality. In this, our second chapter, I should
like to show the complexity special to the deepest kind of life, to
Religion; and to attempt some description of the working harmoni-
zation of this complexity. If Religion turned out to be simple, in the
sense of being a monotone, a mere oneness, a whole without parts, it
could not be true; and yet if Religion be left too much a mere
multiplicity, a mere congeries of parts without a whole, it cannot be
persuasive and fully operative. And the several constituents are there,
whether we harbour, recognize, and discipline them or not; but these
constituents will but hinder or supplant each other, in proportion as
they are not somehow each recognized in their proper place and rank,
and are not each allowed and required to supplement and to stimulate
the other. And though no amount of talk or theory can, otherwise than
harmfully, take the place of life, yet observation and reflection can help
us to see where and how life acts: what are the causes, or at least the
concomitants, of its inhibition and of its stimulation and propagation,
and can thus supply us with aids to action, which action will then, in

its turn, help to give experimental fulness and precision to what otherwise remains a more or less vague and empty scheme.

I. The Three Elements, As They Successively Appear in the Child, the Youth, and the Adult Man

Now if we will but look back upon our own religious life, we shall find that, in degrees and in part in an order of succession varying indefinitely with each individual, three modalities, three modes of apprehension and forms of appeal and of outlook, have been and are at work within us and around.

1. SENSE AND MEMORY, THE CHILD'S MEANS OF APPREHENDING RELIGION

In the doubtless overwhelming majority of cases, there came first, as far as we can reconstruct the history of our consciousness, the appeal to our infant senses of some external religious symbol or place, some picture or statue, some cross or book, some movement of some attendant's hands and eyes. And this appeal would generally have been externally interpreted to us by some particular men or women, a Mother, Nurse, Father, Teacher, Cleric, who themselves would generally have belonged to some more or less well-defined traditional, institutional religion. And their appeal would be through my senses to my imaginative faculty first, and then to my memory of that first appeal, and would represent the principle of authority in its simplest form.

All here as yet works quasi-automatically. The little child gets these impressions long before itself can choose between, or even is distinctly conscious of them; it believes whatever it sees and is told, equally, as so much fact, as something to build on. If you will, it believes these things to be true, but not in the sense of contrasting them with error; the very possibility of the latter has not yet come into sight. And at this stage the External, Authoritative, Historical, Traditional, Institutional side and function of Religion are everywhere evident. Cases like that of John Stuart Mill, of being left outside of all religious tradition, we may safely say, will ever remain exceptions to help prove the rule. The five senses then, perhaps that of touch first, and certainly that of sight most; the picturing and associative powers of the imagination; and the retentiveness of the memory, are the side of human nature specially called forth. And the external, sensible, readily picturable facts and the picturing functions of religion correspond to and feed this side, as readily as does the mother's milk correspond to and feed that same mother's infant. Religion is here, above all, a Fact and Thing.

2. QUESTION AND ARGUMENT, THE YOUTH'S MODE OF APPROACHING
   RELIGION

But soon there wakes up another activity and requirement of human nature, and another side of religion comes forth to meet it. Direct experience, for one thing, brings home to the child that these sense-informations are not always trustworthy, or identical in its own case and in that of others. And, again, the very impressiveness of this external religion stimulates indeed the sense of awe and of wonder, but it awakens curiosity as well. The time of trustful questioning, but still of questioning, first others, then oneself, has come. The old impressions get now more and more consciously sought out, and selected from among other conflicting ones; the facts seem to clamour for reasons to back them, against the other hostile facts and appearances, or at least against those men in books, if not in life, who dare to question or reject them. Affirmation is beginning to be consciously exclusive of its contrary: I begin to feel that *I* hold *this,* and that *you* hold *that;* and that I cannot do both; and that I do the former, and exclude and refuse the latter.

Here it is the reasoning, argumentative, abstractive side of human nature that begins to come into play. Facts have now in my mind to be related, to be bound to other facts, and men to men; the facts themselves begin to stand for ideas or to have the latter in them or behind them. The measuring-rod seems to be over all things. And religion answers this demand by clear and systematic arguments and concatenations: this and this is now connected with that and that; this is true or this need not be false, because of that and that. Religion here becomes Thought, System, a Philosophy.

3. INTUITION, FEELING, AND VOLITIONAL REQUIREMENTS AND EVIDENCES,
   THE MATURE MAN'S SPECIAL APPROACHES TO FAITH

But yet a final activity of human nature has to come to its fullest, and to meet its response in a third side of Religion. For if in Physiology and Psychology all action whatsoever is found to begin with a sense-impression, to move through the central process of reflection, and to end in the final discharge of will and of action, the same final stage can be found in the religious life. Certain interior experiences, certain deep-seated spiritual pleasures and pains, weaknesses and powers, helps and hindrances, are increasingly known and felt in and through interior and exterior action, and interior suffering, effort, and growth. For man is necessarily a creature of action, even more than of sensation and of reflection; and in this action of part of himself against other parts, of himself with or against other men, with or against this or that external fact or condition, he grows and gradually comes to his real self, and gains certain experiences as to the existence and nature and growth of this his own deeper personality.

Man's emotional and volitional, his ethical and spiritual powers, are now in ever fuller motion, and they are met and fed by the third side of religion, the Experimental and Mystical. Here religion is rather felt than seen or reasoned about, is loved and lived rather than analyzed, is action and power, rather than either external fact or intellectual verification.

II. Each Element Ever Accompanied by Some Amount of the Other Two. Difficulty of the Transitions from One Stage to the Other

Now these three sides of the human character, and corresponding three elements of Religion, are never, any one of them, without a trace or rudiment of the other two; and this joint presence of three such disparate elements ever involves tension, of a fruitful or dangerous kind.

1. UTILITY OF THIS JOINT PRESENCE

In the living human being indeed there never exists a mere apprehension of something external and sensible, without any interior elaboration, and any interpretation by the head and heart. We can hardly allow, we can certainly in nowise picture to ourselves, even an infant of a few hours old as working, and being worked upon, by nothing beyond these sense-perceptions alone. Already some mental, abstractive, emotional-volitional reaction and interpretation is presumably at work; and not many weeks or months pass before this is quite obviously the case. And although, on the other hand, the impressions of the senses, of the imagination and the memory are, normally, more numerous, fresh, and lasting in early than in later years, yet up to the end they continue to take in some new impressions, and keep up their most necessary functions of supplying materials, stimulants, and tests to the other powers of the soul.

Thus, too, Religion is at all times more or less both traditional and individual; both external and internal; both institutional, rational, and volitional. It always answers more or less to the needs of authority and society; of reason and proof; of interior sustenance and purification. I believe because I am told, because it is true, because it answers to my deepest interior experiences and needs. And, everything else being equal, my faith will be at its richest and deepest and strongest, in so far as all these three motives are most fully and characteristically operative within me, at one and the same time, and towards one and the same ultimate result and end.

2. THE TWO CRISES OF THE SOUL, WHEN IT ADDS SPECULATION TO INSTI-
   TUTIONALISM, AND MYSTICISM TO BOTH

Now all this is no fancy scheme, no petty or pretty artificial arrangement; the danger and yet necessity of the presence of these three forces, the conflicts and crises within and between them all, in each human soul, and between various men and races that typify or espouse one or the other force to the more or less complete exclusion of the other, help to form the deepest history, the truest tragedy or triumph of the secret life of every one of us.

The transition from the child's religion, so simply naïve and unself-conscious, so tied to time and place and particular persons and things, so predominantly traditional and historical, institutional and external, to the right and normal type of a young man's religion, is as necessary as it is perilous. The transition is necessary. For all the rest of him is growing, — body and soul are growing in clamorous complexity in every direction: how then can the deepest part of his nature, his religion, not require to grow and develop also? And how can it permeate and purify all the rest, how can it remain and increasingly become "the secret source of all his seeing," of his productiveness and courage and unification, unless it continually equals and exceeds all other interests within the living man, by its own persistent vitality, its rich and infinite variety, its subtle, ever-fresh attraction and inexhaustible resourcefulness and power? But the crisis is perilous. For he will be greatly tempted either to cling exclusively to his existing, all but simply institutional, external position, and to fight or elude all approaches to its reasoned, intellectual apprehension and systematization; and in this case his religion will tend to contract and shrivel up, and to become a something simply alongside of other things in his life. Or he will feel strongly pressed to let the individually intellectual simply supplant the institutional, in which case his religion will grow hard and shallow, and will tend to disappear altogether. In the former case he will, at best, assimilate his religion to external law and order, to Economics and Politics; in the latter case he will, at best, assimilate it to Science and Philosophy. In the first case, he will tend to superstition; in the second, to rationalism and indifference.

But even if he passes well through his first crisis, and has thus achieved the collaboration of these two religious forces, the external and the intellectual, his religion will still be incomplete and semi-operative, because still not reaching to what is deepest and nearest to his will. A final transition, the addition of the third force, that of the emotional-experimental life, must yet be safely achieved. And this again is perilous: for the two other forces will, even if single, still more if combined, tend to resist this third force's full share of influence to the uttermost. To the external force this emotional power will tend to appear as akin to revolution; to the intellectual side it will readily seem mere subjectivity and sentimentality ever verging on delusion. And the emotional-experimental force will, in its turn, be tempted to sweep aside both the external, as so much oppressive ballast; and the intellectual, as so much hair-splitting or rationalism. And if it succeeds, a shifting subjectivity, and all but incurable tyranny of mood and fancy, will result, — fanaticism is in full sight.

III. Parallels to This Triad of Religious Elements

If we would find, applied to other matters, the actual operation and co-operation, at the earliest stage of man's life, of the identical powers under discussion, we can find them, by a careful analysis of our means and processes of knowledge, or of the stages of all reflex action.

1. THE THREE CONSTITUENTS OF KNOWLEDGE

Even the most elementary acquisition, indeed the very possibility, of any and all certitude and knowledge, is dependent for us upon the due collaboration of the three elements or forces of our nature, the sensational, the rational, the ethico-mystical.

There is, first, in the order of our consciousness and in the degree of its undeniableness, the element of our actual impressions, the flux of our consciousness as it apprehends particular sights and sounds, smells and tastes and touches; particular sensations of rest and movement, pleasure and pain, memory, judgment, and volition, a flux, "changeless in its ceaseless change." We have so far found neither a true object for thought, nor a subject which can think. And yet this element, and this alone, is the simply, passively received, the absolutely undeniable part of our experience, — we cannot deny it if we would. And again, it is the absolutely necessary prerequisite for our exercise or acquisition, indeed for our very consciousness, of the other two means or elements, without which there can be no real knowledge.

For there is, next in the logical order of the analysis of our consciousness and in the degree of its undeniableness, the element of the
various forms of necessary thought, in as much as these are experienced by us as necessary. We can, with Aristotle, simply call them the
ten categories; or we can, with greater precision and extension, group
them, so far with Kant, under the two main heads of the two pure
"aesthetic" Perceptions of time and space, on the one hand; and of the
various "analytic" Forms of judgment and of the Categories of Unity,
Reality, Substance, Possibility, etc., on the other hand. Now it can be
shown that it is only by means of this whole second element, only
through the co-operation of these "perceptions" and forms of thought,
that any kind even of dim feeling of ordered succession or of system,
of unity or meaning, is found by our mind in that first element. Only
these two elements, found and taken together, present us, in their
interaction, with even the impression and possibility of something to
reason *about,* and something *wherewith* to reason.

The second element then differs from the first in this, that whereas
the first presents its contents simply as actual and undeniable, yet
without so far any necessity or significance: the second presents its
contents as both actual and necessary. By means of the first element
I see a red rose, but without any feeling of more than the fact that a
rose, or at least this one, *is* red; it might quite as well be yellow or blue.
By means of the second element, I think of a body of any kind, not only
as actually occupying some particular space and time, but as
necessarily doing so: I feel that I *must* so think of it.

And yet there is a third and last element necessary to give real value
to the two previous ones. For only on the condition that I am willing
to trust these intimations of necessity, to believe that these necessities
of my subjective thought are objective as well, and correspond to the
necessities of Being, can I reach the trans-subjective, can I have any
real knowledge and experience of anything whatsoever, either within
me or without. The most elementary experience, the humblest something to be granted as really existing and as to be reasoned from, is thus
invariably and inevitably composed for me of three elements, of which
only the first two are directly experienced by me at all. And the third
element, the ethico-mystical, has to be there, I have to trust and
endorse the intimations of necessity furnished by the second element,
if anything is to come of the whole movement.

Thus, here also, at the very source of all our certainty, of the worth
attributable to the least or greatest of our thoughts and feelings and
acts, we already find the three elements: indubitable sensation, clear

thought, warm faith in and through action. And thus life here already consists of multiplicity in unity; and what in it is absolutely indubitable, is of value only because it constitutes the indispensable starting-point and stimulation for the apprehension and affirmation of realities not directly experienced, not absolutely undeniable, but which alone bear with them all the meaning, all the richness, all the reality and worth of life.

2. THE THREE LINKS IN THE CHAIN OF REFLEX ACTION

We can also find this same triad, perhaps more simply, if we look to Psychology, and that most assured and most far-reaching of all its results, the fact and analysis of Reflex Action. For we find here that all the activities of specifically human life begin with a sense-impression, as the first, the one simply *given* element; that they move into and through a central process of mental abstraction and reflection, as the second element, contributed by the mind itself; and that they end, as the third element, in the discharge of will and of action, in an act of free affirmation, expansion, and love.

In this endless chain composed of these groups of three links each, the first link and the last link are obscure and mysterious; the first, as coming from without us, and as still below our own thought; the third, as going out from us, and seen by us only in its external results, never in its actual operation, nor in its effect upon our own central selves. Only the middle link is clear to us. And yet the most mysterious part of the whole process, the effect of it all upon the central self, is also the most certain and the most important result of the whole movement, a movement which ever culminates in a modification of the personality and which prepares this personality for the next round of sense-perception, intellectual abstraction, ethical affirmation and volitional self-determination, — acts in which light and love, fixed and free, hard, soft and cold and warm, are so mysteriously, so universally, and yet so variously linked.

IV. Distribution of the Three Elements Amongst Mankind and Throughout Human History

Let us now watch and see where and how the three elements of Religion appear among the periods of man's life, the human professions, and the races of mankind; then how they succeed each other in history generally; and finally how they exist among the chief types and phases of the Oriental, Classical Graeco-Roman, and Judaeo-Christian religions.

We have already noticed how children incline to the memory-side, to
the external, social type; and it is well they should do so, and they
should be wisely helped therein. Those passing through the storm-
and-stress period insist more upon the reason, the internal, intellectual type; and mature souls lay stress upon the feelings and the will,
the internal, ethical type. So again, women generally tend either to an
excess of the external, to superstition; or of the emotional, to fanaticism. Men, on the contrary, appear generally to incline to an excess
of the intellectual, to rationalism and indifference.

Professions, too, both by the temperaments which they presuppose,
and the habits of mind which they foster, have various affinities. The
fighting, administrative, legal and political sciences and services,
readily incline to the external and institutional; the medical, mathematical, natural science studies, to the internal-intellectual; the po-
etical, artistic, humanitarian activities, to the internal-emotional.

And whole races have tended and will tend, upon the whole, to one
or other of these three excesses: e.g. the Latin races, to Externalism and
Superstition; the Teutonic races, to the two Interiorisms, Rationalism
and Fanaticism.

The human race at large has evidently been passing, upon the whole,
from the exterior to the interior, but with a constant tendency to drop
one function for another, instead of supplementing, stimulating, purifying each by means of the other two.

If we go back as far as any analyzable records will carry us, we find
that, in proportion as religion emerges from pure fetichism, it has ever
combined with the apprehension of a Power conceived, at last and at
best, as of a Father in heaven, that of a Bond with its brethren upon
earth. Never has the sacrifice, the so-to-speak vertical relation between
the individual man and God, between the worshipper and the object
of his worship, been without the sacrificial meal, the communion, the
so-to-speak lateral, horizontal relations between man and his fellow-
man, between the worshippers one and all. Never has religion been
purely and entirely individual; always has it been, as truly and necessarily, social and institutional, traditional and historical. And this
traditional element, not all the religious genius in the world can ever

escape or replace: it was there, surrounding and moulding the very pre-natal existence of each one of us; it will be there, long after we have left the scene. We live and die its wise servants and stewards, or its blind slaves, or in futile, impoverishing revolt against it: we never, for good or for evil, really get beyond its reach.

And yet all this stream and environment of the traditional and social could make no impression upon me whatsoever, unless it were met by certain secret sympathies, by certain imperious wants and energies within myself. If the contribution of tradition is *quantitatively* by far the most important, and might be compared to the contribution furnished by the Vocabulary to the constitution of a definite, particular language, — the contribution of the individual is, *qualitatively* and for that individual, more important still, and might be compared to the contribution of the Grammar to the constitution of that same language: for it is the Grammar which, though incomparably less in amount than the Vocabulary, yet definitely constitutes any and every language.

And there is here no necessary conflict with the claim of Tradition. It is true that all real, actual Religion is ever an act of submission to some fact or truth conceived as not only true but as obligatory, as coming from God, and hence as beyond and above our purely subjective fancies, opinings, and wishes. But it is also true that, if I could not mentally hear or see, I should be incapable of hearing or seeing anything of this kind or of any other; and that without some already existing interior affinity with and mysterious capacity for discriminating between such intimations — as either corresponding to or as traversing my existing imperious needs and instincts — I could not apprehend the former as coming from God. Without, then, such non-fanciful, non-wilful, subjective capacities and dispositions, there is for us not even the apprehension of the existence of such objective realities: such capacities and dispositions are as necessary pre-requisites to every act of faith, as sight is the absolute pre-requisite for my discrimination between black and white. Hence as far back as we can go, the traditional and social, the institutional side of religion was accompanied, in varying, and at first small or less perceptible degrees and forms, by intellectual and experimental interpretation and response.

3. THE THREE ELEMENTS IN THE GREAT RELIGIONS

Even the Greek religion, as largely naturalistic up to the very end, appears, in the centuries of its relative interiorization, as a triad composed of a most ancient traditional cultus, a philosophy of religion, and an experimental-ethical life; the latter element being readily exemplified by the Demon of Socrates, and by the Eleusinian and Orphic Mysteries.

In India and Tibet, again, Brahminism and Buddhism may be said to have divided these three elements between them, the former representing as great an excess of the external as Buddhism does of abstruse reasoning and pessimistic emotion. Mahometanism, while combining, in very imperfect proportions, all three elements within itself, lays special stress upon the first, the external element; and though harbouring, for centuries now and more or less everywhere, the third, the mystical element, looks, in its strictly orthodox representatives, with suspicion upon this mysticism.

Judaism was slow in developing the second, the intellectual element; and the third, the mystical, is all but wholly absent till the Exilic period, and does not become a marked feature till still later on, and in writers under Hellenistic influence. It is in the Book of Wisdom, still more in Philo, that we find all three sides almost equally developed. And from the Hasmonean period onwards till the destruction of Jerusalem by Titus, we find a severe and ardent external, traditional, authoritative school in the Pharisees; an accommodating and rationalizing school in the Sadducees; and, apart from both, more a sect than a school, the experimental, ascetical, and mystical body of the Essenes.

But it is in Christianity, and throughout its various vicissitudes and schools, that we can most fully observe the presence, characteristics, and interaction of these three modalities. We have already seen how the New Testament writings can be grouped, with little or no violence, according to the predominance of one of these three moods, under the heads of the traditional, historic, external, the "Petrine" school; the reasoning, speculative-internal, the Pauline; and the experimental, mystical-internal, the Johannine school. And in the East, up to Clement of Alexandria, in the West up to St. Augustine, we find the prevalence of the first type. And next, in the East, in Clement and Origen, in St. Gregory of Nyssa, in the Alexandrian and the Antiochene school generally, and in the West, in St. Augustine, we find predominantly a combination of the second and third types. The Areopagitic writings of the end of the fifth century still further emphasize and systematize this Neo-Platonic form of mystical speculation, and become indeed the great treasure-house from which above all the Mystics, but also largely the Scholastics, throughout the Middle Ages, drew much of their literary material.

And those six or seven centuries of the Middle Ages are full of the contrasts and conflicts between varying forms of Institutionalism, Intellectualism, and Mysticism. Especially clearly marked is the parallelism, interaction, and apparent indestructibleness of the Scholastic and Mystical currents. Abelard and St. Bernard, St. Thomas of Aquin and the great Franciscan Doctors, above all the often largely latent, yet really ceaseless conflict between Realism and Nominalism, all can be rightly taken as caused by various combinations and degrees, insufficiencies or abnormalities in the action of the three great powers of the human soul, and of the three corresponding root-forms and functions of religion. And whereas, during the prevalence of Realism, affective, mystical religion is the concomitant and double of intellectual religion; during the later prevalence of Nominalism, Mysticism becomes the ever-increasing supplement, and at last, ever more largely, the substitute, for the methods of reasoning. "Do penance and believe in the Gospel" becomes now the favorite text, even in the mouth of Gerson (who died in 1429), the great Nominalist Doctor, the Chancellor of the then greatest intellectual centre upon earth, the University of Paris. A constant depreciation of all dialectics, indeed largely of human knowledge generally, appears even more markedly in the pages of the gentle and otherwise moderate Thomas of Kempen (who died in 1471).

Although the Humanist Renaissance was not long in carrying away many minds and hearts from all deeper consciousness and effort of a moral and religious sort, yet in so far as men retained and but further deepened and enriched their religious outlook and life, the three old forms and modalities reappear, during the earlier stages of the movement, in fresh forms and combinations. Perhaps the most truly comprehensive and Christian representative of the new at its best, is Cardinal Nicolas of Coes, the precursor of modern philosophy. For he combines the fullest adhesion to, and life-long labour for, External Institutional authority, with the keenest Intellectual, Speculative life, and with the constant temper and practice of experimental and Mystical piety. And a similar combination we find in Blessed Sir Thomas More in England, who lays down his life in defence of Institutional Religion and of the authority of the visible Church and its earthly head; who is a devoted lover of the New Learning, both Critical and Philosophical; and who continuously cultivates the Interior Life. A little later on, we find the same combination in Cardinal Ximenes in Spain.

But it is under the stress and strain of the Reformation and Counter-Reformation movements that the depth and vitality of the three currents get specially revealed. For in Germany, and in Continental Protestantism generally, we see (immediately after the very short first "fluid" stage of Luther's and Zwingli's attitude consequent upon their breach with Rome) the three currents in a largely separate condition, and hence with startling distinctness. Luther, Calvin, Zwingli, different as are their temperaments and both their earlier and their later Protestant attitudes and doctrines, all three soon fall back upon some form and fragmentary continuation, or even in its way intensification, of Institutional Religion, — driven to such conservatism by the iron necessity of real life and the irrepressible requirements of human nature. They thus formed that heavy untransparent thing, orthodox Continental Protestantism. Laelius and Faustus Socinus attempt the construction of a purely Rationalistic Religion, and capture and intensify the current of a clear, cold Deism, in which the critical mind is to be supreme. And the Anabaptist and other scattered sects and individuals (the latter represented at their best by Sebastian Frank) attempt, in their turn, to hold and develop a purely interior, experimental, emotional-intuitive, ecstatic Religion, which is warm, indeed feverish and impulsive, and distrusts both the visible and institutional, and the rational and critical.

In England the same phenomenon recurs in a modified form. For in Anglicanism, the most characteristic of its parties, the High Church school, represents predominantly the Historical, Institutional principle. The Latitudinarian school fights for the Rational, Critical, and Speculative element. The Evangelical school stands in close spiritual affinity to all but the Unitarian Nonconformists in England, and represents the Experimental, Mystical element. We readily think of Laud and Andrewes, Pusey and Keble as representatives of the first class; of Arnold, Stanley and Jowett as figures of the second class; of Thomas Scott, John Newton and Charles Simeon as types of the third class. *The Tracts for the Times, Essays and Reviews,* and (further back) Bunyan's Works, would roughly correspond to them in literature.

And this trinity of tendency can also be traced in Catholicism. Whole Religious Orders and Congregations can be seen or felt to tend, upon the whole, to one or the other type. The Jesuits can be taken as predominantly making for the first type, for fact, authority, submission, obedience; the Dominicans for the second type, for thought, a philosophico-speculative, intellectual religion; the Benedictines, in their noble Congregation of St. Maur, for a historico-critical intellectual type; the French Oratory, for a combination of both the speculative (Malebranche) and the critical (Simon, Thomassin); and the Franciscans, for the third, for action and experimental, affective spirituality.

And yet none of these Orders but has had its individuals, and even whole secondary periods, schools, and traditions, markedly typical of some current other than that specially characteristic of the Order as a whole. There are the great Critics and Historians of the Jesuit Order: the Spanish Maldonatus, the New Testament Scholar, admirable for his time, and helpful and unexhausted still; the French Denys Petau, the great historian of Christian Doctrine and of its development; the Flemish Bollandists, with their unbroken tradition of thorough critical method and incorruptible accuracy and impartiality. There are the great Jesuit Mystics: the Spanish Venerable Balthazar Alvarez, declared by St. Teresa to be the holiest mystical soul she had ever known; and the Frenchmen, Louis Lallemant and Jean Joseph Surin. There are those most attractive figures, combining the Scholar and the Mystic: Blessed Edmund Campion, the Oxford Scholar and Elizabethan Martyr; and Jean Nicolas Grou, the French translator of Plato, who died in exile in England in 1800. The Dominicans have, from the first, been really representative of external authority as well as of the speculative rational bent; and the mystical side has never been wanting to them, so amongst the early German Dominicans, Tauler and Suso, and many a Dominican female Saint. The Benedictines from the first produced great rulers; such striking types of external authority as the Pope-Saints, Gregory the Great and Gregory VII (Hildebrand), and the great Benedictine Abbots and Bishops throughout the Middle Ages are rightly felt to represent one whole side of this great Order. And again such great mystical figures as St. Hildegard of Bingen and the two Saints Gertrude are fully at home in that hospitable Family. And the Franciscans have, in the Conventuals, developed representatives of the external authority type; and in such great philosopher-theologians as Duns Scotus and Occam, a combination which has more of the intellectual, both speculative and critical, than of the simply ascetical or even mystical type.

And if we look for individual contrasts, we can often find them in close temporal and local juxtaposition, as in France, in the time of Louis XIV, in the persons of Bossuet, Richard Simon, and Fénelon, so strikingly typical of the special strengths and limitations of the institutional, rational, experimental types respectively. And yet the most largely varied influence will necessarily proceed from characters which combine not only two of the types, as in our times Frederick Faber combined the external and experimental; but which hold them all three, as with John Henry Newman in England or Antonio Rosmini in Italy.

DAISETZ SUZUKI

The Doctrine of Karma

Daisetz Teitarù Suzuki (1870–1966) was the Japanese Buddhist thinker who, as one scholar has put it, "almost singlehandedly introduced Zen to the West," where he worked for a number of years as a writer and editor. The following selections come from the second set of his *Studies in Zen Buddhism,* which were devoted to the task of explaining Zen in terms that were simultaneously faithful to the Buddhist tradition and intelligible to Western readers.

SUPERFICIALLY, passivity does not seem to be compatible with the intellectual tendency of Buddhism, especially of Zen, which strongly emphasizes the spirit of self-reliance as is seen in such passages as "The Bodhisattva-mahāsattva retiring into a solitude all by himself, should reflect within himself, by means of his own inner intelligence, and not depend upon anybody else"; or as we read in the *Dhammapada:*

> By self alone is evil done,
> By self is one disgraced;
> By self is evil undone,
> By self alone is he purified;
> Purity and impurity belong to one;
> No one can purify another.

Besides the four Noble Truths, the Twelvefold Chain of Origination, the Eightfold Path of Righteousness, etc. — all tend towards enlightenment and emancipation, and not towards absolute dependence or receptivity. "To see with one's own eyes and be liberated" is the Buddhist motto, and there is apparently no room for passivity.

* * * * *

There is thus a round of Karma and a round of fruit going on all the time. And who is the bearer of Karma and its fruit?

No doer is there does the deed,
Nor is there one who feels the fruit;
Constituent parts alone roll on;
This view alone is orthodox.

And thus the deed, and thus the fruit
Roll on and on, each from its cause;
As of the round of tree and seed,
No one can tell when they began.

Not in its fruit is found the deed,
Nor in the deed finds one the fruit;
Of each the other is devoid,
Yet there's no fruit without the deed,

Just as no store of fire is found
In jewel, cow-dung, or the sun,
Nor separate from these exists,
Yet short of fuel no fire is known;

Even so we ne'er within the deed
Can retribution's fruit descry.
Not yet in any place without;
Nor can in fruit the deed be found.

Deeds separate from their fruits exist,
And fruits are separate from the deeds;
But consequent upon the deed
Fruit doth into being come.

No god of heaven or Brahma-world
Doth cause the endless round of birth;
Constituent parts alone roll on,
From cause and from material sprung.

* * * * *

Karma may also be regarded as with or without "intimation." An act
with intimation is one the purpose of which is perceptible by others,
while an act without intimation is not at all expressed in physical
movements; it follows that when a strong act with intimation is
performed it awakens the tendency in the mind of the actor to perform
again deeds, either good or bad, of a similar nature.

It is like a seed from which a young plant shoots out and bears fruit by the principle of continuity; apart from the seed there is no continuity; and because of this continuity there is fruition. The seed comes first and then the fruit; between them there is neither discontinuity nor constancy. Since the awakening of a first motive, there follows an uninterrupted series of mental activities, and from this there is fruition. Apart from the first stirring of the mind, there will be no stream of thoughts expressing themselves in action. Thus there is a continuity of Karma and its fruit. Therefore, when the ten deeds of goodness and purity are performed, the agent is sure to enjoy happiness in this life and be born after death among celestial beings.

*   *   *   *   *

"Self" is a very complex and elusive idea, and when we say that one is to be responsible for what one does by oneself, we do not exactly know how far this "self" goes and how much it includes in itself. For individuals are so intimately related to one another not only in one communal life but in the totality of existence — so intimately indeed that there are really no individuals, so to speak, in the absolute sense of the word.

Individuality is merely an aspect of existence; in thought we separate one individual from another and in reality too we all seem to be distinct and separable. But when we reflect on the question more closely we find that individuality is a fiction, for we cannot fix its limits, we cannot ascertain its extents and boundaries, they become mutually merged without leaving any indelible marks between the so-called individuals. A most penetrating state of interrelationship prevails here, and it seems to be more exact to say that individuals do not exist, they are merely so many points of reference, the meaning of which is not at all realizable when each of them is considered by itself and in itself apart from the rest.

Individuals are recognizable only when they are thought of in relation to something not individual; though paradoxical, they are individuals so long as they are not individuals. For when an individual being is singled out as such, it at once ceases to be an individual. The "individual self" is an illusion.

MARTIN LINGS

The Reality of Sufism

Martin Lings, from whose University of London doctoral dissertation this chapter is taken, was a lecturer at the University of Cairo and then "keeper of Oriental manuscripts and printed books" in the British Museum (British Library). His various works on Islam have earned the distinction, rare for books by a Western scholar, of being translated into major languages of the Muslim world, including Arabic, Turkish, Persian, and Urdu.

As a translation of *sufi* the word "mystic" is only adequate if used in its original sense to denote one who has access, or seeks access, to "the Mysteries of the Kingdom of Heaven," for Sufism is the Islamic way of transcending one's own soul, that is, of "letting one's Spirit rise above oneself," and it is where the human self ends that the Heavenly Mysteries begin.

Although the name Sufism only came to be used after two or three generations of Islam, its reality is rooted in the first generation; and one of its roots may be said to reach back across the threshold of Islam to Muhammad's pre-Islamic practice of spiritual retreat which he took from the few scattered hermits of Arabia known as the Hunafā', and in virtue of which he was already, before his mission, a representative of all that was left of the mysticism of his ancestors Abraham and Ishmael. It was in one of his retreats in a cave on Mount Hira at the outskirts of Mecca, when he was about forty years old, that he received the first Qoranic Revelation.

In order to understand what is meant by the doctrine that the Qoran is the Eternal, Uncreated Word of God, it is necessary to make a distinction — one that is familiar to Hindus and Jews as well as to Moslems though it is not immediately so to Christians — between inspiration and revelation. If a work of the highest inspiration may be likened to a spark that is struck from a flint, the flint being man and the striker God, then a Revelation is as a spark struck by God from Himself.

It is an essential point of Islamic orthodoxy that the Qoran is revealed. In reference to its own "naked" potentialities, which are providentially veiled from man, the Holy Book says of itself, speaking with the voice of God: *If We caused this Qoran to descend upon a mountain, thou wouldst see the mountain lying prostrate with humility, rent asunder through fear of God;* and since Revelation confronts time with Eternity, thus eluding the normal conditions of time, it says that the *Lailat al-Qadr,* the night on which the Archangel Gabriel first brought a part of it to the Prophet, *is better than a thousand months.*

The first word to be revealed was the imperative *iqra',* "recite"; and *qur'ān* itself means "recitation." The revealing of a text to be recited necessarily amounts, at the summit of the community which receives it, to the inauguration of a form of mysticism, since to recite such a text is to undergo a Divine "interference," a mysterious penetration of the soul by the Spirit, of this world by the next, and the practice of taking advantage of this possibility becomes, after a certain point, no less than following a mystic path. The Sufis have always sought to take full advantage of the Presence of the Infinite in the finite by "drowning" themselves in the verses (*āyāt,* literally "miraculous signs") of the Revelation. In one of his poems the Shaikh Al-'Alawī says of the Qoran:

"It hath taken up its dwelling in our hearts and on our tongues and is mingled with our blood and our flesh and our bones and all that is in us."

Elsewhere he tells of the exceptional case of a saintly woman who made a vow never to waste another breath with the utterance of anything except the Qoran, a vow which she kept until her death, for a period of over forty years.

In certain passages where the impact of the Qoranic "substance" is given a particular direction by the impact of the meaning there lies, virtually, the entire path of the mystics. Such verses as *God leadeth to His Light whom He will* and *Lead us along the straight path* and *He it is Who hath sent down the Spirit of Peace into the hearts of the faithful that they may increase in faith upon faith* are only limited in so far as the intelligence of one who recites them is limited. They can be, if interpreted in their highest sense, as openings through which the immortal in man may pour itself out in escape from the mortal limitations of the soul. But anything that can be said of this two-fold transcendence of words which are metaphysical in content as well as in "fabric" applies pre-eminently to the Divine Names and above all to the Supreme Name *Allāh* ("God" in the absolute sense of the word). One of the first injunctions revealed to the Prophet was: *Invoke in remembrance the Name of thy Lord, and devote thyself to Him with an utter devotion.* This verse inaugurated for the new religion a practice which has been ever since the Moslem mystic's chief means of approach to God.

The Qoran is the Book of *Allāh* in every sense of the word "of." It comes from Him, it is "of one substance" with Him, and He is its basic theme; and if what might seem to be digressions from this theme do not soon lead up to it, they are abruptly snatched up to it again, as if the Qoran was bent on demonstrating its own continuously repeated words: *Do not all things return to Allāh?* The Name *Allāh* occurs so often that it may be considered as the warp on which the Qoranic text is woven.

The verse: *Verily ye have a fair pattern in the Messenger of God* is full of meaning at every level of Islam, but its highest significance must be understood in the light of an earlier Revelation, another of the very first injunctions received by the Prophet at Mecca: *Prostrate thyself and draw nigh* (to God). The ritual act of prostration, which is an extremity of self-effacement, is implicit in one of Muḥammad's secondary names, *'Abd Allāh,* the Slave of God. Without the complete self-effacement of slavehood it is impossible to *draw nigh* or, in other words, without first being empty of other than God it is impossible to be filled with the ever-present Reality of His Nearness, of which the Qoran says: *We (God) are nearer to him (man) than his jugular vein.* The realization of this Nearness is implicit in another of the Prophet's names, *Habīb Allāh,* the Beloved of God, for the following Tradition, though it is of universal import, refers to him first and foremost:

"My slave ceaseth not to draw nigh unto Me with devotions of his free will until I love him; and when I love him, I am the Hearing wherewith he heareth, and the Sight wherewith he seeth, and the Hand wherewith he smiteth, and the Foot whereon he walketh."

The full range of Sufism, as it has shown itself to be throughout the centuries, lies summed up in this Tradition.

In speaking to his closest followers Christ said: "It is given unto you to know the mysteries of the Kingdom of Heaven, but to them it is not given." In speaking to the whole community of Moslems the Qoran generalizes the same idea in the words: *We exalt in degree whom We will; and above each one that hath knowledge is one that knoweth more.* But none the less, subtly and unobtrusively, the Qoran is elsewhere more explicit. Three times in the earliest Revelations the faithful are divided into two groups. In one chapter the lower group is called *the Companions of the Right* and these are no doubt the generality of believers, since they are said to be *many among the earlier generations and many among the later generations,* and they are contrasted with *the Companions of the Left,* who are the damned. Above *the Companions of the Right* are *the Foremost,* and these are said to be *many among the earlier generations and few among the later generations.* The superlative implicit in their title is confirmed by their definition as *Near* (literally "brought near" by God to Himself), this being the word that is used to distinguish the Archangels from the other Angels. In another chapter *the Near* are represented as drinking at a fountain named *Tasnīm.* Below them are *the Righteous* who have not direct access to this fountain but who are given to drink a draught that has been flavoured at it with the perfume of musk. The same imagery is used in a third chapter where *the Righteous* are represented as drinking a draught which has been flavoured with camphor from a fountain named *Kāfūr,* to which only *the Slaves of God* have direct access. According to the commentary, "slavehood" and "nearness" are two aspects of the one highest spiritual degree, representing respectively extinction in God and Eternal Life in God. The Saints drink at *Kāfūr* inasmuch as they are *Slaves* and at *Tasnīm* inasmuch as they as *Near.*

It must be remembered that what is significant in itself, however unobtrusively it may be set in its context, will lose nothing of its significance for those who are spiritually sensitive and who devote themselves to constant recitation of the Qoran. This point is relevant not only to the passages just mentioned but also to some of the Qoranic formulations of doctrine; for just as Christ spoke to the multitude in parables, the Qoran expresses great mysteries by means of aphorisms which are too elliptic to "cause offence," but which have at the same time an overwhelming directness, as for example the already quoted words *We are nearer to him than his jugular vein.* There can be no question of any divergence of interpretation as regards such statements: the difference here between exoterism and esoterism, between piety which saves and mysticism which sanctifies, is like the difference between two and three dimensions respectively, esoterism's extra dimension being that of "depth" or "height." The same is true as regards the understanding of the Divine Names, and certain Traditions such as the Holy Tradition in which it is said, "I am the Hearing wherewith he heareth and the Sight wherewith he seeth." The difference is as between one who takes such statements as a manner of speaking, allowing them to pass over his head, and one in whom they awaken a "vertical" consciousness which is what the Sufis call *dhauq,* literally "taste." This word is used in view of the directness of such perception, to show that it transcends indirect mental knowledge, being no less than some degree of "Heart-knowledge."

In connection with one of the Prophet's mystical visions, the Qoran says that it was his *Heart* which *saw,* and Baidāwī comments that "other-worldly realities are perceived first by the Heart." What is meant by Heart here, and what the ancients of both East and West mean by saying that the Heart is the throne of the Intellect may be understood with the help of Kāshānī's already quoted commentary, which bases some of its interpretations on the correspondence between outward phenomena and inward faculties. The night corresponds to the soul, the moon to the Heart (which is to the soul what the corporeal heart is to the body) and the sun to the Spirit. Just as the moon is the last outpost of daylight in the darkness of night, so the Heart is the last outpost of Divine Light, that is, direct Knowledge (Gnosis) in the darkness of the soul's knowledge, which even in its highest form, that is, as theoretic understanding of the doctrine, is only mental and therefore indirect. The "Eye of the Heart," which corresponds to the ray of light that connects the moon with the sun, is the Intellect in its true sense — the sense in which *Intellectus* was used throughout the Middle Ages — the organ of transcendent vision.

The aspiration "to let one's Spirit (that is, as here meant, one's centre of consciousness) rise above oneself" presupposes at the very least some remote awareness of the existence of the Heart, which is the point where the human self ends and the Transcendent Self begins. If the clouds in the night of the soul are so thick as to prevent the moon of the Heart from showing the slightest sign of its presence, there can be no such aspiration.

Most of the Qoranic verses quoted so far are among the earliest to be revealed, which is enough to show that a strong mystical element was present from the outset. But coming when it did, as the last religion of this cycle of time, Islam could not be an effective vehicle of the Divine Mercy if it did not take into account the conditions of a world which was long since past its best (the Prophet said: "Naught is left of this world but trial and affliction" and "No time cometh upon you but is followed by a worse"), a world in which *the Foremost* would be in an increasingly small minority. These conditions are implicit in the following passage which was revealed towards the end of the Prophet's life, many years after he and his followers had been forced to emigrate from Mecca to Medina, and after they had returned in triumph to Mecca and had become masters of all Arabia, with an inevitable sacrifice of quality to quantity as regards converts to Islam:

The Arabs of the desert say: "We believe." Say thou (Muḥammad): *"Ye believe not, but say rather: 'We submit,' for faith hath not yet entered your hearts. Yet if ye obey God and His messenger, He will not withhold from you any reward that your deeds deserve. Verily God is Forgiving, Merciful."* We see here as it were the net of Divine Mercy stretched out to find a place in the new religion for some of those who would not have been worthy of the first small Meccan community of Moslems. Yet the growth of Islam throughout the time of the Prophet's mission is not only in this one direction but in all. The Qoran undertakes to answer any questions which might arise during the period of its revelation, and in responding to the needs of the increasingly complex community of Islam as a whole it does not neglect those who follow the path of approach to God; for while it is more and more concerned, in the Medina period, with outward questions — legal, administrative and political — its verses are at the same time more markedly charged with peace and serenity. The much loved and often repeated verse which the Qoran recommends especially for recitation in times of adversity: *Verily we are for God, and verily unto Him are we returning* has a distinctly Medinan flavour. It is significant also that some of those passages which form as it were the crown of the Sufic doctrine of Gnosis were revealed at Medina.

As regards rites, the first Revelations prescribed, both for day worship and for night vigil, litanies of glorification, prostrations, recitations of what had already been revealed of the Qoran, and invocations of the Divine Name. These devotions became voluntary after the obligatory ritual purification and prayer had been established; and other voluntary litanies were revealed at Medina such as the invocation of Divine Blessings upon the Prophet, an orison which is analogous in more than one respect to the Christian *Ave.* Voluntary fasts were also recommended in addition to the obligatory fast of the month of Ramadan. All these devotions, both the obligatory and the voluntary, reinforced by the spiritual retreat, were undoubtedly the practices of Muhammad's greatest Companions; and they are still and have always been the chief devotions of the mystics of Islam, all other practices being purely subsidiary.

It is therefore scarcely possible to speak of any development, after the death of the Prophet, as regards the essentials of Sufism; but during the first six or seven centuries of Islam the tension between the general downstream drifting of the community as a whole and the upstream movement of the mystic path produced a kind of secondary development in Sufism which is neither upward nor downward, and which did not alter the essentials in themselves, but was concerned rather with such questions as varying formulations and disciplines to suit varying needs.

Kalābādhī, a tenth century Sufi of Bukhara, says "Then (after the second generation of Islam) desire diminished and purpose flagged: and with this came the spate of questions and answers, books and treatises."

The inevitable movement from concentrated synthesis to differentiated analysis, which brought about the formation of the four different schools of canon law and, on another plane, the organization of the Sufi brotherhoods, was largely the result of an analogous change that was taking place in human souls. Nicholson is referring to this change — which he clearly did not understand — when he says: "Neither he (the Prophet) nor his hearers perceived, as later Moslems did, that the language of the Qoran is often contradictory."

It would have been less equivocal to say that later Moslems were in general not so well able to make, of two outwardly conflicting statements (as for example the Qoranic affirmations that man is responsible for his actions and that his actions are predestined), a synthesis through which they might perceive the spiritual truth in question. In other words, intellectual activity was giving way to mental activity, and it was to meet the needs of the general rationalistic ferment, and also to counteract certain heresies that had sprung from it, that scholastic theology was developed in Islam; and since those who aspired to follow the mystic path could not help being more mentally dilated than their seventh and eighth century counterparts had been, it was necessary that the Sufi Shaikhs also should make more ample formulations of doctrine in their own domain. But the Sufis have never set too great a store by these attempts to express what is universally admitted to be inexpressible. "Take knowledge from the breasts of men, not from words" and "Whoso knoweth God, his tongue flaggeth" are among the most often repeated of Sufic maxims.

In order to understand how secondary development fits into the structure of Islam, it is necessary to know that after the Qoran and the Prophet the third highest authority is *Ijmā'*, that is, the unanimous opinion of those who are thoroughly versed in the Qoran and the Traditions and who are therefore qualified to establish, by inference and on analogy, precedents about points not definitely and explicitly laid down by the two higher authorities. The deductive process by which they reach their conclusions is called *ijtihād*, (literally "striving"). Below *Ijmā'* there is a certain relative authority in the *ijtihād* of a group of qualified persons or even of a single qualified individual. The differences between the four great schools of Islamic law, for example, are due to the differing *ijtihād*, of four eminent canonists. But each school admits the right of the other schools to hold their own opinions, and it is often said: "In the canonists' differences there lieth a mercy."

The law is not the only plane of the religion, however, as is made clear in the following Tradition which was reported by 'Umar, the second Caliph:

> One day when we were with the Messenger of God there came unto us a man whose clothes were of exceeding whiteness and whose hair was of exceeding blackness, nor were there any signs of travel upon him, although none of us had seen him before. He sat down knee unto knee opposite the Prophet, upon whose thighs he placed the palms of his hands, saying: "O Muḥammad, tell me what is the surrender unto God (*al-islām*)." The Prophet answered: "The surrender is that thou shouldst testify that there is no god but God and that Muḥammad is God's Apostle, that thou shouldst perform the prayer, bestow the alms, fast Ramadan and make, if thou canst, the pilgrimage to the Holy House." He said: "Thou hast spoken truly" and we were amazed that having questioned him he should corroborate him. Then he said: "Tell me what is faith (*īmān*)," and the Prophet answered: "It is that thou shouldst believe in God and His Angels and His Books and His Apostles and the Last Day, and that thou shouldst believe that no good or evil cometh but by His Providence." "Thou hast spoken truly," he said, and then: "Tell me what is excellence (*iḥsān*)." The Prophet answered: "It is that thou shouldst worship God as if thou sawest Him, for if thou seest Him not, verily He seeth thee." . . . Then the stranger went away, and I stayed there long after he had gone, until the Prophet said

to me: "O Umar, knowest thou the questioner, who he was?"
I said: "God and His Prophet know best, but I know not at all."
"It was Gabriel," said the Prophet. "He came to teach you your
religion."

Thus Islam in its fullest sense consists of three planes — surrender
or submission (*islām* in the narrower sense of the word), faith (*īmān*)
and excellence (*ihsān*), and the Shaikh Al-'Alawī points out that there
is scope on all three for the exercise of *ijtihād:* just as the plane of *islām*
crystallized into the different schools of law and the plane of *īman* into
scholastic theology, so also, beneath the *ijtihād* of Junaid and other
Sufis, the plane of *ihsān* became a definitely organized branch of the
religion.

In the Prophet's definition of *ihsān* the word for "worship" (*'abada*)
means literally "to serve as a slave," and indicates not merely a series
of acts but a perpetual state. Thus to worship God "as if thou sawest
Him" implies perpetual remembrance of God, and to achieve this some
form of spiritual guidance and method is, practically speaking, indispensable. Here in fact lies the origin of the Sufic brotherhoods, without
which the plane of *ihsān,* which in the first generations of Islam was
relatively spontaneous and unorganized, could never have been prolonged throughout the centuries.

The Qoran insists without respite on remembrance of God, *dhikr
Allāh,* and this insistence holds the place in Islam that is held in
Christianity by the first of Christ's two commandments. It is the
Qoranic use of the cognitive term "remembrance" rather than "love"
which has, perhaps more than anything else, imposed on Islamic
mysticism its special characteristics.

The predominances, in Christian mysticism of "Love" and in Sufism
of "Knowledge," that is, Gnosis, are so strong that many of the terms
currently used in these two mystical forms are apt to be quite misleading outside their own particular sphere. For example, in the light
of Hinduism, where both perspectives are to be found side by side, it
can be seen at once that the "contemplative" orders of monasticism in
the Roman Catholic Church are closer to the path of Love than to that
of Gnosis. On the other hand what has been termed "the Sufi path of
Love" is far more akin to *jnâna* than to *bhakti,* for it is Love within the
general framework of Knowledge.

Very typical of Sufism is Hasan al-Baśri's saying: "He that knoweth
God loveth Him, and he that knoweth the world abstaineth from it,"

and the saying of another early Sufi: "Intimacy (*uns*) with God is finer and sweeter than longing."

Whereas one aspect of this path of Knowledge reflects the symbolism of light in which the Qoran abounds and also the joyous and often dazzling imagery through which it allows its reader to "taste" the Mysteries of the next world, another aspect reflects not only the stark simplicity of some of the Qoranic formulations but also certain sayings of the Prophet which have an unmistakable "dry" flavour about them, a sober objectivity which puts everything in its proper place, as for example: "Be in this world as a stranger or as a passer-by," and: "What have I to do with this world? Verily I and this world are as a rider and a tree beneath which he taketh shelter. Then he goeth on his way and leaveth it behind him."

These two aspects of Moslem spirituality make themselves felt in varying modes throughout the whole Islamic civilization, and they are especially pronounced in its art, as might be expected, for sacred art is an expression of the Mysteries and therefore springs directly from the deepest layer of its religion. The following passage brings this out very clearly:

> Islamic art is abstract, but also poetical and gracious; it is woven of soberness and splendour . . . uniting the joyous profusion of vegetation with the abstract and pure vigour of crystals: a prayer niche adorned with arabesques holds something of a garden and something of a snowflake. This admixture of qualities is already to be met with in the Qoran where the geometry of the ideas is as it were hidden under the blaze of the forms. Being, if one can so put it, haunted by Unity, Islam has also an aspect of the simplicity of the desert, of whiteness and of austerity which, in its art, alternates with the crystalline joy of ornamentation.

The Shaikh Al-'Alawī, to whose life and teaching this chapter serves as introduction, in no sense belies the roots of the tree on which his spirituality flowered, and his presence, as we feel it from his writings and from the accounts of those who knew him, is fraught now with one, now with the other of these two complementary and alternating aspects of Islam which have their origin at the Fountains of Kāfūr and Tasnīm, in the "slavehood" and the "nearness" of the first representative of the reality of Sufism.

EVELYN UNDERHILL

Mysticism and Theology

> Evelyn Underhill (1875–1941), English mystical writer, came to her scholarly study of the spiritual tradition through a personal conversion experience. Unlike some mystics, however, she did not permit that experience to block the intellectual inquiry into the nature of such experience; on the contrary, as the following discussion brilliantly demonstrates, she looked both at mysticism and at theology critically, each in the light of the other.

IN THE LAST CHAPTER we tried to establish a distinction between the mystic who tastes supreme experience and the mystical philosopher who cogitates upon the data so obtained. We have now, however, to take account of the fact that often the true mystic is also a mystical philosopher; though there are plenty of mystical philosophers who are not and could never be mystics.

Because it is characteristic of the human self to reflect upon its experience, to use its percepts as material for the construction of a concept, most mystics have made or accepted a theory of their own adventures. Thus we have a mystical philosophy or theology — the comment of the intellect on the proceedings of spiritual intuition — running side by side with true or empirical mysticism: classifying its data, criticizing it, explaining it, and translating its vision of the supersensible into symbols which are amenable to dialectic.

Such a philosophy is most usually founded upon the formal creed which the individual mystic accepts. It is characteristic of him that in so far as his transcendental activities are healthy he is generally an acceptor and not a rejector of such creeds. The view which regards the mystic as a spiritual anarchist receives little support from history; which shows us, again and again, the great mystics as faithful sons of

the great religions. Almost any religious system which fosters un-
earthly love is potentially a nursery for mystics: and Christianity,
Islam, Brahmanism, and Buddhism each receives its most sublime
interpretation at their hands. Thus St. Teresa interprets her ecstatic
apprehension of the Godhead in strictly Catholic terms, and St. John
of the Cross contrives to harmonize his intense transcendentalism
with incarnational and sacramental Christianity. Thus Boehme believed to the last that his explorations of eternity were consistent with
the teaching of the Lutheran Church. The Sūfis were good Moham-
medans, Philo and the Kabalists were orthodox Jews. Plotinus even
adapted — though with what difficulty! — the relics of paganism to
his doctrine of the Real.

Attempts, however, to limit mystical truth — the direct apprehension of the Divine Substance — by the formulae of any one religion,
are as futile as the attempt to identify a precious metal with the die
which converts it into current coin. The dies which the mystics have
used are many. Their peculiarities and excrescences are always interesting and sometimes highly significant. Some give a far sharper,
more coherent, impression than others. But the gold from which this
diverse coinage is struck is always the same precious metal: always the
same Beatific Vision of a Goodness, Truth, and Beauty which is *one*.
Hence its substance must always be distinguished from the accidents
under which we perceive it: for this substance has an absolute, and not
a denominational, importance.

Nevertheless, if we are to understand the language of the mystics,
it is evident that we must know a little of accident as well as of
substance: that is to say, of the principal philosophies or religions
which they have used in describing their adventures to the world. This
being so, before we venture to apply ourselves to the exploration of
theology proper, it will be well to consider the two extreme forms
under which both mystics and theologians have been accustomed to
conceive Divine Reality: that is to say, the so-called "emanation-
theory" and "immanence-theory" of the transcendental world.

Emanation and Immanence are formidable words; which though
perpetually tossed to and fro by amateurs of religious philosophy, have
probably, as they stand, little actuality for practical modern men. They
are, however, root-ideas for the maker of mystical diagrams: and his
best systems are but attempts towards their reconciliation. Since the
aim of every mystic is union with God, it is obvious that the vital
question in his philosophy must be the place which this God, the
Absolute of his quest, occupies in the scheme. Briefly, He has been

conceived — or, it were better to say, presented — by the great mystics under two apparently contradictory modes.

(1) The opinion which is represented in its most extreme form by the theory of *Emanations,* declares His utter transcendence. This view appears early in the history of Greek philosophy. It is developed by Dionysius, by the Kabalists, by Dante: and is implied in the language of Rulman Merswin, St. John of the Cross and many other Christian ecstatics.

The solar system is an almost perfect symbol of this concept of Reality; which finds at once its most rigid and most beautiful expression in Dante's "Paradiso." The Absolute Godhead is conceived as removed by a vast distance from the material world of sense; the last or lowest of that system of dependent worlds or states which, generated by or emanating from the Unity or Central Sun, become less in spirituality and splendour, greater in multiplicity, the further they recede from their source. That Source — the Great Countenance of the Godhead — can never, say the Kabalists, be discerned by man. It is the Absolute of the Neoplatonists, the Unplumbed Abyss of later mysticism: the Cloud of Unknowing wraps it from our sight. Only by its "emanations" or manifested attributes can we attain knowledge of it. By the outflow of these same manifested attributes and powers the created universe exists, depending in the last resort on the *latens Deitas:* Who is therefore conceived as external to the world which He illuminates and vivifies.

St. Thomas Aquinas virtually accepts the doctrine of Emanations when he writes: "As all the perfections of Creatures descend in order from God, who is the height of perfection, man should begin from the lower creatures and ascend by degrees, and so advance to the knowledge of God. . . . And because in that roof and crown of all things, God, we find the most perfect unity, and everything is stronger and more excellent the more thoroughly it is one; it follows that diversity and variety increase in things, the further they are removed from Him who is the first principle of all." Suso, whose mystical system, like that of most Dominicans, is entirely consistent with Thomist philosophy, is really glossing Aquinas when he writes: "The supreme and superessential Spirit has ennobled man by illuminating him with a ray from the Eternal Godhead. . . . Hence from out the great ring which represents the Eternal Godhead there flow forth . . . little rings, which may be taken to signify the high nobility of natural creatures."

Obviously, if this theory of the Absolute be accepted the path of the soul's ascent to union with the divine must be literally a transcendence: a journey "upward and outward," through a long series of intermediate states or worlds till, having traversed the "Thirty-two paths of the Tree of Life," she at last arrives, in Kabalistic language, at the Crown: fruitive knowledge of God, the Abyss or Divine Dark of the Dionysian school, the Neoplatonic One. Such a series of worlds is symbolized by the Ten Heavens of Dante, the hierarchies of Dionysius, the Tree of Life or Sephiroth of the Kabalah: and receives its countersign in the inward experience, in the long journey of the self through Purgation and Illumination to Union. "We ascend," says St. Augustine, "thy ways that be in our heart, and sing a song of degrees; we glow inwardly with thy fire, with thy good fire, and we go, because we go upwards to the peace of Jerusalem."

This theory postulates, under normal and non-mystical conditions, the complete separation of the human and the divine; the temporal and the eternal worlds. "Never forget," says St. John of the Cross, "that God is inaccessible. Ask not therefore how far your powers may comprehend Him, your feeling penetrate Him. Fear thus to content yourself with too little, and deprive your soul of the agility which it needs in order to mount up to Him." The language of pilgrimage, of exile, comes naturally to the mystic who apprehends reality under these terms. To him the mystical adventure is essentially a "going forth" from his normal self and from his normal universe. Like the Psalmist "in his heart he hath disposed to ascend by steps in this vale of tears" from the less to the more divine. He, and with him the Cosmos — for to mystical philosophy the soul of the individual subject is the microcosm of the soul of the world — has got to retrace the long road to the Perfection from which it originally came forth; as the fish in Rulman Merswin's Vision of Nine Rocks must struggle upwards from pool to pool until they reach their Origin.

Such a way of conceiving Reality accords with the type of mind which William James called the "sick soul." It is the mood of the penitent; of the utter humility which, appalled by the sharp contrast between itself and the Perfect which it contemplates, can only cry "out of the depths." It comes naturally to the temperament which leans to pessimism, which sees a "great gulf fixed" between itself and its desire, and is above all things sensitive to the elements of evil and imperfection in its own character and in the normal experience of man. Permitting these elements to dominate its field of consciousness, wholly ignoring the divine aspect of the World of Becoming, such a temperament constructs from its perceptions and prejudices the concept of a material world and a normal self which are very far from God.

(2) *Immanence*. At the opposite pole from this way of sketching Reality is the extreme theory of Immanence, which plays so large a part in modern theology. To the holders of this theory, who commonly belong to James's "healthy minded" or optimistic class, the quest of the Absolute is no long journey, but a realization of something which is implicit in the self and in the universe: an opening of the eyes of the soul upon the Reality in which it is bathed. For them earth is literally "crammed with heaven." "Thou wert I, but dark was my heart, I knew not the secret transcendent," says Téwekkul Bég, a Moslem mystic of the seventeenth century. This is always the cry of the temperament which leans to a theology of immanence, once its eyes are opened on the light. "God," says Plotinus, "is not external to anyone, but is present with all things, though they are ignorant that He is so." In other and older words, "The Spirit of God is within you." The Absolute Whom all seek does not hold Himself aloof from an imperfect material universe, but dwells within the flux of things: stands as it were at the very threshold of consciousness and knocks, awaiting the self's slow discovery of her treasures. "He is not far from any one of us, for in Him we live and move and have our being," is the pure doctrine of Immanence: a doctrine whose teachers are drawn from amongst the souls which react more easily to the touch of the Divine than to the sense of alienation and of sin, and are naturally inclined to love rather than to awe.

Unless safeguarded by limiting dogmas, the theory of Immanence, taken alone, is notoriously apt to degenerate into pantheism; and into those extravagant perversions of the doctrine of "deification" in which the mystic holds his transfigured self to be identical with the Indwelling God. It is the philosophical basis of that practice of introversion, the turning inward of the soul's faculties in contemplation, which has been the "method" of the great practical mystics of all creeds. That God, since He is in all — in a sense, *is* all — may most easily be found within ourselves, is the doctrine of these adventurers; who, denying or ignoring the existence of those intervening "worlds" or "planes" between the material world and the Absolute, which are postulated by the theory of Emanations, claim with Ruysbroeck that "by a simple introspection in fruitive love" they "meet God without intermediary." They hear the Father of Lights "saying eternally, without intermediary or interruption, in the most secret part of the spirit, the one, unique, and abysmal Word."

This discovery of a "divine" essence or substance, dwelling, as Ruysbroeck says, at the apex of man's soul is that fundamental experience — found in some form or degree in all genuine mystical religion — which provides the basis of the New Testament doctrine of the indwelling spirit. It is, variously interpreted, the "spark of the soul" of Eckhart, the "ground" of Tauler, the Inward Light of the Quakers, the "Divine Principle" of some modern transcendentalists; the fount and source of all true life. At this point logical exposition fails mystic and theologian alike. A tangle of metaphors takes its place. We are face to face with the "wonder of wonders" — that most real, yet most mysterious, of all the experiences of religion, the union of human and divine, in a nameless *something* which is "great enough to be God, small enough to be me." In the struggle to describe this experience, the "spark of the soul," the point of juncture, is at one moment presented to us as the divine to which the self attains: at another, as that transcendental aspect of the self which is in contact with God. On either hypothesis, it is here that the mystic encounters Absolute Being. Here is his guarantee of God's immediate presence in the human heart; and, if in the human heart, then in that universe of which man's soul resumes in miniature the essential characteristics.

According to the doctrine of Immanence, creation, the universe, could we see it as it is, would be perceived as the self-development, the self-revelation of this indwelling Deity. The world is not projected from the Absolute, but immersed in God. "I understood," says St. Teresa, "how our Lord was in all things, and how He was in the soul: and the illustration of a sponge filled with water was suggested to me." The world-process, then, is the slow coming to fruition of that Divine Spark which is latent alike in the Cosmos and in man. "If," says Boehme, "thou conceivest a small minute circle, as small as a grain of mustard seed, yet the Heart of God is wholly and perfectly therein: and if thou art born in God, then there is in thyself (in the circle of thy life) the whole Heart of God undivided." The idea of Immanence has seldom been more beautifully expressed.

It is worth noticing that both the theological doctrines of reality which have been acceptable to the mystics implicitly declare, as science does, that the universe is not static but dynamic; a World of Becoming. According to the doctrine of Immanence this universe is free, self-creative. The divine action floods it: no part is more removed from the Godhead than any other part. "God," says Eckhart, "is nearer to me than I am to myself; He is just as near to wood and stone, but they do not know it."

These two apparently contradictory explanations of the Invisible have both been held, and that in their extreme form, by the mystics:

who have found in both adequate, and indeed necessary, diagrams by which to suggest something of their rich experience of Reality. Some of the least lettered and most inspired amongst them — for instance, St. Catherine of Siena, Julian of Norwich — and some of the most learned, as Dionysius the Areopagite and Meister Eckhart, have actually used in their rhapsodies language appropriate to both the theories of Emanation and of Immanence. It would seem, then, that both these theories convey a certain truth; and that it is the business of a sound mystical philosophy to reconcile them. It is too often forgotten by quarrelsome partisans of a concrete turn of mind that at best all these transcendental theories are only symbols, methods, diagrams; feebly attempting the representation of an experience which in its fullness is always the same, and of which the dominant characteristic is ineffability. Hence they insist with tiresome monotony that Dionysius must be wrong if Tauler be right: that it is absurd to call yourself the Friend of God if unknowableness be that God's first attribute: that Plato's Perfect Beauty and St. Catherine of Siena's Accepter of Sacrifices cannot be the same: that the "courteous and dear-worthy Lord" who said to Lady Julian, "My darling, I am glad that thou art come to Me, in all thy woe I have ever been with thee," rules out the formless and impersonal One of Plotinus, the "triple circle" of Suso and Dante. Finally, that if God be truly immanent in the material world, it is either sin or folly to refuse that world in order that we may find Him; and if introversion be right, a plan of the universe which postulates intervening planes between Absolute Being and the phenomenal world must be wrong.

Now as regards the mystics, of whom we hold both these doctrines, these ways of seeing truth — for what else is a doctrine but that? — it is well to remind ourselves that their teaching about the relation of the Absolute to the finite, of God to the phenomenal world, must be founded in the first instance on what they know by experience of the relation between that Absolute and the individual self. This experience is the valid part of mysticism, the thing which gives to it its unique importance amongst systems of thought, the only source of its knowledge. Everything else is really guessing aided by analogy. When therefore the mystic, applying to the universe what he knows to be true in respect of his own soul, describes Divine Perfection as very far removed from the material world, yet linked with it by a graduated series of "emanations" — states or qualities which have each of them something of the godlike, though they be not God — he is trying to describe the necessary life-process which he has himself passed through in the course of his purgation and spiritual ascent from the state of the "natural man" to that other state of harmony with the spiritual universe, sometimes called "deification," in which he is able to contemplate, and unite with, the divine. We have in the "Divina Commedia" a classic example of such a twofold vision of the inner and the outer worlds: for Dante's journey up and out to the Empyrean Heaven is really an inward alchemy, an ordering and transmuting of his nature, a purging of his spiritual sight till — transcending all derived beatitude — it can look for an instant on the Being of God.

The mystic assumes — because he tends to assume an orderly basis for things — that there is a relation, an analogy, between this microcosm of man's self and the macrocosm of the world-self. Hence his experience, the geography of the individual quest, appears to him good evidence of the geography of the Invisible. Since he must transcend his natural life in order to attain consciousness of God, he conceives of God as essentially transcendent to the natural world. His description of that geography, however — of his path in a land where there is no time and space, no inner and no outer, up or down — will be conditioned by his temperament, by his powers of observation, by the metaphor which comes most readily to his hand, above all by his theological education. The so-called journey itself is a psychological and spiritual experience: the purging and preparation of the self, its movement to higher levels of consciousness, its unification with that more spiritual but normally unconscious self which is in touch with the transcendental order, and its gradual or abrupt entrance into union with the Real. Sometimes it seems to the self that this performance is a retreat inwards to that "ground of the soul" where, as St. Teresa says, "His Majesty awaits us": sometimes a going forth from the Conditioned to the Unconditioned, the "supernatural flight" of Plotinus and Dionysius the Areopagite. Both are but images under which the self conceives the process of attaining conscious union with that God who is "at once immanent and transcendent in relation to the Soul which shares His life."

He has got to find God. Sometimes his temperament causes him to lay most stress on the length of the search; sometimes the abrupt rapture which brings it to a close makes him forget that preliminary pilgrimage in which the soul is "not outward bound, but rather on a journey to its centre." The habitations of the Interior Castle through which St. Teresa leads us to that hidden chamber which is the sanctuary of the indwelling God: the hierarchies of Dionysius, ascending from the selfless service of the angels, past the seraphs' burning love, to the God enthroned above time and space: the mystical paths of the Kabalistic Tree of Life, which lead from the material world of Malkuth through the universes of action and thought, by Mercy, Justice and Beauty, to the Supernal Crown; all these are different ways of describing this same pilgrimage.

As every one is born a disciple of either Plato or Aristotle, so every human soul leans to one of these two ways of apprehending reality. The artist, the poet, every one who looks with awe and rapture on created things, acknowledges in this act the Immanent God. The ascetic, and that intellectual ascetic the metaphysician, turning from the created, denying the senses in order to find afar off the uncreated, unconditioned Source, is really — though often he knows it not — obeying that psychological law which produced the doctrine of Emanations.

A good map then, a good mystical philosophy, will leave room for both these ways of interpreting our experience. It will mark the routes by which many different temperaments claim to have found their way to the same end. It will acknowledge both the aspects under which the *patria splendida* Truth has appeared to its lovers: the aspects which have called forth the theories of emanation and immanence and are enshrined in the Greek and Latin names of God. *Deus,* whose root means day, shining, the Transcendent Light; and *Theos,* whose true meaning is supreme desire or prayer — the Inward Love — do not contradict, but complete each other. They form, when taken together, an almost perfect definition of that Godhead which is the object of the mystic's desire: the Divine Love which, immanent in the soul, spurs on that soul to union with the transcendent and Absolute Light — at once the source, the goal, the life of created things.

The true mystic — the person with a genius for God — hardly needs a map himself. He steers a compass course across the "vast and stormy sea of the divine." It is characteristic of his intellectual humility, however, that he is commonly willing to use the map of the community in which he finds himself, when it comes to showing other people the route which he has pursued. Sometimes these maps have been adequate. More, they have elucidated the obscure wanderings of the explorer; helped him; given him landmarks; worked out right. Time after time he puts his finger on some spot — some great hill of vision, some city of the soul — and says with conviction, "*Here* have I been." At other times the maps have embarrassed him, have refused to fit in with his description. Then he has tried, as Boehme did and after him Blake, to make new ones. Such maps are often wild in drawing, because good draughtsmanship does not necessarily go with a talent for exploration. Departing from the usual convention, they are hard — sometimes impossible — to understand. As a result, the orthodox have been forced to regard their makers as madmen or heretics: when they were really only practical men struggling to disclose great matters by imperfect means.

Without prejudice to individual beliefs, and without offering an opinion as to the exclusive truth of any one religious system or revelation — for here we are concerned neither with controversy nor with apologetics — we are bound to allow as a historical fact that mysticism, so far, has found its best map in Christianity. Christian philosophy, especially that Neoplatonic theology which, taking up and harmonizing all that was best in the spiritual intuitions of Greece, India, and Egypt, was developed by the great doctors of the early and mediaeval Church, supports and elucidates the revelations of the individual mystic as no other system of thought has been able to do.

We owe to the great fathers of the first five centuries — to Clement of Alexandria and Irenæus, Gregory of Nyssa and Augustine; above all to Dionysius the Areopagite, the great Christian contemporary of Proclus — the preservation of that mighty system of scaffolding which enabled the Catholic mystics to build up the towers and bulwarks of the City of God. The peculiar virtue of this Christian philosophy, that which marks its superiority to the more coldly self-consistent systems of Greece, is the fact that it re-states the truths of metaphysics in terms of personality: thus offering a third term, a "living mediator" between the Unknowable God, the unconditioned Absolute, and the conditioned self. This was the priceless gift which the Wise Men received in return for their gold, frankincense, and myrrh. This solves the puzzle which all explorers of the supersensible have sooner or later to face: *come si convenne l'imago al cerchio,* the reconciliation of Infinite and intimate, both known and felt, but neither understood. Such a third term, such a stepping-stone, was essential if mysticism were ever to attain that active union, that fullness of life which is its object, and develop from a blind and egoistic rapture into fruitful and self-forgetting love.

Where non-Christian mystics, as a rule, have made a forced choice between the two great dogmatic expressions of their experience, (*a*) the long pilgrimage towards a transcendent and unconditioned Absolute, (*b*) the discovery of that Absolute in the "ground" or spiritual principle of the self; it has been possible to Christianity, by means of her central doctrine of the Trinity, to find room for both of them and to exhibit them as that which they are in fact — the complementary parts of a whole. Even Dionysius, the godfather of the emanation doctrine, combines with his scheme of descending hierarchies the dogma of an in-dwelling God: and no writer is more constantly quoted by Meister Eckhart, who is generally considered to have preached immanence in its most extreme and pantheistic form.

Further, the Christian atmosphere is the one in which the individual mystic has most often been able to develop his genius in a sane and fruitful way; and an overwhelming majority of the great European contemplatives have been Christians of a strong, impassioned and personal type. This alone would justify us in regarding it as embodying, at any rate in the West, the substance of the true tradition: providing the "path of least resistance" through which that tradition flows. The very heretics of Christianity have often owed their attraction almost wholly to the mystical element in their teachings. The Gnostics, the Fraticelli, the Brethren of the Free Spirit, the Quietists, the Quakers, are instances of this. In others, it was to an excessive reliance on reason when dealing with the suprarational, and a corresponding absence of trust in mystical intuition that heresy was due. Arius and Pelagius are heretics of this type.

The greatest mystics, however, have not been heretics but Catholic saints. In Christianity the "natural mysticism" which, like "natural religion," is latent in humanity, and at a certain point of development breaks out in every race, came to itself; and attributing for the first time true and distinct personality to its Object, brought into focus the confused and unconditioned God which Neoplatonism had constructed from the abstract concepts of philosophy blended with the intuitions of Indian ecstatics, and made the basis of its meditations on the Real. It is a truism that the chief claim of Christian philosophy on our respect does not lie in its exclusiveness but in its Catholicity: in the fact that it finds truth in a hundred different systems, accepts and elucidates Greek, Jewish, and Indian thought, fuses them in a coherent theology, and says to speculative thinkers of every time and place, "Whom therefore ye ignorantly worship, Him declare I unto you."

The voice of that Truth which spoke once for all on Calvary and there declared the ground plan of the universe, was heard more or less perfectly by all the great seers, the intuitive leaders of men, the possessors of genius for the Real. There are few of the Christian names of God which were not known to the teachers of antiquity. To the Egyptians He was the Saviour, to the Platonists the Good, Beautiful and True, to the Stoics the Father and Companion. The very words of the Fourth Gospel are anticipated by Cleanthes. Heracleitus knew the Energizing Fire of which St. Bonaventura and Mechthild of Magdeburg speak. Countless mystics, from St. Augustine to St. John of the Cross, echo again and again the language of Plotinus. It is true that the differentia which mark off Christianity from all other religions are strange and poignant; but these very differentia make of it the most perfect of settings for the mystic life. Its note of close intimacy, of direct and personal contact with a spiritual reality given here and now — its astonishing combination of splendour and simplicity, of the sacramental and transcendent — all these things minister to the needs of the mystical type.

GERSHOM SCHOLEM

Jewish Mysticism

Gershom G. Scholem (1897–1982), was a professor at the Hebrew University of Jerusalem. His book *Kabbalah* made that enigmatic tradition intelligible to non-Jewish readers, his studies of Jewish apocalypticism related its eschatological visions to those of similar groups, and his examination of *Major Trends in Jewish Mysticism* (the substance of whose opening chapter appears here) probed what was Jewish and what was mystical in these trends.

THE FIRST QUESTION bound to come up is this: what is Jewish mysticism? What precisely is meant by this term? Is there such a thing, and if so, what distinguishes it from other kinds of mystical experience? In order to be able to give an answer to this question, if only an incomplete one, it will be necessary to recall what we know about mysticism in general. I do not propose to add anything essentially new to the immense literature which has sprung up around this question during the past half-century. Some of you may have read the brilliant books written on this subject by Evelyn Underhill and Dr. Rufus Jones. I merely propose to rescue what appears to me important for our purpose from the welter of conflicting historical and metaphysical arguments which have been advanced and discussed in the course of the past century.

It is a curious fact that although doubt hardly exists as to what constitutes the phenomena to which history and philosophy have given the name of mysticism, there are almost as many definitions of the term as there are writers on the subject. Some of these definitions, it is true, appear to have served more to obscure the nature of the question than to clarify it. Some idea of the confusion engendered by these definitions can be gauged from the interesting catalogue of

"Definitions of Mysticism and Mystical Theology" compiled by Dr. Inge as an appendix to his lectures on "Christian Mysticism."

A good starting-point for our investigation can be obtained by scrutinizing a few of these definitions which have won a certain authority. Dr. Rufus Jones, in his excellent "Studies in Mystical Religion" defines his subject as follows: "I shall use the word to express the type of religion which puts the emphasis on immediate awareness of relation with God, on direct and intimate consciousness of the Divine Presence. It is religion in its most acute, intense and living stage." Thomas Aquinas briefly defines mysticism as *cognitio dei experimentalis,* as the knowledge of God through experience. In using this term he leans heavily, like many mystics before and after him, on the words of the Psalmist (Psalm xxxiv, 9): "Oh taste and see that the Lord is good." It is this tasting and seeing, however spiritualized it may become, that the genuine mystic desires. His attitude is determined by the fundamental experience of the inner self which enters into immediate contact with God or the metaphysical Reality. What forms the essence of this experience, and how it is to be adequately described — that is the great riddle which the mystics themselves, no less than the historians, have tried to solve.

For it must be said that this act of personal experience, the systematic investigation and interpretation of which forms the task of all mystical speculation, is of a highly contradictory and even paradoxical nature. Certainly this is true of all attempts to describe it in words and perhaps, where there are no longer words, of the act itself. What kind of direct relation can there be between the Creator and His creature, between the finite and the infinite; and how can words express an experience for which there is no adequate simile in this finite world of man? Yet it would be wrong and superficial to conclude that the contradiction implied by the nature of mystical experience betokens an inherent absurdity. It will be wiser to assume, as we shall often have occasion to do in the course of these lectures, that the religious world of the mystic can be expressed in terms applicable to rational knowledge only with the help of paradox. Among the psychologists G. Stratton, in his "Psychology of Religious Life" (1911), has laid particular stress on this essential conflict in religious life and thought, even in its non-mystical form. It is well known that the descriptions given by the mystics of their peculiar experiences and of the God whose presence they experience are full of paradoxes of every kind. It is not the least baffling of these paradoxes — to take an instance which is common to Jewish and Christian mystics — that God is frequently described as the mystical Nothing. I shall not try now to give an interpretation of this term, to which we shall have to return; I only want to stress the fact that the particular reality which the mystic sees or tastes is of a very unusual kind.

To the general history of religion this fundamental experience is known under the name of *unio mystica,* or mystical union with God. The term, however, has no particular significance. Numerous mystics, Jews as well as non-Jews, have by no means represented the essence of their ecstatic experience, the tremendous uprush and soaring of the soul to its highest plane, as a union with God. To take an instance, the earliest Jewish mystics who formed an organized fraternity in Talmudic times and later, describe their experience in terms derived from the diction characteristic of their age. They speak of the ascent of the soul to the Celestial Throne where it obtains an ecstatic view of the majesty of God and the secrets of His Realm. A great distance separates these old Jewish Gnostics from the Hasidic mystics one of whom said: "There are those who serve God with their human intellect, and others whose gaze is fixed on Nothing. . . . He who is granted this supreme experience loses the reality of his intellect, but when he returns from such contemplation to the intellect, he finds it full of divine and inflowing splendor." And yet it is the same experience which both are trying to express in different ways.

This leads us to further consideration: it would be a mistake to assume that the whole of what we call mysticism is identical with that personal experience which is realized in the state of ecstasy or ecstatic meditation. Mysticism, as an historical phenomenon, comprises much more than this experience, which lies at its root. There is a danger in relying too much on purely speculative definitions of the term. The point I should like to make is this — that there is no such thing as mysticism in the abstract, that is to say, a phenomenon or experience which has no particular relation to other religious phenomena. There is no mysticism as such, there is only the mysticism of a particular religious system, Christian, Islamic, Jewish mysticism and so on. That there remains a common characteristic it would be absurd to deny, and it is this element which is brought out in the comparative analysis of particular mystical experiences. But only in our days has the belief gained ground that there is such a thing as an abstract mystical religion. One reason for this widespread belief may be found in the pantheistic trend which, for the past century, has exercised a much greater influence on religious thought than ever before. Its influence can be traced in the manifold attempts to abandon the fixed forms of dogmatic and institutional religion in favour of some sort of universal religion. For the same reason the various historical aspects of religious mysticism are often treated as corrupted forms of an, as it were, chemically pure mysticism which is thought of as not bound to any particular religion. As it is our intention to treat of a certain definite kind of mysticism, namely Jewish, we should not dwell too much upon such abstractions. Moreover, as Evelyn Underhill has rightly pointed out, the prevailing conception of the mystic as a religious anarchist who owes no allegiance to his religion finds little support in fact. History rather shows that the great mystics were faithful adherents of the great religions.

Jewish mysticism, no less than its Greek or Christian counterparts, presents itself as a totality of concrete historical phenomena. Let us, therefore, pause to consider for a moment the conditions and circumstances under which mysticism arises in the historical development of religion and particularly in that of the great monotheistic systems. The definitions of the term *mysticism,* of which I have given a few instances, lead only too easily to the conclusion that all religion in the last resort is based on mysticism; a conclusion which, as we have seen, is drawn in so many words by Rufus Jones. For is not religion unthinkable without an "immediate awareness of relation with God"? That way lies an interminable dispute about words. The fact is that nobody seriously thinks of applying the term *mysticism* to the classic manifestations of the great religions. It would be absurd to call Moses, the man of God, a mystic, or to apply this term to the Prophets, on the strength of their immediate religious experience. I, for one, do not intend to employ a terminology which obscures the very real differences that are recognized by all, and thereby makes it even more difficult to get at the root of the problem.

The point which I would like to make first of all is this: Mysticism is a definite stage in the historical development of religion and makes its appearance under certain well-defined conditions. It is connected with, and inseparable from, a certain stage of the religious consciousness. It is also incompatible with certain other stages which leave no room for mysticism in the sense in which the term is commonly understood.

The first stage represents the world as being full of gods whom man encounters at every step and whose presence can be experienced without recourse to ecstatic meditation. In other words, there is no room for mysticism as long as the abyss between Man and God has not become a fact of the inner consciousness. That, however, is the case only while the childhood of mankind, its mythical epoch, lasts. The immediate consciousness of the interrelation and interdependence of things, their essential unity which precedes duality and in fact knows nothing of it, the truly monistic universe of man's mythical age, all this is alien to the spirit of mysticism. At the same time it will become clear why certain elements of this monistic consciousness recur on another plane and in different guise in the mystical consciousness. In this first stage, Nature is the scene of man's relation to God.

The second period which knows no real mysticism is the creative epoch in which the emergence, the break-through of religion occurs. Religion's supreme function is to destroy the dream-harmony of Man, Universe and God, to isolate man from the other elements of the dream stage of his mythical and primitive consciousness. For in its classical form, religion signifies the creation of a vast abyss, conceived as absolute, between God, the infinite and transcendental Being, and Man, the finite creature. For this reason alone, the rise of institutional religion, which is also the classical stage in the history of religion, is more widely removed than any other period from mysticism and all it implies. Man becomes aware of a fundamental duality, of a vast gulf which can be crossed by nothing but the *voice;* the voice of God, directing and law-giving in His revelation, and the voice of man in prayer. The great monotheistic religions live and unfold in the ever-present consciousness of this bipolarity, of the existence of an abyss which can never be bridged. To them the scene of religion is no longer Nature, but the moral and religious action of man and the community of men, whose interplay brings about history as, in a sense, the stage on which the drama of man's relation to God unfolds.

And only now that religion has received, in history, its classical expression in a certain communal way of living and believing, only now do we witness the phenomenon called mysticism; its rise coincides with what may be called the romantic period of religion. Mysticism does not deny or overlook the abyss; on the contrary, it begins by realizing its existence, but from there it proceeds to a quest for the secret that will close it in, the hidden path that will span it. It strives to piece together the fragments broken by the religious cataclysm, to bring back the old unity which religion has destroyed, but on a new plane, where the world of mythology and that of revelation meet in the soul of man. Thus the soul becomes its scene and the soul's path through the abysmal multiplicity of things to the experience of the Divine Reality, now conceived as the primordial unity of all things, becomes its main preoccupation. To a certain extent, therefore, mysticism signifies a revival of mythical thought, although the difference must not be overlooked between the unity which is there before there is duality, and the unity that has to be won back in a new upsurge of the religious consciousness.

Historically, this appearance of mystical tendencies is also connected with another factor. The religious consciousness is not exhausted with the emergence of the classic systems of institutional religion. Its creative power endures, although the formative effect of a given religion may be sufficiently great to encompass all genuine religious feeling within its orbit for a long period. During this period the values which such a religious system has set up retain their original meaning and their appeal to the feelings of the believers. However, even so new religious impulses may and do arise which threaten to conflict with the scale of values established by historical religion. Above all, what encourages the emergence of mysticism is a situation in which these new impulses do not break through the shell of the old religious system and create a new one, but tend to remain confined within its borders. If and when such a situation arises, the longing for new religious values corresponding to the new religious experience finds its expression in a new interpretation of the old values which frequently acquire a much more profound and personal significance, although one which often differs entirely from the old and transforms their meaning. In this way Creation, Revelation and Redemption, to mention some of our most important religious conceptions, are given new and different meanings reflecting the characteristic feature of mystical experience, the direct contact between the individual and God.

Revelation, for instance, is to the mystic not only a definite historical occurrence which, at a given moment in history, puts an end to any further direct relation between mankind and God. With no thought of denying Revelation as a fact of history, the mystic still conceives the source of religious knowledge and experience which bursts forth from his own heart as being of equal importance for the conception of religious truth. In other words, instead of the one act of Revelation, there is a constant repetition of this act. This new Revelation, to himself or to his spiritual master, the mystic tries to link up with the sacred texts of the old; hence the new interpretation given to the canonical texts and sacred books of the great religions. To the mystic, the original act of Revelation to the community — the, as it were, public revelation of Mount Sinai, to take one instance — appears as something whose true meaning has yet to unfold itself; the secret revelation is to him the real and decisive one. And thus the substance of the canonical texts, like that of all other religious values, is melted down and given another form as it passes through the fiery stream of the mystical consciousness. It is hardly surprising that, hard as the mystic may try to remain within the confines of his religion, he often consciously or unconsciously approaches, or even transgresses, its limits.

It is not necessary for me to say anything further at this point about the reasons which have often transformed mystics into heretics. Such heresy does not always have to be fought with fire and sword by the religious community: it may even happen that its heretical nature is not understood and recognized. Particularly is this the case where the mystic succeeds in adapting himself to the "orthodox" vocabulary and uses it as a wing or vehicle for his thoughts. As a matter of fact, this is what many Kabbalists have done. While Christianity and Islam, which had at their disposal more extensive means of repression and the apparatus of the State, have frequently and drastically suppressed the more extreme forms of mystical movements, few analogous events are to be found in the history of Judaism. Nevertheless, in the lectures on Sabbatianism and Hasidism, we shall have occasion to note that instances of this kind are not entirely lacking.

We have seen that mystical religion seeks to transform the God whom it encounters in the peculiar religious consciousness of its own social environment from an object of dogmatic knowledge into a novel and living experience and intuition. In addition, it also seeks to interpret this experience in a new way. Its practical side, the realization of God and the doctrine of the Quest for God, are therefore frequently, particularly in the more developed forms of the mystical consciousness, connected with a certain ideology. This ideology, this theory of mysticism, is a theory both of the mystical cognition of God and His revelation, and of the path which leads to Him.

It should now be clear why the outward forms of mystical religion within the orbit of a given religion are to a large extent shaped by the positive content and values recognized and glorified in that religion. We cannot, therefore, expect the physiognomy of Jewish mysticism to be the same as that of Catholic mysticism, Anabaptism or Moslem Sufism. The particular aspects of Christian mysticism, which are connected with the person of the Saviour and mediator between God and man, the mystical interpretation of the Passion of Christ, which

is repeated in the personal experience of the individual — all this is
foreign to Judaism, and also to its mystics. Their ideas proceed from
the concepts and values peculiar to Judaism, that is to say, above all
from the belief in the Unity of God and the meaning of His revelation
as laid down in the Torah, the sacred law.

Jewish mysticism in its various forms represents an attempt to
interpret the religious values of Judaism in terms of mystical values.
It concentrates upon the idea of the living God who manifests himself
in the acts of Creation, Revelation and Redemption. Pushed to its
extreme, the mystical meditation on this idea gives birth to the
conception of a sphere, a whole realm of divinity, which underlies the
world of our sense-data and which is present and active in all that
exists. This is the meaning of what the Kabbalists call the *world of the
"Sefiroth."* I should like to explain this a little more fully.

The attributes of the living God are conceived differently and
undergo a peculiar transformation when compared with the meaning
given to them by the philosophers of Judaism. Among the latter,
Maimonides, in his "Guide of the Perplexed," felt bound to ask: How
is it possible to say of God that He is living? Does that not imply a
limitation of the infinite Being? The words "God is living," he argues,
can only mean that he is not dead, that is to say, that he is the opposite
of all that is negative. He is the negation of negation. A quite different
reply is given by the Kabbalist, for whom the distinction, nay the
conflict, between the known and the unknown God has a significance
denied to it by the philosophers of Judaism.

No creature can take aim at the unknown, the hidden God. In the
last resort, every cognition of God is based on a form of relation
between Him and His creature, i.e. on a manifestation of God in
something else, and not on a relation between Him and Himself. It has
been argued that the difference between the *deus absconditus,* God in
Himself, and God in His appearance is unknown to Kabbalism. This
seems to me a wrong interpretation of the facts. On the contrary, the
dualism embedded in these two aspects of the one God, both of which
are, theologically speaking, possibly ways of aiming at the divinity, has
deeply preoccupied the Jewish mystics. It has occasionally led them
to use formulas whose implied challenge to the religious consciousness of monotheism was fully revealed only in the subsequent development of Kabbalism. As a rule, the Kabbalists were concerned to find
a formula which should give as little offense as possible to the philosophers. For this reason the inherent contradiction between the two
aspects of God is not always brought out as clearly as in the famous

doctrine of an anonymous writer around 1300, according to whom God in Himself, as an absolute Being, and therefore by His very nature incapable of becoming the subject of a revelation to others, is not and cannot be meant in the documents of Revelation, in the canonical writings of the Bible, and in the rabbinical tradition. He is not the subject of these writings and therefore also has no documented name, since every word of the sacred writings refers after all to some aspect of His manifestation on the side of Creation. It follows that while the living God, the God of religion of whom these writings bear witness, has innumerable names — which, according to the Kabbalists, belong to Him by His very nature and not as a result of human convention — the *deus absconditus,* the God who is hidden in His own self, can only be named in a metaphorical sense and with the help of words which, mystically speaking, are not real names at all. The favorite formulae of the early Spanish Kabbalists are speculative paraphrases like "Root of all Roots," "Great Reality," "Indifferent Unity," and, above all, *En-Sof.* The latter designation reveals the impersonal character of this aspect of the hidden God from the standpoint of man as clearly as, and perhaps even more clearly than, the others. It signifies "the infinite" as such; not, as has been frequently suggested, "He who is infinite" but "that which is infinite." Isaac the Blind (one of the first Kabbalists of distinguishable personality) calls the *deus absconditus* "that which is not conceivable by thinking," *not* "He who is not etc." It is clear that with this postulate of an impersonal basic reality in God, which becomes a person — or appears as a person — only in the process of Creation and Revelation, Kabbalism abandons the personalistic basis of the Biblical conception of God. In this sense it is undeniable that the author of the above-mentioned mystical aphorism is right in holding that *En-Sof* (or what is meant by it) is not even mentioned in the Bible and the Talmud. . . . It will not surprise us to find that speculation has run the whole gamut — from attempts to re-transform the impersonal *En-Sof* into the personal God of the Bible to the downright heretical doctrine of a genuine dualism between the hidden *En-Sof* and the personal Demiurge of Scripture. For the moment, however, we are more concerned with the second aspect of the Godhead which, being of decisive importance for real religion, formed the main subject of theosophical speculation in Kabbalism.

The mystic strives to assure himself of the living presence of God, the God of the Bible, the God who is good, wise, just and merciful and the embodiment of all other positive attributes. But at the same time he is unwilling to renounce the idea of the hidden God who remains

eternally unknowable in the depths of His own Self, or, to use the bold
expression of the Kabbalists "in the depths of His nothingness." This
hidden God may be without special attributes — the living God of
whom the Revelation speaks, with whom all religion is concerned,
must have attributes, which on another plane represent also the
mystic's own scale of moral values: God is good, God is severe, God
is merciful and just, etc. As we shall have occasion to see, the mystic
does not even recoil before the inference that in a higher sense there
is a root of evil even in God. The benevolence of God is to the mystic
not simply the negation of evil, but a whole sphere of divine light, in
which God manifests Himself under this particular aspect of benevolence to the contemplation of the Kabbalist.

These spheres, which are often described with the aid of mythical
metaphors and provide the key for a kind of mystical topography of
the Divine realm, are themselves nothing but stages in the revelation
of God's creative power. Every attribute represents a given stage,
including the attribute of severity and stern judgment, which mystical
speculation has connected with the source of evil in God. The mystic
who sets out to grasp the meaning of God's absolute unity is thus faced
at the outset with an infinite complexity of heavenly spheres and
stages which are described in the Kabbalistic texts. From the contemplation of these "Sefiroth" he proceeds to the conception of God
as the union and the root of all these contradictions. Generally
speaking, the mystics do not seem to conceive of God as the absolute
Being or absolute Becoming but as the union of both; much as the
hidden God of whom nothing is known to us, and the living God of
religious experience and revelation, are one and the same. Kabbalism
in other words is not dualistic, although historically there exists a close
connection between its way of thinking and that of the Gnostics, to
whom the hidden God and the Creator are opposing principles. On the
contrary, all the energy of "orthodox" Kabbalistic speculation is bent
to the task of escaping from dualistic consequences; otherwise they
would not have been able to maintain themselves within the Jewish
community.

VIII FAITH AND FREEDOM

Regardless of dogma, or of the lack of dogma, faith and freedom have long existed in an uneasy symbiosis. The Nirvana promised by Buddhism is deliverance from the tyrannies of time and desire; Islam means submission to the will of God, and freedom through that submission; the rituals of primitive religion are a means of liberation from the threatening forces that surround human life. And yet every faith, in its very offer of freedom, simultaneously calls for obedience, the acceptance of authority, and the surrender of the self. Apologists for religion have often likened that complex relation of faith and freedom to the mystery of falling in love, which involves both the loss of freedom to the claims of another and the discovery of authentic freedom through fulfillment in the other.

As that uneasy symbiosis characterizes the relation of faith to spiritual freedom, so it is evident to an even greater extent in the relation between religious faith and social or political freedom. Ever since the shamans and divine chieftains of early peoples, religion has been an instrument for those who rule to dominate their subjects. What the West came to call "the divine right of kings" was one version of a widespread tendency toward developing a political theology. Sometimes the ruler was said to be divine, sometimes the revealed will of God was regarded as an explicit guideline for political policy, and sometimes the kingship and the priesthood were combined in one person. Yet even where kingship and priesthood have been distinguished and church and state have been separated, the sanctions of religion have become a means of enforcing the will of the ruling "powers that be"; in exchange, the ruling powers have accorded special privileges to religious institutions and practices. And yet those very institutions and practices have, more than once, become the seedbeds of revolution against the establishment.

The selections that follow in this section are a documentation of this complex relation. In some of them the impulse to shape the social order in accordance with the divine standard seems to sanctify the existing structures of society, in others it acts to call society to new levels of humanity and compassion. Although religion has for centuries served as a rationale for racial and religious oppression, it has in the twentieth century found its authentic voice as a radical summons to justice and equality, though only after witnessing the sacrifice of millions of human beings. And organized religion, which in so many cultures has provided a justification for international violence or has even made it into a holy cause, has during the modern era begun to rediscover the age-old imperative to find a substitute for war. Thus it has reminded insiders and outsiders alike of one of the most fundamental of all religious convictions (though it has been variously expressed): that because God is the father of all, the entire human race is one family.

BARBARA WARD

Faith and Freedom

Barbara Mary Ward, Lady Jackson (1914–1981) was by
training an economist and by outlook a citizen of the world.
Throughout her life she was in the forefront of the struggle
for social justice, especially also in relation to what eventually came to be called the Third World, but she was more
explicit than most of her colleagues in grounding that
struggle in her religious beliefs, as the following selection
from *Faith and Freedom* shows.

However rational, however compelling, however logical the arguments for Western unity may be, however obvious the benefits of
economic co-operation, however hopeful the promise of amity between the nations, one may still question whether reason or logic, of
themselves, are enough to change the direction of Western development. The vitalities that must be mastered are the fiercest in the world.
They appeal to the ultimate instincts in mankind — the protection of
the tribe and the struggle for physical survival. Reason may be out-
matched in its struggle with such giants. Has Western man other
forces to summon to his aid?

There is, of course, the fact of fear. It is not to be despised. Many
things have been accomplished in recent years — including the
groundwork of the Atlantic alliance — which would never have been
achieved without Soviet pressure. Moreover, even if the Soviets were
outwardly unaggressive, they could still — like their totalitarian
brethren the Nazis — inspire in the West a salutary fear by demonstrating, in its ultimate stages, the rake's progress in which all Western
civilization is to some extent involved. Both these systems of absolute
dictatorship have sprung from the Western world. Both have carried
to an extreme degree principles and policies which have already made

their appearance in the West. The nationalism which Hitler turned to a horror of blood and butchery presides in a sedate form over all Western democracies. The confidence in state action, the glorification of technology, the unlimited faith in science, the centralization of decision, and the subordination of law to so-called mass interests — all these, which in an extreme form have gone to set an inhuman stamp upon Soviet society, have helped in the West to create communities in which the individual citizen feels overwhelmed, isolated, and helpless before the anonymities of public and private bureaucracy. We are right to fear these vast distortions of tendencies already at work in our own society. Both the Soviet and the Nazi systems must stand as dread reminders that in the twentieth century, the line of least resistance in politics tends toward the full apparatus of totalitarian rule. It is not wrong to fear such warnings. It is the beginning of wisdom.

But fear alone is a poor counsellor because it is essentially negative. The Western world cannot combat Communism on such a basis. A people guided only by fear leaves all the initiative and all the advantage with the other side and is reduced to a blind defensive maneuvering in order to counter the other's positive actions, to inferiority, to loss of control, and in all probability to ultimate defeat. Throughout history, the men with a positive goal and a persistent aim have had their way. Like artists at work on the raw material of stone or wood or canvas, they have imposed their vision and drawn the rough vitalities of human existence together into new patterns of society. True, the materials have often proved recalcitrant and the vision has been distorted. Yet such ideals as the Greek *polis,* the "chosen people" of Jewry, the unity of Christendom, the American Republic — or indeed the Dictatorship of the Proletariat — have proved instruments in the hands of men by virtue of which the forces of hunger and power and fear, which are the inchoate stuff of existence, have been molded into something nearer the visionaries' desire. If, in the second half of the twentieth century, the Western peoples have lost all their visions and dreamed all their dreams, then the world is open to the powerful myths of the totalitarians. The society which they picture may be in many respects a nightmare, but nightmares are potent in a world without good dreams.

The West will prove more vulnerable than any other society if it abandons the pursuit of visions and ideals for, more than any other community, it is the product not of geographical and racial forces but of the molding power of the human spirit. Geographically, Europe is no more than the small Western promontory of the land mass of Asia.

It is "Europe" solely because its frontiers mark the frontiers of Christendom. Racially, the United States is a melting pot of every nation under the sun. Only by force of an idea — the "proposition" that men are created equal and possess inalienable rights — has it risen to be the most powerful community in the history of man. Both European society and its extension into the New World have been sustained by a unique faith in man — in his freedom, in his responsibility, in the laws which should safeguard him, in the rights that are his and in the duties by which he earns those rights. So accustomed are we to this view of man that we do not realize the audacity which was needed to bring it into being. At a time when humanity was subject to every physical calamity, when perpetual labor was needed to wring a livelihood from the soil, when the fatalities of tempest and sickness and the general recalcitrance of matter lay heavily upon man's spirit, and when the world, unpenetrated by rational discovery, was a vast unknown — in such a time, the Greek and Jewish forebears of our own civilization made their tremendous acts of faith in man and in his destiny. They declared him to be the crown of the universe. They saw nature as a field open to his reason and his dominion. The Greeks affirmed his power to build a rational order, the Jews proclaimed him a co-worker in the coming reign of righteousness.

It was because this picture of man was so high and so untrammeled and its ambition so vast that it led to the discovery of material instruments of mastery, to science and industry and all the material means of our own day. Man is not master of the universe because he can split the atom. He has split the atom because he first believed in his own unique mastery. Faith led to the material achievement, not the achievement to the faith. In fact, now that the means of mastering the environment, of building — physically — a better world, are more complete than ever before, it is a paradox that the faith is slackening. The men of the West believed in man's high destiny and in his power to remold society in a divine pattern more entirely when their physical means were inadequate and their control marginal than they do today when science and industry offer unlimited opportunities of creation. The reason is that the old audacious view of man and of his destiny was sustained only by faith. Reduce man to a creature of his environment, projected from the fatality of birth by anonymous forces on to the fatality of death — then he is ready to surrender his freedom, his rights, his greatness. He is ready for dictatorship and the slave state.

The human heart has both appetites and despairs which rational codes alone are unable to control. Man is lonely. He is not self-sufficient. He rebels against meaninglessness in life. He is haunted by death. He is afraid. He needs to feel himself part of a wider whole and he has unassuageable powers of dedication and devotion which must find expression in worship and service. If, therefore, there is no other outlet for these powers, then the community in which he lives, the tribe, the state, Caesar, the dictator, become the natural and inevitable objects of his religious zeal. Religion is not abolished by the "abolition" of God; the religion of Caesar takes its place. And since, for a few men, the need to worship is satisfied in *hubris*, in the worship of the self, the multitudes who look for a god can nearly always be certain of finding a willing candidate. In times of crisis, when insecurity, anxiety, loneliness, and the meaninglessness of life become well-nigh insupportable — how can a man tolerate years without work in modern industrial society? — the hunger for godlike leadership, for religious reassurance, for a merging of the self in the security of the whole becomes irresistible. Even when faith in God survives, the desire wells up for strong government. Where religious faith has vanished, all the energies of the soul are poured into the one channel of political faith. In our own day, Communism and National Socialism have proved to be powerful religions and have brought back into the world the identification of state and church, city and temple, king and god which made up the monolithic unity of archaic society and the universal servitude of archaic man.

Few deny the historical role of Christianity in creating a double order of reality and a division of power out of which the possibility of freedom has grown. Even the most doubtful must confront the fact that totalitarian government in its extremest form has returned when the waning of religion left the altars of the soul empty and turned men back to the oldest gods of all — the idols of the tribe. Nor is it easy to conceive of any means other than religious faith for preserving a genuine division of power in society; for if man is no more than the creature of his environment, and a product of his social order, on what foundations can he base claims and loyalties which go beyond the social order? From what source can he draw the strength to resist the claims of society? To what justice can he appeal beyond the dictates of the state? The state is by nature so powerful and compelling and voracious an institution that the citizen, standing alone against it, is all but powerless. He needs counter-institutions, above all the counter-institution of the Church, which of all organized bodies alone can look Caesar in the face and claim a higher loyalty.

It is, however, one thing to argue that a recovery of faith in God is necessary as a safeguard of Western freedom. It is quite another to put forward sociological and political and historical facts as the basis for a revival of faith. Such a procedure runs the risk of resembling the hypocrisy of eighteenth-century cynics who argued that religion was good for the poor because it kept them contented. Faith is not a matter of convenience nor even — save indirectly — a matter of sociology. It is a question of conviction and dedication and both spring from one source only — from the belief in God as a fact, as the supreme Fact of existence. Faith will not be restored in the West because people believe it to be useful. It will return only when they find that it is true.

But can modern man accept such a possibility? The whole trend of four hundred years of rationalism and science has taken him in the opposite direction — toward acceptance of a single material universe which is the sum of all there is and has no place for gods, for supernature, for First Causes or Creators claiming the worship and obedience of man. After so much conditioning in the idea of a single natural system, can man find in his contemporary universe any trace of a supernatural order of reality, any hint that the faith which once sustained his civilization is not a helpful myth but still the essential map of human destiny?

Perhaps the surest starting point for such an inquiry — and it is idle to speak of a recovery of faith unless such an inquiry is undertaken — lies with the fact of the existence of a physical universe. One of the problems that has puzzled mankind ever since man began to reflect upon experience is that of "being" itself. All our knowledge of physical reality, from its minutest atoms and impulses up to its most awesome manifestations in mountain ranges or volcanic eruptions, suggests that each physical phenomenon has a physical cause behind it and that it is not in itself a sufficient explanation of what and why it is. Yet if the whole physical universe is made up of dependent substances, each requiring an explanation, then the sum of reality is still only a sum of dependent things and it does not seem that all dependent substances added together can somehow add the quality of independence to themselves merely, as it were, by huddling together. Logically, they seem to demand a self-explanatory self-subsistent ground to account for their existence. Some scientists, believing the whole of the universe to display evidence of declining energy, hold that a physical act of creation once took place to launch the whole complex phenomenon of physical reality — a theory which seems to imply a Creator behind the act of creation. A more recent theory suggests that the total

universe is maintained by a constant pouring into the system of
interstellar gas out of which are condensed the galaxies, which in their
turn breed stars whose explosions precipitate the planets, on one of
which — our own — we know life exists. But this theory, while
solving the problem of the appearance of the solar system, leaves us
with the problem of the interstellar gas. How does it appear? Has it a
cause? Or alone of all the physical phenomena of which we are aware,
has it no cause? Its supposed continuous creation at least suggests
something behind it which does the creating.

But even if the mind can grasp and be satisfied with the idea of
interstellar gas as the uncaused, self-subsistent ground of physical
reality, this prop breaks down when we turn from matter to mind,
from physical reality to the field of rationality and reason. One of the
great progenitors of our civilization, the Greeks, believed that rationality is evidence of the divine in nature. If it can be shown that the
very notion of rationality can have no place in a single material order
of nature, then the presumption must be that there is more than a
material universe and that any account of reality must include other
than purely material factors. In ordinary daily common sense living we
do, of course, make constant distinctions between purely material
facts and sensations and something else that seems to be beyond and
apart from them. We do not confuse mind with matter. We believe we
understand what we say when we distinguish between rational and
irrational behavior. We think we can see the difference between a valid
and an invalid inference or conclusion. To put the distinction in
concrete terms, a man undergoing a nightmare has vivid mental
images which may cause him to call out, to wave his arms about, to
get up, and even to threaten violence. Similarly, a man overcome by
a fit of rage or under the influence of drugs may commit crimes of
which he would normally be believed incapable. In none of these cases
do we consider the man's mind — his rational nature — to have been
at work: he has been overcome by irrational forces, by the store of
uncontrolled sensory images and desires in his subconscious, by a
flood of sensation, by the physical effect of some narcotic substance.
These material powers have invaded his mind and taken over control.

So strong is this belief that rationality is something apart from
material and emotional causation that the followers of Marx have
mobilized it into a most potent weapon against Western society. It is
their contemptuous charge that Western freedom, Western law, and
Western idealism are all cloaks for the greed and rapacity of Western
economic exploitation. They attack the validity of Western ideas on

the grounds that they are only projections of self-interest and class feeling. In another field, Freud has helped to confuse conventional morality by reducing much of it to the rationalization of unconscious drives and impulses.

But here is the puzzle. If the whole of reality is made up of a single material process, it follows that mind can be only the by-product of the physical brain and that every thought is materially conditioned by the sensations and impulses which have previously been registered in the physical organism. This, briefly, is the view of mind held by those who believe only in a single material order of reality. In fact, it is the view they must hold, for if mind were something else, their theory would be wrong: there would be one point in nature to which material conditioning did not provide the full explanation; mind would be the entry point of another order of reality, the chink, however tiny, through which might stream another radiance, the light of the Logos itself, the fount of truth.

Is mind then the projection of the physical organism? If it is, all our thoughts have at some point physical origins. They are all rooted in what, in our everyday language, we call irrational facts, facts of temperament, physique, heredity, or environment. Each of these facts, used to explain a single happening, would, as we have seen, destroy the credibility of the explanation. Add all the single happenings together to make up the whole universe and is there any more room for reason? By choosing a single material order of reality, we seem to exclude rationality altogether. And this possibility has very serious consequences for thought.

A passion for truth is generally held to be among mankind's noblest aspirations. All the world religions have affirmed that God, in some mysterious fashion, is Truth. At this stage of the argument, we can at least maintain the negative point that in a universe without supernature, without some order of reality apart from material happenings, there can be no such thing as truth. Valid argument, rational deduction, proof itself are alike impossibilities. When Marx says that law and custom and idealism and religion and theories and ideas are all by-products of the material process of production, he clearly means us to believe the statement. But on his own showing, his statement, like that of any other idea, must be the product of a certain stage of economic development. It is no more "rational" than the theories of capitalism it is used to demolish.

Similarly with every other argument, if statements are no more than certain rearrangements of impulses in the speaker's brain; if, as Dr.

Thomas Huxley once said to the British Association, "the thoughts to which I am now giving utterance and your thoughts regarding them are expressions of the molecular changes in the matter of life," then they can be observed and noted but they cannot be said to "prove" something any more than an attack of measles can be looked on as an argument. They simply occur.

Some materialists would attempt to get around this difficulty by saying that thoughts have been rising in human minds for thousands and thousands of years. Some thoughts give their thinkers greater chances of survival than others. Over the millennia ideas have been weeded out by process of elimination — the thinkers of inefficient thoughts succumbing, the thinkers of self-preserving thoughts surviving — until today, the thoughts we call true are really those which have helped the human organism to exist and develop. But this whole argument, to be convincing, depends upon the validity of a chain of argument. It depends upon a number of inferences about the past, it depends upon judgments on the efficacy of heredity and upon deductions based upon the supposed survival of the fittest. But if all these mental processes of judgment, inference, and deduction are simply the mental reflections of material cerebral patterns, of the dance of atoms in the cortex, in what sense can they be said to be true? And if the inferences and the deductions are unprovable, the theory is in the same state.

Some thinkers, faced with these difficulties, have solved them by giving up the idea of truth. They no longer claim that the mind can give a true account of external reality. But it can know that certain things work out according to predetermined physical tests. Some of these help human wellbeing and it is enough to concentrate on them and leave abstruse problems of truth to the philosophers. Yet even the claim that truth cannot be known is, presumably, a statement of fact, a statement about the limitations of the mind, and as such it puts in its claim to be true. If, however, the mind is a physical substance, causally determined by other physical substances, it cannot tell us, one way or the other, which view of its powers is correct. As Professor J. S. Haldane once wrote: "If my mental processes are determined wholly by the motions of atoms in my brain, I have no reason to suppose that my beliefs are true . . . and hence I have no reason for supposing my brain to be composed of atoms." Even if we can in theory dispense with truth — and it is difficult to believe that anyone should seriously consider abandoning one of mankind's deepest and most disinterested pursuits — the claim to truth or the desire for truth seems to re-enter by the very door through which it has been expelled.

Rationality and the pursuit of truth — the great inheritance from the Greek world — can occupy a place in a purely material order of reality only, as it were, by stealth. Strictly, they have no right to be there. Nor does the other deepest element in the Western tradition — the intense Jewish concern with moral righteousness and the sense of God as the supreme Good — find any easier entry point into a closed material world. If there is no more in the universe than material facts and causations, goodness or the Good can be only a by-product of material processes. Great efforts have been made in the last century to trace the meaning of goodness back to its supposedly material source — in individual or collective interest, in emotion, in the desire for self or group preservation. Indeed, such theories are inevitable, if there is no more than a material universe. If goodness cannot be reduced to material interests and emotions, the universe cannot be seen as a single natural process: another loophole opens in nature, another order of reality may obtrude reflecting a transcendent and absolute Perfection.

Yet to believe that goodness is ultimately reduceable to material components is a much more troublesome process than it may seem at first. To go back to our everyday thinking, we distinguish very easily between the good and the self-interested; in fact, it seems part of the essence of goodness to be disinterested. If material causes can be found for supposedly "good" conduct, its goodness begins to fade. For instance, if we say "Miss Smith has given up everything to look after her troublesome and ailing old uncle," we are inclined to applaud her spirit of self-sacrifice. If, however, the rider is added, "She also expects to inherit his large fortune," the goodness of her behavior is open to doubt. Yet if material causes prevent us in individual instances from calling actions or personalities good, where is there place for goodness in a universe which contains nothing but material causes?

An answer can be attempted by moving from the individual to the collective level. It is the wisdom of the race or the tribe bent on self-preservation that has given rise in individual minds to judgments of value. Courage or self-sacrifice are "good" because both are necessary to the survival of the community. The essence of the idea of Good is that it compels obedience. We feel we ought to acquire characteristics or undertake action which we believe to be good. But this reaction is due to the fact that millennia of collective conditioning and disciplining have induced in us this conditioned reflex of obedience. The belief that the good has a claim on us, the whole concept of conscience, duty, and obligation which is inextricably tied up with the idea of the good, can be traced back ultimately to such purely material causes as physical survival and tribal taboo.

But, if this is the case, how has the distinction come about between the good on the one hand and the merely useful or expedient on the other? It is a fact that if we are told that the root of our morals is only expediency, or social use, then the hold of morality on our conscience instantly begins to slacken. We can accept a morality based upon social utility only if we believe the wellbeing of the greater number to be more valuable — to contain a higher good — than our own individual wellbeing. This is itself a moral judgment. But if it is only a reflection of long collective conditioning, it ceases to be binding on our conscience.

The puzzle is to account for "goodness" at all as a powerful factor in our mind if it disappears on being reduced to material interest. If there is no such thing in reality as goodness, how did it ever come to be invented or invoked? When the supposed conditioning of mankind began, why was the appeal made, beyond fear and discipline, to the idea of goodness constraining the conscience? The possibility that "I ought" is more than a Pavlovian reflex is suggested by the fact that the moment I am told it is just a reflex, I cease to feel that I ought to take any notice of it. And yet the notion of goodness and duty exists.

ABRAHAM HESCHEL

The Spirit of Judaism

Abraham Joshua Heschel (1907–1972) was born in Poland and taught in Germany and England before emigrating to the United States. In his thought the mystical and social dimensions of religion were inseparable, as were his devotion to the particularity of Jewish faith and his dedication to the universality of a humanity that had been created in the divine image; all of those themes come to voice in his book *God in Search of Man*.

IS THERE A UNIQUE EXPRESSION for the spirit of Judaism? Is there a term that would convey its singular nature?

Let us turn to the text of the Ten Commandments, the most representative monument of Jewish teaching, and see whether such a term can be found. The Ten Commandments have been translated into all tongues, and its vocabulary has become part of the literature of all nations. Reading that famous text in any translation, Greek, Latin or English, we are struck by a surprising fact. All words of the Hebrew text have been easily rendered by English equivalents. There is a word for *pesel:* a graven image; there are words for *shamayim,* for example, and *erets:* heaven and earth. The whole text has been faithfully translated into English and yet it reads as if it were originally written in English. But, lo and behold! There is one Hebrew word for which no English equivalent has been found and which remained untranslated: *Sabbath.* "Remember the Sabbath Day." In the Greek of the Septuagint we read *Sabbaton;* in the Latin of the Vulgate *Sabbatum;* in Aramaic *Shabbatha;* in the King James version the *Sabbath.*

Perhaps Sabbath is the idea that expresses what is most characteristic of Judaism.

What is the Sabbath? A reminder of every man's royalty; an abolition of the distinction of master and slave, rich and poor, success and failure. To celebrate the Sabbath is to experience one's ultimate independence of civilization and society, of achievement and anxiety. The Sabbath is an embodiment of the belief that all men are equal and that equality of men means the nobility of men. The greatest sin of man is to forget that he is a prince.

The Sabbath is an assurance that the spirit is greater than the universe, that beyond the good is the holy. The universe was created in six days, but the climax of creation was the seventh day. Things that come into being in the six days are good, but the seventh day is holy. The Sabbath is *holiness in time*.

What is the Sabbath? The presence of eternity, a moment of majesty, the radiance of joy. The soul is enhanced, time is a delight, and inwardness a supreme reward. Indignation is felt to be a desecration of the day, and strife the suicide of one's additional soul. Man does not stand alone, he lives in the presence of the day.

The Art of Surpassing Civilization

Lift up your eyes and see: who created these. Six days a week we are engaged in conquering the forces of nature, in the arts of civilization. The seventh day is dedicated to the remembrance of creation and the remembrance of redemption, to the liberation of Israel from Egypt, to the exodus from a great civilization into a wilderness where the word of God was given. By our acts of labor during the six days we participate in the works of history; by sanctifying the seventh day we are reminded of the acts that surpass, ennoble and redeem history.

The world is contingent on creation, and the worth of history depends on redemption. To be a Jew is to affirm the world without being enslaved to it; to be a part of civilization and to go beyond it; to conquer space and to sanctify time. Judaism is *the art of surpassing civilization,* sanctification of time, sanctification of history.

Civilization is on trial. Its future will depend upon how much of the Sabbath will penetrate its spirit.

The Sabbath, as experienced by man, cannot survive in exile, a lonely stranger among days of profanity. It needs the companionship of the other days. All days of the week must be spiritually consistent with the seventh day. Even if we cannot reach a plane where all our life would be a pilgrimage to the seventh day, the thought and appreciation of what the day may bring to us should always be present in our minds. The Sabbath is the counterpoint of living; the melody sustained throughout all agitations and vicissitudes which menace our conscience; our awareness of God's presence in the world. It teaches us to sense the delights of spirit, the joys of the good, the grandeur of living in the face of eternity.

What the Sabbath is among the days, the consecrated man, the *talmid chacham,* is among us, the common people. The consecrated man is he who knows how to sanctify time. Not deceived by the splendor of space, he remains attentive to the divine tangent at the whirling wheel of living.

The Sabbath is more than a day, more than a name for a seventh part of the week. It is eternity within time, *the spiritual underground of history.*

In the language of the Jew, living *sub specie aeternitatis* means living *sub specie Sabbatis.* Every Friday eve we must kindle the lights in the soul, enhance our mercy, deepen our sensitivity.

The Sabbath is one day, *Shabbesdikeit* is what should permeate all our days. *Shabbesdikeit* is spirituality, the epitome and spirit of Judaism.

The great dream of Judaism is not to raise priests, but a people of priests; to consecrate all men, not only some men.

"And why was not the tribe of Levi granted a share in the land of Israel? . . . Because it was dedicated to the worship of God and His ministry. The vocation of the tribe of Levi was to teach the multitude the upright ways of the Lord and His righteous judgments. . . . But not the tribe of Levi alone was consecrated thus. Every human being born into this world whose spirit stirs him and whose intellect guides him to dedicate himself to the Lord in order to minister to Him and worship Him and to come to know Him, and who acts in conformity with God's design and disembarrasses himself of the devious ways which men have sought out, becomes sanctified with supreme sanctity."

The Meaning of Jewish Existence

There is a high cost of living to be paid by a Jew. He has to be exalted in order to be normal in a world that is neither propitious for nor sympathetic to his survival. Some of us, tired of sacrifice and exertion, often wonder: Is Jewish existence worth the price? Others are overcome with panic; they are perplexed, and despair of recovery.

The meaning of Jewish existence, the major theme of any Jewish philosophy, is baffling. To fit it into the framework of personal intellectual predilections or current fashions of our time would be a distortion. The claim of Israel must be recognized *before* attempting an interpretation. As the ocean is more than what we know about it, so Judaism surpasses the content of all philosophies of it. We have not invented it. We may accept or reject, but should not distort it.

It is as an individual that I am moved by an anxiety for the meaning of my existence as a Jew. Yet when I begin to ponder about it, my theme is not the problem of one Jew but of all Jews. And the more deeply I probe, the more strongly I realize the scope of the problem: It embraces not only the Jews of the present but also those of the past and those of the future, the meaning of Jewish existence in all ages.

What is at stake in our lives is more than the fate of one generation. In this moment *we*, the living, are Israel. The tasks begun by the patriarchs and prophets, and carried out by countless Jews of the past, are now entrusted to us. No other group has superseded them. We are the only channel of Jewish tradition, those who must save Judaism from oblivion, those who must hand over the entire past to the generations to come. We are either the last, the dying, Jews or else we are those who will give new life to our tradition. Rarely in our history has so much depended upon one generation. We will either forfeit or enrich the legacy of the ages.

Thinking Compatible with Our Destiny

Understanding Judaism cannot be attained in the comfort of playing a chess-game of theories. Only ideas that are meaningful to those who are steeped in misery may be accepted as principles by those who dwell in safety. In trying to understand Jewish existence a Jewish philosopher must look for agreement with the men of Sinai as well as with the people of Auschwitz.

We are the most challenged people under the sun. Our existence is either superfluous or indispensable to the world; it is either tragic or holy to be a Jew.

It is a matter of immense responsibility that we here and Jewish teachers everywhere have undertaken to instill in our youth the will to be Jews today, tomorrow and for ever and ever. Unless being a Jew is of absolute significance how can we justify the ultimate price which our people was often forced to pay throughout its history? To assess Judaism soberly and farsightedly is to establish it as a good to be preferred, if necessary, to any alternative which we may ever face.

The task of Jewish philosophy today, is not only to describe the essence but also to set forth the universal relevance of Judaism, the bearings of its demands upon the chance of man to remain human. Bringing to light the lonely splendor of Jewish thinking, conveying the taste of eternity in our daily living is the greatest aid we can render to the man of our time who has fallen so low that he is not even capable of being ashamed of what happened in his days.

We were not born by mere chance as a by-product of a migration of nations or in the obscurity of a primitive past. God's vision of Israel came first and only then did we come into the world. We were formed according to an intention and for the sake of a purpose. Our souls tremble with the echo of unforgettable experiences and with the sublime expectation of our own response. To be a Jew is to be committed to the experience of great ideas. The task of Jewish philosophy is to formulate not only these ideas but also the depth of that commitment in vivid, consistent thinking. The task of Jewish philosophy is *to make our thinking compatible with our destiny*.

Life appears dismal if not mirrored in what is more than life. Nothing can be regarded as valuable unless assessed in relation to something higher in value. Man's survival depends on the conviction that there is something that is worth the price of life. It depends upon a sense of the supremacy of what is lasting. That sense of conviction may be asleep, but it awakens when challenged. In some people it lives as a sporadic wish; in others it is a permanent concern.

What we have learned from Jewish history is that if a man is not more than human then he is less than human. Judaism is an attempt to prove that in order to be a man, you have to be more than a man, that in order to be a people we have to be more than a people. Israel was made to be a "holy people." This is the essence of its dignity and the essence of its merit. Judaism is a link to eternity, kinship with ultimate reality.

A sense of contact with the ultimate dawns upon most people when their self-reliance is swept away by violent misery. Judaism is the attempt to instill in us that sense as an everyday awareness. It leads us to regard injustice as a metaphysical calamity, to sense the divine significance of human happiness, to keep slightly above the twilight of the self, enabling us to sense the eternal within the temporal.

We are endowed with the consciousness of being involved in a history that transcends time and its specious glories. We are taught to feel the knots of life in which the trivial is intertwined with the sublime. There is no end to our experience of the spiritual grandeur, of the divine earnestness of human life. Our blossoms may be crushed, but we are upheld by the faith that comes from the core of our roots. We are not deceived by the obvious, knowing that all delight is but a pretext for adding strength to that which is beyond joy and grief. We know that no hour is the last hour, that the world is more than the world.

Israel — a Spiritual Order

Why is our belonging to the Jewish people a sacred relation? Israel is a *spiritual order* in which the human and the ultimate, the natural and the holy enter a lasting covenant, in which kinship with God is not an aspiration but a reality of destiny. For us Jews there can be no fellowship with God without the fellowship with the people Israel. Abandoning Israel, we desert God.

Jewish existence is not only the adherence to particular doctrines and observances, but primarily the living *in* the spiritual order of the Jewish people, the living *in* the Jews of the past and *with* the Jews of the present. It is not only a certain quality in the souls of the individuals, but primarily the existence of the community of Israel. It is neither an experience nor a creed, neither the possession of psychic traits nor the acceptance of a theological doctrine, but the living in a holy dimension, in a spiritual order. Our share in holiness we acquire by living in the Jewish community. What we do as individuals is a trivial episode, what we attain as Israel causes us to grow into the infinite.

The meaning of history is to be a sanctuary in time, and every one of us has his part in the great ritual. The ultimate meaning of human deeds in not restricted to the life of him who does these deeds and to the particular moment in which they occur.

Religious living is not only a private concern. Our own life is a movement in the symphony of ages. We are taught to pray as well as to live in the first person plural. We do a mitsvah "in the name of all Israel." We act both as individuals and as the community of Israel. All generations are present, as it were, in every moment.

Israel is the tree, we are the leaves. It is the clinging to the stem that keeps us alive. There has perhaps never been more need of Judaism than in our time, a time in which many cherished hopes of humanity lie crushed. We should be pioneers as were our fathers three thousand years ago. The future of all men depends upon their realizing that the sense of holiness is as vital as health. By following the Jewish way of life we maintain that sense and preserve the light for mankind's future visions.

It is our destiny to live for what is more than ourselves. Our very existence is an unparalleled symbol of such aspiration. By being what we are, namely Jews, we mean more to mankind than by any particular service we may render.

We have faith in God and faith in Israel. Though some of its children have gone astray, Israel remains the mate of God. We cannot hate what God loves. Rabbi Aaron the Great used to say: "I wish I could love the greatest saint as the Lord loves the greatest rascal."

Israel exists not in order to be, but in order to cherish the vision of God. Our faith may be strained but our destiny is anchored to the ultimate. Who can establish the outcome of our history? Out of the wonder we came and into the wonder we shall return.

The Dignity of Israel

Belonging to Israel is in itself a spiritual act. It is utterly inconvenient to be a Jew. The very survival of our people is a *kiddush hashem* [sanctification of the Divine Name]. We live in spite of peril. Our very existence is a refusal to surrender to normalcy, to security and comfort. Experts in assimilation, the Jews could have disappeared even before the names of modern nations were known. Still we are patient and cherish the will to perpetuate our essence.

We are Jews as we are men. The alternative to our existence as Jews is spiritual suicide, disappearance. It is *not* a change into something else. Judaism has allies but no substitutes. Jewish faith consists of attachment to God, attachment to Torah, and attachment to Israel.

There is a unique association between the people and the land of Israel. Even before Israel becomes a people, the land is preordained for it. What we have witnessed in our own days is a reminder of the power of God's mysterious promise to Abraham and a testimony to the fact that the people kept its promise, "If I forget thee, O Jerusalem, let my right hand wither" (Psalms 137:5). The Jew in whose heart the love of Zion dies is doomed to lose his faith in the God of Abraham who gave the land as an earnest of the redemption of all men.

The people of Israel groaned in distress. Out of Egypt, the land of plentiful food, they were driven into the wilderness. Their souls were dried away; there was nothing at all: no flesh to eat, no water to drink. All they had was a promise: to be led to the land of milk and honey. They were almost ready to stone Moses. "Wherefore hast thou brought us up out of Egypt, to kill us and our children and our cattle with thirst?" they cried. But, after they had worshipped the golden calf — when God had decided to detach Himself from His people, not to dwell any more in their midst, but to entrust an angel with the task of leading them out of the wilderness to the Promised Land — Moses exclaimed: "If Thou Thyself dost not go with us, take us not out of the wilderness" (Exodus 33:15). This, perhaps, is the secret of our history: *to choose to remain in the wilderness rather than to be abandoned by Him.*

Israel's experience of God has not evolved from search. Israel did not discover God. Israel was discovered by God. Judaism in *God's quest for man*. The Bible is a record of God's approach to His people. More statements are found in the Bible about God's love for Israel than about Israel's love for God.

We have not chosen God; He has chosen us. There is no concept of a chosen God but there is the idea of a chosen people. The idea of a chosen people does not suggest the preference for a people based upon a discrimination among a number of peoples. We do not say that we are a superior people. The "chosen people" means a people approached and chosen by God. The significance of this term is genuine in relation to God rather than in relation to other peoples. It signifies not a quality inherent in the people but a relationship between the people and God.

Harassed, pursued with enmity and wrong, our fathers continued to feel joy in being Jews. "Happy we are. How good is our destiny, how pleasant our lot, how beautiful our heritage." What is the source of that feeling?

The quest for immortality is common to all men. To most of them the vexing question points to the future. Jews think not only of the end but also of the beginning. As parts of Israel we are endowed with a very rare, a very precious consciousness, the consciousness that we do not live in a void. We never suffer from harrowing anxiety and fear of roaming about in the emptiness of time. We own the past and are, hence, not afraid of what is to be. We remember where we came from. We were summoned and cannot forget it, as we wind the clock of eternal history. We remember the beginning and believe in an end. We live between two historic poles: Sinai and the Kingdom of God.

> Upon thy walls, O Jerusalem,
> I have set watchmen,
> All the day and all the night
> They shall never be silent.
> Ye that stir the Lord to remember,
> Take no rest,
> And give Him no rest
> Till He establishes Jerusalem,
> And makes it a praise in the earth.
>
> Isaiah 62:6–7

HAMILTON GIBB

The Foundations of
Islamic Thought

Sir Hamilton Alexander Rosskeen Gibb (1895–1971) was,
in the opinion of many, the leading Islamicist in the
English-speaking world. His books, such as *The Arabs* and
Arabic Literature, expressed his wide-ranging scholarship
with force and clarity of expression, and in *Modern Trends
in Islam,* whose opening discussion appears here, he put the
movements of twentieth-century Muslim thought into the
same historical perspective.

IN SETTING OUT to survey the currents of religious thought among
Muslims at the present day, we are faced at the start with a serious
practical difficulty. No movement of thought takes place in a void.
Whether the impulses which affect it from without are many and
powerful or few and weak, they are related in the mind of the subject
to a habit of thought and a system of ideas which are already there. We
cannot hope to follow with any understanding the modern movements in Islam unless we set them against an established background
of Islamic ideas.

It would seem self-evident that the only satisfactory background
must be the state of Islam in the nineteenth century, or, at the earliest,
Islam in the eighteenth century. But these are subjects on which our
knowledge is still limited by immense gaps. The usual practice of
writers on Islam is to concentrate on the early centuries of theological
and legal development and sectarian conflicts and the rise of the Sufi
movement and brotherhoods. After the thirteenth century or so, it is
assumed that, from a religious angle, Islam stayed put — that it
remained fixed in the molds created for it by the scholars, jurists,

doctors, and mystics of the formative centuries and, if anything, decayed rather than progressed.

In some respects this view is apparently justified, and it is, indeed, held by a number of modern Muslim scholars themselves. But no great organization of human belief, thought, and will really stands still over a period of six centuries. It is true that the external formulations of the Muslim faith have shown little development during the whole of these six centuries. Yet, in fact, the inner structure of Muslim religious life was being profoundly readjusted and, as in other religious communities, the process generated an expansive energy which found outlets in several different kinds of activity.

Consider only the external evidences of vitality which Islam showed during this time — the establishment of the Ottoman Empire in the Near East and of the Mogul Empire in India, the revival of Shi'ism in Persia, the expansion into Indonesia and the Malay Peninsula, the growth of the Muslim community in China, the expulsion of the Spanish and Portuguese from Morocco, the extension of the Islamic belt in East and West Africa. The older historians were liable to regard all or most of these as military movements pure and simple; and the element of military power and conquest which they contain must not, of course, be left out of view. Even so, a conquering and expanding faith is a living faith, not a mere dry husk of belief and practice. We now know, too, better than before, the role played by this living faith, first in anticipating and then in helping to build up the military power, in molding the inner structure and organization of empire, and in repairing the ravages of war and reknitting the social fabric.

In the next chapter an attempt will be made to trace in outline the character of the internal evolution in Islam between the thirteenth and the nineteenth centuries. This by itself will not wholly overcome the difficulty with which we are confronted. Yet it may serve the purpose if, leaving detail aside, the general process can be seen in relation to the fundamental terms and categories of Islamic thought. This method of approach to the problem, however, requires, in the first place, some analysis and definition of the concepts and attitudes which underlie the formulation and the religious institutions of Islam. It is all the more important to make this effort, since these characteristic features have a direct bearing not only on the medieval but also on the modern developments within Islam. Modernism itself is the outcome of certain changes in the character of religious thought; and much of the argument for and against modernism is related, consciously or unconsciously, to those first principles which lie at the roots of the Muslim structure of belief and practice.

The basis of all Muslim thought about religion is, of course, the Koran. The Koran is not, like the Bible, a collection of books of widely different dates and by many different hands. It is a volume of discourses delivered by Muhammad during the last twenty years or so of his life, consisting mainly of short passages of religious or ethical teaching, arguments against opponents, commentaries on current events, and some rulings on social and legal matters. Muhammad himself believed that all these utterances were inspired, since they were not shaped by his own conscious thought. By him, as by all Muslims of his own time and of later ages, they were taken to be the direct word of God, dictated to him through the angel Gabriel. After what Professor Duncan Black Macdonald has said about the closeness of the unseen world to the Semitic mind and about the Eastern conception of prophecy, it would be superfluous for me to trace further the psychological presuppositions of this belief.

Yet we should be seriously mistaken if we were to regard it as merely a theological dogma which has been inherited, generation after generation, for thirteen hundred years. On the contrary, it is a living conviction which ever renews and confirms itself in the heart and mind of the Muslim, and more especially the Arab, as he studies the sacred text.

Muslim orthodoxy has generally been opposed to the translation of the Koran even into other Islamic languages, although the Arabic text is sometimes accompanied by interlinear translations in Turkish, Persian, Urdu, and so forth. This attitude is supported by theological reasoning, which is quite self-consistent but possibly rationalizes to some extent objections derived from rather different considerations, for the Koran is essentially untranslatable, in the same way that great poetry is untranslatable. The seer can never communicate his vision in ordinary language. He can express himself only in broken images, every inflection of which, every nuance and subtlety, has to be long and earnestly studied before their significance breaks upon the reader — images, too, in which the music of the sounds plays an indefinable part in attuning the mind of the hearer to receive the message. To paraphrase them in other words can only be to mutilate them, to substitute clay for fine gold, the plodding of the pedestrian intelligence for the winged flight of intuitive perception — at least until long familiarity, as in the case of Latin and English translations of the Hebrew and Greek Scriptures, has given the new words something of the same emotive power, independently of the structure (and sometimes even of the meaning) of the originals.

An English translation of the Koran must employ precise and often arbitrary terms for the many-faceted and jewel-like phrases of the Arabic; and the more literal it is, the grayer and more colorless it must be. In passages of plain narrative, legislation, and the like, the loss may be less great, although not only the unevennesses and the incohesions of the compilation but also the fine shades, the hammer strokes, and the eloquent pauses (if they can be reproduced at all) may have a disconcerting or, as Carlyle said, a "crude and incondite" effect. Even in so simple a sentence as "Verily We give life and death and unto Us is the journeying," it is impossible to present in English (or perhaps any other language) the force of the five-times-repeated "We" in the six words of the original. Allowing for all this, however, we shall still not grasp what the Koran means to the Arab until we make an effort to appreciate the part that language plays in determining his psychological attitudes.

The spring of mental life among the Arabs, as among other peoples, is furnished by the imagination, expressing itself in artistic creation. One often hears it said that the Arabs have no art. If art is confined to such things as painting and sculpture, the charge may be true. But this would be a despotic and unjustifiable limitation of the term. Art is any production in which aesthetic feeling expresses itself, and it is doubtful whether any people is totally devoid of artistic expression in some form or another, whether it be in music or dancing or ceramics or the visual arts. The medium in which the aesthetic feeling of the Arabs is mainly (though not exclusively) expressed is that of words and language — the most seductive, it may be, and certainly the most unstable and even dangerous of all the arts. We know something of the effect of the spoken and written word upon ourselves. But upon the Arab mind the impact of artistic speech is immediate; the words, passing through no filter of logic or reflection which might weaken or deaden their effect, go straight to the head. It is easy, therefore, to understand why Arabs, to whom the noble use of speech is the supreme art — and other Muslims also, to whom by long familiarity the Arab sensitivity to its language has become second nature — should see in the Koran a work of superhuman origin and a veritable miracle.

Further, the Arab artistic creation is a series of separate moments, each complete in itself and independent, connected by no principle of harmony or congruity beyond the unity of the imagining mind.

Western art, especially since the Middle Ages, has developed a whole series of complicating techniques — drama superimposed on romance, mass in place of line, polyphony in place of homophony in music — which make of the artistic creation a harmony or synthesis of multiple elements, appealing to the refined intelligence as well as to the emotions. The art of speech, on the other hand, among ourselves as well as among the Arabs, still retains its simple and discrete (we might even call it "primitive") character; and because of this it exerts a far more intense power of appeal to the imagination both of the individual and of the mass, a power which may even be so great as to inhibit the capacity to form a synthesis.

Among all developing peoples, however, the creative impulses of the imaginative life must be furnished with an intelligible object or direction. This function is assumed by one of two forces, namely, religious intuition and rational thought. I should not like to assert that these alternatives are by necessity mutually exclusive; but it is a matter of experience that, apart from cases of special genius, individuals or societies incline generally to the one or to the other. Nor do I mean to exclude religion from the rational life; but, whereas the intuitive life is directed either by religion or by sheer subjective fantasy (which is to say, by nothing at all), the rational life comprehends religion as only one of its objects.

There could be no question as to which of these two would more immediately attract and move the Arab mind, in view of its inherited awareness of the unseen world and the powerful stimulus of the Koran. Besides all this, the outward simplicity and concreteness of the ideas of the Koran corresponded to the simplicity and concreteness of their imaginative life, and its code of ethics set up a practical ideal, which harmonized with and satisfied their social aspirations. Consequently, all their intellectual powers were directed into the effort to build up the structure of the religious institution of Islam and to make it dominant in every relationship of social life as it already dominated their mental life.

But this endeavor called for the exercise of a different set of faculties. The artistic imagination cannot construct a system. That is the task of reason. Now it is very frequently observed both in individuals and in nations that the very qualities in which they excel entail, and may even be the result of, the defect of other qualities. The student of Arabic civilization is constantly brought up against the striking contrast between the imaginative power displayed, for example, in certain branches of Arabic literature and the literalism, the pedantry, displayed in reasoning and exposition, even when it is devoted to these same productions. It is true that there have been great philosophers among the Muslim peoples and that some of them were Arabs, but they were rare exceptions. The Arab mind, whether in relation to the outer world or in relation to the processes of thought, cannot throw off its intense feeling for the separateness and individuality of the concrete events. This is, I believe, one of the main factors lying behind that "lack of a sense of law" which Professor Macdonald regarded as the characteristic difference in the oriental.

It is this, too, which explains — what it is so difficult for the Western student to grasp — the aversion of the Muslims from the thought-processes of rationalism. The struggle between rationalism and intuitive thought for control of the Muslim mind was fought out, for the first time, over the postulates of Greek speculative philosophy in the early centuries of Islam. The intellectual consequences of that conflict were decisive. They not only conditioned the formulation of the traditional Muslim theology but set a permanent stamp upon Islamic culture; and they still lie behind the conflicts arising in more recent years out of direct contact with modern Western thought. The rejection of rationalist modes of thought and of the utilitarian ethic which is inseparable from them has its roots, therefore, not in the so-called "obscurantism" of the Muslim theologians but in the atomism and discreteness of the Arab imagination.

Consequently, the Arabs — and with them the Muslims generally — were compelled to distrust all abstract or a priori universal concepts, such as the "Law of Nature" or ideal "Justice." Such concepts they branded (and not unjustly) as "dualism" or "materialism," based on false modes of thought which could produce but little good and much evil. The great Muslim revivalist of the nineteenth century, Jamāl ad-Dīn al-Afghāni, emptied the vials of his wrath upon those Indian modernists who tried to prove the truth of Islam by arguing its "conformity with nature." Although the Muslim scholastics found such auxiliary disciplines as logic and mathematics useful, and to that extent adopted and encouraged the "scientific" mode of thought, they kept them closely confined to a subordinate status; and the stricter theologians — like Ibn Taimīya, who wrote a "Refutation of Logic" — were unwilling to concede even so much.

On the other hand — if I may diverge for a moment — the concentration of Arab thought upon the individual events fitted Muslim scholars to develop the experimental method in science to a degree far beyond their predecessors in Greece and Alexandria. This is a subject on which I am not competent to enlarge; but it is, I think, generally agreed that the detailed observations of Muslim investigators materially aided the progress of scientific knowledge and that it was from them that the experimental method was introduced or restored to medieval Europe. In the other aspect of science, however, the combination of the results of observation and experiment and the dovetailing of them into self-consistent ideal structures, held together by the concept of natural laws, the Muslim scientists were, of course, hampered by the very qualities in which they excelled, besides being to some extent inhibited by theological dogmas.

To revert now to Muslim religious thought, we should expect to find these same qualities of imagination and literalism displayed in the development of the theological system and its social applications. We do, in fact, see it very clearly in the interpretation of the Koran; but a simpler example will be found in the treatment of the person, acts, and sayings of Muhammad. Under the impulse of veneration for the Prophet and for his office, the religious imagination begins to elaborate its conception of what a prophet should be — sinless, for example, and endowed with miraculous powers; and as it progressively raises its standards, literalism obediently toils up behind it, producing out of the stores of tradition and by interpretation of koranic verses the evidences and proofs required to consolidate the concept as a theological dogma. The religious imagination, not content with accepting the inspiration of the Koran, insists that the inspiration of the Prophet cannot end there; this would be to allow too much scope to his mere humanity and possibly, therefore, his liability to err. In all that he said and did he must be, at least tacitly, inspired, and every action must be capable of serving as the model for human action in the same sphere. The scholars, intent on expanding the doctrinal and legal systems based on the Koran and needing for these purposes the additional materials supplied by the tradition, formally incorporate it in the theological structure as a second infallible source. Then they build up a vast and intricate science by which spurious traditions can be detected and rejected and the accepted traditions can be classified in categories of "good," "less good," and "weak."

Already in this connection we meet the difficulty that we shall encounter elsewhere about the relation between inner reality and outer form. It is easy to drive a coach and horses through the whole fabric of this elaborate "science of tradition." Many Muslim scholars themselves in the early centuries were uneasy about it. Yet ultimately it was accepted, because (broadly speaking) the external rules were, to a large extent, only a formal method of stabilizing and rationalizing what the conscience of the Muslim community already accepted. Thus and thus is what the Prophet could have been expected to say in given circumstances or in answer to given questions; if traditions existed in the contrary sense, they must be spurious, or at least (if the rules made it impossible to reject them as spurious) they must be "harmonized" or else discarded as having been "abrogated." I have no doubt in my own mind that the older tradition does, in fact, reflect the mind of Muhammad to a greater or less extent, though many who are better qualified to judge than I am hold a different view. But it is precisely because the tradition as a whole has been used to validate, instead, the outlook and opinions of the early generations of Muslims that so many schools of modernists reject its authority altogether and adopt the slogan "Back to the Koran."

The way in which the corpus of tradition was shaped to serve the ends of the Muslim religious consciousness vividly illustrates a third characteristic of Muslim thought. I find it difficult to define its nature precisely, because of the misleading associations of all the relevant words in English. Thus we are frequently told, on the one hand, that Islam is authoritarian, and so in a sense it is. . . . On the other hand, Muslim apologists proclaim with conviction that Islam is democratic, which is true also, provided the political sense of the term is not insisted on. That the ordinary business of secular government is to be controlled by the general body of believers is an idea which was, indeed, formulated in the first century of Islam, but only to be decisively rejected as heretical, because of the excesses of its supporters. Not even the theoretical equality of all Muslims, though supported by several texts of the Koran, is enough to prove its political democracy. But in religious matters the humblest Muslim stands on a level with the caliph of his chief *qadi,* and the ultimate control rests with the conscience of the people as a whole. *Vox populi,* the expressed will of the community — not as measured by the counting of votes or the decisions of councils at any given moment, but as demonstrated by the slowly accumulating pressure of opinion over a long period of time — is recognized in orthodox Islam next after *Vox Dei* and *Vox Prophetae* as a third infallible source of religious truth.

This principle is known as *ijmā*ᶜ, the "consensus of the community." There were those who tried to limit it to the consensus of the learned. But a striking incident in the seventeenth century showed how futile the consensus of the learned was, even when supported by the secular power, against the pressure of public opinion. When the use of coffee began to spread in the Near East the jurists almost unanimously took the view that coffee-drinking was unlawful and punishable with the same penalties as wine-drinking, and a number of persons were actually executed for indulging in this vicious practice. But the will of the community prevailed, and today coffee is freely consumed even by those puritans who reject *ijmā*ᶜ in principle altogether.

It should be clear why *ijmā*ᶜ has always been a subject of controversy between the conservative and the modernizing wings in Islam. Consensus is by no means a liberal principle; on the contrary, it is a principle of authority. What the community says may not be gainsaid. But because its authority is formally invoked only for what is not formally or explicitly authorized by the Koran or by the tradition, and because it is therefore an authority which may and does sanction what are called "innovations," the stricter theologians of all ages from the third century of Islam to the Wahhabis of today reject the claims made for it and confine its validity to the first generation of Muslims only, while the modernists of all ages have relied upon it to provide their eventual justification.

YU-LAN FUNG

The Spirit of Chinese Philosophy

Yu-Lan Fung is the author of the monumental *History of Chinese Philosophy*. But it is in his book *A Short History of Chinese Philosophy*, which his editor Derk Bodde describes as having been "written with the Western reader specifically in mind," that he has defined the most succinctly his interpretation of Chinese religious philosophy.

THE PLACE which philosophy has occupied in Chinese civilization has been comparable to that of religion in other civilizations. In China, philosophy has been every educated person's concern. In the old days, if a man were educated at all, the first education he received was in philosophy. When children went to school, the *Four Books,* which consist of the *Confucian Analects,* the *Book of Mencius,* the *Great Learning,* and the *Doctrine of the Mean,* were the first ones they were taught to read. The *Four Books* were the most important texts of Neo-Confucianist philosophy. Sometimes when the children were just beginning to learn the characters, they were given a sort of textbook to read. This was known as the *Three Characters Classic,* and was so called because each sentence in the book consisted of three characters arranged so that when recited they produced a rhythmic effect, and thus helped the children to memorize them more easily. This book was in reality a primer, and the very first statement in it is the "the nature of man is originally good." This is one of the fundamental ideas of Mencius' philosophy.

Place of Philosophy in Chinese Civilization

To the Westerner, who sees that the life of the Chinese people is permeated with Confucianism, it appears that Confucianism is a religion. As a matter of fact, however, Confucianism is no more a religion than, say, Platonism or Aristotelianism. It is true that the *Four Books* have been the Bible of the Chinese people, but in the *Four Books* there is no story of creation, and no mention of a heaven or hell.

Of course, the terms philosophy and religion are both ambiguous. Philosophy and religion may have entirely different meanings for different people. When men talk about philosophy or religion, they may have quite different ideas in their minds concerning them. For my part, what I call philosophy is systematic, reflective thinking on life. Every man, who has not yet died, is in life. But there are not many who think reflectively on life, and still fewer whose reflective thinking is systematic. A philosopher *must* philosophize; that is to say, he must think reflectively on life, and then express his thoughts systematically.

This kind of thinking is called reflective because it takes life as its object. The theory of life, the theory of the universe, and the theory of knowledge all emerge from this type of thinking. The theory of the universe arises because the universe is the background of life — the stage on which the drama of life takes place. The theory of knowledge emerges because thinking is itself knowledge. According to some philosophers of the West, in order to think, we must first find out what we can think; that is to say, before we start to think about life, we must first "think our thinking."

Such theories are all the products of reflective thinking. The very concept of life, the very concept of the universe, and the very concept of knowledge are also the products of reflective thinking. No matter whether we think about life or whether we talk about it, we are all in the midst of it. And no matter whether we think or speak about the universe, we are all a part of it. Now, what the philosophers call the universe is not the same as what the physicists have in mind when they refer to it. What the philosophers call the universe is *the totality of all that is*. It is equivalent to what the ancient Chinese philosopher, Hui Shih, called "The Great One," which is defined as "that which has nothing beyond." So everyone and everything must be considered part of the universe. When one thinks about the universe, one is thinking reflectively.

When we think about knowledge or speak about knowledge, this thinking and speaking are themselves knowledge. To use an expression of Aristotle, it is "thinking on thinking"; and this is reflective thinking. Here is the vicious circle which those philosophers follow who insist that before we think we must first think about our thinking; just as if we had another faculty with which we could think about thinking! As a matter of fact, the faculty with which we think about thinking is the very same faculty with which we think. If we are skeptical about the capacity of our thinking in regard to life and the universe, we have the same reason to be skeptical about the capacity of our thinking in regard to thinking.

Religion also has something to do with life. In the heart of every great religion there is a philosophy. In fact, every great religion *is* a philosophy with a certain amount of superstructure, which consists of superstitions, dogmas, rituals, and institutions. This is what I call religion.

If one understands the term religion in this sense, which does not really differ very much from common usage, one sees that Confucianism cannot be considered a religion. People have been accustomed to say that there were three religions in China: Confucianism, Taoism, and Buddhism. But Confucianism, as we have seen, is not a religion. As to Taoism, there is a distinction between Taoism as a philosophy, which is called *Tao chia* (the Taoist school), and the Taoist religion (*Tao chiao*). Their teachings are not only different; they are even contradictory. Taoism as a philosophy teaches the doctrine of following nature, while Taoism as a religion teaches the doctrine of working *against* nature. For instance, according to Lao Tzu and Chuang Tzu, life followed by death is the course of nature, and man should follow this natural course calmly. But the main teaching of the Taoist religion is the principle and technique of how to avoid death, which is expressly working *against* nature. The Taoist religion has the spirit of science, which is the conquering of nature. If one is interested in the history of Chinese science, the writings of the religious Taoists will supply much information.

As to Buddhism, there is also the distinction between Buddhism as a philosophy, which is calledo *Fo hsüeh* (the Buddhist learning), and Buddhism as a religion, which is called *Fo chiao* (the Buddhist religion). To the educated Chinese, Buddhist philosophy is much more interesting than the Buddhist religion. It is quite common to see both Buddhist monks and Taoist monks simultaneously participating in Chinese funeral services. The Chinese people take even their religion philosophically.

At present it is known to many Westerners that the Chinese people have been less concerned with religion than other people are. For instance, in one of his articles, "Dominant Ideas in the Formation of Chinese Culture," Professor Derk Bodde says: "They [the Chinese] are not a people for whom religious ideas and activities constitute an all important and absorbing part of life. . . . It is ethics (especially Confucian ethics), and not religion (at least not religion of a formal, organized type), that provided the spiritual basis in Chinese civilization. . . . All of which, of course, marks a difference of fundamental importance between China and most other major civilizations, in which a church and a priesthood have played a dominant role."

In one sense this is quite true. But one may ask: Why is this so? If the craving for what is beyond the present actual world is not one of the innate desires of mankind, why is it a fact that for most people religious ideas and activities constitute an all-important and absorbing part of life? If that craving is one of the fundamental desires of mankind, why should the Chinese people be an exception? When one says that it is ethics, not religion, that has provided the spiritual basis of Chinese civilization, does it imply that the Chinese are not conscious of those values which are higher than moral ones?

The values that are higher than the moral ones may be called super-moral values. The love of man is a moral value, while the love of God is a super-moral value. Some people may be inclined to call this kind of value a religious value. But in my opinion, this value is not confined to religion, unless what is meant here by religion differs from its meaning as described above. For instance, the love of God in Christianity is a religious value, while the love of God in the philosophy of Spinoza is not, because what Spinoza called God is really the universe. Strictly speaking, the love of God in Christianity is not really super-moral. This is because God, in Christianity, is a personality, and consequently the love of God by man is comparable to the love of a father by his son, which is a moral value. Therefore, the love of God in Christianity is open to question as a super-moral value. It is a quasi super-moral value, while the love of God in the philosophy of Spinoza is a real super-moral value.

To answer the above questions, I would say that the craving for something beyond the present actual world is one of the innate desires of mankind, and the Chinese people are no exception to this rule. They have not had much concern with religion because they have had so much concern with philosophy. They are not religious because they are philosophical. In philosophy they satisfy their craving for what is beyond the present actual world. In philosophy also they have the super-moral values expressed and appreciated, and in living according to philosophy these super-moral values are experienced.

According to the tradition of Chinese philosophy, its function is not the increase of positive knowledge (by positive knowledge I mean information regarding matters of fact), but the elevation of the mind — a reaching out for what is beyond the present actual world, and for the values that are higher than the moral ones. It was said by the *Lao-tzu*: "To work on learning is to increase day by day; to work on *Tao* (the Way, the Truth) is to decrease day by day." I am not concerned with the difference between increasing and decreasing, nor do I quite agree with this saying of *Lao-tzu*. I quote it only to show that in the tradition of Chinese philosophy there is a distinction between working on learning and working on *Tao* (the Way). The purpose of the former is what I call the increase of positive knowledge, that of the latter is the elevation of the mind. Philosophy belongs in the latter category.

The view that the function of philosophy, especially metaphysics, is not the increase of positive knowledge, is expounded by the Viennese school in contemporary Western philosophy, though from a different angle and for a different purpose. I do not agree with this school that the function of philosophy is only the clarification of ideas, and that the nature of metaphysics is only a lyric of concepts. Nevertheless, in their arguments one can see quite clearly that philosophy, especially metaphysics, would become nonsense if it did attempt to give information regarding matters of fact.

Religion does give information in regard to matters of fact. But the information given by religion is not in harmony with that given by science. So in the West there has been the conflict between religion and science. Where science advances, religion retreats; and the authority of religion recedes before the advancement of science. The traditionalists regretted this fact and pitied the people who had become irreligious, considering them as having degenerated. They ought indeed to be pitied, if, besides religion, they had no other access to the higher values. When people get rid of religion and have no substitute, they also lose the higher values. They have to confine themselves to mundane affairs and have nothing to do with the spiritual ones. Fortunately, however, besides religion there is philosophy, which provides man with an access to the higher values — an access which is more direct than that provided by religion, because in philosophy, in order to be acquainted with the higher values, man need not take the roundabout way provided by prayers and rituals. The higher values with which man has become acquainted through philosophy are even purer than those acquired through religion, because they are not mixed with imagination and superstition. In the world of the future, man will have philosophy in the place of religion. This is consistent with Chinese tradition. It is not necessary that man should be religious, but it *is* necessary that he should be philosophical. When he is philosophical, he has the very best of the blessings of religion.

Problem and Spirit of Chinese Philosophy

The above is a general discussion of the nature and function of philosophy. In the following remarks I shall speak more specifically about Chinese philosophy. There is a main current in the history of Chinese philosophy, which may be called the spirit of Chinese philosophy. In order to understand this spirit, we must first make clear the problem that most Chinese philosophers have tried to solve.

There are all kinds and conditions of men. With regard to any one of these kinds, there is the highest form of achievement of which any one kind of man is capable. For instance, there are the men engaged in practical politics. The highest form of achievement in that class of men is that of the great statesman. So also in the field of art, the highest form of achievement of which artists are capable is that of the great artist. Although there are these different classes of men, yet all of them are men. What is the highest form of achievement of which a man *as a man* is capable? According to the Chinese philosophers, it is nothing less than being a sage, and the highest achievement of a sage is the identification of the individual with the universe. The problem is, if men want to achieve this identification, do they necessarily have to abandon society or even to negate life?

According to some philosophers, this is necessary. The Buddha said that life itself is the root and fountainhead of the misery of life. Likewise, Plato said that the body is the prison of the soul. And some of the Taoists said that life is an excrescence, a tumor, and death is to be taken as the breaking of the tumor. All these ideas represent a view which entails separation from what may be called the entangling net of the matter-corrupted world; and therefore, if the highest achievement of a sage is to be realized, the sage has to abandon society and even life itself. Only thus can the final liberation be attained. This kind of philosophy is what is generally known as "other-worldly philosophy."

There is another kind of philosophy which emphasizes what is in society, such as human relations and human affairs. This kind of philosophy speaks only about moral values, and is unable to or does not wish to speak of the super-moral ones. This kind of philosophy is generally described as "this-worldly." From the point of view of a this-worldly philosophy, an other-world philosophy is too idealistic, is of no practical use and is negative. From the point of view of an other-worldly philosophy, a this-world philosophy is too realistic, too superficial. It may be positive, but it is like the quick walking of a man who has taken the wrong road: the more quickly he walks the further he goes astray.

There are many people who say that Chinese philosophy is a this-world philosophy. It is difficult to state that these people are entirely right or entirely wrong. Taking a merely superficial view, people who hold this opinion cannot be said to be wrong, because according to their view, Chinese philosophy, regardless of its different schools of thought, is directly or indirectly concerned with government and ethics. On the surface, therefore, it is concerned chiefly with society, and not with the universe; with the daily functions of human relations, not hell and heaven; with man's present life, but not his life in a world to come. When he was once asked by a disciple about the meaning of death, Confucius replied: "Not yet understanding life, how can you understand death?" (*Analects,* XI, 11.) And Mencius said: "The sage is the acme of human relations" (*Mencius,* IVa, 2), which, taken literally, means that the sage is the morally perfect man in society. From a surface point of view, with the ideal man being of this world, it seems that what Chinese philosophy calls a sage is a person of a very different order from the Buddha of Buddhism and the saints of the Christian religion. Superficially, this would seem to be especially true of the Confucian sage. That is why, in ancient times, Confucius and the Confucianists were so greatly ridiculed by the Taoists.

This, however, is only a surface view of the matter. Chinese philosophy cannot be understood by oversimplification of this kind. So far as the main tenet of its tradition is concerned, if we understand it aright, it cannot be said to be wholly this-worldly, just as, of course, it cannot be said to be wholly other-worldly. It is both of this world *and* of the other world. Speaking about the Neo-Confucianism of the Sung Dynasty, one philosopher described it this way: "It is not divorced from daily ordinary activities, yet it goes straight to what antedated Heaven." This is what Chinese philosophy has striven for. Having this kind of spirit, it is at one and the same time both extremely idealistic and extremely realistic, and very practical, though not in a superficial way.

This-worldliness and other-worldliness stand in contrast to each other as do realism and idealism. The task of Chinese philosophy is to accomplish a synthesis out of these antitheses. That does not mean that they are to be abolished. They are still there, but they have been made into a synthetic whole. How can this be done? This is the problem which Chinese philosophy attempts to solve.

According to Chinese philosophy, the man who accomplishes this synthesis, not only in theory but also in deed, is the sage. He is both this-worldly and other-worldly. The spiritual achievement of the Chinese sage corresponds to the saint's achievement in Buddhism, and in Western religion. But the Chinese sage is not one who does not concern himself with the business of the world. His character is described as one of "sageliness within and kingliness without." That is to say, in his inner sageliness, he accomplishes spiritual cultivation; in his kingliness without, he functions in society. It is not necessary that the sage should be the actual head of the government in his society. From the standpoint of practical politics, for the most part, the sage certainly has no chance of being the head of the state. The saying "sageliness within and kingliness without" means only that he who has the noblest spirit should, theoretically, be king. As to whether he actually has or has not the chance of being king, that is immaterial.

Since the character of the sage is, according to Chinese tradition, one of sageliness within the kingliness without, the task of philosophy is to enable man to develop this kind of character. Therefore, what philosophy discusses is what the Chinese philosophers describe as the *Tao* (Way, or basic principles) of sageliness within and kingliness without.

This sounds like the Platonic theory of the philosopher-king. According to Plato, in an ideal state, the philosopher should be the king or the king should be a philosopher; and in order to become a philosopher, a man must undergo a long period of philosophical training before his mind can be "converted" from the world of changing things to the world of eternal ideas. Thus according to Plato, as according to the Chinese philosophers, the task of philosophy is to enable man to have the character of sageliness within and kingliness without. But according to Plato, when a philosopher becomes a king, he does so against his will — in other words, it is something forced on him, and entails a great sacrifice on his part. This is what was also held by the ancient Taoists. There is the story of a sage who, being asked by the people of a certain state to become their king, escaped and hid himself in a mountain cave. But the people found the cave, smoked him out and compelled him to assume the difficult task. (*Lü-shih Ch'un-ch'iu,* I, 2.) This is one similarity between Plato and the ancient Taoists, and it also shows the character of other-worldliness in Taoist philosophy. Following the main tradition of Chinese philosophy, the Neo-Taoist, Kuo Hsiang of the third century A.D., revised this point.

According to Confucianism, the daily task of dealing with social affairs in human relations is not something alien to the sage. Carrying on this task is the very essence of the development of the perfection of his personality. He performs it not only as a citizen of society, but also as a "citizen of the universe," *t'ien min,* as Mencius called it. He must be conscious of his being a citizen of the universe, otherwise his deeds would not have super-moral value. If he had the chance to become a king he would gladly serve the people, thus performing his duty both as a citizen of society, and as a citizen of the universe.

Since what is discussed in philosophy is the *Tao* (Way) of sageliness within and kingliness without, it follows that philosophy must be inseparable from political thought. Regardless of the differences between the schools of Chinese philosophy, the philosophy of every school represents, at the same time, its political thought. This does not mean that in the various schools of philosophy there are no metaphysics, no ethics, no logic. It means only that all these factors are connected with political thought in one way or another, just as Plato's *Republic* represents his whole philosophy and at the same time is his political thought.

For instance, the School of Names was known to indulge in such arguments as "a white horse is not a horse," which seems to have very little connection with politics. Yet the leader of this school, Kung-sun Lung, "wished to extend this kind of argument to rectify the relationship between names and facts in order to transform the world." We have seen in our world today how every statesman says his country wants only peace, but in fact, when he is talking about peace, he is often preparing for war. Here, then, there is a wrong relationship between names and facts. According to Kung-sun Lung, this kind of wrong relationship should be rectified. This is really the first step towards the transformation of the world.

Since the subject matter of philosophy is the *Tao* of sageliness within and kingliness without, the study of philosophy is not simply an attempt to acquire this kind of knowledge, but is also an attempt to develop this kind of character. Philosophy is not simply something to be *known,* but is also something to be *experienced.* It is not simply a sort of intellectual game, but something far more serious. As my colleague, Professor Y. L. Chin, has pointed out in an unpublished manuscript: "Chinese philosophers were all of them different grades of Socrates. This was so because ethics, politics, reflective thinking, and knowledge were unified in the philosopher; in him, knowledge and virtue were one and inseparable. His philosophy required that he live it; he was himself its vehicle. To live in accordance with his philosophical convictions was part of his philosophy. It was his business to school himself continually and persistently to that pure experience in which selfishness and egocentricity were transcended, so that he would be one with the universe. Obviously this process of schooling could not be stopped, for stopping it would mean the emergence of his ego and the loss of his universe. Hence cognitively he was eternally groping, and conatively he was eternally behaving or trying to behave. Since these could not be separated, in him there was the synthesis of the philosopher in the original sense of that term. Like Socrates, he did not keep office hours with his philosophy. Neither was he a dusty, musty philosopher, closeted in his study, sitting in a chair on the periphery of life. With him, philosophy was hardly ever merely a pattern of ideas exhibited for human understanding, but was a system of precepts internal to the conduct of the philosopher; and in extreme cases his philosophy might even be said to be his biography."

WALTER RAUSCHENBUSCH

The Social Principles of Jesus

Walter Rauschenbusch (1861–1918), professor of church history at Rochester Theological Seminary, was perhaps the leading spokesman for the theology of the Social Gospel in American Protestantism, through books such as *Christianity and the Social Crisis* and *Christianizing the Social Order*. Here in "The Social Principles of Jesus" he set forth his reading of the Gospels as the ultimate foundation for his social philosophy.

JESUS CHRIST was the founder of the highest religion; he was himself the purest religious spirit known to us. Why, then, was he in opposition to religion? The clash between him and the representatives of organized religion was not occasional or superficial. It ran through his whole activity, was one of the dominant notes in his teaching, culminated in the great spiritual duel between him and the Jewish hierarchy in the last days at Jerusalem, and led directly to his crucifixion.

I

The opposition of Jesus was not, of course, against religion itself, but against religion as he found it. It was not directed against any departure from the legitimate order of the priesthood; nor against an improper ritual or wrong doctrine of sacrifices. In fact, it did not turn on any of the issues which were of such importance to the church in later times. He criticized the most earnest religious men of his day because their religion harmed men instead of helping them. It was unsocial, or anti-social.

The Old Testament prophets also were in opposition to the priestly system of their time because it used up the religious interest of the people in ceremonial performances without ethical outcome. It diverted spiritual energy, by substituting lower religious requirements for the one fundamental thing which God required — righteousness in social and political life. They insisted over and over that Jehovah wants righteousness and wants nothing else. Their aim was to make religion and ethics one and inseparable. They struck for the social efficiency of religion.

At the time of Jesus the Jewish sacrifices had lost much of their religious importance. During the Exile they had lapsed. They were professional performances of one class. The numerous Jews scattered in other countries perhaps saw the Temple once in a lifetime. Modern feeling in the first century was against bloody sacrifices. The recorded sayings of Jesus hardly mention them. On the other hand, the daily life of the people was pervaded by little prescribed religious actions. The Sabbath with its ritual was punctiliously observed. There were frequent days of fasting, religious ablutions and baths, long prayers to be recited several times daily, with prayer straps around the arm and forehead, and a tasseled cloth over the head. The exact performance of these things seemed an essential part of religion to the most earnest men.

We have seen how Jesus collided with these religious requirements, and on what grounds. If men were deeply concerned about the taboo food that went into their bodies, they would not be concerned about the evil thoughts that arose in their souls. If they were taught to focus on petty duties, such as tithing, the great ethical principles and obligations moved to the outer field of vision and became blurred. The Sabbath, which had originated in merciful purpose toward the poor, had been turned into another burden. Religion, which ought to bring good men into saving contact with the wayward by love, actually resulted in separating the two by a chasm of religious pride and censoriousness. A man-made and artificial religious performance, such as giving toward the support of the Temple, crowded aside fundamental obligations written deep in the constitution of human society, such as filial reverence and family solidarity.

Other reformers have condemned religious practices because they were departures from the holy Book or from primitive custom. Jesus, too, pointed out that some of these regulations were recent innovations. But the real standard by which he judged current religious questions was not ancient authority but the present good of men. The spiritual center on which he took his stand and from which he judged all things, was the kingdom of God, the perfect social order. Even the ordinances of religion must justify themselves by making an effective contribution to the kingdom of God. The Sabbath was made for man, and its observance must meet the test of service to man's welfare. It must function wholesomely. The candle must give light, or what is the use of it? The salt must be salty and preserve from decay, or it will be thrown out and trodden under foot. If the fig tree bears no fruit, why is it allowed to use up space and crowd better plants off the soil? This, then, is Christ's test in matters of institutional religion. The church and all its doings must serve the kingdom of God.

II

The social efficiency of religion is a permanent social problem. What is the annual expense of maintaining the churches in the United States? How much capital is invested in the church buildings? How much care and interest and loving free-will labor does an average village community bestow on religion as compared with other objects? All men feel instinctively that religion exerts a profound and subtle influence on the springs of conduct. Even those who denounce it, acknowledge at least its power for harm. Most of us know it as a power for good. But all history shows that this great spiritual force easily deteriorates. *Corruptio optimi pessima* [There is nothing worse than the corruption of the best].

Religion may develop an elaborate social apparatus of its own, wheels within wheels, and instead of being a dynamic of righteousness in the natural social relations of men, its energies may be consumed in driving its own machinery. Instead of being the powerhouse supplying the kingdom of God among men with power and light, the church may exist for its own sake. It then may become an expensive consumer of social wealth, a conservative clog, and a real hindrance of social progress.

Live religion gives proof of its value by the sense of freedom, peace, and elation which it creates. We feel we are right with the holy Power which is behind, and beneath, and above all things. It gives a satisfying interpretation of life and of our own place in it. It moves our aims higher up, draws our fellow men closer, and invigorates our will.

But our growth sets a problem for our religion. The religion of childhood will not satisfy adolescent youth, and the religion of youth ought not to satisfy a mature man or woman. Our soul must build statelier mansions for itself. Religion must continue to answer all our present needs and inspire all our present functions. A person who has failed to adjust his religion to his growing powers and his intellectual horizon, has failed in one of the most important functions of growth, just as if his cranium failed to expand and to give room to his brain. Being microcephalous is a misfortune, and nothing to boast of.

Precisely the same problem arises when society passes through eras of growth. Religion must keep pace. The church must pass the burning torch of religious experience from age to age, transmitting the faith of the fathers to the children, and not allowing any spiritual values to perish. But it must allow and aid religion to adjust itself. Its inspiring teaching must meet the new social problems so effectively that no evil can last long or grow beyond remedy. In every new age religion must stand the test of social efficiency. Is it passing that test in Western civilization?

Religion is a bond of social coherence. It creates loyalty. But it may teach loyalty to antiquated observances or a dwarfed system of truth. Have you ever seen believers rallying around a lost cause in religion? Yet these relics were once a live issue, and full of thrilling religious vitality.

Society changes. Will religion change with it? If society passes from agriculture and rural settlements to industry and urban conditions, can the customary practices of religion remain unchanged? Give some instances where pre-scientific conceptions of the universe, embodied in religion, have blocked the spread of scientific knowledge among the people. The caste distinctions of Hinduism were the product of a combination between religion and the social organization of the people; can they last when industrialism and democracy are pervading India? The clerical attitude of authority was natural when the Catholic clergy were the only educated class in the community; is it justified today? Protestantism won the allegiance of industrial communities when the young business class was struggling to emancipate itself from the feudal system. It developed an individualistic philosophy of ethics. Today society tends toward solidaristic organization. How will that affect religion and its scheme of duty? Thus religion, by its very virtues of loyalty and reverence, may fall behind and lose its full social efficiency. It must be geared to the big live issues of today if it is to manifest its full saving energies.

How does this problem of the efficiency of religion bear on the foreign missionary movement? How will backward or stationary civilizations be affected by the introduction of a modern and enthusiastic religion?

We may feel the defects of our church life at home, but there is no doubt that the young men and women who go out from our colleges under religious impulses, are felt as a virile and modernizing force when they settle to their work in Turkey or Persia. Christian educational institutions and medical missions have raised the intellectual and humane standards of young China. Buddhism in Japan has felt the challenge of competition and is readjusting its ethics and philosophy to connect with modern social ideals. The historical effects of our religious colonization will not mature for several generations, but they are bound to be very great. The nations and races are drawing together. They need a monotheistic religion as a spiritual basis for their sense of human unity. This is a big modern social task. It makes its claim on men and women who have youth, education, and spiritual power. Is the religious life of our colleges and universities efficient enough to meet the need?

Here are the enormous tasks of international relations, which the Great War has forced us to realize — the prevention of armed conflicts, the elimination of the irritant causes of war, the protection of the small nations which possess what the big nations covet, the freedom of the seas as the common highway of God, fair and free interchange in commerce without any effort to set up monopoly rights and the privilege of extortionate gain, the creation of an institutional basis for a great family of nations in days to come. These are some of the tasks which the men and women who are now young must take on their mind and conscience for life, and leave to their children to finish. What contributions, in your opinion, could the spirit of the Christian religion make to such a program, if it were realized intelligently and pressed home through the agencies of the Christian church? In what ways has American religion shown its efficiency since the war broke out?

Christianity has been a great power in our country to cleanse and fraternalize the social life of simple communities. Can it meet the complex needs of modern industrialism in the same way? It cannot truthfully be claimed that it has done so in any industrial country. Its immense spiritual forces might be the decisive element, but they have been effectively organized against a few only of the great modern evils. On the fundamental ethical questions of capitalism the church has not yet made up its own mind — not to speak of enforcing the mind of Christ. Nor have the specialists in the universities and colleges supplied the leaders of the church with clear information and guidance on these questions. We cannot make much permanent progress toward a just social order as long as the masses of the working people in the industrial nations continue in economic poverty and political helplessness, and as long as a minority controls the land, the tools, and the political power. We shall linger on the borders of the Inferno until a new accession of moral insight and spiritual power comes to the nations. How will it come?

III

What could the churches in an average village community accomplish if they intelligently directed the power of religion to foster the sense of fraternal unity and to promote the institutions which make for unity? How could they draw the new, the strange, and the irregular families into the circle of neighborly feeling? In what way could they help to assimilate immigrants and to prevent the formation of several communities in the same section, overlapping, alien, and perhaps hostile? How would it affect the recreational situation if the churches took a constructive rather than a prohibitive attitude toward amusements, and if they promoted the sociability of the community rather than that of church groups?

With the rise of land prices and the control of transportation and markets, the rural population is moving toward a social crisis like that which transformed the urban population in the industrial revolution. Agriculture will become capitalistic, and the weaker families will drop to the position of tenants and agricultural laborers. Cooperation is their way of salvation. Its effectiveness has been amply demonstrated in older countries. It requires a strong sense of solidarity, loyalty, and good faith to succeed. It has made so little headway in America because our national character has not been developed in these directions. What could the churches do to save the weaker families from social submergence by backing cooperation and developing the moral qualities needed for it?

The strong religious life of our people might be more effective if the churches were less divided. Their economic and human resources are partly wasted by useless competition. Our denominational divisions are nearly all an historical heritage, imported from Europe, and coming down from a controversial age. Their issues all meant something vital and socially important in the midst of the social order of that day; but in many cases the real significance has quietly crumbled away, and they are not really the same issues that deeply engaged our forefathers. We are all "tithing mint, anise, and cummin," and forgetting the weighty matters, such as social justice and Christian fraternity. Everybody is ready to acknowledge this about every denomination except his own. We need a revaluation of our religious issues from the point of view of the kingdom of God. That would bring us into harmony with the judgment of Jesus. Nothing else will.

IV

The social efficiency of religion — what call is there in that to the college men and women of this generation? Shall they cease to worship and pray, seek the salvation of society in ethics and sociology, and abandon religion to stagnation? Or shall they seek a new experience of religion in full sight of the modern world, and work by faith toward that reign of God in which his will shall be done?

JAMES RUSSELL LOWELL

Once to Every Man and Nation

James Russell Lowell (1819–1891), a professor at Harvard,
was an editor, poet, and essayist, and a vigorous foe of
slavery. His most widely distributed piece was this anti-
slavery poem, "The Present Crisis," which he wrote in
December 1844; with some changes (including the substitution of "martyrs" for "heretics") several portions of it
became, as "Once to Every Man and Nation," a battle hymn
in the modern campaign for human rights.

WHEN a deed is done for Freedom, through the broad earth's
    aching breast
Runs a thrill of joy prophetic, trembling on from east to west,
And the slave, where'er he cowers, feels the soul within him climb
To the awful verge of manhood, as the energy sublime
Of a century bursts full-blossomed on the thorny stem of Time.

Through the walls of hut and palace shoots the instantaneous throe,
When the travail of the Ages wrings earth's systems to and fro;
At the birth of each new Era, with a recognizing start,
Nation wildly looks at nation, standing with mute lips apart,
And glad Truth's yet mightier man-child leaps beneath the Future's
    heart.

So the Evil's triumph sendeth, with a terror and a chill,
Under continent to continent, the sense of coming ill,
And the slave, where'er he cowers, feels his sympathies with God
In hot tear-drops ebbing earthward, to be drunk up by the sod,
Till a corpse crawls round unburied, delving in the nobler clod.

For mankind are one in spirit, and an instinct bears along,
Round the earth's electric circle, the swift flash of right or wrong;
Whether conscious or unconscious, yet Humanity's vast frame
Through its ocean-sundered fibres feels the gush of joy or
      shame; —
In the gain or loss of one race all the rest have equal claim.

Once to every man and nation comes the moment to decide,
In the strife of Truth with Falsehood, for the good or evil side;
Some great cause, God's new Messiah, offering each the bloom or
      blight,
Parts the goats upon the left hand, and the sheep upon the right,
And the choice goes by forever 'twixt that darkness and that light.

Hast thou chosen, O my people, on whose party thou shalt stand,
Ere the Doom from its worn sandals shakes the dust against our
      land?
Though the cause of Evil prosper, yet 't is Truth alone is strong,
And, albeit she wander outcast now, I see around her throng
Troops of beautiful, tall angels, to enshield her from all wrong.

Backward look across the ages and the beacon-moments see,
That, like peaks of some sunk continent, jut through Oblivion's
      sea;
Not an ear in court or market for the low foreboding cry
Of those Crises, God's stern winnowers, from whose feet earth's
      chaff must fly;
Never shows the choice momentous till the judgment hath passed
      by.

Careless seems the great Avenger; history's pages but record
One death-grapple in the darkness 'twixt old systems and the Word;
Truth forever on the scaffold, Wrong forever on the throne, —
Yet that scaffold sways the future, and, behind the dim unknown,
Standeth God within the shadow, keeping watch above his own.

We see dimly in the Present what is small and what is great,
Slow of faith how weak an arm may turn the iron helm of fate,
But the soul is still oracular; amid the market's din,
List the ominous stern whisper from the Delphic cave within, —

"They enslave their children's children who make compromise with
    sin."

Slavery, the earth-born Cyclops, fellest of the giant brood,
Sons of brutish Force and Darkness, who have drenched the earth
    with blood,
Famished in his self-made desert, blinded by our purer day,
Gropes in yet unblasted regions for his miserable prey; —
Shall we guide his gory fingers where our helpless children play?

Then to side with Truth is noble when we share her wretched crust,
Ere her cause bring fame and profit, and 't is prosperous to be just;
Then it is the brave man chooses, while the coward stands aside,
Doubting in his abject spirit, till his Lord is crucified,
And the multitude make virtue of the faith they had denied.

Count me o'er earth's chosen heroes, — they were souls that stood
    alone,
While the men they agonized for hurled the contumelious stone,
Stood serene, and down the future saw the golden beam incline
To the side of perfect justice, mastered by their faith divine,
By one man's plain truth to manhood and to God's supreme design.

By the light of burning heretics Christ's bleeding feet I track,
Toiling up new Calvaries ever with the cross that turns not back,
And these mounts of anguish number how each generation learned
One new word of that grand *Credo* which in prophet-hearts hath
    burned
Since the first man stood God-conquered with his face to heaven
    upturned.

For Humanity sweeps onward: where to-day the martyr stands,
On the morrow crouches Judas with the silver in his hands;
Far in front the cross stands ready and the crackling fagots burn,
While the hooting mob of yesterday in silent awe return
To glean up the scattered ashes into History's golden urn.

'T is as easy to be heroes as to sit the idle slaves
Of a legendary virtue carved upon our fathers' graves,
Worshippers of light ancestral make the present light a crime; —

Was the Mayflower launched by cowards, steered by men behind
    their time?
Turn those tracks toward Past or Future, that make Plymouth Rock
    sublime?

They were men of present valor, stalwart old iconoclasts,
Unconvinced by axe or gibbet that all virtue was the Past's;
But we make their truth our falsehood, thinking that hath made us
    free,
Hoarding it in mouldy parchments, while our tender spirits flee
The rude grasp of that great Impulse which drove them across the
    sea.

They have rights who dare maintain them; we are traitors to our
    sires,
Smothering in their holy ashes Freedom's new-lit altar-fires;
Shall we make their creed our jailer? Shall we, in our haste to slay,
From the tombs of the old prophets steal the funeral lamps away
To light up the martyr-fagots round the prophets of today?

New occasions teach new duties; Time makes ancient good
    uncouth;
They must upward still, and onward, who would keep abreast of
    Truth;
Lo, before us gleam her camp-fires! we ourselves must Pilgrims be,
Launch our Mayflower, and steer boldly through the desperate
    winter sea,
Nor attempt the Future's portal with the Past's blood-rusted key.

MAHATMA GANDHI

Autobiography

Mohandas Karamchand Gandhi (1869–1948), called in Sanskrit "Mahatma" (great-souled), was the political and spiritual father of modern India. As these selections from his autobiography, *My Experiments with Truth,* make clear, he based his strategy of passive resistance on a philosophical-religious synthesis that brought together elements of traditional Hinduism, of (Tolstoyan) Christianity, and of other world religions.

Glimpses of Religion

FROM MY SIXTH OR SEVENTH year up to my sixteenth I was at school, being taught all sorts of things except religion. I may say that I failed to get from the teachers what they could have given me without any effort on their part. And yet I kept on picking up things here and there from my surroundings. The term "religion" I am using in its broadest sense, meaning thereby self-realization or knowledge of self.

Being born in the Vaishnava faith, I had often to go to the *Haveli.* But it never appealed to me. I did not like its glitter and pomp. Also I heard rumours of immorality being practised there, and lost all interest in it. Hence I could gain nothing from the *Haveli.*

But what I failed to get there I obtained from my nurse, an old servant of the family, whose affection for me I still recall. I have said before that there was in me a fear of ghosts and spirits. Rambha, for that was her name, suggested, as a remedy for this fear, the repetition of *Ramanama.* I had more faith in her than in her remedy, and so at a tender age I began repeating *Ramanama* to cure my fear of ghosts and spirits. This was of course short-lived, but the good seed sown in childhood was not sown in vain. I think it is due to the seed sown by the good woman Rambha that today *Ramanama* is an infallible remedy for me.

Just about this time, a cousin of mine who was a devotee of the *Ramayana* arranged for my second brother and me to learn *Ram Raksha*. We got it by heart, and made it a rule to recite it every morning after the bath. The practice was kept up as long as we were in Porbandar. As soon as we reached Rajkot, it was forgotten. For I had not much belief in it. I recited it partly because of my pride in being able to recite *Ram Raksha* with correct pronunciation.

What, however, left a deep impression on me was the reading of the *Ramayana* before my father. During part of his illness my father was in Porbandar. There every evening he used to listen to the *Ramayana*. The reader was a great devotee of Rama, — Ladha Maharaj of Bileshvar. It was said of him that he cured himself of his leprosy not by any medicine, but by applying to the affected parts *bilva* leaves which had been cast away after being offered to the image of Mahadeva in Bileshvar temple, and by the regular repetition of *Ramanama*. His faith, it was said, had made him whole. This may or may not be true. We at any rate believed the story. And it is a fact that when Ladha Maharaj began his reading of the *Ramayana* his body was entirely free from leprosy. He had a melodious voice. He would sing the *Dohas* (couplets) and *Chopais* (quatrains), and explain them, losing himself in the discourse and carrying his listeners along with him. I must have been thirteen at that time, but I quite remember being enraptured by his reading. That laid the foundation of my deep devotion to the *Ramayana*. Today I regard the *Ramayana* of Tulasidas as the greatest book in all devotional literature.

A few months after this we came to Rajkot. There was no *Ramayana* reading there. The *Bhagavat,* however, used to be read on every *Ekadashi* day. Sometimes I attended the reading, but the reciter was uninspiring. Today I see that the *Bhagavat* is a book which can evoke religious fervour. I have read it in Gujarati with intense interest. But when I heard portions of the original read by Pandit Madan Mohan Malaviya during my twenty-one days' fast, I wished I had heard it in my childhood from such a devotee as he is, so that I could have formed a liking for it at an early age. Impressions formed at that age strike roots deep down into one's nature, and it is my perpetual regret that I was not fortunate enough to hear more good books of this kind read during that period.

In Rajkot, however, I got an early grounding in toleration for all branches of Hinduism and sister religions. For my father and mother would visit the *Haveli* as also Shiva's and Rama's temples, and would take or send us youngsters there. Jain monks also would pay frequent visits to my father, and would even go out of their way to accept food from us — non-Jains. They would have talks with my father on subjects religious and mundane.

He had, besides, Musalman and Parsi friends, who would talk to him about their own faiths, and he would listen to them always with respect, and often with interest. Being his nurse, I often had a chance to be present at these talks. These many things combined to inculcate in me a toleration for all faiths.

Only Christianity was at the time an exception. I developed a sort of dislike for it. And for a reason. In those days Christian missionaries used to stand in a corner near the high school and hold forth, pouring abuse on Hindus and their gods. I could not endure this. I must have stood there to hear them once only, but that was enough to dissuade me from repeating the experiment. About the same time, I heard of a well known Hindu having been converted to Christianity. It was the talk of the town that, when he was baptized, he had to eat beef and drink liquor, that he also had to change his clothes, and that thenceforth he began to go about in European costume including a hat. These things got on my nerves. Surely, thought I, a religion that compelled one to eat beef, drink liquor, and change one's own clothes did not deserve the name. I also heard that the new convert had already begun abusing the religion of his ancestors, their customs and their country. All these things created in me a dislike for Christianity.

But the fact that I had learnt to be tolerant to other religions did not mean that I had any living faith in God. I happened, about this time, to come across *Manusmriti* which was amongst my father's collection. The story of the creation and similar things in it did not impress me very much, but on the contrary made me incline somewhat towards atheism.

There was a cousin of mine, still alive, for whose intellect I had great regard. To him I turned with my doubts. But he could not resolve them. He sent me away with this answer: "When you grow up, you will be able to solve these doubts yourself. These questions ought not to be raised at your age." I was silenced, but was not comforted. Chapters about diet and the like in *Manusmriti* seemed to me to run contrary to daily practice. To my doubts as to this also, I got the same answer. "With intellect more developed and with more reading I shall understand it better," I said to myself.

Manusmriti at any rate did not then teach me *ahimsa*. I have told the story of my meat-eating. *Manusmriti* seemed to support it. I also felt that it was quite moral to kill serpents, bugs and the like. I remember to have killed at that age bugs and such other insects, regarding it as a duty.

But one thing took deep root in me — the conviction that morality is the basis of things, and that truth is the substance of all morality. Truth became my sole objective. It began to grow in magnitude every day, and my definition of it also has been ever widening.

A Gujarati didactic stanza likewise gripped my mind and heart. Its precept — return good for evil — became my guiding principle. It became such a passion with me that I began numerous experiments in it. Here are those (for me) wonderful lines:

> For a bowl of water give a goodly meal;
> For a kindly greeting bow thou down with zeal;
> For a simple penny pay thou back with gold;
> If thy life be rescued, life do not withhold.
> Thus the words and actions of the wise regard;
> Every little service tenfold they reward.
> But the truly noble know all men as one,
> And return with gladness good for evil done.

*   *   *   *   *

Christian Contacts

The next day at one o'clock I went to Mr. Baker's prayer-meeting. There I was introduced to Miss Harris, Miss Gabb, Mr. Coates and others. Everyone kneeled down to pray, and I followed suit. The prayers were supplications to God for various things, according to each person's desire. Thus the usual forms were for the day to be passed peacefully, or for God to open the doors of the heart.

A prayer was now added for my welfare: "Lord, show the path to the new brother who has come amongst us. Give him, Lord, the peace that Thou hast given us. May the Lord Jesus who has saved us save him too. We ask all this in the name of Jesus." There was no singing of hymns or other music at these meetings. After the supplication for something special every day, we dispersed, each going to his lunch, that being the hour for it. The prayer did not take more than five minutes.

The Misses Harris and Gabb were both elderly maiden ladies. Mr. Coates was a Quaker. The two ladies lived together, and they gave me a standing invitation to four o'clock tea at their house every Sunday.

When we met on Sundays, I used to give Mr. Coates my religious diary for the week, and discuss with him the books I had read and the impression they had left on me. The ladies used to narrate their sweet experiences and talk about the peace they had found.

Mr. Coates was a frank-hearted staunch young man. We went out for walks together, and he also took me to other Christian friends.

As we came closer to each other, he began to give me books of his own choice, until my shelf was filled with them. He loaded me with books, as it were. In pure faith I consented to read all those books, and as I went on reading them we discussed them.

I read a number of such books in 1893. I do not remember the names of them all, but they included the *Commentary* of Dr. Parker of the City Temple, Pearson's *Many Infallible Proofs* and Butler's *Analogy*. Parts of these were unintelligible to me. I liked some things in them, while I did not like others. *Many Infallible Proofs* were proofs in support of the religion of the Bible, as the author understood it. The book had no effect on me. Parker's *Commentary* was morally stimulating, but it could not be of any help to one who had no faith in the prevalent Christian beliefs. Butler's *Analogy* struck me to be a very profound and difficult book, which should be read four or five times to be understood properly. It seemed to me to be written with a view to converting atheists to theism. The arguments advanced in it regarding the existence of God were unnecessary for me, as I had then passed the stage of unbelief; but the arguments in proof of Jesus being the only incarnation of God and the Mediator between God and man left me unmoved.

But Mr. Coates was not the man easily to accept defeat. He had great affection for me. He saw, round my neck, the *Vaishnava* necklace of Tulasi-beads. He thought it to be superstition and was pained by it. "This superstition does not become you. Come, let me break the necklace."

"No, you will not. It is a sacred gift from my mother."

"But do you believe in it?"

"I do not know its mysterious significance. I do not think I should come to harm if I did not wear it. But I cannot, without sufficient reason, give up a necklace that she put round my neck out of love and in the conviction that it would be conducive to my welfare. When, with the passage of time, it wears away and breaks of its own accord, I shall have no desire to get a new one. But this necklace cannot be broken."

Mr. Coates could not appreciate my argument, as he had no regard for my religion. He was looking forward to delivering me from the abyss of ignorance. He wanted to convince me that, no matter whether there was some truth in other religions, salvation was impossible for me unless I accepted Christianity which represented *the* truth, and that my sins would not be washed away except by the intercession of Jesus, and that all good works were useless.

Just as he introduced me to several books, he introduced me to several friends whom he regarded as staunch Christians. One of these introductions was to a family which belonged to the Plymouth Brethren, a Christian sect.

Many of the contacts for which Mr. Coates was responsible were good. Most struck me as being God-fearing. But during my contact with his family, one of the Plymouth Brethren confronted me with an argument for which I was not prepared:

"You cannot understand the beauty of our religion. From what you say it appears that you must be brooding over your transgressions every moment of your life, always mending them and atoning for them. How can this ceaseless cycle of action bring you redemption? You can never have peace. You admit that we are all sinners. Now look at the perfection of our belief. Our attempts at improvement and atonement are futile. And yet redemption we must have. How can we bear the burden of sin? We can but throw it on Jesus. He is the only sinless Son of God. It is His word that those who believe in Him shall have everlasting life. Therein lies God's infinite mercy. And as we believe in the atonement of Jesus, our own sins do not bind us. Sin we must. It is impossible to live in this world sinless. And therefore Jesus suffered and atoned for all the sins of mankind. Only he who accepts His great redemption can have eternal peace. Think what a life of restlessness is yours, and what a promise of peace we have."

The argument utterly failed to convince me. I humbly replied:

"If this be the Christianity acknowledged by all Christians, I cannot accept it. I do not seek redemption from the consequences of my sin. I seek to be redeemed from sin itself, or rather from the very thought of sin. Until I have attained that end, I shall be content to be restless."

To which the Plymouth Brother rejoined: "I assure you, your attempt is fruitless. Think again over what I have said."

And the Brother proved as good as his word. He knowingly committed transgressions, and showed me that he was undisturbed by the thought of them.

But I already knew before meeting with these friends that all Christians did not believe in such a theory of atonement. Mr. Coates himself walked in the fear of God. His heart was pure, and he believed in the possibility of self-purification. The two ladies also shared this belief. Some of the books that came into my hands were full of devotion. So, although Mr. Coates was very much disturbed by this latest experience of mine, I was able to reassure him and tell him that the distorted belief of a Plymouth Brother could not prejudice me against Christianity.

My difficulties lay elsewhere. They were with regard to the Bible and its accepted interpretation.

*   *   *   *   *

Comparative Study of Religions

If I found myself entirely absorbed in the service of the community, the reason behind it was my desire for self-realization. I had made the religion of service my own, as I felt that God could be realized only through service. And service for me was the service of India, because it came to me without my seeking, because I had an aptitude for it. I had gone to South Africa for travel, for finding an escape from Kathiawad intrigues and for gaining my own livelihood. But as I have said, I found myself in search of God and striving for self-realization.

Christian friends had whetted my appetite for knowledge, which had become almost insatiable, and they would not leave me in peace, even if I desired to be indifferent. In Durban Mr. Spencer Walton, the head of the South Africa General Mission, found me out. I became almost a member of his family. At the back of this acquaintance was of course my contact with Christians in Pretoria. Mr. Walton had a manner all his own. I do not recollect his ever having invited me to embrace Christianity. But he placed his life as an open book before me, and let me watch all his movements. Mrs. Walton was a very gentle and talented woman. I liked the attitude of this couple. We knew the fundamental differences between us. Any amount of discussion could not efface them. Yet even differences prove helpful, where there are tolerance, charity and truth. I liked Mr. and Mrs. Walton's humility, perseverance and devotion to work, and we met very frequently.

This friendship kept alive my interest in religion. It was impossible now to get the leisure that I used to have in Pretoria for my religious studies. But what little time I could spare I turned to good account. My religious correspondence continued. Raychandbhai was guiding me. Some friend sent me Narmadashanker's book *Dharma Vichar*. Its preface proved very helpful. I had heard about the Bohemian way in which the poet had lived, and a description in the preface of the revolution effected in his life by his religious studies captivated me. I came to like the book, and read it from cover to cover with attention. I read with interest Max Muller's book, *India — What Can It Teach Us?* and the translation of the *Upanishads* published by the Theosophical Society. All this enhanced my regard for Hinduism, and its beauties began to grow upon me. It did not, however, prejudice me against other religions. I read Washington Irving's *Life of Mahomet and His Successors* and Carlyle's panegyric on the prophet. These books raised Muhammad in my estimation. I also read a book called *The Sayings of Zarathustra.*

Thus I gained more knowledge of the different religions. The study stimulated my self-introspection and fostered in me the habit of putting into practice whatever appealed to me in my studies. Thus I began some of the Yogic practices, as well as I could understand them from a reading of the Hindu books. But I could not get on very far, and decided to follow them with the help of some expert when I returned to India. The desire has never been fulfilled.

I made too an intensive study of Tolstoy's books. *The Gospels in Brief, What to Do?* and other books made a deep impression on me. I began to realize more and more the infinite possibilities of universal love.

About the same time I came in contact with another Christian family. At their suggestion I attended the Wesleyan church every Sunday. For these days I also had their standing invitation to dinner. The church did not make a favourable impression on me. The sermons seemed to be uninspiring. The congregation did not strike me as being particularly religious. They were not an assembly of devout souls; they appeared rather to be worldly-minded people, going to church for recreation and in conformity to custom. Here, at times, I would involuntarily doze. I was ashamed, but some of my neighbours, who were in no better case, lightened the shame. I could not go on long like this, and soon gave up attending the service.

My connection with the family I used to visit every Sunday was abruptly broken. In fact it may be said that I was warned to visit it no more. It happened thus. My hostess was a good and simple woman, but somewhat narrow-minded. We always discussed religious subjects. I was then re-reading Arnold's *Light of Asia.* Once we began to compare the life of Jesus with that of Buddha. "Look at Gautama's compassion!" said I. "It was not confined to mankind, it was extended to all living beings. Does not one's heart overflow with love to think of the lamb joyously perched on his shoulders? One fails to notice this love for all living beings in the life of Jesus." The comparison pained the good lady. I could understand her feelings. I cut the matter short, and we went to the dining room. Her son, a cherub aged scarcely five, was also with us. I am happiest when in the midst of children, and this youngster and I had long been friends. I spoke derisively of the piece of meat on his plate and in high praise of the apple on mine. The innocent boy was carried away and joined in my praise of the fruit.

But the mother? She was dismayed.

I was warned. I checked myself and changed the subject. The following week I visited the family as usual, but not without trepidation. I did not see that I should stop going there, I did not think it proper either. But the good lady made my way easy.

"Mr. Gandhi," she said, "please don't take it ill if I feel obliged to tell you that my boy is none the better for your company. Every day he hesitates to eat meat and asks for fruit, reminding me of your argument. This is too much. If he gives up meat, he is bound to get weak, if not ill. How could I bear it? Your discussions should henceforth be only with us elders. They are sure to react badly on children."

"Mrs. ———," I replied, "I am sorry. I can understand your feelings as a parent, for I too have children. We can very easily end this unpleasant state of things. What I eat and omit to eat is bound to have a greater effect on the child than what I say. The best way, therefore, is for me to stop these visits. That certainly need not affect our friendship."

"I thank you," she said with evident relief.

MARTIN LUTHER KING

Letter from Birmingham City Jail

Martin Luther King (1929–1968), a Baptist minister and theologian, received the Nobel Prize for peace as a recognition of his leadership in the campaign for justice and peace. In this open letter of April 16, 1963, as his editor, James Washington, points out, Dr. King "wanted Christian ministers to see that the meaning of Christian discipleship was at the heart of the African American struggle for freedom, justice, and equality."

My dear Fellow Clergymen,

While confined here in the Birmingham city jail, I came across your recent statement calling our present activities "unwise and untimely." Seldom, if ever, do I pause to answer criticism of my work and ideas. If I sought to answer all of the criticisms that cross my desk, my secretaries would be engaged in little else in the course of the day, and I would have no time for constructive work. But since I feel that you are men of genuine good will and your criticisms are sincerely set forth, I would like to answer your statement in what I hope will be patient and reasonable terms.

I think I should give the reason for my being in Birmingham, since you have been influenced by the argument of "outsiders coming in." I have the honor of serving as president of the Southern Christian Leadership Conference, an organization operating in every southern state, with headquarters in Atlanta, Georgia. We have some eighty-five affiliate organizations all across the South — one being the Alabama Christian Movement for Human Rights. Whenever necessary and possible we share staff, educational and financial resources with our affiliates. Several months ago our local affiliate here in Birmingham invited us to be on call to engage in a nonviolent direct-action program if such were deemed necessary. We readily consented and when the hour came we lived up to our promises. So I am here, along with several members of my staff, because we were invited here. I am here because I have basic organizational ties here.

Beyond this, I am in Birmingham because injustice is here. Just as the eighth century prophets left their little villages and carried their "thus saith the Lord" far beyond the boundaries of their hometowns; and just as the Apostle Paul left his little village of Tarsus and carried the gospel of Jesus Christ to practically every hamlet and city of the Graeco-Roman world, I too am compelled to carry the gospel of freedom beyond my particular hometown. Like Paul, I must constantly respond to the Macedonian call for aid.

Moreover, I am cognizant of the interrelatedness of all communities and states. I cannot sit idly by in Atlanta and not be concerned about what happens in Birmingham. Injustice anywhere is a threat to justice everywhere. We are caught in an inescapable network of mutuality, tied in a single garment of destiny. Whatever affects one directly affects all indirectly. Never again can we afford to live with the narrow, provincial "outside agitator" idea. Anyone who lives in the United States can never be considered an outsider anywhere in this country.

You deplore the demonstrations that are presently taking place in Birmingham. But I am sorry that your statement did not express a similar concern for the conditions that brought the demonstrations into being. I am sure that each of you would want to go beyond the superficial social analyst who looks merely at effects, and does not grapple with underlying causes. I would not hesitate to say that it is unfortunate that so-called demonstrations are taking place in Birmingham at this time, but I would say in more emphatic terms that it is even more unfortunate that the white power structure of this city left the Negro community with no other alternative.

In any nonviolent campaign there are four basic steps: (1) collection of the facts to determine whether injustices are alive, (2) negotiation, (3) self-purification, and (4) direct action. We have gone through all of these steps in Birmingham. There can be no gainsaying of the fact that racial injustice engulfs this community.

Birmingham is probably the most thoroughly segregated city in the United States. Its ugly record of police brutality is known in every section of this country. Its injust treatment of Negroes in the courts is a notorious reality. There have been more unsolved bombings of Negro homes and churches in Birmingham than any city in this nation. These are the hard, brutal and unbelievable facts. On the basis of these conditions Negro leaders sought to negotiate with the city fathers. But the political leaders consistently refused to engage in good faith negotiation.

Then came the opportunity last September to talk with some of the leaders of the economic community. In these negotiating sessions certain promises were made by the merchants — such as the promise to remove the humiliating racial signs from the stores. On the basis of these promises Rev. Shuttlesworth and the leaders of the Alabama Christian Movement for Human Rights agreed to call a moratorium on any type of demonstrations. As the weeks and months unfolded we realized that we were the victims of a broken promise. The signs remained. Like so many experiences of the past we were confronted with blasted hopes, and the dark shadow of a deep disappointment settled upon us. So we had no alternative except that of preparing for direct action, whereby we would present our very bodies as a means of laying our case before the conscience of the local and national community. We were not unmindful of the difficulties involved. So we decided to go through a process of self-purification. We started having workshops on nonviolence and repeatedly asked ourselves the questions, "Are you able to accept blows without retaliating?" "Are you able to endure the ordeals of jail?" We decided to set our direct-action program around the Easter season, realizing that with the exception of Christmas, this was the largest shopping period of the year. Knowing that a strong economic withdrawal program would be the by-product of direct action, we felt that this was the best time to bring pressure on the merchants for the needed changes. Then it occurred to us that the March election was ahead and so we speedily decided to postpone action until after election day. When we discovered that Mr. Connor was in the run-off, we decided again to postpone action so that the demonstrations could not be used to cloud the issues. At this time we agreed to begin our nonviolent witness the day after the run-off.

This reveals that we did not move irresponsibly into direct action. We too wanted to see Mr. Connor defeated; so we went through postponement after postponement to aid in this community need. After this we felt that direct action could be delayed no longer.

You may well ask, "Why direct action? Why sit-ins, marches, etc.? Isn't negotiation a better path?" You are exactly right in your call for negotiation. Indeed, this is the purpose of direct action. Nonviolent direct action seeks to create such a crisis and establish such creative tension that a community that has constantly refused to negotiate is forced to confront the issue. It seeks so to dramatize the issue that it can no longer be ignored. I just referred to the creation of tension as a part of the work of the nonviolent resister. This may sound rather shocking. But I must confess that I am not afraid of the word tension. I have earnestly worked and preached against violent tension, but there is a type of constructive nonviolent tension that is necessary for growth. Just as Socrates felt that it was necessary to create a tension in the mind so that individuals could rise from the bondage of myths and half-truths to the unfettered realm of creative analysis and objective appraisal, we must see the need of having nonviolent gadflies to create the kind of tension in society that will help men to rise from the dark depths of prejudice and racism to the majestic heights of understanding and brotherhood. So the purpose of the direct action is to create a situation so crisis-packed that it will inevitably open the door to negotiation. We, therefore, concur with you in your call for negotiation. Too long has our beloved Southland been bogged down in the tragic attempt to live in monologue rather than dialogue.

One of the basic points in your statement is that our acts are untimely. Some have asked, "Why didn't you give the new administration time to act?" The only answer that I can give to this inquiry is that the new administration must be prodded about as much as the outgoing one before it acts. We will be sadly mistaken if we feel that the election of Mr. Boutwell will bring the millennium to Birmingham. While Mr. Boutwell is much more articulate and gentle than Mr. Connor, they are both segregationists, dedicated to the task of maintaining the status quo. The hope I see in Mr. Boutwell is that he will be reasonable enough to see the futility of massive resistance to desegregation. But he will not see this without pressure from the devotees of civil rights. My friends, I must say to you that we have not made a single gain in civil rights without determined legal and nonviolent pressure. History is the long and tragic story of the fact that privileged groups seldom give up their privileges voluntarily. Individuals may see the moral light and voluntarily give up their unjust posture; but as Reinhold Niebuhr has reminded us, groups are more immoral than individuals.

We know through painful experience that freedom is never voluntarily given by the oppressor; it must be demanded by the oppressed. Frankly, I have never yet engaged in a direct action movement that was "well-timed," according to the timetable of those who have not suffered unduly from the disease of segregation. For years now I have heard the words "Wait!" It rings in the ear of every Negro with a piercing familiarity. This "Wait" has almost always meant "Never." It has been a tranquilizing thalidomide, relieving the emotional stress for a moment, only to give birth to an ill-formed infant of frustration. We must come to see with the distinguished jurist of yesterday that "justice too long delayed is justice denied." We have waited for more than 340 years for our constitutional and God-given rights. The nations of Asia and Africa are moving with jetlike speed toward the goal of political independence, and we still creep at horse and buggy pace toward the gaining of a cup of coffee at a lunch counter. I guess it is easy for those who have never felt the stinging darts of segregation to say, "Wait." But when you have seen vicious mobs lynch your mothers and fathers at will and drown your sisters and brothers at whim; when you have seen hate-filled policemen curse, kick, brutalize and even kill your black brothers and sisters with impunity; when you see the vast majority of your twenty million Negro brothers smothering in an airtight cage of poverty in the midst of an affluent society; when you suddenly find your tongue twisted and your speech stammering as you seek to explain to your six-year-old daughter why she can't go to the public amusement park that has just been advertised on television, and see tears welling up in her little eyes when she is told that Funtown is closed to colored children, and see the depressing clouds of inferiority begin to form in her little mental sky, and see her begin to distort her little personality by unconsciously developing a bitterness toward white people; when you have to concoct an answer for a five-year-old son asking in agonizing pathos: "Daddy, why do white people treat colored people so mean?"; when you take a cross-country drive and find it necessary to sleep night after night in the uncomfortable corners of your automobile because no motel will accept you; when you are humiliated day in and day out by nagging signs reading "white" and "colored"; when your first name becomes "nigger" and your middle name becomes "boy" (however old you are) and your last name becomes "John," and when your wife and mother are never given the respected title "Mrs."; when you are harried by day and haunted by night by the fact that you are a Negro, living constantly at tiptoe stance never quite knowing what to expect next, and plagued with inner fears and outer resentments; when you are forever fighting a degenerating sense of "nobodiness"; then you will understand why we find it difficult to wait. There comes a time when the cup of endurance runs over, and men are no longer willing to be plunged into an abyss of injustice where they experience the blackness of corroding despair. I hope, sirs, you can understand our legitimate and unavoidable impatience.

You express a great deal of anxiety over our willingness to break laws. This is certainly a legitimate concern. Since we so diligently urge people to obey the Supreme Court's decision of 1954 outlawing segregation in the public schools, it is rather strange and paradoxical to find us consciously breaking laws. One may well ask, "How can you advocate breaking some laws and obeying others?" The answer is found in the fact that there are two types of laws: there are *just* and there are *unjust* laws. I would agree with Saint Augustine that "An unjust law is no law at all."

Now what is the difference between the two? How does one determine when a law is just or unjust? A just law is a man-made code that squares with the moral law or the law of God. An unjust law is a code that is out of harmony with the moral law. To put it in the terms of Saint Thomas Aquinas, an unjust law is a human law that is not rooted in eternal and natural law. Any law that uplifts human personality is just. Any law that degrades human personality is unjust. All segregation statutes are unjust because segregation distorts the soul and damages the personality. It gives the segregator a false sense of superiority, and the segregated a false sense of inferiority. To use the words of Martin Buber, the great Jewish philosopher, segregation substitutes an "I-it" relationship for the "I-thou" relationship, and ends up relegating persons to the status of things. So segregation is not only politically, economically and sociologically unsound, but it is morally wrong and sinful. Paul Tillich has said that sin is separation. Isn't segregation an existential expression of man's tragic separation, an expression of his awful estrangement, his terrible sinfulness? So I can urge men to disobey segregation ordinances because they are morally wrong.

Let us turn to a more concrete example of just and unjust laws. An unjust law is a code that a majority inflicts on a minority that is not binding on itself. This is difference made legal. On the other hand a just law is a code that a majority compels a minority to follow that it is willing to follow itself. This is sameness made legal.

Let me give another explanation. An unjust law is a code inflicted upon a minority which that minority had no part in enacting or creating because they did not have the unhampered right to vote. Who can say that the legislature of Alabama which set up the segregation laws was democratically elected? Throughout the state of Alabama all types of conniving methods are used to prevent Negroes from becoming registered voters and there are some counties without a single Negro registered to vote despite the fact that the Negro constitutes a majority of the population. Can any law set up in such a state be considered democratically structured?

These are just a few examples of unjust and just laws. There are some instances when a law is just on its face and unjust in its application. For instance, I was arrested Friday on a charge of parading without a permit. Now there is nothing wrong with an ordinance which requires a permit for a parade, but when the ordinance is used to preserve segregation and to deny citizens the First Amendment privilege of peaceful assembly and peaceful protest, then it becomes unjust.

I hope you can see the distinction I am trying to point out. In no sense do I advocate evading or defying the law as the rabid segregationist would do. This would lead to anarchy. One who breaks an unjust law must do it *openly, lovingly* (not hatefully as the white mothers did in New Orleans when they were seen on television screaming, "nigger, nigger, nigger"), and with a willingness to accept the penalty. I submit that an individual who breaks a law that conscience tells him is unjust, and willingly accepts the penalty by staying in jail to arouse the conscience of the community over its injustice, is in reality expressing the very highest respect for law.

Of course, there is nothing new about this kind of civil disobedience. It was seen sublimely in the refusal of Shadrach, Meshach and Abednego to obey the laws of Nebuchadnezzar because a higher moral law was involved. It was practiced superbly by the early Christians who were willing to face hungry lions and the excruciating pain of chopping blocks, before submitting to certain unjust laws of the Roman Empire. To a degree academic freedom is a reality today because Socrates practiced civil disobedience.

We can never forget that everything Hitler did in Germany was "legal" and everything the Hungarian freedom fighters did in Hungary was "illegal." It was "illegal" to aid and comfort a Jew in Hitler's Germany. But I am sure that if I had lived in Germany during that time I would have aided and comforted my Jewish brothers even though it was illegal. If I lived in a Communist country today where certain principles dear to the Christian faith are suppressed, I believe I would openly advocate disobeying these anti-religious laws. I must make two honest confessions to you, my Christian and Jewish brothers. First, I must confess that over the last few years I have been gravely disappointed with the white moderate. I have almost reached the regrettable conclusion that the Negro's great stumbling block in the stride toward freedom is not the White Citizen's Counciler or the Ku Klux Klanner, but the white moderate who is more devoted to "order" than to justice; who prefers a negative peace which is the absence of tension to a positive peace which is the presence of justice; who constantly says, "I agree with you in the goal you seek, but I can't agree with your methods of direct action"; who paternalistically feels that he can set the timetable for another man's freedom; who lives by the myth of time and who constantly advises the Negro to wait until a "more convenient season." Shallow understanding from people of good will is more frustrating than absolute misunderstanding from people of ill will. Lukewarm acceptance is much more bewildering than outright rejection.

I had hoped that the white moderate would understand that law and order exist for the purpose of establishing justice, and that when they fail to do this they become dangerously structured dams that block the flow of social progress. I had hoped that the white moderate would understand that the present tension of the South is merely a necessary phase of the transition from an obnoxious negative peace, where the Negro passively accepted his unjust plight, to a substance-filled positive peace, where all men will respect the dignity and worth of human personality. Actually, we who engage in nonviolent direct action are not the creators of tension. We merely bring to the surface the hidden tension that is already alive. We bring it out in the open where it can be seen and dealt with. Like a boil that can never be cured as long as it is covered up but must be opened with all its pus-flowing ugliness to the natural medicines of air and light, injustice must likewise be exposed, with all of the tension its exposing creates, to the light of human conscience and the air of national opinion before it can be cured.

In your statement you asserted that our actions, even though peaceful, must be condemned because they precipitate violence. But can this assertion be logically made? Isn't this like condemning the robbed man because his possession of money precipitated the evil act of robbery? Isn't this like condemning Socrates because his unswerving commitment to truth and his philosophical delvings precipitated the misguided popular mind to make him drink the hemlock? Isn't this like condemning Jesus because His unique God-consciousness and never-ceasing devotion to his will precipitated the evil act of crucifixion? We must come to see, as federal courts have consistently affirmed, that it is immoral to urge an individual to withdraw his

efforts to gain his basic constitutional rights because the quest precipitates violence. Society must protect the robbed and punish the
robber.

I had also hoped that the white moderate would reject the myth of
time. I received a letter this morning from a white brother in Texas
which said: "All Christians know that the colored people will receive
equal rights eventually, but it is possible that you are in too great of
a religious hurry. It has taken Christianity almost two thousand years
to accomplish what it has. The teachings of Christ take time to come
to earth." All that is said here grows out of a tragic misconception of
time. It is the strangely irrational notion that there is something in the
very flow of time that will inevitably cure all ills. Actually time is
neutral. It can be used either destructively or constructively. I am
coming to feel that the people of ill will have used time much more
effectively than the people of good will. We will have to repent in this
generation not merely for the vitriolic words and actions of the bad
people, but for the appalling silence of the good people. We must come
to see that human progress never rolls in on wheels of inevitability. It
comes through the tireless efforts and persistent work of men willing
to be co-workers with God, and without this hard work time itself
becomes an ally of the forces of social stagnation. We must use time
creatively, and forever realize that the time is always ripe to do right.
Now is the time to make real the promise of democracy, and transform
our pending national elegy into a creative psalm of brotherhood. Now
is the time to lift our national policy from the quicksand of racial
injustice to the solid rock of human dignity.

You spoke of our activity in Birmingham as extreme. At first I was
rather disappointed that fellow clergymen would see my nonviolent
efforts as those of the extremist. I started thinking about the fact that
I stand in the middle of two opposing forces in the Negro community.
One is a force of complacency made up of Negroes who, as a result of
long years of oppression, have been so completely drained of self-
respect and a sense of "somebodiness" that they have adjusted to
segregation, and of a few Negroes in the middle class who, because of
a degree of academic and economic security, and because at points
they profit by segregation, have unconsciously become insensitive to
the problems of the masses. The other force is one of bitterness and
hatred, and comes perilously close to advocating violence. It is expressed in the various black nationalist groups that are springing up
over the nation, the largest and best known being Elijah Muhammad's
Muslim movement. This movement is nourished by the contemporary

frustration over the continued existence of racial discrimination. It is made up of people who have lost faith in America, who have absolutely repudiated Christianity, and who have concluded that the white man is an incurable "devil." I have tried to stand between these two forces, saying that we need not follow the "do-nothingism" of the complacent or the hatred and despair of the black nationalist. There is the more excellent way of love and nonviolent protest. I'm grateful to God that, through the Negro church, the dimension of nonviolence entered our struggle. If this philosophy had not emerged, I am convinced that by now many streets of the South would be flowing with floods of blood. And I am further convinced that if our white brothers dismiss as "rabble-rousers" and "outside agitators" those of us who are working through the channels of nonviolent direct action and refuse to support our nonviolent efforts, millions of Negroes, out of frustration and despair, will seek solace and security in black nationalist ideologies, a development that will lead inevitably to a frightening racial nightmare.

Oppressed people cannot remain oppressed forever. The urge for freedom will eventually come. This is what happened to the American Negro. Something within has reminded him of his birthright of freedom; something without has reminded him that he can gain it. Consciously and unconsciously, he has been swept in by what the Germans call the *Zeitgeist,* and with his black brothers of Africa, and his brown and yellow brothers of Asia, South America and the Caribbean, he is moving with a sense of cosmic urgency toward the promised land of racial justice. Recognizing this vital urge that has engulfed the Negro community, one should readily understand public demonstrations. The Negro has many pent-up resentments and latent frustrations. He has to get them out. So let him march sometime; let him have his prayer pilgrimages to the city hall; understand why he must have sit-ins and freedom rides. If his repressed emotions do not come out in these nonviolent ways, they will come out in ominous expressions of violence. This is not a threat; it is a fact of history. So I have not said to my people "get rid of your discontent." But I have tried to say that this normal and healthy discontent can be channelized through the creative outlet of nonviolent direct action. Now this approach is being dismissed as extremist. I must admit that I was initially disappointed in being so categorized.

But as I continued to think about the matter I gradually gained a bit of satisfaction from being considered an extremist. Was not Jesus an extremist in love — "Love your enemies, bless them that curse you,

pray for them that despitefully use you." Was not Amos an extremist
for justice — "Let justice roll down like waters and righteousness like
a mighty stream." Was not Paul an extremist for the gospel of Jesus
Christ — "I bear in my body the marks of the Lord Jesus." Was not
Martin Luther an extremist — "Here I stand; I can do none other so
help me God." Was not John Bunyan an extremist — "I will stay in jail
to the end of my days before I make a butchery of my conscience." Was
not Abraham Lincoln an extremist — "This nation cannot survive half
slave and half free." Was not Thomas Jefferson an extremist — "We
hold these truths to be self-evident, that all men are created equal." So
the question is not whether we will be extremist but what kind of
extremist will we be. Will we be extremists for hate or will we be
extremists for love? Will we be extremists for the preservation of
injustice — or will we be extremists for the cause of justice? In that
dramatic scene on Calvary's hill, three men were crucified. We must
not forget that all three were crucified for the same crime — the crime
of extremism. Two were extremists for immorality, and thusly fell
below their environment. The other, Jesus Christ, was an extremist for
love, truth and goodness, and thereby rose above his environment. So,
after all, maybe the South, the nation and the world are in dire need
of creative extremists.

I had hoped that the white moderate would see this. Maybe I was
too optimistic. Maybe I expected too much. I guess I should have
realized that few members of a race that has oppressed another race
can understand or appreciate the deep groans and passionate yearnings of those that have been oppressed and still fewer have the vision
to see that injustice must be rooted out by strong, persistent and
determined action. I am thankful, however, that some of our white
brothers have grasped the meaning of this social revolution and
committed themselves to it. They are still all too small in quantity, but
they are big in quality. Some like Ralph McGill, Lillian Smith, Harry
Golden and James Dabbs have written about our struggle in eloquent,
prophetic and understanding terms. Others have marched with us
down nameless streets of the South. They have languished in filthy
roach-infested jails, suffering the abuse and brutality of angry policemen who see them as "dirty nigger-lovers." They, unlike so many of
their moderate brothers and sisters, have recognized the urgency of
the moment and sensed the need for powerful "action" antidotes to
combat the disease of segregation.

Let me rush on to mention my other disappointment. I have been
so greatly disappointed with the white church and its leadership. Of

course, there are some notable exceptions. I am not unmindful of the fact that each of you has taken some significant stands on this issue. I commend you, Rev. Stallings, for your Christian stance on this past Sunday, in welcoming Negroes to your worship service on a non-segregated basis. I commend the Catholic leaders of this state for integrating Springhill College several years ago.

But despite these notable exceptions I must honestly reiterate that I have been disappointed with the church. I do not say that as one of the negative critics who can always find something wrong with the church. I say it as a minister of the gospel, who loves the church; who was nurtured in its bosom; who has been sustained by its spiritual blessings and who will remain true to it as long as the cord of life shall lengthen.

I had the strange feeling when I was suddenly catapulted into the leadership of the bus protest in Montgomery several years ago that we would have the support of the white church. I felt that the white ministers, priests and rabbis of the South would be some of our strongest allies. Instead, some have been outright opponents, refusing to understand the freedom movement and misrepresenting its leaders; all too many others have been more cautious than courageous and have remained silent behind the anesthetizing security of the stained-glass windows.

In spite of my shattered dreams of the past, I came to Birmingham with the hope that the white religious leadership of this community would see the justice of our cause, and with deep moral concern, serve as the channel through which our just grievances would get to the power structure. I had hoped that each of you would understand. But again I have been disappointed. I have heard numerous religious leaders of the South call upon their worshippers to comply with a desegregation decision because it is the *law*, but I have longed to hear white ministers say, "Follow this decree because integration is morally *right* and the Negro is your brother." In the midst of blatant injustices inflicted upon the Negro, I have watched white churches stand on the sideline and merely mouth pious irrelevancies and sanctimonious trivialities. In the midst of a mighty struggle to rid our nation of racial and economic injustice, I have heard so many ministers say, "Those are social issues with which the gospel has no real concern," and I have watched so many churches commit themselves to a completely other-worldly religion which made a strange distinction between body and soul, the sacred and the secular.

So here we are moving toward the exit of the twentieth century with a religious community largely adjusted to the status quo, standing as a taillight behind other community agencies rather than a headlight leading men to higher levels of justice.

I have traveled the length and breadth of Alabama, Mississippi and all the other southern states. On sweltering summer days and crisp autumn mornings I have looked at her beautiful churches with their lofty spires pointing heavenward. I have beheld the impressive outlay of her massive religious education buildings. Over and over again I have found myself asking: "What kind of people worship here? Who is their God? Where were their voices when the lips of Governor Barnett dripped with words of interposition and nullification? Where were they when Governor Wallace gave the clarion call for defiance and hatred? Where were their voices of support when tired, bruised and weary Negro men and women decided to rise from the dark dungeons of complacency to the bright hills of creative protest?"

Yes, these questions are still in my mind. In deep disappointment, I have wept over the laxity of the church. But be assured that my tears have been tears of love. There can be no deep disappointment where there is not deep love. Yes, I love the church; I love her sacred walls. How could I do otherwise? I am in the rather unique position of being the son, the grandson and the great-grandson of preachers. Yes, I see the church as the body of Christ. But, oh! How we have blemished and scarred that body through social neglect and fear of being noncon-formists.

There was a time when the church was very powerful. It was during that period when the early Christians rejoiced when they were deemed worthy to suffer for what they believed. In those days the church was not merely a thermometer that recorded the ideas and principles of popular opinion; it was a thermostat that transformed the mores of society. Wherever the early Christians entered a town the power structure got disturbed and immediately sought to convict them for being "disturbers of the peace" and "outside agitators." But they went on with the conviction that they were "a colony of heaven," and had to obey God rather than man. They were small in number but big in commitment. They were too God-intoxicated to be "astronomically intimidated." They brought an end to such ancient evils as infanticide and gladiatorial contest.

Things are different now. The contemporary church is often a weak, ineffectual voice with an uncertain sound. It is so often the arch-supporter of the status quo. Far from being disturbed by the presence of the church, the power structure of the average community is consoled by the church's silent and often vocal sanction of things as they are.

But the judgment of God is upon the church as never before. If the church of today does not recapture the sacrificial spirit of the early church, it will lose its authentic ring, forfeit the loyalty of millions, and be dismissed as an irrelevant social club with no meaning for the twentieth century. I am meeting young people every day whose disappointment with the church has risen to outright disgust.

Maybe again, I have been too optimistic. Is organized religion too inextricably bound to the status quo to save our nation and the world? Maybe I must turn my faith to the inner spiritual church, the church within the church, as the true *ecclesia* and the hope of the world. But again I am thankful to God that some noble souls from the ranks of organized religion have broken loose from the paralyzing chains of conformity and joined us as active partners in the struggle for freedom. They have left their secure congregations and walked the streets of Albany, Georgia, with us. They have gone through the highways of the South on tortuous rides for freedom. Yes, they have gone to jail with us. Some have been kicked out of their churches, and lost support of their bishops and fellow ministers. But they have gone with the faith that right defeated is stronger than evil triumphant. These men have been the leaven in the lump of the race. Their witness has been the spiritual salt that has preserved the true meaning of the gospel in these troubled times. They have carved a tunnel of hope through the dark mountain of disappointment.

I hope the church as a whole will meet the challenge of this decisive hour. But even if the church does not come to the aid of justice, I have no despair about the future. I have no fear about the outcome of our struggle in Birmingham, even if our motives are presently misunderstood. We will reach the goal of freedom in Birmingham and all over the nation, because the goal of America is freedom. Abused and scorned though we may be, our destiny is tied up with the destiny of America. Before the Pilgrims landed at Plymouth we were here. Before the pen of Jefferson etched across the pages of history the majestic words of the Declaration of Independence, we were here. For more than two centuries our foreparents labored in this country without wages; they made cotton king; and they built the homes of their masters in the midst of brutal injustice and shameful humiliation — and yet out of a bottomless vitality they continued to thrive and develop. If the inexpressible cruelties of slavery could not stop us, the opposition we now face will surely fail. We will win our freedom because the sacred heritage of our nation and the eternal will of God are embodied in our echoing demands.

I must close now. But before closing I am impelled to mention one other point in your statement that troubled me profoundly. You warmly commended the Birmingham police force for keeping "order" and "preventing violence." I don't believe you would have so warmly commended the police force if you had seen its angry violent dogs literally biting six unarmed, nonviolent Negroes. I don't believe you would so quickly commend the policemen if you would observe their ugly and inhuman treatment of Negroes here in the city jail; if you would watch them push and curse old Negro women and young Negro girls; if you would see them slap and kick old Negro men and young boys; if you will observe them, as they did on two occasions, refuse to give us food because we wanted to sing our grace together. I'm sorry that I can't join you in your praise for the police department.

It is true that they have been rather disciplined in their public handling of the demonstrators. In this sense they have been rather publicly "nonviolent." But for what purpose? To preserve the evil system of segregation. Over the last few years I have consistently preached that nonviolence demands that the means we use must be as pure as the ends we seek. So I have tried to make it clear that it is wrong to use immoral means to attain moral ends. But now I must affirm that it is just as wrong, or even more so, to use moral means to preserve immoral ends. Maybe Mr. Connor and his policemen have been rather publicly nonviolent, as Chief Pritchett was in Albany, Georgia, but they have used the moral means of nonviolence to maintain the immoral end of flagrant racial injustice. T. S. Eliot has said that there is no greater treason than to do the right deed for the wrong reason.

I wish you had commended the Negro sit-inners and demonstrators of Birmingham for their sublime courage, their willingness to suffer and their amazing discipline in the midst of the most inhuman provocation. One day the South will recognize its real heroes. They will be the James Merediths, courageously and with a majestic sense of purpose facing jeering and hostile mobs and the agonizing lone-liness that characterizes the life of the pioneer. They will be old, oppressed, battered Negro women, symbolized in a seventy-two-year-old woman of Montgomery, Alabama, who rose up with a sense of dignity and with her people decided not to ride the segregated buses, and responded to one who inquired about her tiredness with un-grammatical profundity: "My feet is tired, but my soul is rested." They will be the young high school and college students, young ministers of the gospel and a host of their elders courageously and nonviolently sitting-in at lunch counters and willingly going to jail for conscience's sake. One day the South will know that when these disinherited children of God sat down at lunch counters they were in reality standing up for the best in the American dream and the most sacred values in our Judeo-Christian heritage, and thusly, carrying our whole nation back to those great wells of democracy which were dug deep by the Founding Fathers in the formulation of the Constitution and the Declaration of Independence.

Never before have I written a letter this long (or should I say a book?). I'm afraid that it is much too long to take your precious time. I can assure you that it would have been much shorter if I had been writing from a comfortable desk, but what else is there to do when you are alone for days in the dull monotony of a narrow jail cell other than write long letters, think strange thoughts, and pray long prayers?

If I have said anything in this letter that is an overstatement of the truth and is indicative of an unreasonable impatience, I beg you to forgive me. If I have said anything in this letter that is an understatement of the truth and is indicative of my having a patience that makes me patient with anything less than brotherhood, I beg God to forgive me.

I hope this letter finds you strong in the faith. I also hope that circumstances will soon make it possible for me to meet each of you, not as an integrationist or a civil rights leader, but as a fellow clergyman and a Christian brother. Let us all hope that the dark clouds of racial prejudice will soon pass away and the deep fog of misunderstanding will be lifted from our fear-drenched communities and in some not too distant tomorrow the radiant stars of love and brotherhood will shine over our great nation with all of their scintillating beauty.

Yours for the cause of Peace and Brotherhood,
Martin Luther King, Jr.

ALEKSANDR SOLZHENITSYN

Beauty Will Save the World

Aleksandr Isayevich Solzhenitsyn is the author of major works of fiction such as *Cancer Ward* and *The First Circle,* and of several works of history, above all the volumes of *The Gulag Archipelago*. In his lecture accepting the Nobel Prize for literature, he articulated this creed, which goes far beyond the aestheticism of its title (a quotation from Dostoyevsky) to affirm, with Dostoyevsky, a metaphysical and ultimately a religious vision.

LIKE THAT BEWILDERED SAVAGE who has picked up a strange object . . . perhaps something thrown up by the sea, perhaps disinterred from the sands or dropped from the heavens . . . an object intricate in its convolutions, which shines first with a dull glow and then with a bright shaft of light . . . who keeps turning it over and over in his hands in an effort to find some way of putting it to use, seeking some humble function for it, which is within his limited grasp, never conceiving of a higher purpose . . .

So we, too, holding art in our hands vaingloriously considering ourselves to be its master, undertake brazenly to give it direction, to renovate it, to reform it, to issue manifestoes about it, to sell it for money. We use it to play up to those who possess power. We employ it at times for amusement — even in music hall songs and night clubs — and also, at times, grabbing hold of it however we can, for transient and limited political and social needs. But art is not desecrated by our carryings-on. It does not lose sight of its own origins because of them. And each time and in each mode of use it sheds on us a portion of its secret inner light.

But can we embrace *all* that light? Who is there so bold as to proclaim that he has DEFINED art? That he has enumerated all its facets?

Yet perhaps in ages past someone did comprehend and define it for us, but we grew impatient: we listened in passing and paid no heed and discarded it immediately in our eternal haste to replace even the very best with something else just because it is new! And then later on, when what is old is restated, we forget that we heard it before.

One artist imagines himself the creator of an independent spiritual world and takes on his shoulders the act of creating that world and its population, assuming total responsibility for it — but he stumbles and breaks down because there is no mortal genius capable of bearing such a load; just like man, who once declared himself the center of all existence but was incapable of creating a balanced spiritual system. And then, when failure occurs, it is all blamed on the eternal disharmony of the world, on the complexity of the shattered contemporary soul, or on the stupidity of the public.

Another artist realizes that there is a supreme force above him and works away gladly as a small apprentice beneath God's heaven, even though his responsibility for everything he writes or draws and for the souls which perceive it is all the more strict. But still: it was not he who created this world, nor is it he who provides it with direction, and he has no doubts of its foundations. The artist is only given to sense more keenly than others the harmony of the world and all the beauty and savagery of man's contribution to it — and to communicate this poignantly to people. And even in the midst of failure and down at the lowest depths of existence — in poverty, prison, illness — the sensation of a stable harmony will never leave him.

However, all the irrationality of art, its blinding twists and turns, its unpredictable discoveries, its soul-shaking impact on people are too magical to be contained within the world-outlook of an artist, in his conception or in the work of his unworthy fingers.

Archaeologists have not yet discovered any stage of human existence without art. Even in the half-light before the dawn of humanity we received this gift from Hands we did not manage to discern. Nor have we managed to ask: Why was this gift given us and what are we to do with it?

And all those prophets who are predicting that art is disintegrating, that it has used up all its forms, that it is dying, are mistaken. We are the ones who shall die. And art will remain. The question is whether before we perish we shall understand all its aspects and all its ends.

Not all can be given names. Some of them go beyond words. Art opens even the chilled, darkened heart to high spiritual experience. Through the instrumentality of art we are sometimes sent — vaguely, briefly — insights which logical processes of thought cannot attain.

Like the tiny mirror of the fairy tale: you look into it and you see — not yourself — but for one fleeting moment the Unattainable to which you cannot leap or fly. And the heart aches. . . .

Dostoyevsky once let drop the enigmatic phrase: "Beauty will save the world." What does this mean? For a long time it used to seem to me that this was a mere phrase. Just how could such a thing be possible? When had it ever happened in the bloodthirsty course of history that beauty had saved anyone from anything? Beauty had provided embellishment certainly, given uplift — but whom had it ever saved?

However, there is a special quality in the essence of beauty, a special quality in the status of art: the conviction carried by a genuine work of art is absolutely indisputable and tames even the strongly opposed heart. One can construct a political speech, an assertive journalistic polemic, a program for organizing society, a philosophical system, so that in appearance it is smooth, well structured, and yet it is built upon a mistake, a lie; and the hidden element, the distortion, will not immediately become visible. And a speech, or a journalistic essay, or a program in rebuttal, or a different philosophical structure can be counterposed to the first — and it will seem just as well constructed and as smooth, and everything will seem to fit. And therefore one has faith in them — yet one has no faith.

It is in vain to affirm that which the heart does not confirm.

In contrast, a work of art bears within itself its own confirmation: concepts which are manufactured out of whole cloth or overstrained will not stand up to being tested in images, will somehow fall apart and turn out to be sickly and pallid and convincing to no one. Works steeped in truth and presenting it to us vividly alive will take hold of us, will attract us to themselves with great power — and no one, ever, even in a later age, will presume to negate them. And so perhaps that old trinity of Truth, Good, and Beauty is not just the formal outworn formula it used to seem to us during our heady, materialistic youth. If the crests of these three trees join together, as the investigators and explorers used to affirm, and if the too obvious, too straight branches of Truth and Good are crushed or amputated and cannot reach the light — yet perhaps the whimsical, unpredictable, unexpected branches of Beauty will make their way through and soar up TO THAT VERY PLACE and in this way perform the work of all three.

And in that case it was not a slip of the tongue for Dostoyevsky to say that "Beauty will save the world," but a prophecy. After all *he* was given the gift of seeing much, he was extraordinarily illumined.

And consequently perhaps art, literature, can in actual fact help the world of today.

That little which I have managed to discern over the years I shall try to set forth here today.

I have climbed my way up to this lectern from which the Nobel Lecture is read, a lectern not granted to every writer and once only in a lifetime, not just up three or four specially erected steps but hundreds and even thousands of them — unyielding, steep, frozen, out of the dark and the cold where I was fated to survive and where others, who possessed perhaps greater talent and were stronger than I, perished. I met only a few among them in the Gulag Archipelago scattered over a widespread multitude of islands. And beneath the millstone of police surveillance and mistrust I did not speak face to face with all those who were there either. Of some I only heard at second hand and about others I only guessed. Those who fell into that abyss who already had made a name in literature are at least known to us — but how many were unknown, had never been published! And so very few, almost no one, managed to survive and return. A whole national literature remained behind, buried not only without coffins and graves, but even without underwear, naked except for an identification tag on the toe. Russian literature never ceased for one moment! Yet from outside it seemed a desert. Where a thick forest might have grown there remained, after all the timbering, only two or three trees which had missed being cut down.

And today how am I, accompanied as I am by the spirits of those who perished, my head bowed as I let pass before me up to this lectern others who were earlier worthy of it, how am I here today supposed to divine and express that which *they* would have wished to say?

This duty has long weighed upon me, and I have understood it. In the words of Vladimir Soloviev:

> In chains, too, we must close the circle
> Which the gods have drawn for us.

In exhausting camp marches, rows of lanterns lighting the columns of prisoners in the darkness of subzero nights, more than once we felt in our throats what we would have liked to shout out to the whole world, if only the world could have heard some spokesman from among us. At that time it seemed so very, very clear that all our lucky envoy had to do was to raise an outcry and instantly the whole world would respond. Our entire outlook, in terms of both material objects and emotional actions and reactions, was precisely defined. And we sensed no lack of balance in the indivisible world. Those thoughts did not come from books and had not been taken over for the sake of harmony and good order: they had been formulated in prison cells and around timber-camp bonfires in conversations with people long since dead who had emerged tried and true from that life, who had matured in that existence.

When the external pressure lessened, our outlook and my own outlook broadened, and gradually, if only through a peephole, the "whole world" could be seen and discerned. And, surprisingly for us, that "whole world" turned out to be something quite different from what we had expected it to be. It did not live by what we had expected. It was proceeding to a destination we had not anticipated. When it came to a swampy bog, it exclaimed: "What a divine and lovely lawn!" When it encountered stocks made of concrete that were going to be placed around the necks of prisoners, it exclaimed: "What a lovely necklace!" And where unquenchable tears poured forth for some, others danced to lighthearted music.

So how has this come about? Whence has this abyss arisen? Were we all unfeeling? Or was the world unfeeling? Or was it due to the difference in languages? How does it happen that people are unable to understand each other's plain speech? Words resound and flow away like water — without taste, or color, or odor. Without a trace.

To the extent that I have come to understand this, the content, meaning, and tone of my possible speech here have changed over and over again with the years . . . the speech that I am delivering today.

It is by now very little like that speech which I first conceived in the subzero cold of the camp nights.

*   *   *   *   *

However, I am encouraged and emboldened by the vital perception of WORLD LITERATURE as the one great heart which beats for the concerns and misfortunes of our world, even though these are represented and visible in different, separate ways in each of its corners.

Beyond the age-old national literatures there existed from early times the concept of world literature — viewed as a network of connecting lines joining the peaks of national literatures, and as the totality of reciprocal literary influences. But there used to be a time lag: readers and writers learned of writers in other languages only after delays that were sometimes ages long, so that mutual influences were also delayed, and world literature as a network of connecting lines joining national literary peaks did not reach contemporaries, but their descendants only.

But today there is a mutual reaction between the writers of one country and the readers and writers of another which if not immediate is at least close to it. I have felt it myself. My books, as yet unpublished in my own country, notwithstanding hasty and often poor translations swiftly found themselves responsive world readers. Even outstanding Western writers such as Heinrich Böll have undertaken critical analysis of them. And through all these last years, when my work and my freedom never quite collapsed and fell, when they remained suspended in air in violation of all the laws of gravity, seemingly ON NOTHING AT ALL — on invisible, mute, public sympathy — I learned with grateful warmth, quite unexpectedly, of the support also of the world brotherhood of writers. I was astounded when on my fiftieth birthday I received greetings from well-known European writers. No pressure brought on me went unnoticed any longer. In that day, so dangerous for me, of my expulsion from the Writers' Union, A WALL OF DEFENSE was erected by the outstanding writers of the world which saved me from worse persecutions, and Norwegian writers and artists hospitably readied a shelter for me in the event of the expulsion from my motherland which threatened me. And then, in the end, my nomination for the Nobel Prize itself was initiated, not in the country in which I live and write, but by François Mauriac and his colleagues. More than this, national writers' organizations expressed their unanimous support of me.

And this was how I perceived and felt in my own case that world literature was not an abstraction, not something which had not yet crystallized, something created by the scholars of literature, but was a certain common body and common spirit, a living unity of the heart, in which the growing spiritual unity of humanity was expressed. And state boundaries are still being reddened by blood and heated by high-tension wires and by bursts of fire from automatic weapons, and certain ministries of internal affairs still imagine that literature, too, is an "internal affair" of the countries at their disposal, and newspaper headlines still read: "They do not have the right to interfere in our internal affairs!" Meanwhile there is no such thing left on our Earth as INTERNAL AFFAIRS. And the only salvation of humanity lies in everyone concerning himself with everything everywhere: the peoples of the East would then not be totally indifferent to what takes place in the

West; and the peoples of the West would not be totally indifferent to what takes place in the East. Literature, one of the most delicate and responsive instruments of human existence, has been the first to take hold of, to assimilate, to seize upon this feeling of the growing unity of humanity. And so, today, I am appealing to world literature with conviction — to hundreds of friends whom I have never met face to face and whom I perhaps never will see.

Friends! If we are worth anything, let us try to help! In our own countries, torn asunder by the discord of parties, movements, castes, and groups, who is it who has from the earliest ages been a force not for disunity but for unity? This in essence is the position of writers: the spokesmen for their national language — the principal tie binding together a nation, binding together the very Earth occupied by a people, and in fortunate cases their national soul also.

I think that world literature has it within its power in these frightening hours to help humanity know itself truly despite what prejudiced people and parties are attempting to instill; to communicate the condensed experience of one region to another in such a way that we will cease to be split apart and our eyes will no longer be dazzled, the units of measurement on our scales of values will correspond to one another, and some peoples may come to know the true history of others accurately and concisely and with that perception and pain they would feel if they had experienced it themselves — and thus be protected from repeating the same errors. And at the same time we ourselves can perhaps develop within ourselves a WORLD VIEW: seeing with the center of the eye, like every human being, what is close, and with the edge of the eye registering what is happening in the rest of the world. And so we can bring world-wide standards into correlation and adhere to them.

And who, if not the writers, are to express condemnation not only of their own bankrupt rulers (and in some countries this is the easiest way of all to earn a living and everyone except those who are too lazy is occupied with it) but also of their own society, whether it be a matter of its craven humiliation or its complacent weakness, or the feather-brained escapades of youth, or young pirates brandishing knives?

People will ask what literature can do in the face of the pitiless assault of open violence? Well, let us not forget that violence does not have its own separate existence and is, in fact, incapable of having it: it is invariably interwoven with THE LIE. They have the closest of kinship, the most profound natural tie: violence has nothing with which to cover itself except the lie, and the lie has nothing to stand

on other than violence. Once someone has proclaimed violence as his
METHOD, he must inexorably select the lie as his PRINCIPLE. At its birth
violence acts openly and even takes pride in itself. But as soon as it is
reinforced and its position is strengthened, it begins to sense the
rarefied atmosphere around it, and it can go further only when fogged
about with lies, cloaked in honeyed, hypocritical words. It does not
always nor invariably choke its victims; more often it demands of them
only the oath of the lie, only participation in the lie.

Simple is the ordinary courageous human being's act of not participating in the lie, of not supporting false actions! What his stand
says is: "So be it that *this* takes place in the world, that it even reigns
in the world — but let it not be with my complicity." Writers and
artists have a greater opportunity: TO CONQUER THE LIE! In battle with the
lie, art has always been victorious, always wins out, visibly, incon-
trovertibly for all! The lie can stand up and win out over much in the
world — but not over art.

And as soon as the lie is dispersed, the repulsive nakedness of
violence is exposed, and violence will collapse in impotence.

And that is why, my friends, I think that we are capable of helping
the world in its white-hot hour of trial. We must not reconcile
ourselves to being defenseless and disarmed; we must not sink into a
heedless, feckless life — but go out to the field of battle.

In the Russian language there are some favorite proverbs on TRUTH.
They express enduringly the immense folk experience, and are sometimes quite surprising:

"ONE WORD OF TRUTH OUTWEIGHS THE WHOLE WORLD."

And so it is that my own activity is founded on so apparently
fantastic a violation of the law of the conservation of energy and mass,
as is my appeal to the writers of the whole world.

Acknowledgments

"The Unbeliever and Christians" from *Resistance, Rebellion and Death* by Albert Camus, translated by Justin O'Brien. Copyright © 1960 by Alfred A. Knopf, Inc. Reprinted by permission of the publisher and Hamish Hamilton, Ltd.

Excerpt from *Five Stages of Greek Religion* by Gilbert Murray. Reprinted by permission of Oxford University Press.

"God As Cause" from *Lectures on the Essence of Religion* by Ludwig Feuerbach. Copyright © 1967 by Ralph Manheim. Reprinted by permission of Harper & Row, Publishers, Inc.

Selection reprinted from *The Future of an Illusion* by Sigmund Freud, translated by James Strachey. Used with the permission of W. W. Norton & Company, Inc. Copyright 1961 by James Strachey.

Excerpts from *I and Thou* by Martin Buber, translated by Walter Kaufman. Translation copyright © 1970 by Charles Scribner's Sons. Reprinted by permission of Charles Scribner's Sons, an imprint of Macmillan Publishing Co., and T & T Clark.

"Faith As Confession" from *Dogmatics in Outline* by Karl Barth. Copyright © 1959 by Harper & Row, Publishers, Inc. Reprinted by permission of the publisher and SCM Press Ltd.

"The Spiritual Problem of Modern Man" from *Modern Man in Search of a Soul* by Carl Jung. Reprinted by permission of Harcourt Brace Jovanovich, Inc., and Routledge & Kegan Paul Ltd.

Excerpts from *The Screwtape Letters* by C. S. Lewis. Copyright 1943 by William Collins Sons & Co. Ltd. Used by permission.

"The Four Stages of Life" from *The Religion of Man* by Rabindranath Tagore. Copyright 1961 by Unwin Hyman Ltd.

"The Prophet and Prophetic Religion" from *Ideas and Realities of Islam* by Seyyed Hossein Nasr. Copyright 1967 by Unwin Hyman Ltd.

Excerpts from *The Diary of a Country Priest* by Georges Bernanos. Copyright 1937, renewed 1965, by The Macmillan Company.

Excerpts from *Prolegomena to the Study of Greek Religion* by Jane Ellen Harrison. Copyright 1903 by Cambridge University Press.

"The Image of God" from *The Mind of the Maker* by Dorothy L. Sayers. Copyright 1941 by Harcourt Brace Jovanovich, Inc. Published by Gollancz.

"Sacraments of Africa" from *The Golden Bough* by James Frazer. Copyright © 1922 by Macmillan Publishing Company, renewed 1950 by Barclays Bank Ltd. Reprinted with permission of Macmillan Publishing Company and A. P. Watt Ltd. on behalf of Trinity College, Cambridge.

"Strange Is Our Situation Here upon Earth" by Albert Einstein. Reprinted by permission of The Hebrew University of Jerusalem, Israel.

"The New Reformation" from *Adventures of Ideas* by Alfred North Whitehead. Copyright © 1933 by Macmillan Publishing Company, renewed 1961 by Evelyn Whitehead. Reprinted by permission of Macmillan Publishing Company.

Excerpts from *Reverence for Life* by Albert Schweitzer. Copyright © 1969 by Rhena Eckert-Schweitzer. Reprinted by permission of Harper & Row, Publishers, Inc., and SPCK.

"Divinity School Address" from *Collected Works* by Ralph Waldo Emerson. Copyright © 1971 by the President and Fellows of Harvard College. Reprinted by permission of Harvard University Press.

"The Qur'ān" from *Islam,* 2nd ed., by Fazlur Rahman. Copyright © 1966 by Rahman, copyright © 1979 by The University of Chicago. All rights reserved.

"Confession" from *The Long Loneliness* by Dorothy Day. Copyright 1952 by Harper & Row, Publishers, Inc. Reprinted by permission of the publisher.

Excerpts from *Beauty Will Save the World: The Nobel Lecture on Literature* by
Aleksandr Solzhenitsyn. Copyright © 1972 by the Nobel Foundation.
English translation copyright © 1972 by Thomas P. Whitney. Reprinted
by permission of Harper & Row, Publishers, Inc.